D1578671

TEXTBOOK ON
CONTRACT

TEXTBOOK ON
CONTRACT

Sixth Edition

Jill Poole, LLB, LLM, FCI Arb,
of Lincoln's Inn, Barrister

Senior Lecturer and Course Director, LLM Commercial Law,
Cardiff Law School, Cardiff University

 Blackstone Press

Published by
Blackstone Press Limited
Aldine Place
London
W12 8AA
United Kingdom

Sales enquiries and orders
Telephone +44-(0)-20-8740-2277
Facsimile +44-(0)-20-8743-2292
e-mail: sales@blackstone.demon.co.uk
website: www.blackstonepress.com

ISBN: 1-84174-194-9
First edition © T. Antony Downes 1987
Second edition 1991
Reprinted 1992
Third edition 1993
Reprinted 1994
Fourth edition 1995
Fifth edition 1997
Reprinted 1999
Sixth edition © Jill Poole 2001

British Library Cataloguing in Publication Data
A catalogue record for this book is available from the British Library

This publication is protected by international copyright law. All rights reserved. No part of this publication may be reproduced, stored in a retrieval system, or transmitted in any form or by any means, electronic, mechanical, photocopying, recording or otherwise, without the prior permission of the publisher.

Typeset in 10/11pt Plantin by Style Photosetting Ltd, Mayfield, East Sussex
Printed and bound in Great Britain by Ashford Colour Press Ltd,
Gosport, Hampshire

Contents

Preface   ix

Table of Cases   xiii

Table of Statutes   xxxiii

Table of Statutory Instruments   xxxvii

Abbreviations   xxxviii

1 Introduction to the Law of Contract   1

1.1 The nature of contractual liability   1.2 Relationship between contract and tort   1.3 History of contract law   1.4 Role of contract and contract law 1.5 Contract and the sale of goods   1.6 The globalisation of contract law

PART I   FORMATION   25

2 Agreement   26

2.1 Determining the existence of agreement   2.2 Traditional and non-traditional approaches to identifying agreement   2.3 Determining the existence of agreement using offer and acceptance   2.4 Offers and invitations to treat   2.5 Communication of the offer   2.6 Acceptance   2.7 Termination of offers   2.8 Unilateral contracts

3 Agreement Problems   64

3.1 Certainty of agreements   3.2 Agreement mistake   3.3 Types of mistakes negativing agreement   3.4 Mistakes in documents

4 Enforceability Criteria   91

4.1 Introduction   4.2 Intention to create legal relations   4.3 Consideration
4.4 Reliance and estoppel   4.5 Unenforceability by defect of 'form'
4.6 Contractual capacity

PART II CONTENT, INTERPRETATION,
PERFORMANCE AND DISCHARGE   151

5 Content of the Contract and Principles of Interpretation 152

A. Content   5.1 Pre-contractual statements   5.2 Written contracts
5.3 Incorporation of terms   5.4 Promissory and contingent obligations
distinguished   5.5 Implied terms   *B. Interpretation*

6 Exemption Clauses and Unfair Contract Terms   183

6.1 Control of the substantive content of contracts   6.2 Standard form
contracts and the purpose of exemption clauses   6.3 Judicial attitudes to
exemption clauses   6.4 Types and nature of exemption clauses   6.5 Exemption
clauses as defences to liability   6.6 Statutory control of exemption clauses

7 Discharge by Performance, Agreement and Breach   224

7.1 Background   7.2 Discharge by performance   7.3 Discharge by agreement   7.4 Self-terminating contracts   7.5 Breach and repudiatory breach

8 Discharge by Frustration: Subsequent Impossibility   255

8.1 Introduction   8.2 History of the frustration doctrine   8.3 Legal nature
of the frustration doctrine   8.4 Frustrating events   8.5 Contracts concerning land   8.6 Foreseeability and risk allocation   8.7 Fault   8.8 Legal effects
of frustration

PART III METHODS OF POLICING THE MAKING
OF THE CONTRACT   275

9 Non-Agreement Mistake   276

9.1 Introduction   9.2 Categories of common mistake at common law
9.3 Mistake as to quality at common law   9.4 Mistake and allocation of risk
9.5 Common mistake in equity

10   Misrepresentation   292

10.1 Introduction   10.2 Actionable misrepresentations   10.3 Representations
which become terms   10.4 Types of misrepresentation   10.5 Remedies for
misrepresentation   10.6 Excluding or limiting liability for misrepresentation

11   Duress, Undue Influence and Unconscionable Bargains 326

11.1 Duress   11.2 Undue influence   11.3 A doctrine of unconscionable
bargaining?

12   Illegality   348

12.1 Introduction   12.2 Statutory illegality   12.3 Gambling contracts
12.4 Public policy under the common law   12.5 General effect of illegality
12.6 Recovery of money or property   12.7 Contracts in restraint of trade

PART IV   ENFORCEMENT OF CONTRACUAL
OBLIGATIONS   373

13   Damages for Breach of Contract   376

13.1 The aim of contractual damages   13.2 Quantification of loss: lost
expectation   13.3 Quantification of loss: reliance loss   13.4 Quantification
of loss: avoiding double compensation   13.5 Quantification of loss: restitutionary damages   13.6 Consequential loss   13.7 Time for assessment of
loss   13.8 Effect of tax on quantification   13.9 Limitations on the ability to
obtain compensation   13.10 Agreed damages provisions

14   Remedies Providing for Specific Relief
and Restitutionary Remedies   420

14.1 Claim for an agreed sum   14.2 Specific performance   14.3 Injunction
14.4 Restitution

PART V   WHO CAN ENFORCE THE CONTRACT?   439

15   Third Party Rights and the Doctrine of
Privity of Contract   441

15.1 The doctrine of privity of contract   15.2 Criticisms and calls for reform
15.3 The Contracts (Rights of Third Parties) Act 1999   15.4 Means of
circumventing the privity doctrine   15.5 Exceptions to the privity doctrine
15.6 Remedies available to the promisee   15.7 Privity and imposing
obligations upon third parties

16 Assignment and Agency

16.1 Assignment: introduction   16.2 Statutory assignments   16.3 Equitable assignments   16.4 Limits on assignment   16.5 Assignment of the burden of the contract   16.6 Agency: introduction   16.7 Formation of the relationships of agency   16.8 Relationship between principal and third party 16.9 Relationship between principal and agent   16.10 Relationship between agent and third party   16.11 Termination of agency

Index

503

Preface

It is now some fourteen years since Blackstone Press published the first edition of *Textbook on Contract*. At that time it had become clear that traditional textbooks had grown in prominence to such an extent that they were largely being written as comprehensive reference works for other academics rather than to fulfil the needs of students who were often new to the study of law. It is not putting it too strongly therefore, to state that the publication of *Textbook on Contract* was at the forefront of a quiet revolution in legal writing for students being spearheaded by Blackstone Press. Its publication was warmly welcomed by students and those responsible for educating them as a clear, accurate and authoritative account of the law of contract which was highly accessible and reasonably priced, but which also confronted major issues in contract law today in a way that would be comprehensible to those new to the study of contract law. The credit for this quiet revolution must go to Alistair MacQueen, Heather Saward and the team at Blackstone Press but also to those pioneering authors.

My copy of the first edition of *Textbook on Contract* was very well thumbed and I know that the explanations I read as a relatively new academic charged with responsibility for a number of contract 'courses', have greatly influenced my own understanding and appreciation of this subject. As I read through the fifth edition from cover to cover, I was again impressed by its content and, in particular, its treatment of a number of controversial and developing areas of interest. The credit for this belongs to Tony Downes and I am grateful to him for allowing me to retain many sections of the previous editions of this text, especially those with historical and contextual content. There would be little point in changing that which cannot be enhanced or improved upon. I also wish to acknowledge my gratitude to Professor Downes for his support in the writing of this new edition.

In the sixth edition of this *Textbook* I have sought to follow the objectives which underpinned the publication of that first edition, whilst taking this opportunity to expand the treatment of contract law and to present the discussion within a slightly different structure in order to more closely align the *Textbook* with my *Casebook on Contract*.

There have been a number of significant developments since the publication of the fifth edition including the Contracts (Rights of Third Parties) Act 1999, which has allowed for enforcement by third parties in some circumstances, and developments in the context of unfair contract terms, including a decision of the Court of Appeal on the unfairness of a term in a consumer contract under the 1994 Regulations and the replacement of those Regulations by the Unfair Terms in Consumer Contracts Regulations 1999. As always, there has been some interesting (although not always welcome) case law. In particular, the law governing remedies for misrepresentation cries out for a fundamental reappraisal. The potential scope of the decision in *Attorney-General* v *Blake* will inevitably add to the wealth of academic debate surrounding the question of restitutionary damages in contract as an incentive to contractual compliance. This decision, and a vast array of other new cases, is included within the assessment in this edition.

I have also sought to acknowledge the fact that contract law cannot stand still but must develop to meet the needs of our ever-changing society. We are now involved in the study of contract law in a twenty-first century economy with global communications. The impact of the Internet on the process of contracting has a particular interest for students, if the number of e-mails and questions I receive on the topic is a basis for judgment, and therefore I have included discussion of such matters as the legal status of websites, the process of contracting by e-mail and on-line shopping. I have also made reference, where useful and appropriate, to the various sets of principles which have been devised in an attempt to rationalise contract principles at a European and international level. Whilst having no legal force, these principles are likely to be increasingly quoted as offering alternative solutions or confirmation of particular legal principles in English contract law and I am keen to highlight their existence to a wider audience.

In addition to Professor Downes, I would also like to thank everyone at Blackstone Press, especially Heather Saward, Jennifer Cowan and the editorial team for their incredible levels of patience, tolerance and professionalism. I would particularly like to thank Alistair MacQueen for his continuing enthusiasm and to acknowledge his very considerable skills of persuasion. At Cardiff Law School I need to thank Sharron Alldred and James Devenney who have both shielded me from other things and thereby enabled me to find the time to finish this book. I also need to thank Richard Williams, Ph.D. student, for photocopying source materials. It may help current students to know that all my students over the past seventeen years have in some way contributed to my writing, and this book is dedicated to their struggles and many successes.

On the domestic front, I wish to thank my parents, Margaret and Dewi Evans, and my brother, Peter, for their support and for entertaining my son Alex, thereby enabling me to spend hours alone at the computer. Alex deserves a special mention as during these many months he has been deprived of his Internet access, which is a very considerable hardship for any 11 year old. Both children, Becci and Alex, have given me many reasons to be proud of them and I hope that they will also now have some reason to be proud of their mum.

As always, I welcome any comments or questions by e-mail.

Jill Poole
Llandaff, Cardiff
E-mail address: PooleJ@Cardiff.ac.uk

Table of Cases

A. Roberts & Co. Ltd v Leicestershire CC [1961] Ch 555   88
AB Marintrans v Comet Shipping Co. Ltd, The Shinjitsu Maru No. 5
  [1985] 1 WLR 1270   397, 398
AB v South West Water Services Ltd [1993] 1 All ER 609   373
Adams and Brownsword (1990) 53 MLR 536   123
Adams v Lindsell (1818) 1 B & Ald 681   49
Adamson v Jarvis (1827) 4 Bing 66   498
Addis v Gramophone Co. Ltd [1909] AC 488   406, 407, 409, 411
AEG (UK) Ltd v Logic Resource Ltd [1996] CLC 265   166
Aerial Advertising Co. v Batchelors Peas Ltd (Manchester) [1938] 2 All ER 788   411
Ailsa Craig Fishing Co. Ltd v Malvern Fishing Co. Ltd [1983] 1 WLR 964   191, 195
Albazero, The [1977] AC 774   465
Alcher v Rawlins (1872) LR 7 Ch App 259   452
Alder v Moore [1961] 2 QB 57   416
Alderslade v Hendon Laundry Ltd [1945] 1 KB 189   190
Alec Lobb (Garages) Ltd v Total Oil (GB) Ltd [1985] 1 WLR 173   344, 366
Alexander Corfield v David Grant (1992) 59 BLR 102   243
Alexander v Rayson [1936] 1 KB 169   353
Alexander v Rolls Royce Motor Cars [1996] RTR 95   408
Alfred MacAlpine Construction Ltd v Panatown Ltd [2000] 3 WLR 946   467
Alfred Toepfer International GmbH v Itex Itagrani Export SA [1993]
  1 Lloyd's Rep 360   248, 254
Ali v Christian Salvesen Food Services Ltd [1997] 1 All ER 721   173
Allam & Co. Ltd v Europa Poster Services Ltd [1968] 1 All ER 826   495
Allcard v Skinner (1887) 36 ChD 145   337
Allen v Robles [1969] 1 WLR 1193   232
Alliance and Leicester Building Society v Edgestop Ltd [1994] 2 All ER 38   321
Alliance Bank v Broom (1864) 2 Dr & Sm 289   107, 108
Allied Dunbar (Frank Weisinger) Ltd v Weisinger [1988] IRLR 61   363
Allied Maples Group Ltd v Simmons & Simmons (a firm) [1995] 4 All ER 907   385
Allied Maritime Transport Ltd v Vale do Rio Doce Navagacao SA, The Leonidis D
  [1985] 1 WLR 925   29
Allinson v Clayhills (1907) 97 LT 709   496
Alpha Trading Ltd v Dunnshaw-Patten [1981] QB 290   498
Amalgamated Investment & Property Co. Ltd v John Walker & Sons Ltd
  [1977] 1 WLR 164   264, 265, 278
Amalgamated Investment & Property Co. Ltd v Texas Commerce International
  Bank Ltd [1982] QB 84   133

American Cyanamid Co. v Ethicon Ltd [1975] AC 396   371
Anangel Atlas Compania Naviera SA v Ishikawajima-Harima Heavy Industries Co. Ltd
    (No. 2) [1990] 2 Lloyd's Rep 526   106, 121, 124
Anderson Ltd v Daniel [1924] 1 KB 138   351
Andrews Bros (Bournemouth) Ltd v Singer & Co. Ltd [1934] 1 KB 17   188
Andrews v Hopkinson [1957] 1 QB 229   455
Anglia Television Ltd v Reed [1972] 1 QB 60   385, 387
Anglo-Continental Holidays Ltd v Typaldos Lines (London) Ltd
    [1967] 2 Lloyd's Rep 61   205
Antaios Cia Naviera SA v Salen Rederierna AB, The Antaios [1983] 1 WLR 1362
    (affirmed on other grounds [1985] AC 191)   181, 232
Appleby v Myers (1867) LR 2 CP 651   270, 273, 274
Arab Monetary Fund v Hashim [1996] 1 Lloyd's Rep 589   497
Archbolds (Freightage) Ltd v Spanglett Ltd [1961] 1 QB 374   351
Archer v Stone (1898) 78 LT 34   492
Arcos Ltd v Ronassen [1933] AC 470   225
Arctic Shipping Co. Ltd v Mobilia AB [1990] 2 Lloyd's Rep 51   483, 485
Armagas Ltd v Mundogas SA [1986] 1 AC 717   483
Armstrong v Jackson [1917] 2 KB 822   310
Armstrong v Stokes (1872) LR 7 QB 598   493
Associated Japanese Bank (International) Ltd v Credit du Nord SA [1989] 1 WLR 255
                                                            276, 278, 281, 285, 288
Astyanax, The [1985] 2 Lloyd's Rep 109   491
Atkinson v Cotesworth (1825) 3 B & C 647   492
Atlas Express Ltd v Kafco (Importers & Distributors) Ltd [1989] 1 All ER 641   327, 330
Attorney-General for Ceylon v Silva [1953] AC 461   483
Attorney-General of Australia v Adelaide Steamship Co. [1913] AC 781   365
Attorney-General of Hong Kong v Humphreys Estate (Queen's Gardens) Ltd
    [1987] 1 AC 114   134
Attorney-General v Blake [2000] 3 WLR 625   3, 374, 377, 382, 390, 391
Attwood v Lamont [1920] 3 KB 571   362, 369
Attwood v Small (1838) 6 Cl & F 232   301
Australasian Steam Navigation Co. v Morse (1872) LR 4 PC 222   486
Avery v Bowden (1855) E & B 714   253
Avon Finance Co. Ltd v Bridger [1985] 2 All ER 281   90, 336
Avon Insurance plc v Swire Fraser Ltd [2000] 1 All ER (Comm) 573,
    [2000] CLC 665   294, 300, 317
Awwad v Geraghty & Co. (A Firm) [2000] 3 WLR 1041   350

B & S Contracts & Design Ltd v Victor Green Publications Ltd [1984] ICR 419   329
Baden v Société Générale pour Favoriser le Développement du Commerce et de
    l'Industrie en France SA (1982) [1992] 4 All ER 161   89
Baird Textile Holdings Ltd v Marks & Spencer plc (unreported), 28 February 2001   137
Baker v White (1690) 2 Vern 215   354
Balfour Beatty Construction (Scotland) Ltd v Scottish Power plc (1994) 71 BLR 20   401
Balfour v Balfour [1919] 2 KB 571   94, 99, 100
Banco de Portugal v Waterlow [1932] AC 452   405
Banco Exterior Internacional v Mann [1995] 1 All ER 936   341
Bangladesh Export Import Co. Ltd v Sucden Kerry SA [1995] 2 Lloyd's Rep 1   266
Bank Line Ltd v Arthur Capel & Co. [1919] AC 435   260
Bank of Baroda v Rayarel [1995] 2 FCR 631   341
Bank of Credit and Commerce International SA (in liquidation) v Ali (Permission
    to Appeal) (unreported), 4 May 2001 (CA)   385
Bank of Credit and Commerce International SA (in liquidation) v Ali (Stigma Claims)
    [1999] 4 All ER 83   385, 410
Bank of Credit and Commerce International SA v Aboody [1990] 1 QB 923   333
Bank of Cyprus (London) Ltd v Markou [1999] 2 All ER 707   340

Bannerman v White (1861) 10 CB NS 844   155
Banque Bruxelles Lambert SA v Australian National Industries Ltd (1989) 21
  NSWLR 502, noted at [1991] JBL 282   98
Banque Bruxelles Lambert SA v Eagle Star Insurance Co. Ltd [1995] 2 WLR 607,
  [1995] QB 375   395, 403
Banque Financière de la Cité SA v Westgate Insurance Co. Ltd [1989] 2 All ER 952   307
Barber v NWS Bank plc [1996] 1 All ER 906   235
Barclays Bank plc v Boulter [1999] 4 All ER 513   339
Barclays Bank plc v Caplan [1998] FLR 532   308, 338
Barclays Bank plc v Coleman [2000] 3 WLR 405   334, 337, 340, 342
Barclays Bank plc v Fairclough Building Ltd [1995] QB 214   398
Barclays Bank plc v Goff [2001] EWCA Civ 635 (unreported), 3 May 2001   342, 345
Barclays Bank plc v O'Brien [1994] 1 AC 180   333, 334, 336, 339, 340, 342, 345, 347
Barclays Bank plc v Thomson [1997] 4 All ER 816   341
Barron v Fitzgerald (1840) 6 Bing NC 201   498
Barry v Davies (Trading as Heathcote Ball & Co.) [2000] 1 WLR 1962   39
Barton v Armstrong [1976] 1 AC 104   327
Basham, Re [1987] 1 All ER 405   133, 134
Beck & Co. v Szymanowski & Co. [1924] AC 43   188
Behzadi v Shaftesbury Hotels Ltd [1992] Ch 1   238
Belgische Radio en Televisie v SABAM [1974] ECR 51   368
Bell v Lever Bros Ltd [1932] AC 161   280, 281, 283, 284, 286, 287, 288
Bence Graphics International Ltd v Fasson (UK) Ltd [1998] QB 87   380
Bennett v Bennett [1952] 1 KB 249   369
Benyon v Nettlefold (1850) 3 Mac & G 94   354
Beoco Ltd v Alfa Laval Co. Ltd [1994] 4 All ER 464   396
Beswick v Beswick [1966] Ch 538, [1968] AC 58   426, 444, 462, 463, 464, 468
Betterbee v Davis (1811) 3 Camp 70   226
Bettini v Gye (1876) 1 QBD 183   238
BHP Petroleum v British Steel [2000] 2 All ER (Comm) 133   191
BICC plc v Burndy Corporation [1985] 1 All ER 417   419
Bigos v Bousted [1951] 1 All ER 92   353, 358
Birmingham & District Land Co. v LNW Ry Co. (1888) 40 ChD 268   126, 128
Bisset v Wilkinson [1927] AC 177   298
Blackburn Bobbin Co. Ltd v T.W. Allen & Sons Ltd [1918] 2 KB 467   261
Blackpool & Fylde Aero Club v Blackpool Borough Council [1990] 1 WLR 1195
                                                                       38, 39, 61, 73
Blades v Free (1829) 9 B & C 167   485
Bliss v South East Thames Regional Health Authority [1987] ICR 700   407
Bloxsome v Williams (1824) 3 B & C 232   350, 357
Boardman v Phipps [1967] 2 AC 46   496
Bolton Partners v Lambert (1889) 41 ChD 295   488
Bolton v Mahadeva [1972] 1 WLR 1009   244, 246, 247
Boone v Eyre (1779) 1 H Bl 273; 126 ER 160   247
Boston Deep Sea Fishing & Ice Co. Ltd v Farnham [1957] 3 All ER 204   488
Boston Deep Sea Fishing & Ice Co. v Ansell (1888) 39 ChD 339   496
Boulton v Jones (1857) 27 LJ Ex 117   81
Boustany v Pigot (1993) 69 P & CR 298   346
Bowerman v ABTA Ltd [1996] CLC 451   27, 28, 34, 58, 95, 96
Bowmakers Ltd v Barnet Instruments Ltd [1945] KB 65   359
BP Exploration Co. (Libya) Ltd v Hunt (No. 2) [1979] 1 WLR 783 ([1983] 2 AC 352   273
Bradbury v Morgan (1862) 1 Hurl & C 249   55
Brasserie de Haecht v Wilkin (No. 1) [1968] CMLR 26   368
Brasserie de Haecht v Wilkin (No. 2) [1973] CMLR 287   368
Brewer Street Investments Ltd v Barclays Woollen Co Ltd [1954] 1 QB 428   74
Bridge v Campbell Discount Co. Ltd [1962] AC 600   416
Brikom Investments Ltd v Carr [1979] QB 467   126, 129, 133

Brimnes, The [1975] QB 929   52
Brinkibon Ltd v Stahag Stahl und Stahlwarenhandelsgesellschaft mbH GmbH
    [1983] 2 AC 34   52
Bristow v Eastman (1794) 1 Esp 172   148
British & Commonwealth Holdings plc v Quadrex Holdings Inc. [1989] QB 842   237
British Bank for Foreign Trade Ltd v Novinex Ltd [1949] 1 KB 623   67
British Car Auctions Ltd v Wright [1972] 1 WLR 1519   39
British Crane Hire Corporation Ltd v Ipswich Plant Hire Ltd [1975] QB 303   168, 178
British Movietonews Ltd v London & District Cinemas Ltd [1952] AC 166   263
British Steel Corporation v Cleveland Bridge & Engineering Co. Ltd
    [1984] 1 All ER 504   44, 68, 72, 73, 436
British Transport Commission v Gourley [1956] AC 185   394
British Westinghouse Electric and Manufacturing Co. Ltd v Underground Electric
    Railways Co. of London Ltd [1912] AC 673   404, 405
Brogden v Marriot (1836) 3 Bing NC 88   351
Brogden v Metropolitan Railway Co. (1877) 2 App Cas 666   43
Brook's Wharf and Bull Wharf Ltd v Goodman Bros [1937] 1 KB 534   480
Brown v KMR Services Ltd [1995] 4 All ER 598   403
BS & N Ltd (BVI) v Micado Shipping Ltd (Malta) No. 1, The Seaflower
    [2001] 1 Lloyd's Rep 341, [2001] 1 All ER (Comm) 240   241
Bunge Corporation v Tradax Export SA [1980] 1 Lloyd's Rep 294 at 306,
    [1981] 2 All ER 513, [1981] 1 WLR 711   235, 236, 240
Butler Machine Tool Co. Ltd v Ex-Cell-O-Corporation (England) Ltd
    [1979] 1 WLR 401   31, 45
Butwick v Grant [1924] 2 KB 483   490
Byrne & Co. v Van Tienhoven & Co. (1880) 5 CPD 344   57

C & P Haulage v Middleton [1983] 1 WLR 1461   386, 394
C (a debtor), Re (1994) The Times, 11 May   118, 121, 124, 128
C.H. Giles & Co. Ltd. v Morris [1972] 1 All ER 960   427
Calico Printers' Association v Barclays Bank (1931) 145 LT 51   495
Campanari v Woodburn (1854) 15 CB 400   502
Canada Steamship Lines v The King [1952] AC 192   189
Caparo Industries plc v Dickman [1990] 1 All ER 568   305
Car and Universal Finance Co. Ltd v Caldwell [1961] 1 QB 525   309
Carillion Construction Ltd v Felix (UK) Ltd [2001] BLR 1   330
Carlill v Carbolic Smoke Ball Co. [1893] 1 QB 256   34, 47, 58, 94, 103, 152, 351
Carlton Hall Club Ltd v Laurence [1929] 2 KB 153   353
Carney v Herbert [1985] 1 All ER 438   370
Carter and Tolhurst (1996) 10 JCL 264   272
Cartwright v Cartwright (1853) 3 De G M & G 982   354
Casey's Patents, Re [1892] 1 Ch 104   110, 111
Cassell & Co. Ltd v Broome [1972] AC 1027   373
CCC Films (London) Ltd v Impact Quadrant Films Ltd [1985] 1 QB 16   387
Cehave NV v Bremer Handelsgesellschaft mbh, The Hansa Nord [1976] QB 44 235, 247, 254
Cellulose Acetate Silk Co. Ltd v Widnes Foundry (1925) Ltd [1933] AC 20   412
Cenargo Ltd v Empresa Nacional Bazan de Construcciones Navales Militares SA
    (unreported), 30 January 2001   414
Central London Property Trust Ltd v High Trees House Ltd [1947] KB 130
                                       127, 128, 130, 131, 132, 133, 136
Centrovincial Estates plc v Merchant Investors Assurance Company Ltd
    [1983] Com LR 158   30, 79, 80
Chandler v Webster [1904] 1 KB 493   270
Channel Home Centers Division of Grace Retail Corporation v Grossman 795 F 2d 291
    (1986)   70
Chapelton v Barry Urban District Council [1940] 1 KB 532   35, 163
Chaplin v Hicks [1911] 2 KB 786   384, 385

Chaplin v Leslie Frewin (Publishers) Ltd [1965] 3 All ER 764   147
Chappell & Co. Ltd v Nestlé Co. Ltd [1960] AC 87   103, 105, 106
Charge Card Services, Re [1988] 3 All ER 702   36
Charter v Sullivan [1957] 2 QB 117   379
Chaudhry v Prabhakar [1988] 3 All ER 718   494
Cheese v Thomas [1994] 1 WLR 129   338
Chemco Leasing SpA v Rediffusion [1987] 1 FTLR 201, CA   55
Chester Grosvenor Hotel Co. Ltd v Alfred McAlpine Management Ltd
    (1991) 56 BLR 115   201
Chestertons v Barone [1987] 1 EGLR 15   493
Chichester Joinery v John Mowlem & Co. (1987) 42 BLR 100   45
China Pacific SA v Food Corporation of India [1982] AC 939   485, 486
CIBC Mortgages plc v Pitt [1994] 1 AC 200   332, 334, 337, 339, 340
Circle Freight International Ltd v Medeast Gulf Exports Ltd [1988] 2 Lloyd's Rep 427 169
Citibank NA v Brown Shipley & Co. Ltd [1991] 2 All ER 690   86
City and Westminster Properties (1934) Ltd v Mudd [1959] Ch 129   159
Clarion Ltd v National Provincial Institution [2000] 2 WLR 1888   290
Clarke v Dickson (1858) EB & E 148   310
Clarke v Dunraven [1897] AC 59   31
Clarkson, Booker Ltd v Andjel [1964] 2 QB 775   493
Clay v Yates (1856) 1 Hurl & N 73   354
Clea Shipping Corp v Bulk Oil International Ltd, The Alaskan Trader
    [1984] 1 All ER 129   250, 251, 421
Clef Aquitaine SARL v Laporte Materials (Barrow) Ltd [2000] 3 WLR 1760   300, 314
Clifton v Palumbo [1944] 2 All ER 497   33
Clough v London and North Western Railway Co. (1871) LR 7 Ex 26   231
Co-operative Insurance Society Ltd v Argyll Stores (Holdings) Ltd
    [1997] 2 WLR 898   426, 427, 428
Coastal Estates Pty Ltd v Melevende [1965] VR 433   231
Coates v Lewes (1808) 1 Camp 444   493
Collen v Wright (1857) 8 El & Bl 647   501
Collins v Godefroy (1831) 1 B & Ad 950   113, 114
Combe v Combe [1951] 2 KB 215   129, 130, 137
Commercial Bank of Australia Ltd v Amadio (1983) 151 CLR 447   344, 345
Commission for the New Towns v Cooper (GB) Ltd [1995] Ch 259   89, 140
Commonwealth of Australia v Verwayen (1990) 170 CLR 394   124, 136
Compagnie Commerciale Sucres et Denrées v C. Czarnikow Ltd, The Naxos
    [1990] 1 WLR 1337   235, 236
Consten & Grundig v Commission [1966] ECR 299   368
Cook v Lister (1863) 13 CB (NS) 543   120
Cooper v Phibbs (1867) LR 2 HL 149   280, 287, 288
Coote (1990) 3 JCL 23   123
Coral (UK) Ltd v Rechtman [1996] 1 Lloyd's Rep 235   499
Cornish v Midland Bank Ltd [1985] 3 All ER 513   336
Corporacion Nacionale del Cobre de Chile v Sogemin Metals Ltd [1997] 1 WLR 1396   321
Couchman v Hill [1947] KB 554   158, 191
Coulls v Bagot's Executor & Trustee Co. (1967) 119 CLR 460   442, 443
Coulthart v Clementson (1879) 5 QBD 42   55
Countess of Dunmore v Alexander (1830) 9 S 190   51
Countrywide Communications Ltd v ICL Pathway Ltd [2000] CLC 324   73
County Ltd v Girozentrale Securities [1996] 3 All ER 834   395
County Natwest Ltd v Barton [1999] Lloyd's Rep Bank 408   301
Couturier v Hastie (1856) 5 HL Cas 673   279, 486
Crabb v Arun District Council [1976] Ch 179   133, 134
Craven-Ellis v Canons Ltd [1936] 2 KB 403   436
Credit Lyonnais Bank Nederland NV v Burch [1997] 1 All ER 144   342, 345, 346, 347
Cremdean Properties Ltd v Nash (1977) 244 EG 547   323

Cresswell v Potter [1978] 1 WLR 255   346
Cricklewood Property and Investment Trust Ltd v Leighton's Investment Trust Ltd
   [1945] AC 221   264
CTN Cash and Carry Ltd v Gallagher Ltd [1994] 4 All ER 714   331
Cullinane v British 'Rema' Manufacturing Co. Ltd [1954] 1 QB 292   387
Cundy v Lindsay (1878) 3 App Cas 459   83, 85
Currie v Misa (1875) LR 10 Ex 153   101
Curtis v Chemical Cleaning & Dyeing Co. Ltd [1951] 1 KB 805   162, 192, 294
Cutter v Powell (1795) 6 TR 320   244, 246, 270

D & C Builders v Rees [1966] 2 QB 617   131, 327
D & F Estates Ltd v Church Commissioners for England [1989] AC 177   451
Damon Compania Naviera SA v Hapag-Lloyd International SA [1985] 1 All ER 475   417
Darlington Borough Council v Wiltshier Northern Ltd [1995] 1 WLR 68   444, 466, 468
Darlington Futures Ltd v Delco Australia Pty Ltd (1986) 161 CLR 500   191
Dataliner Ltd v Vehicle Builders and Repairers Association (1995) Independent,
   30 August   386, 387
Daulia Ltd v Four Millbank Nominees Ltd [1978] Ch 231   59, 61
Davies v Collins [1945] 1 All ER 247   479
Davis Contractors Ltd v Fareham UDC [1956] AC 696   257, 258, 262, 266
Davis v Churchward (unreported), 6 May 1993   315
De Bussche v Alt (1878) 8 ChD 286   494, 495
De Francesco v Barnum (1890) 45 ChD 430   146, 428
De la Bere v Pearson [1908] 1 KB 280   108
De Meza v Apple [1974] 1 Lloyd's Rep 508   398
Deacons v Bridge [1984] 2 All ER 19   364
Dean v Ainley [1987] 1 WLR 1729   394
Dearle v Hall (1823) 3 Russ 1   477
Debenham's Ltd v Perkins (1925) 133 LT 252   489
Debenham v Mellon (1880) 6 App Cas 24   485
Decro-Wall International SA v Practitioners in Marketing Ltd
   [1971] 1 WLR 361   229, 249
Deepak Fertilisers & Petrochemical Corporation v Davy McKee (London) Ltd
   [1999] 1 Lloyd's Rep 387   160
Denne v Light (1857) DM & G 774   429
Denny, Mott & Dickson v James B. Fraser & Co. Ltd [1944] AC 265   259
Derry v Peek (1889) 14 App Cas 337   303, 312
Devonald v Rosser [1906] 2 KB 728   173
Dick Bentley Productions Ltd v Harold Smith (Motors) Ltd [1965] 1 WLR 623
                                                                           154, 155, 156
Dickinson v Dodds (1876) 2 ChD 463   56
Dies v British & International Mining & Finance Corporation Ltd [1939] 1 KB 724   417
Diggle v Higgs (1872) 2 ExD 422   352
Dillwyn v Llewelyn (1862) 4 De GF & J 517   134
Dimmock v Hallett (1866) LR 2 Ch App 21   295
Dimskal Shipping Co. SA v International Transport Workers' Federation,
   The Evia Luck [1991] 4 All ER 871   327, 329
Director General of Fair Trading v First National Bank plc [2000] 2 WLR 1353
                                                                     23, 218, 220, 223, 345
Donoghue v Stevenson [1932] AC 562   4, 440, 451
Downs v Chappell [1997] 1 WLR 461   313, 315
Doyle v Olby (Ironmongers) Ltd [1969] 2 QB 158   304, 312, 313, 314, 315, 316
Drew v Nunn (1879) 4 QBD 661   502
DSND Subsea Ltd v Petroleum Geo Services ASA [2000] BLR 530   328, 329, 330
Dunbar Bank plc v Nadeem [1998] 3 All ER 876   338, 340, 345
Dunlop Pneumatic Tyre Co. Ltd v New Garage and Motor Co. Ltd
   [1915] AC 79   412, 414, 415

Dunlop Pneumatic Tyre Co. Ltd v Selfridge & Co. Ltd [1915] AC 847
                                                                    102, 441, 442, 444, 455
Dunlop v Lambert (1839) 6 Cl & F 600   465
Durham Bros v Robertson [1898] 1 QB 765   473
Durham Fancy Goods Ltd v Michael Jackson (Fancy Goods) Ltd [1968] 2 QB 839   126
Dyster v Randall & Sons [1926] Ch 932   492

E. Pfeiffer Weinkellerei-Weineinkauf GmbH & Co. v Arbuthnot Factors Ltd
     [1988] 1 WLR 150   475, 477
E.E. Caledonia Ltd v Orbit Valve Co. plc [1994] 1 WLR 1515   190, 191
East Ham Corporation v Bernard Sunley & Sons Ltd [1966] AC 406   393
East v Maurer [1991] 1 WLR 461   314, 315, 316
Eastham v Newcastle United Football Club Ltd [1964] Ch 413   367
Ebrahim Dawood Ltd v Heath (Est. 1927) Ltd [1961] Lloyd's Rep 512   434
Ecay v Godfrey (1947) 80 Lloyd's Rep 286   154
Economides v Commercial Union Assurance Co. plc [1997] 3 WLR 1066   298
Edgington v Fitzmaurice (1885) 24 ChD 459   299, 302
Edmonds v Lawson [2000] QB 501   28, 93, 98, 105
Edmund Murray Ltd v BSP International Foundations Ltd (1992) 33 Con LR 1   192, 212
Edwards v Carter [1893] AC 360   147
Elder, Dempster & Co. v Paterson, Zochonis & Co. Ltd [1924] AC 522   458
Ellis v Torrington [1920] 1 KB 399   478
Entores Ltd v Miles Far East Corporation [1955] 2 QB 327   51, 53
Erlanger v New Sombrero Phosphate Co. (1878) 3 App Cas 1218   310
Errington v Errington [1952] 1 KB 290   59, 60
Esso Petroleum Co. Ltd v Commissioners of Customs & Excise [1976] 1 WLR 1   96
Esso Petroleum Co. Ltd v Harper's Garage (Stourport) Ltd [1968] AC 269   363, 366
Esso Petroleum Co. Ltd v Mardon [1976] QB 801   156, 157, 299, 306, 494
Etherington v Parrot (1703) 1 Salk 118   485
Eugenia, The [1964] 2 QB 226   262, 267, 396
Eurico SpA v Philipp Brothers [1987] 2 Lloyd's Rep 215   265
Euro-Diam Ltd v Bathurst [1988] 2 All ER 23   357
European Asian Bank AG v Punjab and Sind Bank (No. 2) [1983] 3 All ER 508   481
Eurymedon, The see New Zealand Shipping Co. Ltd v A. M. Satterthwaite & Co. Ltd
Evans Marshall & Co. Ltd v Bertola SA [1973] 1 All ER 992   431, 426
Export Credit Guarantee Department v Universal Oil Products Co. [1983] 1 WLR 399   416

F. Drughorn Ltd v Rederiaktiebolaget Trans-Atlantic [1919] AC 203   491
F.A. Tamplin Steamship Co. Ltd v Anglo-Mexican Petroleum Products Co. Ltd
     [1916] 2 AC 397   257, 260
Fairclough Building Ltd v Port Talbot BC (1993) 62 BLR 82   39
Falcke v Scottish Imperial Insurance Co. (1886) 34 ChD 234   486
Famosa Shipping Co. Ltd v Armada Bulk Carriers Ltd [1994] 1 Lloyd's Rep 633   405
Far Eastern Shipping Co. Ltd v Scales Trading Ltd [2001] 1 All ER (Comm) 319   308, 338
Farley v Skinner (No. 2) [2000] PNLR 441, [2000] EGCS 52   408
Federal Commerce and Navigation Ltd v Molena Alpha Inc. [1979] AC 757   253
Felthouse v Bindley (1862) 11 CB NS 869   47, 48
Fercometal SARL v Mediterranean Shipping Co. SA, The Simona [1989] AC 788   249, 252
Ferguson v Davies [1997] 1 All ER 315, 323   107, 128
Fibrosa SA v Fairbairn Lawson Combe Barbour Ltd [1943] AC 32   259, 270, 271, 433
First Energy (UK) Ltd v Hungarian International Bank Ltd [1993] 2 Lloyd's Rep 194   484
Firstpost Homes Ltd v Johnson [1995] 4 All ER 355   139
Firth v Staines [1897] 2 QB 70   487
Fisher v Bell [1961] 1 QB 394   35
Fisher v Bridges (1854) 3 El & Bl 642   357
Fitzgerald v Dressler (1858) 7 CB NS 374   143
Floods of Queenferry Ltd v Shand Construction Ltd [2000] BLR 81   308, 319

Foakes v Beer (1884) 9 App Cas 605   120, 121, 122, 128, 129, 135
Foley v Classique Coaches Ltd [1934] 2 KB 1   70, 111
Foley v Hill (1848) 2 HL Cas 28   497
Ford Motor Co. Ltd v AUEFW [1969] 2 QB 303   98
Forman & Co. Pty Ltd v The Liddesdale [1900] AC 190   486
Forsikringsaktieselskapet Vesta v Butcher [1986] 2 All ER 488   397, 398
Forster v Baker [1910] 2 KB 636   473
Fortescue v Barnett (1834) 3 My & K 36   476
Fraser River Pile & Dredge Ltd v Can-Dive Services Ltd [2000] 1 Lloyd's Rep 199   445, 461
Fray v Voules (1859) 1 El & El 839   494
Frederick E. Rose (London) Ltd v William H. Pim Junior & Co. Ltd
   [1953] 2 QB 450   88, 283
Freeman & Lockyer v Buckhurst Park Properties (Mangal) Ltd [1964] 2 QB 480   482, 483
Frost v Knight (1872) LR 7 Ex 111   248
Fry v Lane (1888) 40 ChD 312   184, 346, 347

G. Percy Trentham Ltd v Archital Luxfer Ltd [1993] 1 Lloyd's Rep 25   67
Gallie v Lee [1971] AC 1004   90
Galloway v Galloway (1914) 30 TLR 531   277
Galoo Ltd v Bright Grahame Murray [1995] 1 All ER 16   394
Gamerco SA v ICM/Fair Warning (Agency) Ltd [1995] 1 WLR 1226   258, 272
Gamerco v ICM   273
Garnac Grain Co. Inc. v H.M.F. Faure & Fairclough Ltd [1968] AC 1130   393
Geier v Kujawa Weston and Warne Bros (Transport) Ltd [1970] 1 Lloyd's Rep 364   164
General Bill Posting Co. Ltd v Atkinson [1909] AC 118, HL   364
George Mitchell (Chesterhall) Ltd v Finney Lock Seeds Ltd
   [1983] 2 AC 803   187, 191, 195, 207, 208, 209
Gibbons v Proctor (1891) 64 LT 594   41, 42
Gibson v Manchester City Council [1978] 1 WLR 520, [1979] 1 WLR 294   31, 33
Gill & Duffus SA v Berger & Co. Inc. [1984] AC 382   229
Gillatt v Sky Television Ltd [2000] 1 All ER (Comm) 461   71
Gillett v Holt [2001] Ch 210   134, 135
Giumelli v Giumelli (1999) 163 ALR 473   136
Glasbrook Brothers Ltd v Glamorgan County Council [1925] AC 270   113
Glegg v Bromley [1912] 3 KB 474   475
Goldsoll v Goldman [1915] 1 Ch 292   369
Goldsworthy v Brickell [1987] 1 All ER 853   332
Gordon v Gordon (1819) 3 Swan 400   297
Gordon v Sellico (1986) 278 EG 53   294
Gore v Van der Lann [1967] 2 QB 31   463
Goss v Chilcott [1997] 2 All ER 110   433, 434
Gould v Gould [1970] 1 QB 275   99
Government of Zanzibar v British Aerospace (Lancaster House) Ltd [2000] 1 WLR 2333,
   [2000] CLC 735   308, 310, 319, 324, 325
Grainger & Sons v Gough [1896] AC 325   34
Gran Gelato Ltd v Richcliff (Group) Ltd [1992] Ch 560   321, 322
Gray v Barr [1971] 2 QB 554   354
Gray v Southouse [1949] 2 All ER 1019   359
Great Northern Railway Co. v Witham (1873) LR 9 CP 16   58, 62
Greer v Downs Supply Co. [1927] 2 KB 28   491
Greig v Insole [1978] 1 WLR 302   366
Griffith v Brymer (1903) 19 TLR 434   278
Griffith v Tower Publishing Co. Ltd [1897] 1 Ch 21   479
Grist v Bailey [1967] Ch 532   288, 290
Grogan v Robin Meredith Plant Hire [1996] CLC 1127   162, 164, 168
Grover & Grover v Mathews [1910] 2 KB 401   487

H. Parsons (Livestock) Ltd v Uttley Ingham & Co. Ltd [1978] 1 QB 791   6, 402, 403
Hadley v Baxendale (1854) 9 Exch 341   153, 399, 402, 423
Halifax Mortgage Services Ltd v Stepsky [1996] Ch 207   341
Hallett's Estate, Re (1880) 13 ChD 696   497
Hannah Blumenthal, The [1983] 1 AC 854, [1983] 1 All ER 34   27, 29, 118, 227
Harbutts' 'Plasticine' Ltd v Wayne Tank and Pump Co. Ltd [1970] 1 QB 447   194
Harding v Harding (1886) 17 QBD 442   473
Hardman v Booth (1863) 1 H & C 803   81
Hardwick Game Farm v Suffolk Agricultural Poultry Producers Association
    [1969] 2 AC 31   167
Hargreaves Transport Ltd v Lynch [1969] 1 WLR 215   169
Harris v Nickerson (1873) LR 8 QB 286   39
Harris v Sheffield United Football Club Ltd [1987] 2 All ER 838   114
Harse v Pearl Life Assurance Co. [1904] 1 KB 558   359
Hart v O'Connor [1985] AC 1000   145
Hartog v Colin & Shields [1939] 3 All ER 566   30, 37, 79, 80
Harvela Investments Ltd v Royal Trust Co. of Canada [1986] AC 207   37, 38, 61, 62
Harvey v Facey [1893] AC 552   33
Harvey v Ventilatorenfabrik Oelde GmbH (1988) 8 Tr LR 138   162
Hayes v James & Charles Dodd [1990] 2 All ER 815   408
Head v Tattersall (1871) LR 7 Ex 7   169
Heald v Kenworthy (1855) 10 Ex 739   490
Hedley Byrne & Co. Ltd v Heller & Partners Ltd [1964] AC 465
    109, 153, 304, 306, 307, 315, 316, 317, 321, 495
Heilbut, Symons & Co. v Buckleton [1913] AC 30   153, 154, 156
Henderson v Arthur [1907] 1 KB 10   157, 159
Henderson v Merrett Syndicates Ltd [1994] 3 All ER 506, [1995] 2 AC 145
    4, 5, 171, 305, 306, 495
Henthorn v Fraser [1892] 2 Ch 27   49
Herbert Morris Ltd v Saxelby [1916] AC 688   362, 363
Hermann v Charlesworth [1905] 2 KB 123   354
Herne Bay Steam Boat Co. v Hutton [1903] 2 KB 683   264
Heron II, The [1969] 1 AC 350   6, 400, 402
Heywood v Wellers [1976] QB 466   407
Hill v William Hill (Park Lane) Ltd [1949] AC 530   352
Hillas & Co. Ltd v Arcos Ltd (1932) 147 LT 503   64, 65, 67, 171
Hine Brothers v Steamship Insurance Syndicate Ltd (1895) 72 LT 79   490
Hirachand Punamchand v Temple [1911] 2 KB 330   120
Hirji Mulji v Cheong Yue Steamship Co. Ltd [1926] AC 497   258, 269
Hitchens, Harrison, Woolston & Co. v Jackson & Sons [1943] AC 266   500
Hobbs v London & South Western Railway Co. (1875) LR 10 QB 111   406
Hochster v De La Tour (1853) 2 E & B 678, 118 ER 922   248, 251
Hoenig v Isaacs [1952] 2 All ER 176   245, 247
Hollier v Rambler Motors (AMC) Ltd [1972] 2 QB 71   168, 187
Holman v Johnson (1775) 1 Cowp 341   355, 357
Holt v Heatherfield Trust Ltd [1942] 2 KB 1   474
Holwell Securities Ltd v Hughes [1974] 1 WLR 155   50, 56
Home Counties Dairies Ltd v Skilton [1970] 1 WLR 526   364
Hong Kong Fir Shipping Co. Ltd v Kawasaki Kisen Kaisha Ltd [1962] 2 QB 26
    234, 239, 240, 241, 254
Horsfall v Thomas (1862) 1 H & C 90   294, 295, 300
Horton v Horton (No. 2) [1961] 1 QB 215   107
Hotel Services Ltd v Hilton International Hotels (UK) Ltd [2000] 1 All ER
    (Comm) 750   401
Houghton v Trafalgar Insurance Co. Ltd [1954] 1 QB 247   188
Hounslow London Borough Council v Twickenham Garden Developments Ltd
    [1971] Ch 233   249, 250

Household Fire and Carriage Accident Insurance Co. Ltd v Grant (1879) 4 ExD 216   49
Howard Marine & Dredging Co. Ltd v A. Ogden & Sons (Excavations) Ltd
   [1978] QB 574   307, 323
Howard v Baillie (1796) 2 H Bl 618   481
Howard v Sheward (1866) LR 2 CP 148   481
Howard v Shirlstar Container Transport Ltd [1990] 3 All ER 366   356
Howe v Smith (1884) 27 ChD 89   416
Howell v Coupland (1876) 1 QBD 258   261
Huddersfield Banking Co. Ltd v Henry Lister & Son Ltd [1895] 2 Ch 273   287
Hudson v Shogun Finance Ltd [2001] EWCA Civ 100, (2001) The Times, 4 July   85
Hughes v Asset Managers plc [1995] 3 All ER 669   351
Hughes v Clewley (No. 2) [1996] 1 Lloyd's Rep 35   356
Hughes v Greenwich London Borough Council [1993] 3 WLR 821   173
Hughes v Liverpool Victoria Legal Friendly Society [1916] 2 KB 482   359
Hughes v Metropolitan Railway Co. (1877) 2 App Cas 439
   125, 126, 127, 128, 129, 130, 131, 132
Humble v Hunter (1848) 12 QB 310   491
Hummingbird Motors Ltd v Hobbs [1986] RTR 276   298
Hunt v Silk (1804) 5 East 449   435
Hussey v Eels [1990] 2 QB 227   318
Hutton v Warren (1836) 1 M & W 466   170, 177
Huyton SA v Peter Cremer GmbH & Co. [1999] 1 Lloyd's Rep 620   330, 332
Hyde v Wrench (1840) 3 Beav 334   42
Hydraulic Engineering Co. Ltd v McHaffie, Goslett & Co. (1878) 4 QBD 670   387
Hyman v Hyman [1929] AC 601   354
Hyundai Heavy Industries Co. v Papadopolous [1980] 1 WLR 1129   417

Imperial Loan Co. v Stone [1892] 1 QB 599   145
Industrie Chimiche Italia Centrale v Alexander G. Tsavliris & Sons Maritime Co.
   [1990] 1 Lloyd's Rep 516   481
Ingram v Little [1961] 1 QB 31   84, 85, 86
Inntrepreneur Pub Co. v East Crown Ltd [2000] 2 Lloyd's Rep 611
   153, 154, 159, 160, 324, 325
Interfoto Picture Library Ltd v Stiletto Visual Programmes Ltd
   [1989] 1 QB 433   22, 161, 162, 166, 187
Investors Compensation Scheme Ltd v West Bromwich Building Society
   [1998] 1 All ER 98   180, 182
Inwards v Baker [1965] 2 QB 507   135
Ireland v Livingston (1872) LR 5 HL 395   481
Irvani v Irvani [2000] 1 Lloyd's Rep 412   345
Irvine & Co. v Watson & Sons (1880) 5 QBD 414   490, 493
Isaac Cooke and Sons v Eshelby (1887) 12 App Cas 271   493
Israel Cocoa Ltd v Nigerian Produce Marketing Co. Ltd [1972] AC 741   128

J. Evans & Son (Portsmouth) Ltd v Andrea Merzario Ltd [1976] 1 WLR 1078   158, 159, 191
J. Lauritzen AS v Wijsmuller BV, The Super Servant Two [1990] 1 Lloyd's Rep 1
   255, 261, 268, 269
J. Murphy & Sons Ltd v ABB Daimler-Benz Transportation (Signal) Ltd (unreported),
   2 December 1998   68
J. Spurling Ltd v Bradshaw [1956] 1 WLR 461   162
J.A. Mont (UK) Ltd v Mills [1993] IRLR 172   370
Jackson v Horizon Holidays Ltd [1975] 1 WLR 1468   407, 464, 465, 468
Jackson v Rotax Motor and Cycle Co. [1910] 2 KB 937   244
Jackson v Union Marine Insurance Co. Ltd (1874) LR 10 CP 125   260, 261
Jacob & Youngs v Kent (1921) 230 NY 239   381, 382, 383
Jacobs v Morris [1902] 1 Ch 816   480
James McNaughton Papers Group Ltd v Hicks Anderson & Co. [1991] 1 All ER 134   306

James v Evans [2000] 42 EG 173   142
Janred Properties Ltd v Ente Nazionale Italiano per il Turismo [1989] 2 All ER 444   393
Jarvis v Swans Tours Ltd [1973] QB 233   407, 409
Jayaar Impex Ltd v Toaken Group Ltd [1996] 2 Lloyd's Rep 437   43
Jobson v Johnson [1989] 1 WLR 1026   413, 418
Johnson v Agnew [1980] AC 367   229, 392, 431
Johnson v Gore Wood & Co. [2001] 2 WLR 72   407, 408, 411
Johnson v Unisys Ltd [2001] UKHL 13, [2001] 2 WLR 1076   408, 409, 410
Johnstone v Bloomsbury Health Authority [1992] 1 QB 333   171, 172
Jones v Daniel [1894] 2 Ch 332   42
Jones v Padavatton [1969] 1 WLR 328   100
Jones v Vernon's Pools Ltd [1938] 2 All ER 626   96
Jorden v Money (1854) 5 HL Cas 185   128
Joscelyne v Nissen [1970] 2 QB 86   87, 88
Joseph Constantine Steamship Line Ltd v Imperial Smelting Corporation Ltd
    [1942] AC 154   268
Junior Books Ltd v Veitchi Co. Ltd [1983] 1 AC 520   451

Kaines (UK) Ltd v Osterreichische Warrenhandelsgesellschaft Austrowaren GmbH
    [1993] 2 Lloyd's Rep 1   393, 405
Kall-Kwik Printing (UK) Ltd v Rush [1996] FSR 114   362
Kalsep Ltd v X-Flow BV (2001) The Times, 3 May   285, 346
Kearley v Thomson (1890) 24 QBD 742   358
Keates v The Earl of Cadogan (1851) 10 CB 591   295
Keighley, Maxsted & Co. v Durant [1901] AC 240   487, 490
Keir v Leeman (1846) 6 QB 308   354
Kelly v Cooper [1993] AC 205   496
Kelner v Baxter (1866) LR 2 CP 174   487, 499
Kennedy v Panama, New Zealand and Australian Royal Mail Co.
    (1867) LR 2 QB 580   281
Kerr v Morris [1986] 3 All ER 217   364
King's Norton Metal Co. Ltd v Edridge, Merrett & Co. (1897) 14 TLR 98   82
Kingston v Preston (1773) 2 Doug 689   241
Kleinwort Benson Ltd v Birmingham CC [1997] QB 380   433
Kleinwort Benson Ltd v Lincoln CC [1998] 4 All ER 513   433
Kleinwort Benson Ltd v Malaysia Mining Corporation Bhd [1989] 1 WLR 379   95, 97, 98
Kpohraror v Woolwich Building Society [1996] 4 All ER 119   401, 403, 411
Krell v Henry [1903] 2 KB 740   264, 278

L. Schuler AG v Wickman Machine Tools Sales Ltd [1974] AC 235   234
L'Estrange v E. Graucob Ltd [1934] 2 KB 394   27, 161, 162
Lake v Simmons [1927] AC 487   82
Lambert v Co-operative Insurance Society Ltd [1975] 2 Lloyd's Rep 485   297
Lampleigh v Brathwait (1615) Hob 105   110
Lansing Linde Ltd v Kerr [1991] 1 All ER 418   371
Lasky v Economy Grocery Stores 65 NE 2d 305 (1946)   36
Lawrence David Ltd v Ashton [1991] 1 All ER 385   371
Lazenby Garages Ltd v Wright [1976] 1 WLR 459   379
Leaf v International Galleries [1950] 2 KB 86   282, 284, 310
Lease Management Services Ltd v Purnell Secretarial Services Ltd
    (1993) 13 Tr LR 337   192, 212, 482
Lee v GEC Plessey Telecommunications [1993] IRLR 383   106
Lefkowitz v Great Minneapolis Surplus Store, 86 NW 2d 689 (1957)   34, 36
Leigh and Sillavan Ltd v Aliakmon Shipping Co. Ltd [1986] AC 785   457
Lemenda Trading Co. Ltd v African Middle East Petroleum Co. Ltd
    [1988] 1 All ER 513   355
Les Affréteurs Réunis SA v Leopold Walford (London) Ltd [1919] AC 801   455

Lewis v Averay [1972] 1 QB 198   81, 82, 83, 84, 85
Lewis v Clay (1897) 67 LJ QB 224   89
Lewis v Samuel (1846) 8 QB 685   498
Lilley v Rankin (1887) 56 LJ QB 248   352
Linden Gardens Trust Ltd v Lenesta Sludge Disposals Ltd [1994] 1 AC 85
                                                         465, 466, 467, 478
Lipkin Gorman v Karpnale Ltd [1987] 1 WLR 987, [1991] 2 AC 548   105, 388, 397, 432
Lips Maritime Corporation v President of India, The Lips [1987] 1 All ER 957,
   [1988] AC 395   400, 423
Lister v Romford Ice and Cold Storage Co. Ltd [1957] AC 555   176
Liverpool City Council v Irwin [1977] AC 239   172, 173, 174, 177, 178, 226, 242
Living Design (Home Improvements) Ltd v Davidson [1994] IRLR 69   370
Lloyd's v Harper (1880) 16 ChD 290   455, 464, 468
Lloyd's Bank Ltd v Bundy [1975] QB 326   336, 343, 344
Lloyd's Bank plc v Waterhouse [1991] Fam Law 23   90
Lock International v Beswick [1989] 1 WLR 1268   371
Lodder v Slowey [1904] AC 442   437
Logicrose Ltd v Southend United Football Club Ltd [1988] 1 WLR 1256   495
Lombard North Central plc v Butterworth [1987] 1 QB 527   234
London, Chatham and Dover Railway Co. v South Eastern Railway Co.
   [1893] 1 AC 429   422
London Drugs Ltd v Kuehne & Nagel International Ltd (1993) 97 DLR (4th) 261
                                                              445, 460, 461
Long v Lloyd [1958] 1 WLR 753   309
Lord Strathcona Steamship Co. Ltd v Dominion Coal Co. Ltd [1926] AC 108   469, 470
Lovell & Christmas Ltd v Wall (1911) 104 LT 85   180
Lumley v Gye (1853) 2 E & B 216   469
Lumley v Ravenscroft [1895] 1 QB 683   147
Lumley v Wagner (1852) 1 De GM & G 604   428
Luxor (Eastbourne) Ltd v Cooper [1941] AC 108   61, 497, 498
Lynch v DPP for Northern Ireland [1975] AC 653   329

Macdonald v Green [1951] 1 KB 594   353
Mackay v Dick (1881) 6 App Cas 251   169
Magee v Pennine Insurance Co. Ltd [1969] 2 QB 507   288
Mahesan v Malaysia Government-Officers' Cooperative Housing Society Ltd
   [1979] AC 374   496
Mahkutai, The [1996] 3 All ER 502   446, 460
Mahmoud and Ispahani, Re [1921] 2 KB 716   350, 357
Mahmud v BCCI, Re see Malik v Bank of Credit and Commerce International SA
Mahoney v Purnell [1996] 3 All ER 61   338
Malik v Bank of Credit and Commerce International SA (in liquidation)
   [1998] AC 20   409, 410
Manchester Diocesan Council of Education v Commercial & General Investments Ltd
   [1970] 1 WLR 241   50
Mann v Nunn (1874) 30 LT 526   159
Mannai Investment Co. Ltd v Eagle Star Life Assurance Co. Ltd [1997] 2 WLR 945 180
Marcan Shipping (London) Ltd v Polish Steamship Co. [1989] 2 Lloyd's Rep 138   498
Maritime National Fish Ltd v Ocean Trawlers Ltd [1935] AC 524   268
Marshall v Harland & Wolff Ltd [1972] 2 All ER 715   259
Marshall v NM Financial Management Ltd [1995] 4 All ER 785   370
Martin-Baker Aircraft Co. Ltd v Canadian Flight Equipment Ltd [1955] 2 QB 556 502
Mason v Provident Clothing and Supply Co. Ltd [1913] AC 724   362, 364
Massey v Midland Bank plc [1995] 1 All ER 929   336, 341
Matthews v Baxter (1873) LR 8 Ex 132   146
May & Butcher v R [1934] 2 KB 17n   69, 70, 71
McArdle, Re [1951] Ch 669   110, 111, 475

McCausland v Duncan Lawrie Ltd [1997] 1 WLR 38   140, 141
McCullagh v Lane Fox and Partners Ltd [1996] 1 EGLR 35   305
McCutcheon v David MacBrayne Ltd [1964] 1 WLR 125   167
McInerny v Lloyd's Bank Ltd [1974] 1 Lloyd's Rep 246   294
McRae v Commonwealth Disposals Commission (1951) 84 CLR 377   279, 285, 384, 385
Mears v Safecar Securities Ltd [1983] QB 54   171
Mendelssohn v Normand Ltd [1970] 1 QB 177   192
Merritt v Merritt [1970] 1 WLR 1211   99
Metropolitan Asylums Board Managers v Kingham & Sons (1890) 6 TLR 217   488
Metropolitan Water Board v Dick Kerr & Co. Ltd [1918] AC 119   266
Midland Bank plc v Shephard [1988] 3 All ER 17   335
Mihalis Angelos, The [1971] 1 QB 164   236, 248
Millar v Radford (1903) 19 TLR 575   497
Minter (F.G.) v Welsh Health Technical Services Organization (1980) 13 BLR 1 422
Mohamed v Alaga & Co. (A Firm) [2000] 1 WLR 1815   350
Monarch Airlines Ltd v London Luton Airport Ltd [1997] CLC 698   189, 209, 210
Mondial Shipping and Chartering BV v Astarte Shipping Ltd [1995] CLC 1011   52
Montgomerie v United Kingdom Mutual Steamship Association Ltd
    [1891] 1 QB 370   489
Moorcock, The (1889) 14 PD 64   178
Morgan Crucible Co. plc v Hill Samuel Bank Ltd [1991] 1 All ER 148   306
Morley v Loughnan [1893] 1 Ch 736   334
Morley v United Friendly Insurance plc [1993] 1 WLR 996   188
Morris v Baron & Co. [1918] AC 1   227
Morris v C.W. Martin & Sons Ltd [1966] 1 QB 716   470
Motor Oil Hellas (Corinth) Refineries SA v Shipping Corporation of India,
    The Kanchenjunga [1990] 1 Lloyd's Rep 391, HL   230

Napier v National Business Agency [1951] 2 All ER 264   369
Nash v Inman [1908] 2 KB 1   146
National Carriers Ltd v Panalpina (Northern) Ltd [1981] AC 675   265
National Oilwell (UK) Ltd v Davy Offshore Ltd [1993] 2 Lloyd's Rep 582   487
National Westminster Bank Ltd v Morgan [1985] AC 686   333, 335, 336, 343, 344
Naughton v O'Callaghan [1990] 3 All ER 191   317
Nelson v Nelson (1995) 184 CLR 538   356
New Zealand Shipping Co. Ltd v A.M. Satterthwaite & Co. Ltd, The Eurymedon
    [1975] AC 154   30, , 58, 62, 115, 123, 445, 457, 459, 461, 471
Newbigging v Adam (1886) 34 ChD 582   320
Nicholson & Venn v Smith-Marriott (1947) 177 LT 189   283, 284
Nickoll & Knight v Ashton, Edridge & Co. [1901] 2 KB 126   260
Nicolene Ltd v Simmonds [1953] 1 QB 543   68
Nissan UK Ltd v Nissan Motor Manufacturing (UK) Ltd (unreported),
    26 October 1994   45
Nordenfelt v Maxim Nordenfelt Guns and Ammunition Co. Ltd [1894] AC 535 361, 365
North Ocean Shipping Co. Ltd v Hyundai Construction Co. Ltd, The Atlantic Baron
    [1979] QB 705   117, 331, 332
North Western Railway v McMichael (1850) 5 Ex 114   147
Northern Electric Ltd v Econofreight Heavy Transport Ltd (unreported),
    21 December 2000   470
Northwestern Salt Co. Ltd v Electrolytic Alkali Co. Ltd [1914] AC 461   348
Norwich and Peterborough Building Society v Steed (No. 2) [1993] Ch 116   90
Norwich City Council v Harvey [1989] 1 All ER 1180   460, 461
Nurdin and Peacock plc v D.B. Ramsden and Co. Ltd [1999] 1 WLR 1249   433
Nutt v Read (2000) 32 HLR 761, (1999) The Times, 3 December   290

O'Shea, Re [1911] 2 KB 981   353

O'Sullivan v Management Agency and Music Ltd [1985] QB 428   338
Occidental Worldwide Investment Corporation v Skibs A/S Avanti,
    The Siboen and The Sibotre [1976] 1 Lloyd's Rep 293   327, 331
Ocean Chemical Transport Inc. v Exnor Craggs Ltd [2000] 1 All ER (Comm) 519
                                                                              162, 166, 167
Office Overload Ltd v Gunn [1977] FSR 39   371
Offord v Davies (1862) 12 CB NS 748   55
Olley v Marlborough Court Ltd [1949] 1 KB 532   109, 164
Olympia & York Canary Wharf Ltd (No. 2), Re [1993] BCC 159   238
Orion Insurance Co. plc v Sphere Drake Insurance plc [1992] 1 Lloyd's Rep 239   98
Oscar Chess Ltd v Williams [1957] 1 WLR 370   28, 155, 156
Oswald Hickson Collier & Co. v Carter-Ruck [1984] 2 All ER 15   364
Overbrooke Estates Ltd v Glencombe Properties Ltd [1974] 1 WLR 1353   324, 484
Overseas Medical Supplies Ltd v Orient Transport Services Ltd [1999] CLC 1243   211

Page One Records Ltd v Britton [1968] 1 WLR 157   428
Pagnan SpA v Tradax Ocean Transportation SA [1987] 3 All ER 565   266
Pan Atlantic Insurance Co. Ltd v Pine Top Insurance Co. Ltd [1994] 3 All ER 581   297
Pan Ocean Shipping Co. Ltd v Creditcorp Ltd [1994] 1 WLR 161   477
Pao On v Lau Yiu Long [1980] AC 614   112, 115, 116, 132, 328, 329, 343, 344
Paradine v Jane (1647) Al 26, 82 ER 897   256
Parker, Re (1882) 21 ChD 408   498
Parker v Clark [1960] 1 WLR 286   101
Parker v South Eastern Railway (1877) 2 CPD 416   164, 165
Parker v Winlow (1857) 7 El & Bl 942   489, 500
Parkin, Re [1892] 3 Ch 510   430
Parkinson v College of Ambulance Ltd [1925] 2 KB 1   355
Partridge v Crittenden [1968] 2 All ER 421   33
Payzu Ltd v Saunders [1919] 2 KB 581   405
Pearce v Brooks (1866) LR 1 Ex 213   354
Peek v Gurney (1873) LR 6 HL 377   300
Pegler v Wang (UK) Ltd [2000] BLR 218   202
Penn v Bristol and West Building Society [1997] 1 WLR 1356   501
Perera v Vandiyar [1953] 1 All ER 1109   374
Perry v Sidney Phillips & Son [1982] 1 WLR 1297   406
Peter Lind & Co. Ltd v Mersey Docks and Harbour Board [1972] 2 Lloyd's Rep 234   44
Peters v General Accident and Life Assurance Corporation Ltd
    [1937] 4 All ER 628   478
Petrotrade Inc. v Texaco Ltd [2000] CLC 1341   167, 168
Peyman v Lanjani [1985] Ch 457   231, 232
Pharmaceutical Society of Great Britain v Boots Cash Chemists (Southern) Ltd
    [1953] 1 QB 401   35, 36
Philips Hong Kong Ltd v Attorney-General of Hong Kong (1993) 61 BLR 49   414, 415
Philips v Ward [1956] 1 WLR 471   383
Phillips Products Ltd v Hyland [1987] 1 WLR 659   204, 207
Phillips v Brooks Ltd [1919] 2 KB 243   83, 84, 85
Phillipson v Hayter (1870) LR 6 CP 38   485
Photo Production Ltd v Securicor Transport Ltd [1980] AC 827
                      16, 186, 187, 194, 204, 208, 209, 211, 224, 228, 229, 364, 376
Pilkington v Wood [1953] Ch 770   404
Pilmore v Hood (1838) 5 Bing NC 97   300
Pinnel's Case (1602) 5 Co Rep 117a   120, 121, 127, 227
Pioneer Container, The [1994] 2 AC 324   470
Pioneer Shipping Ltd v BTP Tioxide Ltd [1982] AC 724   259
Pitt v PHH Asset Management Ltd [1994] 1 WLR 327   38, 69, 140
Planche v Colburn (1831) 8 Bing 14   436
Pole Properties Ltd v Feinberg (1982) 43 P & CR 121   263

Polhill v Walter (1832) 3 B & Ad 114   500
Port Jackson Stevedoring Pty Ltd v Salmond & Spraggon (Australia) Pty Ltd,
  The New York Star [1981] 1 WLR 138   459
Port Line Ltd v Ben Line Steamers Ltd [1958] 2 QB 146   469
Portman Building Society v Dusangh [2000] 2 All ER (Comm) 221   343, 345, 346, 347
Posner v Scott-Lewis [1986] 3 All ER 513   427
Possfund Custodian Trustee Ltd v Diamond [1996] 1 WLR 1351   301
Potts v Bell (1800) 8 TR 548   355
Poussard v Spiers (1876) 1 QBD 410   238
Prager v Blatspiel, Stamp and Heacock Ltd [1924] 1 KB 566   486
Prenn v Simmonds [1971] 1 WLR 1381   180
Prentis Donegan & Partners Ltd v Leeds & Leeds Co. Inc. [1998] 2 Lloyd's Rep 326   495
Presentaciones Musicales SA v Secunda [1994] 2 All ER 737   487
President of India v La Pintada Cia Navegacion SA [1985] AC 104   422, 423
President of India v Lips Maritime Corporation [1988] AC 395   423
Price v Easton (1833) 4 B & Ad 433   441
Price v Strange [1978] Ch 337   147, 430
Priestly v Fernie (1865) 3 Hurl & C 977   489, 490, 492
Printing & Numerical Registering Co. v Sampson (1875) LR 19 Eq 462   353, 361
Pritchard v Cook & Red Ltd (unreported), 4 June 1998   154, 155, 156
Production Technology Consultants Ltd v Bartlett [1988] 1 EGLR 182   312
Pym v Campbell (1856) 6 E & B 370   169

Quadrant Visual Communications Ltd v Hutchinson Telephone (UK) Ltd
  [1993] 1 BCLC 442   429
Quebec & Richmond Railroad Co. v Quinn (1858) 12 Moo PC 232   494

R & B Customs Brokers Co. Ltd v United Dominions Trust Ltd
  [1988] 1 WLR 321   199, 200, 201, 215
R. Leslie Ltd v Sheill [1914] 3 KB 607   148
R v Andrews [1973] QB 422   354
R v Clarke (1927) 40 CLR 227   41, 62, 103
R v Secretary of State for Trade and Industry, ex parte Consumers' Association
  (unreported), 28 February 1996   222
R.W. Green Ltd v Cade Brothers Farms [1978] 1 Lloyd's Rep 602   210
Radford v De Froberville [1977] 1 WLR 1262   382, 392, 407
Raffaella, The [1985] 2 Lloyd's Rep 36   483
Raffles v Wichelhaus (1864) 2 Hurl & C 906, 159 ER 375   66, 77
Rainbow Estates Ltd v Tokenhold Ltd [1998] 2 All ER 860   427
Rama Corporation Ltd v Proved Tin and General Investments Ltd [1952] 2 QB 147   483
Ramsgate Victoria Hotel Co. Ltd v Montefiore (1866) LR 1 Ex 109   54
Rayner v Grote (1846) 15 M & W 359   501
Reardon Smith Line Ltd v Hansen Tangen [1976] 3 All ER 570   237, 239, 240
Record v Bell [1991] 4 All ER 471   139, 141
Redgrave v Hurd (1881) 20 ChD 1   301, 321, 322
Regalian Properties plc v London Dockland Development Corporation
  [1995] 1 WLR 212   73, 74, 436
Regazzoni v Sethia (1944) Ltd [1958] AC 301   355
Regent OHG Aisestadt v Francesco of Jermyn Street Ltd [1981] 3 All ER 327   243
Remco, The [1984] 2 Lloyd's Rep 205   501
Reynolds v Atherton (1921) 125 LT 690   55
Rice (T/A The Garden Guardian) v Great Yarmouth Borough Council
  (2000) The Times, 26 July   234, 240, 243
Richardson v Mellish (1824) 2 Bing 229   218, 353
Riverlate Properties Ltd v Paul [1975] Ch 133   88
Roberts v Gray [1913] 1 KB 520   147
Roberts v Leicestershire CC   89

Robinson v Davison (1871) LR 6 Ex 269   259
Robinson v Harman (1848) 1 Ex 850   377
Robophone Facilities Ltd v Blank [1966] 1 WLR 1423   414
Robson v Drummond (1831) 2 B & Ad 303   478
Rock Refrigeration Ltd v Jones [1997] 1 All ER 1   364
Rolls Razor Ltd v Cox [1967] 1 QB 552   499
Roscorla v Thomas (1842) 3 QB 234   109, 110
Rose & Frank Co. v J.R. Crompton & Bros [1925] AC 445   96, 97, 98
Rosenbaum v Belsen [1900] 2 Ch 267   481
Routledge v Grant (1828) 4 Bing 653   56
Rover International Ltd v Cannon Film Sales Ltd (No. 3) [1989] 1 WLR 912   417, 434, 436
Rowland v Divall [1923] 2 KB 500   19, 148, 435
Roxburghe v Cox (1881) 17 ChD 520   477
Royal Bank of Scotland v Etridge (No. 2) [1998] 4 All ER 705   334, 340, 342, 347
Royscot Trust Ltd v Rogerson [1991] 2 QB 297   316, 317, 321
Ruxley Electronics and Construction Ltd v Forsyth [1996] 1 AC 344   382, 407
Ryan v Mutual Tontine Westminster Chambers Association [1893] 1 Ch 116   427

S. Pearson & Son Ltd v Dublin Corporation [1907] AC 351   301, 323
Said v Butt [1920] 3 KB 497   492
Salomon v A. Salomon & Co. Ltd [1897] AC 22   149
Salvage Association v CAP Financial Services Ltd [1995] FSR 654   202
Saunders v Anglia Building Society [1971] AC 1004   90
Saunders v Edwards [1987] 2 All ER 651   349, 356
Sauter Automation Ltd v Goodman (Mechanical Services) Ltd (1986) 34 BLR 81   45
Scally v Southern Health and Social Services Board [1992] 1 AC 294   175
Scammell & Nephew Ltd v Ouston [1941] AC 251   66, 67
Scandinavian Trading Tanker Co. AB v Flota Petrolera Ecuatoriana
    [1983] 2 All ER 763   419
Scarf v Jardine (1882) 7 App Cas 345   492
Schawel v Reade [1913] 2 IR 81   154, 155
Schebsman, Re [1944] Ch 83   443, 456
Schenkers Ltd v Overland Shoes Ltd [1998] 1 Lloyd's Rep 498   210
Schmaltz v Avery (1851) 16 QB 655   501
Schroeder Music Publishing Co. Ltd v Macaulay [1974] 1 WLR 1308
                                                      185, 343, 362, 363, 367
Schuler v Wickman Machine Tool Sales Ltd [1974] AC 235   182
Scotson v Pegg (1861) 6 Hurl & N 295   114, 115
Scott v Avery (1855) 5 HL Cas 811   354
Scriven Bros & Co. v Hindley & Co. [1913] 3 KB 564   77, 78
Scruttons Ltd v Midland Silicones Ltd [1962] AC 446   458, 460, 461
Sears Investment Trust Ltd v Lewis's Group Ltd [1992] RA 262   496
Seatrade Groningen BV v Geest Industries Ltd [1996] 2 Lloyd's Rep 375   489, 500
Selectmove Ltd, Re [1995] 1 WLR 474   48, 118, 121, 122, 124, 127, 129, 227
Seven Seas Properties Ltd v Al-Essa (No. 2) [1993] 3 All ER 577   399
Shadwell v Shadwell (1860) 9 CB NS 159   115
Shanklin Pier Ltd v Detel Products Ltd [1951] 2 KB 854   454
Shearson Lehman Hutton Inc. v Maclaine Watson & Co. Ltd (No. 2)
    [1990] 3 All ER 723   378
Shell UK Ltd v Lostock Garage Ltd [1976] 1 WLR 1187   171, 173, 174, 429
Sherwood v Walker 33 NW 919 (1887)   283
Shiloh Spinners Ltd v Harding [1973] AC 691   419
Shirlaw v Southern Foundries (1926) Ltd [1939] 2 KB 206   173, 257
Shuey v United States 92 US 73 (1875)   62
Simpson v London and North Western Railway Co. (1876) 1 QBD 274   384
Singh v Ali [1960] AC 167   359
Siu Yin Kwan v Eastern Insurance Co. Ltd [1994] 1 All ER 213   491, 492

Skilton v Sullivan (1994) The Times, 25 March   357
Sky Petroleum Ltd v VIP Petroleum Ltd [1974] 1 All ER 954   425
Slade's Case (1602) 4 Co Rep 92a, 76 ER 1072   8
Slater v Hoyle & Smith Ltd [1920] 2 KB 11   380
Slowey v Lodder (1901) 20 NZLR 321   437
Smith New Court Securities Ltd v Scrimgeour Vickers (Asset Management) Ltd
    [1997] AC 254   312, 315, 316, 317, 396
Smith v Butler [1900] 1 QB 694   169
Smith v Chadwick (1884) 9 App Cas 187   300
Smith v Eric S. Bush [1990] 1 AC 831   196, 204, 208, 212
Smith v Hughes (1871) LR 6 QB 597   28, 77, 78, 80
Smith v Land & House Property Corporation (1884) 28 ChD 7   298
Snelling v John G. Snelling Ltd [1973] 1 QB 87   463
Société Commerciale de Reassurance v ERAS (International) Ltd [1992] 2 All ER 82, 85   7
Société des Industries Metallurgiques SA v The Bronx Engineering Co. Ltd
    [1975] 1 Lloyd's Rep 465   425
Société Italo-Belge pour le Commerce et l'Industrie SA v Palm & Vegetable Oils
    (Malaysia) Sdn Bhd, The Post Chaser, [1982] 1 All ER 19   130, 131
Society of Lloyds, The v Twinn (2000) The Times, 4 April   43
Solle v Butcher [1950] 1 KB 671   28, 283, 284, 286, 288, 290, 299
South Australia Asset Management Corporation v York Montague Ltd [1997] AC 191
                                                                          315, 395
South Tyneside Metropolitan Borough Council v Svenska International plc
    [1995] 1 All ER 545   433
Southern Water Authority v Carey [1985] 2 All ER 1077   460, 461
Spence v Crawford [1939] 3 All ER 271   310
Spencer v Harding (1870) LR 5 CP 561   37
Spice Girls Ltd v Aprilla World Service BV [2000] EMLR 478   294, 295, 307
Spice Girls Ltd v Aprilla World Service BV (Damages) [2001] EMLR 8   316
Spiro v Glencrown Properties Ltd [1991] 1 All ER 600   140
Sport International Bussum BV v Inter-Footwear Ltd [1984] 2 All ER 321   419
Spring v Guardian Assurance plc [1995] 2 AC 296   175, 306
St Albans City and District Council v International Computers Ltd [1995] FSR 686;
    [1996] 4 All ER 481   200, 202, 212
St John Shipping Corporation v Joseph Rank Ltd [1957] 1 QB 267   351
St Paul Fire and Marine Insurance Co. (UK) Ltd v McConnell Dowell Constructors Ltd
    [1996] 1 All ER 96   297
Staffordshire Area Health Authority v South Staffordshire Waterworks Co.
    [1978] 3 All ER 769   228, 263
Standard Chartered Bank v Pakistan National Shipping Corporation (Reduction of
    Damages) [2001] QB 167 (reported as (No. 4) [2000] 3 WLR 1692, (No. 2)
    [2000] CLC 1575 and as (No. 3) [2000] 2 All ER (Comm) 929)   313, 322
State Trading Corporation of India Ltd v Golodetz Ltd
    [1989] 2 Lloyd's Rep 277   231, 235
Steinberg v Scala (Leeds) Ltd [1923] 2 Ch 452   147
Stent Foundations Ltd v Gleeson plc [2001] BLR 134   190
Stevenson, Jacques & Co. v McLean (1880) 5 QBD 346   44
Stevenson v Rogers [1999] 2 WLR 1064   201, 424
Stewart Gill Ltd v Horatio Myer & Co. Ltd [1992] 1 QB 600   196, 209, 213
Stilk v Myrick (1809) 2 Camp 317, 6 Esp 129   116, 117, 120, 327
Stockloser v Johnson [1954] 1 QB 476   417, 419
Stocks v Dobson (1853) 4 De GM & G 11   476
Stocks v Wilson [1913] 2 KB 235   148
Stocznia Gdanska SA v Latvian Shipping Co. [1996] 2 Lloyd's Rep 132,
    [1997] 2 Lloyd's Rep 228, [1998] 1 WLR 574   250, 251, 252, 417, 434
Stoddart v Union Trust Ltd [1912] 1 KB 181   477
Storer v Manchester City Council [1974] 3 All ER 824   26, 33

Strickland v Turner (1852) 7 Ex 208   277, 288
Strongman (1945) Ltd v Sincock [1955] 2 QB 525   357
Strover v Harrington [1988] 1 All ER 769   300
Stubbs v Holywell Railway Co. (1867) LR 2 Ex 311   259
Sudbrook Trading Estate Ltd v Eggleton [1983] 1 AC 444   71, 72, 437
Suisse Atlantique Société d'Armement Maritime SA v NV Rotterdamsche Kolen
    Centrale [1967] 1 AC 361   193, 194, 412
Suleyman Stalskiy, The [1976] 2 Lloyd's Rep 609   459
Sumpter v Hedges [1898] 1 QB 673   245, 435
Surrey County Council v Bredero Homes Ltd [1993] 1 WLR 1361
                                               374, 376, 377, 388, 389, 390
Sutton & Co. v Gre [1894] 1 QB 285   143
Swan, The [1968] 1 Lloyd's Rep 5   500
Swiss Bank Corporation v Lloyds Bank Ltd [1979] Ch 548   469
Sze Hai Tong Bank Ltd v Rambler Cycle Co. Ltd [1959] AC 576   191

Tai Hing Cotton Mill Ltd v Liu Chong Hing Bank Ltd [1986] AC 80   171, 175
Tailby v Official Receiver (1888) 13 App Cas 523   475
Tamplin v James (1880) 15 ChD 215   78, 79
Tancred v Delagoa Bay and East Africa Railway Co. (1889) 23 QBD 239   473
Tate v Williamson (1866) LR 2 Ch App 55   296
Taylor v Bowers (1876) 1 QBD 291   358
Taylor v Caldwell (1863) 3 B & S 826   256, 257, 258, 268, 278
Taylor v Chester (1869) LR 4 QB 309   359
Taylor v Webb [1937] 2 KB 283   242
Teheran-Europe Co. Ltd v S. T. Belton (Tractors) Ltd [1968] 2 All ER 886   490
Tettenborn [1996] JBL 602   445
Thacker v Hardy (1878) 4 QBD 685   498
Thackwell v Barclays Bank plc [1986] 1 All ER 676   356
Thake v Maurice [1984] 2 All ER 513   28
Thomas Bates & Son Ltd v Wyndham's (Lingerie) Ltd [1981] 1 WLR 505   89
Thomas v Thomas (1842) 2 QB 851   102, 103, 104
Thomas Witter Ltd v TBP Industries Ltd [1996] 2 All ER 573
                                        298, 303, 310, 317, 319, 320, 323
Thompson (W.L.) Ltd v R. Robinson (Gunmakers) Ltd [1955] Ch 177   379
Thompson v London, Midland & Scottish Railway [1930] 1 KB 41   164
Thompson v T. Lohan (Plant Hire) Ltd [1987] 1 WLR 649   205, 207
Thornton v Shoe Lane Parking Ltd [1971] 2 QB 163   162, 165, 166, 187
Thoroughgood's Case (1584) 2 Co Rep 9a, 76 ER 401   8, 89
Times Newspapers Ltd v Weidenfeld & Nicolson Ltd (unreported),
    28 March 2001   172
Tinn v Hoffman (1873) 29 LT 271   42
Tinsley v Milligan [1994] 1 AC 340   349, 355, 356, 357, 360
Tito v Waddell (No. 2) [1977] Ch 106   382, 388
Tool Metal Manufacturing Co. Ltd v Tungsten Electric Co. Ltd
    [1955] 1 WLR 761   128, 132, 133
Toomey v Eagle Star Insurance Co. Ltd (No. 2) [1995] 2 Lloyd's Rep 88   322
Tootal Clothing Ltd v Guinea Properties Management Ltd (1992) 64 P & CR 452   140
Torkington v Magee [1902] 2 KB 427   474
Torvald Klaveness A/S v Arni Maritime Corporation, The Gregos
    [1994] 1 WLR 1465   236, 239, 240
Traill v Baring (1864) 4 D J & S 318   296
Trendtex Trading Corporation v Credit Suisse [1982] AC 679   478
Trentham Ltd v Archital Luxfer Ltd [1993] 1 Lloyd's Rep 25   27, 31
Tribe v Tribe [1996] Ch 106   358, 360
Trident General Insurance Co. Ltd v McNiece Brothers Proprietary Ltd
    (1988) 165 CLR 107   443, 446, 460

Triffit Nurseries (a firm) v Salads Etcetera Ltd [1999] 1 All ER (Comm) 110;
  aff'd [2000] 1 All ER (Comm) 737   502
Trueman v Loder (1840) 11 Ad & El 589   502
Tsakiroglou & Co. Ltd v Noblee Thorl GmbH [1962] AC 93   262
TSB Bank plc v Camfield [1995] 1 WLR 430   308, 311, 337
Tudor Grange Holdings Ltd v Citibank NA [1992] Ch 53   206
Tulk v Moxhay (1848) 2 Ph 774   468
Tweddle v Atkinson (1861) 1 B & S 393   442, 443, 444, 448

Union Eagle Ltd v Golden Achievement Ltd [1997] AC 514   235, 419
United Bank of Kuwait Ltd v Hammoud [1988] 1 WLR 1051   484
United Bank of Kuwait plc v Sahib [1997] Ch 107   141
United Dominions Trust Ltd v Parkway Motors [1955] 2 All ER 557   478
United Kingdom Mutual Steamship Assurance Association Ltd v Nevill
  (1887) 19 QBD 110   491
United Scientific Holdings Ltd v Burnley Borough Council [1978] AC 904 235, 237
Universal Bulk Carriers Ltd v Andre et Cie SA [2000] 1 Lloyd's Rep 459 237
Universal Corporation v Five Ways Properties Ltd [1979]1 All ER 552   418
Universal Steam Navigation Co. Ltd v J. McKelvie & Co. [1923] AC 492 500
Universe Tankships Inc. of Monrovia v International Transport Workers' Federation,
  The Universe Sentinel [1983] 1 AC 366   329, 330
Upton-on-Severn RDC v Powell [1942] 1 All ER 220   31

Vadasz v Pioneer Concrete (SA) Pty Ltd (1995) 130 ALR 570   308, 338
Vanbergen v St Edmund Properties [1933] 2 KB 223   120
Vandepitte v Preferred Accident Insurance Corporation of New York [1933] AC 70 456
Vaswani v Italian Motors (Sales and Services) Ltd [1996] 1 WLR 270 253, 254
Victoria Laundry (Windsor) Ltd v Newman Industries Ltd [1949] 2 KB 528
                                          380, 399, 400, 401, 402, 403
Vitol SA v Norelf Ltd, The Santa Clara [1996] AC 800   230, 251
Voyle v Hughes (1854) 2 Sm & G 18   476

W.J. Alan & Co. Ltd v El Nasr Export & Import Co. [1972] 2 QB 189   130
W.J. Tatem Ltd v Gamboa [1939] 1 KB 132   267
Wadsworth v Lydall [1981] 2 All ER 401   423
Wagon Mound (No. 1), The [1961] AC 388   315
Wakeham v Wood (1982) 43 P & CR 40   431
Wales v Wadham [1977] 1 WLR 199   296
Walford v Miles [1992] 2 AC 128   23, 38, 69
Walker, Re [1905] 1 Ch 160   145
Walters v Morgan (1861) 3 DF & J 718   429
Walton Stores (Interstate) Ltd v Maher (1988) 164 CLR 387   124, 135, 136, 137
Ward v Byham [1956] 1 WLR 496   114
Warlow v Harrison (1859) 1 E & E 309   39
Warner Brothers Pictures Incorporated v Nelson [1937] 1 KB 209 428, 429
Warren v Mendy [1989] 1 WLR 853   428
Watford Electronics Ltd v Sanderson CFL Ltd [2001] EWCA Civ 317,
  [2001] 1 All ER (Comm) 696   203, 208, 210
Watson v Davies [1931] 1 Ch 455   488
Watteau v Fenwick [1893] 1 QB 346   481, 483
Watts v Morrow [1991] 1 WLR 1421   383, 406, 408
Waugh v H.B. Clifford & Sons [1982] 1 Ch 374   481
Webster v Cecil (1861) 30 Beav 62   78, 79, 429
West of England Bank v Batchelor (1882) 51 LJ Ch 199   498
Westdeutsche Landesbank Girozentrale v Islington BC [1994] 4 All ER 890 433
Western Webb Offset Printers Ltd v Independent Media Ltd [1996] CLC 77 381
Westerton, Re [1919] 2 Ch 104   474

Whincup v Hughes (1871) LR 6 CP 78   434
White & Carter (Councils) Ltd v McGregor [1962] AC 413   249, 250, 251, 252, 421
White v Bluett (1853) 23 LJ Ex 36   106
White v John Warwick & Co. Ltd [1953] 1 WLR 1285   189
Whittington v Seal-Hayne (1900) 82 LT 49   320
Whitwham v Westminster Brymbo Coal and Coke Co. [1896] 2 Ch 538   389
Wilkie v London Passenger Transport Board [1947] 1 All ER 258   31
William Brandt's Sons & Co. v Dunlop Rubber Co. Ltd [1905] AC 454   472, 474
William Sindall plc v Cambridgeshire County Council [1994] 1 WLR 1016
                                                             285, 289, 318, 319, 320
Williams v Bayley (1886) LR 1 HL 200   327
Williams v Carwardine (1833) 5 C & P 566   41
Williams v Natural Life Health Foods Ltd [1998] 2 All ER 577   306
Williams v Reynolds (1865) 6 B & S 495   378
Williams v Roffey Bros & Nicholls (Contractors) Ltd [1991] 1 QB 1   56, 102, 105,
   106, 110, 113, 116, 117, 118, 119, 121, 123, 124, 127, 129, 132, 136, 227, 327, 328, 330
Williams v Williams [1957] 1 WLR 148   114, 116
Wilson v Best Travel Ltd [1993] 1 All ER 353   176, 177
Wilson v Tumman (1843) 6 Man & G 236   486
Wilson v United Counties Bank Ltd [1920] AC 102   411
With v O'Flanagan [1936] Ch 575   295, 303
Wolverhampton Corporation v Emmons [1901] 1 KB 515   427
Woodar Investment Development Ltd v Wimpey Construction (UK) Ltd
   [1980] 1 WLR 277   248, 249, 253, 254, 265, 444, 464
Woodhouse A.C. Israel Cocoa SA v Nigerian Produce Marketing Co. [1972] AC 741   129
Woolcott v Sun Alliance & London Insurance Ltd [1978] 1 All ER 1253   297
Workers Trust and Merchant Bank Ltd v Dojap Investments Ltd [1993] AC 573 417, 419
Wroth v Tyler [1974] Ch 30   392, 395, 405
Wrotham Park Estate Co. Ltd v Parkside Homes Ltd [1974] 1 WLR 798   388, 390
Wyatt v Kreglinger and Fernau [1933] 1 KB 793   364

Yaxley v Gotts [2000] Ch 162   141
Yeoman Credit Ltd v Latter [1961] 1 WLR 828   143
Yianni v Edwin Evans & Sons [1981] 3 All ER 593   300
Yonge v Toynbee [1910] 1 KB 215   502
Young v Kitchin (1878) 3 ExD 127   477
Yukong Line Ltd of Korea v Rendsburg Investments Corporation of Liberia
   [1996] 2 Lloyd's Rep 604   231, 247, 251, 254
Yule v Little Bird Ltd (unreported), 5 April 2001   74

Table of Statutes

Administration of Justice Act 1982 424

Bills of Exchange Act 1882   453
  s.3(1)   143
  s.8(1)   453
  s.17(2)   143
  s.27   112
  s.27(1)(b)   454
  s.27(2)   454
  s.29(1)   454
  s.30(2)   454
  s.31(3)-(4)   454
  s.38(2)   454
Bills of Lading Act 1855   457
Bills of Sale Act 1878   143
  s.4   143
Bills of Sale Act (1878) Amendment Act
  1882   143
  s.9   143

Carriage of Goods by Sea Act 1992   457
  s.2   457
  s.5   457
Children Act 1989
  s.2(9)   354
Companies Act 1985   149, 473
  s.36C   499
Companies Act 1989   149
Competition Act 1980   367, 368
Competition Act 1998   365, 368
  s.2(2)(a)   365
Consumer Credit Act 1974   218–19, 326,
  343, 418
  s.60   142
  s.100(1)-(2)   418
Consumer Protection Act 1987
  s.20-s.26   37

Contracts (Rights of Third Parties) Act 1999
  102, 426, 430, 443, 446, 447–50, 461,
  468, 471, 490
  s.1   450
  s.1(1)   447, 448
  s.1(1)(a)   448
  s.1(1)(b)   448, 461, 462
  s.1(2)   447, 448
  s.1(3)   447, 448, 461
  s.1(5)   447
  s.1(6)   447, 461
  s.2(1)-(7)   449
  s.3   447
  s.3(6)   447
  s.4-s.5   449
  s.6   450
  s.7(1)-(2)   450
  s.7(4)   450
County Courts Act 1984
  s.38   371
  s.69   424
Criminal Law Act 1967
  s.5(1)   354

Electronic Communications Act 2000   22,
  203
  s.7   144, 161
  s.7(1)   144
  s.8   138, 144
  s.15(2)   144
European Communities Act 1972
  s.2(2)   177

Factors Act 1889
  s.2(1)   19

Gaming Act 1710   352, 353

Gaming Act 1835   352, 353
Gaming Act 1845   352
  s.18   352, 432
Gaming Act 1892
  s.1   353
Gaming Act 1968   353
  s.16   353

Honours (Prevention of Abuses) Act 1925
  355
Human Fertilisation and Embryology Act
  1990
  s.36   354

Infants Relief Act 1874
  s.2   148

Judicature Act 1873   287, 472, 474
  s.25(6)   472
Judicature Act 1875   451, 472

Late Payment of Commercial Debts
  (Interest) Act 1998   424
  s.5   424
  s.14   424
Law of Property Act 1925
  s.40   139
  s.41   237
  s.49(2)   417, 418
  s.49(3)   418
  s.52   138
  s.53(1)(c)   476
  s.54   138
  s.136(1)   472–3, 474
  s.146   126
Law of Property (Miscellaneous Provisions)
  Act 1989   139
  s.1   92, 138
  s.1(2)-(3)   138
  s.2   134, 139, 140, 141
  s.2(1)   139, 140
  s.2(2)-(3)   139
  s.2(4)   140
  s.2(8)   140
  s.4   140
Law Reform (Contributory Negligence) Act
  1945   321, 322, 396, 397, 398
  s.1(1)   321
  s.4   396, 398
Law Reform (Frustrated Contracts) Act
  1943   271–4, 278
  s.1(2)   271, 272, 273, 274
  s.1(3)   272, 273, 274
  s.1(3)(b)   274
  s.1(4)   271
  s.2(3)-(4)   274
  s.2(5)(a)-(c)   274

Limitation Act 1980   6
  s.5(1)   138
  s.8(1)   138
  s.11   6
Limited Liability Partnerships Act 2000
  s.1   149
  s.5   149
  s.6   149

Marine Insurance Act 1906
  s.20(4)   294
  s.21-s.24   143
Married Woman's Property Act   1882
  s.11   456
Matrimonial Causes Act 1973
  s.34   354
Mental Health Act 1983
  Part VII   145
Minors' Contracts Act 1987   146, 147, 148
  s.3(1)-(2)   148
Misrepresentation Act 1967   153, 317, 323
  s.1   302
  s.2(1)   153, 303, 304, 306–7, 308, 316,
    317, 319, 320, 321
  s.2(2)   153, 308, 311, 318, 319–20
  s.2(3)   319
  s.3   160, 323, 325

National Minimum Wage Act 1998   98

Policies of Assurance Act 1867   473
Powers of Attorney Act 1971
  s.10   480
Property Misdescriptions Act 1991   293

Rent Act 1977
  s.125   358
Restrictive Practices Act 1956   367
Restrictive Trade Practices Acts   368
Road Traffic Act 1988
  s.148(7)   456

Sale of Goods Act 1893   279
  s.8   70
Sale of Goods Act 1979   18, 41, 179
  s.2(1)   18
  s.3   146, 147
  s.6   278, 279
  s.8   70, 437
  s.8(1)   70
  s.8(2)   71
  s.11(4)   232, 245
  s.12   198
  s.12(3)-(5)   199
  s.12(5A)   179
  s.13   179, 199, 225
  s.14   109, 175, 179, 198, 199, 201

Sale of Goods Act 1979 – *continued*
  s.14(1) 16
  s.14(2) 16, 170, 175, 216, 245, 281
  s.14(2A) 175
  s.14(2B) 175
  s.14(2B)(e) 176
  s.14(2C) 176
  s.14(3) 176, 245
  s.14(6) 179, 233
  s.15 179, 199
  s.15A 179, 233
  s.15A(1)-(2) 179
  s.18 422
  s.21(1) 19
  s.23 20, 311
  s.28 242
  s.31(2) 243
  s.35(1)-(2) 232
  s.35(4) 232
  s.35(6)(a)-(b) 232
  s.35A(1) 232
  s.49 422
  s.49(1) 422
  s.50(3) 378
  s.51(3) 378, 392
  s.55 195
  s.55(3) 209
  s.57(2) 39
  s.57(4)-(5) 40
Sale and Supply of Goods Act 1994 175, 176, 179
Statute of Frauds 1677
  s.4 143
Supply of Goods (Implied Terms) Act 1973 195
Supply of Goods and Services Act 1982 198
  s.2 199
  s.4 176
  s.7 199
  s.13 176, 179, 205, 226
  .15 437
  s.17(2) 199
Supreme Court Act 1981
  s.35A 424
  s.36(4) 113
  s.37(1) 371
  s.49 431
  s.50 430

Trade Descriptions Act 1968 200, 293
Trade Union and Labour Relations Act 1974 330
Trade Union and Labour Relations (Consolidation) Act 1992
  s.11 367
  s.179 98

Trade Union and Labour Relations (Consolidation) Act 1992 – *continued*
  s.236 428
Trading with the Enemy Act 1939 259, 355

Unfair Contract Terms Act 1977 5, 12, 160, 162, 194, 195, 196–214, 215, 218, 219–20, 256, 323, 324, 415, 424, 450
  s.1(1) 197
  s.1(3) 196, 200
  s.2 196, 197, 215
  s.2(1) 197, 206, 220, 450
  s.2(2) 197, 220, 450
  s.3 160, 196, 198, 200, 201, 202, 203, 215, 450
  s.3(1) 201, 204, 205, 216
  s.3(2)(a) 203
  s.3(2)(b) 204, 205
  s.3(2)(b)(i) 204, 205, 218
  s.3(2)(b)(ii) 204
  s.4 196, 205
  s.5 200
  s.5(2) 200
  s.6 198, 199, 201, 209
  s.6(1)(a) 198–9
  s.6(2) 16, 171, 200, 201, 216
  s.6(2)(a) 199
  s.6(3) 16, 199, 215
  s.6(4) 196, 198
  s.7 197, 198, 201, 209
  s.7(2) 199
  s.7(3) 199, 215
  s.7(3A) 199
  s.7(4) 199
  s.8 323
  s.10 206
  s.11 160, 206
  s.11(1) 207, 213, 323
  s.11(2) 209
  s.11(4) 208
  s.11(5) 207
  s.12 200, 201
  s.12(1) 199, 201, 215
  s.12(1)(c) 200
  s.12(2)-(3) 199
  s.13(1) 196, 215
  s.13(2) 196
  s.14 196, 200
  s.26 197
  sch.1
  para.1 196–7
  para.2 197
  para.4 197
  sch.2 209, 217, 343, 424
Unsolicited Goods and Services Act 1971 48

International Conventions
Vienna Convention on Contracts for the
   International Sale of Goods 1980
   21, 53
  art. 15.1   40
  art. 19(3)   46
Warsaw Convention   216

European legislation
Directive 1986/653/EC (commercial agents)
   488
Directive 1990/314 (package holidays)
   177
Directive 1993/13/EC (unfair terms in
   consumer contracts)   22, 177, 195,
   214
  art. 7   221
Preamble   215–16, 217
Directive 1997/7/EC (direct selling directive)
   22, 142, 177
Directive 1999/93/EC (electronic signatures
   directive)   22, 138, 144

Directive 2000/31/EC (e-commerce
   directive)   22, 54, 138, 144–5
  art. 9(1)   144
  art. 9(2)   144
  art. 9(2)(a)   144
  art. 9(2)(c)   144
  art. 11   54
EC Treaty (post-Amsterdam renumbering)
  art. 81   365, 367, 368
  art. 81(2)-(3)   367
  art. 82   367, 368
Regulation 2790/1999   368

New Zealand legislation
Contracts (Privity) Act 1982   445
  s.4   448

United States legislation
Restatement (2d) Contracts
  s.90   21
  s.90(1)   136
Uniform Commercial Code   46, 56, 261,
344

Table of Statutory Instruments

Civil Procedure Rules
  r.24 421
Commercial Agents (Council Directive)
  Regulations 1993 (SI 1993/3053) 488
Competition Act 1998 (Land and Vertical
  Agreements Exclusion) Order 2000
  (SI 2000/310) 368
Consumer Credit (Agreements) Regulations
  1983 (SI 1983/1553) 142
Consumer Protection (Cancellation of
  Contracts Concluded away from
  Business Premises) Regulations 1987
  (SI 1987/2117) 326
Consumer Protection (Distance Selling)
  Regulations 2000 (SI 2000/2334) 22,
  54, 142, 177, 326
  r.3(1) 142
  r.5 142
  r.7(1) 142
  r.8 142
  r.11-r.12 142
  r.24 48

Package Travel, Package Holidays and
  Package Tours Regulations 1992
  (SI 1992/3288) 177, 293
  r.4 293

Unfair Terms in Consumer Contracts
  (Amendment) Regulations 201
  (SI 2001/1186) 222
Unfair Terms in Consumer Contracts
  Regulations 1994 (SI 1994/3159) 195,
  214, 217, 222
  r.4(2) 217
  r.8 222
  r.15 222
  sch.2 217, 222

Unfair Terms in Consumer Contracts
  Regulations 1999 (SI 1999/2083) 5,
  22, 23, 104, 162, 177, 195, 214–23,
  323, 324, 343, 344, 450
  r.3(1) 215
  r.4(1) 215
  r.4(2) 215, 220
  r.4(2)(a) 215
  r.4(2)(b) 216
  r.5(1) 217, 220
  r.5(2)-(3) 216
  r.5(5) 217
  r.6(1) 217
  r.6(2) 104, 215, 216, 220
  r.7(1) 221
  r.7(2) 188–9, 220, 221
  r.8(1) 220, 221
  r.8(2) 221
  r.10(1) 222
  r.10(2)-(3) 223
  r.11(1) 222
  r.11(2) 223
  r.12 220, 223
  sch.1 222
  sch.2 218, 220, 345
    para.1 220
    para.1(a) 215, 220
    para.1(b) 215
    para.1(c) 220
    para.1(e) 413, 416
    para.1(g) 218
    para.1(j) 218, 220
    para.1(k) 220
    para.1(n) 324
    para.1(o) 220

Abbreviations

A	agent
CPR	Civil Procedure Rules 1998
DGFT	Director General of the Office of Fair Trading
LR(FC)A	Law Reform (Frustrated Contracts) Act 1943
P	principal
para.	paragraph
paras	paragraphs
PECL	*Principles of European Contract Law*
r.	rule
reg.	regulation
s.	section
ss.	sections
sch.	schedule
SGA	Sale of Goods Act 1979
UCC	Uniform Commercial Code (United States)
UCTA	Unfair Contract Terms Act 1977
UNCITRAL	United Nations Commission on International Trade Law
UNIDROIT	International Institute for the Unification of Private Law
UTCC	Unfair Terms in Consumer Contracts Regulations 1999

ONE

Introduction to the law of contract

1.1 THE NATURE OF CONTRACTUAL LIABILITY

Major legal concepts, such as 'contract', are notoriously difficult to define. All that will be attempted here is a generalisation, which admittedly is subject to exceptions and incomplete, but which it is believed gives an adequate indication of the core of the concept. Contracts are *legally enforceable agreements*. Liability for breach of contract is, therefore, liability for failure to keep to the terms of such an agreement. To say that an agreement is 'legally enforceable' is merely a shorthand way of saying that it is one to which the law gives its sanction, as opposed to mere social arrangements which exist outside the framework of the law and which are binding only in the sense of moral obligation or social convention.

This definition of contract implies (at least) three distinct fields of legal rule relating to contracts. There must be rules relating to the formation and content of agreements, rules relating to the enforcement of agreements, and rules distinguishing those agreements which are legally enforceable from those which are not.

1.1.1 Essential ingredients of enforceability

The rules determining whether an agreement is to be regarded as enforceable are the subject of Chapter 4. They embrace three separate elements: intention (4.2), consideration (4.3), and form (4.5). Thus, an agreement will be classed as a contract only if the parties intend legal consequences to result from it, if it satisfies the requirements of consideration, and if it meets any special rules of evidence which are applicable.

Of the above elements the most important is consideration, which is a distinguishing feature of the common law contract not found in civil law systems. Consideration will be defined below (4.3.1) as the action, inaction or promise thereof by one party which induces the action, inaction or promise of another. Consideration for one promise may therefore be provided by another promise, and so a contract may be constituted out of nothing more than an exchange of promises. There are good functional reasons for the enforceability of promises which have induced the reliance of another, but it has sometimes been suggested that liability upon a promise which has not yet induced another's reliance is an unnecessary feature of the law. The reason for that suggestion is that where there has been no reliance, no harm will be caused by failure to keep the promise. Despite the apparent logic of this reasoning, the law has rightly rejected it for practical reasons of evidence. That is, it may in some circumstances be extremely difficult to prove reliance on a promise. For example, if A promises to sell to B 100 tonnes of grain, and B agrees to buy it, but before A commences delivery or B makes any payment one of them backs out of the agreement, it might be said that no harm will be done by cancellation of the contract since neither party has done anything in reliance on it. However, what if B has already sold the grain to C, or A has turned down the opportunity to sell the grain to D, on account of the contract? Rather than put the parties to the proof of their reliance, the law assumes that promises have a tendency to induce reliance, and so liability attaches to the mere act of reciprocal promising. Contracts in which performance on both sides remains in the future are described as 'executory', and the binding nature of such agreements is an important element in the commercial value of the device of contract.

1.1.2   Agreement

The rules relating to the formation and the substance of agreements are the subjects respectively of Chapters 2 and 5. In defining contracts as being based on agreements, it is implicit that we are concerned with obligations which are consensually (or voluntarily) undertaken. Moreover, it follows from the description of consideration given above (1.1.1) that agreements usually consist of reciprocal promises. It is important, however, to give an early warning about the limits of the notion of agreement.

In the first place, not all undertakings are completely voluntary, in that the law imposes certain obligations on those who enter particular types of agreement (see 5.5). Thus, the fact of entering the agreement may be voluntary, but the substance of the agreement is to some extent dictated by law (e.g., undertakings as to the quality of goods sold). Secondly, not all agreements are consensual if by that term we are to understand a precise symmetry between the real intentions of the parties. It was once common to speak of agreements being formed by a 'meeting of the minds' of the parties, which suggests that their *subjective* intentions must coincide. It is of course almost impossible to discover a person's real or subjective intentions, and for this reason the law regards agreements as formed by a coincidence of *objectively ascertained* intentions. That is, what each party actually intended is irrelevant if to all outward appearances the parties are in agreement. The objective test of formation of contracts, and especially the meaning of 'objectivity' in this context, is considered in more detail below (2.1).

1.1.3 Enforcement

When we consider the necessity of enforcing the obligations created by those agreements which qualify as contracts, it is inevitable that our attention will primarily be focused on those remedies for breach of contract which are available in the ordinary courts. Our understanding of the rules of the law of contract, including those rules relevant to enforcement, is largely derived from judicial statements. The enforcement of contractual obligations by legal proceedings is the subject of Chapters 13 and 14. It is necessary here only to summarise what is explained in more detail in the introduction to Part IV (p. 373–75).

Although we speak of the enforcement of contractual obligations, the paradigm remedy for breach of contract is compensation for non-performance rather than compulsion of the performance promised in the contract. Moreover, although in the field of criminal law the idea of 'law enforcement' involves the imposition of penalties for non-compliance, the law of contract denies any role to penalties in securing performance of contracts (although see *Attorney General* v *Blake* [2000] 3 WLR 625 and the remedy of accounting for profits in exceptional circumstances).

It is important, however, not to be misled by the concentration on judicial remedies for breach of contract into believing that the courts are the most important element in the enforcement of contracts. For the practising lawyer, litigation is the last resort. The lawyer's first thought is often towards restoring the relationship between the parties (especially in long-term or relational contracts), thereby securing performance. Failing that, he or she will seek a negotiated settlement of the dispute. In that case the legal rules may play a part, but the terms of the settlement will probably owe less to the legal rules than to a compromise between the parties (although it must be recognised that such a compromise is itself a contract: see 4.3.2.2). Even where compromise is not possible, litigation in the ordinary courts is not the only means of dispute resolution. The parties may agree at the time of making the contract, or subsequently, that disputes be submitted to arbitration, which may have advantages of cost, time and informality of procedure over the ordinary courts (*cf.* Kerr [1980] JBL 164). Commercial disputes are frequently settled in this way. Disputes involving small sums of money are determined by arbitration under the county court small claims procedure. Mediation or conciliation may also be an appropriate dispute resolution mechanism depending on the particular facts. (Mediation is a process whereby an impartial third party seeks to facilitate the resolution of a dispute by means of agreement between the parties. Conciliation is similar, although the third party is commonly far more interventionist and may be required to make recommendations to the parties on how they might settle their dispute.) However, the key feature of mediation is that it is non-binding on the parties in the sense that an external body does not impose a settlement upon them. Lastly, it may sometimes be more appropriate to invoke the powers and assistance of the trading standards officer, or the Office of Fair Trading, both of which have regulatory powers over contracts.

1.2   RELATIONSHIP BETWEEN CONTRACT AND TORT

English law maintains a fairly strict division between contract and tort, which represents one of the major divisions of legal classification between obligations voluntarily assumed and obligations imposed by law. Contractual obligations are voluntarily assumed, in that they derive from agreements which individuals are free to make or refrain from making. Tortious obligations arise independently of the will of those involved, and derive from standards of behaviour imposed by law. In this section reference will be made exclusively to the tort of negligence, which imposes an obligation not to breach the duty of care (i.e., the duty to behave as would a reasonable person in the circumstances) which the law says is owed to those who may foreseeably be injured by any particular conduct or activity. The leading case on the law of negligence is *Donoghue* v *Stevenson* [1932] AC 562, which involved the notorious snail in the bottle of ginger beer. The manufacturer and bottler of the ginger beer was held to owe to consumers a duty of care (see further 15.4.1).

It is ironic that a marked distinction is maintained between contract and tort, since the action for breach of contract was originally a sub-species of an early form of action for tort (see 1.3). The strictness of the distinction appears to owe much to nineteenth-century developments. The prevailing philosophy of the time, sometimes summarised under the epithet *'laissez-faire'*, regarded man as master of his own destiny, and believed that, if given free rein, man's intelligence would operate to the benefit of all. This philosophy gave rise to two specific legal notions relevant to contracts. The first, and more important, is 'freedom of contract' (1.4.2.2). The second was that, being based in free will, contract was the *superior* norm. That is, contractual obligations were supposedly superior to all others because of the manner of their generation. Thus, obligations which might otherwise be imposed by law, would give way to obligations contractually agreed between the parties. Modern writers have been deeply sceptical of this second notion. Some have gone as far as to talk of the 'death of contract' (*cf.* G. Gilmore, *The Death of Contract*, Ohio State Univ. Press, 1986), suggesting that the law is moving progressively to a system of imposed obligations even in those fields traditionally regarded as the exclusive domain of the law of contract. Reports of the death of contract are no doubt greatly exaggerated, but there is no denying that there has been a marked retreat from the high point of contractual superiority. More recently, in *Henderson* v *Merrett Syndicates Ltd* [1994] 3 All ER 506, 532, Lord Goff, deprecating analysis which 'involves treating the law of tort as supplementary to the law of contract', affirmed the modern trend, saying that 'the law of tort is the general law, out of which the parties can, if they wish, contract'.

1.2.1   Overlap of contract and tort

That there is nothing which makes contractual obligations necessarily superior to tortious obligations appears to be a logical conclusion from the fact that there are many instances where the two may overlap. A simple example should suffice to demonstrate that the same factual situation may give rise to both contractual and tortious liability. A student (A) arranges with a haulier (B) to send his case of belongings to a college, paying in advance for the service to be provided. In the course of performance of this service, the case is placed in an open truck and, as the truck goes round a sharp bend, one side comes down and the case falls off the truck into the river. A has a contract with B. There are reciprocal, voluntarily assumed obligations (A to pay: B to deliver the case). A may therefore bring an action for breach of contract against B. Alternatively, if A can prove negligence on B's part (which may not be difficult, since the assumption must be that it is not normal for a case to be lost in this way), A may sue in tort, since B will be in breach of a duty to take proper care of A's case. Thus, the same facts may give rise to a claim either for breach of contract, or for breach of a duty of care arising in tort.

At first sight it may seem curious to regard the contractual obligation in this situation as superior to that arising in tort, since they are identical. It is possible, however, because contractual obligations are agreed, to agree to modify the nature of the obligation by contract, for example by inserting an exemption clause in the contract which limits or excludes B's liability (see generally 6.4 and 6.5). It is the potential for the parties to stipulate the substance of the obligation which led to the belief in the superiority of contractual obligations. So, in *Henderson* v *Merrett Syndicates Ltd* (above), Lord Goff said:

> Approached as a matter of principle, therefore, it is right to attribute to that assumption of responsibility, together with its concomitant reliance, a tortious liability, and then to enquire whether or not that liability is excluded by the contract because the latter is inconsistent with it.

To this extent Lord Goff acknowledges the superiority of contract.

Nevertheless, the potential for a contractual term to exclude liability is today seriously diminished. For example, a clause purporting to limit B's liability in the above situation would be valid only if it were reasonable under the Unfair Contract Terms Act (UCTA) 1977 (see 6.6.2), and the exclusion may also be an unfair term under the Unfair Terms in Consumer Contracts Regulations 1999 (SI 1999 No. 2083) (see 6.6.3). Thus, absolute freedom of contract, if it ever existed, has given way to a much more limited freedom which must coexist with many rules of contract law which impose obligations on the parties and limit the substance of a contract.

1.2.2   Remaining significance of the division

Despite the blurring of the distinction between contract and tort which has taken place in recent years, it is easy to identify ways in which contract and tort remain separate.

An obligation of positive performance some time in the future can normally be created only by contract, even if some of the substance of that obligation will be defined by legal imposition. The standard of performance required under a contract is often strict (see 7.2.1), while liability for the tort of negligence depends upon the claimant being able to prove that the defendant acted unreasonably. Nevertheless, the blurring of the distinction between contract and tort has led to the disappearance of, or uncertainty over, differences traditionally regarded as fundamental.

1.2.3 Measure of loss recoverable

The traditional distinction between damages for breach of contract and damages for negligence was that, in the case of the former, damages for loss of profit might be recovered (see p. 375); while in the latter, lost profit (or pure economic loss) could not be recovered, and the claimant was limited to the recovery of reliance loss (the amount necessary to restore the claimant to the position he or she was in before the tort took place). It has been accepted for some time that a claimant bringing proceedings for breach of contract may claim reliance losses rather than lost profits in some circumstances (see 13.3). If he or she is unable to establish what that profit would have been, because it is too speculative, he or she may even be forced to claim reliance loss damages (13.2.3).

Although English law has flirted with the converse rule, that a person bringing a claim in tort may recover expectation loss (or 'pure economic loss'), it has now repudiated such a doctrine. The rule has important repercussions for subcontractors. In this field, at least, the notion that contract is the superior norm still prevails to some extent.

1.2.4 Remoteness of damage

In both contract and tort, damages may not be recovered for losses which are too remote a consequence of the breach of contract or breach of duty. It has been traditional to assert that the test of remoteness is stricter in relation to contract claims than it is in relation to claims in tort, in that the test in contract is one of reasonable contemplations whereas the test in tort is reasonable foreseeability (*The Heron II* [1969] 1 AC 350). However, in *H. Parsons (Livestock) Ltd v Uttley Ingham & Co. Ltd* [1978] 1 QB 791, the members of the Court of Appeal were unable to agree whether there was any difference at all in the remoteness tests of contract and tort, or whether such difference as there was lay not between contract and tort but between expectation (profit) and reliance (physical) losses. The respective merits of these potential rules, and the policies they may be taken to represent, are discussed below (see generally 13.9.2).

1.2.5 Limitation of actions

Under the Limitation Act 1980, a standard limitation period of six years applies to claims both in contract and in tort, with the exception of personal injury cases in tort when the period is three years (s. 11 of the 1980 Act).

Nevertheless, a distinction remains between contract and tort, since the time at which the limitation period begins to run varies. In contract it begins to run at the time of breach. In tort it does not begin to run until some damage occurs, because there is no cause of action up to this time. This difference was roundly condemned by Mustill LJ in *Société Commerciale de Reassurance v ERAS (International) Ltd* [1992] 2 All ER 82, 85:

> The different treatment for limitation purposes of claims in contract and in tort is already unsatisfactory because: (1) whatever the legal logic, the fact that claims in contract and in tort between the same parties arising out of the same facts become time-barred on dates which may well be years apart offends common sense; . . . (3) so far as limitation is concerned, the rules regarding the accrual of the cause of action tend to push the evolution of substantive law in the wrong direction. In most if not all cases a plaintiff will be better off framing his action in tort, whereas, in our judgment, if a contract is in existence this is the natural vehicle for recourse.

1.3 HISTORY OF CONTRACT LAW

The history of the law of contract is complex and contentious, and those who seek a comprehensive account must refer to specialist works (e.g., A.W.B. Simpson, *A History of the Common Law of Contract*, OUP, 1987; Simpson also wrote the historical introduction to M.P. Furmston, *Law of Contract* (Cheshire, Fifoot and Furmston), 13th edn, Butterworth, 1996). The intention in this section is to provide a brief historical explanation of some elements of the law of contract, since it is an inevitable feature of the common law, based as it is in the system of precedent, that ancient doctrines sometimes return to haunt the modern law.

Two periods of history are especially significant in the development of the law of contract. The first, which is examined here, covers a period of some three hundred years, ending in the early years of the seventeenth century, when the action for breach of contract first developed. The second period covers the late eighteenth and nineteenth centuries, which saw the climax of the philosophy of freedom of contract and which laid the foundations upon which our modern law is built.

At the beginning of the thirteenth century the royal courts did not hear actions relating to contracts. Of course, many transactions took place which we would today recognise as contracts, such as sales and loans, but they were left to be regulated by the many specialist or local jurisdictions which existed at the time. The first common law action for breach of contract was that of *covenant*. However, it was unable to develop into a general law of contract, because it was restricted to contracts made under seal (*cf.* 4.1). A further action of *debt* was developed which applied in the case of informal agreements, and which enabled the recovery of a specific sum of money owed to the claimant on the fiction that the claimant was recovering his own money. Debt nevertheless had its limitations. It did not allow the recovery of an unliquidated sum by way of damages for failure to perform a promised action (as opposed to the mere payment of money). In addition, trial procedures for debt were open to abuse by defendants, making success in such actions something of a lottery.

When the royal courts finally sought to expand their jurisdiction by taking control over contract actions, they did not seek to develop either of the existing writs (or claims) which today we recognise as contractual in nature. Rather, they turned to a more flexible writ, which was the forerunner of the modern tort of negligence, known as *trespass on the case*. The advantage of the trespass action was that the procedure was far more secure against abuse than was the case for the action of debt. By the end of the fourteenth century the courts would allow claims based on trespass for defective performance of an undertaking, which in the medieval Latin of court pleadings was known as an *assumpsit*. Assumpsit is the real foundation of the law of contract, but it developed relatively slowly, since in the early period it was available only for defective performance of an undertaking, and was not available for non-performance. This discrepancy can be explained in terms of formal procedure, but in practical terms was clearly illogical, and it was finally removed in *Thoroughgood's Case* (1584) 2 Co Rep 9a, 76 ER 401. The remaining obstacle to the development of assumpsit as a complete contract doctrine was the action for debt, since some courts would not allow an action to recover a specific sum of money on assumpsit, but insisted on the action being brought in debt, with its associated procedural difficulties. This obstacle was removed, and the law of informal contracts brought within the unified cause of action of assumpsit, by *Slade's Case* (1602) 4 Co Rep 92a, 76 ER 1072.

In the peculiar way of the common law, the establishment of a unified remedy for all types of contract action was the catalyst for the development of general principles of contract law. The most important, and yet the most baffling to scholars, was the development of the doctrine of consideration. There are broadly two schools of thought as to how consideration came into English law. The first attributes it to the doctrine of *causa* found in Roman and civil law, and which is said to have made its way into the common law via Canon law and then the Chancery court. The second attributes it to an analogous (but far from identical) requirement of the action of debt, and the requirement of detriment in the action of trespass, which were somehow transferred to the action of assumpsit to give it form. Whichever may be the true explanation, the precise mechanics of the development of the doctrine of consideration are obscure. All that may be said with confidence is that by the seventeenth century the requirement of consideration in informal contracts was in place, and the law of contract began to take on a shape which we still recognise today.

1.4 ROLE OF CONTRACT AND CONTRACT LAW

The central role of contract in our legal and economic systems is not accidental. If lawyers, judges and (latterly) Parliament have worked at refining, honing and polishing the law, and litigants continue to rely on it, it is because contract serves important purposes in society. Indeed, it appears that the device of contract is put to important uses in many diverse societies, and it would be wrong to assume that contract law as we know it is the only model, or is of universal application. It is essential to distinguish between the device of contract, which has universal qualities, and the law of contract, which is the vehicle for adapting those universal qualities to the particular needs of a given society.

1.4.1 Role of contract

All societies require a vehicle through which *planned exchanges* can be made. Societies which have moved beyond hunting and subsistence farming require methods of ordering existence so that such cooperation as is deemed necessary may take place. The role of planning embraces the need people have to project into the future reliable courses of action. The idea of *exchange* includes not only 'one-off' contracts, but also long-term business relationships comprising perhaps many hundreds of individual contracts; it may also include interpersonal relationships, and even the individual's relationship with the state. There is a relationship of mutual support between societal stability, the idea of planning and the existence of exchange. The ability to plan ahead is an important factor in creating stability, while a stable society, in which it can be predicted that exchanges will take place, is an essential ingredient of reliable planning.

What may seem to be an entirely theoretical description of the role of contract may be put into context by a simple example. For many readers, the only experience of contracting will be as an ultimate consumer, so that each contract made seems isolated and discrete. In that sort of situation the planning element in contracts is not self-evident. So, when a student purchases a book in a shop there is no doubt that the machinery by which the purchase is executed is a contract, but there is little sense of being merely one link in a chain, since the student is the last link. A moment's consideration will reveal, however, that the particular contract of sale can be achieved only within a complex matrix of other contracts. If it is an academic textbook, it is likely to have been commissioned by a publisher from the author. Both parties derive planning benefits from such a contract. The author knows that the time spent labouring on the book will be rewarded by publication and (he or she hopes) the payment of royalties on sales. The publisher is able to fill a gap in the list of books it publishes, in the secure knowledge that it will have such a book to offer to booksellers after a certain period. Before the decision to go ahead with the book is made, the publisher's employees will probably have carried out some market research, and a decision will have been reached on the price at which such a book will sell. The publisher will seek to meet that price target by making contracts with printers and binders which will keep costs at the estimates made when fixing the price of the book. The printers and binders will in turn make long-term contracts with their raw material suppliers, so that they too may be sure that their costs remain within estimates. Delivery services, wholesalers and retail bookshops will all be involved in the process of delivering the book to the ultimate consumer.

Businessmen do not assume that the link between author and reader will be achieved by a catalogue of fortunate accidents: they plan every stage of the marketing of a book, and they achieve confidence in the planning by securing it with contracts. This matrix of contractual relationships, against which any particular contract must be viewed, explains why the first instinct of contract lawyers is to seek to preserve an agreement under threat, since much more is at stake when one contract fails than just the relationship between the two contracting parties.

1.4.2   Role of contract law

If the role of the device of contract is to provide for confident planning of exchanges, the role of contract law is to mould those planned exchanges to the particular society the law serves. Thus, English contract law reflects the politico-economic philosophy prevailing in this country. Theories of the law of contract, which in recent years have been a fashionable subject of academic debate, are simply the reflection of these politico-economic philosophies. Just as few claim that any single such philosophy has a monopoly of the right answers for any given society, so it is difficult to claim that any single contract theory provides all the right answers as far as the development of the law of contract is concerned. But that does not mean that contract theory is without value.

1.4.2.1   The significance of theory   There are many judges and practising lawyers who would deny the existence of any theory underlying the common law of contract, or who would dismiss theory as unrelated to the real world. This attitude may be understandable, since judges and lawyers must decide individual cases on their merits in accordance with the law, and are not primarily concerned with the elaboration of theory. Nevertheless, it may also be shortsighted. The law does not stand still, but rather has its own internal dynamism. In particular, changes in the law may result from judicial reasoning by reference to values where the court perceives the need to make a choice of how the law should develop to meet a situation not previously encountered, or where the scope of a particular rule has not been precisely defined. Consistent development of the law, so that such changes 'fit' within the existing scheme of things, assumes that judges have a sense of what the scheme of things is. Thus, an understanding of the theory of contract is essential to rational choices in developing the law, and should provide the student of law with criteria by which to assess the appropriateness of choices made. A satisfactory theory must explain how the law has developed to the point it is at today, and must provide the basis for establishing how the law may develop in the future by indicating general principles capable of giving rise to specific rules. Dissatisfaction with theory in general may have been caused by the growing inability of classical theory, which until now has dominated, to account for the existing rules of the law of contract. The question remains whether there is any more satisfactory theory which can take its place.

The discussion in this section inevitably refers to the substance of the law, which is examined later in this book. Readers may therefore find it beneficial to return to this section after completing their study of the substantive law.

1.4.2.2 Classical theory The roots of classical theory go back at least as far as the eighteenth century. In seeking to explain the somewhat adventitious development of contract law in England, nineteenth-century commentators borrowed from the writings of French legal theorists, who by 1804 had succeeded in embodying in the French civil code a highly individualist conception of contract. The parties were regarded as having the power and the unrestricted freedom to determine how their relationship was to be governed. This French approach, which was the product of the political liberalism of the eighteenth century, fell in with the economic liberalism of nineteenth-century England to produce an equally individualist theory of contract law in this country. Nevertheless, the realities of the process of adjudication meant that the substantive law was obliged to move away from a purely individualist or subjective approach to contract, so that the much vaunted sanctity of individual autonomy in contracting, which made contract immune from judicial interference, was much more a theoretical ideal than a rule of law.

When we talk about the classical theory of contract today (see C. Fried, *Contract as promise: a theory of contractual obligation*, Harvard University Press, 1981), we must consider a modified form of the theory which has tried to account for the way the law has developed. Nevertheless, at the core of this 'modern' classical theory is the binding nature of the promise which has been voluntarily made. The crucial element in contract, which marks it out as different from most other areas of the law of obligations, is that it is more than reactive: it is creative. It does not merely provide the means of resolving disputes which may arise when certain events happen: it provides the mechanisms whereby things can be made to happen. For early contract scholars it was a crucial observable phenomenon that without any reliance by either party the law regarded the mutual exchange of promises as, without more, sufficient to create a binding obligation (see 4.3.1.1). Tort and restitution were obligations produced by a reaction to events; but contract produced obligation as the result of the mere *exercise of will* in the form of promise. It was not surprising, therefore, that promise became the core of the theory, since it appears to be the essential ingredient marking contract out as separate from the rest of the law of obligations.

Before we examine how classical theory fits with the law of contract, we should examine why the mere fact of promise (or voluntary undertaking) produces obligation. A first explanation, which owes much to political liberal theory, is that there is a *moral obligation* inherent in promising which is derived from the social convention of creating expectations by one's undertaking (Fried, *op cit.*, pp. 14–17). The social convention came into being because the liberal ideal of respect for persons and property could be achieved only if reliable cooperation could be established. There is support for this idea in the rule that the measure of damages for breach of contract is the amount necessary to put the non-breaching party into the position he or she would have been in had the contract been performed (13.1), which is generally regarded as protecting that party's expectation under the contract. We know that this protection of expectation is restricted by rules relating to remoteness (13.9.2) and the fact that it is not possible to recover for loss of expectation where that expectation loss is too speculative (13.2.3). However, a cogent argument can be made that these doctrines are no more than necessary limits to cope with procedural problems such as the fallibility of the means of proof, and do not take away from the basic premise that the promisee's actual expectation is to be protected. A more serious objection arises out of the fact that the objectivisation of contract apparent in the formation of contracts (2.1) and in remedies for breach of contract (13.2) appears to be more than procedural, and seems to substitute for the actual expectation a collective appraisal of what the expectation should have been.

A second explanation of the binding nature of promise, not entirely distinct from the first, derives from the liberal economic theories of the nineteenth century. Here, individual autonomy is not the goal itself, but it is a pivotal tool in the achievement of the actual goal of *maximisation of wealth* to the greater good of all in society. Maximisation of wealth is achieved by market exchanges, where both or all the parties involved count themselves as benefited by the exchange which has taken place. The concept of market depends upon the binding nature of bargains made in the market, so that the individual's promise is required to be binding for the market system to work. Support for this version of classical theory can be found in the existing English rules relating to exemption clauses in genuinely freely negotiated contracts (see 6.2). The purpose of such devices is said by economists to be to provide a mechanism whereby the parties may allocate the risks of the enterprise between them: if they are both wealth-maximisers they may be assumed to have allocated those risks in a mutually beneficial way. To refuse to enforce exemption clauses in such circumstances would be wrong, since the effect would be to reallocate the risk away from what the parties had calculated was mutually beneficial. Nevertheless, classical theory is ill equipped to account for such intervention in freedom of contract as is provided, for example, by the UCTA 1977 (6.6.2).

It is not surprising that classical theory provides a coherent explanation of the rules of formation of agreement (Chapter 2). Promise is the essence of the theory. Promises create expectation, and can only do so if clear lines of communication are established. These rules do no more than set out the means whereby promises are made. Nevertheless, the fact that the rules are consistent with the theory cannot hide the fact that there is increasing doubt, even among the judiciary, about whether the existing rules really conform to what business people do in practice (see below).

It is perhaps surprising that classical theory should cavil at the doctrine of consideration (Fried, *op cit.*, pp. 28–39, especially at p. 35). After all, the paradigm of consideration is usually said to be the mutual exchange of promises. Perhaps the consideration doctrine is no more than a trace of the Protestant work ethic in the common law: a rule against getting something for nothing! More probably, it shows that the common law idea of contract is founded in economic rather than political liberalism: wealth maximisation results from mutual exchange, and there is no exchange involved in gratuitous promising.

Beyond the rules relating to the formation of contracts the position of classical theory is less secure. Where the law must react to events which are outside the scope of the will of the parties, or to which the parties have for whatever reason given no attention, the insistence of classical theory on the autonomy of the will of the parties is inconsistent with the rules of the law of contract as they exist today. Thus, we shall see that in relation to mistake (Chapter 3), illegal contracts (Chapter 12), implied terms (5.5) and frustration (Chapter 8), the approach of contemporary law is to impose a solution, often on the criterion of what is reasonable in the circumstances, and to abandon the fiction of searching for and complying with the will of the parties. That is not to say that classical theory is wholly without relevance. There is no doubt that it shaped the law in a crucial period of its development, and that it draws attention to an important element in modern contract law, the binding nature of mutual promises. However, it cannot be regarded as a satisfactory theory when it is unable to account for important areas of the law. Its failure in this regard probably reflects the fact that the politico-economic philosophy which inspired it, is no longer the philosophy underlying our contemporary law. Nevertheless, the doctrine of binding precedent ensures that cases decided during the period when the classical concept of contract was at its height remain influential today, and it is for this reason that classical theory continues to make a significant contribution to existing law.

In recent years two separate perceptions have generated the belief among many commentators that classical theory is unable to explain the entirety of modern contract law. The first is that contract law is not merely a response to the exercise of will by the contracting parties. Contract law also responds to events, often by imposing an obligation generally regarded as nevertheless contractual, or by modifying an already existing obligation. In each case the reaction of the law is independent of the will of the parties. Examples of this response to events may be found in the law relating to promissory estoppel (see generally 4.4.2) and other areas of law.

The second perception is that the limited empirical evidence available (see Beale and Dugdale (1975) 2 Br J Law Soc 45) suggests that in practice business people do not behave in a manner consistent with the classical conception of contract. For example, only in a formal sense could their contractual undertakings be regarded as promises, or the product of an exercise of will, since they frequently had little knowledge of the detailed undertakings contained in contractual documents. Moreover, business people frequently do not seek to avail themselves of the full remedy available for breach of contract (damages for lost profit) in cases of mutual exchange of promises but no performance. Thus, where an order was cancelled before any work had been done, most of the firms surveyed would accept the cancellation without seeking compensation. Where there had been some, but not complete, performance by the time of cancellation, a charge would be made, usually based on the cost of work actually done, and an allowance for profit related not to the entire contract but solely to the means of computing actual costs incurred.

1.4.2.3 Reliance-based theories The most significant post-classical theory of contract is based on the notion that obligation results from the fact of reliance (and its most eloquent exponent has been Professor Atiyah: see especially (1978) 94 LQR 193). Both the practice of business people and some of the legal doctrines noted above (especially promissory estoppel) suggest that the important factor is not the promise made, but the fact of reliance on it. Promise remains important in providing evidence of what has been undertaken, but it is not the source of obligation. Even in the field of formation of agreements, where classical theory is relatively secure, the analysis is sometimes improved by considering reliance as the source of obligation. This view is certainly a more rational explanation of the cases relating to what are known respectively as the 'battle of forms' (2.6.3.2) and 'agreements to agree' (3.1.3).

In general it seems that our instinct of obligation (or its absence) lies not in the mere fact of promise, but in the quality of the reaction to the promise. Consider this well-known example: A says to B, 'Let's go out for dinner. I'll pay for the meal: you buy the wine.' B agrees, and they arrange to meet at the restaurant. A does not keep the date, preferring to go to the cinema with C. It is almost universally accepted that A's behaviour should not be regarded as a breach of contract actionable in the courts. For classical theory that conclusion presents a problem, since there appears to be no difference in moral terms between this promise and a promise of a more commercial nature (e.g., to deliver goods for payment). The social convention of keeping promises applies equally to both. Neither is there an absence of exchange: A's promise is not gratuitous, and therefore appears to meet the wealth-maximising criterion. Why then is it our first instinct that A's promise did not give rise to a contractual obligation? The answer appears to lie in the quality of our reaction to the promise, which involves weighing the extent and nature of the reliance placed upon it. Thus serious consequences are likely to result from the failure to deliver goods which have been promised in return for payment, but it is not easy to predict very serious consequences resulting from the failure to keep a dinner date. Notice, however, that our reaction is not in terms of what actually happened: it is a generalised reaction based upon what in our experience would normally be the case, or what would be reasonable in the circumstances.

It seems clear, therefore, that in some circumstances reliance may provide a better explanation of the source of contractual obligations than does classical theory. Nevertheless, it also seems that, like classical theory, reliance cannot alone account for the whole of the law of contract. In the first place, there is the problem of wholly executory contracts, which are enforceable after the mere exchange of promises. They may be less significant in real life than the place given to them in the textbooks, but there is no denying that the law does enforce contracts which exist in the absence of any reliance. Secondly, there is the problem of promissory estoppel, which although a source of obligation is only a qualified source: it does not create any new obligations where none existed previously (4.4.3.2). How can reliance be the major source of obligation when the principal reliance-based doctrine does not itself create active obligations? Lastly, there is the problem of those rules of contract law which are based on criteria independent of the parties to the contract. A weakness of the reliance theory is that it is as much based in the relationship between the contracting parties as is classical theory. In respect of classical theory it was suggested that one flaw was its inability to cope with those rules of contract law which permit judicial intervention in the agreement between the parties according to what is reasonable rather than according to what is presumed to have been their intention. The same criticism applies to reliance theory, in that it is unable to account for the court's intervention in the contract on grounds of reasonableness which do not derive from the dealings between the parties but from a collective or community sense of what is right in the circumstances.

1.4.2.4 A collective theory of contract A somewhat different response to the inadequacy of classical theory has been the suggestion that contractual obligation is derived from the need to protect reasonable or legitimate expectation (e.g., B. Reiter and J. Swan, 'Contracts and the protection of reasonable expectation', in *Studies in Contract Law*, Toronto: Butterworths, 1980, pp. 1–23 and Steyn, 'Contract Law: Fulfilling the Reasonable Expectations of Honest Men' (1997) 113 LQR 433). This theory is similar to classical theory in seeing expectation as the essence of contract, but it goes beyond classical theory in recognising that promise is not the only means of creating expectation. Indeed, it assumes that in many circumstances society (through the courts) will regard one party's expectation as reasonably held and so deserving of protection irrespective of the will of the other party. So, some expectation will be created by promise, some by reliance, some by other means, including perhaps the protection of certain classes within society and 'fairness'. The essence of the collective approach to contract and its basis in reasonable expectation is that it endeavours to be sufficiently flexible to account for most, if not all, observable instances of contractual obligation.

This theory rests heavily on the roles both of the device of contract and of contract law. Contract law, it was suggested above, is the vehicle which adapts the device of contract, which is important for its facilitation of planned exchanges, to the need of a particular society. Classical contract law, therefore, reflected the use made of planned exchanges in the aggressively free enterprise society of the nineteenth century. It would not be surprising to find classical ideas of contract law unsatisfactory if the nature of society had itself changed. Most people accept that there has indeed been a change in the nature of society since the nineteenth century, from out-and-out free enterprise to mixed economy. That is, in our society today resources are allocated partly through the decisions of private individuals and companies, and partly through the decisions of government (including the courts). The precise balance of the mixture changes from time to time, and since the 1980s there has been a swing away from a more collectivist approach to one which is more individualist.

In this context 'allocation of resources' involves the redistribution of wealth between the more and less powerful in society by means other than taxation and welfare legislation. Thus, the law administered by the courts does not strive only for allocative efficiency, as a free-market approach would prescribe. It also contains an element of distributive justice which cannot be explained in terms of market economics. The law, whether it is a judicial creation or the creation of Parliament, attempts to redress the balance between the weak and strong elements in society, protecting the former against the latter. On the other hand, the very idea of a *mixed* economy means that where the functions of balance and protection are not required, the legal system must enable private ordering of exchange. Thus, the law must assess the level of intervention required according to the type of contract confronting it. It is able to do so by amending the nature of what it deems to be a reasonable expectation according to the circumstances of the case.

The relevant circumstances to be consulted in evaluating what are the reasonable expectations in any given situation will include the nature of the parties, and especially their relative positions. However, they will also include the nature of the subject-matter of the contract, the manner in which the contract was entered into, and relevant public policies of the society in which the contract was made. The result is that we should have general principles of the law of contract, but also specific rules tailored to particular types of contractual activity.

This theoretical breaking down of contractual activity into distinct groups, to which distinct rules may apply because of the different assumptions we make about what would be a reasonable expectation within each particular type of activity, appears to have been reflected in recent developments in the substantive law. Although there is still a common core of principles of contract law, many discrete areas of contractual activity have developed their own specialised rules. Employment contracts, contracts for the sale of goods (see 1.5), contracts made by consumers, contracts of insurance, contracts of international trade, are all examples where it is necessary to proceed from an understanding of the general law of contract to more specific rules relevant to the particular context alone. A detailed example will serve to illustrate the point. In contracts for the sale of goods there is no blanket implied term guaranteeing the quality of goods sold, but there is such an implied term where the seller is selling 'in the course of a business' (s. 14(1) and (2), Sale of Goods Act 1979; see 5.5.3.2). This implied term about quality can be excluded by express words in the contract of sale where the buyer is also in business, but it is not possible to exclude the guarantee of quality in the case of a sale to a consumer (s. 6(2) and (3), UCTA 1977; see 6.6.2.4). Thus we find that within the law relating to the sale of goods there are differing rules which apply according to the nature of the contracting parties. The rules which apply between business people exist to enforce the bargain made between them by their express promises (see, e.g., *Photo Production Ltd* v

Securicor Transport Ltd [1980] AC 827 and case law on reasonableness under UCTA 1977 in the context of commercial contracts), but the rules applicable in the case of contracts with consumers impose standards of 'fair' contractual behaviour intended to prevent the stronger party taking advantage of the weaker, and those standards reflect the collective values of society as a whole.

1.4.2.5 Formalism and realism One further theory merits some mention here, which also reflects the practical distinction in approach to commercial and consumer contracts. J. N. Adams and R. Brownsword ('The Ideologies of Contract' (1987) 7 LS 205, *Understanding Contract Law*, 3rd edn, Sweet & Maxwell, 2000, and R. Brownsword, *Contract Law: Themes for the Twenty-First Century*, Butterworths, 2000, Chap. 6) argue that there are competing ideologies in the approach of the judiciary to contract cases. They believe that these competing ideologies assist both in explaining contract decisions and in predicting future decisions, although they lead to tensions in what Adams and Brownsword refer to as the contract 'rule book'.

Formalism regards the rule book as a closed system of principles which are to be mechanically applied, and it is therefore divorced from the results in individual cases. However, most modern judges tend to adopt a realist approach which may involve challenges to the rule book where it stands in the way of achieving justice. The realist approach can itself be broken down into market-individualism and consumer-welfarism. The philosophy behind the market-individualist approach is essentially commercial and focuses on contract as the means to facilitate competitive exchanges. Therefore certainty is a vital influencing factor for market-individualists, who in this context seek to defend the reasonable assumptions of the parties. On the other hand, the consumer-welfarist approach is more interventionist (e.g., consumer protection) and focuses on questions of fairness and reasonableness. As a result it is far more flexible and protectionist in its approach compared to market-individualism. As Brownsword states in *Contract Law: Themes for the Twenty-First Century* (at p. 124):

> Putting the contrast very generally, whereas the former ideology insists upon contractors being held to their freely agreed exchanges, the latter seeks to ensure a fair deal for consumer contractors and, more generally, to relieve against harsh or unconscionable bargains.

It is possible to identify these differing approaches in individual judgments and *ratios* of cases: see Adams and Brownsword, *Understanding Contract Law*.

1.4.2.6 Conclusion If any single theory can explain the disparate elements of current contract law, it is perhaps the chameleon-like theory of protection of reasonable expectations. It has been argued that the theory rests on a circular argument, since the expectation exists only by virtue of the fact of its protection, and so the theory is no more than a self-fulfilling prophecy. This argument neglects the importance of the role of the device of contract (see 1.4.1), which suggests that the function of confident forward planning which is facilitated by contract would continue to be used by the great majority of contracting parties whether or not contracts were legally enforceable. Equally, the mere fact that contracts are enforceable would not cause parties to contract unless the device of contract was perceived to be socially useful. In other words, like classical theory, the theory of protection of reasonable expectations derives its sense of obligation from social convention, from the socially practised habit of contracting in order to provide for planned exchanges. The important difference between classical, promise-based theory and the protection of reasonable expectation is that under the latter theory the content of the expectation may be dictated by something other than an individual's voluntary undertaking. Of course, in many contracts, especially those of a commercial nature, the law allows the dimension of individual autonomy to govern the expectation, and in those situations this theory may be little different from classical theory. Thus, in commercial matters the law must be the servant and not the master of those engaged in business. But in many other types of contract the law imposes limits on the dimension of individual autonomy in contracting, and contractual expectations are shaped by collective evaluations of what the content of obligations should be.

1.5 CONTRACT AND THE SALE OF GOODS

Contracts for the sale of goods are amongst the most common types of contract encountered. For many readers, their main experience of contracting will have been in purchasing goods. For that reason, many of the hypothetical examples of contracts used in this text are based on simple sales transactions. Nevertheless, it is important to enter a note of caution about contracts for the sale of goods. Such contracts have developed as a distinct category, to which the general principles of contract law apply, but on top of which have been grafted special rules applicable to sales transactions alone. This law was originally codified in 1893, and subsequent amendments have been consolidated in the Sale of Goods Act (SGA) 1979. A detailed study of these rules requires a separate book (e.g., P. S. Atiyah, J. N. Adams and H. MacQueen, *The Sale of Goods*, 10th edn, Longman, 2001). Particular rules applicable to the sale of goods are noted throughout this text, but it is necessary here to explain the important impact of the notion of 'property' which is central to such contracts.

1.5.1 The central role of property rights

Section 2(1) of the SGA 1979 defines a contract of sale of goods as a 'contract by which the seller transfers or agrees to transfer the property in goods to the buyer for a money consideration'. 'Property' here means ownership, and so the legal effect of a sales transaction is to transfer the ownership of the goods from seller to buyer. When dealing with sales contracts it is important to keep that legal effect in mind, since it has important consequences for the rest of the law. It is also important to realise that the parties' reasons for entering a sale transaction may only incidentally coincide with the legal purpose of the transaction. In litigation, however, the parties' motives will take second place to the legal purpose.

The overriding importance of the transfer of ownership is well demonstrated by the decision in *Rowland* v *Divall* [1923] 2 KB 500. The plaintiff had bought a car from the defendant. He then resold the car to a third party. The police repossessed the car after a period of four months, the car having been stolen by a person who had sold it to the defendant. The plaintiff repaid the money he had received from the third party, and then claimed back the price he had paid to the defendant, on the ground of total failure of consideration (14.4.2). That is, he claimed that he had received nothing of what he was entitled to receive under the contract of sale. The defendant sought to resist this claim by saying that the failure of consideration was not total, since the plaintiff had had the (potential) use of the car for four months. His defence failed, because the plaintiff was entitled under a contract of sale not merely to use of the car but to legal ownership. Since the car was stolen, the defendant was not in a position to transfer legal ownership and this meant that the whole contract failed.

1.5.2 The power to transfer ownership

The general rule is that the seller can transfer only such title to goods as he himself enjoys (s. 21(1), SGA 1979). Therefore, where the seller is not the owner, he cannot transfer ownership to the buyer. Unfortunately, lawyers and judges often still refer to this rule by its Latin name, so it is necessary to give it here: *nemo dat quod non habet*. The rule is subject to a number of important exceptions, which are of particular importance in the law of agency. The operation of the rule can be demonstrated by reference to the facts of *Rowland* v *Divall* [1923] 2 KB 500 (above). The plaintiff was obliged to refund the money to the third party to whom he thought he had sold the car, because he had not been able to pass the ownership of the car to that third party. The reason for his inability to pass on ownership was that he had not been the owner, since the defendant, who had purported to sell the car to him, was also not the owner at the time of the sale. Thus, a defect early in the chain of sales (the defendant did not acquire ownership when he unwittingly bought the car from a thief) caused all the subsequent sales to be defective because ownership was not transferred by the transaction.

Of course, had one of the exceptions to the general rule applied to any one of the chain of transactions, ownership would have been transferred even if the seller had not himself been the owner, and from that point on subsequent sales would not have been defective. For example, if the thief had been a mercantile agent who was known regularly to sell cars on behalf of others, and had been in possession of the car with the consent of the owner before he misappropriated it, the defendant would have acquired good title (s. 2(1), Factors Act 1889) and the subsequent sales in the chain would have been unaffected by the early defect in title.

The *nemo dat* rule is clearly an obstacle to the free flow of goods in commerce, especially where it necessitates the unravelling of complex chains of sales, and the exceptions to the rule have been developed precisely to avoid, if possible, the need to unravel contracts which at the time of the transaction neither contracting party knew to be affected by a defect in title to the goods purportedly sold.

1.5.3 Void and voidable contracts and sales to third parties

The rule relating to the power to transfer ownership is further complicated by the distinction which must be made between void and voidable contracts. A void contract is automatically no contract at all; it is treated as if it had never been made, so that a void contract can have no effect. An agreement which is affected by 'common mistake' is, for example, void: the contract fails from the very beginning and no consequences can ensue from it (9.1). On the other hand, a voidable contract remains a valid contract until the party who has the right to complain takes steps to have it set aside. Should that party choose not to have the contract set aside, the contract is valid and all the usual effects of contract flow from it. An example of a voidable contract is an agreement affected by misrepresentation (Chapter 10).

These differences of effect between void and voidable contracts have an impact on the power to transfer ownership. Since a void contract can have no effect, it is impotent to transfer ownership between the purported seller and buyer. Thus, if a contract of sale from A to B is void, a third party (C) who subsequently purports to buy the goods from B cannot obtain ownership of the goods since B is not the owner. This consequence can be avoided only if one of the exceptions to the rule about transfer of ownership applies (see 1.5.2). On the other hand, since a voidable contract is of full effect until actually set aside, it can transfer ownership between seller and buyer. Thus, if a contract of sale from A to B is merely voidable, a third party (C) who subsequently purports to buy the goods from B does obtain ownership of the goods provided the sale by B to C takes place before A takes steps to have the contract set aside. This rule is embodied in s. 23 of the SGA 1979. A close corollary of the rule is that once third-party rights have intervened in the case of a voidable contract, the party who had the right to have the contract set aside (rescind it) loses that right (see, for example, 3.2.2 and 10.5.2.4).

1.6 THE GLOBALISATION OF CONTRACT LAW

There are a number of international influences on the principles of English contract law which have had an impact on its development over recent years. These developments have in the first place meant that some changes to substantive principles have been necessary, e.g., to implement European legislation. In addition, English contract law needs to adapt to the demands of contracting in an electronic age which is necessarily international. The growth of e-commerce poses considerable challenges for existing principles.

Alongside these developments, there have been a number of projects the objective of which has been the harmonisation of contract and commercial law principles. Given the increasingly international dimension of contracting, it is seen as important to address differences in principles and treatment of specific issues arising in contractual formation, performance and breach.

1.6.1 Harmonised statements of principle

In the latter part of the twentieth century, there were a number of attempts to harmonise or produce statements of principles in an effort to rationalise the distinctions apparent between jurisdictions. In the context of international sales contracts, the United Nations Commission on International Trade Law (UNCITRAL) was responsible for the 1980 Vienna Convention on Contracts for the International Sale of Goods (CISG). As an international Convention, this can have effect only if ratified by the country concerned. To date the Vienna Convention has not been ratified by the UK, although it has been ratified by most other significant trading nations and now forms part of the legal principles applicable to international sales contracts within those jurisdictions.

In 1994, UNIDROIT, the International Institute for the Unification of Private Law, produced its *Principles of International Commercial Contracts* in an attempt to provide a uniform set of principles (or articles) which might be adopted for use in any jurisdiction. The intention is that they can be adopted by the parties as governing their contractual dealings. The Principles are truly international, in the sense that the participants to the discussions who devised the Principles come from a range of backgrounds: common law, civil law and socialist traditions. (See M. P. Furmston, 'Unidroit General Principles for International Commercial Contracts' (1996) 10 JCL 11.)

At the same time the Lando Commission produced a set of contract law principles for Europe which might be used as the basis for harmonisation of contract and commercial law within the European Union (experience with the implementation of relevant European directives having highlighted the fundamental differences between the legal backgrounds in Member States) and, in the meantime, might also be explicitly adopted by the parties. These *Principles of European Contract Law* (PECL) were published in two parts and now form part of a single volume (O. Lando and H. Beale, *Principles of European Contract Law, Parts I and II*, Kluwer Law International, 2000). As we shall see, there are many similarities between the UNIDROIT Principles and PECL. However, both have no legal force and their use will depend upon adoption by the parties.

It is anticipated that these Principles will become increasingly important as examples of how the law might develop, and it is therefore important that students should both be aware of their existence and have some exposure to examples of the Principles in individual instances. For this reason, individual articles are referred to on occasions in this text.

Where relevant and of interest, this book also highlights some decisions of Commonwealth courts, e.g., the High Court of Australia and the Supreme Court of Canada, and principles of substantive law, e.g., § 90 of the American Restatement of Contracts, for the purposes of indicating how these jurisdictions have approached a particular issue or legal dilemma, e.g., alteration promises (4.4.7) and privity (15.2 and 15.5.4). It has become common practice for judges to refer to a range of sources as justifying their decisions. This factor alone is further evidence of the internationalisation of contract law.

1.6.2 European directives

The European Union has introduced a number of measures, essentially in the field of consumer protection, as directives, which have required implementation by Member States. These have had considerable influence on the law of consumer protection and, less directly, on general approaches to contracting. Examples include Directive 1993/13/EC on unfair terms in consumer contracts (implemented and now in force as the Unfair Terms in Consumer Contracts Regulations 1999 (SI 1999 No. 2083) (discussed at 6.6.3)). Although the central importance of this Directive is its scope and challenge to the fairness of terms in consumer contracts, it also introduced the concept of 'good faith' as a principle of English contract law (see below 1.6.3). Other examples of directives discussed in this text are the Distance Selling Directive 1999/7/EC, which protects consumers in distance sales or services contracts (implemented as the Consumer Protection (Distance Selling) Regulations 2000 (SI 2000 No. 2334)). This Directive is relevant to contracts concluded through the electronic medium, e.g., Internet contracts. There have also been more recent directives aimed at achieving an effective basis for e-commerce in the European Union, namely the Electronic Signatures Directive 1999/93/EC (implemented in part by the Electronic Communications Act 2000) and the E-Commerce Directive 2000/31/EC (discussed at 4.5.5).

The 'Europeanisation' of contract law (in the sense of general principles) has been quite limited because it has largely been aimed at consumer transactions (although the Directive on Self-Employed (Commercial Agents), 1986/653/EC, has a more general impact on agency law in the commercial context). (For further discussion see H. Beale, 'The "Europeanisation" of Contract Law', in R. Halson (ed.), *Exploring the Boundaries of Contract*, Dartmouth, 1996.) Arguably the most significant contribution made to general contractual principles has been the introduction of the concept of 'good faith'.

1.6.3 Good faith in English contract law

(For an excellent discussion of the issues and arguments, see R. Brownsword, *Contract Law: Themes in the Twenty-First Century*, Chap. 5. The discussion here is merely intended to give some background to the current debate.)

Traditionally, unlike civil law jurisdictions and several common law jurisdictions, English law has not recognised any general concept of good faith contracting, in terms of negotiation, content or performance of contracts. It was recognised by Bingham LJ in *Interfoto Picture Library Ltd* v *Stiletto Visual Programmes Ltd* [1989] 1 QB 433 as being 'in essence a principle of fair and open dealing'. However, many commentators regard its major deficiency to be the inability to provide a clear definition of what it encompasses.

While English law has not recognised any general principle of good faith, it has, to use the words of Bingham LJ, 'developed piecemeal solutions in response to demonstrated problems of unfairness'. For example, the regulation of exemption clauses (Chapter 6), the penalty rule (13.10), duress and undue influence, and the rule governing incorporation of onerous and unusual terms (5.3.3.2). However, this is not the same thing as adoption of a general principle.

There has been some scepticism about the desirability of adopting a general principle of good faith in English contract law (e.g., Lord Ackner in *Walford v Miles* [1992] 2 AC 128, 138, who, in the context of negotiations, regarded such a concept as too vague and 'inherently repugnant to the adversarial position of the parties when involved in negotiations'). Commercial lawyers, concerned to ensure that England retains its primary role in the resolution of international commercial disputes, have worried about the inherent uncertainty of such a general concept and the restrictions that it may impose on commercial dealings. Of course, this may be unduly to underestimate the ability of the English courts to give effect to vague principles and notions. For example, it is accepted that English law gives effect to 'reasonable expectations' of the contracting parties, which some would argue can be equally difficult to identify with precision. In any event, it would appear to be easier for English contract lawyers to accept a concept of good faith in relation to performance of a contract than in relation to its negotiation, and it is in this context that the concept of good faith has now been explicitly incorporated into English law in the Unfair Terms in Consumer Contracts Regulations 1999. Some assistance in defining the concept was given by the Court of Appeal in *Director General of Fair Trading v First National Bank plc* [2000] 2 WLR 1353, when it expressly equated good faith with 'fair and open dealing' and the prevention of 'unfair surprise and the absence of real choice'. (Good faith is discussed further in relation to the Regulations at 6.6.3.3.) It therefore appears that, in one case at least, English judges have experienced fewer difficulties with the concept than the sceptics would have anticipated.

Given that the concept of good faith appears to be an integral element of European consumer protection, we are likely to see its significance grow in this context in particular. Its relevance in the context of commercial contracts will always be more controversial. Both PECL and the UNIDROIT *Principles of International Commercial Contracts*, contain a general principle requiring that the parties act in accordance with fair dealing and good faith (Article 1.7, UNIDROIT; Article 1:201, PECL). This broad principle is applied in other articles throughout each set of principles, and the good faith requirement applies to formation, performance and enforcement. The concept is therefore seen as an essential underlying principle against which the parties' dealings are to be judged and in the light of which future principles will need to develop.

PART I   FORMATION

This Part examines issues concerning the formation of contracts. A contract is a legally binding agreement and this has a number of elements: there must be agreement and that agreement must be legally enforceable.

Chapter 2 examines the process of determining whether an agreement has been reached between the parties. This involves the question of how we determine the existence of agreement and the interrelationship of the legal principles for assessing agreement, including the issue of communication in an electronic age. One of the most interesting — and commercially essential — questions for contract formation is whether the existing principles can be adapted to the needs of electronic contracting, especially as English contract law has taken some time to devise principles governing communications by facsimile and telephone; even now there remains uncertainty in terms of contracting through these media. In the wider context, the contract formation principles contained in the *Principles of European Contract Law* (PECL) and the UNIDROIT *Principles of International Commercial Contracts*, may suggest that some of the tensions in the law of formation in English law might be better addressed by other principles.

The negotiation process can be protracted, and on occasions the parties may well fail to reach agreement on all the terms of their contract, or may agree to negotiate or deliberately leave gaps in their agreement. Chapter 3 examines those principles which determine when an agreement is sufficiently certain to be capable of enforcement and what happens when no agreement has been reached. It also examines mistakes which prevent agreement between the parties and mistakes whereby the contractual document fails accurately to reflect what the parties agreed.

The factors determining the enforceability of agreements and promises are examined in Chapter 4, namely intention to create legal relations, consideration and formalities. The consideration requirement is relevant both to formation and alterations to existing contracts, but both are examined within this Part for ease of understanding and to avoid excessive repetition. Chapter 4 also explains the capacity restrictions; in particular, contracts entered into by minors (persons under the age of 18).

TWO

Agreement

2.1 DETERMINING THE EXISTENCE OF AGREEMENT

In order to be able to conclude that there is a contract, giving rise to enforceable obligations, we must first identify the existence of a binding *agreement* between the parties.

It is the fact that the obligations are voluntarily agreed which distinguishes contract from other areas of law, such as tort, where the obligations are imposed by law. However, although it is often said that for agreement there must be a *consensus ad idem* (or meeting of minds), this does not mean that subjectively the parties' intentions must coincide. The existence (and indeed the content) of an agreement, and whether that agreement was intended to be legally binding, are not determined on the basis of what the parties themselves thought or intended. Instead, the courts look at external evidence (what the parties said and did at the time) as objectively indicating the parties' intentions and ask whether, on the basis of this evidence, the reasonable man would say that the parties were in agreement. As Lord Denning stated in *Storer* v *Manchester City Council* [1974] 3 All ER 824, 828:

> In contracts you do not look into the actual intent in a man's mind. You look at what he said and did. A contract is formed when there is, to all outward appearances, a contract. A man cannot get out of a contract by saying: 'I did not intend to contract', if by his words he has done so.

It is clear that the objective approach is preferable to a purely subjective approach for a number of reasons:

(a)   A subjective approach would create uncertainty. It would not be safe to rely on any promise if the promisor could later deny that he ever intended to make such a promise.

(b)   It would be totally impractical. As the parties may later say whatever suits their purpose at that time, it is clearly preferable to look only at what the parties said and did at the time of the agreement.

As J. N. Adams and R. Brownsword (*Understanding Contract Law*, 3rd edn, Sweet & Maxwell, 2000, p. 50) have stated: 'To found contract on a subjective approach, therefore, would impede commerce, invite fraud, and unfairly defeat good faith reliance on the natural meaning of a promise'.

It is clear, therefore, that determining the existence and content of an agreement — and whether it is intended to be legally binding — depends not on the parties' subjective intentions but on the impression which they have given by their words and actions. Steyn LJ, in *Trentham Ltd* v *Archital Luxfer Ltd* [1993] 1 Lloyd's Rep 25, 27, said, 'the governing criterion is the reasonable expectations of honest men' or what a reasonable man has been led to believe the position to be. Of course, this gives rise to a further question: Whose views determine the impression given? Who is the reasonable man for this purpose? There is no agreed view on this issue.

2.1.1   The objective approach interpreted

Howarth ('The Meaning of Objectivity in Contract' (1984) 100 LQR 265) argued that there are three different interpretations of what is meant by objectivity depending upon the standpoint of the reasonable man:

(a)   'promisor objectivity', which involves an assessment from the point of view of the reasonable promisor;
(b)   'promisee objectivity', which involves an assessment from the point of view of a reasonable promisee to whom the words were conveyed;
(c)   'detached objectivity', involving an assessment of the position from the point of view of an independent external person (so-called 'fly on the wall' objectivity).

In particular, 'promisee objectivity' must be understood as referring to a reasonable promisee in the context of the actual promisee, e.g., business-person or consumer (*Butterworth's Law of Contract*, M. P. Furmston (ed), Butterworths, 1999, p. 288). For example, in *Bowerman* v *ABTA* [1996] CLC 451, the majority of the Court of Appeal held that the ABTA notice would reasonably have been read by a member of the public (in the position of the promisee) as containing an offer of protection.

There has been much academic disagreement on this question of the meaning of objectivity. For example, J. R. Spencer, 'Signature, Consent and the Rule in *L'Estrange* v *Graucob*' [1973] CLJ 104 and J. P. Vorster, 'A Comment on the Meaning of Objectivity in Contract' (1987) 103 LQR 274, support promisee objectivity; whereas Howarth ((1984) 100 LQR 265 and (1987) 103 LQR 527) supported detached objectivity.

Lord Brightman's statement in *The Hannah Blumenthal* [1983] 1 All ER 34, at 55 (see 2.1.2 below), may be interpreted as supporting promisee objectivity; and the classic statement of Blackburn J in *Smith* v *Hughes* (1871) LR 6 QB 597 ('If, whatever a man's real intention may be, he so conducts himself that a reasonable man would believe he was assenting to the terms proposed by the other party, and that other party upon that belief enters into the contract with him, the man thus conducting himself would be equally bound as if he had intended to agree to the other party's terms') is often cited as supporting promisee objectivity, but seems equally capable of being cited to support detached objectivity.

On the other hand, there are also a number of statements by Lord Denning (e.g., in *Solle* v *Butcher* [1950] 1 KB 671, at 691, and *Oscar Chess Ltd* v *Williams* [1957] 1 WLR 370, at 373, references to 'an intelligent bystander') which appear to support detached objectivity. In *Thake* v *Maurice* [1984] 2 All ER 513 (at first instance), Peter Pain J stated (at 519): 'The test as to what the contract in fact was does not depend on what the plaintiffs or the defendant thought it meant, but on what the court objectively determines that the words used meant.' It is not surprising that judges who favour greater judicial intervention in the formation of contracts tend also to be those who advocate the 'fly on the wall' approach to objectivity, since it gives greater scope for a creative approach to interpreting the contract.

Interestingly, the Court of Appeal, in *Thake* v *Maurice* [1986] 1 All ER 497, adopted the more orthodox approach of promisee objectivity, and recent case law indicates that the courts appear to favour this approach (e.g., *Bowerman* v *ABTA Ltd* [1996] CLC 451 and *Edmonds* v *Lawson* [2000] QB 501).

The truth of the matter is almost certainly that the courts have not wished to be tied down to a single meaning on objectivity and wish to be able to choose between promisee and detached objectivity according to the court's perception of the merits of the case, albeit that promisee objectivity might be regarded as the usual or orthodox approach.

It is interesting also that both the *Principles of European Contract Law* (PECL) and the UNIDROIT *Principles of International Commercial Contracts* resolve the question of whether agreement has been reached (where there is an absence of common intention) by applying a general test of intention of the parties, interpreted 'according to the meaning that reasonable persons of the same kind as the parties would give to [the contract] in the same circumstances' (Article 4.1(2), UNIDROIT; Article 5:101(3), PECL). This test is essentially detached objectivity, but limiting the detachment so that the reasonable person is deemed to have the skills and knowledge possessed by these parties when making this judgment. This appears to be appropriate in the context of interpretation of a contract which already exists, but does not seem to be drafted to apply to the question of whether an agreement has resulted in the first instance.

In addition, there is a further provision in PECL (although omitted by UNIDROIT) identifying how an intention to be legally bound is to be determined (as opposed to the factual issue of agreement or interpretation in general). Article 2:102 provides that intention to be legally bound 'is to be determined from the party's statements or conduct as they were reasonably understood by the other party', thereby applying promisee objectivity to this issue.

There is much confusion over the applicable test of intention, and it is submitted that intention in terms of formation should not be judged (as in the case of the UNIDROIT principles) in accordance with a broad test of interpretation of content. For further discussion of the meaning of contractual intention, see A. De Moor, 'Intention in the Law of Contract: Elusive or Illusory?' (1990) 106 LQR 632, and the distinction between 'substantive' and 'formal' intention. It may therefore be appropriate to apply detached objectivity to general interpretation questions; but promisee objectivity would appear to be more appropriate to determining the issue of whether there is agreement and intention to be legally bound.

2.1.2   The residual subjective element

Of course, subjective intentions are relevant in the general sense that they may well coincide with the objectively ascertained intentions of the parties. However, does subjective intention have any other relevance?

In *The Hannah Blumenthal* [1983] 1 All ER 34, the issue to be determined was whether an arbitration had been abandoned by agreement based on a failure by the parties to take any active steps to progress the arbitration. Lord Diplock's formulation of the test for determining the existence of agreement stated that it was necessary that 'the intention of each as it has been communicated to and understood by the other (even though that which has been communicated does not represent the actual state of mind of the communicator) should coincide'. This appeared to introduce a subjective element into the test by requiring that *each* party's actual understanding of the other's intention had to coincide with the understanding of a reasonable man.

However, this formulation was not followed by the Court of Appeal in *The Leonidas D (Allied Maritime Transport Ltd v Vale do Rio Doce Navagacao SA)* [1985] 1 WLR 925, the Court preferring the formulation of Lord Brightman in *The Hannah Blumenthal*. Robert Goff LJ in *The Leonidas* D explained Lord Brightman's formulation in the following terms (at 936):

[I]f one party, O, so acts that his conduct, objectively considered, constitutes an offer, and the other party, A, believing that the conduct of O represents his actual intention, accepts O's offer, then a contract will come into existence, and on those facts it will make no difference if O did not in fact intend to make an offer, or if he misunderstood A's acceptance, so that O's state of mind is in such circumstances irrelevant.

Thus, whereas the conduct of the promisor is judged objectively and what the promisor may subjectively have intended is irrelevant, the actual assumptions made by the promisee are relevant where the promisee either knows, or ought reasonably to know, that the promisor did not intend to make an offer (or did not intend to make an offer in those terms). There will therefore be no contract where the promisee actually knows that the promisor has no intention to contract with him on those terms. It is only in this sense that subjective considerations are relevant to determining the existence of agreement. Treitel (*The Law of Contract*, 10th edn, Sweet & Maxwell 1999, p. 1) makes clear the reasoning for this exception when he states that the purpose of the objective approach 'is to protect B (the promisee) from the prejudice which he might suffer as a result of relying on a false appearance of agreement. There is clearly no need in this way to protect a party who knows that the objective appearance does not correspond with reality'. Of course, this reference is to positive actual knowledge of a different intention, when clearly there will be no prejudice to the promisee. However, will something less than actual knowledge suffice? Will it suffice that the promisee 'could not have been unaware' of the true position, or 'ought reasonably to have known'? Is it also the case that the promisee is not considered as prejudiced in this situation? In *Hartog* v *Colin & Shields* [1939] 3 All ER 566 (for facts see 3.3.2) it was held that on the basis of the pre-sale negotiations the plaintiff could not reasonably have supposed that the offer contained the offeror's true intention. However, this decision is difficult to reconcile with that of the Court of Appeal in *Centrovincial Estates plc* v *Merchant Investors Assurance Company Ltd* [1983] Com LR 158 (for facts see 3.3.2). It can be argued that the defendants, the tenants, ought to have known of the plaintiffs' mistake because the rent review clause indicated that in no circumstances should the rent fall when reviewed. However, the Court of Appeal did not consider that the plaintiffs had satisfied the necessary burden of proof on this issue. (In this situation the person making the offer alleges that he made a mistake with regard to the contract terms which the other ought to have known about and so cannot be allowed to 'snap it up'. It is discussed in the context of agreement mistake in Chapter 3, at 3.3.2).

2.2   TRADITIONAL AND NON-TRADITIONAL APPROACHES TO IDENTIFYING AGREEMENT

The objective approach looks for external evidence of agreement. Traditionally, agreement must be demonstrated by an unequivocal offer made by one party (the offeror) and by complete acceptance of that offer by the other party (the offeree). This approach is, of course, neat and designed to promote certainty. However, it is clearly artificial and inflexible, and may well ignore the reality of the situation by dictating that no agreement has been reached for purely technical reasons. As a result, there have long been instances of the courts either 'finding' the necessary offer and acceptance, or ignoring the traditional approach and simply recognising the existence of agreement by means of other external evidence.

Lord Wilberforce, in *New Zealand Shipping Co. Ltd* v *A.M. Satterthwaite & Co. Ltd, The Eurymedon* [1975] AC 154 (for facts see 4.3.4.2), admitted that this first method was a recognised practice when he said (at 167): 'English law, having committed itself to a rather technical and schematic doctrine of contract, in application takes a practical approach, often at the cost of forcing the facts to fit uneasily into the marked slots of offer, acceptance and consideration.'

This statement was later used by Lord Denning to support his view that on occasion a different approach to determining the existence of agreement was called for. In *Butler Machine Tool Co. Ltd v Ex-Cell-O-Corporation (England) Ltd* [1979] 1 WLR 401, Lord Denning suggested that the circumstances as a whole (i.e., all the documents and the parties' conduct) should be examined in an attempt to discover agreement. It seems that he wished to replace what was a question of law (subject to precise and sometimes detailed rules) with a pure question of fact. Although Lord Denning applied this approach in both *Butler Machine* and in the Court of Appeal in *Gibson v Manchester City Council* [1978] 1 WLR 520, the House of Lords in *Gibson* ([1979] 1 WLR 294; see the judgment of Lord Diplock at 297) made it clear that offer and acceptance remained the normal analysis and applied it to the facts before them (involving a contract said to have been entered into as a result of exchange of correspondence).

Of course, this does mean that the House of Lords was accepting that offer and acceptance was the only mechanism for determining the existence of a contract. Lord Diplock said 'there may be certain types of contract, though I think they are exceptional, which do not fit easily into the normal analysis of a contract as being constituted by offer and acceptance'. In what circumstances, therefore, might a different analysis of agreement be appropriate?

Steyn LJ, in *Trentham Ltd v Archital Luxfer Ltd* [1993] 1 Lloyd's Rep 25, considered that the normal analysis would apply 'in the vast majority of cases', and specifically gave a contract alleged to be made by exchange of correspondence as an example of the application of this approach. However, he added that this 'is not necessarily so in the case of a contract alleged to have come into existence during and as a result of performance'. Therefore, agreement may be found to exist using other means, where the alleged agreement is based on the conduct of both parties (i.e., executed agreement), despite the inability to analyse the performance in terms of offer and acceptance. This appears to be part of a more general policy-based approach to recognise executed agreements wherever possible (see 3.1.2), so that it cannot be said that the decision in *Trentham* provides unqualified general support for the alternative analysis determining the existence of agreement.

However, there is clear acceptance in the statements of Principles of the fact that agreement can be reached without the traditional analysis of offer and acceptance (e.g., Article 2:211, PECL; Article 2.1, UNIDROIT), and there are recognised situations in case law where the offer and acceptance analysis does not work very well and may come to be abandoned. These are situations which involve one or more third parties in the negotiating process (see *Clarke v Dunraven* [1897] AC 59), or instances where an offer is made more generally than to a single, identified offeree (see *Wilkie v London Passenger Transport Board* [1947] 1 All ER 258) or instances where the court is using the vehicle of contract to impose an obligation (see *Upton-on-Severn RDC v Powell* [1942] 1 All ER 220).

2.3 DETERMINING THE EXISTENCE OF AGREEMENT USING OFFER AND ACCEPTANCE

Determining the existence of agreement using offer and acceptance is inevitably to some extent a technical process. It is important, therefore, to determine both the issue of whether there has been an event which is capable of constituting a valid offer, acceptance or revocation, and the issue of whether and when communication of it took place.

The first question to address is whether the offeror has made an 'offer' (which involves an examination of what can constitute an offer; see 2.4). Other questions then arise, such as: did the offeree accept that offer (and what is needed to constitute an acceptance) (see 2.6), or was the offer withdrawn before acceptance could occur? (See 2.7.) There is a further complication in the need to determine whether the correspondence in question, be it offer, acceptance or revocation, has been effectively communicated since, until such time, it cannot take effect (see 2.5 and 2.6.4). This involves identifying the applicable principle for communication, for example, the need for the communication to have been actually communicated to the recipient, and then determining whether this in fact happened and, if so, at what point in time it occurred?

2.4 OFFERS AND INVITATIONS TO TREAT

2.4.1 Introduction

An offer is an expression of willingness to contract on the specified terms without further negotiation, so that it requires only acceptance for a binding agreement to be formed. It must be distinguished from all other statements made in the course of negotiations towards a contract (so called 'invitations to treat') since only an offer is capable of immediate translation into a contract by the fact of acceptance. A technical definition of an invitation to treat would be restricted to statements indicating the maker's willingness to receive offers. However, the expression is commonly used to describe any negotiating statement falling short of an offer which furthers the bargaining process, e.g., 'Would you be interested in buying my car?' is an invitation to treat and not an offer. Such statements may take the form of attempts to stimulate interest, requests for the supply of information, or any other stage in the sometimes lengthy progress to agreement.

Obviously, on many occasions offers and invitations to treat are easy to distinguish. On the other hand, there are times when the distinction is a fine one. In practice the courts look to the individual facts of each case in making the distinction, although there are recognised instances when a communication is more likely to be regarded as only an invitation to treat (discussed below at 2.4.2). The starting point for any determination of this issue must be that in order to constitute an offer the communication must be:

(a)   sufficiently specific in terms of the main obligation and price to be capable of immediate acceptance; and
(b)   made with an intention to be bound by the mere fact of acceptance.

This intention to be bound by the mere fact of acceptance is determined objectively, so that it amounts to examining the language used. In *Gibson* v *Manchester City Council* [1979] 1 WLR 294, the House of Lords examined the language of the correspondence to determine whether there was the necessary intention to be bound.

The Council had a policy of selling council houses to tenants. Mr Gibson was such a tenant and he applied for details. The city treasurer had replied that the Council 'may be prepared to sell the house to you' and invited Mr Gibson to complete an application form if he wished to buy. Mr Gibson did this, but the Council changed its policy and the question arose as to whether there was already a concluded contract of sale between Mr Gibson and the Council.

The House of Lords held that there was no concluded contract because the language of the city treasurer's letter made it clear that the Council did not intend to make a binding promise to be bound. The letter was not an offer which Mr Gibson had accepted, rather it was inviting Mr Gibson to make an offer to buy. Although Mr Gibson had made such an offer, his offer had not been accepted at the time of the change of policy. This decision is normally contrasted with that of the Court of Appeal in *Storer* v *Manchester City Council* [1974] 3 All ER 824, where the Court held that a binding contract had been concluded because the language used — namely, '[i]f you will sign the Agreement and return it to me, I will send you the Agreement signed on behalf of the [Council] in exchange' — indicated that it was the Council's intention to be bound and therefore constituted an offer.

A further useful illustration is provided by the decision in *Harvey* v *Facey* [1893] AC 552, where the plaintiffs had asked the defendants whether they would sell a particular property and requested that the defendants telegraph their lowest price. The defendants' reply, stating that the lowest price was £900, was held not to constitute an offer but only an indication of the minimum price if the defendants decided to sell. This case also illustrates that in contracts for the sale of land the courts will look for clear evidence that the process of negotiation is complete and that a definite promise to be bound is being made, before it determines that there is an offer capable of being accepted. (See also *Clifton* v *Palumbo* [1944] 2 All ER 497: 'I am prepared to offer you my estate for £600,000' was not an offer.)

2.4.2   Examples of the distinction in practice

Case law has established that there are some recognised instances when a particular communication is more likely to be regarded either as an offer, or as an invitation to treat. These operate as a starting point for consideration by the court, but it is quite possible that the normal principle may be found to be inappropriate, being at odds with the intention of the parties as revealed by the facts and the language used.

2.4.2.1   Advertisements, brochures and price lists   In *Partridge* v *Crittenden* [1968] 2 All ER 421, the appellant had placed an advertisement

indicating that he had certain wild birds for sale. It was an offence to offer such birds for sale. The advertisement did state a price, but gave no details about delivery or quantities available. On appeal the appellant's conviction was quashed, because the Court held that the advertisement did not amount to an offer but was merely an invitation to treat. In the words of Lord Parker, there was 'business sense' in treating such an advertisement as no more than an invitation to treat. Such a conclusion makes 'business sense' because construing such an advertisement as an offer would mean that the seller might find himself unable to supply all those who replied to the advertisement ('the limited stocks argument'). In *Grainger & Sons* v *Gough* [1896] AC 325, a wine merchant's catalogue and price list were considered to constitute no more than an invitation to treat on precisely that ground. If, however, the catalogue had been addressed to a limited group of customers, or had made it clear that unlimited supplies were available then, other things being equal, it might have been sufficiently specific to amount to an offer.

In addition, if a reward is advertised for the performance of a specified act, such as supplying information, that advertisement will constitute an offer of a unilateral contract (see 2.8), assuming that the language is sufficiently definite to be viewed as such. The acceptance of such an offer is the performance of that act and it cannot be accepted by making a promise (which is the position in bilateral contracts such as simple sale of goods contracts).

In *Carlill* v *Carbolic Smoke Ball Co.* [1893] 1 QB 256, the defendants had placed an advertisement in which they promised to pay £100 to any person catching influenza after using their smoke ball remedy three times a day for two weeks. The advertisement stated that £1,000 had been placed in a separate bank account in order to meet any claims made. The plaintiff had caught influenza after using the smoke ball in the required manner. The Court of Appeal treated the deposit of money as an indication of a willingness to be bound by the terms of the advertisement, thus making it an offer.

Similarly, in *Bowerman* v *ABTA* [1996] CLC 451, the majority of the Court of Appeal held that an ABTA notice, which was displayed on the premises of travel agents who were ABTA members, constituted an offer (or promise) of ABTA protection for customers performing an act, namely booking holidays with those ABTA members. This was because the notice was intended to be read, and would reasonably have been read, as an offer. It also requested the performance of an act as the acceptance, namely booking a holiday through an ABTA member.

The fact that such advertisements are regarded as offers makes practical sense, in that if a notice of a reward for performance of a particular act were to be regarded as an invitation to treat, the response (namely performing the act) would be the offer which could be accepted or rejected at will. People offering a reward would therefore have the benefit of seeing the requested act performed and yet not necessarily have to pay the reward.

That an advertisement requesting perform of an act constitutes an offer can be seen by examining the American decision in *Lefkowitz* v *Great Minneapolis Surplus Store*, 86 NW 2d 689 (1957). Here the advertisement was in the following terms: 'Saturday 9 am sharp: 3 brand new fur coats, worth to $100. First come first served. $1 each.' This was held to be an offer. Such an advertisement is requesting the performance of an act (being one of the first three customers on Saturday morning) as constituting the acceptance and entitling the customer to purchase one of these fur coats at this sale price. (By comparison, and for amusement, see the terms of the Pepsi promotion in the United States, discussed in S. Graw, 'Puff, Pepsi and "That Plane" — The John Leonard Saga' (2000) 15 JCL 281.)

2.4.2.2 Shop displays — shop windows or supermarket shelves   In *Fisher* v *Bell* [1961] 1 QB 394, it was held that to display a flick-knife with a price marker in a shop window did not amount to commission of the offence of offering such a knife for sale. In *Pharmaceutical Society of Great Britain* v *Boots Cash Chemists (Southern) Ltd* [1953] 1 QB 401, it was held that the display of goods on shelves in a self-service store did not amount to an offer of the goods for sale, so that no contract was formed merely by the customer removing the goods from the shelf. The facts were as follows:

There was a legal requirement that certain drugs and medicines only be sold under the supervision of a registered pharmacist. Boots had introduced self-service stores where the cash desks were supervised by such a person. Therefore an offence was committed if any sale contract relating to these drugs and medicines was formed before the customer reached the cash desk, e.g., if the sale contract was formed when the goods were removed from the shelves, since there was no supervision at that point.

It was held that no offence had been committed because the display of goods on supermarket shelves constituted an invitation to treat and not an offer. The court explained its decision in terms of the inconvenience to customers of not being able to remove goods from the shelves, put them in baskets and subsequently change their minds about the purchase, which would be the situation in theory if removing the goods from the shelves amounted to acceptance of an offer. In addition, in an ordinary shop, such as a bookshop, the shopkeeper reserves the right to refuse to sell, and that option is exercised in each case by the cashier on his behalf when the goods are presented for payment at the cash desk. To achieve this objective (of shopkeeper's freedom of contract) the offer to buy must come from the customer.

Nevertheless, it is possible to imagine a situation in which the display of goods in a shop would amount to an offer, for example, if it were made clear that the shopkeeper was willing to sell to anyone paying the displayed price. In this way it is also possible to explain the conclusion in *Chapelton* v *Barry Urban District Council* [1940] 1 KB 532, that a display of deckchairs constituted an offer. It also enables commercial sense to be realised by accepting the conclusion that in a self-service petrol station the customer accepts the garage's offer of petrol by putting petrol into the vehicle's petrol tank and is therefore liable to pay the amount shown on the pump (*Re Charge Card Services* [1988] 3 All ER 702).

As a final point on displays, it can be argued that it would have been perfectly possible for the court in the *Boots* case to have found that the display was an offer but that the offence was not committed because there would be supervision prior to acceptance of that offer by the customer, constituted by the customer's act of handing the goods to the cashier at the check-out (see the American case of *Lasky* v *Economy Grocery Stores* 65 NE 2d 305 (1946)). The courts in the *Boots* case appear to have assumed that if they found the display to be an offer then the customer's acceptance would have been the act of removing the goods from the shelves.

2.4.2.3   Websites   It would seem that websites are the electronic equivalent of displays, advertisements or catalogues of products for sale. This should mean that, in general, a website constitutes an invitation to treat. From a practical perspective this is important, since, as discussed above, the result is that that the site provider will retain freedom to contract because the offer will come from the customer. The site provider can therefore avoid entering into contracts with on-line buyers in excluded jurisdictions. In addition, the provider's stock may be limited and if the website is an invitation to treat so that customers make offers to buy, the provider can manage its stock and will not find itself bound to supply all those on-line buyers who seek to place orders.

A particular problem for website providers is mispricing of goods. In this context the status of the website, and whether a binding contract has been made, will be highly relevant. If a website constitutes no more than an invitation to treat, mispricing will not result in the supplier having to fulfil a contract at the misquoted price. For example, in September 1999, Argos advertised Sony television sets on its website at £2.99 instead of £299. The legal position would seem to differ depending upon what happened to individual customers: some orders were placed and also confirmed by Argos; while, on discovering the mistake, Argos advised other customers trying to place orders that there had been a mistake and that no orders could be accepted at the stated price. In the case of customers whose orders were not accepted or confirmed, there could be no binding contract of sale if the website constituted an invitation to treat. These on-line buyers would need to argue that the website was an offer, which would be a theoretical possibility only if performance of an act is requested (see 2.4.2.1 above). However, a normal sale of goods contract is bilateral, involving an exchange of promises and not the performance of an act. Something similar to the factual scenario in *Lefkowitz* would be required, e.g., a television set at £2.99 to the first ten on-line buyers after 6 am GMT on Thursday, 1 March.

The difficulty facing those customers whose orders had been confirmed was the fact that Argos had made a very clear mistake as to the price term, which on-line buyers either knew or ought reasonably to have known had been made. This was surely the whole point of the attempts to secure the television sets at the bargain price; on-line buyers knew very well that a mistake had been made and were seeking to 'snap it up'. The case law establishes that there will be no binding contract in this situation (*Hartog* v *Colin & Shields* [1939] 3 All ER 566; see 2.1.2 and 3.3.2).

It should not be assumed, however, that there is no liability on suppliers in this situation of mispricing goods (see Consumer Protection Act 1987, ss. 20–26). The important point is that there will be no contractual liability (and hence no compensation with which to purchase the television set which has been denied).

2.4.2.4 Tenders   The request for tenders is a negotiating device common in the world of major commercial contracts. A company seeking to purchase a major item or service, such as a piece of equipment or some construction work, will invite tenders from those interested in supplying the goods or service sought. Such an invitation may be published generally or in a trade journal, or circulated to companies likely to be interested. In normal circumstances the invitation for tenders is not treated as an offer, since the company issuing it may have criteria other than price which they wish to take into account in awarding the contract. In that case the tenders themselves are the first offers made (see *Spencer* v *Harding* (1870) LR 5 CP 561) and the person requesting the tenders has the freedom to determine which (if any) he or she will accept.

On the other hand, it is always possible that a request for tenders can be both specific and intended to be turned into a contract by mere acceptance, in which case it will be an offer. The usual case is where the expression 'highest bidder' or 'lowest bidder' is used, indicating a system of competitive tendering under which the person issuing the invitation to tender has declared himself or herself willing to be bound by the most competitive tender. There are *obiter* statements to this effect in *Spencer* v *Harding* (above).

The process of competitive tendering ran into a particular difficulty in the case of *Harvela Investments Ltd* v *Royal Trust Co. of Canada (CI) Ltd* [1986] AC 207. The vendors of a plot of land sought a 'single offer' for the whole plot from each of two interested parties, promising to accept the highest offer received provided it met other conditions stipulated. Both parties submitted bids complying with the conditions, but while one merely stated a price it was prepared to pay, the other stated both a concrete sum and a referential bid (i.e., '$101,000 in excess of any other offer'). The question for the House of Lords was which of the two bids was the higher, thus constituting the acceptance necessary for the formation of the agreement.

In one sense the referential bid was the higher offer, but such a conclusion was possible provided only one party made such a bid. The view taken was based on the fact that one of the main purposes of competitive tender bargaining is to ensure that negotiations come safely to fruition. To allow unrestricted use of referential bids was to risk such bargaining being abortive. The House of Lords therefore implied into the request for bids a stipulation that referential bids would not be accepted. In the opinion of Lord Templeman, with whom all their Lordships agreed, it was open to the vendors to initiate a process of bargaining by referential bids (which would be a form of auction), but such an interpretation would not be placed on a request for competitive tenders in the absence of express words to that effect.

The implied unilateral contract   In *Harvela Investments Ltd* v *Royal Trust Co. of Canada (CI) Ltd* (see above), Lord Templeman faced a conceptual difficulty in respect of the implied stipulation against referential bids, in that there was no contract immediately apparent into which the stipulation could be implied. It could not be implied into any eventual contract to buy the land, since such a term would be too late and would bind only one party. Lord Diplock overcame the problem by describing the tendering process as being governed by a unilateral contract (see 2.8) under which the invitation to submit tenders was a unilateral offer to accept the highest bid and to abide by the other tendering conditions, which was accepted by submitting a bid.

A fictional contract was also used in *Blackpool and Fylde Aero Club Ltd* v *Blackpool Borough Council* [1990] 1 WLR 1195, to provide a means of managing the tendering process, although somewhat surprisingly the court was not referred to the speech of Lord Diplock in the *Harvela Investments* case. The council ran an airport, and granted a single concession to operate pleasure flights from the airport. For a number of years that licence had been held by the plaintiff club. When the concession came up for renewal, the council determined to invite competitive tenders for it. Tenders were to be submitted by 12 noon on a given day. The council's letter-box was not cleared between the time of the club posting its tender and the closing time for bids, with the result that the club's tender was not considered. The club claimed that the council was in breach of an implied obligation to consider all tenders received before the deadline.

The Court of Appeal upheld the club's claim. There was a contract governing the conduct of the tendering process, and it was an implied term of that contract that all bids arriving before the deadline would be considered. This was a unilateral offer to consider conforming bids, which was accepted by submitting such a bid. Bingham LJ acknowledged that contracts are not lightly to be implied, but it is clear that in this case such judicial reluctance was outweighed by the opportunity to do substantive justice, which the implied contract was perceived to offer. In particular, it was recognised that no one would go to the trouble and expense of preparing a tender and submitting it in time if he thought that it would not even be considered, so that in recognising the implied contract the Court of Appeal was giving effect to the reasonable expectations and reliance of those submitting bids. However, the Court also stressed that the only contractual obligation was to consider the bid. (The House of Lords has since confirmed that an agreement to agree, or an agreement to negotiate, would be unenforceable for uncertainty (*Walford* v *Miles* [1992] 2 AC 128; see 3.1.3). On the other hand, an agreement not to negotiate with anyone else for a limited period is potentially enforceable in some circumstances (*Pitt* v *PHH Asset Management Ltd* [1994] 1 WLR 327).)

Whereas in *Harvela* the obligation forming the basis of the unilateral contract was an express promise to accept the highest bid, in *Blackpool Aero*

Club the obligation to consider confirming tenders was implied from the circumstances, namely the fact that only a limited number of contractors were invited to tender and that there was a detailed procedure to be followed for the submission of tenders. These factors were said to justify the implication of a promise to consider conforming tenders. Since they are hardly exceptional, it is likely that such an implication can be made in the vast majority of situations.

The analysis of an implied contract regulating the tendering process was accepted by the Court of Appeal in *Fairclough Building Ltd* v *Port Talbot BC* (1993) 62 BLR 82, but the *Blackpool Aero Club* case was distinguished on its facts. In *Blackpool Aero Club*, the council had wholly failed to consider the bid, whereas in *Fairclough* the bid was ruled out after preliminary consideration because of a risk of conflict of interest. As a result, no breach of the implied unilateral contract had occurred.

2.4.2.5   Auctions   A request for bids or an advertisement that an auction will be held amounts only to an invitation to treat (*Harris* v *Nickerson* (1873) LR 8 QB 286), even if the auction advertisement refers to lots being 'offered for sale' (*British Car Auctions Ltd* v *Wright* [1972] 1 WLR 1519). Therefore, each bid is an offer, and acceptance occurs when the auctioneer indicates acceptance of a bid with the fall of his hammer (SGA s. 57(2) 1979).

Harris v *Nickerson* is authority for the fact that if an advertised auction fails to take place, or if the lots advertised are withdrawn from the sale, because the advertisement was only an invitation to treat, the auctioneer will incur no liability. However, the position is different where an auction is advertised as being 'without reserve' (i.e., involving a promise to sell to the highest bidder and not to apply any reserve price or allow the vendor to bid in order artificially to push up the price). In *Warlow* v *Harrison* (1859) 1 E & E 309, the court dealt *obiter* with the question of whether the next highest bidder has any remedy where the owner successfully bids for the property at a without reserve auction. The court stated that there would be a remedy for breach of contract. The basis for this appears to be the implication of a unilateral contract based on the promise that it will be an auction without reserve. This promise constitutes a unilateral offer, which is accepted by the highest bona fide bidder at the auction. If the promise not to apply a reserve is broken then the auctioneer would be liable in damages to this person. (Another possible analysis would be that the offer is accepted by all those who turn up and bid at the auction without reserve, but only the highest bidder will suffer loss and be entitled to a remedy if the contract is broken — although this is not the analysis in the case law.) However, the highest bona fide bidder would not be entitled to the property sold, because his offer had not been accepted by the fall of the auctioneer's hammer.

Warlow v *Harrison*, and this analysis, was recently applied by the Court of Appeal in *Barry* v *Davies (Trading as Heathcote Ball & Co.)* [2000] 1 WLR 1962. The case concerned an auction without reserve applicable to the sale of two machines. The plaintiff was the only bidder for the two machines, worth about £14,000 each. The auctioneer withdrew the machines from the sale on the basis that the bids (of £200 for each machine) were too low. The plaintiff claimed damages representing the cost to purchase the machines elsewhere, less the amount of his auction bids.

The Court of Appeal allowed this damages award (of £27,600) on the basis that there was a collateral contract between the auctioneer and the highest bidder that the auctioneer would sell to that bidder, and the auctioneer had breached this contract by withdrawing the machines from the sale. The consideration for this contract was the detriment suffered by the bidder whose bid was open to be accepted by the auctioneer, and it was a benefit to the auctioneer through increased attendances pushing the bidding up (although on the facts in *Barry* v *Davies* this clearly did not have the desired effect since the plaintiff was the only bidder). The other consequence of this decision, as explained by Stuart-Smith LJ, is that by withdrawing the goods, the auctioneer was bidding on behalf of the seller, which was unlawful under s. 57(4) of the SGA 1979. This may have consequences for the seller and, by s. 57(5), the buyer may treat a sale in contravention of s. 57(4) as fraudulent.

2.5 COMMUNICATION OF THE OFFER

An offer does not take effect unless and until it is actually communicated to the offeree; and it is not possible to an offeree to accept unless he or she had knowledge of the offer (see 2.6.2). The point of communication of the offer is important because it is only then that the offer can be accepted. This gives rise to the question of what will constitute 'actual communication' (which is also a question of relevance when considering acceptances and revocations). What, for example, would the position be if the offer letter (or e-mail) were delivered to the offices of the offeree but not immediately opened by the offeree? This issue is considered below at 2.6.4.3 and 2.6.4.4, but it is interesting to note that the Vienna Convention on Contracts for the International Sale of Goods 1980, has a 'receipt' rule for offers (Article 15.1) and helpfully defines 'receipt' as occurring when an offer 'is made orally' to the offeree or is 'delivered by any other means to him personally, to his place of business or mailing address' (see also Article 2.3(1) and Article 1.9(3), UNIDROIT; Article 1:303, PECL). Where a person has no mailing or business address then receipt will occur when the offer is delivered to his or her 'habitual residence'. Therefore, 'receipt', in these contexts, does not require that the communication should actually have been read by the person to whom it is addressed.

2.6 ACCEPTANCE

2.6.1 Introduction

Acceptance is what turns a specific and comprehensive offer, made with the intention to be bound, into an agreement. How do we identify whether such an acceptance has occurred? The general principles applying to acceptances are as follows:

(a)   to constitute acceptance (and thus agreement), the offeree's expression of intention and assent must be made in response to, and must exactly match, the terms of the offer;

(b)   the matching acceptance must be communicated to the offeror.

These principles are so well established as to need little general comment. Such difficulties as exist arise out of the application of the principles to the realities of everyday contract negotiation. In simple consumer transactions it is common enough that only one offer is made, and acceptance is straightforward. No detailed negotiation of terms is involved. Taking the example of a sale in a self-service shop (see 2.4.2.2), the customer takes a price-marked item off the shelf and presents it to the cashier, thus making an offer to buy it for the marked price. The cashier accepts the offer on behalf of the shop, payment is instantaneous, and terms as to quality are left to be implied under the SGA 1979 (see 5.5.3.2). The role of acceptance in this case is crucial but without legal difficulty. Commercial contracts, especially for non-standard goods, may be very different. Frequently more than one offer will be made before negotiations are complete, and the language of 'acceptance' may be used before a technical legal analysis would identify acceptance as having been made.

2.6.2   Acceptance in response to the offer

The rule that acceptance must be made in response to the offer is a close relative of the rule which defines consideration as that which induces the promise of the other party. Thus, it will be suggested later that the decision that a claimant was not entitled to a reward when his performance of the act requested took place in ignorance of the reward offer, could be explained either in terms of an absence of consideration or in terms of an absence of agreement (see 4.3.1.1: *R* v *Clarke* (1927) 40 CLR 227). That is, either the performance was not induced by the offer, or the acceptance (which in such a contract is constituted by the performance: see 2.8 below) was not made in response to the offer.

However, it is clear from the decision in *Williams* v *Carwardine* (1833) 5 C & P 566, that as long as the offeree did have knowledge of the offer, and thus accepted in response to it, his or her motive in so doing is irrelevant. The decision in *Gibbons* v *Proctor* (1891) 64 LT 594 might be considered to be at odds with the principle that there must be knowledge of the offer in order to be able to claim the reward. However, it has been explained as turning on the particular requirements of the offer, which required the information to be given to a particular person, Superintendent Penn. Although the information was initially given to another colleague at a time when there was no knowledge of the reward, the offeree had the necessary knowledge at the time when the information reached Superintendent Penn.

The rule that acceptance must be in response to, and with knowledge of, the offer, has a number of unfortunate consequences. First, it may leave parties who are in fact subjectively agreed on all matters without a contract if they cannot objectively be shown to have gone through the process of agreement. If two parties both make offers to each other more or less simultaneously (i.e., before receiving the other's offer) then even if the offers are made in identical terms there is no contract. The offers may correspond, but there is no agreement because there is no acceptance made in response to the other's offer (*Tinn* v *Hoffman* (1873) 29 LT 271). It should be pointed out that the apparent harshness of this rule is mitigated by the fact that any small act of performance by one party may well be regarded as acceptance by conduct sufficient to seal the agreement (see 2.6.3). The finding of no contract in the absence of some act of performance was explained in *Tinn* v *Hoffman* as a rule of convenience to avoid uncertainty over whether a contract had come into existence. Secondly, as Hudson (1968) 84 LQR 503 has argued in the context of rewards and the decision in *Gibbons* v *Proctor*, an offeror could obtain the benefit of performance of an act and yet not have to pay the reward simply because the particular offeree happened not to see the offered reward.

2.6.3   The mirror image rule

An acceptance must be unconditional and correspond with the exact terms proposed by the offeror. Therefore, if when responding in a form purporting to be an acceptance, the offeree alters the terms contained in the offer or adds a new term, that response will itself constitute a counter-offer. This counter-offer cannot constitute an acceptance of the original offer. Instead, as the counter-offer is itself an offer on the revised terms being made by the offeree, agreement will result only if there is acceptance of the counter-offer by the original offeror. The further effect of a counter-offer is to operate in the same way as a rejection, namely to cause the original offer to lapse and prevent the original offeree from changing his mind and accepting that original offer. This effect is clearly demonstrated in relation to a price term in the case of *Hyde* v *Wrench* (1840) 3 Beav 334. A offered to sell land to B for £1,000. B replied offering £950. Clearly that was not an acceptance but a counter-offer. A rejected the counter-offer, whereupon B purported to accept the original offer of £1,000. A denied that any contract had been made, and the court agreed. It was not open to B to revive A's offer unless A was willing to revert to those terms.

Where the variation in terms is in relation to something less central than the price clause, it is common for the reply to the offer to be described as an 'acceptance'. However, in this situation the reply is also only a counter-offer. In *Jones* v *Daniel* [1894] 2 Ch 332, A offered £1,450 for land belonging to B. Purporting to accept the offer, B sent a document for signature to A containing terms additional to those proposed by A, relating to method of payment, proof of title and final performance. Although there was nothing unreasonable about the terms, they could not be part of an agreement until A had assented to them. Since A did not agree, there was no contract.

Thus, even where there is agreement on the major terms (e.g., price and subject-matter) there may still be no contract because of failure to agree on the ancillary terms. For this reason, courts have sometimes suggested that acceptance of all essential terms is sufficient to give rise to a contract, even when no agreement has been reached in respect of non-essential terms (see 2.6.3.2). However, in most cases the counter-offer rule prevails, because terms relating to method of payment and mode of performance are often crucial. Nevertheless, the rule can lead to difficulty where the parties are not particularly concerned about the details of the ancillary terms, and fail to notice discrepancies between the offer and the purported acceptance.

The difficulty is illustrated by *Brogden v Metropolitan Railway Co.* (1877) 2 App Cas 666. The appellant had for some time supplied coal as required to the respondent company. The parties decided to enter into a more formal long-term agreement. After negotiations, a draft contract was drawn up by the respondent and sent to the appellant. The appellant filled in the name of an arbitrator, marked the draft as 'approved' and returned it to the respondent. In technical terms the appellant's communication was a counter-offer, but the respondent's manager, being satisfied with it, merely put it in a file. He did not communicate his acceptance of the additions made. The parties then commenced performance under the agreement. Subsequently, a dispute arose in which it was questioned whether in fact any long-term contract had come into existence. The House of Lords held that the commencement of performance by the respondent, which had ordered and taken delivery of coal consistently with the terms of the alleged agreement, was acceptance by conduct of the appellant's counter-offer. However, it must be the case that such acceptance can be established only when the conduct is 'only referable to the contract document' in question (*per* Rix J in *Jayaar Impex Ltd v Toaken Group Ltd* [1996] 2 Lloyd's Rep 437, 446). In this case it was argued that one party had agreed to a proposed modification of an existing contract, and that their acceptance was constituted by performance of their part of the agreement. The judge refused to accept the argument, since the performance was equally referable to the terms of the original contract, so that no conclusion could be drawn in respect of the proposed modification.

An interesting question recently arose for decision in *The Society of Lloyds v Twinn* (2000) *The Times*, 4 April. The case turned on whether an acceptance was sufficiently unconditional. The defendants alleged that they had not accepted a Reconstruction and Renewal Settlement Agreement offered to Lloyd's Names in July 1996, and therefore could not be in breach of the agreement because, although they had completed the application forms, their covering letter had asserted that they would not be able to pay the sums that would be due from them under the terms of the Settlement. The Court of Appeal rejected this argument and concluded that there was an unconditional acceptance of the offer in the form of the completed application forms. The covering letter sought to obtain a concession, but it was separate and collateral to the concluded contract rather than a condition of the acceptance, and this fact was borne out by subsequent correspondence in which the defendants clearly accepted that they had signed and returned valid acceptances of the offer. Scott V-C expressed the position as follows:

> An acceptance which seeks an indulgence will be effective if it is clear that the offeree was unconditionally accepting the offer. In a case where the

terms of the offer held out a considerable benefit to the offeree, the offeree might well want to accept notwithstanding that in some respect or other he, the offeree, would not be able to perform. Suppose an offer with a stipulation requiring performance by a specified date. . . . Why should the offeree not give an unconditional acceptance but, at the same time, try to agree an extension of time, warning the offeror that his (the offeree's) performance would anyway take place later than the specified date?

He added that the question of whether there was an unconditional acceptance and a collateral counter-offer, or a counter-offer preventing acceptance, would depend on the facts of the particular case, and that 'the intended effect of a purported acceptance' would need to be 'judged objectively from the language used and the surrounding circumstances'.

2.6.3.1 Requests for further information
A counter-offer, which purports to accept but in fact operates to reject the original offer, must be distinguished from a request for further information before the offeree decides whether to accept. In this situation the offer will remain available for acceptance.

Stevenson, Jacques & Co. v *McLean* (1880) 5 QBD 346, concerned negotiations for the sale of a quantity of iron. The defendant had offered to sell at a price of '40s net cash per ton'. The plaintiffs had replied asking whether the defendant would accept '40 for delivery over 2 months, or if not, the longest limit you could give'. It was held that this reply did not operate to reject the defendant's offer but was only an inquiry to determine whether there was any flexibility in the offer terms. Therefore, it remained possible for the plaintiffs to accept that offer.

It is not too difficult to make the distinction between counter-offer and request for more information on these facts, since the plaintiffs had not reached the stage where they were purporting to accept and their response could not be interpreted as sufficiently specific and definite to constitute a counter-offer.

2.6.3.2 The battle of forms
With the increasing use of often conflicting standard terms of business, each party to a sale or supply contract will send its own terms in an effort to ensure that those terms and conditions prevail. The question in such a case is to determine whose terms govern in this 'battle of forms'. The problem here is that if the traditional analysis of offer, counter-offer and acceptance is applied, there may well be no contract at all, because of the absence of a matching offer and acceptance, or a contract referable to the last set of terms to be sent before performance. In both situations it may be that neither party appreciated this legal effect, although, if there is no contract, it may be possible to obtain payment for goods or services on a restitutionary basis (*Peter Lind & Co. Ltd* v *Mersey Docks and Harbour Board* [1972] 2 Lloyd's Rep 234 and *British Steel Corporation* v *Cleveland Bridge & Engineering* [1984] 1 All ER 504, see 3.1.4).

Despite the consequences that can result from the application of the traditional analysis, the courts have tended to follow it. For example, it was adopted by the majority of the Court of Appeal in *Butler Machine Tool Co. Ltd v Ex-Cell-O Corporation (England) Ltd* [1979] 1 WLR 401, although Lord Denning MR suggested a more radical approach. In *Butler Machine*, the sellers sent a quotation for the supply of a machine to the buyers. This quotation was issued on the basis of the sellers' conditions which were to 'prevail over any terms and conditions in the buyer's order', and which included a price variation clause. The buyers placed an order, and their letter contained conflicting conditions which, in particular, contained no price variation clause. At the bottom of the order was a tear-off confirmation slip expressly subject to the buyers' terms, which the sellers completed and returned. The sellers claimed to be entitled to vary the contract price.

The Court of Appeal rejected that claim on the basis that the sellers had expressly accepted the buyers' terms when they completed and returned the acknowledgement slip. In other words, the sellers had accepted the buyers' 'last shot'. However, whereas Lawton and Bridge LJJ analysed this last shot as a counter-offer, Lord Denning MR adopted a different approach, which involved separating the question of formation of a contract from the determination of its content. He considered that a contract was formed where the parties were agreed on the material points even if there were conflicting terms in their forms. He then turned to the question of whose terms would govern, and stated:

> In some cases, the battle is won by the man who gets the blow in first. If he offers to sell at a named price on the terms and conditions stated on the back: and the buyer orders the goods purporting to accept the offer — on an order form with his own different terms and conditions on the back — then if the difference is so material that it would affect the price, the buyer ought not to be allowed to take advantage of the difference unless he draws it specifically to the attention of the seller. There are yet other cases where the battle depends on the shots fired on both sides. There is a concluded contract but the forms vary. The terms and conditions of both parties are to be construed together. If they can be reconciled so as to give a harmonious result, all well and good. If differences are irreconcilable — so that they are mutually contradictory — then the conflicting terms may have to be scrapped and replaced by a reasonable implication.

The 'last shot' invariably appears to be the significant document in determining who wins (or loses) the battle because of the possibility of acceptance of this counter-offer by conduct, e.g., *Sauter Automation Ltd v Goodman (Mechanical Services) Ltd* (1986) 34 BLR 81, *Chichester Joinery v John Mowlem & Co.* (1987) 42 BLR 100 and *Nissan UK Ltd v Nissan Motor Manufacturing (UK) Ltd* (unreported), 26 October 1994. Although in *Butler Machine* the sellers had tried to ensure that their terms were paramount by drafting a clause stating that their terms and conditions would prevail over those in the buyers' order, this proved ineffective in the face of their express acceptance of the buyers' counter-offer (the last shot). They had also claimed that their terms were in fact the last document, because in sending the acknowledgement slip they had again referred to their quotation. This argument failed because the Court of Appeal regarded this reference as relevant only to the issue of the price and not as an attempt to incorporate the sellers' standard terms of supply.

Lord Denning's approach — and, in particular, his suggestion for determination of content in cases of conflicting terms by replacing such terms with terms based on reasonable implication — would seem to be far ahead of what is currently acceptable to English law, and we shall have to go some way further down the road to judicial intervention in the process of contracting before the courts will construct a contract on behalf of the parties out of the conflicting terms and conditions in the various documents passing between them (but see § 2-207 of the Uniform Commercial Code in the United States; discussed in M. Furmston, T. Norisada and J. Poole, *Contract Formation and Letters of Intent*, John Wiley & Sons, 1998).

Article 2.22, UNIDROIT and Article 2:209 of PECL both broadly accept that a contract is formed in a battle of forms situation unless one party has explicitly notified the other (either in advance, or without delay) that it does not intend to be bound if there are conflicting terms. Where a contract is formed despite the conflicting terms, its content will comprise those terms which are common in substance, and the implication is that the courts will fill any gaps. Each set of Principles also contains a provision addressing 'modified acceptances' (Article 2.11, UNIDROIT; Article 2:208, PECL). These Articles state the general rule, i.e. that a modified acceptance is a counter-offer. However, modified acceptances 'which do not materially alter the terms of the offer' will be acceptances unless the offeror makes speedy objection to the discrepancy (UNIDROIT and PECL), or the offer expressly limited acceptance to the terms of the offer (PECL), or the offeree's acceptance was conditional upon the offeror's assent to the differing terms and the assent was not received within a reasonable time (PECL). Where there is such an acceptance, the terms of the contract will be the offer terms as modified by the acceptance.

Lord Denning's approach to formation of the contract, like the formulations in the UCC (Uniform Commercial Code (United States)), Vienna Convention, UNIDROIT and PECL, placed great emphasis on material terms or terms which 'materially alter' the offer. This raises the question of identification of 'material terms' and hence 'material alterations'. Article 19(3) of the Vienna Convention on Contracts for the International Sale of Goods defines 'material alterations'. However, this definition is extremely broad and only the most trivial of alterations would be regarded as not materially altering the offer. In particular, if the response contains any changes to price, payment terms, delivery, liability and any dispute mechanism, the response would constitute a rejection. There is some explanation of 'material' terms and modifications in the commentary to the UNIDROIT Principles and PECL, but the idea of a list as in Article 19(3) of the Convention is expressly rejected by PECL in favour of the retention of flexibility, given that any list could not be exhaustive. Article 1:301(5) of PECL contains a definition of 'material' as a matter 'which a reasonable person in the same situation as one party ought to have known would influence the other party in its decision whether to contract on the proposed terms or to contract at all'.

2.6.4 Communication of acceptance

The second general principle of acceptance is that the acceptance needs to be communicated to the offeror.

There are two important exceptions to this general rule. The first concerns implied waiver of the communication requirement in the case of unilateral contracts; and the second is concerned with acceptances by post where the parties are necessarily not in each other's presence.

2.6.4.1 Implied waiver of the need to communicate acceptance in unilateral contracts

In a unilateral contact, performance of the act constitutes the acceptance and there is therefore no need to communicate the fact that you are attempting to perform that act. Authority for this principle is the decision in *Carlill* v *Carbolic Smoke Ball Co.* [1893] 1 QB 256 and, in particular, the statement by Bowen LJ:

> In the advertisement cases it seems to me to follow as an inference to be drawn from the transaction itself that a person is not to notify his acceptance of the offer before he performs the condition, but if he performs the condition notification is dispensed with.

Bowen LJ gave the example of a reward for the return of a lost dog to a particular place. The acceptance is the act of returning the dog to that place and there is no need to communicate an intention to perform the act. Of course, the particular offer may expressly provide that communication is a necessary part of the acceptance (requested act), as where there is a reward for supplying information. In addition, although it may not be necessary to communicate an intention to seek to perform the requested act, it may still be necessary at a practical level to communicate the fact of that performance in order to notify the offeror that the reward is being claimed. However, that is not part of the acceptance itself.

Silence in bilateral contracts In standard bilateral negotiations, the general rule is that the offeror cannot waive the need for communication and stipulate that silence will constitute acceptance. The authority for this is said to be the decision in *Felthouse* v *Bindley* (1862) 11 CB NS 869. An uncle and nephew had been negotiating the sale of the nephew's horse to his uncle, but they could not agree on the price. In the end the uncle had written, saying that if he heard no more he would assume that the nephew agreed to his proposal of a price of £30 15s. The nephew appears to have been satisfied with this arrangement, since he instructed an auctioneer to withdraw the horse in question from a sale. However, he did not communicate this fact to his uncle. When the auctioneer mistakenly sold the horse, the uncle sued him for conversion, claiming to be the owner of the horse under a contract with his nephew. The court did not accept his claim, stating as one of its reasons that 'the uncle had no right to impose upon the nephew a sale . . . unless he chose to comply with the condition of writing to repudiate the offer'.

However, it is certainly not the case that silence can never be acceptance (see, for example, the comments by Peter Gibson LJ in *Re Selectmove Ltd* [1995] 1 WLR 474, 478, suggesting that an offeree will be bound by his silence where he has given an undertaking to speak). In some contexts, especially where there has been a continuing course of dealing, silence can be sufficient acceptance. If A operates a coal delivery round, and regularly delivers two bags of coal to B, either collecting the money on delivery or leaving an invoice to be paid later, without any formal order being placed, B would be unable to deny the existence of a contract for coal actually delivered. B would be bound by his own silence, which would constitute a sufficient acceptance. Equally, many people rely on the automatic annual renewal of their insurance policies to ensure that the required cover starts as soon as the previous year's cover comes to an end. Yet it is not uncommon, at the crucial date, for the policyholder not to have replied to the company's proposal, which is no more than an offer needing acceptance. What the courts will not countenance is that an offeror should, without any previous course of dealing, force upon an offeree the need to reply in order to avoid the formation of a contract. In the case of such inertia selling to consumers, reg. 24 of the Consumer Protection (Distance Selling) Regulations 2000 (SI 2000 No. 2334) (discussed at 4.5.3.3) now applies, so that unsolicited goods sent to consumers become an unconditional gift with immediate effect. It is also an offence to demand payment for such unsolicited goods, or to threaten proceedings or to place the recipient on a blacklist if payment is not made. The previous legislation aimed at deterring inertia selling, the Unsolicited Goods and Services Act 1971, will continue to apply in the business context.

Even in *Felthouse* v *Bindley* itself, the particular form of the action (against the auctioneer) may have been significant. Miller ((1972) 35 MLR 489) would argue that if the facts had been different, and it had been the uncle who had refused to take delivery of the horse on the basis that there had been no communication of acceptance to him, his nephew should have been able to rely on the uncle's stipulation and his own silence as establishing the existence of the contract (see Treitel, *The Law of Contract*, 10th edn, Sweet & Maxwell, 1999 pp. 32–33). Thus, in this situation the offeror would be bound by the offeree's silence, and arguably the basis for this would be estoppel (i.e., the fact that the offeror expressly formulated his offer so that silence should be acceptance and therefore cannot deny this position where the offeree has relied on it).

2.6.4.2 The postal rule of acceptance When the parties negotiate to a conclusion in each other's presence there is little problem. There is little danger of uncertainty as to whether agreement has been reached, although recollections may differ as to its content if it has not been recorded. The general rule is that words of acceptance must not only be spoken, they must be heard by the offeror. Thus, if words of acceptance are drowned by a loud noise they must be repeated before the contract is concluded. However, when the parties are not in each other's presence communication becomes a more critical issue, especially when the agency of a third party, such as the Post Office, or of a machine is involved. The law has developed a distinction of potentially fundamental importance between instantaneous and non-instantaneous communication. The former is treated more or less as if the parties are in each other's presence, whereas special rules apply to the latter.

The problem with contract negotiation by post is that letters may either be delayed or lost. Those are risks inherent in the use of the post, and the real question is who should bear that risk. In *Adams v Lindsell* (1818) 1 B & Ald 681, the defendants offered to sell wool to the plaintiffs, asking for a reply 'in course of post'. The defendants' letter was misdirected, so that the plaintiffs' reply was delayed beyond the normal course of post, and the defendants sold the wool to someone else. Nevertheless, the plaintiffs had sent a letter of acceptance on the same day that they had received the offer, and they claimed that there was an enforceable contract. The court upheld that claim, and since this case the rule has been that where acceptance is communicated by post the contract is formed as soon as the letter is sent, without need for it ever to reach the offeror. The rule applies equally to all potential consequences, both procedural matters (such as time and place of making the contract) and substantive matters (such as non-performance by an offeror ignorant of the fact of acceptance): *Household Fire and Carriage Accident Insurance Co. Ltd v Grant* (1879) 4 ExD 216. The postal rule therefore places the risk of loss or delay squarely on the offeror.

Attempts have been made to justify the rule on all kinds of grounds. It is said that without such a rule offerees would never know whether a contract had been formed. It is also suggested that such a rule prevents offerees from speculating by writing an acceptance and then (if the market changes) withdrawing it by speedier means (e.g., telephone). It could be argued that the offeror, unlike the offeree, will not be prejudiced by delays or loss in the post, since the offeror is expecting a response and will check if a reply is not received. Alternatively, it is argued that if the offeror indicates that use of the post is permissible then he or she should bear the risks of that system. This last explanation is borne out by *Henthorn v Fraser* [1892] 2 Ch 27, in which it was made clear that the postal rule is applicable only where it was reasonable in all the circumstances for the offeree to have used the post; such would most obviously be the case where the offer had been sent by post.

The truth of the matter is almost certainly that whenever one of the risks of the use of the post materialises, whatever conclusion the court reaches will be harsh on one of the parties. The postal rule is no more than a rule of convenience adopted in the interests of certainty. The basic argument is that offerors should know the risks inherent in use of the post and can protect themselves if they so wish. Indeed, the fact that the postal rule can be avoided in practice is often used as a reason to justify its existence!

Avoiding the postal rule   In *Household Fire and Carriage Accident Insurance Co. Ltd v Grant* (1879) 4 ExD 216, there was a powerful dissent by Bramwell LJ, who would have preferred the ordinary rule of communication to apply equally to acceptance by post. The most significant part of his judgment is where he says that the harm he perceives in the postal rule 'will be obviated only by the rule being rendered nugatory by every prudent man saying: "Your answer by post is only to bind if it reaches me."' This statement reveals an important limitation on all non-instantaneous negotiations, namely that the offeror enjoys a legal power to stipulate the medium by which communication is to be made.

This in itself raises another question: What is the position if the offeror has prescribed a particular method of acceptance and the offeree has used a different method? In *Manchester Diocesan Council of Education* v *Commercial & General Investments Ltd* [1970] 1 WLR 241, Buckley J sought to answer this question as follows:

(a) If the stipulation is entirely for the benefit of the offeror, and the offeree communicates by some other means, the offeror may waive the stipulation, making the acceptance effective.

(b) Where a method of acceptance is prescribed, but acceptance is not expressly limited to that method alone, then an equally efficacious method of acceptance will also be valid if it fulfils the purpose in prescribing the method. For example, if the offeror wants a quick response and prescribes acceptance by fax, then as long as this method is not mandatory, any acceptance that is just as quick as a fax acceptance will suffice.

The result of the operation of the postal rule is that the offeror could discover that he or she is bound by a contract of which he or she has no knowledge because the postal acceptance was lost in the post. Thus, it is sensible for the offeror to seek protection against this risk by stipulating that he or she requires a particular means of acceptance (other than the post), or wording the offer so that he or she is requiring actual communication of any acceptance. This is precisely what the offeror achieved in *Holwell Securities Ltd* v *Hughes* [1974] 1 WLR 155. There, the defendant granted the plaintiff an option for the purchase of certain land, which was said to be exercisable by notice in writing to the defendant at a given address within six months. An option is no more than an offer, and although the plaintiff posted a letter accepting the offer in question within the six-month period, it failed to arrive.

The Court of Appeal held that the option had not been validly exercised and, accordingly, there was no contract. The main finding was that the mere words 'notice in writing to' were sufficient to override the postal rule. These words amounted instead to a stipulation that notice must reach the offeror, thus reinstating the general principle of actual communication. It would seem relatively straightforward, in the light of this interpretation of what are fairly common words, to avoid the operation of the postal rule. Thus, its significance as a practical principle may well be overstated. In his judgment Lawton LJ referred to football pools coupons as an example of a familiar situation where the postal rule is ousted.

The postal rule can therefore be ousted by *express* words. However, Lawton LJ also stated that the postal rule 'probably does not operate if its application would produce manifest inconvenience and absurdity', and he interpreted this to mean that the rule can be ousted if it is clear from the subject-matter and the circumstances that the parties cannot have intended that there should be a binding agreement until there had been actual communication of an acceptance. This again provides ample scope for the avoidance of the postal rule in practice.

Retraction of a postal acceptance   Is it possible to retract a postal acceptance before it reaches the offeror? There is no English case authority; and a Scottish case (*Countess of Dunmore* v *Alexander* (1830) 9 S 190) is highly dubious authority, although it is sometimes cited in support of the conclusion that it is possible to overtake a postal acceptance. Despite the absence of authority, there has been much academic discussion of this question.

It might be assumed that if the postal rule is in fact a 'rule' then logic would dictate that it would not be possible to retract a postal acceptance since it would be binding on posting. This conclusion is frequently supported by asserting that to allow any other conclusion would permit the offeree to be able to 'play the market' i.e., to accept an offer to purchase goods at one price and later to withdraw that offer by a quicker method if market conditions make the contract less profitable to him or her. On the other hand, it can also be argued that the postal 'rule' is nothing more than a rule of convenience to determine who should bear the risk of loss or delay in the post. As such, its operation should focus on the question of inconvenience, and it can be argued that logically any offeror will accept and act upon the communication he or she receives first, so that as long as a postal acceptance is retracted before that postal acceptance arrives, the offeror suffers no disadvantage, (see A. H. Hudson, 'Retraction of Letters of Acceptance' (1966) 82 LQR 169). Not only does the offeror suffer no disadvantage, but it might equally be unreasonable for him or her to rely upon a postal acceptance which he or she knows has been retracted. A further justification for allowing the offeree this latitude is the fact that the offeror can always oust the operation of the postal rule if he or she so wishes.

2.6.4.3   Other forms of distant dealing — the distinction between instantaneous and non-instantaneous communications   The post is very obviously a form of non-instantaneous communication, and therefore the law has recognised that there needs to be a principle to determine who should bear the risks of transmission. On the other hand, it is generally accepted that telephone negotiation is a form of instantaneous communication, so that the parties are treated as if in each other's presence and no contract will be formed unless the words of acceptance are clearly heard by the offeror ('the receipt rule'). A similar approach was taken to telex communications (*Entores Ltd* v *Miles Far East Corporation* [1955] 2 QB 327); but even in *Entores*, Denning LJ had recognised that there were occurrences which could affect the instantaneous nature of the transmission, e.g., if the line went dead during transmission but the offeree was unaware of this fact and thought his message had gone through. If the offeror, knowing that a message was being sent, did not ask for it to be repeated, Denning LJ (at 333) considered that 'the offeror . . . is clearly bound, because he will be estopped from saying that he did not receive the message of acceptance. It is his own fault that he did not get it'.

That there are instances when the actual communication would be non-instantaneous, despite the use of an instantaneous method of communication, was explicitly recognised in *Brinkibon Ltd v Stahag Stahl und Stahlwarenhandelsgesellschaft mbH GmbH* [1983] 2 AC 34. Lord Wilberforce stated that today telex machines frequently send messages out of business hours, leaving messages stored until the following day, and the same can be said of fax communications and e-mail. In such non-instantaneous cases, he stated (at 42) that 'No universal rule can cover such cases: they must be resolved by reference to the intentions of the parties, by sound business practice and in some cases by a judgment where the risks should lie'. In effect Lord Wilberforce was saying that there is no rule for such cases. However, a general principle appears to be identifiable, namely that if the offeree has done all that he might reasonably be expected to do to get his message through, that acceptance should take effect when the offeree might reasonably expect it to be communicated to the offeror. Therefore, if an acceptance has been communicated to a business during office hours, the offeree could reasonably expect the offeror to be monitoring the (say) fax machine, and would expect communication to occur when the message was received by the machine. Accordingly, in this situation, communication to the machine would suffice. Authority for this is the decision in *The Brimnes* [1975] QB 929, (although the case itself concerned a notice of withdrawal rather than an acceptance), and comments by Lord Fraser in *Brinkibon Ltd v Stahag Stahl* that messages would be at the risk of the recipient if he failed to man his machine.

The converse position was considered by Gatehouse J in *Mondial Shipping and Chartering BV v Astarte Shipping Ltd* [1995] CLC 1011. The judge suggested that receipt of a contractual notice should be deemed to occur at the start of the next working day if it was in fact received and stored outside normal working hours (in this case the opening for business on the following Monday, since the message was sent and received at 23.41 hours on a Friday). Gatehouse J also indicated that he viewed this result as consistent with Lord Wilberforce's approach, which was to consider each case on its particular facts. This, of course, raises a difficult question concerning the definition of 'ordinary business hours' and how this will be determined. Will it, for example, vary according to the knowledge of the parties in any particular case, or should this question be determined objectively and a general definition provided? The first solution would fit more easily with the principles set out by Lord Wilberforce, although those who seek certainty in their commercial dealings would probably regard a more objective formulation as preferable.

Even these principles leave open some difficult questions, such as when is there communication of an acceptance message left on a telephone answering machine? If we apply the general principle of what the offeree could reasonably expect, the conclusion might be that the message will not be communicated until actually played back, since anyone leaving a message should reasonably assume that, since the machine is switched on, the message will not be communicated immediately. (This ignores the practice of using an answering machine to screen calls.) On the other hand, Coote ((1971) 4 NZULR 331) argued, by analogy with the postal rule, that where the machine appears to be working, in leaving the message the offeree has put the matter out of his control so that this should be the point of communication. This might be preferable for evidential reasons since many machines will record the time of receipt of the message; and it is also a good deal more convenient for the offeree since it avoids the possibility of numerous repeat telephone calls.

2.6.4.4 Electronic means of communicating It is vitally important to decide whether the postal rule ('the dispatch rule') or 'the receipt rule' applies to these communications, because this will in turn determine the place of contracting.

E-mail E-mail messages raise complex questions, since messages are sent via a server and may not be immediately received. It can be argued, therefore, that such messages are similar to postal acceptances. The sender of the message puts it out of his or her control by pressing the 'send message' key and there will inevitably be some, albeit very short, interval before the message reaches its destination. If the postal rule applied, the e-mail contract would be binding the moment the message of acceptance was sent. This would be important, assuming the customer makes the offer, for suppliers of goods or services who send acceptances by e-mail, since the contract would then be formed in the jurisdiction of that seller or supplier.

However, given the complexities of individual e-mail systems, it would seem preferable to apply an actual communication (or 'receipt' rule), especially because the sender will know if the message has not been sent and can resend it. By analogy with *Entores*, that ought to mean that responsibility for getting the message through to its destination should lie with the sender. There are two obvious problems with such a solution. In the first place, it will mean that if the customer makes the offer, the contract will be formed in the customer's jurisdiction, which may suit the customer but will be too risky for suppliers. The second problem with such a solution is the same difficulty that affects all communications to which the receipt rule applies, namely to determine what is meant by 'receipt' or 'actual communication'. Is it communication to the mail server, to the computer, or when it is actually read? As mentioned at 2.5, the Vienna Convention, UNIDROIT Principles and PECL, all adopt a definition of 'receipt' to assist with certainty, and a similar rule might be usefully devised to cover electronic communications if the receipt principle is adopted. It is possible with e-mail to determine when a message is read by the recipient, so that there may not be the same evidential problems as with other communications in this respect. However, it might more logically be argued that the crucial time is when the message is downloaded from the server on to the computer.

Once the E-Commerce Directive 2000/31/EC (see 4.5.5) is implemented there may be greater certainty, since Article 11 states that (unless the parties are businesses and agree otherwise) any electronic order and acknowledgement of that order 'are deemed to be received when the parties to whom they are addressed are able to access them'. This would suggest that the receipt rule is appropriate for all electronic contracts and that, in the case of e-mail communications, receipt will occur when the message has been downloaded from the server and is therefore capable of being accessed.

Internet contracting   Internet contracting (i.e., offer and acceptance at the website) is instantaneous so that the receipt rule should apply. In practical terms, the transmission of messages is controlled by clicking on various responses to messages. The on-line buyer initially clicks on a 'checkout' or 'send order' button. The retailer then checks stock availability and will usually confirm this by message. This is not intended to constitute acceptance, because it is clear to the customer that further action on his or her part is required by entering credit or debit card details. Only after these details have been transmitted and accepted does the retailer send a message of acceptance confirming that the order has been received. Even this may not be an acceptance but merely an offer by the site provider, which must be accepted by the on-line buyer via clicking to indicate the intention to be bound.

Electronic communications are covered by the Consumer Protection (Distance Selling) Regulations 2000 (SI 2000 No. 2334), so that certain information must be provided to the consumer before the conclusion of the contract. This makes it important to determine when the contract is concluded. Confirmation (containing the required information) also needs to be given in a 'durable medium' prior to delivery. It is therefore common practice amongst reputable on-line providers to send such a confirmatory e-mail message.

2.7   TERMINATION OF OFFERS

To be capable of acceptance an offer must not only be specific and comprehensive, and have been made with the intention of being bound (see 2.4.1), it must also be current. Acceptance made after an offer has ceased to be valid is ineffective to form a contract. This section examines the means by which offers terminate, other than by the offeree making a counter-offer or a rejection (see 2.6.3).

2.7.1   Lapse of time

Where an offer is left open indefinitely, there may come a time when the offeree can no longer accept. In *Ramsgate Victoria Hotel Co. Ltd* v *Montefiore* (1866) LR 1 Ex 109, the defendant had applied for shares in the plaintiff company in early June 1864. Shares were allotted to him in late November 1864. The defendant refused to pay for the shares, although he had not withdrawn his application at the time when the shares were allotted. It was held that he was not obliged to go through with the purchase of the shares. The company's response to the defendant's offer had not been made within a reasonable time (see also *Chemco Leasing SpA v Rediffusion* [1987] 1 FTLR 201, CA).

It is not possible to give any indication of what is a reasonable time, which will be a question of fact in each case. Where the offer is expressly stipulated to be open for a limited period, that is an exercise of the offeror's power to stipulate a particular mode of acceptance and the offeree must comply with it (subject to the principles discussed at 2.6.4.2).

2.7.2 Death

The death of either party may terminate an offer, although the English authorities are far from clear as to the precise circumstances in which an offer will lapse on death.

Where the contract is for the performance of a personal service by the offeror, which depends upon some skill which is exclusive to the offeror, the offeror's death automatically terminates the offer. Thus, an offer by a concert pianist to perform at a concert could not be accepted after the death of the pianist. Where the subject-matter is something available in an open market, there is no difficulty about obtaining substitute performance of what had been offered. The issue is then whether the executor of the dead offeror's estate should have to arrange such substitute performance. The orthodox view is that the burden should not fall upon the executor provided notice of the death of the offeror has been given to the offeree, so that in the case of an offer to give a guarantee it has been held that an offeree cannot accept it after he has been informed of the death of the offeror (*Coulthart v Clementson* (1879) 5 QBD 42). But where the offeree has no notice of the death of the offeror at the time when the acceptance is made, the deceased's estate will be bound. There are *obiter dicta* to this effect in *Bradbury v Morgan* (1862) 1 Hurl & C 249.

In the case of death of the offeree, although there are *obiter* statements in *Reynolds v Atherton* (1921) 125 LT 690 suggesting that the offer ceases to be an offer at all, the position is probably that the offeree's representatives can accept the offer if it is of a non-personal nature.

2.7.3 Revocation

In negotiations towards a bilateral contract, the general rule is that the offeror is at liberty to withdraw the offer at any time before acceptance (*Offord v Davies* (1862) 12 CB NS 748). Revocation of an offer is not effective until communicated to the offeree.

2.7.3.1 'Firm offers' It is not uncommon for an offer to be expressed as 'open' for a given period of time, which is no more than a promise not to revoke the offer before that period has elapsed. This kind of promise is sometimes called a 'firm offer'. English law is clear that such a promise is no different from any other promise and is unenforceable unless supported by separate, valuable consideration (e.g., an option: see *Holwell Securities Ltd* v *Hughes* [1974] 1 WLR 155). There is authority to this effect in *Routledge* v *Grant* (1828) 4 Bing 653.

In *Routledge* v *Grant* the defendant offered to take a lease of premises belonging to the plaintiff, at the same time promising to hold his offer open for six weeks. After only three weeks the defendant purported to revoke this offer, while at the end of the six weeks the plaintiff purported to accept it. The court held that there was no contract. In the absence of consideration to support the promise to keep the offer open for a specified period, the offer may be withdrawn at any time even before expiry of that period.

The English rule on firm offers is not accepted by most other legal systems. Even most American states, whose contract law is derived from English law, have abandoned the rule, at least in the case of firm offers made by those in business in relation to potential sales of goods (see Uniform Commercial Code, § 2-205). The firm offer is a valuable tool in forward planning, especially where a firm wishes to be able to rely on prices quoted by potential subcontractors when tendering for a major contract. It might therefore be thought desirable for the English rule to be abandoned. Such a reform might be achieved simply by identifying a very small reciprocal benefit to the offeror, such as might amount to consideration under the approach adopted in the context of alteration promises to pay more in *Williams* v *Roffey Bros & Nicholls (Contractors) Ltd* [1991] 1 QB 1 (described as a 'practical' or 'factual' benefit; see 4.3.5.2). There might, for example, be some factual benefit to the offeror in having an identified offeree carefully considering his offer, even if it may not be converted into the benefit of an actual contract. However, the *Williams* v *Roffey* principle cannot be applied in this context because it applies only to promises altering existing contracts (see 4.3.5).

Article 2.4, UNIDROIT and Article 2:202, PECL provide that an offer cannot be revoked if it states a fixed time for acceptance. It is clear from the commentary to PECL that this would cover the firm offer.

2.7.3.2 Impact of acceptance Revocation of an offer after the time of acceptance is ineffective. Indeed, since the contract is formed from the moment of acceptance, attempted revocation after that time might amount to breach by anticipatory repudiation (see 7.5.6). In all types of negotiation, whether instantaneous or not, revocation is ineffective until actually communicated to the offeree, and until that time the offer is open to acceptance. On the other hand, to be effective a communication of revocation need not be authorised by the offeror, provided the offeree ought reasonably to believe it. In *Dickinson* v *Dodds* (1876) 2 ChD 463, the defendant had offered to sell a house to the plaintiff, and had promised to leave the offer open for three days, although the plaintiff had given no consideration for the promise. The plaintiff had decided to accept the offer, but had taken no steps to communicate his decision to the defendant when he was informed by Berry, an apparently reliable person, that the defendant had been offering or agreeing to sell the property to a third party. The plaintiff then attempted to communicate his acceptance to the defendant, and claimed that there had been no effective revocation of the offer before his communication of acceptance.

The Court of Appeal held that the manner of communication of revocation was irrelevant, provided that the plaintiff knew that the defendant no longer intended to sell the property to him by the time his purported acceptance was made. This conclusion means that an offeree will have to decide whether to believe revocation information which is communicated by a third party. There is a risk that the source is unreliable and the information is incorrect. The safest course of action, if possible, will be for the offeree to check directly with the offeror in such circumstances.

2.7.3.3 Communication of a revocation The fact that the postal rule applies in the case of acceptance (see 2.6.4.2) but does not apply in the case of revocation (see 2.7.3 above) means that the courts must pay close attention to the timing of communications. If an acceptance is posted after a revocation has been posted, but before it is received, that acceptance will be effective to form a binding contract. This exactly what happened in *Byrne & Co.* v *Van Tienhoven & Co.* (1880) 5 CPD 344. A letter of revocation of an offer was sent from Cardiff to New York on 8 October. Acceptance of the original offer was telegraphed on 11 October from New York to Cardiff, followed on 15 October by a letter of confirmation, each being sent before the letter of revocation had arrived. The court held that a contract had come into existence on 11 October (the postal rule also applying to acceptances by telegram), because the revocation was ineffective until communicated to the offeree.

The UNIDROIT Principles and PECL both contain potentially useful provisions which aim to protect the offeree in the case of postal acceptances, given that both apply the receipt rule to postal acceptances. Although an acceptance is not effective until it reaches the offeror (Article 2:205, PECL; Article 2:6(2), UNIDROIT), the offeror can revoke only if the revocation reaches the offeree before he has dispatched his acceptance (Article 2:202, PECL; Article 2.4(1), UNIDROIT). However, this rule as to revocations will have no effect in the case of oral acceptance.

2.8   UNILATERAL CONTRACTS

It was suggested at 2.2 that the traditional offer and acceptance analysis of the formation of agreements may not always be appropriate in situations other than conscious negotiation between two identified parties. A unilateral contract is a contract where one party (the promisor) binds himself to perform a stated promise upon performance of a stated condition by the promisee, but under which the promisee gives no commitment to perform the condition but rather is left free to choose whether to perform or not. Such contracts are sometimes referred to as 'if contracts', since they take the form of the following well-known example first cited in *Great Northern Railway Co.* v *Witham* (1873) LR 9 CP 16: 'If you will go to York, I will give you £100.' Examples of unilateral contracts are option contracts, estate agency contracts and reward contracts (which can include rewards for information, return of property and for collecting tokens in an advertising promotion). This kind of bargain is outside the standard contracting situation, usually described as bilateral or synallagmatic. Unilateral contracts can be explained in terms of offer and acceptance, but sometimes only with difficulty. It was in the context of just such a contract that Lord Wilberforce commented upon the artificiality of offer and acceptance analysis in *The Eurymedon* [1975] AC 154 (see 2.2).

2.8.1 Offer

Little need be added to what has already been said about offers in the context of bilateral contracts (see 2.4.2.1). In unilateral contracts, two essentially different offers may be made. In the first place, an offer may be made to an identified individual. In *Great Northern Railway Co.* v *Witham* (1873) LR 9 CP 16, the defendant argued that an offer in the form of a conditional promise to the plaintiff could not result in a contract because there was no reciprocity from the promisee. That argument was roundly rejected by the court, which saw such offers as a matter of everyday practice.

Alternatively, the offer may be made to the public at large, or to a particular class of persons. The classic example of such offers is the offer of a reward in return for the performance of some service, such as the apprehension of a criminal or the finding of lost property. In *Carlill* v *Carbolic Smoke Ball Co.* [1893] 1 QB 256 (the facts are given at 2.4.2.1), the defendants sought to avoid having to pay the promised sum, although the plaintiff had caught influenza after apparently proper use of the smoke ball, by saying that there could be no contract because there would otherwise have been a unilateral contract with the whole world. Bowen LJ rejected this argument, saying:

> It is not a contract made with all the world. There is the fallacy of the argument. It is an offer made to all the world; and why should not an offer be made to all the world which is to ripen into a contract with anybody who comes forward and performs the condition? It is an offer to become liable to anyone who, before it is retracted, performs the condition, and, although the offer is made to the world, the contract is made with that limited portion of the public who come forward and perform the condition on the faith of the advertisement.

There is still force in this authority. It was relied on by the majority of the Court of Appeal in *Bowerman* v *ABTA Ltd* [1996] CLC 451, in deciding that an ABTA notice displayed by a travel agent containing a promise to reimburse the cost of holidays when ABTA members ceased to operate, constituted an offer to customers which was accepted by anyone booking a holiday with an ABTA member.

2.8.2   Acceptance and consideration

It has already been noted with regard to acceptance in bilateral contracts that such acceptance must be made in response to the offer made (see 2.6.2). The rule is of particular application to unilateral offers made to the whole world, such as rewards, and much of the case law is concerned with these offers.

The general rule is that in unilateral contracts acceptance and consideration are constituted by the same thing, namely, performance of the condition stipulated in the offeror's promise. Thus, in *Daulia Ltd* v *Four Millbank Nominees Ltd* [1978] Ch 231, Goff LJ said: '[T]he true view of a unilateral contract must in general be that the offeror is entitled to require full performance of the condition which he has imposed and short of that he is not bound.' However, there is an argument (P. H. Winfield, *Pollock's Principles of Contract*, 13th edn, Stevens, 1950, p. 19, and adopted by the Law Revision Committee in its Sixth Interim Report in 1937) which suggests that for some purposes acceptance may be constituted by commencing performance of the stipulated condition, so that any attempt to revoke the offer after the commencement of performance will be too late (see 2.8.3.2 below). However, no reward would be payable until the complete performance of the act (i.e., the consideration for the promise of the reward). There are considerable difficulties in accepting this analysis which are discussed at 2.8.3.2 below.

2.8.3   Revocation

Revocation presents particular difficulty in the case of offers of unilateral contracts, as a result of the rule that acceptance is constituted by performance of the condition stated in the offer. In theory it would be open to the offeror to revoke the offer at any time before completion of performance, even where the offeree had gone to effort or expense in attempting performance, since the revocation would have been made before the moment of acceptance (see 2.7.3). It has long been recognised that application of the normal rule in this situation can cause hardship and injustice, but attempts to overcome the rule have run into conceptual difficulties. It is generally accepted that it would be more desirable for the power to revoke to be lost once the offeror has notice that an offeree has unequivocally embarked upon performance. Loss of the power to revoke would not affect the rule that acceptance is constituted only by full performance of the condition in the offer. There are *dicta* to that effect from Goff LJ in *Daulia Ltd* v *Four Millbank Nominees Ltd* [1978] Ch 231. The difficulty is in finding a conceptual explanation for such a rule.

2.8.3.1 Promissory estoppel Perhaps the most obvious explanation lies in the doctrine of promissory estoppel (see 4.4.2), since it is not difficult to identify both a representation that the offer would be held open long enough for performance to be completed and a reliance by the other party on that representation. In *Errington* v *Errington* [1952] 1 KB 290, a father had bought a house for his son and daughter-in-law to live in, promising that although the house and accompanying mortgage were in his name he would transfer the house to their names once they had paid off all the mortgage instalments. The father died and the son left the daughter-in-law, who continued to live in the house and to pay the instalments. The question arose of whether the daughter-in-law could be forced to surrender possession of the house. Denning LJ said:

> The father's promise was a unilateral contract — a promise of the house in return for their act of paying the instalments. It could not be revoked by him once the couple entered on performance of the act but it would cease to bind him if they left it incomplete and unperformed . . . They have acted on the promise and neither the father nor his widow, his successor in title, can eject them in disregard of it.

There is a hint in the passage quoted that Denning LJ viewed the inability to revoke the promise as based on estoppel, since he referred expressly to the fact that the couple had acted on the promise. In many cases, however, such analysis will not work, because there is no pre-existing legal relationship and because in English law the doctrine cannot currently be used to found a cause of action (see 4.4.3.2). Since *Errington v Errington* involved the expenditure of money on land belonging to another, it may be justified on the basis of the analogous doctrine of proprietary estoppel (see 4.4.6), but that places a serious limitation on the case as explaining the loss of the power to revoke.

2.8.3.2 Acceptance upon commencement   An alternative explanation is to question the usual rule that in unilateral contracts acceptance and consideration are synonymous and simultaneous (see above, 2.8.2). However, the main difficulty with such a simple rule is that it has always been accepted that an offeree is entirely free whether to perform or not, and indeed free to commence performance and then stop before completion without fear of any penalty other than the loss of the opportunity to earn the promised reward. If acceptance were to be constituted by starting performance then the contract would, of course, be in existence from that moment. The offeree would then be obliged to complete performance or face a claim for breach of contract should he fail. To tie the offeree in by such a rule would be to defeat one of the objects of the unilateral contract, which is to avoid the need for initial reciprocity inherent in the consideration doctrine as applied to bilateral contracts.

2.8.3.3 Collateral contract   A third explanation rests on the identification of two contracts in such cases. The first is the main unilateral contract, with acceptance and consideration furnished in the orthodox way by performance of the condition, stipulated in the offer, and until complete performance of the condition no reward would be payable. However, there is an additional collateral (or ancillary) unilateral contract. It consists of an offer not to revoke the main offer once the offeree has commenced performance of the condition, and this offer would be accepted by that act of commencing this performance (see McGovney (1914) 27 Harv LR 644, 659). There would then be an enforceable promise to keep open the main offer (and not to revoke).

There is no real conceptual difficulty with this explanation, since commencing performance can be the consideration for the collateral contract not to revoke because it is the performance impliedly requested in the offer. However, this explanation is highly artificial and bears no resemblance to the manner in which unilateral offers are in fact made. It also possesses one significant drawback, namely that this mechanism will not actually prevent revocation of the main unilateral offer. It only means that there will be a breach of the collateral contract and the remedy would be damages for that breach. Nevertheless, recent developments in respect of implied contracts (see, for example, *Harvela Investments* v *Royal Trust Co. of Canada Ltd* [1986] AC 207 and *Blackpool & Fylde Aero Club* v *Blackpool Borough Council* [1990] 1 WLR 1195 (2.4.2.4)) may lend support to this approach to the problem. In addition, both *Luxor* v *Cooper* and *Daulia* v *Four Millbank Nominees* consider the question of whether revocation is possible against a background where there is an implied promise not to revoke once performance has commenced. *Luxor (Eastbourne) Ltd* v *Cooper* [1941] AC 108 involved an estate agency contract on terms whereby the agent was to be paid £10,000 on completion of the sale of two cinemas to a purchaser for at least £185,000. Although such a purchaser was found, the sale did not take place. The House of Lords refused to imply a term to the effect that the owners had undertaken not to prevent the sale (i.e., there was no implied term not to revoke) on the basis that the terms of the offer made it clear that it was to be freely revocable at any time before completion.

2.8.3.4 Conclusion None of the above explanations is entirely satisfactory. The one involving least conceptual difficulty involves an undesirable resort to legal fiction. Of the other two, promissory estoppel appears best to describe what actually happens and to leave the unilateral contract device intact for the functions for which it is so useful. It seems fairly safe to predict that, at least where the offer contemplates that the offer may be freely revoked, the courts will continue to find offers of unilateral contracts irrevocable after performance has begun. However, there are instances where the offer may make it clear that the parties intended that revocation might occur at any time before complete performance of the act, as in *Luxor (Eastbourne) Ltd* v *Cooper* [1941] AC 108. It is likely that future courts will continue their reticence to explain why they are prepared to hold that an offer is irrevocable once performance has commenced. On the other hand, it may be that in the promissory estoppel explanation (and the removal of some of its current limitations) lie the seeds of the wider development of that doctrine into a principle of full liability.

2.8.4 Communication of revocation of a unilateral offer

In relation to offers made to the whole world, there are particular problems in applying a rule which states that a revocation of an offer must be communicated to the offeree since the offerees will be unidentified. Practical considerations would therefore suggest that it would be appropriate to follow the approach taken in the American case of *Shuey v United States* 92 US 73 (1875). Here, it was held to be sufficient that the 'same notoriety be given to the revocation that was given to the offer'. Therefore, if the same channel is used and the same level of publicity achieved, the fact that an individual offeree had not seen the revocation would be irrelevant.

2.8.5   Function of unilateral contracts

The typical unilateral contract is usually regarded as being the offer of a reward for the performance of some service (see *R v Clarke* (1927) 40 CLR 227), or the repeat option for the supply of goods provided in a long-term contract to deliver goods as and when ordered (see *Great Northern Railway Co. v Witham* (1873) LR 9 CP 16). These functions are well known and well documented, and require no further comment. In addition to these typical functions, as we have seen throughout this chapter (e.g., 2.4.2.4), unilateral contracts are sometimes used by the courts to manipulate the facts of situations of negotiation into binding contracts where instinct suggests that a contractual relationship exists but the facts do not lend themselves to a conventional analysis of a bilateral contract. Two House of Lords cases will serve to illustrate the point.

The facts of *The Eurymedon* [1975] AC 154 are related elsewhere (see 4.3.4.2 and 15.5.4). The essential point is that the court found a contract to exist between a shipper and a stevedore, although the two had not dealt directly with each other but each had a separate contract with the carrier in the case. Lord Wilberforce explained the existence of the contract between shipper and stevedore in the following way:

> The bill of lading brought into existence a bargain initially unilateral but capable of becoming mutual, between the shippers and the stevedore, made through the carrier as agent. This became a full contract when the stevedore performed services by discharging the goods. The performance of these services for the benefit of the shipper was the consideration for the agreement by the shipper that the stevedore should have the benefit of the exemptions and limitations contained in the bill of lading.

There is little doubt that this analysis owes more to the court's legitimate desire at that time to avoid the doctrine of privity of contract than it does to any genuine description of the nature of the negotiations between the three parties.

The facts of *Harvela Investments Ltd v Royal Trust Co. of Canada* [1986] AC 207 are stated above (see 2.4.2.4). The essential issue was whether a referential bid was permissible following a request for single bids for the purchase of property. Lord Templeman's speech is couched in terms of an implied stipulation by the offeror about the nature of any acceptance. Lord Diplock, however, appeared to believe that the decision could be explained on the basis of a 'business efficacy' implied term (see 5.5.4), which at first sight is a little surprising since, at the time of the request for bids, by any conventional analysis no contract had come into force. Lord Diplock saw a contract into which a term might be implied in the following way:

> It was not a mere invitation to negotiate for the sale of the shares . . . Its legal nature was that of a unilateral or 'if' contract, or rather of two unilateral contracts in identical terms to one of which the vendors and Harvela were the parties as promisor and promisee respectively, while to the other the vendors were promisor and Sir Leonard was promisee.

Lord Diplock's approach is further evidence of the way the unilateral contract device can be used to 'find' a contract where by a conventional analysis none exists. It seems highly probable that the implication of such unilateral contracts will continue as a pragmatic means of solving existing deficiencies in English contract law.

THREE
Agreement problems

Despite the apparent existence of agreement between the parties, the agreement may be void as a contract (automatically of no effect from the very beginning) due to uncertainty in its terms, or because the parties have made a fundamental mistake as to a term of the agreement. However, because the effect of a contract being void is so drastic, the courts have limited the circumstances in which an allegation of mistake will lead to this result on the basis that 'mistake is not to be used as an excuse to escape from bad bargains, and nor is it to be allowed to jeopardise the security of market transactions' (J. N. Adams and R. Brownsword, *Understanding Contract Law*, 3rd edn, Sweet & Maxwell, 2000, p. 69). The same principle can be seen in relation to curable uncertainty. The courts are keen, recognising the need for precision in business contracts, to find a concluded contract despite allegations of uncertainty where they are able to determine the meaning of vague terms or resolve a problem of a missing term, especially where the agreement in question has been executed by the parties. As Lord Tomlin stated in *Hillas & Co. Ltd* v *Arcos Ltd* (1932) 147 LT 503, at 512, the purpose is to ensure that 'the dealings of men may so far as possible be treated as effective, and that the law may not incur the reproach of being the destroyer of bargains'.

3.1 CERTAINTY OF AGREEMENTS

3.1.1 General

More complex than the issue of mere existence of agreement is the problem raised where the existence of an agreement in formal terms is not disputed, but one party alleges either that important terms have not been agreed upon or that a term or terms is or are too vague, so that the contract is unenforceable. In practice there is considerable overlap between these possibilities, since if an essential term is omitted, the agreement will necessarily be vague; and if certain terms are vague, in the sense that their meaning is unclear, this will lead to uncertainty as to the meaning of what has been agreed.

This is clearly an area where there is at least potential for conflict between the relational nature of contracting and the once-and-for-all focus inherent in judicial intervention in contracts. To adopt the words of Lord Wright in *Hillas & Co. Ltd v Arcos Ltd* (1932) 147 LT 503, at 516, it is accepted that when business people make 'big forward contracts for future goods over a period . . . in general in such contracts it must be impossible . . . to specify in advance all the details of a complicated performance'. Parties sometimes leave trivial details to be worked out later, or in long-term contracts leave the price to be agreed from time to time, or otherwise consciously leave gaps in their agreements because the information and transaction costs of negotiating an agreed allocation of any particular risk are out of proportion to the likelihood of the risk maturing. Sometimes, as a safety net, they put in an arbitration clause for the resolution of matters which cannot be worked out amicably between them. In nearly all cases they rely on their goodwill at the time of contracting and their mutual interest in maintaining the relationship (which almost certainly extends beyond the individual contract in question) to iron out any problems not covered by the agreement.

It can be the case that loosely drafted contracts may be some way into performance before this vagueness or lack of provision is appreciated or considered an issue. At that point, any court which becomes involved will be left with an invidious task. If asked to enforce the agreement between the parties where they have left some matters deliberately unspecific, the court may feel that it has nothing tangible to enforce. At that stage, of course, if the matter has got as far as litigation, there is a danger that the goodwill on which the parties once relied may have evaporated. Yet, if there has been more than trifling performance by one or both of the parties, it is a drastic step to say that the matter is too vague for there to be any real agreement, and thus that there is no contract.

The task of the court is to walk the narrow line between writing the parties' agreement for them (which has traditionally been viewed as beyond the power of the judges and an infringement of freedom of contract) and maintaining the contract by supplying 'reasonable' terms to be implied from the perceived intentions of the parties (on the implication of terms, see generally 5.5).

Turning again to *Hillas & Co. Ltd v Arcos Ltd*, Lord Wright makes it clear that the role of the court (at least where there has already been some performance) is to preserve the contract whenever possible. Lord Wright also said (at 514):

[T]he court is [not] to make a contract for the parties . . . except in so far as there are appropriate implications of law, as for instance, the implication of what is just and reasonable to be ascertained by the court as a matter of machinery where the contractual intention is clear but the contract is silent on some detail. Thus in contracts for future performance over a period, the parties may neither be able nor desire to specify many matters of detail.

. . . Save for the legal implication I have mentioned, such contracts might well be incomplete or uncertain.

As with the rest of the area of formation of agreements, much depends upon the facts of each case. There are no clear lines dividing certain agreements from uncertain agreements. Rather it is often a question of degree coupled with the extent of the willingness of the particular court to intervene to rescue the contract. The general principle can probably be stated as follows: to be enforceable as a contract an agreement must be sufficiently precise (taking into account the whole context of the negotiations) for the court to be confident that what it is enforcing complies with the parties' actual intentions (objectively ascertained, of course: see 2.1) rather than any imputed to them by the court itself. The problem, ironically, is that this principle is itself vague and an invitation to the exercise of a considerable amount of judicial discretion. It is possible, however, to discern certain guidelines.

3.1.2   Agreements where essential terms are vague

In *Raffles* v *Wichelhaus* (1864) 2 Hurl & C 906, 159 ER 375, the level of ambiguity was such that there could be no agreement between the parties. The plaintiff had promised to sell and deliver to the defendants 125 bales of cotton at a given price 'to arrive ex *Peerless* from Bombay'. There were two ships called *Peerless*, and one left Bombay in October while the other left Bombay in December. When the defendants refused to accept the plaintiff's cotton which had been shipped on the December ship, the plaintiff brought an action against the defendants alleging breach of contract. The defendants alleged that they understood the ship in the agreement to be the ship sailing in October. At the time of contracting, the fact that there were two ships of this name sailing from Bombay within this time period seems not to have been known by either party.

The court found for the defendants. Understanding the case is not easy, since the court gave no reason for its decision. The case is cited by some as one of the last vestiges of a subjective approach to intention (see 2.1). The real intentions of the parties (assuming the court had discovered their real intentions) did not coincide, so that there was never really any agreement. On the other hand, it seems likely that neither a detached bystander, nor a reasonable man in the defendants' shoes would have had any way of knowing from the words used between the parties which of the two ships was intended. The court expressly recognised the existence of latent ambiguity, which in this case could not be resolved by resort to any objective standard. The court was therefore left with no alternative other than to conclude that there was no contract.

Even where there is no total ambiguity, it must be possible to ascertain a meaning which would satisfy the objective bystander. In *Scammell & Nephew Ltd* v *Ouston* [1941] AC 251, the House of Lords was faced with an agreement to purchase a van on 'hire purchase terms', but details of these hire purchase terms, such as amount of any deposit and the amount and frequency of repayments, had not been agreed. The House of Lords consider-ed that there were so many possible interpretations of this expression that it was impossible to say which one the parties had intended, and it was necessary for the parties in each case to agree upon the relevant terms. However, it is equally clear that where a court can resort to clear commercial practice or to previous dealings between the parties in order to ascertain the meaning of a particular contractual expression, it will do so thereby giving effect to what must have been the 'obvious' intentions of the parties. For example, Lord Wright, in *Scammell* v *Ouston* (at 273), referred to the example of a sale contract 'on cif terms', which he regarded as having 'a definite and complete meaning under the law merchant'. By contrast, there are a number of different meanings of a contract made on 'fob' terms.

The existence of expert evidence as to the recognised meaning of 'fair and reasonable specification' was regarded as one of the factors rescuing an option in *Hillas & Co.* v *Arcos Ltd* (1932) 147 LT 503. The plaintiffs had agreed to buy '22,000 standards of softwood goods of fair specification' from the defendants during the 1930 season, and had also been granted an option to enter into a contract 'to purchase 100,000 standards for delivery during 1931'. The option clause did not specify the kind, size or quality of goods to be supplied. The plaintiffs made a valid exercise of the option, but the defendants had already sold their entire season's production of timber and so claimed that there was no option contract because it was too vague to be enforceable. However, the House of Lords held that the option contract was complete and binding. Their Lordships were forced to go to considerable lengths in implying terms in order to make sense of the agreement. This was achieved by implication from the terms of the 1930 contract, which had already been performed, and by expert evidence regarding recognised com-mercial practice in interpreting 'fair specification'. The option clause had been part of what the plaintiffs had paid for, and to have found it unenforce-able as too vague would have been to deprive the plaintiffs of part of their bargain. Therefore the preferable course was clearly to rescue this agreement if at all possible.

The other significant factor in *Hillas* v *Arcos* was the fact that part of the contract, relating to supply in the 1930 season, had already been performed and, in general, case law suggests that there is a reluctance to come to the conclusion that there is no valid agreement where there has been perform-ance. Instead, in such circumstances, the courts strive to maintain a contract whenever possible. After all, if the parties have managed to perform an apparent agreement it would appear odd for a court to conclude that it is too vague to be capable of performance. Where there has been no performance (and the agreement is executory) a different attitude prevails. The importance of the 'executed agreement' factor in influencing the decision of courts was recognised by Cohen LJ in *British Bank for Foreign Trade Ltd* v *Novinex Ltd* [1949] 1 KB 623, 629–30, quoting Denning J, the judge at first instance. It was also more fully articulated by Steyn LJ in *G. Percy Trentham Ltd* v *Archital Luxfer Ltd* [1993] 1 Lloyd's Rep 25, at 27, when he stressed that where both parties have partly or fully performed the apparent agreement it will be 'unrealistic' to argue that an apparent agreement is void for vagueness or uncertainty. He added that 'the fact that the transaction is executed makes it easier to imply a term resolving any uncertainty, or, alternatively, it may make it possible to treat a matter not finalised in negotiations as inessential'.

However, it must be clear from the decision in *British Steel Corporation* v *Cleveland Bridge & Engineering Co. Ltd* [1984] 1 All ER 504 (see 3.1.3 below) that this 'executed factor' will enable a court to avoid a conclusion of vagueness or uncertainty only where there is a sufficient basis for 'gap filling'. Robert Goff J had concluded that there was too much which had still to be agreed on the facts. A similar conclusion was reached in *J. Murphy & Sons Ltd* v *ABB Daimler-Benz Transportation (Signal) Ltd* (unreported), 2 December 1998, where the defendant had authorised the plaintiff subcontractor, to commence a phase of the works and this work had been carried out. Nevertheless, the judge concluded that there was no agreement because at least two material terms remained to be settled between the parties.

It is important also to note that where a particular inessential term is vague, it may be possible to sever that term and enforce the rest of the agreement. For example, in *Nicolene Ltd* v *Simmonds* [1953] 1 QB 543, the agreement in question referred to acceptance as being on 'the usual conditions of acceptance' when there were no such 'usual conditions of acceptance'. The plaintiffs, the buyers in the case, sought damages for breach of contract by the seller, and the seller argued that no contract had been concluded because of the uncertainty as to this term. However, the Court of Appeal rejected this argument, holding that as this clause was meaningless, it could be severed from the rest of the agreement. Denning LJ expressly distinguished a meaningless clause (capable of being severed) from a clause on which agreement had not yet been reached (see 3.1.3 below). There is a discernible policy objective in this decision, namely that without the application of severance in such circumstances, a party would be able to insert a meaningless clause in order to allow for a later escape route from the contract.

3.1.3 Agreements where essential terms are missing

As a general principle, there needs to be agreement on all important terms or the agreement will be too uncertain to be enforceable. If important matters have still to be agreed between the parties, the assumption must be that the parties are still negotiating and do not yet intend to be legally bound. For example, in *British Steel Corporation* v *Cleveland Bridge & Engineering Co. Ltd* [1984] 1 All ER 504, important terms had still to be agreed between the parties so that the court held there to be no concluded agreement. Negotiations were entered into in anticipation of concluding a contract whereby the plaintiffs would manufacture steel nodes for the defendants. Although all the elements of the contract had not been agreed, both parties confidently expected that a contract would result. The defendants requested the plaintiffs to commence the work before complete agreement was reached. However, agreement was never reached on some matters and no formal contract was concluded. The plaintiffs had delivered all but one of these nodes and so sued the defendants for the value of the nodes on the basis of a *quantum meruit* (reasonable value). The defendants counterclaimed for breach of contract.

Robert Goff J found that so much remained to be agreed (such as price, delivery dates and liability for consequential loss and delay) that it was 'very difficult to see' how a contract had been formed. Accordingly, there could be no counterclaim for breach of contract. This is probably explained by the fact that the judge clearly considered the defendants largely responsible for the failure to agree. To have found a contract in the circumstances might have exposed the plaintiffs to an action for breach of contract by the defendants, penalising the plaintiffs for something which, in the judge's view, was not their fault. However, it was held that the plaintiffs could recover on a *quantum meruit* because the defendants would otherwise have been unjustly enriched at the plaintiffs' expense (see 3.1.4).

If a matter is left to later agreement between the parties then it will lack the necessary certainty. In *May & Butcher* v *R* [1934] 2 KB 17n, an agreement had been made for the sale of surplus war equipment to the plaintiffs, the price being left to be agreed between the parties 'from time to time'. The parties were unable to agree, and the plaintiffs sought to enforce the agreement at a 'reasonable price' to be determined by the court. The House of Lords refused to do this. The point was not articulated as part of the reasoning, but there can be little doubt that the court's conclusion that no contract had come into existence was made much easier by the fact that no performance under the agreed terms had taken place.

A further example of the reluctance of the English courts to enforce 'agreements to agree' where there has been no performance under the terms of the alleged contract, is provided by the decision of the House of Lords in *Walford* v *Miles* [1992] 2 AC 128. The parties, negotiating for the sale and purchase of a business, had entered into a 'lock-out agreement', the purported effect of which was to prevent the respondent prospective sellers from negotiating with anyone other than the appellants. Negotiations were unsuccessful, and after a time the respondents decided to sell to a third party. The appellants then brought an action for breach of the 'lock-out agreement'. The agreement was found to be unenforceable. According to Lord Ackner, who gave the only substantial speech in the House of Lords, the fatal weakness of the agreement was that it was indefinite in length. It was a bare agreement to negotiate, and therefore without legal force. The House of Lords rejected the argument that such an agreement could be made sufficiently certain because there was an implied duty placed on a party who had agreed to a lock-out to negotiate with the other party and reach agreement. Such a position was regarded as 'irreconcilable with the adversarial nature of the parties when involved in contract negotiations' (*per* Lord Ackner at 138). On the other hand, had the 'lock-out agreement' stipulated a period of time during which exclusive negotiations were to take place, it would have been enforceable, because the element of uncertainty would have been removed. Lord Ackner's *dictum* was followed by the Court of Appeal in *Pitt* v *PHH Asset Management Ltd* [1994] 1 WLR 327, in relation to a 'lock-out' agreement for a two-week period.

Thus English law does not recognise a general duty to negotiate in good faith (although see comments by Lord Steyn in 'Contract Law: Fulfilling the Reasonable Expectations of Honest Men' (1997) 113 LQR 433 at 439). This position may usefully be compared with the recognition of a duty to negotiate in good faith in other jurisdictions, e.g. Germany, and the provisions of attempted codifications of contractual principles (see 1.6.1). Article 2:301 of PECL states that although a party is free to negotiate and is not liable for failure to reach agreement, 'a party who has negotiated or broken off negotiations contrary to good faith and fair dealing is liable for the losses caused to the other party'. Article 2:301(3) continues by specifying one such instance where it is 'contrary to good faith and fair dealing' as being where a party enters into or continues negotiations 'with no real intention of reaching an agreement with the other party'. Article 2.15 of the UNIDROIT *Principles of International Commercial Contracts* is in the same terms. A contract to negotiate in good faith is also recognised in the United States (see *Channel Home Centers Division of Grace Retail Corporation* v *Grossman* 795 F 2d 291 (1986)).

However, in English law, even where there is only an agreement between the parties to agree a price, it seems that the courts will enforce that agreement if they possibly can once performance has begun. In *Foley* v *Classique Coaches Ltd* [1934] 2 KB 1, the parties had made an agreement for the supply of the defendants' petrol requirements, at a price to be agreed from time to time. The contract included an arbitration clause, and was linked to a deal whereby the defendants purchased a parcel of land from the plaintiff. Performance continued without incident for three years before the defendants argued that the requirements contract was unenforceable because the price clause was uncertain. The Court of Appeal found that the agreement was enforceable, the defendants having to pay a 'reasonable price' for petrol supplied. What was reasonable in the circumstances might be determined, if necessary, by arbitration. In part it seems that it was the fact of actual performance, including the conveyance of the parcel of land, and the danger of depriving the plaintiff of one important element of the bargain, which persuaded the Court. It is interesting to note that the Court did not allow the decision of the House of Lords in *May & Butcher* v *R* (above) to dissuade it from reaching this conclusion.

It seems, therefore, that uncertainty as to price is not as a matter of law always fatal to an agreement; rather, it is a question of construction of the contract in each case. The most obvious distinguishing feature between the two cases, however, is the lack of performance in one and the substantial performance in the other.

Section 8 of the SGA 1979 (substantially reproducing the same section of the 1893 Act) provides:

(1)   The price in a contract of sale may be fixed by the contract, or may be left to be fixed in a manner agreed by the contract, or may be determined by the course of dealing between the parties.

(2)   Where the price is not determined as mentioned in subsection (1) above the buyer must pay a reasonable price.

In *May & Butcher* v *R*, Lord Dunedin suggested that s. 8(2) applies only where the contract is silent as to price, and does not apply where a price-fixing mechanism has failed to work. Such an interpretation seems to be unduly narrow and to fly in the face of logic. To say nothing at all about price is surely less certain than to attempt to make a flexible provision, which takes into account the changing value of money through time.

This interpretation also appears to be inconsistent with the common law (a possible but unlikely and undesirable conclusion). In *Sudbrook Trading Estate Ltd* v *Eggleton* [1983] 1 AC 444, a lease contained an option to purchase the land in question at a price to be agreed by two valuers, one to be nominated by each party. The lessors refused to appoint a valuer and claimed that the option clause was unenforceable because the price term was uncertain. The House of Lords refused to find the clause unenforceable and held that if the parties have provided sensible but subsidiary and non-essential machinery for fixing a fair price, and that machinery had for some reason broken down, then the court should attempt to take the place of that machinery by identifying a fair and reasonable price which was reasonable in all the circumstances. Lord Diplock's judgment distinguishes this position from a case where an individual is specifically named in the clause as being given the responsibility to determine the important matter, where the contract would be frustrated if that person was then unable to make a determination through no fault of either of the parties, e.g., death of the person named.

No doubt their Lordships were influenced in their conclusion that this clause was inessential by the fact that there had been considerable performance of the main contract and there was a danger of the lessee being deprived of an important part of its bargain had a contrary result been reached. Lord Fraser also stressed the fact that it was the lessors who, in not making the appointment, were preventing the machinery from operating thereby deriving the lessees of this benefit. In addition, as Lord Fraser stressed, although it might appear logical for the courts to refuse to substitute their own machinery for that provided by the parties, such a practice would be commercially inconvenient as the inevitable consequence would be that such an agreement would be void.

However, *Sudbrook* v *Eggleton* was distinguished in the context of an argument to enforce a single payment provision, by the Court of Appeal in *Gillatt* v *Sky Television Ltd* [2000] 1 All ER (Comm) 461. The Court of Appeal in this case had no such incentive to substitute its own machinery since the agreement itself would not be rendered void. In addition, the party requesting the court to substitute its own machinery had the ability (but had failed) to make the necessary appointment itself.

In *Gillatt*, by an agreement Sky had acquired shares in Tele-Aerials Satellite Ltd (TAS), and by clause 6 it had been agreed that if Sky sold or disposed of this shareholding then Sky would pay '55 per cent of the open market value of such shares . . . as determined by an independent chartered accountant' to Mallard Ltd. Mallard Ltd had subsequently assigned this right to Gillatt. Sky had transferred the shares to a wholly-owned subsidiary, and Gillatt claimed that clause 6 applied so that he was entitled to the payment. However, neither Gillatt, nor Sky nor Mallard had taken any steps to appoint the independent accountant to determine the value of the shares and, since a reasonable time had elapsed, it was no longer possible to do so.

Gillatt argued that this requirement was only intended as a description of the machinery to be applied if there was any dispute between the parties as to entitlement under the clause and was not an essential pre-condition to the existence of any entitlement under the clause. He relied on *Sudbrook* as authority to support the principle that 'where the machinery is not essential, if it breaks down for any reason the court will substitute its own machinery'. However the Court of Appeal concluded that the valuation requirement in *Gillatt* was both integral and essential, and the clause did not contain any other objective criteria in order to determine the value of the shares as there was no definition of 'open market value' (despite the fact that there were many ways of calculating this). This indicated that the parties had agreed to leave this to the independent chartered accountant, and it was the duty of the court to give effect to this intention rather than to make its own valuation. This was also not a case involving a breakdown of the contractual machinery, since the claimant had not attempted to make the necessary appointment.

It would seem that the principle in *Sudbrook* will in future be confined to cases where the breakdown in the machinery is attributable to the fault of one of the parties in not cooperating. It had also been thought that where a particular person was not named in the clause, that machinery was more likely to be regarded as non-essential on the basis that a decision to name a person indicated that this machinery was regarded as essential because certain skills, which this individual possessed, were required by the parties. This was strongly argued by counsel for Mr Gillatt, but was not regarded as significant by the Court of Appeal in the light of the other evidence.

These cases indicate that it would seem ultimately to be a question of fact in each case whether the contract is sufficiently clear for the court to be able to enforce by reasonable implication the apparent agreement between the parties.

3.1.4 Recovery where a contract fails to materialise

As was seen in *British Steel Corporation* v *Cleveland Bridge & Engineering* [1984] 1 All ER 504 (at 3.1.3), even where the court concludes that no agreement was reached between the parties because essential terms are missing, it may still be prepared to order that the recipient should pay a sum to cover the reasonable value of the performance he or she received where that performance was requested by that party. The basis for this award is restitution, namely, that to allow the recipient to retain the promised performance would result in that party being unjustly enriched at the expense of the performing party.

However, this possibility of recovery does not apply generally to expenses incurred during the negotiation process in preparation for the contract. This is the result of the decision of Rattee J in *Regalian Properties plc* v *London Dockland Development Corp.* [1995] 1 All ER 1005. The judge made it clear that, in the absence of a express contractual undertaking to cover such costs, the words 'subject to contract' made it clear that each party was free to withdraw from negotiations at any time and that each party incurred pre-contractual costs at his or her own risk. In addition, it was possible to distinguish *British Steel Corporation* v *Cleveland Bridge* on the basis that in that case the plaintiffs had sought to recover for the 'accelerated performance of the anticipated contract' where that performance had been requested by the defendants. However, in *Regalian* the plaintiffs had incurred expenses in the form of payment of professional fees for designs to enable them to obtain and perform the contract so that there was not the same benefit to the defendant.

On the facts in *Regalian*, the judge also found that the contract did not materialise because of the failure to agree on the price and not, as had been alleged by the plaintiffs, because the defendant decided to abandon the project. The judge did not deal with the position where the negotiations were not 'subject to contract' and where they broke down because of the unilateral decision by one party to abandon the project.

In *Countrywide Communications Ltd* v *ICL Pathway Ltd* [2000] CLC 324, there was fault. The plaintiff had carried out public relations work in connection with a successful bid which had been made by the defendant to supply a system for the payment of benefits to the Benefits Agency and Post Office Counters Ltd. The plaintiff had been assured that it would be appointed if the bid succeeded, but on the success of the bid the defendant appointed another consultancy. It was held that the plaintiff was entitled to payment (£38,370) for the time it had spent and to cover its costs on the basis that there was fault on the part of the defendant and the services in question were of benefit to the defendant. The judge, Nicholas Strauss QC, stressed that this did not allow for any general recovery of costs incurred in tendering or preparing for a hoped for contract (although see *Blackpool & Fylde Aero Club* v *Blackpool Borough Council* [1990] 1 WLR 1195, at 2.4.2.4, where an obligation to consider conforming tenders was implied, and in the event of breach of this promise, contractual damages would be available which might be based on reliance loss). However, the judge in *Countrywide Communications* identified a number of factors to consider in deciding whether it was possible on a particular set of facts (referred to as 'exceptional cases') to recover for expenditure incurred in anticipation of a contract which did not materialise (at 349):

(a) Whether the services were of a kind which would normally be given free of charge.

(b) The terms in which the request to perform the services was made may be important in establishing the extent of the risk (if any) which the plaintiffs may fairly be said to have taken that such services would in the end be unrecompensed. This was linked to the issue of whether the parties were expressly or impliedly negotiating 'subject to contract', or whether one party had given an assurance that he would not withdraw in these circumstances.

(c)   Whether the services were of real benefit to the defendant so that he could be said to be unjustly enriched at the plaintiff's expense (clearly important in the light of *Regalian Developments*, although Denning LJ in *Brewer Street Investments Ltd* v *Barclays Woollen Co Ltd* [1954] 1 QB 428 had regarded the fact that the services were requested as being a benefit in itself).

(d)   The circumstances in which the contract failed to materialise (i.e., any fault on the part of the defendant so that the circumstances are outside the risk undertaken by the plaintiff).

In addition, the judge stressed that recovery was unlikely if the expense was not incurred in the course of providing services requested by the defendant, and that the weight to be given to each of these factors would vary from case to case. This decision is helpful in rationalising existing case law to provide a set of guiding principles concerning when recovery may be possible.

A further recent example of an award of a *quantum meruit* occurred in *Yule* v *Little Bird Ltd* (unreported), 5 April 2001. The claimant alleged that he had been engaged to direct a documentary film by the defendant and had worked on the project for some months before being dropped and replaced by another director. It was found as a fact that no formal contract had ever materialised between the parties and that this practice was usual in the industry. However, as the defendant had requested, or at least accepted, services from the claimant in furtherance of the project, he could not expect the services of the claimant to go unrewarded and a *quantum meruit* was therefore appropriate.

Therefore, although English law does not expressly recognise any general duty of good faith in contract negotiations, there are clear indicators here that there is some recognition of principles of fair dealing through the use of restitutionary principles to recompense a party who has performed services at the request of the other party, where that party has been expressly led to believe that he or she will be awarded the contract to which those services relate.

3.2   AGREEMENT MISTAKE

By agreement mistake we mean that one or both of the parties made a fundamental mistake which prevents the formation of an agreement, although the parties may well subjectively believe that they are in agreement. Treitel (*The Law of Contract*, 10th edn, Sweet & Maxwell, 1999, p. 262) refers to these mistakes as negativing consent. There is another category of mistake in English law which does not relate to the issue of reaching agreement. This occurs where both parties do not deny that they reached agreement but allege that this agreement is impossible to perform because they both made a fundamental mistake (see common or shared mistake, Chapter 9).

3.2.1   The doctrine of mistake in English law

The single word 'mistake' may be misleading if it is taken to indicate a single coherent doctrine. It indicates no more than a loose association of doctrines often connected in no other way than that they are called into play in factual contexts in which one or both parties may in everyday language be said to have been mistaken. In fact, it has been argued that English law really knows no independent doctrine of mistake, and that those cases in which apparent mistake has resulted in a contract being set aside involve the application to the particular situation of established rules of the law of contract, such as the rules of offer and acceptance. Such a conclusion almost certainly overstates the case, but it does at least reflect the fact that English law has only a limited doctrine of mistake. Much of what passes for mistake can be explained in terms of other rules of English law, which have been dressed up in language borrowed from the civil law and arguably inappropriate to the common law conception of contract.

The reason for this civil law influence appears to be that the writing of systematic legal treatises began in France much earlier than it did in England, and at the end of the eighteenth century and the beginning of the nineteenth century the writings of the celebrated French lawyer Pothier gained a certain currency in England. The transference of the notion of mistake from one legal system to the other was misguided, however, since French law at the time was committed to a much more subjective approach to the formation of contracts than ever prevailed in England. An allegation of mistake is inevitably much more serious where the test of agreement is subjective.

3.2.2   The effect of mistake

One reason for the limited doctrine of mistake in English law is that where mistake operates it usually makes the contract void. More precisely, the effect is that there is no contract and the law takes the view that there never has been a contract. The wider impact of this conclusion is such that the courts appear to have been unwilling to extend the mistake doctrine.

The fact that the contract is void is of fundamental importance in the context of sale of goods. If no contract ever existed, title to the property which is the subject-matter of the sale cannot have passed between seller and buyer. By contrast, if a sale contract is voidable, i.e. valid until set aside, as for example in the case of a contract induced by misrepresentation (see generally Chapter 10), title does pass. It is the fact that title does not pass under contracts which are void for mistake that has made mistake an attractive doctrine to claimants but left the courts uneasy about its application. The reason is that a seller who has not lost title to the goods in question is entitled to the return of the actual goods, by virtue of his or her rights of ownership. The seller may well be entitled to the return of the actual goods even where they have passed out of the hands of the original buyer into the hands of a third party who knows nothing of the dealings between seller and buyer (a so-called 'innocent' third party). However, if the contract were merely voidable, and before the time of the seller's claim the buyer had disposed of the goods to an innocent third party, the third party would be protected from recovery of the goods by the original seller.

Where the original buyer remains present and solvent, the impact of the fact that a contract affected by mistake is void is slight, since if, for example, the original seller seeks redress then it is unlikely in most circumstances to matter whether he or she recovers the actual goods or their monetary equivalent. Where, however, the original buyer has disappeared, or is insolvent, the seller will seek a remedy by recovering the actual goods, if entitled to do so. It is true that both the original seller and the third party into whose hands the goods have passed are 'innocent', so that it is unfortunate that either should suffer. Nevertheless, it is considered that the original seller is in a better position to guard against mistake than the third party, who played no part in the transaction between seller and buyer. It would be somewhat harsh therefore, for the third party to be the person who suffers. However, this will be the inevitable result where the original seller retains title to the goods because the contract was void. It is probably for this reason that the English courts have been unwilling to extend the doctrine of mistake beyond its current narrow bounds.

3.3   TYPES OF MISTAKES NEGATIVING AGREEMENT

Agreement mistakes occur where, despite what one or other party may assert, it is impossible to identify objective evidence of agreement from what has passed between the parties (see 2.1). For that reason they are sometimes called 'mistakes negativing consent'. If both parties are willing to recognise that they have failed to come to any final agreement, they may usually extricate themselves without recourse to the courts. Problems occur, and litigation ensues, when one of the parties asserts that an agreement exists on the basis of the terms as *that party* understood them. Cases fall into two categories:

  (a)   those where the parties are genuinely at cross-purposes, so that each party makes a mistake but they are different mistakes (3.3.1); and
  (b)   unilateral mistakes, where only one party is mistaken but the other either knows of the mistake or ought to know of it (3.3.2).

Instances of both kinds of mistake being claimed successfully are rare, and the conclusion must be that in this context mistake is a very narrow doctrine unlikely to afford relief.

3.3.1   Cross-purposes mistake

Mistakes of the kind where the parties are at cross-purposes are sometimes referred to as 'mutual mistakes', although care must be taken with this expression because it has also been used, especially by nineteenth-century courts, to describe shared or common mistakes. The essence of the problem created by cross-purpose mistakes is that although one or both parties may assert that a contract exists, each on terms favourable to that party, on an objective interpretation it is impossible to resolve the ambiguity over what was agreed, so that the only possible conclusion is that there is no contract. In fact, when stated in this way, it is clear that the rule is not peculiar to the law on mistake. It is the same rule as was examined in relation to the formation of agreements and certainty of terms (see 2.1). Thus, the famous old case of *Raffles* v *Wichelhaus* (1864) 2 Hurl & C 906 is often treated as an instance of cross-purposes mistake (for a full discussion, see 3.1.2).

In *Scriven Bros & Co.* v *Hindley & Co.* [1913] 3 KB 564, two lots taken from the cargo of a single ship were put up for sale by auction. Inspection would have revealed that one was hemp and one was tow, but the auction catalogue did not reveal this. The lots carried the same shipping marks, and the custom of the trade was that different cargoes would not normally have the same marks. The buyers bid for both lots, having inspected the hemp but not the tow, in the mistaken belief that both lots were hemp. The buyers had therefore agreed to pay well over the market price for the lot which was tow. The sellers brought an action against the buyers to recover the price of the tow, and the buyers alleged that they had not agreed to buy the tow and that the tow had been knocked down to them as a result of a mistake. After considering the evidence, the court allowed the defendants to avoid the contract on the basis that there had been no agreement. The court considered that the auctioneer realised only that the defendants had made a mistake as to the value of the goods being sold, and did not accept that the auctioneer realised the defendants' mistake as to the subject-matter of the sale at the time of contracting.

3.3.1.1 The objective test The above decision may become easier to understand once it is remembered that the courts apply the objective test to the question of the existence of agreement. The leading case on the meaning of objectivity is *Smith* v *Hughes* (1871) LR 6 QB 597 (see 3.3.2), which involved an allegation of cross-purposes mistake.

In *Smith* v *Hughes*, the plaintiff offered to sell oats to the defendant. The defendant examined a sample, and agreed to take the whole consignment. On delivery it was discovered that the oats were 'new', and thus of no use to the defendant who required 'old' oats (that is, the previous season's oats). The defendant then refused to pay, claiming that the contract was void for mistake. The court rejected this defence. The mere fact that one party had deluded himself into entering into a contract, which was of no advantage to him, did not enable the court to say that there was no contract in the absence of any express mention by the defendant that he required 'old' oats. Symmetry between what was offered and what was accepted was apparent from an objective standpoint, and so the contract was upheld.

Applying that objective test to *Scriven Bros & Co.* v *Hindley & Co.* (above), a reasonable person in the position of the buyers might have been misled into believing that both lots on offer were hemp. Since it was impossible to say what should have been understood from the lots on display, the decision that there was no contract is quite justified.

3.3.1.2 A fault doctrine? It is difficult in relation to these cases to resist the inference that the courts apply a sometimes (but not always) unarticulated fault doctrine. Where a genuine situation of cross-purposes is seen to exist and one party is seen as responsible for provoking the mistake, the court will decide in favour of the other party. In *Scriven Bros & Co.* v *Hindley & Co.* [1913] 3 KB 564, the auctioneer who sought to enforce the contract had provoked the mistake by failing to make clear the distinction between the bales of hemp and tow, although they had the same shipping marks, and producing a catalogue which was unclear and misleading. The court refused to enforce the contract, Lawrence J stating:

> [I]t was peculiarly the duty of the auctioneer to make it clear to the bidder . . . which lots were hemp and which lots were tow. . . . [A] contract cannot arise when the person seeking to enforce it has by his own negligence, or by that of those for whom he is responsible, caused, or contributed to cause, the mistake.

Of course, the defendants had not investigated both lots, but the court recognised that the defendants owed no *duty* to examine the samples of tow.

The decision to enforce the alleged contract in *Smith* v *Hughes* (1871) LR 6 QB 597 can be explained in similar terms. The party seeking to resist enforcement of the contract had contributed to, or provoked, the mistake, and could not then be heard to say that there was no contract.

3.3.1.3 Refusal of specific performance in equity

In some circumstances the remedy for breach of contract is the equitable remedy of specific performance (for detailed treatment, see 14.2). Since equitable remedies generally are not available as a matter of right, but only when the court considers it appropriate that they be granted, the courts of equity would sometimes refuse to award specific performance in circumstances in which the objective test of agreement was satisfied. In *Webster* v *Cecil* (1861) 30 Beav 62, for example, the objective evidence revealed a contract of sale at a price of £1,250. Since the defendant had already refused to sell at £2,000, it seemed clear that the defendant had made a careless mistake. In fact he intended to sell at £2,250. The court refused to grant specific performance of the contract against him because it would be inequitable to do so.

Nevertheless, it is probably the case that the principle is of limited value beyond those situations in which the contract would in any case be void under the common law. The contract in *Webster* v *Cecil* would be void under the ordinary rule (see below, 3.3.2). In other cases it is likely that the fault doctrine described above (3.3.1.2) would prevent the court finding enforcement of the contract to be inequitable. Thus, in *Tamplin* v *James* (1880) 15 ChD 215, the defendant clearly misunderstood the offer which he accepted. He thought he was buying an inn and adjoining gardens of a property well known to him. In fact, the sale particulars were clear that the gardens were not included in the property on offer, but the defendant had not bothered to examine the particulars of the sale. At first instance Baggallay LJ granted specific performance against the defendant, saying:

> [W]here there has been no misrepresentation, and where there is no ambiguity in the terms of the contract, the defendant cannot be allowed to

evade the performance of it by the simple statement that he has made a mistake. Were such to be the law the performance of a contract could rarely be enforced upon an unwilling party who was also unscrupulous.

The Court of Appeal ((1880) 15 ChD 219) explained *Webster* v *Cecil* as a case where permitting specific performance would have been unreasonable because of the 'injustice' which would have resulted on the facts. Arguably, *Webster* v *Cecil* is a case where the buyer cannot have been unaware that a mistake as to a fundamental term was being made by the defendant seller. (See 3.3.2 below, *Centrovincial Estates plc* v *Merchant Investors Assurance Co. Ltd* [1983] Com LR 158 and *Hartog* v *Colin & Shields* [1939] 3 All ER 566).

However, in *Tamplin*, the plaintiff was unaware of the mistake being made by the defendant and if, as the Court of Appeal suggested, it was necessary to examine 'the hardship on the other side' before refusing specific performance, the sellers in *Tamplin* would be at a clear disadvantage in that they would have to find another buyer as a result of the reckless conduct of the defendant buyer. *Tamplin* v *James* clearly marked a recognition that the courts would no longer focus solely on whether it was 'oppressive and unjust' to the mistaken party to allow enforcement of the contract.

3.3.2 Unilateral mistake

In some situations it is said that only one of the parties is mistaken. However, as can be seen from the discussion of the case law concerning cross-purposes mistake (at 3.3.1), this is in fact no more than another way of saying that one party's understanding and the objectively observed agreement coincide, and the other party's understanding is out of line.

In such circumstances, the objectivity principle determines that there is a contract on the objectively observed terms, which will be enforced by the courts. However, the courts will ignore the objectivity principle where it appears that the party whose understanding coincides with the objective agreement was aware that the other party was labouring under a mistake and failed to draw his or her attention to it. Indeed, the courts will go further and assume that a party is aware of the other's mistake where a reasonable person in that party's place would have been so aware. As discussed above (3.3.1.3), this is why in relation to *Webster* v *Cecil* (1861) 30 Beav 62 it was said that although the case is regarded as an example of equity refusing specific performance, the contract would also have been void under the common law since the buyer ought to have realised the seller's mistake, and drawn it to his attention.

This very limited mistake doctrine applies where:

(a)   one party is genuinely mistaken as to a term of the contract and the mistake is one without which that party would not have entered into the contract;

(b)   that mistake ought reasonably to have been known to the other party; and

(c)   the mistaken party is not in any way at fault.

Condition (a) is particularly important since, if the mistake does not relate to a term of the contract but affects a so-called 'collateral' matter, such as a quality of the subject-matter, it will not prevent agreement as it is not a mistake relating to what has been offered and accepted. In *Smith v Hughes* (3.3.1.1), in the absence of an express stipulation for 'old' oats, whether the oats supplied were 'old' or 'new' was only a collateral matter concerning a quality of the oats.

Examples of all the conditions being met are rare. In *Hartog v Colin & Shields* [1939] 3 All ER 566, the defendants offered to sell to the plaintiffs certain hare skins at ten pence farthing per pound. In fact, the defendants intended to sell at the same price per piece. The trade custom was to sell by the piece, and there were about three pieces to the pound, so that the defendants' offer was at about one third of the normal price. The plaintiffs claimed to have accepted the offer so that there was a binding agreement based on the contract price as mistakenly offered. They claimed to be entitled to damages when the defendants failed to perform. The court found for the defendants. Singleton J made it clear that the crucial element for any defendant to establish was that the other party must have realised the mistake. In other words, a party cannot 'snap up' an offer when he or she is aware that the other has made a mistake relating to the offer terms. This is recognition of a principle of fair dealing in contractual negotiations in English law which prevents a party taking advantage of an obvious error by the other party.

However, in many instances the impact of the mistake will be much less clear, in which case the mistaken party may find it impossible to satisfy the burden of proof. This occurred in *Centrovincial Estates plc v Merchant Investors Assurance Company Ltd* [1983] Com LR 158. The defendants were tenants of offices with an annual rental of £68,320, subject to review from 25 December 1982. The rent review clause provided that on that date the rent should be increased to the current market rental value, as agreed between the parties, and in no circumstances should the rent be lower than the figure payable immediately before the review. Agreement was reached on a figure of £65,000 before the plaintiffs realised that they had made a mistake, since they claimed that they had intended to propose a figure of £126,000. The Court of Appeal refused to grant a declaration to the effect that there was no legally binding agreement on the ground of a figure of £65,000 on the ground that it had not been established that the defendants knew or ought reasonably to have known of the plaintiffs' error when they reached agreement on the figure of £65,000. The Court appears to have considered it 'at least arguable' that the defendants considered that the rent might be reduced, despite the existence of the proviso in the rent review clause.

3.3.3   Unilateral mistake: mistake as to identity

The situation in which unilateral mistake has most often been relied upon is that of mistake of identity. It should be made clear that nearly always a mistake as to identity has been provoked by conduct on the part of the other party which amounts to fraudulent misrepresentation (see 10.4.1). The disadvantage of misrepresentation is that its effect is to make the contract merely voidable, so that a remedy may be sought only against the person making the representation because rescission is a purely personal remedy. In mistake of identity cases the usual situation is that property is acquired and immediately resold to a third party. The dishonest party (the 'rogue') then disappears, making the misrepresentation remedy worthless and leaving the original owner trying to recover the property from the third party. The result is that the courts are faced with having to decide which of two 'innocent parties' should suffer as a result of the fraud by the rogue. If mistake can be proved the contract is void (see 3.2.2) and the original owner will succeed in recovering the property from the third party, even though that third party may be wholly innocent. In order to avoid this conclusion, Lord Denning suggested that the effect of mistake of identity ought to be to make the contract voidable (see *Lewis v Averay* [1972] 1 QB 198), on the basis that the innocent third party is generally more 'innocent' than the mistaken party and in need of greater protection. This suggestion has its attractions, and had been recommended by the Law Reform Committee in its *Twelfth Report on Transfer of Title to Chattels* (Cmnd 2958, 1966, para. 15). However, each case must still be assessed on its own facts, although it is clear that, as a general principle, it is extremely difficult to establish that a contract is void for mistake as to identity.

3.3.3.1 General rule Applying the unilateral mistake formula (see 3.3.2) to the particular context, if A believes himself to be contracting with B and regards B's identity as crucially important, when in fact he is dealing with C, the contract will be void, provided that C is aware of A's mistake and that A is not at fault in making the mistake.

In *Boulton v Jones* (1857) 27 LJ Ex 117, the defendant sent an order for goods to the shop of Brocklehurst. The same day Brocklehurst had sold his business, including current stock, to the plaintiff, his former foreman. The plaintiff supplied the goods, but the defendant was unwilling to pay for them on the basis that he had ordered from Brocklehurst because he had a set-off against him. The court found for the defendant, because it was not open to the plaintiff to substitute himself for the original offeree without first inform-ing the offeror (which would amount to making a counter-offer). The identity of the contracting party was vitally important to the defendant because of the existence of the right of set-off. The defendant was not at fault in believing he was dealing with someone else, and the plaintiff was aware that the defendant intended to deal with his predecessor.

Identity will also be important where a person wishes to contract with a particular company, but ends up contracting with a bogus official in the belief that he is the genuine representative of the company (see *Hardman v Booth* (1863) 1 H & C 803). In such circumstances the mistaken party will clearly intended to deal only with the company and not with the representative in a personal capacity.

Where, however, the mistake is only as to an attribute of the party with whom the contract is made, the contract will not be void. The most common mistake of this kind is a mistake as to creditworthiness (although Treitel, *The Law of Contract*, 10th edn, Sweet & Maxwell, 1999, p. 278, argues that a mistake as to creditworthiness should not be categorised as an attributes mistake but as a business risk). Nevertheless, this distinction between true identity mistake and mistake as to attributes has been used by the courts as the mechanism for giving effect to the policy that generally the contract will be voidable, as it will be extremely difficult to establish a true mistake as to identity because mistakes can invariably be classified as concerning attributes. Indeed, in *Lewis v Averay* [1972] 1 QB 198, 206, Lord Denning argued that such a distinction between identity and attributes was a 'distinction without a difference' because a person is identified by means of his attributes (see, for example, 'the wife of Van der Borgh' in *Lake v Simmons* [1927] AC 487). Lord Denning considered that a person's name was one such attribute and concluded that 'such fine distinctions do no good to the law'.

In *King's Norton Metal Co. Ltd v Edridge, Merrett & Co.* (1897) 14 TLR 98, a rogue, named Wallis, established a bogus business called 'Hallam & Co.', and had written to the plaintiffs on headed paper depicting a large factory and suggesting that it was a well-established and thriving firm. The plaintiffs supplied goods to Hallam & Co. on credit. These goods were immediately sold to the defendants, innocent purchasers. The plaintiffs claimed that the contract was void for mistake and sought to recover the goods from the defendants. The Court of Appeal rejected their claim. The plaintiffs had intended to deal with the writer of the letter, whoever that was. In order for a mistake as to identity to operate, one existing entity had to be mistaken for another existing entity. In fact, there was only one existing identity here (the rogue using an alias) and the plaintiffs must have intended to deal with that person. The mistake made by the plaintiffs was as to the writer's ability or willingness to pay for the goods. In other words, it was merely a mistake as to creditworthiness, or an error of judgment, which will not negative agreement.

In a practical sense, if not in a technical sense, it is arguable that if a person believes he or she is dealing with an existing entity and then discovers he or she has dealt with a person using that identity as an alias, that person will still feel that he or she has made a mistake in contracting with a person who is different to the person intended. It therefore ought not to make a difference whether the one entity actually exists (see Hall (1995) 24 Anglo-Am L Rev 493, 505). Of course, on the facts in *King's Norton*, the mistake would still not operate to render the contract void because it is categorised as a mistake as to creditworthiness rather than identity.

3.3.3.2 Intention to deal with some other person regarded as crucial   The greatest difficulty confronting a claimant in mistake of identity cases is establishing the intention to deal with an identified person other than the party with whom agreement has apparently been reached. Where the parties negotiate at a distance it may be easier to establish such a mistake,

because the identity of the person placing an order has to be known in order to dispatch the goods and it is therefore easier to prove that it was of crucial importance to the making of the contract.

In *Cundy* v *Lindsay* (1878) 3 App Cas 459, the rogue set up business under the name Blenkarn at 37 Wood Street. A very respectable company called Blenkiron & Co. traded at 123 Wood Street. The rogue ordered goods from the plaintiffs, making his signature look as though it read Blenkiron. The plaintiffs sent the goods without payment to 'Blenkiron & Co.' at the rogue's address, and the rogue sold them to the defendants, innocent purchasers. The success of the plaintiffs' plea of mistake, and thus their ability to recover the goods from the defendants, depended upon whether they intended to deal with whichever firm traded at 37 Wood Street, or whether they intended to deal specifically with Blenkiron & Co. The court of first instance took the former view, but the Court of Appeal and the House of Lords took the latter, so that the plaintiffs succeeded in establishing that the contract was void for mistake. It seems a reasonable inference from the facts that the plaintiffs intended to deal with a particular firm by name, as opposed to dealing with an address, which would be of no great significance to them. However, this gives rise to the question why the name of the firm would be important to them. It may well be because they thought they were dealing with the respectable Blenkiron & Co. which was likely to pay for the goods supplied on credit. The decision may also be questionable because of the emphasis placed on the need for a subjective meeting of minds in the judgments of their Lordships. The implication of the finding that the contract was void for mistake as to identity was that it was the defendants, as innocent third-party purchasers, who suffered the loss because they were found to have converted goods to which they had no title.

Where the parties negotiate in each other's presence, however, it will be much harder to resist the inference that the allegedly mistaken party intended to deal with the person present, without concern about who that person was. For example, in *Phillips* v *Brooks Ltd* [1919] 2 KB 243, a rogue went into a jewellery shop and examined some jewellery. He wrote out a cheque for some pearls and a ring, and announced that he was Sir George Bullough, giving an address in St James's Square. He was allowed to take away a ring without paying for it after the plaintiff had checked that the name and address tallied. The court was unwilling to allow the plaintiff to recover the ring from the third party to whom it had been pledged, since in its view the contract was not void. The plaintiff had intended to contract with the person who had been present in the shop. It was a judgment as to creditworthiness, rather than the person's identity, which had persuaded the plaintiff in this case to allow the contract to proceed on credit terms.

The same rationale explains *Lewis* v *Averay* [1972] 1 QB 198. The plaintiff had advertised his car for sale. The rogue offered to buy it. He said that he was the well-known actor, Richard Greene, and wrote out a cheque, signing it 'R.A. Green'. The plaintiff was unwilling to allow him to take the car away until the cheque had cleared, but the rogue showed him an official pass for Pinewood Studios with his photograph on it in the name of 'Richard A.

Green'. At that point the plaintiff allowed the rogue to take the car and the log-book. The rogue sold the car to the defendant (an innocent purchaser), and his cheque proved to be worthless. The plaintiff was unable to recover the car from the defendant. Lord Denning's reasoning in the case has already been explained (see 3.3.3.1). Megaw LJ proceeded by a more orthodox analysis to the same conclusion. He felt that the plaintiff had not been concerned about the identity of the person with whom he was dealing. He had been misled by the rogue into believing that he was dealing with a person of substance, but this was a mistake as to creditworthiness.

In both *Phillips* v *Brooks* and *Lewis* v *Averay* the presumption of an intention to contract with the person physically present had not been rebutted. In addition, in both cases it can be argued that the decision to contract had already been made before the issue of identity was raised, and in neither case was the sale 'called off' when the purchaser proposed to pay on credit. In both cases it is possible to argue, therefore, that the raising of the question of identity concerned only the issue of creditworthiness relating to the decision to allow the person present to take the goods away on credit before the cheque payment had cleared. It may be that these cases can be distinguished from the decision in *Ingram* v *Little* [1961] 1 QB 31 on this basis, because in *Ingram* v *Little* the plaintiff initially made it clear that she was not prepared to let the car be taken away before the cheque had cleared and changed her mind only after checking identity. On this reasoning, it is at least arguable that, even in face-to-face contracts, if the rogue introduces himself at the outset as someone else, this might make that identity crucial to the decision to contract. On the other hand, all three cases appear essentially to turn on a judgment about ability to pay and creditworthiness, and so ought to have reached the same basic conclusion on the effect of the mistake. In addition, the reports of *Phillips* v *Brooks Ltd* are ambiguous as to the precise point at which the rogue mentioned that he was Sir George Bullough.

In *Ingram* v *Little* [1961] 1 QB 31, two spinster sisters had negotiated for the sale of their car to a rogue masquerading as one Hutchinson. At first they would not accept his cheque, but they later relented having checked the name, initials and address he had given them against a telephone directory entry. They then allowed him to take the car away immediately, and later sought to recover it from the innocent third party to whom it had been sold. The majority in the Court of Appeal appears to have been satisfied, on rather flimsy evidence, that the plaintiff had intended to deal with the person the rogue had pretended to be rather than with whomever was present before her. In the light of the very limited check on his identity made by the plaintiff the decision is a little surprising. The reasoning rested on concluding that the offer to sell had been made only to the real Hutchinson so that only he could accept it.

In *Lewis* v *Averay*, *Ingram* v *Little* is treated as anomalous (even though strictly binding on the court). Lord Denning stated that he considered the 'material facts' in all three cases to be 'quite indistinguishable'. It may be that the decision is explicable as one based on policy in that, in normal circumstances, where an allegation of mistaken identity is made, the courts are concerned to protect the innocent third-party purchaser who acquired the goods from the rogue. However, in *Ingram* v *Little* that innocent third party was a car dealer, and the Court of Appeal may have felt more sympathy towards the elderly plaintiff. More recently in *Hudson* v *Shogun Finance Ltd* [2001] EWCA Civ 100, (2001) *The Times*, 4 July, the majority of the Court of Appeal rejected an argument based on the application of the presumption that a contracting party intends to contract with the person in front of him or her in face-to-face negotiations. (In this case the contract between the rogue and the finance company had been entered into at the premises of a car dealer.) The majority reached their conclusion on the basis that the car dealer was not acting as agent for the finance company so that this was not a face-to-face contract. However, more generally, the majority also considered that the face-to-face presumption only applied to oral contracts, when the contract in question was written. This seems a startling conclusion and there was a strong dissent from Sedley LJ who considered that the presumption applied so that the finance company had contracted with the rogue. The other potentially disturbing aspect of this decision is the reliance placed by the majority on the analysis used by the majority of the Court of Appeal in *Ingram* v *Little*, i.e. focusing on the question of 'to whom should the offeree (the rogue) reasonably have interpreted the offer as having been made?' Sedley LJ advocated that Parliament should look at this area of the law because development at common law was effectively curtailed by the decision of the House of Lords in *Cundy* v *Lindsay*.

3.3.3.3 No fault by the mistaken party

Where the claimant is able to establish an intention to deal with some person other than the one with whom agreement has apparently been made, he or she must go on to show that he or she was not at fault in making the mistake. In most cases this rule results in the onus falling on the claimant to show that he or she took reasonable steps to check the identity of the person with whom he or she was dealing. The decision in *Phillips* v *Brooks Ltd* [1919] 2 KB 243 (see 3.3.3.2) may alternatively be explained on this ground. Merely to have checked in a directory that Sir George Bullough lived at the address given did not establish that the man in the jewellery shop was in fact Sir George Bullough. However, again this does not explain the different conclusion on the effect of the mistake in *Ingram* v *Little* [1961] 1 QB 31, where the plaintiff had checked that the person who the rogue purported to be lived at the address given, but no more. In *Lewis* v *Averay* [1972] 1 QB 198, checking the pass to Pinewood Studios, displaying a photograph of the rogue, ought arguably to be regarded as reasonable steps to confirm identity, since there is then a connection between the identity claimed and the evidence to establish that the person in question has that identity. This would seem to be fairly typical as a means of checking identity. However, on the facts, the Court of Appeal regarded this as insufficient.

As a final point on this matter, it can be argued that where a contract is concluded by post there is no such requirement to check identity, since this failure was not considered by the House of Lords in *Cundy* v *Lindsay* (see

3.3.3.2). Such a check might have considerably delayed the process of reaching agreement on the facts of this case, because at the time communications at a distance could not be achieved via instantaneous methods. Of course, nowadays, no such argument could be sustained and it would seem to be appropriate practice to carry out some sort of check before dispatching goods on credit. Inevitably, however, this may necessarily be a credit check rather than a check to establish identity.

The existence of fault on the part of the mistaken party was clear in the case of *Citibank NA v Brown Shipley & Co. Ltd* [1991] 2 All ER 690. A rogue had persuaded Citibank to issue a banker's draft on a particular account held with that bank, by pretending to be a signatory on that account. The rogue had asked that the draft be handed to a messenger in exchange for the company's letter of authority. The rogue acquired possession of this draft by representing that he was the messenger and handing over a forged letter of authority. He then presented the draft to Brown Shipley to pay for foreign currency. Before paying, Brown Shipley had checked with Citibank that the draft was genuine and had been assured that it was. Citibank credited Brown Shipley with the amount of the draft but, on discovering the fraud, sought damages for conversion of the draft by Brown Shipley. The court therefore had to consider whether the contract between the rogue and Citibank was void for mistake as to identity, and this turned on whether the identity of the rogue was crucial.

The court concluded that the identity of the messenger was unimportant as he was 'a mere conduit', so that title to the draft passed directly from Citibank to Brown Shipley. The mistake was merely a mistake as to attributes, namely whether the rogue had the authority of the bank's customer to debit the account. In terms of fault, it would clearly be wrong for Citibank to transfer the risk of this transaction to Brown Shipley when Brown Shipley had checked whether the draft was genuine before paying against it and been assured by Citibank that it was.

3.3.3.4 Conclusion

Although there is no rule to the effect that mistakes as to identity will always render the contract voidable, thus protecting innocent third-party purchasers, it is clear from the case law that it will be very difficult to establish that the contract is in fact not voidable but void for mistake as to identity.

The problem with the current position is that there is a good deal of uncertainty, and arguably the void/voidable distinction is not the most appropriate one since it is an 'all or nothing' approach, i.e. either the contract is void for mistake so that the mistaken party can recover the goods (and the innocent third-party purchaser suffers the loss), or the contract is voidable for fraud so that the innocent third party can keep the goods (and the mistaken party suffers the loss). An alternative suggestion of apportioning the loss between these two innocent parties in accordance with their respective degrees of fault was suggested by Devlin LJ in *Ingram v Little* [1961] 1 QB 31. However, this solution did not find favour when it was considered by the Law Reform Committee, *Twelfth Report on Transfer of Title to Chattels* (Cmnd

2958, 1966). The reason given was that apportionment was considered to leave too much to judicial discretion and was too complex, thereby leading to uncertainty.

For further academic discussion of mistake as to identity, see Goodhart (1941) 57 LQR 228 and Williams (1945) 23 Can Bar Rev 271.

3.4 MISTAKES IN DOCUMENTS

The remedy of rectification of a written document may be available in some limited instances where a transcription mistake has been made in recording the parties' oral agreement in writing (see 3.4.1). Another type of mistake relating to a document may raise the question of the applicability of the plea of *non est factum*. It is important to appreciate that this plea will be applicable only in exceptional cases. It involves a party asserting that, although a document contains that party's signature, it is not the document that that party thought he or she was signing so that it should not be binding upon him or her (see 3.4.2). This plea of *non est factum*, although in one sense reflecting a mistake by the party signing, also bears some relationship to fraud (see 10.4.1).

3.4.1 Rectification

3.4.1.1 Operation of the doctrine   Rectification was defined above as providing a remedy where there has been a simple transcription mistake in recording an oral agreement in writing. The remedy is normally available only when the document said to incorporate the agreement fails to reproduce the *common intentions* of the parties. The operation of the doctrine is well illustrated by *Joscelyne* v *Nissen* [1970] 2 QB 86.

A daughter owned a house, which was also occupied by her father and mother. Her mother became seriously ill, and her father could not afford the time to run his car hire business. Her father had agreed to transfer the business to the daughter, and in return she had agreed to pay him a weekly sum and to pay household expenses, including the gas, electricity and coal bills and the cost of a home help. However, the eventual written agreement referred to the payment of the pension and that the daughter was to 'discharge all expenses in connection with the whole premises'. Although at first the daughter had paid these household expenses, a dispute had arisen and she had stopped paying the fuel bills and costs of home help. The father sought rectification of the document containing their agreement to make explicit their original intention that such bills should be paid by the daughter.

The court was satisfied that the father's version of the agreement did reflect what had actually been agreed between the parties. Indeed, the daughter's defence focused more on pursuing a legal argument against rectification (see below) than on denying the terms of this agreement. The contract was rectified in line with the interpretation originally placed on the contractual document by the daughter.

The most difficult obstacle confronting a claimant seeking rectification is to prove that the document does not truly reflect what was agreed. Courts are understandably reluctant to change the terms of a written agreement, since in the great majority of cases the contractual document is the most secure evidence there is of what was agreed by the parties. In *Joscelyne v Nissen*, the Court of Appeal said that 'convincing proof' would be required, indicating that by this expression they intended a high burden of proof to fall on the claimant.

If all the objective evidence is that the parties did agree in the terms used in the document, it will not avail the claimant to insist that he or she misunderstood the meaning of the words used. This point is well illustrated by the decision in *Frederick E. Rose (London) Ltd v William H. Pim Junior & Co. Ltd* [1953] 2 QB 450. There, the plaintiffs were asked to supply 'Moroccan horse beans described as "feveroles"'. The plaintiffs did not know what feveroles were, and asked the defendants, who said they were simply horse beans. The plaintiffs therefore entered into a contract to purchase the requisite number of horse beans from the defendants. They then discovered that 'feveroles' were a superior type of horse bean, and the buyers of these 'feveroles' sought damages from the plaintiffs. The plaintiffs sought rectification of their agreement with the defendants. However, the Court of Appeal refused rectification on the basis that the contract as written down reflected what had been agreed orally. (In fact, both parties had mistakenly thought that 'feveroles' were the same as horse beans, but on the facts there was no remedy in mistake; see 9.3.)

It was once thought that rectification would be available only where there was already an 'antecedent concluded contract' on the basis of the oral negotiations between the parties, and that rectification would not be available where the document itself represented the first point of contracting between the parties. However, this theory was rejected in *Joscelyne v Nissen*. The Court of Appeal in this case held that firm agreement short of contract was sufficient, provided that the common intention of the parties continued up to the moment of recording their agreement in writing.

3.4.1.2 Rectification if the contractual document fails to accurately record the intentions of only one party

There were authorities, culminating in *A. Roberts & Co. Ltd v Leicestershire CC* [1961] Ch 555, which suggested that even where the document failed to record the intentions of only one of the parties, rectification might be available. It was sometimes suggested that the other party might choose in those circumstances between rectification and rescission i.e., the complete unravelling of the agreement. However, those authorities were largely overruled by *Riverlate Properties Ltd v Paul* [1975] Ch 133.

In *Riverlate Properties*, a lessor had made a mistake in drafting a document containing a proposed lease, and subsequently sought to amend it in a way that would have increased the burden on the lessee. The Court of Appeal refused to rectify the lease in those circumstances, although this decision was explicable, as the court was at pains to point out, by the fact that at the time of contracting the lessee did not know about the lessor's mistake, still less had there been any kind of sharp practice.

The significance of these factors was made clear in *Thomas Bates & Son Ltd* v *Wyndham's (Lingerie) Ltd* [1981] 1 WLR 505. Tenants had taken a lease from the plaintiffs on two previous occasions, and on each occasion an option for renewal in the lease contained a price term leaving the matter to be agreed between the parties, or to be fixed by arbitration. A further lease omitted provision for arbitration in the event of any dispute over fixing the rent, a fact noted by the tenants but not drawn to the attention of the plaintiffs. The plaintiffs sought rectification of the lease after it had been executed. The Court of Appeal dismissed the tenants' appeal against the trial judge's order for rectification. Rectification would be allowed even where the mistake was one-sided, provided the other party knew of the mistake but failed to draw it to the attention of the mistaken party; and provided there was some inequitable benefit to the party conscious of the other's mistake (not necessarily amounting to sharp practice). *Roberts* v *Leicestershire CC* was good law because it rested on precisely this principle.

This line of authority was considered again in *Commission for New Towns* v *Cooper* [1995] Ch 259, where Stuart-Smith LJ suggested that rectification in the one-sided mistake cases turned upon the existence of 'unconscionable conduct'. That in turn raised the subsidiary question of whether rectification could ever be granted in such circumstances if the party seeking to rely upon the terms as written did not know of the other's mistake. Stuart-Smith LJ was satisfied that the existence of unconscionable conduct would be established if it could be shown that a party intended the other to be mistaken, and so conducted himself as to divert that other's attention from discovering the mistake. He was also satisfied that in such circumstances the suspicion that the other may indeed be mistaken would be sufficient to amount to actual knowledge of the mistake. In so deciding he relied upon the classification of Peter Gibson J in *Baden* v *Société Générale pour Favoriser le Développement du Commerce et de l'Industrie en France SA (1982)* [1992] 4 All ER 161, 235, which treats as actual knowledge 'wilfully shutting one's eyes to the obvious'.

3.4.2 The plea of *non est factum*

The Latin phrase *non est factum* literally means 'It is not my deed'. As a rule of the law of contract, it affords a defence to a party against whom a claim is brought in reliance upon a signed written agreement, where that party is able to show that he or she was unaware of the true meaning of the document when signing it. It is a very limited exception to the rule that a person's signature on a document irrevocably binds the person to its contents (see 5.3.1).

The rule developed at a time when adult literacy was far from commonplace (*cf. Thoroughgood's Case* (1584) 2 Co Rep 9a). The classic example of the operation of the rule is *Lewis* v *Clay* (1897) 67 LJ QB 224. The plaintiff asked the defendant to witness some deeds for him. He showed the defendant some papers, over which he held a piece of blotting-paper with a number of holes cut in it, his explanation being that the content of the deeds must remain private. The defendant signed in the spaces. In fact, the papers were promissory notes made out to the plaintiff, to the value of £11,000. It was found as a fact that the defendant had not been negligent, and he was therefore able to resist the plaintiff's action.

Later, the advent of universal education and general adult literacy put the continued existence of the rule in doubt. The matter eventually came before the House of Lords in *Saunders* v *Anglia Building Society* (also known as *Gallie* v *Lee*) [1971] AC 1004. An elderly aunt intended to give her house to her nephew, so that he could use it as security for a loan, on condition that she be allowed to remain living there. A friend of the nephew, known to be assisting him to obtain a loan, asked her to sign a document, which he said was a deed of gift of the house to the nephew. The aunt had broken her glasses, and so signed without reading the document, which turned out to be a deed conveying the house to the friend. The friend then mortgaged the property but defaulted on the payment of the mortgage instalments, so that the building society sought possession of the house. The aunt's plea of *non est factum* failed.

The House of Lords declined to abolish the plea of *non est factum*. The narrow *ratio* of their Lordships' decision is that the difference between what the aunt signed and what she thought she was signing was not so great as to establish beyond doubt that she did not consent to it. She thought she was signing a document transferring ownership of the house, which is precisely what she signed. Thus, the *non est factum* defence is not available except in cases where 'the transaction which the document purports to effect is essentially different in substance or in kind from the transaction intended' (*per* Lord Wilberforce). Their Lordships did, however, consider the extent of the rule. Lord Wilberforce thought it would be rare today for a literate adult to succeed in a plea of *non est factum*. In the case of those who were illiterate, or blind or lacking in understanding, the position was less clear. According to Lord Wilberforce (p. 1027):

> The law ought . . . to give relief if satisfied that consent was truly lacking but will require of signers even in this class that they act responsibly and carefully according to their circumstances in putting their signature to legal documents.

That the rule has been severely restricted by the decision in *Saunders* v *Anglia Building Society* is confirmed by the peremptory dismissal of the plea of *non est factum* by the Court of Appeal in *Avon Finance Co. Ltd* v *Bridger* [1985] 2 All ER 281 (and for continuing evidence of judicial reluctance to invoke the doctrine, see *Norwich and Peterborough Building Society* v *Steed (No. 2)* [1993] Ch 116).

On the other hand, the doctrine is not quite dead. It was relied upon by two members of the Court of Appeal in *Lloyds Bank plc* v *Waterhouse* [1991] Fam Law 23, in a decision which emphasised the close links between *non est factum*, misrepresentation (Chapter 10), undue influence (11.2) and unilateral mistake (3.3.2).

FOUR

Enforceability criteria

4.1 INTRODUCTION

In Chapter 1, a contract was defined as a legally enforceable agreement (see 1.1). We have already considered the process of finalising agreement (see Chapter 2) and problems relating to uncertain terms and agreement mistakes, which may result in the agreement having no effect (Chapter 3). Later we shall also be examining factors which may vitiate consent and which relate to the actual making of the agreement, such as misrepresentation (Chapter 10) and duress and undue influence (Chapter 11).

It is an implicit assumption of the definition, however, that not all agreements are contracts. There must therefore be a body of legal rules by which it is possible to determine whether or not an agreement amounts to a contract. This chapter examines the principles determining the circumstances in which an agreement will be treated as enforceable (i.e., treated as a legally binding contract).

It was suggested in Chapter 1 that, in its formative period, English law developed by the curious means of first identifying remedies and then inductively developing the rights which gave rise to those remedies. In the case of contract, the result was that once a remedy for breach of an undertaking was identified, the courts still had to develop a test for distinguishing enforceable agreements from those which the courts were unwilling to enforce (see 1.3). The major indicator of enforceability adopted by the common law was that of mutual exchange of (at very least) promises of value. In the terminology of the law, where a promise in an agreement was given in return for something of value (including another promise), the first promise was given for *consideration* and could be enforced by legal action.

A promise given without consideration (gratuitous promise) was unenforceable unless made in a deed under seal. This strange expression means no more than that the promise had to be contained in a document on which the promisor had fixed an impression in wax of some identifying mark, such as a crest. Right up to the present day, documents have been made under seal, particularly for the conveyance of land which has been sold, but the traditional wax seal has given way to a modern red sticker, and sometimes not even as much as that. The formal requirements for the form of deeds were altered by s. 1 of the Law of Property (Miscellaneous Provisions) Act 1989. Deeds no longer require a seal to be valid, and need no longer be written on parchment, although there are stricter requirements for the attestation of signatures, and the deed must be 'delivered' by the person making it (which does not require physical transfer, but merely recognition that it legally binds the deliverer).

It is easy to understand how consideration became the cornerstone of the common law contract, since those seeking to make promises enforceable could avoid quite considerable formality simply by providing evidence of an exchange of things of value. On the other hand, for two reasons, consideration has frequently been the source of much academic debate.

In the first place, many legal systems in the world have efficient and just rules of contract law without any requirement of consideration as a precondition of enforceability. Secondly, some agreements which are acknowledged to satisfy the requirement of consideration are said nevertheless to be unenforceable, either because the court is unwilling to believe that the parties ever intended that they should be enforced by legal action (see 4.2 below), or because the court is not satisfied that there is adequate evidence of the alleged agreement (see 4.5 below). In consequence, some commentators have suggested that the requirement of consideration should be abandoned, on the ground that the task of sorting enforceable from unenforceable agreements is already achieved by principles requiring that an intention to create legal relations be established and by essential formalities for certain types of contract. (Intention is recognised as the applicable criterion in PECL, Articles 2:101 and 2:102. Article 3.2 of the UNIDROIT *Principles of International Commercial Contracts* makes it clear that the only requirement for a contract is agreement (in determining whether there is agreement, intention to be bound is regarded as relevant; Article 2.2) and Article 3.2 expressly excludes consideration or the continental requirement of 'cause' as requirements of enforceability.) Other commentators, such as Williston in the United States, have suggested that rules on intention to create legal relations and evidential formality are themselves redundant since the consideration doctrine ('the test of bargain') embraces such functions. Nevertheless, the orthodox view remains that intention to create legal relations, consideration and (in some cases) evidential formality are all essential ingredients of enforceability.

4.2 INTENTION TO CREATE LEGAL RELATIONS

4.2.1 General

It is generally accepted that legal systems must have some means of identifying those agreements which, although to all outward appearances qualify as contracts, are regarded as being beyond the reach of legal remedies. In essence, therefore, the concept of 'intention to create legal relations' is used by the courts as a device to enable them to deny enforceability to those agreements which they consider should not be legally enforced.

Consider the following simple example: Tom is a 19-year-old student, living at home with his parents during the vacation. He has no money, and approaches his father, Dick, for an allowance. Dick says that if Tom will clean the family car once a week, do the shopping and keep the garden tidy, he will give him £15 per week. Tom agrees. Not many people would disagree with the conclusion that despite the outward appearance of agreement and *consideration* (a promise to do the various odd jobs about the house in exchange for a promise to pay an allowance), this arrangement should not be regarded as a contract, in the sense that the courts ought to be unwilling to enforce trivial family agreements.

For much of the nineteenth century, the period of development of modern contract law, the underlying theory was (as discussed in Chapter 1, at 1.4.2.2) that contracts were built upon the will of the parties. It is not surprising, therefore, that the test for identifying those contracts beyond the reach of the law was framed in terms of whether the parties intended legal relations. Nevertheless, today it is accepted that reference to the parties' intentions may be no more than a convenient short way of describing a test which is rather more complex than that. In fact, it is notoriously difficult to prove intention, since there is often no objective evidence which may be produced as conclusive proof. If every party seeking a legal remedy under a contract were put to the burden of establishing that both parties positively intended legal consequences to their agreement, it would be a major stumbling block to the formation of valid contracts and commercially inefficient. For this reason the law has had to accept a much more restricted test of intention.

4.2.2 Presumed intention

The conventional view of intention to create legal relations is that agreements divide for these purposes into two general types: commercial agreements and social/domestic agreements. For each type there is a corresponding presumption (although for evidence of a recent broader contextual approach, see the decision of the Court of Appeal in *Edmonds* v *Lawson* [2000] QB 501, at 4.2.3.2). For commercial agreements, the presumption is that there is an intention to create legal relations; for social/domestic agreements, the presumption is that no such intention exists. One difficulty with this otherwise straightforward scheme lies in the nature of presumptions, which are technical devices of the law of evidence. A presumption may be displaced by any actual evidence to the contrary. Such a precarious status is inconsistent with the role the particular presumptions are called upon to play in relation to intention to create legal relations, which is precisely to avoid instability of contracts caused by parties finding it too easy to avoid liability by denying the relevant intention.

From the cases which are discussed here, it should be apparent that in this particular context the presumptions are by no means easily displaced, and indeed it may seem that they are at times impossible to displace. The true situation seems to be that the term 'presumption' is not being used in its technical evidential sense here. Rather, when we say intention is presumed in relation to commercial agreements, we mean that a reasonable person in this situation would have expected legal consequences to flow from this agreement and, in the absence of some reason of policy against it, the court will enforce that reasonable expectation. Equally, when we say that there is a presumption of an absence of intention to create legal relations in social or domestic agreements (like Tom and Dick's, above), we mean that the reasonable expectation is that no legal consequences would flow from the agreement. It is true that some aspects of normal presumptions are present in those in use here, notably the fact that a presumption in favour of one conclusion places the burden of proof on the party seeking to establish the opposite. In other words, any party seeking to establish that a commercial agreement was not intended to be legally binding must persuade the court that that is the case, and failure to persuade results in the opposite conclusion prevailing. The difference is that here persuading the court may be very difficult; in legal terms, the burden of proof is very high.

The truth of the matter seems to be that the rules of presumed intention and presumed absence of intention are really based on a judicial policy of unwillingness to interfere in domestic disputes. In the words of Atkin LJ in the leading case of *Balfour* v *Balfour* [1919] 2 KB 571, 579: 'In respect of these promises each house is a domain into which the King's writ does not seek to run.'

4.2.3 Commercial agreements

It was suggested earlier (see 1.4) that one of the main economic purposes of contracts is to stimulate exchange. It would be undesirable, therefore, for the intention to create legal relations doctrine to become a further hurdle in the way of a party seeking to enforce a commercial contract. For this reason, the presumption that intention exists in such contracts is extremely difficult to displace, so that only a party with solid evidence of a contrary intention would risk litigation.

4.2.3.1 Advertising In relation to commercial agreements, advertisers may seek to rely on an absence of intention to create legal relations in order to avoid being held to the exact words of advertisements. If a beer producer chooses to promote its product by claiming that it enables those who drink it to achieve impossible feats beyond the reach of ordinary mortals, it is no doubt seen by reasonable people as a joke, and not as a serious claim to be elevated into a contractual promise or as having any contractual consequences. Such a statement is a mere advertising gimmick or 'puff'. Nevertheless, it may be possible to establish that an advertisement amounts to a promise because on the facts there is evidence of an intention to be legally bound. This is what happened in *Carlill* v *Carbolic Smoke Ball Co.* [1893] 1 QB 256. The company had claimed that their smoke ball, when used three times a week for two weeks, would provide infallible protection against influenza, and had promised to pay £100 to anyone able to show that they had contracted influenza after use of their smoke ball despite having used it in the prescribed manner. To demonstrate the good faith of this promise, the company stated that it had placed £1,000 in a specific bank account. Particularly in the light of this last fact, the Court of Appeal was unwilling to accept that the promise was no more than an advertising gimmick which was not intended to attract legal consequences. Accordingly, the plaintiff, who had contracted influenza despite using the smoke ball as instructed, was able to enforce the promise.

More recently, a similar argument of no intention to be bound in relation to an ABTA notice of protection was rejected by the majority of the Court of Appeal in *Bowerman* v *ABTA* Ltd [1996] CLC 451. The plaintiffs had booked a holiday through a tour operator, which was an ABTA member. The tour operator had become insolvent and the question that arose for decision was whether the ABTA notice displayed on the premises of the tour operator amounted to a binding offer of protection so that customers were entitled to be reimbursed the full cost of the holiday.

The majority of the Court of Appeal (Waite and Hobhouse LJJ) rejected an argument that this notice was non-promissory and therefore not binding. The majority considered that the notice was intended to be read, and would reasonably be read by customers, as constituting a binding offer which a customer could accept by booking a holiday with the tour operator. Hobhouse LJ stated that the document 'is clearly intended to have an effect on the reader and to lead him to believe that he is getting something of value'. He added that, given this reasonable interpretation by the public, ABTA could not deny that it intended to accept any legal obligation to the customer, or say that it was not making any promise. If ABTA had wished to deny legal effect, it should have done so by the use of express words to this effect. However, as Hobhouse LJ recognised, from a commercial perspective ABTA would not have wished to do this, because 'to have included such words would have destroyed the value of the document in the eyes of the public and nullified the very effect which ABTA intended it to, and which it did, achieve — to induce the public to book with and entrust their money to ABTA members'.

This approach can be compared with the denial of legal effect contained in the dissenting judgment of Hirst LJ. He considered that this was a non-promissory notice intended only to reassure the public. He placed emphasis on the language used as indicating a lack of contractual commitment, and considered that this position was supported by the decision of the Court of Appeal in *Kleinwort Benson* v *Malaysia Mining Corporation Bhd* [1989] 1 WLR 379 (4.2.3.2 below).

These cases indicate that whether a particular advertisement is regarded as promissory, and as intended to have legal effects, will depend upon the particular facts. As the difference of opinion in *Bowerman* indicates, judges may be in total agreement about the law applicable, but unable to agree upon its application to the facts.

A similar difference of opinion occurred in the House of Lords in *Esso Petroleum Co. Ltd* v *Commissioners of Customs & Excise* [1976] 1 WLR 1. The company had organised a promotion in conjunction with the 1970 World Cup, whereby purchasers of four gallons of petrol received a free 'World Cup Coin'. The coins had no real value, but those collecting the coins would presumably buy Esso petrol in preference to other brands for the duration of the promotion. The Commissioners for Customs & Excise sought to recover purchase tax on the coins on the ground that they had been produced for general sale. In the House of Lords one argument was that the coins could only be 'for sale' if there was an intention to create legal relations in respect of the transfer of the coins between garage proprietors and customers purchasing petrol. Lords Simon and Wilberforce considered that there was such an intention, relying on the business context and the large commercial advantage Esso expected to derive from the scheme. On the other hand, Viscount Dilhorne and Lord Russell came to the opposite conclusion, relying on the language of the offer, the trivial value of the coins and the fact that it was unlikely that any motorist denied a coin would bring an action in the belief that a legal remedy was available to him.

4.2.3.2   Rebutting the presumption   As was indicated in the decision of the majority in *Bowerman* v *ABTA Ltd* (4.2.3.1), the presumption of intention to create legal relations in commercial agreements may be rebutted by express words denying that the agreement is to have legal consequences and to be enforceable in the courts, e.g., football pools coupons contain such a statement (see *Jones* v *Vernon's Pools Ltd* [1938] 2 All ER 626).

The leading case accepting the validity of such honour clauses is *Rose & Frank Co.* v *J.R. Crompton & Bros* [1925] AC 445. The plaintiffs were to be the defendants' agents to sell a certain kind of paper in the United States, and the document setting out the agency agreement contained a term usually referred to as the 'honourable pledge clause'. It purported to provide that the agreement was to be viewed as a definite expression of intention, but not as a formal or legal agreement subject to the jurisdiction of the courts. The parties continued their relationship for some time, and from time to time the plaintiffs would place a specific order which was met by the defendants. The defendants then suddenly announced that they would fulfil no more orders, and the plaintiffs sued to enforce the general agency agreement.

The House of Lords upheld the 'honourable pledge clause', effectively saying that in the main agency agreement there was no intention to create legal relations and no legally binding contract. On this basis, there could be no obligation on the plaintiffs to place orders and no obligation on the defendants to fulfil those orders. However, their Lordships treated actual transactions under this agency agreement as giving rise to 'ordinary legal rights', so that there was an obligation to deliver goods where orders had been accepted and an obligation to pay for those goods on delivery.

The presumption of intention can be seen as having been rebutted by the express clause in the agreement, but there is some logical difficulty about this view since ironically it would seem that the clause could have no legal force if the agreement in which it was contained was found not to be a contract. On its face the agreement, which had been signed by both parties, was perhaps good objective evidence of intention, but there must be some doubt about that, since the purpose of the clause appears to have been to avoid the impact of American laws on restrictive practices. As it seems clear that the main agency agreement would have been regarded as a contract but for this clause, it is also slightly surprising that the clause did not fall foul of the rule against ousting the jurisdiction of the courts (see 12.4.2).

The question of intention to create legal relations in commercial agreements was considered again in *Kleinwort Benson Ltd v Malaysia Mining Corporation Bhd* [1989] 1 WLR 379. There, the plaintiff bank agreed to make a loan facility available to M, a wholly-owned subsidiary of the defendants. In the course of negotiations the parties had not been able to agree upon any security to be given for the loan, but the defendants had provided a 'letter of comfort', containing the key sentence: 'It is our policy to ensure that the business of M is at all times in the position to meet its liabilities to you under the above arrangements'. When the tin market collapsed, M ceased trading and went into liquidation, without paying its very considerable debt to the plaintiffs. The plaintiffs then sued the defendants, claiming that this sentence in the 'letter of comfort' was a contractual promise, which had been breached.

At first instance the judge had approached the question of whether there was a contractual promise by considering whether there was an intention to create legal relations. He had applied the presumption applicable to commercial agreements in concluding that there was. However, the Court of Appeal considered that the correct approach was first to consider whether, on the construction of the statement, it was promissory in its nature. On these facts the particular statement was no more than a statement of present intention and not a promise about the future conduct of the defendants. Therefore it had no contractual force. In coming to this conclusion the Court noted the fact that the parties had been unable to agree upon more formal security, and that the notion of a comfort letter was known by both sides to describe a document by which the defendants gave comfort to the plaintiffs, 'by assuming, not a legal liability to ensure repayment of the liabilities of the subsidiary, but a moral responsibility only'.

It might seem that there is little difference between this approach and that followed in respect of intention to create legal relations in *Rose & Frank Co. v J.R. Crompton & Bros*. However, although it was said to be of no practical significance in the outcome of this case, the Court of Appeal suggested that in its approach of relying simply on the construction of the words used, the onus of proof lay on the plaintiffs to show that it should be treated as a contractual promise. This ruling reverses the position described above in relation to legal intention in commercial contracts, and introduces a critical and difficult distinction into an already murky area of the law of contract, between clauses which state that commercial agreements will not be legally enforceable (where the burden of proof is on the party denying legal force), and statements made without legal force (where the burden of proof is on the party asserting legal force). It is perhaps for this reason that the decision in *Kleinwort Benson* has been criticised in some quarters, because it makes it all too easy for firms to avoid legal responsibilities (see *Banque Bruxelles Lambert SA* v *Australian National Industries Ltd* (1989) 21 NSWLR 502, noted at [1991] JBL 282).

In many cases direct evidence of intention will not be available, and the courts must draw such implications as they may from the surrounding circumstances. In both *Rose & Frank Co.* v *J.R. Crompton & Bros* and *Kleinwort Benson Ltd* v *Malaysia Mining Corporation Bhd*, there existed a document which on its face indicated an apparent absence of legal intention, respectively in the 'honourable pledge clause' and the designation of the document containing the relevant assurances as a 'comfort letter'. In *Orion Insurance Co. plc* v *Sphere Drake Insurance plc* [1992] 1 Lloyd's Rep 239, agreement was reached orally and subsequently recorded in writing. The plaintiffs, who sought to prove that the agreement was not legally enforceable, argued that the oral agreement had been agreed to be no more than a matter of goodwill, although no mention of this element was to be found in the written record. The Court of Appeal nevertheless upheld the trial judge's findings of fact, which led to the conclusion that there had been no intention to create legal relations. It was quite permissible to admit parol evidence (see 5.2) to show an absence of such intention. Moreover, although the presumption of legal intention is said not to be easily rebutted in commercial cases, it is clear that in the Court of Appeal's view the appropriate burden of proof remains the usual civil test of balance of probabilities.

Often it seems that a decision on the question of intention to create legal relations is a cloak for a more pressing question of policy. In *Ford Motor Co. Ltd* v *AUEFW* [1969] 2 QB 303, the court was faced with the question of whether a collective bargaining agreement between management and the union was legally binding. The matter was clearly commercial, and so the burden lay on the union, which sought to deny contractual intention. The court found in the union's favour. In so doing it relied on evidence from industrial relations experts, which was general rather than relevant to the particular agreement. Thus the actual intentions of the parties seem to have been less relevant than the court's view that it was desirable as a matter of policy to keep such agreements out of the courts. The matter is now governed by s. 179 of the Trade Union and Labour Relations (Consolidation) Act 1992, which reverses the presumption otherwise prevailing in commercial cases.

More recently, the Court of Appeal, in *Edmonds* v *Lawson* [2000] QB 501, considered the question of intention to create legal relations in the context of a claim by a pupil barrister that her pupillage constituted a contract of employment for the purposes of the National Minimum Wage Act 1998. The judge at first instance had found for the claimant, having concluded that there was an intention to create legal relations in relation to an offer of pupillage because it was a business arrangement. This decision was potentially of great significance to the operation of the pupillage system. However, the Court of Appeal, while holding that there was an intention to create legal relations, and hence a binding contract, held that the pupillage was not a contract of apprenticeship so that pupil barristers were not covered by the legislation. The approach adopted by the Court of Appeal is interesting in that, rather than tackling the argument that, based on the non-payment of the pupil, this was an educational and not a commercial agreement, which would then have led on to the application of the applicable presumption, the Court of Appeal focused on the specific context to determine whether objectively there was the necessary contractual intention. In particular, it seems that the Court was focusing on the seriousness of the arrangement for all the parties concerned as indicating the necessary intent. It emphasised the process leading up to the making of an offer of pupillage and the benefit of recruiting the ablest pupils who might later go on to be considered for tenancy. Lord Bingham (at 515) specifically stressed that whether either the pupil or chambers would sue in the event of default made no difference to the conclusion of whether there was the necessary intention to be legally bound.

4.2.4 Social and domestic arrangements

The law relating to intention to create legal relations is most difficult in the case of non-commercial agreements. The difficulty stems partially from identifying social and domestic arrangements, and partially from the desire to be able to enforce certain agreements even if they are social or domestic in character. It was in the case of *Balfour* v *Balfour* [1919] 2 KB 571 (see 4.2.2) that Atkin LJ first clearly articulated the test based upon the intentions of the parties.

In *Balfour*, the husband worked overseas, and it became clear that for reasons of health his wife could no longer live where he worked. They agreed that she would return to England and he would pay her £30 per month for her living expenses. Subsequently they became estranged, and the wife sued to enforce the promise of financial support. The Court of Appeal held that the promise was not legally enforceable because there had been no intention to create legal relations. There is no doubt, as subsequent cases have shown (see *Merritt* v *Merritt* [1970] 1 WLR 1211), that if the maintenance agreement had been made upon breakdown of the marriage, rather than prior to breakdown when relations between the parties were entirely amicable, the agreement would have been enforceable even though entered into between husband and wife. It is not disputed that legal relations are intended in the latter situation on the basis that the fact of breakdown takes the agreement outside the sphere of domestic arrangements, although it will still be necessary for the language of a promise made on separation to be sufficiently certain if it is to be enforced (see *Gould* v *Gould* [1970] 1 QB 275, promise of payment 'so long as I can manage it').

These cases are further examples of the way in which many potential contractual rights crystallise at the time of formation of the agreement and cannot be affected by subsequent events. In *Balfour* v *Balfour*, the only relevant intention was that existing at the time of making the agreement, and the fact that subsequently the marriage had broken down and the wife intended to enforce the agreement could not change it from being beyond the scope of the law.

4.2.4.1 Rebutting the presumption
In the case of the presumption against intention to create legal relations, it is unlikely that courts would find any express statement of the parties to be conclusive, since it is here that the policy element of the doctrine is at its strongest. Thus, in the example of Tom and Dick (see 4.2.1), it is unlikely that we would be any happier about the legal enforceability of their agreement had it contained a clause stating that it was intended to create legal relations. The policy against judicial intervention in such agreements would still prevail. Nevertheless, the courts have been willing to find social/domestic agreements enforceable in some cases. It is not always easy to see what is the evidence which caused the presumption to be rebutted. Factors such as certainty of terms and reliance appear to be important.

An instructive case is *Jones* v *Padavatton* [1969] 1 WLR 328. The plaintiff sought to persuade her daughter to take up a new career by offering to pay her fees and provide her with a living allowance while she pursued studies to become a barrister. The plaintiff also bought a house, in which the daughter had rooms, the rest being let to tenants. Eventually, after more than one unsuccessful attempt at the examinations, mother and daughter fell out, and the mother sought to evict the daughter from the house. The majority of the Court of Appeal (Danckwerts and Fenton Atkinson LJJ) found that the daughter had no right to stay in the house because there was no contract between her and her mother. The majority relied on the speech of Atkin LJ in *Balfour* v *Balfour* [1919] 2 KB 571, in concluding that this was a domestic agreement and that the presumption of no intention to create legal relations had not been rebutted. Although there was clear reliance by the daughter on the mother's promise, the terms of their arrangement were regarded as not being sufficiently certain. Salmon LJ agreed with the overall conclusion of the majority but for different reasons. In particular, Salmon LJ considered that when the agreement was entered into it was intended to have contractual force. He considered that it was impossible to think that the daughter had given up her secure and lucrative career without the protection of an enforceable promise of financial support. However, this agreement was only to last for a reasonable period of time, and he felt that this had elapsed so that the mother was entitled to possession of the house.

There is much to commend the reasoning of Salmon LJ in this case. It suggests that while families' trivial agreements are beyond the scope of the law, when families come to agreements which will have a serious impact on the lives of their members they are as entitled to the remedies of the courts as everybody else. Such a principle would seem to be inconsistent with the decision in *Balfour* v *Balfour*, however, in that it is difficult not to admit that the agreement between the Balfours had a serious impact on their lives. Nevertheless, other cases do seem to support the idea that where the subject-matter of the dispute is more than trivial, the courts will be more willing to find the requisite intention for a contractual remedy to be available.

In *Parker* v *Clark* [1960] 1 WLR 286, the defendants, an elderly couple agreed with another couple (their niece and her husband, who were some years younger than them) that if the younger couple would sell their home and move in with them, sharing household expenses, the defendants would leave their house to the niece, her sister and daughter. The younger couple, the plaintiffs, sold their own home and moved in with the older couple. However, the two couples later fell out, and the plaintiffs were told to find alternative accommodation. They sought damages for breach of contract. Devlin J held that the language of the correspondence, the surrounding circumstances and the precise details governing the arrangement, indicated that the parties intended to create legal relations. The presumption normally applicable in domestic arrangements had been rebutted. In particular, the judge could not believe that the plaintiffs would have taken the drastic step of selling their own house without the security of a legal right to live in the home of the other couple. On these facts there was seriousness, certainty of terms and reliance.

4.2.4.2 Intention and reasonable expectation The major difficulty with the view that social/domestic agreements will be held enforceable where they are more than trivial and have a serious impact on the parties, is that while it appears to coincide with what the courts often do, it is not entirely consistent with what the judges say they are doing. On the other hand, the orthodox language of intention appears to be based on a legal fiction, in that few (if any) parties turn their minds at the time of forming such agreements to the question of whether legal rights are being created. This is hardly surprising since such agreements are entered into in confident anticipation of continued good relations. It would be undesirable if the nobler feelings of parties to serious social or domestic agreements became an impediment to legal recourse in situations where their good relations have broken down. For this reason the courts must put themselves in the place of the parties at the time of the agreement, and ask whether it would have been reasonable to expect legal relations to result from the agreement in the undesirable event of amicable relations ending. In this way it is possible to avoid the 'rose tinted' view of the parties at the time of making the agreement. It is not surprising, therefore, that the courts' willingness to find intention increases the more serious are the promises made in the agreement, the more precisely they are expressed and the greater the reliance on the agreement.

4.3 CONSIDERATION

4.3.1 Definitions

Consideration is the principal ingredient determining enforceability of agreements. Traditional analysis has usually considered the existence of consideration to be demonstrated by proof of a benefit and/or a detriment. For example, in *Currie* v *Misa* (1875) LR 10 Ex 153, at 162, Lush J stated that:

A valuable consideration, in the sense of the law, may consist either in some right, interest, profit or benefit accruing to the one party, or some forbearance, detriment, loss or responsibility, given, suffered, or undertaken by the other.

Although the same promise may be both a detriment to the promisor and a corresponding benefit to the promisee, it is not necessary to have both benefit and detriment, as was made clear in the statement by Lush J. Traditionally it was also considered that the consideration had to move from the promisee (which was itself interpreted to mean that the consideration had to move from the claimant — see *Thomas* v *Thomas* (1842) 2 QB 851). However, in the light of the Contracts (Rights of Third Parties) Act 1999 and the comments by the Law Commission in its Report, *Privity of Contract: Contracts for the Benefit of Third Parties* (Cm 3329, 1996, Part VI), it seems that consideration need not be provided by a claimant (15.1.2). If the position were otherwise, a third party would be unable to utilise the right to enforce a contractual promise which is given to him in this legislation. It is equally clear, however, that consideration for such a promise must be provided by someone (i.e., the promisee) if it is to be a contractually binding promise which either the promisee, or the third party (under the legislation) can enforce.

Modern English law has largely abandoned the benefit/detriment analysis, preferring the definition of consideration provided by Sir Frederick Pollock (in *Pollock's Principles of Contract*, Sir Percy Winfield, 13th edn, Stevens, 1950, p. 133) to the effect that consideration is constituted by 'an act or forbearance of one party, or the promise thereof,' being 'the price for which the promise of the other is bought'. This statement was adopted by Lord Dunedin in *Dunlop Pneumatic Tyre Co. Ltd* v *Selfridge & Co. Ltd* [1915] AC 847. It is, of course, still possible to detect elements of benefit and detriment in this definition, but what is most important is the emphasis upon exchange. Simple benefit and detriment analysis cannot account for some of the decisions of the courts (see 4.3.2.1), but it is important to be familiar with the formulation given above, in part because some of the cases still use the language of benefit and detriment, but more especially because some sub-rules of the doctrine of consideration owe their existence to the traditional formulation (see 4.3.2, below).

A good example of the continuing influence of the language of benefit and detriment is the decision of the Court of Appeal in *Williams* v *Roffey Bros & Nicholls (Contractors) Ltd* [1991] 1 QB 1, which caused a thorough re-evaluation of the doctrine of consideration (see especially 4.3.5.2). However, in analysing in a contemporary problem whether consideration exists in an agreement, it would be much better to rely on the notion of exchange. The essential test is whether what is provided by the one party (be it action, inaction or merely a promise thereof) induced the action, inaction or promise of the other.

4.3.1.1 Promise or act given in exchange for the promise which it is sought to enforce Consideration has been defined both in terms of acts done or not done and in terms of promises, so that there are two ways in which the other's promise is 'bought'. The great value of contract as a commercial device is that it provides for liability on an obligation even where performance on both sides remains in the future (see 1.1.1). It is in this facility that the strength of contract as an instrument of planning lies. Thus consideration can consist of such an exchange of promises in a bilateral contract. The classic example of consideration involving an exchange of promises is a contract for the sale of goods, where the seller agrees to deliver the goods at some time in the future and the buyer agrees to pay for them either on delivery, or by some credit arrangement. At the time of the agreement neither side has done anything towards the performance of the promises made, but the agreement still has contractual force. Both parties have subjected themselves to a potential claim for breach of contract in the event that they fail to perform, and in this sense there is a clear benefit or detriment at the time the promises are given. This type of consideration is described as *executory*.

Where consideration consists of an exchange of a promise for an act then it is described as *executed*. The classic example of such contracts, sometimes described as unilateral contracts (see 2.8), is promises of rewards. For example, in *R v Clarke* (1927) 40 CLR 227, the government of Western Australia offered a reward for information leading to the arrest of certain criminals. Clarke gave information which led to a conviction, and sued to recover the reward, although he admitted that at the time of giving the information his only motive had been to clear his own name. It was held that he was unable to recover. The case is usually described as being an example of the impossibility of giving assent to an offer of which one has no knowledge. Clarke, however, had seen the reward offer but had forgotten about it. The better view may therefore be that his action was not induced by the promise of reward, and therefore consideration was absent. The element of exchange is vital. Executed consideration consists of a promise followed by an act. Care must be taken to distinguish the situation where an act is followed by a promise, which does not amount to consideration (see 4.3.3: past consideration).

4.3.1.2 Consideration distinguished from conditions imposed upon the recipient of a gift
This distinction can be difficult to explain. Treitel, *The Law of Contract*, 10th edn, Sweet & Maxwell, 1999, p. 68, argues that in *Carlill v Carbolic Smoke Ball Co. Ltd* [1893] 1 QB 256, the consideration provided by the plaintiff was her use of the smoke ball as requested by the defendants. The need to catch influenza was interpreted as only a condition enabling her to enforce the promise. This may be because catching influenza cannot be controlled directly by the plaintiff, and therefore cannot be seen as something of value provided by the plaintiff. Similarly, in *Thomas v Thomas* (1842) 2 QB 851, the requirement that the widow should remain a widow and not remarry was a condition entitling her to enforce the promise, assuming it to be supported by consideration.

These examples of conditions are very different in nature to the requirement to supply three chocolate wrappers in *Chappell & Co. Ltd v Nestlé Co. Ltd* [1960] AC 87 (for facts, see 4.3.2.1 below). The House of Lords rejected an argument to the effect that the wrappers were not part of the consideration but merely a condition for the supply of the record for 1s 6d. As Lord Reid stated, they were supplied by the applicant at the request of the defendants and were of benefit (albeit in the loosest sense of this word) to the defendants. On the other hand, in the case of conditional gifts there is no direct benefit to the requestor from performance of the condition entitling the party to enforce the promise, e.g., catching influenza or remaining a widow.

4.3.2 Value, exchange and inducement

The exchange theory of consideration also requires the offering up, in exchange for a promise, of something of value, so that mere motive in making a promise, unattached to any element of value, is not sufficient consideration.

In *Thomas* v *Thomas* (1842) 2 QB 851, a dying man had expressed the wish to the executors of his will that his wife should be able to live in his house for as long as she should wish to and remained a widow. On the strength of this wish the executors promised the house to the widow. The court was unanimous in its view that, whatever the moral obligation, in such a situation the mere motive of satisfying the wishes of the deceased testator could not constitute consideration.

Once something of value can be shown, however, the court makes no inquiry into whether the thing offered is a genuine equivalent of the promise made. At some early point in its history the doctrine of consideration might have developed as a means to police bargains between parties, requiring the exchange of things of equivalent value. As such it would have been part of the law's armour against duress and fraud (see 4.3.4 below, and Chapter 11). In fact, the doctrine of freedom of contract, and no doubt the mere practical difficulty of proving equivalence, intervened to prevent such a development. There is no investigation of whether the value given in return for the promise is any real benefit to the promisor or any real detriment to the promisee, let alone of whether the promises exchanged are of equivalent value. All that is required is that actual value be given. Thus, in *Thomas* v *Thomas*, the widow to whom the house was promised had in turn promised to pay £1 per annum as ground rent, and to maintain the property in good and tenantable repair. This return promise was found to be of actual value, and thus to amount to sufficient consideration. This rule finds frequent expression in the provision in leases for peppercorn rents.

Although the Unfair Terms in Consumer Contracts Regulations 1999 (SI 1999 No. 2083; for the scope, origin and general impact of the Regulations, see Chapter 6, at 6.6.3) give a broad jurisdiction to overturn contract terms which are unfair, they do not apply to terms which concern the adequacy of the price or remuneration as against the goods or services sold or supplied, provided such terms are in plain, intelligible language (reg. 6(2)). So this basic principle of the common law is largely unaffected by the new law, provided the consumer contract is drafted in clear terms.

4.3.2.1 Benefit detriment and value In saying that in *Thomas* v *Thomas* (1842) 2 QB 851 there was an exchange of things of value, it is possible,

though not particularly revealing, to analyse that exchange in terms of benefit and detriment. Such analysis fails altogether in the case of *Chappell & Co. Ltd v Nestlé Co. Ltd* [1960] AC 87.

The case involved an offer to the public of records at a very low price as a promotional scheme for a brand of chocolate. Copies of a particular dance record could be obtained for 1*s* 6*d* (7.5p) and three chocolate wrappers, whereas the normal price was 6*s* 6*d* (32.5p). Manufacture and sale of the records constituted a breach of copyright in the song unless royalties were paid to the copyright owners, who in this case were the plaintiffs. Under a statutory scheme a copyright owner was not entitled to object if informed and paid a royalty of 6.25 per cent of the ordinary retail selling price. The defendant gave notice, stating the ordinary retail selling price to be 1*s* 6*d*, and the plaintiffs objected.

The House of Lords took the view that whether the chocolate wrappers were part of the price paid depended upon whether they were part of the consideration for the sale of the records to the public. A minority of the House found in the promotional scheme evidence of motive but not of consideration. Lord Reid, making the leading speech for the majority, conceded that the wrappers could not be seen as either benefit or detriment in one sense: the chocolate company threw them away as soon as they arrived, and no doubt the consuming public would have thrown them away before that but for the offer. What mattered was that the company saw fit to require the delivery of the wrappers in exchange for its delivery of the record. Its motive for so doing was of no interest to the court, but the requirement of exchange demonstrated the existence of consideration. By comparison, in *Lipkin Gorman v Karpnale Ltd* [1991] 2 AC 548, gaming chips were held not to constitute consideration for the money paid for the chips by a member of a gaming club on the basis that they were 'worthless'. It seems that the chips were regarded as merely facilitating the gambling process, and therefore not as having any value to the parties involved. This is difficult to justify, and the true basis of the decision would seem to be the desire to protect the victim of the theft of the money in question who was trying to recover it from the gaming club.

This minimalist approach to benefit in *Chappell v Nestlé* was again evident in *Williams v Roffey Bros & Nicholls (Contractors) Ltd* [1991] 1 QB 1 (the facts are given at 4.3.5.2). The Court of Appeal had to decide whether a promise to pay more money to achieve performance under an existing contract was enforceable, despite the fact that the plaintiff had apparently given nothing additional in return for this promise. Two members of the Court of Appeal (Glidewell and Purchas LJJ) were willing to find consideration, despite its absence on a legal and objective analysis, in the subjective (factual) benefit to the promisor arising from making the promise. Detriment was not a required part of the equation (and this position has subsequently been confirmed by the recognition of consideration only in the form of benefit in *Edmonds v Lawson* [2000] QB 501). Russell LJ took a more radical, normative approach and considered that the existence of consideration was to be determined in the light of the view one takes of the desirability of enforcing the promise in question. In this case, he was influenced by the commercial nature of the relationship between the parties, and the unconscionable result of not enforcing the promise.

The majority reasoning in *Williams* v *Roffey Bros & Nicholls (Contractors) Ltd* was followed by Hirst J in *Anangel Atlas Compania Naviera SA* v *Ishikawajima-Harima Heavy Industries Co. Ltd (No. 2)* [1990] 2 Lloyd's Rep 526. This was another case involving a promise altering a term of the existing contract, and the judge found that consideration was constituted by the 'practical conferment of benefit or a practical avoidance of disbenefit'. Despite the existing contract between the parties, the judge found the defendants to have admitted that there was a practical (or subjective) benefit to them in holding the plaintiffs to the original delivery date under the contract, in market conditions in which many clients were seeking to cancel contracts or to postpone delivery dates. By promising amendments to the contract advantageous to the plaintiffs, in return for their taking delivery on the due date, the defendants hoped to influence other clients to keep to their contracts. Consequently, the amendments were legally enforceable. (See also *Lee* v *GEC Plessey Telecommunications* [1993] IRLR 383.)

The definition of consideration in *Chappell* v *Nestlé* and in *Williams* v *Roffey Bros & Nicholls (Contractors) Ltd*, may be regarded as coinciding with Sir Frederick Pollock's definition of consideration as 'the price for which the promise of the other is bought' (see 4.3.1), provided it is realised that price here means anything of actual subjective value to the promisor.

It is worth giving some attention to the test by which the courts determine whether something is of sufficient value to amount to consideration. It appears to embody elements of both law and fact. There seems to be a rule excluding mere sentiment from constituting consideration, and consideration cannot involve a promise to give up a right which is not possessed (see *White* v *Bluett* (1853) 23 LJ Ex 36; son's promise not to complain about his father's distribution of his property could not be consideration because the son had no right to complain). The objectivisation of contract (see 2.1) means that the court is the ultimate arbiter of each party's intentions (see, in particular, the discussion of the meaning of practical benefit in M. Chen-Wishart, 'Consideration: Practical Benefit and the Emperor's New Clothes' in Beatson and Friedmann (eds), *Good Faith and Fault in Contract Law*, OUP, 1995 at 131–32). Subject to these obvious legal limitations, however, it seems that anything may be of sufficient value to amount to consideration if the party receiving it regards it at the time as a sufficient inducement to give his return promise, which is an essentially factual test. This idea of mutual inducement as the most basic kind of exchange is at the heart of the majority opinion in *Chappell* v *Nestlé*, and many of the more difficult English cases on consideration fit more comfortably with that analysis than with any other.

4.3.2.2 Settlement of claims

When a legal claim is settled out of court the settlement is binding on the parties by virtue of the law of contract, and if no contract can be shown to exist then the settlement is not binding. Consideration exists, on the one hand, in a promise not to sue, or to drop any claim which has already commenced, and on the other hand in the payment of a sum of money as final settlement of the claim. It is important (and not always easy) to distinguish this situation from payment to meet an acknowledged liability, which is not consideration for a promise (often based only on inference) not to pursue the balance of the claim: see *Ferguson v Davies* [1997] 1 All ER 315 (and see promises to accept less: 4.3.5.2).

Identification of consideration is even less easy where a true legal analysis reveals that the original claim, which has been settled, would without doubt have been unsuccessful. In that case, a promise not to pursue the claim in the courts is worthless. In *Horton v Horton (No. 2)* [1961] 1 QB 215 the husband agreed to pay the wife £30 per month maintenance, and in return she was not to bring legal action for maintenance. He did not deduct income tax from the sum paid. Some time later, when the issue of tax arose, he promised instead to pay such sum as would leave £30 after deduction of tax. When presented by the Inland Revenue authorities with a claim for tax notionally deducted by him, he stopped the payments claiming that his second promise was not supported by any fresh consideration.

If consideration existed it was in the settlement of the wife's claim for rectification of the original agreement. Rectification is a remedy aimed at making a document, which does not express the actual intention of the parties, into a correct version of their common intention (see 3.4.1). In this case it seems possible that a claim for rectification would not have succeeded. Upjohn LJ held that whether it would have succeeded was irrelevant to the question of whether the settlement of the wife's claims was enforceable. Provided she believed she had some good claim, consideration was present.

This decision makes little sense in terms of an analysis of benefit and detriment, since there is scant benefit in a promise not to pursue a worthless claim. On the other hand, the promise of £30 per month free of tax induced the relinquishment of the claim (and *vice versa*). In that sense there was consideration. There remains a quite separate issue, unrelated to consideration, of whether the wife was being fraudulent; that is, did she genuinely believe that her claim was legally valid or at least a debatable legal point? If not, her behaviour might amount to fraud, and it makes little difference for most purposes whether we say there is no contract on that ground or because there is no consideration (other than for the purposes of drafting a statement of case). If her belief was genuine, there is consideration arising out of inducement.

4.3.2.3 Forbearance

In *Alliance Bank v Broom* (1864) 2 Dr & Sm 289, the defendant owed an unsecured debt of £22,000 to the plaintiff bank. The plaintiff asked for security for the loan, and the defendant promised to provide security in the form of goods he was about to receive from a third party. When the defendant failed to fulfil this promise, the plaintiff sued to obtain the title documents to the goods in question.

The promise was enforceable only if part of a valid contract supported by consideration. In such cases consideration is normally found in a promise by the creditor not to call in the debt for a certain period of time, but in this particular case no such promise was given. The court was obviously anxious nevertheless to make the promise of security enforceable, presumably because such arrangements were common and a necessary bulwark of the credit system. It found consideration to be constituted by the fact of actual forbearance from suing by the bank, even in the absence of any promised period of grace.

Without a promise not to sue (or a promise not to foreclose on the security given for a stated period), forbearance fits uneasily into an analysis of benefit and detriment, since the fact that the bank may if it chooses foreclose tomorrow means that it may suffer no detriment and the debtor derive no benefit. But there is no doubt that the bank was induced actually to forbear by the promise of security, while in turn that promise was induced by the bank's actual forbearance, which created a not unreasonable expectation on the part of the defendant that the bank would continue to forbear. The truth of the matter is that the whole arrangement was a commercial 'bargain' between parties who had been dealing amicably with each other in attempting to cope with the changing financial position of one of them. In the circumstances the court was unwilling to allow a technicality to interfere with their arrangement.

4.3.2.4   The fiction of value   Cases such as *Alliance Bank* v *Broom* (1864) 2 Dr & Sm 289 (above) strain even the more flexible modern version of the doctrine of consideration to the limit, raising the suspicion that where a court is determined to make a promise enforceable it can always 'find' something of value for which the promise is exchanged (so called 'invented consideration'; see Treitel, *The Law of Contract*, 10th edn, Sweet & Maxwell, 1999, pp. 67–68). It must be remembered that the modern law of contract developed somewhat earlier than the modern law of torts, especially in relation to liability for negligent misstatements (see 10.4.3.1) and for extra-contractual economic loss (see 1.2.3). It is not surprising, therefore, that some (especially nineteenth-century) courts have attempted to squeeze cases into the category of contract in order to found a liability which otherwise would be avoided. *De la Bere* v *Pearson* [1908] 1 KB 280 appears to be just such a case.

A newspaper offered free financial advice, and the plaintiff wrote asking for the name of a good stockbroker in order to make an investment. The newspaper negligently gave the name of a man who was an undischarged bankrupt and who subsequently misappropriated money sent to him. (At the time, in the absence of contract the newspaper would have escaped liability altogether.) In the judgments of the Court of Appeal little discussion is devoted to the existence of a contract, and most of this limited discussion is addressed to the questions of offer and acceptance. Only Vaughan Williams LJ addressed the question of consideration, finding it on the one hand in the advice given and on the other in 'the tendency to increase the sale of the paper'. Since the plaintiff was already a reader, it is impossible to say that he was induced to purchase the paper in order to obtain the financial advice. Equally, he gave nothing of value over and above what he normally paid for the paper. It seems most likely that today such a case would not be regarded as raising a contractual liability at all. It may be that there would be liability in tort for negligent misrepresentation (see *Hedley Byrne & Co. Ltd v Heller & Partners Ltd* [1964] AC 465; and see 10.4.3.1).

4.3.3 The necessity for exchange: past consideration

It was suggested at 4.3.1.1 that where it is alleged that a contract exists on the basis of an act followed by a promise, the courts will not enforce such a promise. In such cases the consideration is described as 'past', and the rule is easily explained by the theory of exchange. It is well illustrated by the classic case of *Roscorla v Thomas* (1842) 3 QB 234.

The plaintiff had negotiated the purchase of a horse from the defendant for a given price. When the negotiations had been completed and the contract had formed, the defendant assured the plaintiff that the horse was sound and free from vice. The horse failed to match that description, and the issue was whether any enforceable warranty (i.e. promise) had been given that the horse was sound.

At the time courts were very unwilling to imply terms into contracts unless strong evidence of actual intention of the parties was available (see 5.5). No implied warranty was found in this case; today the case might well be decided differently on this point under s. 14 of the SGA 1979. In the absence of an implied warranty, the plaintiff's only remedy lay in the express warranty given, which could be enforceable only if of contractual force. Since no new consideration had been given subsequent to the assurance of the fitness of the horse, the express warranty could be binding only if in some way it could be brought within the original contract. The court refused to allow such an extension of the consideration through time, and indeed it can be seen that the promise that the horse was sound and free from vice was not given in exchange for the payment made for the horse.

This decision is consistent with the rules on incorporation of terms into contracts (see 5.3). If this express promise had been found to be included within the contract, it is difficult to see how existing rules preventing the incorporation into contracts of clauses excluding or limiting liability might be maintained. The current position is that a clause not brought to the attention of the promisee at the time of contracting, but brought to the promisee's attention before the time of the defective performance giving rise to any claim, is not part of the contract (*Olley v Marlborough Court* [1949] 1 KB 532, see 5.3.3). A promise relating to quality and an exemption clause are legally identical however functionally different, and the same rule must apply to the question of whether either type of term is part of the exchange between the parties. To put the same argument in commercial terms, the price of a horse guaranteed sound is greater than the price of a horse given without any guarantee as to quality, and for the court to have resolved the question in any other way in this case would have been to interfere in the bargain between the parties.

A note of caution must be entered about past consideration cases like *Roscorla v Thomas*. This was not a case where all the performance preceded any promise. There was a contract, followed by an additional promise. Such a promise might be classed as a variation of the contract (4.3.5). As such, until recently the outcome would have been the same, because contract variations were not legally binding unless supported by fresh consideration. However, as a result of the decision of the Court of Appeal in *Williams* v *Roffey Bros & Nicholls (Contractors) Ltd* [1991] 1 QB 1, such a variation might be regarded as binding if a factual benefit could be said to arise to the promisor from making the promise. If that were the case then *Roscorla* v *Thomas* might be decided differently today on this ground. On the other hand, a case like *Re McArdle* [1951] Ch 669 (4.3.3.2) would not be affected because there was no pre-existing contract in respect of which the subsequent promise was made.

4.3.3.1   The requested performance device   There is a device which can be used to avoid the past consideration rule in cases in which it can be said that there was an understanding that goods or services were to be paid for, but no express agreement had been reached as to the amount payable before the time for performance. In such cases, a subsequent promise to pay a stated sum might well appear to be past consideration. On the other hand, it would be undesirable as a matter of policy for such understandings not to be enforceable, not least because many professional people such as account-ants and solicitors operate on the basis that their services are to be paid for but that a fee will not be stated until after performance. This example makes it clear that this device is not an exception to the past consideration rule. The subsequent promise to pay is no more than quantification and evidence of an obligation to pay, which had already arisen by virtue of a simple contract between the parties. As we saw in Chapter 3, s. 8 of the SGA 1979 makes express provision for the price to be left unspecified in a sale of goods contract and fixed at a subsequent date.

The earliest example of the device is *Lampleigh* v *Brathwait* (1615) Hob 105. Brathwait killed a man, and asked Lampleigh to intercede with the King to get him a pardon. Lampleigh did as he was asked, and was successful in obtaining the pardon. Brathwait then promised him £100. There is no doubt that Lampleigh's performance was executed before the promise was made, but the court said that the fact that the service had been requested meant that the promise was nevertheless supported by consideration, namely the per-formance by Lampleigh. In other words, in making the request Brathwait must be taken impliedly to have promised to pay for the service rendered, and in relation to that promise consideration was not past. The later express promise merely fixed the amount of the reward. This explanation of *Lamp-leigh* v *Brathwait* was put forward in *Re Casey's Patents* [1892] 1 Ch 104 by Bowen LJ (at 115–6):

> Even if it were true . . . that a past service cannot support a future promise, you must look at the document and see if the promise cannot receive a proper effect in some other way. Now, the fact of a past service raises an implication that at the time it was rendered it was to be paid for, and, if it

was a service which was to be paid for, when you get in the subsequent document a promise to pay, that promise may be treated either as an admission which evidences or as a positive bargain which fixes the amount of that reasonable remuneration on the faith of which the service was originally rendered.

A positive bargain here might be one of two kinds. It might be the settlement of a quasi-contractual claim for the value of services rendered (*quantum meruit*: see 3.1.4). Alternatively, it might be an enforceable implied agreement to agree the price in the future (see *Foley* v *Classique Coaches Ltd* [1934] 2 KB 1; and see 3.1.3).

4.3.3.2 Distinction between commercial and domestic agreements

It may be that in relation to past consideration it is also valid to make a distinction between commercial and domestic agreements, although it is doubtful whether the distinction is as clear as it is in the case of intention to create legal relations (see 4.2.2). Nevertheless, there is some evidence that a court may be more willing to imply a promise to pay in the case of a commercial relationship than in a domestic one.

In *Re McArdle* [1951] Ch 669, the children of a family were by their father's will entitled to a house after their mother's death. During the life of the mother one of the married children lived in the house and his wife paid for several improvements to be made. Subsequently, all the children signed a document in which they promised that the wife should be repaid £488 out of the estate for the work done. This promise was held to be unenforceable because the work had been executed before the promise was made, so that the promise was made for past consideration. The court did not find in this domestic situation any implied promise to pay dating from before the time when the work was done. There could be no earlier implied promise to compensate because there had been no request by the promisors that the work be carried out.

However, if the context is domestic, even where a request can be found, it will inevitably be more difficult to argue that the request carries with it an implied promise to pay for the services. For example, if I ask my neighbour to help me to take out my rubbish for the rubbish collection, although I have made a request we would not anticipate any remuneration for this service, in the absence of some express promise. In the commercial context, where there is a request of some kind, it will be much easier to establish an implied promise to pay for the services simply because in the commercial context people do not generally do things for nothing.

One example of such a commercial situation is *Re Casey's Patents* [1892] 1 Ch 104 (see 4.3.3.1 above). A manager promoted a particular invention for the owners of the patent rights for a two-year period. The owners then promised him a share in those rights in consideration for his previous services for them. In finding that promise enforceable and not merely supported by past consideration, Bowen LJ found evidence on which to base the implication of a promise to pay in the entirety of the circumstances.

In *Pao On* v *Lau Yiu Long* [1980] AC 614 (another commercial case), Lord Scarman provided the following definition of the conditions for operation of the exception:

> The act must have been done at the promisor's request, the parties must have understood that the act was to be remunerated either by a payment or the conferment of some other benefit, and payment, or the conferment of some other benefit, must have been legally enforceable had it been promised in advance.

These conditions were held to have been met on the facts in this case. It concerned the enforceability of a promise of indemnity in favour of the plaintiffs, which had been made by the defendants, the majority shareholders in the Fu Chip Investment Company. This indemnity document referred to the main agreement between the Fu Chip company and the plaintiffs, whereby the plaintiffs had promised not to sell 60 per cent of their shares in Fu Chip before 30 April 1974. It was clear that the plaintiffs' promise in the main agreement had been made at the request of the defendants who wished to ensure the stability of the market price for shares in Fu Chip. The Privy Council considered that the promise had been made on the understanding that the plaintiffs were to be compensated by the defendants for agreeing to this restriction on their ability to sell their shares. Accordingly, the plaintiffs' promise in the main agreement, whereby they promised to retain the shares, constituted a valid consideration for the defendants' implied promise to compensate them. The later indemnity promise merely fixed the nature of that protection. Lord Scarman, giving the judgment of the court, laid great stress upon the fact that this case involved businessmen bargaining at arm's length ([1980] AC 614 at 634).

It seems clear, therefore, that where the whole arrangement is couched in terms of commercial exchange, the courts may be more willing to interpret circumstances as amounting to a request to perform a service, despite the absence of anything as express between the parties, and they may be more willing to find that the request carries with it an implied promise to pay.

4.3.3.3 Genuine exception for negotiable instruments

A negotiable instrument is a document containing a promise of payment which when transferred gives the transferee for value a right to enforce the promise against the promisor free of any defences which have been available to the promisor against the transferor (see 15.4.4). A good example is a cheque. Section 27 of the Bills of Exchange Act 1882 provides that valuable consideration for a bill may be constituted either by consideration as normally defined in contract law, or by 'an antecedent debt or liability'. Thus, a bank receiving a third party's cheque from a customer whose account with the bank is overdrawn is a transferee for value of the cheque, since by this section the customer's pre-existing debt to the bank is consideration for the transfer by him to the bank. This rule is a genuine exception to the past consideration rule.

4.3.4 Sufficiency and performance of existing duties

It has traditionally been the case that in most circumstances the performance of an existing duty cannot be consideration for a further promise. In terms of our definition of consideration the reason is relatively clear. Where I am already under a legal duty to perform an act or make a promise, I cannot be said to have been induced to do that thing by the further promise made by another, since the obligation to do it already existed.

It is traditional to subdivide the rule into three different types of case:

(a) performance of a public duty;
(b) performance of a contractual duty owed to a third party;
(c) performance of an existing contractual duty owed to the promisor (the context for which will necessarily be a promise to alter an existing contract between the parties).

Until recently, the rule was consistently applied in categories (a) and (c), while category (b) was already established as an exception. As a result of *Williams* v *Roffey Bros & Nicholls (Contractors) Ltd* [1991] 1 QB 1, category (c) may also be an exception to the rule in some circumstances, at least in the context of a commercial relationship. For ease of exposition, the traditional divisions are maintained here.

4.3.4.1 Public duties The leading case in the area of public duties is *Collins* v *Godefroy* (1831) 1 B & Ad 950. The plaintiff was promised payment in return for his undertaking to give expert evidence at a trial at which he was in any case obliged to attend to give evidence because he had been summoned by subpoena. In those circumstances the promise of payment was unenforceable because the plaintiff had given no consideration for it. He had an existing public duty to attend the trial, and accordingly had done no more than he was already legally obliged to do. Although the broad principle in this case still stands, there is now a statutory exception to the rule in the case of payment of expenses to expert witnesses, which merely reflects what had long been the practice (see s. 36(4) of the Supreme Court Act 1981).

A more modern statement of the rule was given by the House of Lords in *Glasbrook Brothers Ltd* v *Glamorgan County Council* [1925] AC 270. This case involved a claim by a local authority to recover payment for the provision of police to guard a mine during a strike. The defendants argued that the police were charged with a public duty to guard the mine as part of their general duty to keep the peace, prevent crime, and protect persons and property from criminal injury. However, at the time of the strike the colliery owners had insisted on a greater level of manning than the local police had deemed necessary. The House of Lords, by a bare majority, decided that the only duty on the local authority was to provide such policing as was considered necessary by the police authority. The decision as to what was necessary was not open to review by the courts in a case of this kind. Provision of policing beyond what was deemed necessary was not therefore performance of an existing duty, and could amount to consideration for a promise to pay for the service provided (see also *Harris* v *Sheffield United Football Club Ltd* [1987] 2 All ER 838).

The notion of performance of something more than the bare existing legal duty is thought by some commentators to explain the otherwise difficult case of *Ward* v *Byham* [1956] 1 WLR 496. The father of an illegitimate child agreed to pay the mother £1 per week to maintain the child, provided the mother was able to show that the child was 'well looked after and happy' and that the child was allowed to choose for herself whether to go to live with her mother or to carry on being cared for by a neighbour of the father's, which had been the previous arrangement. The child went to live with the mother, but the father stopped the payments when the mother married. Denning LJ treated the case as one of performance of an existing duty because the mother was under a statutory duty to look after the child properly. Nevertheless, he would have enforced the promise of maintenance, because in his view a promise to perform an existing duty should be a good consideration on the basis that it was in fact a benefit to the father. However, the majority of the Court of Appeal, Morris and Parker LJJ, while acknowledging that the mother did owe an existing duty, found 'ample consideration' for the promise in the mother's undertakings to keep the child happy and to allow her to choose where to live. A similar approach was taken by the majority of the Court of Appeal in *Williams* v *Williams* [1957] 1 WLR 148, although Denning LJ maintained his argument that 'a promise to perform an existing duty is, I think, sufficient consideration to support a promise, so long as there is nothing in the transaction which is contrary to the public interest' (for example, to enforce a promise such as that in *Collins* v *Godefroy* would clearly be contrary to the public interest).

One way, as these cases illustrate, to avoid the restrictive approach to sufficiency of consideration which the existing duty rule represents and hence to enforce the promise, was for the courts to seek to find something beyond the duty in a party's performance (additional benefit or detriment), and this type of interpretation became popular for this reason. In theory, at least, it involved no direct challenge to the traditional rules, whereas Denning LJ's approach focused on factual benefits as opposed to recognising something additional to the benefit recognised in law.

4.3.4.2 Duty owed to a third party The performance of an existing contractual duty owed to a third party may be consideration for a promise. For example, if B owes an existing contractual duty to A, B can use the performance of this duty to A (or his promise to perform it) as consideration to support a promise by C to pay B a sum of money. (In relation to the contract B/C, A is clearly a third party.) Early evidence of this exception may be found in *Scotson* v *Pegg* (1861) 6 Hurl & N 295.

A entered into a contract with B to deliver coal to C. C then said to A that if A would deliver the coal to him, C would unload the coal at a fixed rate per day. C failed to keep his promise, and in response to legal action by A claimed that his promise was unsupported by consideration since A was already bound by his contract with B to deliver the coal to C. C was nevertheless found liable, and the court expressed the view that performance of an existing contractual duty might be consideration for a separate promise by a third party. It is not clear, however, whether this was the basis of the decision, or whether, on account of facts not disclosed in the report, A's promise to C carried an extra burden by comparison with his promise to B.

There is also a trace of the exception in *Shadwell* v *Shadwell* (1860) 9 CB NS 159, where a nephew had supplied consideration to support a promise to pay him £150 yearly by marrying his fiancée, whom he was under an existing contractual duty to marry because breach of promise to marry actions existed at this time. However, this decision is of doubtful authority on several grounds, including a possible absence of intention to create legal relations since it was a family agreement.

Whatever the authority of the earlier cases, the exception was subsequently confirmed by two Privy Council decisions, which are generally accepted as representing English law on the matter. In *New Zealand Shipping Co. Ltd* v *A.M. Satterthwaite & Co. Ltd, The Eurymedon* [1975] AC 154, Lord Wilberforce, giving the majority opinion, said (at 168):

> An agreement to do an act which the promisor is under an existing obligation to a third party to do, may quite well amount to valid consideration and does so in the present case: the promisee obtains the benefit of a direct obligation which he can enforce. This proposition is illustrated and supported by *Scotson* v *Pegg* . . . which their Lordships consider to be good law.

In *The Eurymedon* the carrier of goods had by contract validly limited its liability to the shipper of the goods. It was the carrier's responsibility to procure a stevedore to unload the goods, but the court found that the stevedores enjoyed a quite independent contract with the shippers (on this aspect of the case, see 15.5.4). The clause in the carrier's contract with the shippers, which limited its liability, purported also to limit the liability of any independent contractor employed by the carrier. Even assuming that the clause was part of the agreement between shipper and stevedores, the question arose of whether sufficient consideration had been given for it to be enforceable by the stevedores, since the only action of the stevedores which could constitute consideration was their act of unloading the goods, and this was a duty which they were already bound by their contract with the carrier to perform. The Privy Council considered that the performance of this contractual duty owed to the carrier (a third party in relation to the contract between the shippers and stevedores) was a good consideration for the shippers' promise of exemption.

The basis of the exception   In *Pao On* v *Lau Yiu Long* [1980] AC 614, the Privy Council followed *The Eurymedon* on the question of consideration and performance of a duty owed to a third party. As discussed at 4.3.3.2 above, the Privy Council held that the plaintiffs had provided consideration for the promise of indemnity by the defendants by promising to perform their existing contractual duty to the Fu Chip company to retain 60 per cent of their shares. The case is therefore significant as an example of a situation where promising to perform an existing duty owed to a third party was held to be a valid consideration.

However, the main interest of the case may lie in the discussion by Lord Scarman of the purpose of the 'pre-existing duty' rule. Although the court was not prepared to commit itself to any particular view, it appeared sympathetic to the idea that it might be based in the prevention of duress by contracting parties against those to whom they owed contractual obligations (see [1980] AC 614 at 634; and see 4.3.4.3 below). It might be thought that in the case of promises by third parties the risk of such coercion would be considerably diminished, so that no such public policy need for the rule would exist in this type of case. The Privy Council, however, went further. Lord Scarman said:

> Where businessmen are negotiating at arm's length it is unnecessary for the achievement of justice, and unhelpful in the development of the law, to invoke such a rule of public policy . . . If a promise is induced by coercion of a man's will, the doctrine of duress suffices to do justice.

In fact, the *Pao On* case was an important stage in the recent development of a doctrine of economic duress (see 11.1.2), which has made the possibility of success on a claim of duress much greater. For this reason, Lord Scarman's argument above was broad enough in scope to apply not only to pre-existing duties as consideration for third party promises, but also to the pre-existing duty cases in which traditionally there has been said to be no consideration. This proposal had already been made by Denning LJ in *Williams* v *Williams* [1957] 1 WLR 148 (see 4.3.4.1, above), when he stated that performance of existing duties should be a good consideration 'so long as there is nothing in the transaction which is contrary to the public interest'. The development of the modern doctrine of economic duress, and the decision of the Court of Appeal in *Williams* v *Roffey Bros & Nicholls (Contractors) Ltd* [1991] 1 QB 1 (4.3.4.3), may have combined to make Denning LJ's proposal an accurate statement of the current law.

4.3.4.3 Contractual duties owed to the promisor Traditionally, the rule was that performance of an existing contractual duty could not be consideration for a further promise from the party to whom the existing duty was owed because there was no additional legal benefit or detriment. The leading case was *Stilk* v *Myrick* (1809) 2 Camp 317.

A crewman had contracted to work a vessel on a voyage for a fixed sum, promising to do all needed in all the emergencies of the voyage. During the voyage, two men deserted. The master offered extra payment to those remaining if they would work the ship home, and then on arrival refused to pay. The promise of extra payment was unenforceable, because desertion of crewmen was an emergency of the voyage so that there was already a duty to work the ship home in such a case. Therefore there was no consideration for the promise of further payment.

Most commentators accept that there is a considerable element of policy in the decision: to have enforced the promise was perceived to have been to risk exposing ships' masters to blackmail by the crew when far from England. Indeed, this was stated to be the *ratio* for the decision in Espinasse's report of *Stilk* v *Myrick* ((1809) 6 Esp 129), and although Espinasse was not regarded as the most reliable of reporters, the need to prevent extortion is a clear factor in both reports. Therefore, in *Stilk* v *Myrick*, the doctrine of consideration performed the function of a rule to prevent economic duress (see 11.1.2).

In order to avoid this restrictive interpretation of existing duties as insufficient consideration, the courts sought to find additional contractual performance in order to be able to conclude that there was the necessary additional benefit or detriment to render the promise enforceable (*North Ocean Shipping Co. Ltd* v *Hyundai Construction Co. Ltd, The Atlantic Baron* [1979] QB 705). However, a more direct attack was made on the restrictive approach to existing contractual duty in the decision of the Court of Appeal in *Williams* v *Roffey Bros & Nicholls (Contractors) Ltd* [1991] 1 QB 1 (for facts, see 4.3.5.2 below), which effectively overruled *Stilk* v *Myrick* (although this was denied and Glidewell LJ preferred to describe his approach as being to 'refine and limit the application of that principle'). In a commercial setting (and in the absence of duress), where it is possible to infer from all the circumstances that the parties both intended the further promises made to have legal force, the courts will give effect to that intention without being constrained by the rigid approach to the concept of consideration found in *Stilk* v *Myrick*. No single majority emerges from the three judgments in the Court of Appeal, but three strands of reasoning can be identified:

(a)   The policy element in *Stilk* v *Myrick*, which resulted in the consideration doctrine being applied in a very strict and formal way, is no longer present because of the emergence of the doctrine of economic duress, which allows for a more substantive appraisal of potentially unconscionable contracts (see 11.1.2).

(b)   The necessary consideration in a commercial case of this kind might be constituted by a factual benefit to the promisor, if the promisor was in fact induced to make the promise by the benefit he perceived himself to be receiving.

(c)   By analogy with the second category of pre-existing duty cases (performance of a duty owed to a third party may be consideration for a contract with a separate promisor: 4.3.4.2), no further consideration is required for the modification of an existing contract provided there is sufficient evidence of an intention that the alteration be legally binding.

Arguments (b) and (c) are conceptually very different, but it would be wrong to make much of this in the light of the ease with which a court may find a factual benefit if it so requires; consequently, the two arguments are functionally very closely related. Although some doubts have been cast upon interpretations of *Williams* v *Roffey*, which have proposed a very wide scope for the *ratio* of the case, it has not been suggested that the narrow *ratio* is in any sense unreliable. Indeed, in distinguishing *Williams* v *Roffey* by restricting it to the context of extra payment for the originally agreed amount of work (so-called 'promises to pay more'), two differently constituted Courts of Appeal appear to have accepted the correctness of the decision in this respect (see *Re Selectmove Ltd* [1995] 1 WLR 474; *Re C (a debtor)* (1994) *The Times*, 11 May).

The conclusion must therefore be that, at least in the context of alteration promises to pay more, consideration can be found in the factual benefit to the promisor arising from the alteration promise to pay more. In this situation, therefore, it should not be too difficult to establish the existence of a binding variation.

4.3.5   Binding alteration promises

4.3.5.1   The consideration requirement   As we can see from the discussion of contractual duties owed to the promisor, the role of consideration is not limited to the initial formation of contracts. The most secure way for any agreement between the parties to take effect is by contract. Agreements between contracting parties not to continue with the contract, or to change (or alter) its terms, are normally unenforceable in the courts unless themselves contracts (see, for example, *The Hannah Blumenthal* [1983] 1 AC 854), which means that consideration must be present. In practice what happens may be very different. Parties on very good terms, and who regularly contract with each other, may be willing to uphold non-contractual variations and terminations of contracts. The problem with relying on the good relationship between the parties rather than on a legally enforceable agreement is that unforeseen circumstances may intervene to sour the good relationship, or to make its impact irrelevant. This is especially true where the original party is replaced by a trustee who is under a legal obligation to insist on strict legal rights, irrespective of any changes made by friendly arrangement. The classic situations of replacement by a trustee (or equivalent) are bankruptcy, receivership or death of one of the parties.

Termination   As far as the termination of agreements is concerned, it is fairly easy to establish consideration in those cases where the contract is wholly or partially executory, i.e. where both parties still have some or all of their performance under the agreement left to execute. In this situation, if both parties give up their right to receive the remaining performance from the other party then there is in that fact an exchange amounting to consideration. It does not matter that the performances outstanding are disproportionate, since the rule that consideration must be sufficient but need not be adequate (see 4.3.2) prevents examination of the equivalence of the exchange. Where one party has performed fully, however, a release of the other party requires further consideration to be binding in contract.

Variation (or alteration)   Variation of the terms of a contract presents greater difficulty. A variation intended to be advantageous to both sides is automatically supported by consideration, since there is a mutual exchange of benefits (see 4.3.1). Sometimes what appears at first to be a one-sided variation can nevertheless, when properly analysed, be brought within the consideration doctrine. Consider the following example: A agrees to sell to B ten boxes of biscuits, ten packets of tea and ten loaves of bread for £20. Before either party has performed, B asks A to substitute five jars of coffee for five of the packets of tea. A agrees, saying that the price will remain the same. Is the variation enforceable? It might seem that the variation lacks consideration, since A is to perform something other than what was first agreed while B is only to pay what was originally asked. However, if the variation is seen as a two-stage (rather than single-stage) process, it is possible to discern consideration for the change being made. The first stage is where B agrees not to receive five packets of tea, in return for which A agrees not to receive whatever proportion of the total price is represented by the five packets. That stage represents one contract. Then A agrees to supply five jars of coffee, in return for which B agrees to pay whatever balance brings the total price back to £20. This is a second contract, and the variation is thereby enforceable. The court may not consider whether a packet of tea is in fact worth the same as a jar of coffee, again because of the rule that consideration must be sufficient but need not be adequate.

Where, however, a variation benefits only one of the parties, some consideration additional to that of the original contract has traditionally been regarded as necessary for the variation to be binding. It is this rule which has been modified in some circumstances by the decision of the Court of Appeal in *Williams* v *Roffey Bros & Nicholls (Contractors) Ltd* [1991] 1 QB 1 (see especially 4.3.5.2) so that, in these circumstances, the legal requirements for contract variation will be rather less demanding because it should be easier to find the necessary consideration to support the variation promise.

4.3.5.2 Alteration promises to pay more and alteration promises to accept less
Problems over consideration in contract variation cases are of two kinds: either one party wishes to provide the same performance but to obtain something greater than was originally agreed from the other party; or one party wishes to obtain the agreed performance from the other party while giving something less than was agreed in return.

Promises to pay more   *Williams* v *Roffey Bros & Nicholls (Contractors) Ltd* [1991] 1 QB 1 was a case involving the enforceability of an alteration promise to pay more (see also 4.3.4.3). The defendants were main contractors on a building contract, and they identified that the plaintiffs, who were subcontractor carpenters on the job, were in financial difficulty and at risk of not completing the work. Had the plaintiffs failed to complete the work, the defendants would have become liable for liquidated damages (apparently not a penalty: 13.10). The defendants therefore took the initiative to avoid the problem, by offering extra payments if the job were to be finished on time.

The plaintiffs accepted that offer, and then, when the additional payments were not made as promised, sought damages relying on the promise to pay more as being an enforceable promise.

The problem confronting the plaintiffs, arising out of *Stilk v Myrick* (1809) 2 Camp 317, was that they had given nothing in return for the promise of extra payment other than the performance they had undertaken to provide under the original contract. On the other hand, the commercial sense of the agreement was that the promise should be enforceable, and this view prevailed with the Court of Appeal. There was a real benefit to the defendants in avoiding having to pay the sums due under the main contract in the event of late completion, and so the avoidance of the risk of breach by the subcontractors clearly induced the defendants to make their promise. In addition, the defendants achieved a further factual benefit by avoiding the difficulties of finding another subcontractor to complete the carpentry work.

Promises to accept less   Promises to accept less than owed under the existing contract have long troubled English courts. The problem is easily illustrated: A sells his book to B for £10, payable next Tuesday; on Tuesday B has not got £10, but offers £8 which A accepts, promising that he will not seek to recover the remaining £2 from B. In *Pinnel's Case* (1602) 5 Co Rep 117a, it was held that a promise to accept less and not to sue for the balance (such as that made by A) was unenforceable unless B gave some new consideration for it. On the other hand, provided something was given, the court was not entitled to enquire whether what was given was equal in value to the promise made (see 4.3.2). For example, the courts accepted that payment in kind ('a horse, a hawk or a robe'), if accepted by the creditor, could constitute the necessary consideration (*Pinnel's Case*). In addition, if additional benefit was conferred and/or detriment suffered, that would also constitute consideration for a promise to accept less, e.g., payment in advance at the creditor's request (*Pinnel's Case*) or at a different place at the creditor's request (although not if simply to suit the debtor, because there would be no additional benefit or detriment: *Vanbergen v St Edmund Properties* [1933] 2 KB 223). Promises to accept less are also enforceable either if part of a composition agreement (e.g., agreement amongst all the creditors of a particular debtor to accept a certain percentage of their debts in full satisfaction: *Cook v Lister* (1863) 13 CB (NS) 543), or if the part payment is made by a third party and accepted in full settlement (*Hirachand Punamchand v Temple* [1911] 2 KB 330). The basis for these last two exceptions seems to be that it would be a fraud (on the other creditors, or on the third party) to go back on the promise.

The rule in *Pinnel's Case* was confirmed by the House of Lords in *Foakes v Beer* (1884) 9 App Cas 605, although Lord Blackburn opposed it (at 622), arguing:

All men of business . . . do every day recognise and act on the ground that prompt payment of a part of their demand may be more beneficial to them than it would be to insist on their rights and enforce payment of the whole. Even where the debtor is perfectly solvent, and sure to pay at the last, this is often so. Where the credit of the debtor is doubtful it must be more so.

Such reasoning recognises that there may be a factual benefit in promising to accept less. Promises to accept less might seem to be no different in their nature to promises to pay more for the same performance, as in *Williams* v *Roffey Bros & Nicholls (Contractors) Ltd* (see J. W. Carter, A. Phang and J. Poole, 'Reactions to *Williams* v *Roffey*' (1995) 8 JCL 248; although compare J. O'Sullivan 'In Defence of *Foakes* v *Beer*' (1996) 55 CLJ 219). If *Williams* v *Roffey Bros & Nicholls (Contractors) Ltd* had been held to be applicable to such promises, consideration might more easily have been found (arising from the factual benefit to the promisor) in a promise to accept less than the sum owed and promising not to claim for the balance. Nevertheless, in two cases heard by the Court of Appeal concerning promises to accept less, *Williams* v *Roffey Bros* has been rejected in favour of adherence to the old-established authority of the House of Lords in *Foakes* v *Beer*. In *Re Selectmove Ltd* [1995] 1 WLR 474, Peter Gibson LJ (*obiter*), with whom the other judges agreed, was clearly reluctant in conceding that he was bound by *Foakes* v *Beer*, but might otherwise have reached a different conclusion. In *Re C (a debtor)* (1994) *The Times*, 11 May, Bingham MR, again speaking for the whole court, simply did not accept that, in the face of *Pinnel's Case* and *Foakes* v *Beer*, the *Williams* v *Roffey Bros* approach could be extended to promises to accept less than contractually owed. These cases both involved debts to public bodies rather than variation of commercial contracts. Nevertheless, in the face of the doctrine of precedent, they clearly restrict further extension of *Williams* v *Roffey Bros* and have led to an unfortunate and arbitrary distinction, in terms of applicable principle and resultant enforceability, between contractual variations involving a promise to pay more and those contractual variations involving a promise to accept less.

It is as well to note that *Foakes* v *Beer* was not applied in one first instance decision where factual benefit was recognised. In *Anangel Atlas Compania Naviera SA* v *Ishikawajima-Harima Heavy Industries Co. Ltd (No. 2)* [1990] 2 Lloyd's Rep 526, the plaintiffs entered a contract to purchase a ship built by the defendants. The world shipping market fell into recession, and the plaintiffs discovered that the defendants were offering more advantageous terms to other clients. They sought and obtained the defendants' agreement that they should be accorded 'most favoured customer' status, so that in all respects, including price and terms of payment, they would be treated as favourably as any other customer. They subsequently sought to enforce this agreement, alleging that another customer had paid a lower price on more favourable payment terms. The defendants argued that the agreement was not supported by consideration.

There was no suggestion that the plaintiffs' request for more favourable terms constituted economic duress. *Foakes* v *Beer* was not referred to in the judgment, but the practical effect of the agreement was to allow the plaintiffs to pay less than the sum originally agreed. By enforcing this agreement in express reliance on *Williams* v *Roffey* and the notion of factual or subjective benefit, Hirst J seems to have avoided the problem posed by *Foakes* v *Beer*.

This apart, the reluctance of courts below the House of Lords to go against the clear authority of *Foakes* v *Beer* is understandable and proper. It has, nevertheless, had the effect of preserving the viability of the doctrine of promissory estoppel and has ensured that the law governing the enforceability of alteration promises is extremely complicated. It may be as well to summarise the current position: *Williams* v *Roffey Bros* applies to alteration promises to pay more money so that (given the absence of economic duress) if there is a factual benefit to the promisor arising from the promise, consideration to support that alteration promise can be found. However, in stating that *Foakes* v *Beer* must apply to alteration promises to accept less, *Re Selectmove* and *Re C (a debtor)* have ruled out the possibility of finding consideration from a factual benefit to a creditor in agreeing to accept a smaller sum in full satisfaction. It will therefore be necessary to look elsewhere for the consideration to support a promise to accept less (see discussion above), or, in the absence of consideration, the promise may have limited enforceability if the defence of promissory estoppel can be invoked.

4.3.6   Conclusions: the future of consideration

Although consideration appears to be firmly established in a central role in the English law of contract, and indeed appears to be the single element which distinguishes the common law contract from its continental civilian cousin, it would be wrong to conclude this section without acknowledging that for much of the twentieth century consideration was under attack from various quarters. In 1937, the Law Revision Committee (see its Sixth Interim Report, Cmd 5449) recommended a number of amendments to the detailed rules. Some of these proposals would have wrought a major change in our law, and could not be achieved without parliamentary intervention. For example, it was proposed that a promise in writing should be enforceable even if not supported by consideration. But other proposals have been at least partially achieved (see, for example, the pre-existing duty rule (4.3.4); the rule that promisors in unilateral contracts should not be allowed to revoke once a promisee has started to perform (2.8.3); and the suggestion that where a promise is relied upon by the promisee it should be binding on the promisor (see generally 4.4 below)), and these changes have been brought about by judicial development, which is testimony to the continuing internal dynamism of the common law.

Professor Atiyah has argued that there are historical grounds for saying that consideration is not the sole test used by the courts to determine whether a promise shall be enforceable, and that where justice required the courts have enforced promises on the basis of reliance by the promisee (see P. S. Atiyah, *Consideration in Contracts: A Fundamental Restatement*, Australian National University Press, 1971, in Atiyah, *Essays in Contract Law*, OUP, 1986). Such a notion, as we shall see (4.4.7, below), is consistent with developments in the United States.

These criticisms made by the Law Revision Committee and Professor Atiyah may be amongst the most eloquent, but they do not stand alone. The decision in *Williams* v *Roffey Bros* highlights the pragmatic approach to finding consideration which some courts are prepared to take in order to hold a particular promise to be binding in the light of the general context in which it was made. As Professor Downes suggested in the first edition of this book, there was likely to be a gradual progression away from the technical analysis of benefit and detriment towards the more impressionistic notion of inducement, thereby allowing the judges greater freedom to decide according to the flavour of the transaction whether agreements and promises should be treated as binding. The way forward was pointed by Lord Wilberforce in *The Eurymedon* [1975] AC 154 (see 4.3.4.2), where he said of the transaction in dispute (at 167):

> If the choice, and the antithesis, is between a gratuitous promise, and a promise for consideration, . . . there can be little doubt which, in commercial reality, this is. The whole contract is of a commercial character, involving service on one side, rates of payment on the other, and qualifying stipulations as to both. The relations of all parties to each other are commercial relations entered into for business reasons of ultimate profit. To describe one set of promises, in this context, as gratuitous, or *nudum pactum*, seems paradoxical and is *prima facie* implausible. It is only the precise analysis of this complex of relations into the classical offer and acceptance, with identifiable consideration, that seems to present difficulty.

In the immediate aftermath of the decision in *Williams* v *Roffey Bros & Nicholls (Contractors) Ltd* [1991] 1 QB 1, there appeared to be clear evidence of such a practice and the pragmatic nature of the decision, if not its technical basis, was warmly welcomed (see Adams and Brownsword (1990) 53 MLR 536 and *Coote* (1990) 3 JCL 23). The only issue at that time appeared to be to assess just how much the foundations of the doctrine of consideration had been shaken by this important decision. The variety of reasons given for enforcing the promise of extra payment (4.3.2.1 and 4.3.4.3) makes it possible to identify both a narrow and a wide principle emanating from the decision. At the narrowest, it seems that the law relating to binding alterations of contracts has changed, so that a post-contractual promise relating to the main agreement (other than a promise to accept as full payment an amount less than the originally agreed price) will be enforced, subject to proof of the necessary intention and the absence of duress. It also seems likely that other areas of the law of contract, where the requirement of consideration may be said to be simply 'technical', will no longer be troublesome, because the identification of a 'factual benefit' will always be possible when the commercial context makes it implausible for the promise not to be regarded as binding (see, for example, Coote (1990) 3 JCL 23, who argued that nobody would promise to pay more to achieve performance unless they regarded such a promise as beneficial to them on the basis that no one would 'throw good money after bad').

Of course, *Williams* v *Roffey Bros* is confined to the context of alteration promises. All three members of the Court of Appeal made it clear that they believed the particular context, which so influenced their reasoning, to be distinct from that of the formation of initial contracts. Accordingly, this principle will not be of any assistance in the context of the rule that a promise to keep an offer open is binding only if it is supported by consideration (see 2.7.3.1). Consequently, it is impossible to argue that the result of *Williams* v *Roffey Bros* will be that the doctrine of consideration will be abandoned altogether. Indeed, it would have been astonishing if such an interpretation were to have been suggested. There is no reason to think that English law should suddenly wish to make all gratuitous promises enforceable. The restrictive comments of the Court of Appeal in this important case were clearly designed to bring home the point that the doctrine of consideration remains central to mainstream contracts, and the decision reinforces the need to find consideration, albeit making it easier to establish in the context of promises to pay more. The Court of Appeal was at pains to stress this and would not otherwise have had to go to such lengths to identify the required consideration. Nevertheless, in *Anangel Atlas Compania Naviera* v *Ishikawajima-Harima Heavy Industries Co. Ltd (No. 2)* [1990] 2 Lloyd's Rep 526 at 545, Hirst J rejected the argument that *Williams* v *Roffey Bros* 'should be read as having only a very narrow ambit', although in the context the judge does not extend the *ratio* beyond the question of variation of an existing contract.

In subsequent cases (*Re Selectmove Ltd* [1995] 1 WLR 474; *Re C (a debtor)* (1994) *The Times*, 11 May), the Court of Appeal sought to place a limit on the scope of the *ratio*. These decisions appear to indicate that the courts are reluctant to abandon traditional rules of consideration, at least as far as release from debts is concerned. As a result, the developments since the 1950s in the field of promissory estoppel seem likely to continue to be of relevance (see 4.4.2); and much of the recent academic argument (such as M. Chen-Wishart, 'Consideration: Practical Benefit and the Emperor's New Clothes' in Beatson and Friedmann (eds), *Good Faith and Fault in Contract Law*, OUP, 1995; and N. J. Hird and A. Blair, 'Minding your own Business — *Williams* v *Roffey* Revisited: Consideration Reconsidered' [1996] JBL 254) has focused on arguments that, because of the technical difficulties in rationalising the decision in *Williams* v *Roffey Bros*, the preferable approach to ensure the enforceability of alteration promises would be to adopt a flexible concept of estoppel as in the High Court of Australia (see *Waltons Stores (Interstate) Ltd* v *Maher* (1988) 164 CLR 387 and *Commonwealth of Australia* v *Verwayen* (1990) 170 CLR 394, discussed at 4.4.7 below). This approach involves a fundamental shift of emphasis away from the consideration doctrine and towards a more limited enforceability by means of the estoppel doctrine (discussed at 4.4).

It is as well to end this section with a note of caution about the developments which arise out of *Williams* v *Roffey Bros & Nicholls (Contractors) Ltd*. Although the tone of the preceding analysis may have been to regard these developments as beneficial, any benefit is achieved at a price. The traditional consideration rules had the virtue of simplicity and the absence of difficult judgmental issues. The new rule invests the judges with an enormous discretion over such cases, especially in ascertaining intention and in determining whether behaviour amounted to illegitimate pressure and consequently economic duress (11.1.2). Before the old rules, and the occasional hard cases they engendered, are abandoned, we should be sure that the greater discretion of the new rule is in the best interests of the commercial community it must serve. In addition, it is important to consider whether there is, or should be, any *objective* evaluation of whether a benefit can be said to be a factual benefit where it is of subjective benefit to the party seeking to enforce an alteration promise to pay more.

4.4 RELIANCE AND ESTOPPEL

4.4.1 Equitable estoppel

4.4.1.1 Development of the doctrine Towards the end of the nineteenth century the courts developed a doctrine intended to prevent injustice arising out of the kind of situation described above. The application of this doctrine meant that one-sided variations of contract might be enforceable in some circumstances despite the absence of consideration to support them. The best example of the operation of the doctrine is the leading case: *Hughes* v *Metropolitan Railway Co.* (1877) 2 App Cas 439.

A lease contained a covenant requiring the lessee to repair upon notice from the lessor. Hughes, the lessor, gave notice requiring repair within six months. The railway company, the lessee, responded by offering to sell back to the lessor the company's remaining interest in the property under the lease. Negotiations continued for some two months before breaking down. Hughes subsequently claimed to be entitled to possession of the property on the basis that, since the company had failed to carry out the required repairs within six months of the original date of the notice requiring repair, the lease had been forfeited. The company claimed that there was a tacit understanding (or an implied promise) that the repairs need not be carried out if the negotiations came to a successful conclusion, and that in the meantime the period of notice would not start to run.

In the House of Lords the existence of that implied promise was not really in doubt. Nevertheless, it was unsupported by consideration and therefore arguably unenforceable. The House of Lords refused to accept that argument, and the basis of their Lordships' decision is contained in the following, now famous, passage from the judgment of Lord Cairns LC (at 448):

It is the first principle upon which all Courts of Equity proceed, that if parties who have entered into definite and distinct terms involving certain legal results . . . afterwards by their own act or with their own consent enter upon a course of negotiations which has the effect of leading one of the parties to suppose that the strict rights arising under the contract will not be enforced or will be kept in suspense or held in abeyance, the person who might otherwise have enforced those rights will not be allowed to enforce them where it would be inequitable, having regard to the dealings which have thus taken place between the parties.

Thus there is, in the name of equity, a doctrine which makes certain promises enforceable despite the absence of consideration. However, the nature and exact limits of this doctrine remain unclear. It should be noted that in some of the cases discussed in the following sections the expression 'promissory estoppel' is used, rather than 'equitable estoppel'. The change in terminology came about because of developments in the law starting in 1947. Those developments are discussed below (see 4.4.2).

4.4.1.2 Scope of equitable estoppel Lord Cairns expressed the doctrine as applying to variations of contractual obligations. Since the decision in *Hughes* v *Metropolitan Railway Co.* (1877) 2 App Cas 439, attempts have been made both to narrow and to extend the scope of the doctrine. In *Birmingham & District Land Co.* v *LNW Ry Co.* (1888) 40 ChD 268, it was argued for the appellants that the doctrine applied only to cases where penal rights in the nature of forfeiture were sought to be enforced. Forfeiture occurs where all the outstanding obligations owing to a party under a contract are lost by virtue of some failure by that party. Equity provides relief from forfeiture in limited circumstances where what might be lost would be disproportionate to a merely technical breach (see now s. 146 of the Law of Property Act 1925 and 13.10.5.3). There are statements in *Hughes* v *Metropolitan Railway Co.* that might have given rise to the belief that the doctrine expounded was limited to such cases, but in the *Birmingham & District Land Co.* case, Bowen LJ rejected this argument. In his opinion (at 286), the doctrine applied where the belief is induced that contractual rights 'will either not be enforced or will be kept in suspense or abeyance for some particular time'.

In *Durham Fancy Goods Ltd* v *Michael Jackson (Fancy Goods) Ltd* [1968] 2 QB 839, the doctrine was said to apply not only to a pre-existing contractual relationship, but to any pre-existing legal relationship that could, in some circumstances, give rise to liabilities and penalties. The relationship in question was statutory in nature. This first instance opinion was implicitly, but not expressly, doubted in *obiter* statements in the Court of Appeal in *Brikom Investments Ltd* v *Carr* [1979] QB 467. Roskill LJ cited with approval a passage in Spencer Bower and A. K. Turner, *The Law Relating to Estoppel by Representation*, Butterworths, 1977, in which it was stated that *Hughes* v *Metropolitan Railway Co.* cannot be cited in support of any wider proposition than that strict rights under contracts may not be enforced in given situations. In *Brikom Investments* v *Carr*, Roskill LJ in fact found that the strict rights in question were not enforceable because of a collateral contract between the parties by which it was agreed for consideration that such rights should be unenforceable. Thus the issue was treated as one of contract. On the other hand, Lord Denning MR took the view that the facts also supported an argument based on 'promissory' estoppel, although he was alone in this view. Roskill and Cumming Bruce LJJ nevertheless believed that the case fell within the *Hughes* v *Metropolitan Railway Co.* principle.

It may therefore be said with confidence that the doctrine applies to variations of pre-existing contractual duties, but beyond that the scope of the doctrine is unclear and awaits authoritative clarification by the courts.

4.4.2 The development of promissory estoppel

In the 1940s, the equitable doctrine established in *Hughes* v *Metropolitan Railway Co.* (1877) 2 App Cas 439 was taken into ground in which, some would argue, it had not been intended to operate. The doctrine originally applied to variation of terms, but promissory estoppel has taken its application into the context of part payment of contract debts.

4.4.2.1 The extension of the doctrine It was explained at 4.3.5.2 that the payment of a smaller sum than that owed cannot on its own be consideration for a promise not to enforce payment of the whole sum. Such an agreement would fall foul of the rule that consideration cannot consist of performance of an existing duty. There is early authority to that effect in *Pinnel's Case* (1602) 5 Co Rep 117a. Although the doctrine of consideration is going through a period of evolution, started by the decision of the Court of Appeal in *Williams* v *Roffey Bros & Nicholls (Contractors) Ltd* [1991] 1 QB 1, the rule in *Pinnel's Case* has recently been confirmed by the Court of Appeal (*Re Selectmove Ltd* [1995] 1 WLR 474).

Nevertheless, the courts had already made a limited attack upon the rule that, in the absence of consideration, a part payment promise is unenforceable. This attack was led by Denning J in *Central London Property Trust Ltd* v *High Trees House Ltd* [1947] KB 130. In this case, Denning J suggested in an *obiter dictum* that where the conditions of promissory estoppel were satisfied, a creditor could not go back on a promise to accept less (and not to sue for the balance) where it would be inequitable to do so. In other words, he could not go back on a promise not to enforce payment of the whole sum.

The case arose out of the classic situation (see 4.3.5.1 above) of a variation of strict contractual terms between parties enjoying a friendly relationship. The tenant company was a subsidiary of the landlord company. The property in question was a block of flats over which the defendant tenant company had a 99-year lease, for which it paid a rent of £2,500 per year. At the outbreak of the Second World War many of the flats remained vacant, and the tenant company was unable to pay the full rent. The landlord company agreed to halve the rent (to £1,250 per year), and the tenant company paid that amount from 1940 onwards. By the beginning of 1945 the flats were fully let again. The landlord company was in receivership. The receiver believed that the company was entitled to arrears of rent for the whole period of the war, but brought a test case claiming full rent for the last two quarters of 1945.

Denning J, relying on *Hughes* v *Metropolitan Railway Co.*, said that as a result of the equitable doctrine, 'a promise to accept a smaller sum in discharge of larger sum, if acted upon, is binding notwithstanding the absence of consideration'. He noted with some satisfaction that his interpretation of the authorities achieved that which had been recommended by the Law Revision Committee in 1937, namely that a creditor's promise to accept part payment as full settlement should be binding.

4.4.2.2 Assessment of the *High Trees* decision In one sense there is little that is startling about this proposition. Contractual provisions as to price and payment are only terms like any others, and it might be argued that as such they are open to variation by the parties by valid means in the same way as any other terms. Nevertheless, it had previously been thought that there were clear authorities against the validity of post-contracting price variations unsupported by consideration. One authority we have already noted; in *Foakes v Beer* (1884) 9 App Cas 605, the House of Lords refused to enforce a promise not to seek interest on a debt when the promise was given without consideration (see 4.3.5.2). *Foakes v Beer* was decided only seven years after *Hughes v Metropolitan Railway Co.*, without reference being made to that earlier decision.

Although it can be argued that estoppel must be pleaded before the court may rely on it, it seems inconceivable that counsel in *Foakes v Beer* would have overlooked the decision in *Hughes* had counsel considered it relevant. In courts below the House of Lords there is a continuing reluctance to disregard the authority of *Foakes v Beer*: (see *Re Selectmove Ltd* [1995] 1 WLR 474 and most recently *Ferguson v Davies* [1997] 1 All ER 315, 323, *per* Henry LJ).

The other major obstacle to the *High Trees* case was *Jorden v Money* (1854) 5 HL Cas 185, in which the House of Lords ruled that the common law estoppel principle (which prevents a person from going back on a statement made once it has been relied upon) applied only to misrepresentations of *existing* fact, and did not apply to promises of *future* conduct. On the other hand, this objection applies equally to *Hughes v Metropolitan Railway Co.* If that case is accepted as a valid exception to the rule in *Jorden v Money*, there would appear to be no reason why the *High Trees* case could not also be an exception.

It is possible to explain away these inconsistencies by ingenious arguments, as Denning J did in the *High Trees* case itself, resorting respectively to 'the fusion of law and equity' and an absence of intention to be legally bound. The truth of the matter appears to be that, as originally conceived in *Hughes v Metropolitan Railway Co.*, equitable estoppel was not intended to apply to variations of price unsupported by consideration. Once, however, Bowen LJ had stated in *Birmingham & District Land Co. v LNW Ry Co.* (1888) 40 ChD 268 that the doctrine was not limited to forfeiture cases but applied to all variations of contractual rights, no meaningful distinction could be made between price terms and any others (although from the reasoning in *Re C (a debtor)* (1994) *The Times*, 11 May, it appears that Sir Thomas Bingham MR would not agree). Denning J exploited this fact to the full by extending the equitable estoppel doctrine to its logical conclusion. Nevertheless, the subsequent cases are peppered with statements suggesting that the extension made by the *High Trees* decision is by no means firmly established in English law. Indeed, the House of Lords has not yet given its blessing to the doctrine of promissory estoppel. In both *Tool Metal Manufacturing Co. Ltd v Tungsten Electric Co. Ltd* [1955] 1 WLR 761 (*per* Lord Tucker at 784; see 4.4.5) and *Woodhouse A.C. Israel Cocoa Ltd v Nigerian Produce Marketing Co. Ltd* [1972] AC 741 (*per* Lord Hailsham at 758; see 4.4.3.1), the House of Lords expressly reserved the question of the existence, or at least the extent, of the doctrine.

Of course, the *Williams* v *Roffey Bros* approach to consideration would make promissory estoppel redundant if it extended to all types of alteration promises; and in *Re Selectmove Ltd* [1995] 1 WLR 474, Peter Gibson LJ appeared to favour such an approach being taken either by the House of Lords or by Parliament, although he was compelled to follow *Foakes* v *Beer* on the facts before him.

4.4.3 Requirements for promissory estoppel

4.4.3.1 The necessary representation The doctrine operates only where there is a clear and unequivocal representation that strict rights will not be enforced. Nevertheless, it is apparent from *Hughes* v *Metropolitan Railway Co.* (1877) 2 App Cas 439 itself that the representation need not be express, since in that case it was implied from the conduct of the lessor. In *Woodhouse A.C. Israel Cocoa SA* v *Nigerian Produce Marketing Co.* [1972] AC 741, Lord Hailsham said (at 756):

> The meaning is to exclude far-fetched or strained, but still possible, interpretations, while still insisting on a sufficient precision and freedom from ambiguity to ensure that the representation will . . . be reasonably understood in the particular sense required.

It seems that what is required is that only one reasonable meaning should be apparent from the representation made.

4.4.3.2 Defence and not a cause of action The major limitation on the promissory estoppel doctrine is that it cannot be used to found a cause of action; that is, it may not be used in legal proceedings brought to force someone to uphold a promise. It can only be used to prevent someone going back on their promise and insisting on enforcement of their strict rights. In *Combe* v *Combe* [1951] 2 KB 215, during divorce proceedings the husband had promised to pay the wife a certain sum by way of maintenance. The wife gave no reciprocal promise to refrain from applying to the court for mainten-ance, so that (unusually) the husband's promise was not supported by consideration. The wife attempted to enforce the promise on the basis of 'promissory' estoppel, but her claim was refused by the Court of Appeal. Denning LJ said (at 219–220):

> Much as I am inclined to favour the principle . . . it is important that it should not be stretched too far, lest it should be endangered. That principle does not create new causes of action where none existed before. . . . The doctrine of consideration is too firmly fixed to be overthrown by a side-wind. Its ill-effects have been largely mitigated of late, but it still remains a cardinal necessity of the formation of a contract, though not of its modification or discharge.

In *Brikom Investments Ltd* v *Carr* [1979] QB 467, Roskill LJ again stressed that 'it would be wrong to extend the doctrine of promissory estoppel, whatever its precise limits at the present day, to the extent of abolishing in this back-handed way the doctrine of consideration'. This limitation is sometimes expressed in the maxim that equitable or promissory estoppel is 'a shield not a sword' (*per* Birkett LJ in *Combe* v *Combe*). As an image the expression makes the point quite well, but it should not lead to the mistaken belief that the doctrine is available only to defendants and not to claimants. Promissory estoppel cannot found a cause of action where none would otherwise exist, but it may be used by a claimant in support of a cause of action which has an independent existence. Thus, if in *Hughes* v *Metropolitan Railway Co.* (1877) 2 App Cas 439 the lessor had actually retaken possession of the property, and upon breakdown of negotiations the lessee had sued to regain possession, the lessee would still have been able to rely on equitable estoppel to defeat the lessor's defence based on the lessee's failure to repair, since the cause of action would be based not on the implied promise to defer the time for repair, but on the right under the original lease to occupy the premises undisturbed for the agreed period.

4.4.3.3 Reliance   The promissory estoppel doctrine depends upon some act of reliance by the promisee before it operates. There are those who believe that reliance demands that the promisee must have been induced by the promise to have acted to his or her detriment in some way (based arguably on the doctrine of strict estoppel, where such a requirement exists). Such a definition is suspiciously reminiscent of now outmoded definitions of consideration (see 4.3.1), and may arise out of a confusion with proprietary estoppel (see 4.4.6). In fact, it is not easy to see that the promisees in either *Hughes* v *Metropolitan Railway Co.* or *High Trees* acted to their detriment, other than that they acted in accordance with the subsequent promise rather than the original contract. The suspension of the strict rights under the contracts was, on the contrary, a benefit to the promisees.

In *W.J. Alan & Co. Ltd* v *El Nasr Export & Import Co.* [1972] 2 QB 189, Lord Denning MR stated that he could find no support in the authorities for the view that there must be a detriment, and that all that was required was that the promisee must have 'conducted his affairs on the basis' of the promise so that 'it would not now be equitable to deprive him of its benefit'.

The one sense in which detriment is relevant to the doctrine is that there would be a detriment if the original contract were to be enforced unamended by the subsequent promise. Here, however, the sense of 'detriment' is nowhere near the same as that once used to define consideration. It does no more than contribute to the sense of justice inherent in the requirement that enforcement of the strict rights under the contract be 'inequitable' in the circumstances. Indeed, it may be that even the requirement of reliance is no more than the most likely way of demonstrating inequity, and is not in itself sufficient to trigger the doctrine. In *Société Italo-Belge pour le Commerce et l'Industrie SA* v *Palm & Vegetable Oils (Malaysia) Sdn Bhd, The Post Chaser*, [1982] 1 All ER 19, Robert Goff J insisted that the only requirement was that inequity be demonstrated. He said (at 27):

But it does not follow that in every case in which the representee has acted or failed to act, in reliance on the representation, it will be inequitable for the representee to enforce his rights, for the nature of the action, or inaction, may be insufficient to give rise to the equity, in which event a necessary requirement stated by Lord Cairns LC for the application of the doctrine would not have been fulfilled.

In this case the promisees did rely on the representation made, but the promisors withdrew the suspension of strict rights very soon afterwards and before any real harm had been done, so that in the particular circumstances the judge found that it would not be inequitable to enforce the strict rights (and the promisors could therefore go back on their representation despite the fact that it had been acted upon).

These comments reflect what must be the functions of reliance as a requirement. One function must be evidential; the existence of reliance tends to confirm that the promise was made and was taken seriously. A second function reflects the statement by Lord Cairns LC in *Hughes v Metropolitan Railway Co.* (1877) 2 App Cas 439, that the doctrine applies to prevent the enforcement of strict rights where to enforce them 'would be inequitable having regard to the dealings which have thus taken place between the parties'. In other words, as indicated by the comments in *The Post Chaser*, the fact of reliance is at least one element to be taken into account in assessing whether enforcement would in all the circumstances be inequitable. Where the reliance is detrimental, it should be easier to establish that it would be inequitable to allow the promisor to go back on the promise.

4.4.4 Duress against creditors

It has already been suggested that a probable reason for the rule that consideration cannot be provided by the performance of an existing duty is the fear of duress by debtors against creditors (see 4.3.4.3). The decision in *Central London Property Trust Ltd v High Trees House Ltd* [1947] KB 130 results in the enforcement of a promise to accept the diminished performance of an existing obligation in final settlement of a debt. These circumstances raise the possibility that the promise to accept less may have been obtained as a result of duress. This problem was confronted in *D & C Builders v Rees* [1966] 2 QB 617, where the debtor exploited the straitened circumstances of the creditor to extort a promise to accept immediate part-payment of the debt in final settlement. (The evidence was that the debtor's wife was aware of the creditor's circumstances.) The plaintiff creditor then claimed the balance, and the question facing the Court of Appeal was whether there was a binding settlement.

Lord Denning MR (who was in a minority on this reasoning, but not in the result of the case) found for the plaintiff creditor by relying on the statement of the doctrine by Lord Cairns LC in *Hughes v Metropolitan Railway Co.* Lord Denning MR said (at 625):

> The creditor is only barred from his legal rights when it would be *inequitable* for him to insist upon them . . . Where there has been a *true accord* . . .

then it is inequitable for the creditor afterwards to insist on the balance
. . . In the present case, on the facts as found by the judge, it seems to me
that there was no true accord. The debtor's wife held the creditor to
ransom.

In simple terms, there is nothing inequitable about not enforcing such a
promise when the promise was obtained by duress. This approach matches
that of Lord Scarman in *Pao On* v *Lau Yiu Long* [1980] AC 614, who said
that there was no harm in allowing consideration to be constituted by
performance of an existing duty provided that there was protection against
duress (see 4.3.4.2). Similar reasoning was used to justify a more liberal
approach to the doctrine of consideration in *Williams* v *Roffey Bros & Nicholls
(Contractors) Ltd* [1991] 1 QB 1 (4.3.4.3).

4.4.5　Effect of promissory estoppel

It seems that the effect of the doctrine is only to suspend strict legal rights
and not, at least in the first instance, to extinguish them. In *Hughes* v
Metropolitan Railway Co. (1877) 2 App Cas 439, such a consequence was
inevitable, since it was impossible in the factual context to extinguish the
property owner's right to have the property repaired. All that was in issue was
the date by which the lessee needed to have complied with the duty to repair.
Subsequent cases suggest, however, that in any situation a party making a
promise not to enforce strict rights may withdraw that promise upon giving
reasonable notice to the promisee.

In *Tool Metal Manufacturing Co. Ltd* v *Tungsten Electric Co. Ltd* [1955] 1
WLR 761, the respondents were bound to pay royalties to the appellants
under an agreement made in 1938 for the import, manufacture, use and sale
of hard metal alloys. They were also to pay compensation if the material
manufactured exceeded a stated volume. At the outbreak of the Second
World War, the appellants agreed to suspend the right to compensation. In
1945 the appellants claimed to have revoked that suspension, and to be
entitled once more to receive it. That claim failed on the basis that reasonable
notice needed to be given in order to resume the strict legal rights under the
contract. In the later case this earlier action was held by the House of Lords
to be sufficient notice to the respondents of termination of the suspension of
the right to compensation.

In the *High Trees* case (4.4.2.1), the promissory estoppel which Denning J
found to exist on the facts, was stated to operate only for as long as the
wartime conditions prevailed. It seems that the right to enforce the strict
rights under the contract revived automatically once those conditions ceased
to exist. It is not easy to see why that did not also happen in *Tool Metal*,
although it might be argued that the giving of reasonable notice is a suitable
mechanism to ensure that the other party is aware that the strict rights are to
be revived and to ensure that it is therefore no longer inequitable to go back
on the promise. It would also appear to generate more certainty (if only we
knew what might constitute a period of 'reasonable' notice) and less injustice

than a rule whereby estoppel might automatically come to an end, especially if there were to be disagreement about whether the estoppel conditions had ceased to exist. The safest way to resume strict legal rights must therefore be to give reasonable notice.

The suspensory nature of the estoppel means that in cases involving single debt obligations, the operation of the estoppel merely gives the debtor more time to pay the balance. However, it may well be that where strict rights are suspended in a contract calling for repeated performances over a period of time, rights accruing during the period of suspension are not enforceable, and in that sense are extinguished. Thus, in the *Tool Metal Manufacturing* case, it seems to have been assumed that, after termination of the suspension, the appellants were not entitled to claim for compensation which would otherwise have been payable during the suspension of the right to compensation. Moreover, in the leading case of *Central London Property Trust Ltd v High Trees House Ltd* [1947] KB 130 (see 4.4.2.1), there are *obiter dicta* of Denning J to the effect that periodic performances falling due during the period of suspension of rights cannot be recovered once the suspension of rights has come to an end. From statements he made in *Brikom Investments Ltd v Carr* [1979] QB 467 (at 484–485), it seems that he believed that in some circumstances it might be impossible for the promisor to go back to the strict rights under the contract.

Nevertheless, it seems unlikely that the courts will find that promissory estoppel extinguishes strict rights except where the context demands it. On the other hand, the enforceability of joined promises, both not to enforce strict rights and not to withdraw that first promise, has not been tested in the courts.

4.4.6 Proprietary estoppel

Proprietary estoppel may best be regarded as having little or nothing to do with the law of contract (in *Re Basham* [1987] 1 All ER 405, the judge described it as 'properly to be regarded as giving rise to a species of constructive trust'), but it is undoubtedly similar to the equitable estoppel doctrine, and developments in relation to the formal requirements for contracts for the sale of land (see 4.5.3.1) have demonstrated that it now plays a role in this context, either in its own right or as a device similar to the constructive trust. For this reason, the general principles of the doctrine will be outlined here.

It has been suggested that the distinction between promissory and proprietary estoppel is not helpful (*per* Scarman LJ in *Crabb v Arun District Council* [1976] Ch 179), and that the proprietary estoppel doctrine is 'an amalgam of doubtful utility' (*per* Goff J in *Amalgamated Investment & Property Co. Ltd v Texas Commerce International Bank Ltd* [1982] QB 84 at 103). Nevertheless, the fact that under the doctrine of proprietary estoppel new rights giving rise to a cause of action may be created is sufficient to distinguish it from promissory estoppel, which is limited to a purely defensive mode of operation.

Proprietary estoppel gives rise to an equitable right under which a non-owner may become entitled to land. The estoppel was originally regarded as being created by expenditure on, or use of, land with the acquiescence of the owner, in the mistaken belief, by the person making the expenditure or using the land, that he or she is the owner (*Dillwyn v Llewelyn* (1862) 4 De GF & J 517). More recently, the doctrine has been extended to provide a remedy where the non-owner is encouraged by the true owner to believe that he or she has an interest in the land, or that the true owner will grant him or her an interest in the land in due course (*Crabb v Arun District Council* [1976] Ch 179).

In this last form it is possible to see that proprietary estoppel may allow the achievement of a legal result which could in other circumstances be achieved by contract. Where there is a contract, that will prevail; but proprietary estoppel may fill a gap in the law's remedial armoury where contract is unavailable (for example, where the formal requirements under s. 2 of the Law of Property (Miscellaneous Provisions) Act 1989 are not satisfied: see 4.5.3.1).

In *Re Basham* [1987] 1 All ER 405, the judge (at 410) described the doctrine in these terms:

> Where one person (A) has acted to his detriment on the faith of a belief, which was known to and encouraged by another person (B), that he either has or is going to be given a right in or over B's property, B cannot insist on his strict legal rights if to do so would be inconsistent with A's belief.

There must be knowledge or encouragement of A's belief, and in practice this must amount to a representation upon which it is reasonable for A to rely, even if the representation is to be implied from conduct. The identification of such a representation raises issues which are largely the same as in the case of promissory estoppel (4.4.3.1). For an example of a case where such reliance would not be reasonable, see *Attorney-General of Hong Kong v Humphreys Estate (Queen's Gardens) Ltd* [1987] 1 AC 114; reliance was not reasonable because the party said to have made the representation had made clear at all times that its statements were 'subject to contract', so that when no contract could be agreed, no liability based upon proprietary estoppel could be imposed. The existence of an assurance will suffice; it is not necessary that there should be an irrevocable promise to transfer the interest (*Gillett v Holt* [2001] Ch 210).

Secondly, there must be detrimental reliance as a result of this encouragement. Here the requirement appears to be strict, and not as fluid as it appears to be in the case of promissory estoppel (4.4.3.3). For a clear case of detriment, see *Gillett v Holt*, where the plaintiff worked for a period exceeding 30 years, had in effect been a surrogate family to the landowner and had taken no other action to benefit himself on the basis of the repeated assurances that the farm business would be his. In addition, in *Crabb v Arun D.C*, the plaintiff sold part of his land, relying on a representation by the defendant that he had a right of access over the defendant's land to reach the land retained by him. No right of access was granted so that the land was landlocked. The Court of Appeal held that the plaintiff had clearly acted to his detriment in reliance on the representation, and the defendant was therefore estopped from denying the right of access.

Where the conditions for the establishment of proprietary estoppel are fulfilled, the court has a wide discretion to satisfy the equity (i.e., to determine a remedy). It may order the full ownership (fee simple) to be transferred to the party encouraged to believe an interest was to be granted; but where appropriate, a more limited form of remedy may be granted (see *Inwards* v *Baker* [1965] 2 QB 507: right to occupy property for life). In *Gillett* v *Holt*, compensation in money (for being excluded from the farm business) formed part of the remedy.

The doctrine of proprietary estoppel is not without difficulty. In particular, it is not clear why it should create a cause of action when promissory estoppel does not. Neither is it clear whether it applies only to real property (land), or whether it extends to other property. It is hard to resist the conclusion that these difficulties stem as much from the hard cases arising out of the doctrine of consideration, as they do from the proprietary estoppel doctrine itself.

4.4.7 Conclusion: the future of promissory estoppel

Despite doubts expressed about the doctrine in the House of Lords (see 4.4.2.2), and fears that it might abolish in a back-handed way the doctrine of consideration (see 4.4.3.2 above), promissory estoppel appears now to be well established as a doctrine of English law. Suggestions that it might become largely redundant by virtue of developments in relation to consideration (4.3.6), which avoid the restriction afflicting promissory estoppel (i.e., that it cannot be used as a cause of action), have subsided as a result of the continuing significance of the decision of the House of Lords in *Foakes* v *Beer*. In fact, it appears that the emphasis has shifted towards promissory estoppel and the possibility that the Australian lead might be followed to develop a broader category of estoppel, or at least to relax the existing doctrine of promissory estoppel in English law.

In the Australian courts a general category of estoppel has been used to prevent unconscionable conduct. This estoppel has been utilised where there was no pre-existing relationship between the parties and to enforce a promise directly. In *Walton Stores (Interstate) Ltd* v *Maher* (1988) 164 CLR 387, negotiations had taken place between the respondent and the appellant whereby the respondent was to demolish an existing building on land owned by the respondent and then build a new building, in accordance with the appellant's specifications, which would be leased to the appellant. The respondent thought that the agreement only needed to be executed and that this was to take place. The respondent therefore began the work of demolition. The appellant failed to execute the agreement, but did not inform the respondent until a considerable amount of the work had taken place. The respondent argued that the appellant was estopped from going back on its implied promise to complete the contract. The appellant argued that estoppel could not operate because there was no pre-existing legal relationship and because estoppel could not be used as a cause of action.

The High Court of Australia held that the appellant knew that the respondent was exposed to a detriment in acting in reliance on the representation that the contract would be executed, and it was unconscionable to act in a way which encouraged that detriment. Accordingly, the appellant was estopped from denying that it was bound.

The decision (and hence this estoppel) is based on preventing 'detrimental reliance' and so would not be appropriate, in this form, in relation to cases where there was no detriment (e.g., *High Trees* itself). In addition, the estoppel will not necessarily lead to enforcement of the promise. The remedy available will be limited to the 'minimum equity needed to avoid the detrimental reliance'. (See also the support for the 'minimum equity' principle in *Commonwealth of Australia* v *Verwayen* (1990) 170 CLR 395.) As the estoppel in *Walton Stores* protects against detrimental reliance through the unconscionable conduct of a promisor, it might be thought that reliance damages would be the appropriate remedy rather than fulfilling the promisee's expectations, although there could be no universal rule (see A. Robertson, 'Reliance and expectation in estoppel remedies' (1998) 18 LS 360). However, in *Giumelli* v *Giumelli* (1999) 163 ALR 473 (see Edelman (1999) 15 JCL 179), the High Court of Australia took the view that estoppel is not based solely on a requirement of detrimental reliance. The Court therefore suggested that *prima facie* the expectation measure was appropriate in order to ensure that the promise is fulfilled. Only in instances of detrimental reliance would a reliance-based remedy be appropriate. There are signs, therefore, of an even greater relaxation of this 'estoppel' in the Australian courts, although further clarification is required on the details and the theoretical underpinning for this doctrine.

It should be noted that there are some dangers associated with such a general estoppel, since it will inevitably be uncertain and may cause problems in its application. However, even the Australia courts deny the existence of a single unified estoppel, while effectively merging the existing estoppels to such an extent that this is the inevitable conclusion.

§ 90(1) of the American Restatement (2d) Contracts (1979) also recognises that promissory estoppel may give rise to a cause of action, and gives the courts a discretion to determine the appropriate remedy:

A promise which the promisor should reasonably expect to induce action or forbearance on the part of the promisee or a third person and which does induce such action or forbearance is binding if injustice can be avoided only by enforcement of the promise. *The remedy granted for breach may be limited as justice requires.* (emphasis added)

In *Williams* v *Roffey Bros* [1991] 1 QB 1, both Glidewell LJ and Russell LJ (more explicitly) raised the possibility that estoppel might have been pursued as an argument on the facts. On the facts, counsel for the plaintiff clearly considered that an argument based on practical benefit was more likely to succeed than an argument based on estoppel as giving rise to a cause of action so that the plaintiff could seek to rely on the promise to pay more. Russell LJ commented, however, that he would have 'welcomed' such an argument based on estoppel. It must be noted, however, that this was a very pragmatic Court of Appeal, and that another court might not be willing to entertain an argument which appears to directly conflict with *Combe v Combe*. Certainly, *Combe v Combe* was relied upon by the Court of Appeal in *Baird Textile Holdings Ltd v Marks & Spencer plc* (unreported), 28 February 2001, in reaching its conclusion that Baird could not successfully argue that there was an estoppel which gave it a right to require Marks & Spencer to continue to place orders for garments. (The estoppel argument also failed because of the uncertainty of any representation.) Counsel for Baird argued that *Walton Stores* should be followed in order to create a cause of action. The argument was rejected and Mance LJ indicated expressly that the reasoning in *Walton Stores* was unlikely to be followed by the English courts, although he could foresee that English courts might reach the same result on the facts. He identified the problem in *Walton Stores* as relating to formalities, i.e. there was agreement but it had not been executed. Given the existence of agreement, he considered that using estoppel in this situation might not constitute 'giving a cause of action in itself'; rather it operated to prevent Maher objecting to the binding nature of what was an agreed lease.

4.5 UNENFORCEABILITY BY DEFECT OF 'FORM'

4.5.1 General

Where the law states that a contract is enforceable only if recorded in a particular way, the rule is described as a requirement of form. It is one of the commonest misconceptions of contract law among lay people that contracts are enforceable only if in writing. It is true that the job of the courts, and of lawyers advising clients, would be much easier if we were to insist that all contracts be put in writing. If we pause and consider the implications of this, it will soon be realised, however, that this would mean that each time anyone bought a loaf of bread or a drink in a pub, they would be obliged to countersign an invoice. There would be an intolerable burden on daily consumer intercourse. For that reason, the general rule is that there is no requirement that contracts be made in writing, and the parties are left to their own good sense as to whether written evidence is necessary.

In commercial dealings written evidence is almost inevitably available, but for the most part that is a matter of choice, not a matter of law. Where complex obligations of great value are undertaken on each side, so that any dispute may involve liability for very large sums of money, parties will inevitably choose to keep an accurate record of their agreement (and see 3.4.1 on rectification).

In the seventeenth century the law required a large number of contracts to be made in writing. Today, it may generally be said that the law insists on writing only where the subject-matter or nature of the contract requires either absolutely certain evidence or some cautionary element to bring home to one of the parties the seriousness of the legal agreement being entered into. Thus, some consumer credit, hire-purchase and distance selling agreements (defined in 4.5.3.3) require a particular form of writing as a means of protecting consumers. There are differing consequences for non-compliance with formalities, e.g., the contract may be void, ineffective, unenforceable or deprive the transaction of the consequences which would normally follow.

Requirements of form are of three types:

(a) contracts required to be made by deed (4.5.2);
(b) contracts required to be in writing (4.5.3);
(c) contracts required to be evidenced in writing (4.5.4).

It is vital to consider the implications of both s. 8 of the Electronic Communications Act 2000 (implementing in part the Directive on Electronic Signatures 1999/93/EC (OJ 2000 L 13/12)) and Directive 2000/31/EC (OJ 2000 L 178/1 on certain legal aspects of information society services, 'the E-Commerce Directive', to be implemented by 17 January 2002) for current formalities requirements.

4.5.2 Contracts required to be made by deed

The common law made provision for a particularly formal kind of legal writing by means of the document made under seal. The more picturesque formalities associated with such documents have now disappeared, but these deeds must still be made in accordance with certain formal requirements, as set out in s. 1 of the Law of Property (Miscellaneous Provisions) Act 1989. These include the requirement of properly attested signature and delivery (s. 1(3)). The document must also make it clear on its face that it is intended to be a deed (s. 1(2)), but this can be achieved by the document being signed and witnessed in accordance with the requirements for a valid deed.

The most common transaction which must be made in the form of a deed, is the conveyance of a legal estate in land (see ss. 52 and 54 of the Law of Property Act 1925). A deed is also the means by which to make enforceable a gratuitous promise which otherwise would have no legal effect (see 4.1). It has the advantage that a longer limitation period applies to contracts made in a deed (12 years from the date of the breach of contract; s. 8(1), Limitation Act 1980), whereas the period applicable to a simple contract (i.e., not contained in a deed) is six years (s. 5(1)). Although this form of enforceable promise is not often used for commercial transactions, there can be tax reasons which dictate its use, e.g., covenants to make gifts to charity.

4.5.3 Contracts required to be made in writing

For some contracts it is an additional condition of enforceability, beyond the fact of consideration and intention to create legal relations, that the contract be in writing. In practical terms, among the most important of these are the following:

(a) contracts for the sale or disposition of an interest in land;

(b)   consumer credit agreements;
(c)   distance selling contracts;
(d)   marine insurance contracts; and
(e)   bills of exchange and bills of sale.

4.5.3.1   Contracts for the sale or disposition of an interest in land   Such contracts must be made in writing, signed by both parties (as to signature, see the discussion of electronic signatures below, at 4.5.5).

The Law of Property (Miscellaneous Provisions) Act 1989 repealed s. 40 of the Law of Property Act 1925, which required contracts for land to be evidenced in writing, and replaced it with a requirement that such contracts be made in writing incorporating all the terms. Section 2(1) of the 1989 Act provides:

> A contract for the sale or other disposition of an interest in land can only be made in writing and only by incorporating all the terms which the parties have expressly agreed in one document or, where contracts are exchanged, in each.

Incorporation of the terms can be achieved by setting them out in the contract document, or by reference to another document (s. 2(2)). There has been a growing body of case law determining which transactions fall within s. 2, how the requirements of s. 2 can be satisfied, and the position where the s. 2 formalities are not complied with.

In *Record* v *Bell* [1991] 4 All ER 471, it was held that where incorporation is alleged to have been achieved by reference to another document, the contract of sale which both parties have signed must refer to and identify the other document for incorporation for the purposes of s. 2 in order to be effective. In *Record* v *Bell*, the plaintiff had attached agreed supplementary terms to one contract document but not to the other. The judge ruled that physical attachment of additional terms to the contract document was ineffective as incorporation unless they were attached to both the documents exchanged. Each party must sign a document incorporating the terms, and it is important that the principal document be signed, rather than the secondary document the terms of which are to be incorporated. So, in *Firstpost Homes Ltd* v *Johnson* [1995] 4 All ER 355, the document, which it was claimed contained the contract between the parties, referred to an attached plan. The purchaser signed the plan but not the principal document, and the Court of Appeal found that the requirements of s. 2 were not satisfied. The Court of Appeal also ruled that the old law, under which the appearance of a typed or printed name might satisfy the requirement of signature, had no application to s. 2 of the 1989 Act, at least where the typed name figured only in an address at the top of a letter. It need not be the same document which bears both signatures, especially where there is to be an exchange of contract documents (s. 2(3)).

The grant of an option to purchase land would fall within the scope of the section, but the exercise of such an option would not and so need not be signed by both parties (*Spiro* v *Glencrown Properties Ltd* [1991] 1 All ER 600). Equally, an agreement made in the course of negotiations for the sale of a house, not to enter into negotiations with any rival purchaser for a period of time (a 'lock-out' agreement), is not a disposition of an interest in land, and so does not fall within the scope of s. 2(1): *Pitt* v *PHH Asset Management Ltd* [1994] 1 WLR 327. However, a variation of a contract for the sale or other disposition of an interest in land must satisfy the requirements of s. 2 just as much as the original contract (*McCausland* v *Duncan Lawrie Ltd* [1997] 1 WLR 38), with the possible exception of the variation of terms which are deemed to be immaterial (*per* Morritt LJ at 49). Since the reference in s. 2(1) to an exchange of documents involves a further step after agreement has been reached, it cannot be satisfied by the correspondence which constitutes the offer and acceptance (*Commission for the New Towns* v *Cooper (GB) Ltd* [1995] Ch 259).

A purported contract made in contravention of these rules would be without effect. The former rule making enforceable an oral contract of which there was a memorandum in writing (which might record only the barest details) no longer applies. Prior to the enactment of s. 2 of the 1989 Act, a contract for the sale or other disposition of an interest in land which did not satisfy the requirement of being evidenced in writing, might nevertheless be enforceable by virtue of the doctrine of part performance. That doctrine, which was said to exist in order to prevent fraud by parties who knew they had entered into a contract and merely sought to take advantage of the formal defect to get out of that bargain, was also repealed, by s. 2(8) and s. 4 of the 1989 Act.

The question, then, is whether any protection against such fraud now remains. The Law Commission, which proposed these changes to the law in its Report No. 164, *Formalities for Contracts for Sale etc. of Land* (1987), suggested that some possible means of protection remain available:

(a) *Rectification*, which is provided for expressly by s. 2(4), is possible by order of the court where it results in the contract fulfilling the s. 2 requirements. This could not be achieved if there had to be a concluded contract before rectification since that would be impossible through failure to fulfil s. 2; however, as discussed in 3.4.1.1, for rectification there need only be evidence that the written agreement does not reflect the terms actually agreed by the parties.

(b) *Collateral contract.* A collateral contract might be available to provide for aspects of the contract not covered by the written document, although presumably such aspects could not be interests in land. An example might be a house sale, in which it had been agreed that carpets would be included in the purchase price but where the sale of the carpets was not recorded in the contract document. That part of the sale might be regarded as a collateral contract, without doing violence to the principle established by s. 2. In *Tootal Clothing Ltd* v *Guinea Properties Management Ltd* (1992) 64 P & CR 452, the Court of Appeal found, as an alternative ground for its decision, that an agreement by which a landlord undertook to contribute to the cost of shop

fitting work to be carried out by the tenant was 'supplemental' to the main
tenancy agreement, as designated by the parties, and was not, therefore, one
of the terms which had to be recorded in writing. Perhaps more surprisingly,
in *Record* v *Bell* [1991] 4 All ER 471, a warranty of title, given in order to
induce exchange of contracts on the date previously anticipated because
proper documentation from the Land Registry was not available, was said to
be a collateral warranty not forming part of the contract of sale and not
therefore required to be part of the writing provided for in s. 2 of the 1989
Act.

(c) *Proprietary estoppel.* The doctrine of proprietary estoppel is thought to
provide protection from fraud. It applies, in particular, where one party has
been encouraged by another to believe that he or she will be granted an
interest in the property in question, and has acted to his or her detriment in
reliance on that belief. The doctrine affords such a party a new cause of action
to protect his or her interest, which might go as far as the court ordering the
property to be conveyed to that party. However, it is not expressly provided
for in the statute, so that its application may risk being excluded as contrary
to the Parliamentary intent (see, e.g., *McCausland* v *Duncan Lawrie Ltd*
[1997] 1 WLR 38 and *United Bank of Kuwait plc* v *Sahib* [1997] Ch 107).
The doctrine is considered in more detail at 4.4.6.

(d) *Constructive trust.* This device has the advantage of being expressly
included in the legislation. By s. 2(5), the constructive trust is specifically
excluded from the s. 2 requirements and ought therefore to provide a way
around a failure to comply with s. 2 formalities. *Yaxley* v *Gotts* [2000] Ch 162
illustrates that both proprietary estoppel and the constructive trust may be
relevant on a particular set of facts, and that the simplest course would then
be to utilise the constructive trust as provided for in s. 2. The case concerned
an oral agreement to transfer the ground floor of a house in exchange for
renovation work and acting as managing agent. The judge at first instance
had awarded an order for a lease on the basis of proprietary estoppel. The
appeal was based on the argument that any oral contract was void as it did
not comply with the s. 2 formalities and proprietary estoppel was therefore
inappropriate. The Court of Appeal held that the agreement could be
enforced using the constructive trust based on the common intentions of the
parties and to avoid unconscionability, which was a similar remedy to
proprietary estoppel. Robert Walker LJ stated that '[a] constructive trust of
that sort is closely akin to, if not indistinguishable from, proprietary estoppel.
Equity enforces it because it would be unconscionable for the other party to
disregard the claimant's rights'.

The advantage of the constructive trust was that there was no potential
conflict with s. 2 and the underlying policy because it was expressly provided
for in the section. Since a constructive trust will almost certainly arise if
proprietary estoppel applies, it is likely that this device will take on greater
prominence in the future as a means of avoiding the unconscionability that
may follow from a failure to comply with s. 2. However, it is important to
note that *Yaxley* v *Gotts* does 'not seek fully' to equate the two doctrines
(Moore (2000) 63 MLR 912). An argument based on proprietary estoppel

and constructive trust was put in *James* v *Evans* [2000] 42 EG 173, but failed because the negotiations had been conducted 'subject to contract'.

4.5.3.2 Consumer credit agreements Other important contracts required to be made in a particular form of writing are consumer hire-purchase and credit sales agreements, which are regulated agreements under the Consumer Credit Act 1974 s. 60. Such contracts must be in the form prescribed by regulation (Consumer Credit (Agreements) Regulations 1983 (SI 1983 No. 1553)). Failure to comply with this form may not be fatal to such an agreement but it will require a court order if it is to be enforced, and this will not be issued if the consumer did not sign the agreement, or did not receive a copy of the agreement or notice of his right to cancel. The underlying purpose of the rule is to provide protection for consumer debtors, in particular by providing them with information such as the details of the annual percentage rate charged for the credit, without permitting the formal requirement to become a technical defence operating to protect suppliers from legal action by consumer claimants.

4.5.3.3 Distance selling contracts The Consumer Protection (Distance Selling) Regulations 2000 (SI 2000 No. 2334) (in force 31 October 2000), implement the EC Distance Selling Directive, 97/7/EC (OJ 1997 L 144/19). The Regulations apply to any contract (except those excluded by reg. 5)

> concerning goods or services concluded between a supplier and a consumer under an organised distance sales or service provision scheme run by the supplier who, for the purposes of the contract, makes exclusive use of one or more means of distance communication up to and including the moment at which the contract is concluded. (reg. 3(1)).

This includes contracts made by letter, press advertising with order forms, catalogues, telephone, fax, e-mail and Internet contracts.

Formalities are required for the conclusion of such contracts in that certain information must be given to the consumer prior to the conclusion of the contract (reg. 7(1)), such as the supplier's identity, price, delivery costs and the existence of the right to cancel. This information can be given in a form 'appropriate to the means of distance communication used', e.g., telephone call or e-mail. Regulation 8 requires much the same information to be given in writing or in another 'durable medium' (e-mail should suffice, but a phone call would not) before or at the time of delivery of the goods or during the performance of the contract for services. The cancellation period is seven working days from the date of receipt of the goods or, in the case of services, from the date on which the contract was made (regs 11 and 12).

Certain contracts are excluded from the operation of the 2000 Regulations, namely contracts for the sale of an interest in land, including for construction of a building on land (although rental agreements are covered), financial services contracts, contracts concluded by means of automated machines and contracts concluded at an auction.

4.5.3.4 Marine insurance contracts By ss. 21 to 24 of the Marine Insurance Act 1906, a contract of marine insurance will not be admitted in evidence unless contained in a document ('policy') signed by the insurer. Thus the whole contract must be in writing.

This is not strictly a condition of validity of such a contract, but only of its admissibility in evidence in trial proceedings. In fact, the contract itself is regarded as formed by assent given before the policy is drawn up. However, inadmissibility in evidence may be an insurmountable obstacle to enforcement.

4.5.3.5 Other instances A bill of exchange must be in writing and signed (ss. 3(1) and 17(2) of the Bills of Exchange Act 1882). A typical example of a bill of exchange is a cheque (see 15.4.4). If the instrument is not in writing it will not be a bill of exchange and the usual characteristics of that instrument will be lost, e.g., negotiability.

A bill of sale is void unless made in a particular form (s. 9, Bills of Sale Act (1878) Amendment Act 1882). A bill of sale is a document recording a transaction transferring title to goods to someone else, but not possession (see s. 4 of the 1878 Act). The Acts of 1878 and 1882 were passed to prevent people obtaining credit on the security of goods which were in their possession but which they no longer owned.

4.5.4 Contracts required to be evidenced in writing

Contracts of guarantee are required to be evidenced in writing. There must be 'some memorandum or note thereof' in writing, which is signed by the party to be charged.

A guarantee is defined by s. 4 of the Statute of Frauds 1677 as a 'promise to answer for the debt, default or miscarriage of another person'. In other words, there is a promise by one person to meet the liabilities of another should that other become liable and fail to pay. This definition is important because the rule is said not to apply to contracts of indemnity. Contracts of indemnity are defined as promises to pay for another whether or not there is liability on that other. Thus, in the case of indemnities the guarantor is taking on primary liability, whereas s. 4 applies only where the guarantor takes on secondary liability. However, the distinction has been subject to severe criticism (*cf. Yeoman Credit Ltd* v *Latter* [1961] 1 WLR 828).

The requirement of writing for contracts of guarantee does not apply where the undertaking is only part of or incidental to a larger transaction (see *Sutton & Co.* v *Gre* [1894] 1 QB 285). Neither does it apply where the guarantee promise is given in order to protect property (see *Fitzgerald* v *Dressler* (1858) 7 CB NS 374). For example, if A wishes to purchase property from B in which C has a security interest on a debt owed by B, A may promise C that A will meet B's debt should B fail to honour it, in order to obtain the property free from C's prevailing interest. Such a promise need not be evidenced in writing. These exceptions may be explained by the argument that the requirement of writing is less strong when the surrounding circumstances of

other transactions provide some evidence of the promises made. Nevertheless, the policy of the law seems to have been buried in a mound of fine
distinctions so that this area cries out for reform.

4.5.5 Electronic signatures and the implications of e-commerce

Electronic signatures have been given legal recognition by the Electronic
Communications Act 2000, s. 7 (implementing aspects of the Electronic
Signatures Directive 1999/93 EC, OJ 2000 L 13/12). Section 7 came into
force on 25 July 2000 (SI 2000 No. 1798). Section 7(1) refers to the
admissibility of an electronic signature 'incorporated into or logically associated with a particular electronic communication or particular electronic
data' and certification of that signature, as evidence in relation to the
authenticity or integrity of the communication or data. In other words, an
electronic signature may fulfil the same function as a hand-written signature
in relation to electronic communications, which is vitally important for the
effectiveness of Internet contracting. Authenticity is explained in s. 15(2) as
relating to questions of whether the communication comes from that person,
whether the communication is 'accurately timed and dated' and whether it is
intended to have legal effect. The integrity issue relates to the question of
whether the communication has been interfered with in any way.

Section 8 of the Act is also significant, because it gives the Secretary of
State the power by statutory instrument to remove restrictions in any other
legislation which impede the effectiveness of electronic commerce (e.g.,
formalities requirements, such as deeds or other writing, or a requirement
that the post be used). This is potentially of great significance for the future
of formalities requirements.

In addition, the E-Commerce Directive (2000/31/EC, see 2.6.4.4) contains
a more specific indication of these potential problems. Article 9(1) of the
Directive provides that Member States must ensure that their legal system
allows contracts to be concluded by electronic means, and that this means
ensuring that any legal requirements which apply to the contractual process
'neither create obstacles for the use of electronic contracts nor result in such
contracts being deprived of legal effectiveness and validity on account of their
being made by electronic means'. This represents a direct challenge to many
of the formality requirements. However, exceptions from this provision are
possible (Article 9(2)). In particular, Article 9(2)(a) allows for exemptions in
relation to 'contracts that create or transfer rights in real estate except for
rental rights'. The problem with this is that it does not appear to exempt
leases, so that in future leases may need to be capable of being created or
transferred electronically. There is also an exemption in Article 9(2)(c) for
'contracts of suretyship granted and on collateral securities furnished by
persons acting for purposes outside their trade, business or profession', which
would take some guarantees outside the electronic requirements. However,
the provision specifies that the exemption will apply only if the guarantor was
'acting outside their trade, business or profession'. Therefore, business
guarantees will also need to be capable of being effected electronically. This

Directive must be implemented by 17 January 2002, and the Department of Trade and Industry is due to consult on implementation.

4.6 CONTRACTUAL CAPACITY

4.6.1 Capacity of individuals

The paradigm of contractual capacity is embodied in the living adult of sound mind, and any deviation from that state is cause to question a party's capacity to contract.

4.6.1.1 Mentally disordered and drunken persons Persons of unsound mind cannot, for the most part, enter into contracts, since they are incapable of giving any real consent to an agreement. The exception to this basic rule is that mentally disordered persons may be liable to pay for necessaries (see the discussion of the same rule in the context of minors' contracts, at 4.6.1.2).

The main difficulty in this area is to know when the mental disorder is such as to impair the ability to give informed consent. Where a person has been declared a 'patient' for the purposes of Part VII of the Mental Health Act 1983 by the Court of Protection, it seems likely that such a person is absolutely incapable of entering into contracts (*cf. Re Walker* [1905] 1 Ch 160). The authorities relate to previous legislation, which is now repealed, but there is no reason to think that the same rule will not apply. In other circumstances, mentally disordered persons are treated as having contractual capacity, but may be able to have a contract set aside at a later date if it can be shown that at the time of contracting the person was incapable of understanding the nature of the actions in question and the other contracting party knew, or ought to have known, of this incapacity at the relevant time (see *Imperial Loan Co.* v *Stone* [1892] 1 QB 599).

Imperial Loan Co. v *Stone* was confirmed as good law by the Judicial Committee of the Privy Council in *Hart* v *O'Connor* [1985] AC 1000. Lord Brightman stressed that the validity of a contract entered into by a mentally disordered person who is at the time of contracting ostensibly sane, is to be judged by the same standards as apply to a contract made by a person of sound mind. The fact that the contract appears 'unfair' is irrelevant, except in so far as it would be relevant to a contract made by a person of sound mind. Thus, the law has to strike a balance between protecting those of limited mental capacity from exploitation, and protecting the integrity of contracts entered into without knowledge of the other party's incapacity. It seems after *Hart* v *O'Connor* that in most cases this latter interest will prevail.

Similar rules apply to contracts entered into by drunken persons, but there is a serious question of fact in each case as to whether the party's reason was sufficiently impaired to invalidate the contract. The presumption is to the contrary, and the courts are unlikely to be sympathetic to a party pleading his or her own excessive drinking as a reason to escape contractual liability. In the case of both drunks and those suffering from temporary periods of mental disorder, a contract ratified during sober or lucid moments is valid (*Matthews* v *Baxter* (1873) LR 8 Ex 132). From this fact it is clear that the effect of such incapacity is to make the contract merely voidable, not void.

4.6.1.2 Minors A minor is a person under 18 years of age. Contracts by minors are governed by a mix of common law and statutory rules, particularly the Minors' Contracts Act 1987. A contract made by a minor is not void; and although the minor is not normally bound, the other party will be. There are, however, some exceptions to this principle where the minor will be bound, e.g., contracts for necessaries. In addition, there are some contracts which are binding on the minor *unless* repudiated by him before he reaches 18, or within a reasonable time of doing so. These might be referred to as 'voidable' contracts. It is also open to the minor to ratify a non-binding contract on attaining his majority.

Contracts for necessaries A minor must pay a reasonable sum for necessaries, defined by s. 3 of the SGA 1979 as 'goods suitable to the condition in life of the minor . . . and to his actual requirements at the time of the sale'. Necessaries are more than just what may be needed to keep body and soul together and reflect a minor's 'condition in life'. The classic case is *Nash* v *Inman* [1908] 2 KB 1, where the defendant, while still a minor, purchased clothing, including 11 fancy waistcoats, from the plaintiff. It was established that he already had a supply of clothing sufficient for his condition in life, and so the clothing purchased could not be regarded as necessaries.

The case illustrates the two difficulties inherent in the rule. In the first place, the court has to make invidious judgments about what is appropriate to any particular 'condition of life'. More seriously, a salesperson may well be unable to judge, when confronted with a minor wishing to make a purchase, whether the good in question is a necessary in the case of the particular minor before him or her. In cases of doubt, that salesperson's wisest course would be to refuse to part with the goods except for cash. The Law Commission once suggested that the concept of necessaries should be abandoned and replaced with a more narrowly defined concept of necessities (see Working Paper No. 81). This suggestion was not pursued by the final report (Law Comm. No. 134).

Contracts of employment, or of apprenticeship or for instruction are also treated as contracts for necessaries. They are binding on minors unless more burdensome than beneficial. For example, in *De Francesco* v *Barnum* (1890) 45 ChD 430, the plaintiff brought an action for an injunction to prevent wrongful interference with his contract (under seal) with a minor who was apprenticed to him as a stage dancer. The contract provided that she was not to be paid unless actually employed by the apprentice master, and that she should not accept other employment without his consent. The girl took employment with the defendant, and the plaintiff's action to restrain this interference in the contract of apprenticeship failed because the contract was invalid as unduly burdensome. It is accepted that such contracts will contain onerous terms for minors. The rule is that such terms must not be out of proportion to the benefit accruing to the minor.

Trading contracts do not fall within the class of necessaries, although it is not easy to defend their exclusion. It may rest on the belief that minors are not mature enough to judge the risks inherent in trading.

The liability of minors to pay for necessaries has generally been regarded as resting not on contract but on quasi-contract: it is payment for a benefit received. In that case, an executory contract (i.e., unperformed) for necessaries would be unenforceable against a minor. The wording of s. 3 of the SGA 1979 is consistent with that conclusion. In the case of contracts of employment, however, the rule may be different. In *Roberts* v *Gray* [1913] 1 KB 520, the defendant entered a contract to work for the plaintiff in what would today be called a billiards 'circus'. The defendant was still a minor. Shortly before the tour began the defendant withdrew, in breach of his contract. The plaintiff brought an action on the contract to recover expenses incurred in preparation for the tour. The contract was found to be enforceable against the minor although still executory.

Contracts valid unless repudiated at majority   Certain contracts made by minors are voidable but become valid when the minor attains majority unless repudiated at that time. The rules governing these contracts are unaffected by the Minors' Contracts Act 1987, and they continue to be governed by the common law rules. The most common types of contract within this category are contracts to acquire either shares in a company, or an interest in land. In each case, what is acquired is an enduring benefit to which certain obligations attach. To be effective, the repudiation must be accompanied by a surrender of the interest in question (see *North Western Railway* v *McMichael* (1850) 5 Ex 114). The contract must be repudiated either before attaining majority, or within a reasonable time of attaining majority, although what is a reasonable time is a question of fact in each case (see *Edwards* v *Carter* [1893] AC 360). Money actually paid is not recoverable in such a case, except where there has been a total failure of consideration (see *Steinberg* v *Scala (Leeds) Ltd* [1923] 2 Ch 452).

Other contracts   Contracts which are not for 'necessaries' and which are not 'voidable' are unenforceable against the minor, although they are binding on the other party. It is sometimes said that specific performance is not available to a minor, but that rule was probably based on the principle of mutuality and the fact that a contract cannot be specifically enforced against a minor (*Lumley* v *Ravenscroft* [1895] 1 QB 683). The principle of mutuality no longer requires the possibility of specific performance against both parties, provided the party seeking specific performance has entirely performed his side of the contract (*Price* v *Strange* [1978] Ch 337, see 14.2.3.2). On that basis, a minor who has wholly executed the performance due from him or her ought now to be able to obtain specific performance against the other party in circumstances where the remedy would otherwise be available.

Although these contracts are unenforceable against the minor, property may pass from the minor to the other party under them (*Chaplin* v *Leslie Frewin (Publishers) Ltd* [1965] 3 All ER 764). Moreover, the minor may not recover property or money which has passed under an unenforceable contract, except in circumstances where such recovery would be available to a person of full contractual capacity, such as total failure of consideration. Since property also passes to the minor under such contracts, in the case of contracts for goods such failure will not occur (*cf. Rowland* v *Divall* [1923] 2 KB 500). By contrast, there is the possibility of recovering property, which has passed under the unenforceable contract from the other party to the minor (see below).

Despite the general rule that other contracts are not binding on the minor, as the rule exists to protect minors and not to prevent contracts, since the repeal of s. 2 of the Infants Relief Act 1874, the minor can choose to ratify the contract, expressly or impliedly, on reaching 18. Although express ratification is likely to present few problems, there may be difficulties in establishing that an alleged ratification is to be implied from conduct.

Misrepresentation of age   A difficult problem arises where the minor represents that he or she is of full age. The law's policy of protecting minors still applies, so that the contract is unenforceable. It would be undesirable, however, for the minor to take advantage of his or her own wrongdoing. A rule of equity therefore requires the minor to restore goods acquired. The same rule cannot provide for the repayment of money loaned. In *R. Leslie Ltd* v *Sheill* [1914] 3 KB 607, when still a minor the defendant had borrowed £400 from the plaintiff moneylenders, but had misrepresented that he was of the age of contractual capacity. The plaintiffs brought an action to recover the principal sum and interest. The plaintiffs were unable to obtain restitution because that would have been equivalent to enforcing the contract and was not possible. Where goods are acquired and sold, the proceeds of sale may be recovered by a tracing remedy (see *Stocks* v *Wilson* [1913] 2 KB 235).

Restitutionary remedy against minors   Before the Minors' Contracts Act 1987, restitution was available against a minor in the case of fraud (see above) or in quasi-contract for so-called 'waiver of tort' (*Bristow* v *Eastman* (1794) 1 Esp 172). These rules are preserved by s. 3(2) of the 1987 Act, but are less favourable to a party seeking restitution against a minor than the new discretionary rule introduced by s. 3(1). The provision will particularly benefit traders who supply goods to minors on credit, and who are then unable to obtain payment because the contract is unenforceable by virtue of the minor's age. Under s. 3(1), the court may order the minor to return the property acquired if it is just and equitable to do so. 'Property' is not defined in this section, and so it is not clear whether it includes money obtained under such a contract. However, s. 3(1) applies to property acquired or any property representing it, and if property acquired has been converted into something else it is likely to have been converted into money. If that may be recovered under the Act, it would be strange if money acquired directly could not be. Another difficulty with the notion of property representing property acquired under the contract is where the proceeds are money, and it has been paid into a bank account from which withdrawals have been made, or where other goods have been purchased the value of which is greater than merely the proceeds of the property originally acquired. No doubt the resolution of these problems will be clouded by the exercise of the court's discretion over whether to order restitution at all.

4.6.2 Companies incorporated under the Companies Act 1985 and limited liability partnerships

A company incorporated under the Companies Act 1985 has separate corporate personality, i.e. it is a legal entity independent of the identity of its respective members (see *Salomon v A. Salomon & Co. Ltd* [1897] AC 22). In the context of the corporate group, each company within the group has separate legal personality. (This can be compared with partnerships, which have no separate legal capacity and whose contracts are governed by general agency principles: see further, Chapter 16.) The capacity of the company to contract is therefore separate from that of the individual owners or directors.

A company's ability to contract was affected by the *ultra vires* rule, i.e. a company lacked the capacity to enter into contracts which were inconsistent with its *objects* as set out in its memorandum of association; these were *ultra vires* contracts. Originally, third parties contracting with the company were deemed to know what its objects clause said, and so were not able to enforce such *ultra vires* contracts. Protection of third parties was introduced in 1972, but it was thought not to go far enough and the Companies Act 1989 effected further, more radical reform. In general terms, the 1989 Act maintains the *ultra vires* rule within the company (that is, in respect of relations between the directors and the shareholders) but removes its effect in respect of relations between the company and third parties. Therefore, as far as the law of contract is concerned, the *ultra vires* doctrine of company law is unlikely to present problems in the future.

Limited liability partnerships are bodies corporate (s. 1, Limited Liability Partnerships Act 2000), i.e. they have separate legal personality. However, contracts entered into by members are governed by agency law (s. 6), as are the terms of the agreement between the members (s. 5). In other words, for this purpose they are in the same position as partnerships.

PART II CONTENT, INTERPRETATION, PERFORMANCE AND DISCHARGE

The essence of a bilateral contract is the existence of obligations owed by each contracting party to the other. Most disputes about contracts, and in turn most litigation, are not concerned with whether a contract has come into existence, but involve questions relating to the performance of the obligations created by the contract. Has a relevant pre-contractual statement become one of the 'promises' of the contract? Are the parties subject to obligations other than those expressed in the terms of their agreement? What standard of performance is demanded? What are the consequences of breach of the terms of the contract? Is it possible to avoid the consequences of breach? What happens to the parties' obligations if, after the contract is made, some event occurs which is outside the control of the parties, but which makes further performance impossible? All these questions are extremely important and are examined in Part II of this book (Chapters 5 to 8).

FIVE

Content of the contract and principles of interpretation

A. CONTENT

5.1 PRE-CONTRACTUAL STATEMENTS

5.1.1 Introduction

The important question here is whether pre-contractual statements (which are often oral) have become terms of the contract. Pre-contractual statements are of three types: puffs, representations, and terms. The most common type of puff is the advertising gimmick. Puffs are statements which give rise to no legal consequences. They are statements which are not meant to be taken literally and there is no intention to be legally bound (see 4.2). *Carlill* v *Carbolic Smoke Ball Co.* [1893] 1 QB 256 is an example of an advertising gimmick where the statement was more than a puff, because there was evidence of an intention to be bound in the company's statement that £1,000 had been deposited with its bank.

The basic distinction between a representation and a term is that a term involves a promise as to the truth of the statement, whereas a representation involves no such promise as to truth, although the statement in question does induce the making of the contract. Both representations and terms give rise to legal consequences if the representation is false (misrepresentation, discussed in Chapter 10) or if the term is broken (breach of contract, discussed in Chapter 7). It is significant, however, that the legal consequences for misrepresentation and breach of contract are not the same.

Prior to the mid-1960s, the distinction between representations and terms was vitally important, because the remedy of damages for misrepresentation could be obtained only if it was established that the misrepresentation was fraudulent. Therefore, it was often vital to establish that a false pre-contractual statement was a term. However, since the House of Lords decision in *Hedley Byrne & Co. Ltd* v *Heller & Partners Ltd* [1964] AC 465 (10.4.3.1) and, in particular, the Misrepresentation Act 1967, damages have been available for non-fraudulent misrepresentations. Nevertheless, there is still a distinction between a claim for misrepresentation and for breach of contract in relation to both the ability to claim damages and, more especially in a practical context, the measure of those damages. For example, there is an automatic right to claim damages on proof of a breach of a term of the contract (see 7.5.1), whereas damages for misrepresentation may be *claimed* only on proof of fault (i.e., where the statement maker was fraudulent or negligent in making the statement). Damages cannot be *claimed* for innocent misrepresentation, although they may be awarded at the discretion of the court (s. 2(2), Misrepresentation Act 1967; see 10.5.3.4).

The most important distinction, however, remains the different measure of damages. In the event of a breach of contract, the normal measure of damages will be the expectation measure, i.e. the claimant is put into the position that he or she would have been in had the contract been properly performed (and the breach not occurred) (13.1). On the other hand, the measure of damages for misrepresentation is tortious, i.e. it aims to put the claimant into the position that he or she would have been in had the contract not been made (10.5.3). This is not the only difference in terms of measure of damages, since the ability to recover for losses (the remoteness rule) is also very different. The applicable remoteness rule in the context of a claim for breach of contract (*Hadley* v *Baxendale* (1854) 9 Exch 341, see 13.9.2) is much stricter, because it requires that the loss in question be within the reasonable contemplation of the parties when they made the contract as the probable result of its breach. The remoteness rule for fraudulent misrepresentation (and under s. 2(1) of the Misrepresentation Act 1967 for negligent misrepresentation) is considerably more generous (although controversial in the context of negligent misrepresentation), since all direct loss, regardless of foreseeability, is recoverable (10.5.3.2 and 10.5.3.3). This difference may therefore be an important one where there are a number of consequential losses resulting from the making of a false pre-contractual statement.

5.1.2 Distinguishing representations and terms

The test of whether a representation has become a term is very imprecise. It is essentially a question of the statement maker's intention, as objectively judged (2.1) (see Lightman J in *Inntrepreneur Pub Co.* v *East Crown Ltd* [2000] 2 Lloyd's Rep 611, at 615). In other words, was it the statement maker's intention to make a binding promise as to the truth of his or her statement so that if the statement were inaccurate it would result in automatic breach of the contract? (See *Heilbut, Symons & Co.* v *Buckleton* [1913] AC 30.) Another way of putting this question is simply to ask whether the intention of the statement maker was to guarantee the truth of his or her statement.

The problem is that there is often very little external evidence from which to identify this intention. In addition, there is an added complexity in the case law, because a statement can also amount to a contractual promise on the basis that it is a collateral warranty; a promise that reasonable care and skill has been exercised, as opposed to a guarantee of a particular result.

Although the existence of the intention necessary for a representation to be incorporated into the contract is regarded as a question of fact, some guiding principles emerge from examination of the cases. As a starting point, where the agreement between the parties has been reduced into writing soon after the representation was made, and the representation is not part of the writing, there is a not unnatural presumption that the representation was not intended to be part of the contract (*Heilbut, Symons & Co.* v *Buckleton* [1913] AC 30). Lightman J in the *Inntrepreneur* case went as far as referring to this as a '*prima facie* assumption . . . that the written contract includes all the terms the parties wanted to be binding between them'. Lightman J also stressed that 'the longer the interval' between the statement and the contract, 'the greater the presumption must be that the parties did not intend the statement to have contractual effect'.

However, this 'presumption' can be rebutted by reference to specific guidelines. Unfortunately, the application of these guidelines does not always lead to the predicted result, and it is submitted that this is because the courts have generally tended to focus on only *one* of these guidelines instead of applying them all to a particular set of facts (although compare the decision in *Pritchard* v *Cook & Red Ltd* (unreported), 4 June 1998). Certainly, although the statement in *Dick Bentley* v *Harold Motors* [1965] 1 WLR 623 (see below) was held to amount to a term because of the special knowledge of the statement maker, it was also the case that the buyer had made it clear that he wished to purchase a 'well vetted' car, so that the 'importance attached' test would also appear to have been satisfied (see below).

5.1.2.1 Accepting responsibility or advising on verification If the statement maker accepts responsibility for the truth of a statement, the statement is likely to be regarded as a term, because in accepting responsibility the statement maker is guaranteeing its truth (*Schawel* v *Reade* [1913] 2 IR 81). On the other hand, if the statement maker asks or advises the other to check the reliability of the statement, e.g., by recommending that a survey be carried out or that the accounts be examined, that statement should be interpreted as a representation, because in such circumstances that person cannot be making a binding promise that the statement is true (*Ecay* v *Godfrey* (1947) 80 Lloyd's Rep 286).

5.1.2.2 Importance attached test If the statement was so important to the recipient that it is clear that he or she would not have contracted had that statement not been made, that statement is likely to be interpreted as a term (or binding promise that the statement is true). It is important to appreciate that it is not merely a matter of the importance of the statement to the recipient; it must also be the case that this importance is clear to the

statement maker before he or she makes the statement, either because the recipient expressly makes the importance clear or because its significance is clear from the circumstances of contracting.

In *Bannerman* v *White* (1861) 10 CB NS 844, the defendant asked whether sulphur had been used in the production of hops he was considering buying, stating that he was not interested in buying them if it had. He was assured that no sulphur had been used. However, the hops were found to contain sulphur, and the defendant claimed to be entitled to reject them, arguing that this amounted to a breach of term (i.e., breach of contract). His argument prevailed. Without the false statement there would have been no contract. This meant that the statement was not merely a pre-contractual inducement but amounted to a description of the subject-matter of the sale, and was thus a term.

An appropriate general test would therefore be to ask whether the statement maker is taking personal responsibility for the statement. If the term satisfies the importance attached test, that will be a factor indicating such personal responsibility. For example, in *Pritchard* v *Cook & Red Ltd* (unreported), 4 June 1998, the plaintiff had purchased a rally car from the defendant after having asked to see the specification for the car. The defendant had produced the specification, which had been supplied to him by the car's manufacturer, but had copied the details on to his own headed notepaper. The written contract made no reference to this technical specification. Since the car did not accord with the specification, the plaintiff claimed damages alleging breach of contract. The Court of Appeal held that the technical specification was a term of the contract on the importance attached test, i.e. the plaintiff had specifically asked to see it and the evidence was that he would not have purchased the car without these details contained in the specification.

5.1.2.3 Statement maker's special knowledge of the subject-matter

Where the person making the statement has special knowledge of the subject-matter of the contract, or holds himself or herself out as having such knowledge, the courts may also be more willing to treat the statement as a term of the contract. A party may hold himself or herself out as having special knowledge by suggesting that there is no need to check the accuracy of the statement made (*Schawel* v *Reade* [1913] 2 IR 81).

The relevance of special knowledge is well illustrated by contrasting two cases in which material facts about second-hand cars were falsely stated. In *Oscar Chess Ltd* v *Williams* [1957] 1 WLR 370, a private seller represented his car to be a 1948 Morris. It was in fact a 1939 version of the same model, worth substantially less. The statement of the car's age was held not to be a term. The private seller had no special knowledge and had relied on the registration book for his belief. In addition, the buyers in this case were car dealers and were therefore in at least as good a position to discover the truth of the statement.

In *Dick Bentley Productions Ltd* v *Harold Smith (Motors) Ltd* [1965] 1 WLR 623, a car dealer stated that a car had an engine which had done only 20,000 miles. This was in fact untrue. The buyer sought damages alleging breach of contract. That statement was treated as a term.

The apparent distinction between the cases is the status of the person making the representation. A private seller did not have the special knowledge which indicated an intention that the statement be treated as a contractually binding promise, but a car dealer did. This distinction led Lord Denning MR to suggest in *Dick Bentley Productions Ltd* v *Harold Smith (Motors) Ltd* that the presence of fault was the basis for the distinction. However, it seems wrong to suggest that fault is the only test, and arguably what Lord Denning was stating was simply that the obligation broken was an obligation to exercise reasonable care and skill. The true test ought therefore to be that the dealer was in a better position to discover the truth and therefore impliedly took personal responsibility for the truth of statements made.

It was argued in *Pritchard* v *Cook & Red Ltd* (see 5.1.2.2) that the defendant was selling in a personal capacity and that *Oscar Chess* v *Williams* therefore applied to any statements made. However, the Court of Appeal distinguished *Oscar Chess* on the basis that in that case the seller had indicated that his statement was derived from the registration book so that he could not be taking personal responsibility for it. However, in *Pritchard* v *Cook & Red Ltd*, the defendant had clearly taken personal responsibility for the manufacturer's specification by copying it on to his own paper and not issuing a disclaimer.

5.1.3 Collateral warranties

When a person with special knowledge of the subject-matter makes a statement, that statement is likely to be interpreted as a contractual promise on the basis that it constitutes a collateral warranty. This is because statements by such 'experts' tend to be forecasts inducing the contract rather than binding promises of a particular position or result. Such a forecast does, however, contain an implied promise that the forecast was made with reasonable care and skill. If this implied promise is broken (i.e., there is a failure to exercise reasonable care and skill), there will be a breach of a contractual promise.

This device was used in the past in order to allow recovery of damages where a statement had been made negligently. It was adopted by the Court of Appeal in *Dick Bentley* v *Harold Motors* (above), where the statement was held to amount to a collateral warranty, giving rise to a remedy of damages for its breach. The 'fault' to which Lord Denning MR was referring in his judgment is the failure to exercise reasonable care and skill in making the statement about mileage.

In *Heilbut, Symons & Co.* v *Buckleton* [1913] AC 30, the House of Lords had stated that the courts should not be quick to find such collateral warranties, and that there must be clear evidence of an intention that the representations made should have contractual force. Despite these strictures, the courts found the collateral warranty to be a useful device for achieving what they believed to be a just result, especially in the period before damages for negligent misrepresentation became available. Lord Denning admitted as much in his judgment in *Esso Petroleum Co. Ltd* v *Mardon* [1976] QB 801.

In *Esso* v *Mardon*, the court held that a forecast by a person with 40 years' experience of the potential throughput of a petrol station, which was intended to induce the defendant to take a tenancy of that petrol station, amounted to a collateral warranty that the forecast had been given using reasonable care and skill. The Court of Appeal also held that the forecast amounted to a negligent misstatement (10.4.3.1).

5.1.4 Conclusion

It is difficult to predict with any certainty which pre-contractual statements will be incorporated as terms and which will be regarded only as representations. It is hard to resist the conclusion that the courts enjoy the element of discretion which the current vague guidelines provide, and would not like to see them replaced by anything more certain. The basic test of contractual intention allows the court to pick and choose those representations which are to have contractual status without reference to tight identifiable criteria. Predictability suffers as a consequence of this rule, but it may be a price we are willing to pay for the element of fairness it may import.

5.2 WRITTEN CONTRACTS

5.2.1 The parol evidence rule

If a contract is wholly in writing, there is no difficulty in ascertaining its express terms — although there may be difficulties interpreting them (see 5.2 below). However, a situation can arise where, although there is a written document, one party alleges that this is not the whole contract and that there is either some orally agreed term, or a term in some other written document. Thus it is claimed that this first written document does not contain the entire contract.

The parol evidence rule states that if the contract is written then that writing is the whole contract and the parties cannot adduce extrinsic evidence, and especially oral evidence, to 'add to, vary or contradict that writing' (e.g., *Henderson* v *Arthur* [1907] 1 KB 10). A related rule prevents use of extrinsic evidence of negotiations and subsequent conduct to prove the meaning of words used in a written contract (see 5(B)).

However, the parol evidence rule applied only to express terms, and did not operate to prevent the implication of terms into the contract (5.5). Neither did it operate to prevent proof by extrinsic evidence of such defects in the contract as mistake (Chapter 3) and misrepresentation (Chapter 10). In disallowing any terms other than those recorded in writing, the rule contributed greatly to contractual certainty, since others could rely on the written document as representing the entire agreement between the parties. Nevertheless, it often did so at the expense of apparent justice, since it was often clear that further terms had been agreed but had not been included in the writing. For this reason, the courts developed a series of exceptions to the rule, to the extent that it can no longer be said that the general rule is that extrinsic evidence is inadmissible to prove further terms. The most important exceptions are considered below.

5.2.2 Rectification

Rectification is an equitable remedy which allows a document to be revised where there has been a transcription mistake in recording in writing a previous oral agreement (3.4.1). The doctrine could not apply without there being an exception to the parol evidence rule, since extrinsic evidence must be introduced to prove the content of the original oral agreement.

5.2.3 Contract partly written and partly oral

If it is held that the contract was intended to be partly written and partly oral, this necessarily means that it is not a wholly written contract, and therefore the parol evidence rule does not apply. It is perfectly permissible to introduce extrinsic evidence of oral terms in order to determine whether the contract is a contract wholly in writing to which the parol evidence rule applies. This means that the parol evidence rule has little substance, since it can always be avoided by introducing evidence of oral terms and concluding that the contract is not a written one. This led Professor Wedderburn ([1959] CLJ 58) to conclude that the rule was no more than a 'self evident tautology', i.e. it is always true.

In *J. Evans & Son (Portsmouth) Ltd* v *Andrea Merzario Ltd* [1976] 1 WLR 1078, the parties had been doing business together for some time. The plaintiffs shipped goods on trailers with the defendants, the trailers always being stored below deck on the ship. The defendants wanted to change to container transport, and the plaintiffs would agree to the change only provided the containers were also shipped below deck. The defendants gave an oral assurance to that effect. The written contract purported to allow the defendants complete freedom in the handling and transportation of the goods. One container was stored on deck, and while in transit fell into the sea. The Court of Appeal had no doubt that there had been a breach of contract. As Roskill LJ stated, where the contract is partly written and partly oral, 'The court is entitled to look at and should look at all the evidence from start to finish in order to see what the bargain was that was struck between the parties'.

Significantly, having accepted evidence that there was an oral term that the goods would be shipped below deck, the Court also held that the oral term overrode the inconsistent term of the written contract (allowing the defendants complete freedom in determining transportation of the goods). This was also the approach taken by the Court of Appeal in *Couchman* v *Hill* [1947] KB 554, where an oral assurance that a heifer was 'unserved' was held to override an exemption printed in the auctioneers' catalogue to the effect that there was to be no responsibility for the correct description, or any fault or defect in a lot.

5.2.4 Collateral contract

The courts have also been willing to allow the use of collateral contracts to side-step the parol evidence rule. The parol evidence rule will apply to the written contract, but there is also an oral second (collateral) contract which exists in parallel, shares the same subject-matter, and was the reason why the main contract was entered into. Since this collateral contract is a separate oral contract, the parol evidence rule cannot apply to it.

In theory, such a contract will be found to exist only if the promise it is alleged to contain is independent of the subject-matter of the major contract (*Mann v Nunn* (1874) 30 LT 526). Equally, a collateral contract is supposed not to contradict the terms of the major contract (*Henderson v Arthur* [1907] 1 KB 10). Nevertheless, it seems clear that the courts have not allowed these limitations to restrict the operation of this device as a means to avoid the parol evidence rule.

In *City and Westminster Properties (1934) Ltd v Mudd* [1959] Ch 129, a representation was made that a landlord would not enforce a covenant in a lease preventing the tenant from residing in the premises. The tenant would not have entered into the contract without that assurance. The oral assurance was held to be a contractual promise (on the basis of the importance attached test). The court found this promise to have been incorporated in a separate collateral contract, overriding the inconsistent covenant against residence in the main contract.

Lord Denning in the Court of Appeal in *J. Evans & Son (Portsmouth) Ltd v Andrea Merzario Ltd* [1976] 1 WLR 1078, concluded that the oral assurance (that goods would not be shipped below deck) constituted a separate collateral contract inducing the written contract. The term of this collateral contract overrode the inconsistent term of the main written contract.

It should be possible to avoid the kind of argument which prevailed in the above case by inserting what is known as an 'entire agreement clause' in the written agreement. Such a clause states that the document is intended and agreed to contain the entirety of the contract between the parties, and each party acknowledges that it has not relied upon any promise or undertaking in entering into the agreement which is not expressly contained in the written document.

The inclusion of such a clause ought to be sufficient to indicate the parties' intentions on the matter, namely that the contract is a purely written contract to which the parol evidence rule applies, so that it is not possible to adduce evidence of alleged oral terms in order to add to, vary or contradict the written document. Certainly, the inclusion of such a clause should operate to prevent an allegation that the contract is partly written and partly oral. However, it is suggested (see *Chitty on Contracts*, 28th edn, Sweet & Maxwell, 1999, Vol. 1, at para [12–102]) that such a clause would not prevent extrinsic evidence of a collateral contract or warranty because 'the parol evidence rule does not extend to such cases'. Nevertheless, it is submitted that there can be only one purpose behind the inclusion of such a clause, and this was acknowledged by Lightman J in the recent decision in *Inntrepreneur Pub Co.*

v *East Crown Ltd* [2000] 2 Lloyd's Rep 611 (see MacDonald [1999] CLJ 413).

In *Inntrepreneur*, the claimant sought to enforce against the defendant a covenant in a lease for a public house, by which the defendant had agreed to purchase its supply of beer from the claimant (a 'beer tie'). The defendant alleged that a collateral warranty had been given by the claimant whereby it had agreed to release the tie by 28 March 1998, and so it counterclaimed that there was no such tie in existence after this date. One of the defences of the claimant to this allegation was that the contract contained an entire agreement clause, and the question was whether the clause prevented the defendant from relying on the alleged collateral warranty.

Lightman J held (following *Deepak Fertilisers & Petrochemical Corporation* v *Davy McKee (London) Ltd* [1999] 1 Lloyd's Rep 387) that even if a collateral warranty could be established, it was deprived of legal effect by the entire agreement clause. The clause made it clear that the terms which the parties had agreed to were only those contained in the written agreement. He said (at 614) that 'any promises or assurances made in the course of the negotiations (which, in the absence of such a clause, might have effect as a collateral warranty) shall have no contractual force save in so far as they are reflected and given effect in that document'. The clause precluded a party to a written agreement 'from threshing through the undergrowth and finding, in the course of negotiations, some (chance) remark or statement (often long forgotten or difficult to recall or explain) upon which to found a claim . . . to the existence of a collateral warranty'. It is interesting to note that the judge did not deal with the question of whether such a clause fell within s. 3 of the UCTA 1977 (6.6.2.4) and so was subject to the requirement of reasonableness in s. 11. One can only assume that he regarded the clause as outside the scope of s. 3 of the 1977 Act. (It is important to note that an entire agreement clause as such does not extend to prevent a claim for misrepresentation, since it is merely a denial of contractual force. However, it is possible to draft a provision which sets out to exclude liability for misrepresentation, although this would be subject to the reasonableness requirement in UCTA 1977 by virtue of s. 3 of the Misrepresentation Act 1967 (see 10.6). Section 3 of the 1967 Act relates only to misrepresentation, and therefore has no application to an entire agreement clause relating to contractual terms.)

5.2.5 Reform

In the absence of an appropriately drafted entire agreement clause, both the collateral contract and the device of finding that the document is not intended to embody the entire agreement, make such substantial inroads into the parol evidence rule that it may be doubted whether much of it remains to be preserved. It seems that there is ample scope for a court which wishes to avoid the rule to do so. The Law Commission in its 1986 Report (Law Com. No. 154, Cmnd 9700) decided that there was no need for legislation to abolish the rule since its effect was already widely understood to be minimal. The Law Commission formulated the rule as follows (at para. 2.7):

[W]hen it is proved or admitted that the parties to a contract intended that all the express terms of their agreement should be as recorded in a particular document or documents, evidence will be inadmissible (because irrelevant) if it is tendered only for the purpose of adding to, varying, subtracting from or contradicting the express terms of the contract.

In other words, the Law Commission concluded that the question of whether a document represented the whole of the parties' agreement rested simply on whether the parties intended the written document to contain their whole contract.

5.3   INCORPORATION OF TERMS

The law on the question of incorporation of terms has evolved almost entirely through litigation in respect of clauses excluding or limiting liability (see Chapter 6), especially those contained in standard form contracts. Nevertheless, the principles are equally applicable to all express terms. In relation to exclusion and limitation clauses, the law on incorporation of terms is less crucial than it once was because other means of control of such devices now exist (see 6.6) which make it less important for a claimant to establish that the clause in question was not part of the agreement. However, analysis of this kind was used in *Interfoto Picture Library Ltd* v *Stiletto Visual Programmes Ltd* [1989] 1 QB 433 to exclude a clause which purported to impose a severe penalty for late performance, on the basis that it had not been incorporated into the contract.

Any statements which it is claimed have been incorporated as terms must be made prior to the conclusion of the contract, and it is for this reason that the rules of offer and acceptance are important in this context (see Chapter 2).

There are various means of achieving incorporation — by signature, by reasonable notice, on the basis of a consistent course of dealing or on the basis of the common understanding of the parties. In addition, of course, as we have already seen at 5.1.2.2 and 5.2.4, a pre-contractual statement can be incorporated as a term of the contract by means such as the importance attached test and the collateral contract device.

5.3.1   Written documents which have been signed

Signature includes a hand-written signature and, in the context of electronic communications, electronic signatures (Electronic Communications Act 2000, s. 7, discussed at 4.5.5).

In *L'Estrange* v *E. Graucob Ltd* [1934] 2 KB 394, Scrutton LJ stated (at 403): 'When a document containing contractual terms is signed, then, in the absence of fraud, or, I will add, misrepresentation, the party signing it is bound, and it is wholly immaterial whether he has read the document or not.' This rule is an important buttress of contractual certainty and is a reflection of the objective approach to contract formation, since if the parties sign a document they are objectively to be taken to be agreeing to its terms. However, its unbending application has sometimes appeared to cause hardship. In part that is because unscrupulous businessmen have exploited the rule to take advantage of others, particularly consumers. In *L'Estrange v E. Graucob Ltd*, the plaintiff had bought a cigarette vending machine from the defendants. She had signed the defendants' order form, which contained a broad exemption from liability in very small print on poor quality paper. It was held that as the plaintiff had signed the written document, she was bound by its terms, including the exemption, although she had not read it.

The traditionally strict approach to signed documents was, however, disregarded in *Harvey v Ventilatorenfabrik Oelde GmbH* (1988) 8 Tr LR 138. In a contract of sale there was the usual exchange of documents comprising the contract. One half of what was otherwise a duplicate set contained additional terms in German. This document was signed by the plaintiff and returned to the defendants. The question arose whether the terms in German formed part of the contract. The Court of Appeal found that the circumstances, and especially the difference between the documents, justified the court enquiring whether the plaintiff had in fact assented to the German terms, even when he had signed the document. The Court took the view that its decision was consistent with *L'Estrange v E. Graucob Ltd*, in which it had been suggested that the strict approach to signed documents would not apply where the party claiming not to be bound was misled.

It is also important to bear in mind that there are some limitations on this principle in *L'Estrange v Graucob Ltd*, in addition to the limitation of instances of fraud or misrepresentation (see *Curtis v Chemical Cleaning and Dying Co.* [1951] 1 KB 805). Statute now regulates exemption clauses and, more generally, unfair terms in consumer contracts (see the Unfair Contract Terms Act 1977 (6.6.2), and the Unfair Terms in Consumer Contracts Regulations 1999 (6.6.3)). In addition, the document which is signed must be a document which one would expect to contain contractual conditions (e.g., *Grogan v Robin Meredith Plant Hire* [1996] CLC 1127 — signing a time sheet containing clauses could not amount to a binding variation of the contract terms because a time sheet was not a document which might be expected to contain such clauses).

On more than one occasion Lord Denning suggested that, in the case of particularly sweeping exclusion clauses, the law ought to impose on the offeror a more positive obligation to draw the attention of the offeree to the clause in question before being prepared to hold the offeree bound by it. In *Thornton v Shoe Lane Parking Ltd* [1971] 2 QB 163, he said: 'In order to give sufficient notice, it would need to be printed in red ink with a red hand pointing to it, or something equally startling.' (See also *J. Spurling Ltd v Bradshaw* [1956] 1 WLR 461.) It has always been assumed that in the context of signed written documents, this should mean that such unusual or onerous terms might need to be presented in a large size print or be placed in a box. However, in *Ocean Chemical Transport Inc. v Exnor Craggs Ltd* [2000] 1 All ER (Comm) 519 (MacDonald [1999] CLJ 413), the Court of Appeal had the opportunity to address the argument that the *Interfoto* test had to be applied even where the other party had signed the terms. The Court of Appeal suggested that that this would be the position only in an extreme case 'where a signature was obtained under pressure of time or other circumstances' *and* where the clause was particularly onerous or unusual in relation to the contract. However, on the facts of this case there was an express acknowledgement of the fact of incorporation, so that it could not be said that the party seeking to rely on the term had failed to bring it sufficiently to the notice of the other party. In addition, and probably most significantly, Evans LJ (with whose judgment the other members of the Court agreed) did not consider that the clause in question was 'in any way extreme or totally unexpected' in such a contract.

5.3.2 Incorporation of written terms into an oral contract

The practical difficulty is to establish precisely what terms have been agreed by the parties to an oral contract.

It may be alleged that terms on unsigned written documents (e.g., on a ticket or order form) have been incorporated as terms of an oral contract. In order for such terms to be effectively incorporated, they must be set out in a document which would be expected to contain contractual terms, and reasonable notice of the existence of the terms must have been given.

Contractual document In *Chapelton v Barry UDC* [1940] 1 KB 532, tickets for the hire of deckchairs were obtainable from the deckchair attendant. The plaintiff obtained tickets from the attendant. He did not notice that the tickets contained a clause purporting to exempt the council from any liability for accidents or damages arising from the hire of the deckchairs. The Court of Appeal held that this term on the ticket could not be relied on by the council since the ticket was a mere voucher or receipt for money paid rather than a contractual document.

There are two important factors to bear in mind when seeking to assess whether a written document, such as a ticket, constitutes a contractual document. First, the fact that a ticket or other document is called a receipt is not conclusive of the fact that it is non-contractual. Secondly, the time of the making of the contract appears to be important, since a document can constitute a contractual document only if it is delivered before the contract is formed. On the facts in *Chapelton*, there was a binding contract when the deckchair was removed from the pile. Since the ticket was not part of this contractual process and might be obtained some time later, it could only be a receipt for money paid. Of course, if the ticket were obtained from the attendant before selecting and removing the deckchair, it would seem to be a contractual document and its terms duly incorporated. This sort of distinction is unhelpful in terms of determining the terms of a contract.

It is recognised that some documents record performance of an existing contractual obligation rather than forming part of the making of the contract and evidencing its terms. Such documents are therefore not regarded as contractual documents, essentially because the contract has already been made. In *Grogan* v *Robin Meredith Plant Hire* [1996] CLC 1127, it was stated that invoices, time sheets or statements of account are not normally documents forming part of the making of a contract. However, it may well be the case that, rather than recording the existence of a contract, a particular invoice constitutes the offer to contract and clearly, in these circumstances, that invoice would be a contractual document.

5.3.3   Reasonable notice of the existence of the terms

It is a question of whether reasonable notice (in an objective sense) of the existence of the terms was given to the offeree before the time of accepting the offer. However, it is important to appreciate that the offeree does not need actual subjective knowledge of the terms in question. If the person receiving the ticket (or other written document) knows that it contains writing, he or she will be bound by the terms contained in the document, provided that it is a contractual document and provided that it is common knowledge that such writing contains terms and conditions (*per* Mellish LJ in *Parker* v *South Eastern Railway* (1877) 2 CPD 416). Nowadays it is common knowledge that tickets and similar documents generally do contain such conditions, and the test will therefore be whether notice of the conditions has been provided to people in general (*Thompson* v *London, Midland & Scottish Railway* [1930] 1 KB 41). No account will therefore be taken of the fact that the individual claimant is illiterate or unable to understand the language in which the terms are drafted, at least where this factor is not known to the party supplying the ticket or other document (*Geier* v *Kujawa Weston and Warne Bros (Transport) Ltd* [1970] 1 Lloyd's Rep 364).

It is also clearly recognised that terms can be incorporated by reference to another document in which they can be found, e.g., in the *Thompson* case the face of the ticket said 'see back', and on the back it stated that the ticket was issued subject to conditions set out in the timetables, available for purchase at 6*d*. These conditions were held to be incorporated. Although this is an extreme case, because the timetables were extremely bulky and relatively expensive to purchase, the principle of incorporation by reference remains a valid one.

Due to the need for reasonable notice to be given 'in time', the principles of offer and acceptance are important in this context. In *Olley* v *Marlborough Court Ltd* [1949] 1 KB 532, a hotel sought to exclude its liability for the loss of valuable personal possessions by a guest at the hotel by reference to an exclusion notice on the back of the hotel bedroom door. The contract had been made at the hotel reception desk before the offeree had any possible means of knowing about the purported exclusion of liability. The court found the notice to be ineffective because it was too late to be incorporated as a term of the contract.

Similarly, in *Grogan* v *Robin Meredith Plant Hire* [1996] CLC 1127, the agreement for the hire of a driver and machine was made over the telephone, whereas the Contractors' Plant Association Conditions were not introduced until two weeks later when the driver presented his time sheet, which referred to the work as being undertaken on the basis of these conditions. The Court of Appeal held that this notice was too late.

5.3.3.1 Tickets It has been suggested that printed notices contained in tickets are an exception to the general principle, in that they may be effective to exclude liability although not actually delivered to the purchaser until after the moment of agreement between the parties. Certainly the nineteenth-century ticket cases are not easy to explain. In *Parker v South Eastern Railway* (1877) 2 CPD 416, the railway company operated a left luggage office in which the plaintiff left a bag, paying the required fee and receiving in return a ticket. On the ticket were the words 'See Back', and on the back was a clause purporting to limit the company's liability in the case of lost luggage to £10. The plaintiff's bag was lost; its contents were worth more than £10. The court found the clause on the ticket sufficient to limit the company's liability as stated.

As discussed above, Mellish LJ took the view that printing on a ticket would be incorporated into a contract provided that a reasonable person would appreciate that there was writing containing conditions on the ticket. This view appears to neglect the issue of whether such notice as there was came too late, since it is common for the point of offer and acceptance to precede the issuing of the ticket. However, in *Thornton v Shoe Lane Parking Ltd* [1971] 2 QB 163, Lord Denning explained the process of offer and acceptance in ticket cases so that the result could coincide with the position in *Parker v S.E. Railway* and other nineteenth-century ticket cases where incorporation was achieved. According to Lord Denning, the issue of the ticket is the offer, and acceptance occurs when the customer takes the ticket and retains it without objection. On this basis there is incorporation in time of any terms printed on the ticket. Lord Denning acknowledged that this interpretation was based on a 'fiction', because it assumes that the customer will examine the ticket and decide whether to accept the terms or return it without incurring any liability. Of course, there must be the possibility in theory for the terms to be examined in advance of conclusion of the contract if this principle is to apply.

In *Thornton v Shoe Lane Parking Ltd*, there was a notice at the entrance to a barrier-operated car park which stated that parking was to be 'at owner's risk'. An automatic barrier controlled entry to the car park. When the motorist drove up to the barrier, a machine dispensed a ticket. This ticket stated that it was 'issued subject to conditions displayed on the premises'. Inside the car park there was a notice excluding liability for personal injury to customers. The Court of Appeal held that the exemption on the ticket was too late, because the contract for the use of the car park was concluded when the motorist drove up to the barrier and activated the machine. Lord Denning said he was not prepared to apply the nineteenth-century ticket cases in the context of a ticket issued by an automatic machine. Instead, he stated that the machine is making a standing offer which the customer accepts when he does whatever is required to activate the machine, e.g., by putting money into a slot. The net effect of this analysis was that anything on the ticket dispensed by the machine would not be incorporated because it would be too late.

5.3.3.2 The stricter approach for onerous or unusual terms In *Thornton v Shoe Lane Parking* the notice at the entrance ('parking at owner's risk') was in time, but it was construed so as not to extend to exempt the car park from liability in respect of personal injury. This was because it was said to be an unusual liability to exclude in these circumstances and therefore needed explicitly to be drawn to the customer's attention in order to be incorporated (see 5.3.1 and Lord Denning's suggestion of the use of red ink with a red hand pointing to the unusual term).

This approach involves applying different standards of incorporation to different terms, and it was adopted by the Court of Appeal in *Interfoto Picture Library Ltd v Stiletto Visual Programmes Ltd* [1988] QB 433. The term in question involved a fee of £5 per day per transparency for their late return. The Court of Appeal regarded the clause as particularly onerous and unusual, and argued that such a clause would not be regarded as fairly brought to the notice of the other party 'unless it was drawn to his attention in the most explicit way'. However, whereas Dillon LJ concluded that for this reason the clause was not incorporated, Bingham LJ considered that, although it was incorporated, it could not have any effect in the circumstances of the case.

The difficulties of this approach of differing standards of incorporation are well illustrated by the decisions of the members of the Court of Appeal in *AEG (UK) Ltd v Logic Resource Ltd* [1996] CLC 265. The majority (Hirst and Waite LJJ) held that in a purchase contract to supply goods for export, a clause which stated that the purchaser was to return defective goods at his own expense was an onerous and unusual term, so that it would be incorporated only if 'fairly and reasonably brought to the attention' of the purchaser. However, Hobhouse LJ gave a dissenting judgment on this issue on the basis that this type of clause was commonly found in printed conditions. Hobhouse LJ considered (at 277) that the correct approach would be to consider 'the kind of clause' in issue and to consider whether a particular clause was onerous or unusual only in the context of this kind of clause. He considered it wrong to apply the *Interfoto* test to the specific terms of the particular clause in question, on the basis that this amounted to 'completely distorting the contractual relationship between the parties and the ordinary mechanisms of making contracts'. He therefore distinguished both *Interfoto*, which was described as 'an extortionate clause', and *Thornton v Shoe Lane Parking*, where the clause related to personal injuries, regarded as something totally different to the subject-matter of a car parking contract.

Therefore, the real difficulty with this approach will be to decide whether a clause is onerous and unusual so that the higher standard of incorporation is required. The result of such a vague test will inevitably be much uncertainty over appropriate drafting of terms. These problems were highlighted by a statement in the judgment of Evans LJ (with whose judgment the other members of the Court of Appeal agreed) in *Ocean Chemical Transport Inc. v Exnor Craggs Ltd* [2000] 1 All ER (Comm) 519 (at 529):

> It seems to me that the question of incorporation must always depend upon the meaning and effect of the clause in question. It may be that the type of clause is relevant. It may be that the effect of the particular clause in the

particular case is relevant. That, of course, was the division of opinion in the *AEG* case.

In the *Ocean Chemical* case, Evans LJ suggested (at 530) what he referred to as a broad formulation applying to all clauses, namely 'the question is whether the defendants have discharged the duty which lies upon them of bringing the existence of the clause upon which they rely (and if [counsel] is right, of the effect of that particular clause) to the notice of the other party in the circumstances of the particular case'. This applies one test, but it is inevitably no more certain in terms of outcome. It is also significant that Evans LJ rejected the approach of Hobhouse LJ in *AEG* v *Logic Resources* and required the *particular* clause to be unusual or onerous rather than that any clause of this type would statisfy this test.

5.3.3.3 Internet contracts Before leaving this section, it is as well to consider the question of incorporation of terms and conditions into contracts concluded on the Internet. A supplier will need to ensure that the customer had reasonable notice of applicable terms and conditions before contracting. Normally this will be achieved by requiring the customer to click on an icon to signal his agreement to the terms and conditions which are displayed (but seldom read). The same need to ensure a higher degree of notice for unusual terms will also apply.

5.3.4 Consistent course of dealing

Where the parties deal with each other on a regular basis, on standard terms and conditions, even if notice of the terms was not given on the particular occasion, they may be incorporated into the particular contract on the basis of previous course of dealing between the parties (*Hardwick Game Farm* v *Suffolk Agricultural Poultry Producers Association* [1969] 2 AC 31). Nevertheless, the party seeking to rely on a course of dealing for the incorporation of terms will have to sustain the burden of proving that the course of past conduct has been *sufficiently consistent* to give rise to the implication that in similar circumstances a similar contractual result will follow. In *McCutcheon* v *David MacBrayne Ltd* [1964] 1 WLR 125, the plaintiff had used the defendants' ferry service for his car on several occasions in the past. Sometimes he had been asked to sign a note containing an exclusion clause, but sometimes he had not. On the occasion in question the ferry sank, and no note had been signed. The defendants were unable to rely on the course of dealing to incorporate an exclusion clause into the contract since it was inconsistent.

A recent example of incorporation based on previous course of dealing is provided by the decision of the Court of Appeal in *Petrotrade Inc.* v *Texaco Ltd* [2000] CLC 1341. The contract was entered into by telephone and the basic terms agreed. Subsequently, a telex was sent which contained Petrotrade's standard terms, which included a clause providing for payment to be made without deduction or set-off. It was alleged that these terms were incorporated on the basis of the previous dealings between the parties. The Court of

Appeal found that over the 13 months prior to this contract there had been five other contracts between the parties for the sale of the same or similar products by Petrotrade, and where the transactions had been confirmed on the same terms including this anti-set off clause. Accordingly, given this previous course of dealing, both parties made the agreement on the basis that the contract would again be subject to these terms.

The decisions in course of dealing cases turn on their particular facts, but it should be easier to establish the necessary consistency in the course of dealing between commercial parties (as in *Petrotrade* v *Texaco*) than as against a consumer. For example, in *Hollier* v *Rambler Motors (AMC) Ltd* [1972] 2 QB 71, the Court of Appeal held that a garage's standard terms were not incorporated into a repair contract with a customer because there was not a consistent course of dealing between the parties using these terms. The customer had used the garage for repairs on only three or four occasions in a five-year period.

5.3.5 Common knowledge

In very limited circumstances the courts may be willing to incorporate a term into a contract without actual notice and without any prior course of dealing. The courts will incorporate terms in these circumstances only where there is some common basis shared by the parties which justifies the presumption that the parties have a common understanding that the terms will apply. The common basis will usually be supplied by the fact that both parties belong to and are familiar with the terms of a particular trade, and indeed the terms in question may need to be standard conditions issued by a trade association.

An example of incorporation in this form can be found in *British Crane Hire Corporation Ltd* v *Ipswich Plant Hire Ltd* [1975] QB 303. This case involved a clause in a standard form hire contract between two businesses, which were both in the plant hire business. Although notice was given too late in relation to the particular contract, the terms were held to be incorporated because both parties knew of these printed conditions which were in common use in the plant hire business.

This case can usefully be compared with *Grogan* v *Robin Meredith Plant Hire* [1996] CLC 1127, where the judge rejected an argument to the effect that although notice of the terms had been given too late on this occasion (5.3.3), they could be incorporated based on the common understanding of the parties. The judge appeared to regard the terms in question as not being used so frequently and commonly as to be common knowledge within the industry. This seems doubtful in view of the decision in *British Crane Hire*, and the significant distinguishing factor may be the fact that the parties in *Grogan* were not operating in the same business. Only one party was in the business of hiring plant, the other party laid pipes.

5.3.6 Incorporation of written terms in practice

It is convenient for the purposes of presentation to treat the various means of incorporation of terms as conceptually distinct categories. In practice, the lines between categories may be blurred, and the courts may be willing to treat a term as incorporated because an argument may be made for that conclusion under more than one head. A good example is *Circle Freight International Ltd* v *Medeast Gulf Exports Ltd* [1988] 2 Lloyd's Rep 427, 428–33. Taylor LJ found an exemption clause to have been incorporated on three distinct grounds: incorporation by reference to the standard conditions of the Institute of Freight Forwarders; a course of dealing over 11 previous transactions; and trade usage known to everybody in the particular business.

5.4 PROMISSORY AND CONTINGENT OBLIGATIONS DISTINGUISHED

In ordinary language a condition is a stipulation of something which must be fulfilled before further action will take place or results will be achieved. The law has attributed more specific meanings to the word, and it is important to distinguish between these meanings.

A *condition precedent* is a stipulation of a state of affairs which must be achieved before any contractual liability, or possibly any further contractual liability, will be incurred. In some circumstances the parties agree that a contract shall come into existence between them upon the occurrence of some event which is uncertain, but remain free to withdraw from that agreement until the event occurs (*Pym* v *Campbell* (1856) 6 E & B 370). More usually, however, the main contractual obligations do not come into force until the condition is satisfied, but the parties are contractually bound not to withdraw from the conditional agreement (*Smith* v *Butler* [1900] 1 QB 694). In these circumstances the parties may be under an obligation not to impede the occurrence of the condition (*Mackay* v *Dick* (1881) 6 App Cas 251). Sometimes there may even be an obligation to use reasonable efforts to cause the event upon which the contract is conditioned to occur, and failure to use such efforts is a breach (*Hargreaves Transport Ltd* v *Lynch* [1969] 1 WLR 215).

A *condition subsequent* is a stipulation of a state of affairs which will cause existing contractual obligations to terminate (*Head* v *Tattersall* (1871) LR 7 Ex 7). A modern example of such a condition might be a provision in a long-term supply agreement that the contract should terminate when the price of the goods in question reaches a stated amount.

Conditions precedent and subsequent, which are sometimes collectively called 'contingent' conditions, impose no positive obligation to ensure absolutely that the condition does (or does not) materialise. They must, therefore, both be distinguished from *promissory conditions*, under which one party undertakes that a certain result will be achieved, and guarantees that undertaking by his or her promise. Failure to achieve the promised result is a breach. Thus, a promissory condition is the type of condition which is used to express a primary obligation of the contract. Where the word 'condition' is used without qualification, it is almost certainly being used in the sense of a promissory condition, and it is in that sense that it is being referred to in this chapter and in Chapter 7, where breach of contract is discussed.

Promissory obligations can be classified as being conditions, innominate (or intermediate) terms or warranties. The significance of this distinction concerns the remedies available for breach of each type of obligation, and this issue is therefore considered in detail in Chapter 7 ('Discharge on Breach'). However, in the broadest terms, conditions are important terms which are said 'to go to the root of the contract'; and if they are broken, the non-breaching party will have the option of terminating the contract for the future or affirming it, in addition to the remedy of damages. Conditions can be directly contrasted with warranties, which are less important terms; and the breach of such a term can be adequately compensated with a remedy of damages so that there is no option for the non-breaching party to terminate or affirm. Innominate (or intermediate) terms lie somewhere between these two, in that the breach of such a term may or may not give rise to a right to terminate depending on the seriousness of the effects of the breach. If the effects are serious, there is an option to terminate or affirm; whereas if the effects are not serious, the remedy is limited to damages only.

5.5   IMPLIED TERMS

5.5.1 Introduction

In many contracts, although the main primary obligations are contained in express terms, the parties do not express all the primary obligations or do not provide for every eventuality. The device of the implied term is used to fill the gaps in the parties' contract, or to achieve some form of protection for a party as a matter of policy.

Terms may be implied in fact or in law, and may be implied by the courts or by statute. To take a simple example, when a student goes into a shop to buy a new textbook, the bookseller and the student do not discuss or express any terms relating to the quality of the book to be sold. Nevertheless, if the book proved to have been bound with an important section missing, the student would less than happy if he or she had no remedy against the bookseller. On the contrary, it is understood that what is being sold must be a book which is in the state a book of that description would normally be in. That understanding is incorporated into the contract by means of an implied term (in the particular case, a term derived from statute: s. 14(2) of the SGA 1979, imposing an obligation that the goods will be of satisfactory quality — see 5.5.3.2).

The device of implying terms into contracts to fill gaps in the express terms has existed since at least the early nineteenth century (*cf. Hutton* v *Warren* (1836) 1 M & W 466). It is something of an embarrassment to the classical theory of contract, which attributes the source of all contractual obligations to the expression of the will of the parties. At first it was maintained that the implication of terms was only ever an exercise of construction of the facts to seek the parties' intentions. In other words, implied terms were consistent with classical theory since they merely filled gaps where the parties' will had operated but had not been expressed. However, it is no longer possible to accept that terms are implied only when the parties had intended such terms but have simply failed to express them. It is true that some terms are implied as 'one-off' terms which seem inevitably to have been intended to supplement the express terms of the contract (5.5.2). It is equally clear, however, that some terms are implied irrespective of the intentions of the parties (5.5.3). In the example above of the sale of a book, the obligation to meet a certain quality standard is said to derive from an implied term, but it may not be certain that the bookseller intended such a term. Indeed, it may be more honest simply to say that in that situation a positive obligation of the law of contract is imposed on the seller, whatever his intentions (*cf.* Stephenson LJ in *Mears* v *Safecar Securities Ltd* [1983] QB 54). The notion of an *imposed* obligation is all the more persuasive because in our example it will be impossible for the seller to exclude liability for the obligation as against a consumer (s. 6(2), UCTA 1977; 6.6.2.4).

In practice, in many cases the courts do not distinguish between terms implied in fact and terms implied in law, and some categories of implied term, which once might have been regarded as implied in fact, are probably now treated as types of imposed obligation (5.5.4).

This development has taken on greater significance since the Privy Council asserted, in *Tai Hing Cotton Mill Ltd* v *Liu Chong Hing Bank Ltd* [1986] AC 80, that the law should not seek to develop tortious duties where the parties are in a contractual relationship (although in this same decision Lord Scarman doubted whether implied terms of the contract were properly to be regarded as 'imposed' obligations). The Privy Council's view on the relationship between contracts and tortious duties was adopted for English law by the Court of Appeal in *Johnstone* v *Bloomsbury Health Authority* [1992] 1 QB 333. It should be noted, however, that the House of Lords has rejected the idea that there cannot be a tortious duty of care where there is a contractual relationship between the parties (*Henderson* v *Merrett Syndicates Ltd* [1995] 2 AC 145). A question which remains to be explored more fully is the extent to which tortious duties and contractual implied terms may in such circumstances differ in scope. The answer may depend upon the type of implied term in question (see 5.5.2 and 5.5.3).

Whatever the conceptual basis of implied terms of this type (and no doubt the prevailing political philosophy of the 1980s discouraged courts from wishing to appear to regulate market-based transactions by imposing terms), in practice the courts have inevitably been drawn into a practice of seeking to ensure that contracts of a recognisable and frequently occurring type conform to general expectations of what obligations such contracts should contain. It is important to realise, however, that while the courts today may be more willing to imply terms than once they were, there are important limits on the implied term device. In the first place, the greater the number of gaps in an alleged contract, the more reluctant the court may be to 'write the parties' contract' for them (*cf.* Lord Wright in *Hillas & Co. Ltd* v *Arcos Ltd* (1932) 147 LT 503: see 3.1.1). Secondly, and perhaps paradoxically, where the parties' contract consists of a detailed set of written terms, the courts may be unwilling to add to those terms by implication, except in so far as the law generally imposes obligations in the type of situation in question (*Shell UK Ltd* v *Lostock Garage Ltd* [1976] 1 WLR 1187).

This also raises the question of the relationship between express and implied terms. An implied term cannot co-exist with an express term which flatly contradicts it; but where the exact scope of an express term leaves some latitude in its application (such as in the form of a discretion), it may be narrowed or widened by an implied term (*per* Browne-Wilkinson V-C in *Johnstone* v *Bloomsbury Health Authority* [1992] 1 QB 333 at 350–51).

In *Times Newspapers Ltd* v *Weidenfeld & Nicolson Ltd* (unreported), 28 March 2001, it was held that a court should not be too ready to imply terms where care had been taken over the drafting of a written agreement with reference to another written agreement. The case concerned an alleged breach of contract by the defendant publisher, which had purchased the publication rights in the proposed memoirs of Sir Edward Heath. The claimant had bought the serialisation rights from the defendant but, by the time the memoirs were ready, the defendant had terminated its agreement to purchase the memoirs from Sir Edward's company. The claimant argued that the serialisation agreement contained an implied term that the defendant would do nothing in relation to the main publishing agreement which would put *The Times* serialisation beyond its power. However, this was held to be too wide, because it amounted to saying that the claimant had to be given the serial rights in any book of Heath memoirs, irrespective of the identity of the publisher. This was also inconsistent with the express provisions of the serialisation agreement, which defined the serial rights as limited to rights in a book to be published by the defendant in accordance with the publishing agreement. Accordingly, no such term could be implied.

5.5.2   Terms implied in fact

Terms are implied in fact on the basis of an intention imputed to the parties from the actual circumstances. Thus, there is no question of imposing a legal obligation irrespective of the parties' intentions. Such a term will be implied only if the contract would be incomplete without it. In the words of Lord Cross in *Liverpool City Council* v *Irwin* [1977] AC 239, at 258:

> What the court is being in effect asked to do is to rectify a particular — often a very detailed — contract by inserting in it a term which the parties have not expressed. Here it is not enough for the court to say that the suggested term is a reasonable one the presence of which would make the contract a better or fairer one; it must be able to say that the insertion of the term is necessary.

In the Court of Appeal, Lord Denning MR had suggested that such a term might be implied where it was just and reasonable in the circumstances. The House of Lords rejected his suggestion, although some of their Lordships applied a similar test to the separate category of terms implied in law (5.5.3).

The very strict approach to implied terms based on the particular circumstances of the contractual relationship was confirmed by the House of Lords in *Hughes* v *Greenwich London Borough Council* [1993] 3 WLR 821. According to Lord Lowry, such an implied term will be found to exist only where there is a compelling reason, or, put another way, where it is essential; quoting Farwell LJ in *Devonald* v *Rosser* [1906] 2 KB 728 at 743, the term will be implied only where it is one 'such as the parties, being businessmen, must have intended to make'.

The classic test for the implication of a term in fact is often known as 'the officious bystander test' and derives from *Shirlaw* v *Southern Foundries (1926) Ltd* [1939] 2 KB 206. MacKinnon LJ said:

> Prima facie that which in any contract is left to be implied and need not be expressed is something so obvious that it goes without saying; so that, if, while the parties were making their bargain, an officious bystander were to suggest some express provision for it in their agreement, they would testily suppress him with a common 'Oh, of course!'.

The nature of those terms which may be implied in fact is very varied, although in practice the number of terms so implied is relatively few. Any term which although not expressed is obviously necessary to make the contract work may be implied, and it is impossible to give any guidelines on what is or is not likely to be accepted by the courts. On the other hand, it must be recognised that the so-called 'officious bystander' test stated above imposes a very strict standard for the imposition of terms (*cf.* Lord Wilberforce in *Liverpool City Council* v *Irwin*). Attempts to have terms implied on this basis often fail on the simple ground that while one of the parties would clearly have assented to the term if it had been proposed, the same cannot unquestionably be said of the other party (see *Shell UK Ltd* v *Lostock Garage Ltd* [1976] 1 WLR 1187). Another reason why the suggested term was not implied in the *Shell* case was that it could not 'be formulated with sufficient precision', and this may be an inherent problem with terms implied in fact. Alternatively, attempts to imply terms on this basis may fail because of the rule of construction, referred to above (5.5.1), that where the contract consists of a carefully negotiated and detailed set of written terms, any omission must be deemed to be deliberate and to reflect the parties' intentions (e.g., *Ali* v *Christian Salvesen Food Services Ltd* [1997] 1 All ER 721).

5.5.3   Terms implied in law

Terms implied in law do not depend upon any intention imputed to the parties. They consist of legal obligations generally imposed on one of the parties in a common contractual relationship, without reference to the particular circumstances (except perhaps to determine whether a contrary intention has been expressed). Some such legal obligations are imposed by the courts; many, although originally imposed by the courts, have now been given statutory force.

5.5.3.1 Terms implied in law by the courts Lord Denning MR described the process of implication of terms in law in *Shell UK Ltd* v *Lostock Garages Ltd* [1976] 1 WLR 1187. He said that it occurs in all common contractual relationships, such as seller and buyer, master and servant, landlord and tenant, and so on. He continued at 1196:

> In such relationships the problem is not solved by asking: what did the parties intend? Or, would they have unhesitatingly agreed to it, if asked? It is to be solved by asking: has the law already defined the obligation or the extent of it? If so, let it be followed. If not, look to see what would be reasonable in the general run of such cases . . . and then say what the obligation shall be.

The basis for the implication of terms in this way appears to be the desire to regulate certain common types of contract. It is done so that one party does not take unfair advantage of another, and so that adequate protection is given to both parties even when, as is often the case with such common contracts, little time is spent on detailed negotiation of the terms. Thus, the common contracts have taken on a standard content, by implication of terms in law. As is apparent from the passage quoted from Lord Denning MR above, in the case of terms implied in law, the finding of a term in one case may be binding in terms of precedent in subsequent cases. Such a position would be inconceivable in the case of terms implied in fact.

The leading case on legal obligations imposed on a contracting party by the courts is *Liverpool City Council* v *Irwin* [1977] AC 239. The Council let flats and maisonettes in a tower block to tenants. The lifts and rubbish chutes of the tower block constantly broke down. The tenancy agreement imposed certain obligations on tenants, but was silent about the obligations of the Council to maintain the building. The appellants withheld their rent in protest at the Council's failure to maintain the building properly. The Council brought an action to obtain possession of the appellants' maisonette, and the appellants counter-claimed for breach of an implied obligation to keep the block in proper repair.

As was noted earlier (5.5.2), the House of Lords was unwilling to imply a term in fact into the particular agreement. But their Lordships were willing to imply, as a necessary incident of all tenancy agreements in which the tenants are granted the use in common of stairways, corridors, lifts, etc., an obligation on the landlord 'to take reasonable care to keep in reasonable repair and usability' the common parts (*per* Lord Wilberforce).

According to Lord Cross, the test to be applied in deciding whether to imply such a term generally in all contracts of a particular type is 'whether in the general run of such cases the term in question would be one which it would be reasonable to insert'. Lord Wilberforce suggested that the test was one of necessity, but the term which he implied was not absolutely necessary, although the tenancy agreements would have been unreasonable without it. Lord Cross's test was followed in *Shell UK Ltd* v *Lostock Garages Ltd* (above), as appeared logical since the distinction between necessary on the particular facts and reasonable in a particular category of contracts seemed to embody the distinction between terms implied in fact and terms implied in law. However, subsequent authority suggests that it is Lord Wilberforce's test of necessity that has prevailed. Lord Scarman in *Tai Hing Cotton Mill Ltd v Liu Chong Hing Bank Ltd* [1986] AC 80 at 107 and Lord Bridge in *Scally* v *Southern Health and Social Services Board* [1992] 1 AC 294 at 307, both refer to terms which are a 'necessary incident' of a ('definable category of', *per* Lord Bridge) contractual relationship. Lord Bridge's formulation was warmly approved by Lord Woolf in *Spring* v *Guardian Assurance plc* [1995] 2 AC 296.

Despite what may be seen as an unfortunate parallelism of language, it seems that 'necessary on the facts' and 'necessary incident of a definable category of contractual relationship' must have different meanings. The notion of 'necessary incident' draws upon a much wider set of criteria to determine its meaning, and it must be supposed that ultimately terms implied in law on the basis of being a necessary incident of such contracts are founded upon reasonable expectation (see further, A. Phang, 'Implied terms in English law' [1993] JBL 242). Lord Woolf's short speech in *Spring* v *Guardian Assurance plc* provides an excellent demonstration of the implication of a term under this rule. He refers expressly to what is 'normal practice' in contracts of the particular kind, and to the fact that it would not be right to expect the party to enter into an engagement of that kind except on the basis of the proposed implied term. This is very much the language of reasonable expectation.

5.5.3.2   Terms imposed by statute

Certain obligations, which were at one time imposed by the courts, have now been given statutory force. Most important among these are terms relating to quality in the case of sale or supply of goods, and those relating to the standard of care in contracts for services. The SGA 1979, s. 14 (as amended by the Sale and Supply of Goods Act 1994) provides:

> (2)   Where the seller sells goods in the course of a business, there is an implied term that the goods supplied under the contract are of satisfactory quality.
> (2A)   For the purposes of this Act, goods are of satisfactory quality if they meet the standards that a reasonable person would regard as satisfactory, taking account of any description of the goods, the price (if relevant) and all the other relevant circumstances.
> (2B)   For the purposes of this Act, the quality of goods includes their state and condition and the following (among others) are in appropriate cases aspects of the quality of goods—
> (a)   fitness for all the purposes for which goods of the kind in question are commonly supplied,
> (b)   appearance and finish,
> (c)   freedom from minor defects,
> (d)   safety, and
> (e)   durability.

(2C)   The term implied by subsection (2) above does not extend to any matter making the goods unsatisfactory—
    (a)   which is specifically drawn to the buyer's attention before the contract is made,
    (b)   where the buyer examines the goods before the contract is made, which that examination ought to reveal, or
    (c)   in the case of a contract for sale by sample, which would have been apparent on a reasonable examination of the sample.

Section 14(2B)(e) introduces an element of durability into quality, which it could not be said was always present under the old law.

Under s. 14(3), where the buyer makes known to the seller a particular (as opposed to the common) purpose for buying the goods in question, there is a further implied term that the goods be fit for that particular purpose. Similar implied terms apply to contracts for the supply of goods other than by way of sale (e.g., goods to be incorporated into building work being done) under s. 4 of the Supply of Goods and Services Act 1982 (which was also amended by the 1994 Act).

Contracts for the supply of services were until comparatively recently the domain of the common law as far as implied terms governing standards of performance were concerned (*cf. Lister* v *Romford Ice and Cold Storage Co. Ltd* [1957] AC 555). However, such contracts are now also regulated by statute. Under s. 13 of the Supply of Goods and Services Act 1982, there is an implied term that the supplier of services will carry out the service with reasonable care and skill. It should be noted that this standard is different from that applying to the sale or supply of goods. In the case of the latter the obligation to meet the required standard is absolute, and it will not be a defence to a claim of breach of the implied term of, for example, satisfactory quality, that the seller did his best to supply goods of that quality. In the case of the supply of services, however, the performance obligation will be met if the person performing the services uses reasonable care and skill. There is no guarantee that a particular result will be achieved (see 7.2.1). The exact scope of the obligation of reasonable care and skill depends upon the obligations expressly undertaken by contract.

In *Wilson* v *Best Travel Ltd* [1993] 1 All ER 353, the defendant tour operator advertised a holiday in Greece in its brochure, which indicated that the tour operator inspected all accommodation offered as part of package holidays. The plaintiff was seriously injured in a fall against a glass door, which met Greek but not British safety standards. Phillips J rejected the notion that there was a general duty to provide 'safe' accommodation to be implied into every package holiday contract. But where the contract included the service of inspection of properties offered in the brochure, such inspection must be carried out with reasonable care and skill with a view to matters of safety, amongst other things. In this case the judge found the duty to have been satisfied. It seems, however, that the judge was willing to contemplate that no such duty would have arisen if the contract had not expressly indicated that such inspection would take place. It should be noted that obligations of suppliers of package holidays are affected and largely increased by the Package Travel, Package Holidays and Package Tours Regulations 1992 (see below).

5.5.3.3 The increasing significance of statutory duties

Regulation of contracts belonging to definable categories, and which occur frequently, by means of statutory imposition of terms, appears to be an increasing phenomenon. Although Parliament only rarely finds time for the kind of law reform such legislation requires, there is no doubt that the particular policy of consumer protection is more likely to be accommodated within the Parliamentary timetable than more arcane matters, not least because electors take an interest in it.

There is a further source of law reform the importance of which must not be overlooked. As part of the programme of harmonisation of the law of Member States in order to ensure that there is a single market for goods and services, the European Union is addressing the question of the content of typical contracts throughout the Member States, essentially with a view to protecting consumers. So, for example, the United Kingdom Package Travel, Package Holidays and Package Tours Regulations 1992 (SI 1992 No. 3288) implement EC Directive 90/314. The aim of this Directive was to standardise the law relating to package holidays and the contracts governing them in all Member States. (It should be noted that law reform of this kind, implementing EU directives in the field of consumer protection, is achievable by statutory instrument (by virtue of s. 2(2) of the European Communities Act 1972).) Other examples of relevant European directives include Directive 1993/13/EC on unfair terms in consumer contracts (now implemented as the Unfair Terms in Consumer Contracts Regulations 1999 (SI 1999 No. 2083); 6.6.3) and Directive 1997/7/EC relating to consumer protection in distance selling contracts (implemented by the Consumer Protection (Distance Selling) Regulations 2000 (SI 2000 No. 2334)).

5.5.4 Blurring the categories

Although two distinct categories of implied terms (in fact and in law) are now recognised by high authority (cf. *Liverpool City Council* v *Irwin* [1977] AC 239), it may be that the categories are not as distinct as the courts make out. For example, in *Wilson* v *Best Travel Ltd* [1993] 1 All ER 353, Phillips J expressed agreement with the judge in an unreported case who had found implication of a particular term 'neither necessary nor obvious nor reasonable', without specifying the proper test for implying a term in the particular circumstances.

Two particular types of implied term appear to embody elements of both categories. The earliest forms of implied term were those implied by custom. Thus, in *Hutton* v *Warren* (1836) 1 M & W 466, the court implied a term into an agricultural lease that upon quitting tenants were entitled to an allowance for seed and labour, on the basis of a custom which was said to be incorporated into all such contracts unless altered by them. It was once thought that such terms were incorporated by virtue of what it might be assumed in all the circumstances must have been the intention of the parties, treating them as a species of term implied in fact. Today, the incorporation of customary terms, especially those in general use in a particular trade, may owe more to the courts' desire to regulate the content of contracts by encouraging the use of standardised terms. Such an approach would be more closely akin to that of terms implied in law. For example, in *British Crane Hire Corporation Ltd* v *Ipswich Plant Hire Ltd* [1975] QB 303 (see also 5.3.5), the Court of Appeal held that the contract was subject to terms not seen by the offeree before the time of contracting but which were a version of the 'Contractors' Plant Association' terms which were customarily used in the particular trade, and with which both parties would have been familiar since they were both in the plant hire business. The term in question related to liability for the cost of recovering a crane if it got bogged down in soft ground. It is doubtful, however, whether it would have satisfied the strict test for implication of terms in fact (see 5.5.2).

A fruitful source of implied terms has been the so-called 'business efficacy' rule, first articulated in *The Moorcock* (1889) 14 PD 64. The plaintiffs had agreed with the defendants that the plaintiffs' ship should load and unload at the defendants' wharf on the Thames. Both parties knew that the ship would settle on the riverbed at low tide, but the defendants had not expressly guaranteed the good condition of the riverbed. The ship was damaged while at the wharf when it settled on hard ground rather than on mud. The question was whether there was an implied term in the contract to take reasonable care to see that the berth at the wharf was safe. The Court found such a term to exist. Bowen LJ said (at 68):

> An implied warranty, or as it is called a covenant in law, as distinguished from an express contract or express warranty, really is in all cases founded upon the presumed intention of the parties, and upon reason. The implication which the law draws from what must obviously have been the intention of the parties, the law draws with the object of giving efficacy to the transaction and preventing such a failure of consideration as cannot have been within the contemplation of either side.

These 'business efficacy' implied terms have always been regarded as examples of terms implied in fact, and the references to what is necessary to make the transaction work, and to presumed intention, support that idea (see 5.5.2). However, Bowen LJ said that such terms are also based on 'reason', which is the test normally associated with terms implied in law, and which has specifically been rejected in the case of terms implied in fact (*cf. Liverpool City Council* v *Irwin* [1977] AC 239).

5.5.5   Classification of implied terms

Just as express terms may be classified according to their relative importance (5.4 and 7.5.3), so some implied terms are more important than others. The

SGA 1979 employs the expression 'implied term', but it goes on to specify more precisely the type of obligation. So, the implied terms of satisfactory quality and fitness for purpose in s. 14 are said to be conditions (s. 14(6)). If s. 15A of the 1979 Act (inserted by the Sale and Supply of Goods Act 1994) applies to the sale, the position may be different. Section 15A can be expressly or impliedly ousted (s. 15A(2)). Section 15A(1) provides that where the buyer is a non-consumer and there is a breach of ss. 13, 14 or 15 (so-called breaches of condition), such a breach *may* instead be treated as a breach of warranty (so that the only remedy will be damages) if the breach is so slight that it would be unreasonable to reject the goods (i.e., unreasonable to exercise the normal remedy of terminating the contract). Putting convoluted drafting into plain language: in consumer contracts these implied terms are conditions; in non-consumer contracts they may be treated as warranties if the breach is so slight that it would be unreasonable to reject the goods. (For a discussion of the definition of 'consumer', see 6.6.2.4.)

Not all implied obligations in the sales legislation are conditions; for example, the implied term that the goods in question are free of any charge or encumbrance and that the buyer has a right to quiet possession is expressed to be a 'warranty' (s. 12(5A)). On the other hand, s. 13 of the Supply of Goods and Services Act 1982, which imposes an obligation of reasonable care and skill in the supply of services, refers only to an 'implied term'. It must be assumed that the statutory intention was for this term to be treated by the courts as innominate, on the basis that it is the type of term where breach may sometimes result in serious damage and sometimes trivial damage. Except in the case of statutory implied terms, there is no reason for prior classification of implied terms, since the terms are not known to the parties until the time of litigation. There is, therefore, no requirement of certainty or predictability of the effect of breach of such terms, since, being implied, they cannot be relied upon in the course of a party's planning. The court is free simply to indicate the type of term when specifying the term to be implied in any given case. It seems likely that in practice the courts will do so only after considering the consequences of the breach which has been found to have occurred (see generally, 7.5.3).

B.   INTERPRETATION

Just as statutes inevitably require interpretation by the courts to overcome the inherent inability of language to capture a single meaning representing the intention of Parliament, so for similar reasons the parties' contract may also require interpretation in order to ascertain its meaning before it is capable of being enforced. Since the modern rules of interpretation are based on the law of the nineteenth century, which in turn was based on a theory of contractual liability created by the will of the parties (1.4.2.2), the basic rule is that the court must find the intention of the parties. Traditionally, it was considered that, as a result of the parol evidence rule, the courts were, in general terms, limited in the search for intention to consideration of the contract document alone. In particular, as a general rule it is not possible to have regard to the parties' negotiations or subsequent conduct.

In *Lovell & Christmas Ltd* v *Wall* (1911) 104 LT 85, at 88, Cozens-Hardy MR said

> It is irrelevant and improper to ask what the parties, prior to the execution of the instrument, intended or understood . . . [U]nless the case can be brought within some or one of [the] exceptions, it is the duty of the court, which is presumed to understand the English language, to construe the document according to the ordinary grammatical meaning of the words used therein, and without reference to anything which has previously passed between the parties to it.

The reason for not allowing recourse to the negotiations to establish intention was explained in *Prenn* v *Simmonds* [1971] 1 WLR 1381. Lord Wilberforce said that 'such evidence is unhelpful' because only when the contract is finally made is there a consensus, and until that time the parties' respective intentions may change, or be refined. There can be no guarantee, therefore, that an intention appearing during negotiations has remained constant until the time of contracting. In those circumstances it is thought safer to rely on the words of the document alone.

Traditionally, however, there were three recognised exceptions where it was permissible to go outside the document and introduce extrinsic evidence to establish meaning. The first exception is perhaps the most obvious, namely where the words in question have a technical (or other special) meaning. It is clear that this remains the position. The other exceptions required an examination of the purpose and background to the document (the so-called 'matrix') either in order to resolve a clear ambiguity, or where the literal meaning of the words used would lead to absurdity.

In *Prenn* v *Simmonds* [1971] 1 WLR 1381 at 1385, Lord Wilberforce stated that if the interpretation of the words used would destroy the very purpose of the contract and undermine it, 'that may be a strong argument for an alternative interpretation, if that can reasonably be found'. Although Lord Wilberforce appeared to make this comment in the context of the limitations of the so-called 'absurdity' exception, this comment was taken by the House of Lords in *Investors Compensation Scheme Ltd* v *West Bromwich Building Society* [1998] 1 All ER 98 to allow a more liberal interpretation of contracts according with principles of commercial common sense (see Lord Steyn in *Mannai Investment Co. Ltd* v *Eagle Star Life Assurance Co. Ltd* [1997] 2 WLR 945).

Lord Hoffmann stated the current legal principles in the *Investors Compensation Scheme* case as follows (at 114–15):

> (1)   Interpretation is the ascertainment of the meaning which the document would convey to a reasonable person having all the background knowledge which would reasonably have been available to the parties in the situation in which they were at the time of the contract.
> (2)   The background was famously referred to by Lord Wilberforce as the 'matrix of fact' . . . Subject to the requirement that it should have been

reasonably available to the parties and to the exception to be mentioned next, it includes absolutely anything which would have affected the way in which the language of the document would have been understood by a reasonable man.

(3) The law excludes from the admissible background the previous negotiations of the parties and their declarations of subjective intent. They are admissible only in an action for rectification. The law makes this distinction for reasons of practical policy and, in this respect only, legal interpretation differs from the way we would interpret utterances in ordinary life . . .

(4) The meaning which a document . . . would convey to a reasonable man is not the same thing as the meaning of its words. The meaning of words is a matter of dictionaries and grammars; the meaning of the document is what the parties using those words against the relevant background would reasonably have been understood to mean. The background may not merely enable the reasonable man to choose between the possible meanings of words which are ambiguous but even . . . to conclude that the parties must, for whatever reason, have used the wrong words or syntax. . . .

(5) The 'rule' that words should be given their 'natural and ordinary meaning' reflects the commonsense proposition that we do not easily accept that people have made linguistic mistakes, particularly in formal documents. On the other hand, if one would nevertheless conclude from the background that something must have gone wrong with the language, the law does not require judges to attribute to the parties an intention which they plainly could not have had.

Lord Hoffmann justified this approach by relying on what he described as 'the fundamental change which has overtaken this branch of the law, particularly as a result of the speeches of Lord Wilberforce'. However, the approach is far-reaching because it completely removes the traditional constraints of the parol evidence rule.

The approach now would appear to be that, unless the words have a technical meaning, they are to be construed in their natural and ordinary meaning set in the context of the contract as a whole. The contract must then be construed against the 'matrix of facts', i.e. all the information and background available to the parties at the time they made the contract, such as previous dealings and their contractual purpose, but excluding evidence of their negotiations.

The prevailing guideline where the meaning is unclear appears to be to give such a meaning as reflects 'business common sense'. As Lord Diplock stated in *Antaios Cia Naviera SA* v *Salen Rederierna AB, The Antaios* [1985] AC 191, 201: 'If detailed semantic and syntactical analysis of words in a commercial contract is going to lead to a conclusion that flouts business common sense, it must yield to business common sense.' In other words, if the contract as construed would lead to an unreasonable result, the assumption must be that the parties cannot have intended it. (This approach is similar to the much-criticised approach taken by the House of Lords in *Schuler* v *Wickman Machine Tool Sales Ltd* [1974] AC 235.)

The *Investors Compensation Scheme* approach to contractual interpretation is open to criticism on a number of grounds; but in particular, because of its vagueness it will inevitably lead to the much-dreaded uncertainty in the context of commercial contracts, especially for third parties. There is clearly no universal understanding, even among commercial judges, of what will constitute 'business common sense'. In addition, as Sir Christopher Staughton wrote ('How do the Courts Interpret Commercial Contracts?' [1999] CLJ 303, 307), the need to examine the matrix of facts when determining contractual interpretation means that '[i]t is hard to imagine a ruling more calculated to perpetuate the vast cost of commercial litigation'.

SIX

Exemption clauses and unfair contract terms

6.1 CONTROL OF THE SUBSTANTIVE CONTENT OF CONTRACTS

This chapter focuses on legal regulation of 'substantive unfairness' in contracts. In other words, the parties' ability to control the content of their contracts is not unrestricted, and both the courts and Parliament — most recently in order to implement European Directives — have interfered to prevent the inclusion and use of terms that are regarded as 'unfair'.

Clauses which purport to exclude or to limit liability for breach of contract are the most common form of what are referred to in this chapter as 'exemption clauses'. It is important to note, however, that exemption clauses come in many different forms (6.4). The applicable rules remain generally the same. Exemption clauses are an important feature of modern contracts, and in recent years have been the focus of much judicial, legislative and academic attention. More recently, in the context of consumer contracts, there has been legislative regulation of both specific terms (e.g., the consumer credit legislation) and the broader category of terms on the basis of 'unfairness'. This broader regulation, contained in the Unfair Consumer Contracts Regulations 1999 (SI 1999 No. 2083), is particularly interesting because the intervention is expressly linked to the concept of 'good faith', which has long been recognised as an essential feature of contracting in many jurisdictions, although not in England and Wales. (There are specialist texts examining this area of law, most notably, E. Macdonald, *Exemption Clauses and Unfair Terms*, Butterworths, 1999; and R. Lawson, *Exclusion Clauses and Unfair Terms*, 6th edn, Sweet & Maxwell 2000.) This chapter examines the reasons for, and the mechanisms of, control of exemption clauses and other mechanisms for the control of the fairness of contractual terms.

It is also important to appreciate that the restraint of trade doctrine and measures controlling anti-competitive agreements (discussed in detail in Chapter 12) are further examples of the control of the content of contracts. This control is based both on reasonableness as between the parties and broader considerations of public policy, i.e. what is reasonable in the public interest. In addition, there may be a broader doctrine of unconscionability (based on the principle in *Fry* v *Lane* (1888) 40 ChD 312, discussed in Chapter 11) which will affect contractual content; and the 'penalty rule' and rules governing relief from forfeiture (discussed in Chapter 13) also represent an attempt to regulate contractual content.

6.2 STANDARD FORM CONTRACTS AND THE PURPOSE OF EXEMPTION CLAUSES

Since classical contract law saw contractual liability as something created by the operation of the will of the parties, rather than as liability imposed by law, it was inevitable that the classical law should accept the power of the parties to modify as they saw fit the nature of the liability created. Thus, while the usual result of the breach of a promise, which had been duly incorporated in a valid contract, was, at the very least, to create a secondary obligation to pay damages in compensation of any loss suffered, it was open to the parties to agree to contractual 'promises' that did not have this usual result. The more common means of modifying the usual liability were to exclude any obligation to pay compensation, or to limit the amount of compensation payable.

It should not be thought that exemption clauses are necessarily bad, or that the classical law was excessively naive in allowing parties to abdicate all responsibility for their promises. The classical law *assumed* (in a way which today most lawyers would challenge) that all parties to contractual negotiations would be bargaining freely, would be best placed to know their own interests, and would agree to such terms only if some, not necessarily immediately apparent, benefit would accrue from so doing.

These assumptions remain valid where the parties do in fact deal with each other on an equal footing. In that situation, typified by the commercial contract, the exemption clause is an important device for allocating the risks of the contract between the parties. Imagine a contract for the supply of machinery which depends upon the availability of raw materials from abroad. Both parties know that there is a slight risk that the usual, low-cost supplier will be slow to supply because of the unstable political conditions in its country. Alternative supplies are available at much higher cost. The seller of the machinery may quote two prices: let us say £2,500 for a guaranteed delivery date, by using the high-cost raw materials; and let us say £1,500 using the low-cost raw materials, but subject to an exclusion of liability for late delivery. The buyer may then choose which contract he or she prefers, knowing that the seller will not agree to bear the risk of late delivery if the cheaper contract is chosen. There is no reason for the law to interfere with this kind of use of exemption clauses, and indeed to do so would be to undermine the economic basis of the parties' agreement.

Nevertheless, it is generally accepted today that there are situations in which exemption clauses are not freely negotiated, at which point the law may seek to interfere. These situations usually involve standard form contracts. Such contracts are entered into on the basis of a standard set of contractual terms contained in a document drawn up by one of the parties. Standard form contracts are not necessarily bad. They represent the reaction of lawyers to the increase in contractual activity engendered by the industrial revolution. Just as goods were mass produced, so too it became much more convenient to use 'mass produced' contracts, since the circumstances of one sale were normally very similar to another, and so the costs of individual drafting could be avoided. It became normal practice to include one or more exemption clauses in such standardised contracts.

Sometimes the inclusion of these clauses reflected the practice of a particular trade in the allocation of risks between buyers and sellers, and so was entirely legitimate. The problem of standard form contracts, however, is that they may present little choice to the party who has not drawn up the document. If he or she wants the product, he or she may have to accept the terms; if the terms are unacceptable, that party will have to resign himself or herself to not obtaining the product. For this reason they are sometimes called 'contracts of adhesion'. Thus, standard form contracts may be used to *impose* an exclusion or limitation of liability which has not been negotiated, and for which the person whose normal contractual rights are diminished has received no alternative benefit. The imposition of such exemption clauses may be particularly harmful in consumer contracts, where the disequilibrium between the bargaining positions of the parties may be substantial, and where the consumer may have no alternative but to accept the terms if such exemptions are commonplace throughout the particular industry, as is often the case.

6.3 JUDICIAL ATTITUDES TO EXEMPTION CLAUSES

Judicial attitudes to exemption clauses have hardened over the last hundred years. It is still the case that individually negotiated contracts containing exemption clauses are generally assumed not to be harmful. The attitude to standard form contracts may be summarised by reference to the speech of Lord Diplock in the House of Lords in *Schroeder Music Publishing Co. Ltd* v *Macaulay* [1974] 1 WLR 1308. Standard form contracts which are used for convenience to express common commercial agreements, and which do so in terms normal to such contracts, are presumed to be fair and reasonable. Standard form contracts in consumer transactions, and in other situations in which one party is said to have no alternative but to contract on the terms offered if he or she is to contract at all, are not presumed to be fair and reasonable. Rather, they are viewed as the product of the superior bargaining position of one of the parties. The courts often suspect that that superior bargaining position is being exploited to the cost of the other party, and for that reason will do everything in their power to avoid the consequences of such clauses.

It is sometimes suggested that the judicial attitude to exemption clauses in this last category is over-simplistic (*cf.* M. J. Trebilcock in *Studies in Contract*

Law, B. Reiter and J. Swan (eds), Butterworths, 1981, at p. 481). The assertion that consumers have no alternative but to contract on such terms has been challenged, and it has been suggested that consumers do get (an admittedly non-negotiated) benefit from such contracts in the form of lower prices than would prevail if each contract had to be individually negotiated. Nevertheless, there is growing evidence that such clauses have been used in consumer contracts precisely in order to frighten off complainants, even when there is little or no prospect of the clause being upheld in a court of law. In these circumstances it seems likely that, whatever the economists may say about the reasonableness and utility of exemption clauses in all types of contract, judicial attitudes will remain unsympathetic to their use in consumer contracts. That position has been reinforced by legislation (see 6.6).

6.4   TYPES AND NATURE OF EXEMPTION CLAUSES

It would be impossible, and fruitless, to catalogue every known type of exemption clause. The wit and invention of contracts' draftsmen have been fuelled by the courts' attempts to control such clauses into the regular discovery of new and ingenious forms, to which subsequently the courts have to react. Most common are the total exclusion of liability for part at least of what would otherwise be included in the contractual undertaking (e.g., implied terms of quality; but see 6.6.2.4), and the limitation of liability to a particular sum (e.g., the price payable under the contract). Other common forms are those which limit the remedy available either by imposing a short time-limit during which claims for breach must be made, or by imposing onerous conditions on obtaining the remedy (such as payment of costs of transport of defective goods to and from the supplier's place of business).

More difficult to control are clauses which, rather than exempting liability for breach, purport to modify the performance obligation, so that no breach occurs (*cf.* discussion of terms which modify expected contractual obligations; see 6.6.2.4).

Before examining the approach to legal regulation of such clauses, it is essential to first consider their nature. It is possible, and arguably more logical, to treat an exemption clause like any other term of the contract so that it operates to define the obligations of the parties. This was the approach adopted by Lord Diplock in *Photo Production Ltd* v *Securicor Transport Ltd* [1980] AC 827. However, the generally accepted view is that such clauses may operate as a defence to the liability which would otherwise exist. This is artificial in that it involves construing all of the other terms of the contract in order to identify the contractual obligations and duties owed, and then separately considering whether the exemption clause operates to exclude or limit that liability (see D. Yates, *Exclusion Clauses in Contracts*, 2nd edn, Sweet & Maxwell, 1992, pp. 123–33).

6.5   EXEMPTION CLAUSES AS DEFENCES TO LIABILITY

The common law provides no rule or doctrine whereby an exemption clause may simply be declared unenforceable on the ground that it is unfair or unreasonable (*Photo Production Ltd v Securicor Transport Ltd* [1980] AC 827; see 6.5.3). For many years, therefore, the courts' hostility to such clauses found expression in the application, often in strict or strained terms, of devices of the general law of contracts to the particular problem of exemption clauses. The more common of such devices are described below. In theory, they are still applicable despite the enactment of statutory controls on certain exemption clauses; in practice, the courts have been able to adopt a more realistic and less artificial approach to the application of these devices because of the existence of the more direct means of control where these are available.

It is recognised that in order to be able to rely upon an exemption clause as a defence to liability, the party seeking to rely upon it needs to establish that it was incorporated and covers the liability which has occurred in the circumstances in which it occurred. The final step is to establish that the clause is not rendered unenforceable by statute.

6.5.1 Incorporation

The rules governing the incorporation of written terms into agreements have already been examined (5.3). As was noted there, the law on incorporation had developed almost exclusively through judicial attempts to avoid the impact of exemption clauses. Any clause which has not reasonably been brought to the notice of the offeree before the time of acceptance of the offer (and thus the making of the contract) will not be incorporated into the contract (see, for example, *Thornton v Shoe Lane Parking Ltd* [1971] 2 QB 163, at 5.3.3.1). By means of this rule the courts have been able to prevent reliance upon contract terms which were printed in receipts or invoices and which had not come to the attention of the party in question when entering the agreement. The courts have also used the requirement that a higher degree of notice is required for unusual or onerous terms, in order to prevent reliance on such terms which were not brought to the attention of the other party (*Interfoto Picture Library Ltd v Stiletto Visual Programmes Ltd* [1989] QB 433, at 5.3.3.2; notably, Bingham LJ considered this to be an aspect of English law developing 'piecemeal solutions to demonstrated problem of unfairness' in a way which achieved the same result as the doctrine of good faith (or 'fair and open dealing') in other jurisdictions.

6.5.2 Construction

6.5.2.1 Devices of interpretation   At one time, this was the final mechanism open to a court which sought to protect the consumer from the consequences of an exemption clause in a contract. On occasions, therefore, there is clear evidence of rather strained and artificial constructions of such clauses; the classic example being the decision of the Court of Appeal in *Hollier v Rambler Motors (AMC) Ltd* [1972] 2 QB 71. Such artificial interpretations are no longer required because of the existence of statutory provisions to regulate the use of such clauses, and the basic construction test propounded by Lord Bridge in *George Mitchell (Chesterhall) Ltd v Finney Lock*

Seeds [1983] 2 AC 803, at 811, namely, 'whether the relevant condition, on its true construction in the context of the contract as a whole' is effective to exclude or limit the liability in question. In other words, it is only necessary to construe the clause on its natural and ordinary meaning to see if it covers what has happened.

However, this said, there are a number of interpretation devices which indicate that the basic approach to construction is a strict one. A party seeking to avoid liability must be able to prove the common intention of the parties by clear words, since the courts will otherwise assume that the normal incidents of contractual liability were intended. This strict interpretation takes several forms.

In the first place, the courts will not imply any exemption greater than that contained in the words used. So, in *Andrews Bros (Bournemouth) Ltd* v *Singer & Co. Ltd* [1934] 1 KB 17, the plaintiffs contracted to purchase 'new' cars from the defendant company. The contract contained a clause excluding 'all conditions, warranties and liabilities implied by common law statute or otherwise'. One of the cars was found to have done a substantial mileage on delivery to the plaintiffs and therefore clearly was not 'new'. The exclusion clause did not protect the defendants. It excluded implied terms, while the requirement that the cars be 'new' was an express term of the contract.

Secondly, the courts operate what is known as the *contra proferentem* rule. Where the meaning of an exemption clause is ambiguous, that ambiguity will be resolved against the party seeking to rely on the clause (the *proferens*). In other words, the courts will adopt the meaning which is unfavourable to that party. In *Beck & Co.* v *Szymanowski & Co.* [1924] AC 43, the contract provided that goods delivered were deemed to be in satisfactory condition unless complaint was made within 14 days of receiving them. The clause was ineffective to exclude liability for short delivery (i.e., for goods not delivered) even though complaint was made more than 14 days after receiving the goods.

Although this rule rests on the existence of ambiguity in the meaning of the exemption clause, the courts have been resourceful in finding such ambiguity when it has suited them to be able to cut down the impact of a clause. For example, in *Houghton* v *Trafalgar Insurance Co. Ltd* [1954] 1 QB 247, a car insurance policy did not give protection to cover damage occurring when the car was conveying 'any load in excess of that for which it was constructed'. An accident occurred when the car, designed to carry five people, was carrying six. The Court of Appeal considered that 'load' was ambiguous, and construed it against the insurers to limit it to excess weight rather than excess passengers. A modern example of this approach may be found in *Morley* v *United Friendly Insurance plc* [1993] 1 WLR 996. An insurance policy excluded claims resulting from 'wilful exposure to needless peril'. The Court of Appeal held that an intentional and risky act did not fall within the scope of the clause where the risk was modest and the party affected did not have time to assess the peril involved.

The *contra proferentem* rule is expressly contained in reg. 7(2) of the Unfair Terms in Consumer Contracts Regulations 1999 (SI 1999 No. 2083), which provides that 'If there is doubt about the meaning of a written term, the interpretation which is most favourable to the consumer shall prevail'. However, this principle is excluded from operation in respect of pre-emptive challenges to clauses in standard forms (see discussion at 6.6.3.7).

Thirdly, in what is a particular and common example of the operation of the *contra proferentem* rule, the policy of the courts is to limit the scope of exclusion clauses (as opposed to limitation clauses) by restricting their application to exclude or limit contractual liability. Therefore, the courts have shown themselves unwilling to extend the scope of an exclusion clause to other liabilities (unless expressly stated to cover them), thereby ensuring that the claimant has an alternative remedy in tort to which the clause does not apply.

This policy is given effect in the test proposed by Lord Morton in *Canada Steamship Lines* v *The King* [1952] AC 192 at 208:

> (ii)   If the clause contains language which expressly exempts the person in whose favour it is made (hereafter called 'the *proferens*') from the consequence of the negligence of his own servants, effect must be given to that provision . . .
>
> (iii)   If there is no express reference to negligence, the court must consider whether the words are wide enough, in their ordinary meaning, to cover negligence on the part of the servants of the *proferens* . . .
>
> (iv)   If the words used are wide enough for the above purpose, the court must then consider whether 'the head of damage may be based on some ground other than that of negligence' . . . The 'other ground' must not be so fanciful or remote that the *proferens* cannot be supposed to have desired protection against it; but subject to that qualification . . . the existence of a possible head of damage other than that of negligence is fatal to the *proferens* even if the words are *prima facie* wide enough to cover negligence on the part of his servants.

The classic example of the application of this rule of construction is *White* v *John Warwick & Co. Ltd* [1953] 1 WLR 1285. The plaintiff was injured when the saddle on a bicycle hired from the defendants tipped and he fell on the road. The contract of hire exempted the defendants from liability for any personal injuries to the hirers of bicycles. Without the clause, the plaintiff might have succeeded against the defendants either for breach of contract, or for the defendants' negligence. The Court of Appeal ruled that the exemption clause was effective to exclude liability in contract only, so that the plaintiff's action in the tort of negligence succeeded despite the clause.

Although this is a rule of construction, and so each case must be treated on its particular facts, some common threads emerge. In accordance with Lord Morton's first test in the *Canada Steamship* case, to exclude liability for negligence as well as liability for breach of contract, express words ('negligence' or a synonym of negligence) must be used (see, for example, *Monarch Airlines Ltd* v *London Luton Airport Ltd* [1997] CLC 698, where the words 'neglect or default' extended to exclude liability for negligence and breach of statutory duty). Of course, as Steyn LJ made clear in *E.E. Caledonia Ltd* v *Orbit Valve Co. plc* [1994] 1 WLR 1515, at 1523, it might not make commercial sense to insert such a reference as it would tend to frighten off the other party. Thus, '[o]missions of express reference to negligence tend to be deliberate'.

Since the policy of the courts is to require very clear words indeed before permitting a party to avoid liability for the consequences of his or her own negligence, a strict interpretation is evident both in relation to express references to negligence and whether the clause is capable, on the basis of the words used, of applying to negligence liability. For example, in *Stent Foundations Ltd* v *Gleeson plc* [2001] BLR 134, the clause provided as follows: 'The Sub-Contractor shall be responsible for and indemnify the Contractor against any claims in respect of plant or tools of the Sub-Contractor or his workmen which may be lost or damaged by fire or any other cause . . .' The judge dismissed an argument that the words used covered negligence liability. There was no express reference to negligence and, in addition, the words were not wide enough to cover such liability. The words 'any other cause' had to be interpreted restrictively in the light of the preceding words 'lost or damaged by fire', and fire was neutral on the question of fault. It would therefore not have been necessary to apply the third element of Lord Morton's test before concluding that negligence liability was not covered.

Another example of this strict interpretation of clauses as not excluding liability for negligence can be seen in the decision of the Court of Appeal in *E.E. Caledonia Ltd* v *Orbit Valve Co. plc* [1994] 1 WLR 1515. The plaintiffs made a payment to the estate of an engineer following his death in a fire on the plaintiffs' oil platform. The plaintiffs sought to recover this payment from the defendants (the engineer's employers) under the terms of an indemnity. The indemnity applied in respect of any claim, demand, cause of action, loss, expense or liability arising from the death of such an employee in the performance of the contract. The death had been found to be the result of the plaintiffs' negligence and as a result of their breaches of health and safety regulations (i.e., breach of statutory duty). The Court of Appeal held that the indemnity did not expressly cover negligence and that very clear words would be required in order for it to operate to protect a party from the consequences of his own negligence. In addition, as there was another liability (breach of statutory duty), the indemnity could not extend to cover the negligence. (On the facts, the Court of Appeal also held that the indemnity did not cover the breach of statutory duty because it amounted to a provision allocating full responsibility to each party for the consequences of its own actions.)

The clause must be construed to cover negligence liability, despite the absence of any express reference to negligence, if the words of the clause are wide enough to cover negligence and negligence is the only liability which has arisen on the facts. For example, in *Alderslade* v *Hendon Laundry Ltd* [1945] 1 KB 189, the plaintiff sent items to the laundry which were not returned. The contract contained a clause restricting recovery for lost items to 20 times the laundering charge. Since the laundry's only liability for lost items lay in negligence, the limitation clause was redundant unless applicable to such liability. Therefore, the Court of Appeal held that the defendant was able to rely on the clause.

Generally speaking, the approach of the courts to limitation clauses has been more generous and such clauses tend to be construed more favourably. In particular, in order to limit liability for negligence the test is only that the clause should be 'most clearly and unambiguously expressed' (*per* Lord Wilberforce, *Ailsa Craig Fishing Co. Ltd* v *Malvern Fishing Co. Ltd* [1983] 1 WLR 964, at 966). Lord Wilberforce set out the basis for this favourable treatment:

> Clauses of limitation are not regarded by the courts with the same hostility as clauses of exclusion: this is because they must be related to other contractual terms, in particular to the risks to which the defending party may be exposed, the remuneration which he receives, and possibly also the opportunity of the other party to insure.

This distinction in treatment has subsequently been endorsed at the highest level, e.g., by Lord Bridge in *George Mitchell* v *Finney Lock Seeds* [1983] 2 AC 803 at 814, by Steyn LJ in *E.E. Caledonia Ltd* v *Orbit Valve plc* [1994] 1 WLR 1515 at 1521 and by Evans LJ in *BHP Petroleum* v *British Steel* [2000] 2 All ER (Comm) 133 at 143. However, there are a large number of assumptions made about the circumstances in which limitation amounts are determined. It may be that it is at the stage of legislative regulation (and, in particular, the reasonableness and circumstances of drafting the clause) that the more favourable treatment should be given, rather than at the construction stage. It is possible to envisage a position where the limitation amount is drafted at such a low figure that it is not substantially different in effect to a total exclusion clause (see, for example, comments by the High Court of Australia in *Darlington Futures Ltd* v *Delco Australia Pty Ltd* (1986) 161 CLR 500). It would be sensible, therefore, to avoid any blanket rule applicable to limitation clauses and leave examination of such clauses to the context of the legislation.

Lastly, out of the strict interpretation approach has emerged the 'repugnancy' or 'total non-performance' rule, which is closely related to what was once the main common law means of controlling exclusion clauses (see 6.5.3). The courts will be very unwilling to construe an exemption clause as depriving a main undertaking of the contract of any legal value by making it unenforceable (*J. Evans & Son (Portsmouth) Ltd* v *Andrea Merzario Ltd* [1976] 1 WLR 1078, see 5.2.3 — oral undertaking that the goods would be stored below deck overrode the inconsistent printed conditions which would have rendered the oral promise illusory; and see also *Couchman* v *Hill* [1947] KB 554). In *Sze Hai Tong Bank Ltd* v *Rambler Cycle Co. Ltd* [1959] AC 576, the respondents had contracted to deliver a consignment of bicycles to Singapore, to be delivered to sub-purchasers on production of correct documentation. The carriers released the consignment to the original buyers (rather than to the sub-purchasers) without production of proper documentation, with the effect that the sellers were not paid. The sellers' contract with the carriers provided that the carriers' responsibility was to be deemed to

'cease absolutely' once the goods were discharged from the ship. The carriers
(or rather their indemnifiers, the appellants in the action) argued that the
effect of this clause was to exclude liability for the wrongful release of the
bicycles to the original buyers. The Privy Council refused to accept such an
argument. For the Privy Council Lord Denning said:

> There is . . . an implied limitation on the clause, which cuts down the
> extreme width of it: and, as a matter of construction, their Lordships
> decline to attribute to it the unreasonable effect contended for. But their
> Lordships go further. If such an extreme width were given to the exemption
> clause, it would run counter to the main object and intent of the contract
> . . . It would defeat this object entirely if the shipping company was at
> liberty, at its own will and pleasure, to deliver the goods to somebody else,
> to someone not entitled at all, without being liable for the consequences.
> The clause must therefore be limited and modified to the extent necessary
> to enable effect to be given to the main object and intent of the contract.

In *Mendelssohn* v *Normand Ltd* [1970] 1 QB 177, there was an implied
promise by a car park attendant to see that the contents of a car were safe
because he had expressly promised to lock it. The Court of Appeal held that
this implied promise took priority over the printed exemption because it was
inconsistent with it.

The rationale of this approach is clear: it is disingenuous to promise by
contract a particular performance while in the same breath (or perhaps under
it) disclaiming any liability should you simply prefer not to keep your
promise. Nevertheless, this approach is only a rule of *construction*, and there
can be no doubt that by carefully chosen words such an effect could be
achieved (see 6.5.3). It has been suggested that there is no scope for the
repugnancy approach where the statutory controls under the UCTA 1977
apply (*Edmund Murray Ltd* v *BSP International Foundations Ltd* (1992) 33
Con LR 1). In practice, however, the courts will be most unwilling to find a
clause which could be described as 'repugnant' to be reasonable under the
Act (see *Lease Management Services Ltd* v *Purnell Secretarial Services Ltd* (1993)
13 Tr LR 337).

6.5.2.2 Fraud or misrepresentation As we saw in Chapter 5, at 5.3.1,
a party will be unable to rely on an exemption clause if he or she has induced
the other party to enter the contract by misrepresenting, fraudulently or
otherwise, the meaning and effect of the clause. In *Curtis* v *Chemical Cleaning
and Dyeing Co.* [1951] 1 KB 805, the defendants sought to rely on a clause
exempting liability for 'any damage, however arising', which had been
represented to the plaintiff as only excluding liability for particular risks,
namely the beads and sequins on a dress. The Court of Appeal held that the
defendants could not rely on the clause to avoid liability when the dress was
returned with a stain which appeared during cleaning, since that was damage
of a type not listed in their representation to the plaintiff.

6.5.3 Fundamental breach

In the 1950s there developed out of the strict interpretation approach to exemption clauses, a doctrine suggesting that *as a matter of law* the courts would not allow an exemption clause to exclude or limit liability for a breach which deprived the non-breaching party of the main performance owing to him or her under the contract. Sometimes it was said that there were certain 'fundamental terms', liability for breach of which could never be exempted. Alternatively, it was said that certain types of breach were 'fundamental', in that they were so serious that liability for them could not be exempted. The authority for such a rule, or rules, was never very clearly explained, and such interference with the intentions of the parties as expressed in their contract was out of character for the common law.

In *Suisse Atlantique Société d'Armement Maritime SA* v *NV Rotterdamsche Kolen Centrale* [1967] 1 AC 361, the House of Lords attempted to put an end to this alleged rule of law. The case involved the charter of a ship for two years' consecutive voyages between the United States and Europe. The owners were to be paid according to the number of voyages made. Eight round-trips were made in all, and the owners alleged that but for breach of the terms of the contract relating to loading and unloading a further six trips could have been made. The charterers said that the owners' damages were limited by a clause fixing compensation for delay to $1,000 per day. The owners claimed not to be bound by that clause because the charterers had committed a fundamental breach of the contract. Viscount Dilhorne said (at 392):

> In my view, it is not right to say that the law prohibits and nullifies a clause exempting or limiting liability for a fundamental breach or breach of a fundamental term. Such a rule of law would involve a restriction on freedom of contract and in the older cases I can find no trace of it.

There can be little doubt that the other judges in the House of Lords agreed with this statement, and intended their remarks to be consistent with it. Nevertheless, their attempt to bury the fundamental breach doctrine was not entirely successful. In the first place, their remarks were strictly *obiter*, since it was found that the clause in question was not an exemption clause at all but a liquidated damages clause (see 13.10.1). Moreover, several passages in their Lordships' speeches suggested that there might be a residual rule of law applicable in the case of fundamental breach, especially where the non-breaching party elected to treat the contract as repudiated. Lord Wilberforce said that it might be correct to say that there is a rule of law against the application of exemption clauses the effect of which is to deprive one party's stipulations of all contractual force, reducing the contract to 'a mere declaration of intent'. And Lord Reid suggested that an election to treat a contract as repudiated caused the whole contract to cease to exist, including the exclusion clause, so that it would be ineffective to exclude loss.

Out of these fragments the Court of Appeal, led by Lord Denning MR, contrived to revive the doctrine of fundamental breach, at least in the case where the effect of breach was so serious that the non-breaching party had no real alternative but to elect to treat the contract as repudiated (see *Harbutts' 'Plasticine' Ltd* v *Wayne Tank and Pump Co. Ltd* [1970] 1 QB 447).

The House of Lords was given a further opportunity to clarify the law in *Photo Production Ltd* v *Securicor Transport Ltd* [1980] AC 827. This time there could be no doubt that the issue of the effect of fundamental breach on an exemption clause was squarely raised. Under the contract in question, Securicor were to make patrol visits at night and at weekends to the premises of Photo Production. The contract contained a clause exempting Securicor from liability for the acts of its employees unless they could have been prevented by due diligence on the part of Securicor; and exempting Securicor from liability for loss caused by fire unless the loss was solely attributable to the negligence of a Securicor employee acting within the course of his employment. One night the duty patrolman deliberately started a fire, and although it was not found that his intention was to destroy the factory, his action caused a loss of £615,000.

The House of Lords overruled *Harbutts' 'Plasticine' Ltd* v *Wayne Tank and Pump Co. Ltd* [1970] 1 QB 447. It said that the question of whether an exemption clause applied in the case of a very serious or 'fundamental' breach was no more than a question of the proper construction of the particular clause. It found that in this case the clause was drafted in such terms that liability was in fact excluded. The decision was justified on the basis that this was a commercial contract between parties in equal bargaining positions and the clause was therefore a risk allocation provision placing the burden of insurance on Photo Production.

The last vestiges of the fundamental breach rule of law were demolished by a careful analysis of the effect of a breach of condition or a serious breach of an innominate term, since the House of Lords (*per* Lord Diplock) took the view that the latter and fundamental breach were one and the same thing. As we have already seen (5.4), the effect of such breach is to give the non-breaching party the option of treating the contract as repudiated, so that there is no longer any need to perform the primary obligations. However, the contract itself does not come to an end. The secondary obligations (e.g., to pay damages for loss caused by breach) remain in existence, as would any exemption clause. The Court of Appeal in *Harbutts' 'Plasticine'* (and perhaps Lord Reid in *Suisse Atlantique*) had confused the ending of the primary obligations with the ending of all obligations.

The facts of *Photo Production* pre-dated the UCTA 1977, although the Act had been passed by the time the case reached the House of Lords. Lord Wilberforce indicated what he believed should be the policy of the common law towards exemption clauses after the passing of the Act, saying:

> It is significant that Parliament refrained from legislating over the whole field of contract. After this Act, in commercial matters generally, when the parties are not of unequal bargaining power, and when risks are normally borne by insurance, not only is the case for judicial intervention undemon-strated, but there is everything to be said, and this seems to have been

Parliament's intention, for leaving the parties free to apportion the risks as they think fit and for respecting their decisions.

The position at common law seems to be, therefore, that the only control over the use of exemption clauses duly incorporated into the contract is to determine whether as a matter of construction they apply to the breach in question. There is little doubt that in the past the courts were willing to find ambiguity and difficulty simply in order to have a means of eliminating oppressive exemption clauses. It now seems that since oppressive clauses may be dealt with under the legislation, there is no reason to adopt any artificial constructions or to stray beyond merely seeking the ordinary meaning of the words used. There are indications that the House of Lords has recognised that strict construction should not be 'strained construction' (*per* Lord Wilberforce in *Ailsa Craig Fishing Co. Ltd* v *Malvern Fishing Co. Ltd* [1983] 1 WLR 964; approved by Lord Bridge in *George Mitchell (Chesterhall) Ltd* v *Finney Lock Seeds Ltd* [1983] 2 AC 803).

6.6 STATUTORY CONTROL OF EXEMPTION CLAUSES

6.6.1 The nature of the statutory control

The enactment of the Unfair Contract Terms Act (UCTA) 1977 introduced a major addition to the mechanisms for controlling exemption clauses. The power to override exemption clauses found to be unreasonable had been introduced in the case of implied terms in the sale of goods by the Supply of Goods (Implied Terms) Act 1973 (see now s. 55 of the SGA 1979). The 1977 Act, however, applied more extensive controls to a wide range of categories of contract, so that, for contracts within the scope of the Act, the courts for the first time had a general and direct means of control of the use of exemption clauses. The application of UCTA 1977 may render an exemption clause either totally unenforceable, or unenforceable unless shown to be reasonable.

Further changes to this statutory regime of control of exemption clauses were introduced by adoption by the Council of Ministers of Directive 93/13/EC on Unfair Terms in Consumer Contracts, now implemented in the Unfair Terms in Consumer Contracts Regulations 1999 (SI 1999 No. 2083) (replacing the original implementing regulations of 1994, SI 1994 No. 3159). In general terms, the Regulations provide that 'unfair terms' in a contract concluded between a 'seller or supplier' and a 'consumer' will not be binding on the consumer. Thus, the Regulations apply only in the context of 'consumer contracts' (defined at 6.6.3.1), but their application extends beyond exemption clauses to 'unfair terms' in general.

A detailed assessment of the differences between the scope of these two legislative measures can be found at 6.6.3.4. This chapter will focus on an examination of UCTA 1977 before embarking upon a detailed examination of the Unfair Terms in Consumer Contracts Regulations 1999 (at 6.6.3).

6.6.2   The Unfair Contract Terms Act 1977

6.6.2.1   Scope of the Act   The UCTA 1977 applies (subject to certain exceptions) in the case of both contract and tort to 'business liability', which means liability for things done or to be done in the course of a business, and liability arising from the occupation of business premises (s. 1(3), UCTA 1977). 'Business' is given a broad definition by the Act (s. 14, UCTA 1977), so that it embraces not only the normal meaning of commercial activity, but also the professions, government departments and local or public authorities. The intention appears to have been to exclude from the general scope of the Act by this expression only private, occasional contracts. In the case of sale and hire purchase, the Act applies irrespective of whether the liability arises in the course of a business (s. 6(4), UCTA 1977), although this exception is not as major as it may appear (see below at 6.6.2.4).

It must be stressed that UCTA 1977 does not provide a general power to strike out any term which the court considers to be unreasonable or unfair. Its main targets are exemption clauses; that is, clauses excluding or limiting liability. This definition is extended by s. 13(1) to include clauses making the enforcement of liability subject to compliance with a condition, clauses excluding or limiting any right or remedy that would otherwise be available, and clauses restricting or excluding rules of evidence or procedure.

Stewart Gill Ltd v *Horatio Myer & Co. Ltd* [1992] 1 QB 600, provides an example of a clause which purported to restrict a right or remedy otherwise available, and therefore fell within the ambit of UCTA 1977. The clause in question purported to prevent the buyer from withholding payment by reason of a set-off or counter-claim in the event of a breach of contract by the supplier. It was claimed on behalf of the supplier that the reference in s. 13(1) to restrictions of rights or remedies and rules of procedure brought such clauses within the scope of the Act only where they achieved indirectly an exclusion or limitation of liability which, if expressly stipulated, would be subject to control under the Act; whereas in this case the restriction on the right of set-off did not exclude or limit the liability of the supplier, but only required the buyer to prosecute his claim in relation to defective goods in separate legal proceedings. This argument was unanimously rejected by the Court of Appeal, which held that the clause excluded the buyer's 'right' to set off its claims against the seller's claim for the price and also excluded the procedural rules applicable to a set-off.

The Act also applies to clauses which purport to modify the expected contractual obligation or duty, rather than to exempt liability for breach (s. 13(1), UCTA 1977). For example, in *Smith* v *Eric S. Bush* [1990] 1 AC 831, the House of Lords held that a disclaimer clause in a mortgage valuation which stipulated that the valuation was provided without any acceptance of responsibility, fell within s. 13(1) of UCTA 1977 because it purported to prevent any duty of care from arising. The 1977 Act does not, however, apply to arbitration clauses (s. 13(2), UCTA 1977).

Certain important categories of contracts are excluded from the scope of the major provisions of the Act. Schedule 1, para. 1 excludes from ss. 2–4 and s. 7 contracts of insurance, contracts relating to interests in land, contracts relating to intellectual property, contracts relating to companies (whether or not incorporated) and contracts relating to securities. Schedule 1, para. 2, excludes contracts of marine salvage, charterparties and contracts of carriage of goods by sea from the same provisions other than s. 2(1), except where the provisions operate in favour of a person dealing as a consumer (see 6.6.2.4). Employment contracts are excluded by sch. 1, para. 4, on similar terms. Lastly, under s. 26, the Act does not apply to international supply contracts as defined in that section.

6.6.2.2 Liability for negligence 'Negligence' is defined by the 1977 Act as breach of an obligation to take reasonable care or to exercise reasonable skill arising out of the express or implied terms of a contract (i.e., qualified contractual liability, 7.2.1), or existing as a common law duty (i.e., in tort) or arising out of the Occupiers' Liability Act 1957 (s. 1(1), UCTA 1977).

As far as the law of contract is concerned, it should be remembered that many obligations arising out of contracts are strict. That is to say, the standard of performance demanded is not merely to take reasonable care or to exercise reasonable skill in attempting to achieve the purpose of the contract. Rather, the party performing can avoid breach only by actually achieving that purpose. Therefore, exemption clauses relating to such contractual terms are not subject to the controls applying to clauses which purport to exclude or limit liability for 'negligence' contained in s. 2 of the Act (but see 6.6.2.4). Nevertheless, some contractual obligations are not strict. Where the achievement of the result is dependent to some appreciable extent on factors beyond the control of the person providing the service, it would be nonsensical to *guarantee* that the result will be achieved (7.2.1). Thus a lawyer cannot guarantee that his or her client will escape conviction when prosecuted; he or she can only undertake to use reasonable skill in seeking to prevent conviction. Breach of such obligations is what is meant by 'negligence' liability in the context of contracts, and exemption clauses relating to such liability are governed by s. 2, UCTA 1977.

Section 2(1) of the 1977 Act provides:

(1) A person cannot by reference to any contract term or to a notice given to persons generally or to particular persons exclude or restrict his liability for death or personal injury resulting from negligence.

It should be noted that the section applies to more than exemption clauses contained in contracts. It would apply, for example, to a notice erected by the owner of land at an entrance to that land through which members of the public pass. Section 2(1) renders totally unenforceable any exclusions and limitations of liability for death or personal injury caused by negligence. Section 2(2) UCTA 1977 provides that liability for other loss or damage (i.e., other than death or personal injury) resulting from negligence may be excluded, provided the contract term or notice satisfies the requirement of reasonableness (see 6.6.2.6). 'Other loss or damage' includes property damages and financial loss.

6.6.2.3 Guarantees of consumer goods Sometimes manufacturers (and possibly distributors) of consumer goods issue a 'guarantee' of goods sold by the retailer to the consumer. Often the guarantee purports to limit, or even exclude, the liability of the party issuing it for negligence which leads to the goods being defective. Such an exemption may take effect as a non-contractual notice, or may constitute a separate contract between manufacturer and consumer (although not a contract of sale). The danger of such guarantees is that, while they may offer an easier remedy for trivial defects than can be had by taking the goods back to the seller, such advantage is often gained by the sacrifice of more important rights in the case of serious loss such as might result from a defect causing personal injury. For this reason purported exemptions contained in consumer guarantees are of no effect (s. 5, UCTA 1977). Therefore, although s. 5 may overlap with s. 2 in some instances, the protection offered is such that the clause will always be totally unenforceable. The section does not apply to exemptions contained in contracts of sale, hire purchase, work and materials or hire, which are provided for elsewhere (see 6.6.2.4).

6.6.2.4 Contractual liability In the case of attempted exemptions of strict contractual obligations (i.e., obligations which must be performed completely and precisely to an absolute standard), the 1977 Act contains two provisions which may be applicable. In the first place, there are specific provisions designed to deal with attempts to exclude or limit liability for breaches of the implied obligations relating to the goods in sale and supply contracts (ss. 6 and 7, UCTA 1977). Secondly, there is also a general provision which may apply to attempts to exempt from liability for breaches of strict contractual obligations, but it will be applicable only if one of the qualifying conditions is met (s. 3, UCTA 1977).

The sale or supply of goods As mentioned above, the Act contains special provisions, additional to those in s. 3, which apply to clauses purporting to exempt liability for breach of the terms relating to the goods which are implied by statute into contracts for the sale or supply of goods (see 5.5.3.2). Section 6 applies to implied terms in the sale of goods. It should be noted that this section applies to all liability, and not merely to that incurred in the course of a business (s. 6(4), UCTA 1977). However, the important implied terms of quality in s. 14 of the SGA 1979 arise only in the case of sales made in the course of a business. The Supply of Goods and Services Act 1982 implies terms similar to those of the 1979 Act into contracts for the supply of goods, that is, contracts under which title to goods passes but not by way of sale (e.g., work and materials contracts, such as a building contract under which goods are to be incorporated into the finished structure as part of the contract performance, see 5.5.3.2). Attempted exemptions of liability for breach of these implied terms are governed by s. 7, UCTA 1977.

In the context of a sale of goods contract, the implied condition that the seller has or will have the right to sell the goods (s. 12, SGA 1979) cannot in any circumstances be excluded by reference to a contract term (s. 6(1)(a),

UCTA 1977). It should be noted, however, that the parties may define the seller's obligation in a more limited way, so that he or she is obliged only to transfer such title as he or she has (s. 12(3)–(5), SGA 1979). Section 7(3A) of the 1977 Act provides that liability for breach of s. 2 of the Supply of Goods and Services Act 1982 (relating to the transfer of goods in a work and materials contract) cannot be exempted (s. 17(2), Supply of Goods and Services Act 1982). However, liability for breach of s. 7 of the 1982 Act (implied obligation concerning the right to transfer possession of goods in a hire contract) can be exempted, but only if the clause satisfies the reasonableness requirement (s. 7(4), UCTA 1977).

In the case of attempts to exempt liability for breaches of ss. 13–15 of the SGA 1979 (covering sale by description, satisfactory quality, fitness for purpose and sale by sample), the position under s. 6, UCTA 1977 is different depending upon whether or not one of the parties *deals as consumer* (s. 12, UCTA 1977). Where one party deals as consumer, liability for breach of these implied terms cannot be exempted (s. 6(2)(a), UCTA 1977). Where the party seeking to enforce liability is not a consumer, liability for breach of the implied terms may be exempted, but only in so far as the exemption clause satisfies the requirement of reasonableness (s. 6(3), UCTA 1977).

The same distinction applies in the context of attempts to exclude the same obligations relating to description, satisfactory quality, fitness for purpose and correspondance with sample in contracts for work and materials and hire contracts, i.e. these obligations cannot be excluded as against a consumer (s. 7(2)) but may be excluded as against a person dealing otherwise than as consumer where the clause in question is shown to be reasonable (s. 7(3), UCTA 1977).

The Act therefore contains an important distinction between those dealing as consumers and others.

'*Dealing as consumer*'   A party *deals as consumer* if he or she does not make (or hold himself or herself out as making) the contract in the course of a business while the other party does, and, in the case of a contract for goods, the goods are of a type ordinarily supplied for private use or consumption (s. 12(1), UCTA 1977). Section 12(2) also provides that a buyer in a sale by auction or by competitive tender will never be dealing as a consumer. By s. 12(3), if a person claims that the other is not dealing as consumer, that person has the burden of establishing this.

The mere fact that a party is a business (e.g., a partnership or a corporation) will not necessarily mean that particular contracts which it enters into are made in the course of business. In *R & B Customs Brokers Co. Ltd* v *United Dominions Trust Ltd* [1988] 1 WLR 321, the Court of Appeal held that a transaction would be made in the course of a business where it was integral to the nature of the business or, if only incidental to the carrying on of the relevant business, where there was a degree of regularity in entering into such transactions.

The plaintiff company was a small company and operated as a freight forwarding agent. The company was owned and managed by a husband and wife. The company purchased a car under a conditional sale agreement from the defendant finance company. The car was to be used for both business and private use. However, it proved to be defective and the plaintiff company brought an action against the defendant. The defendant sought to rely on an exemption clause in the contract excluding the implied conditions as to the quality of the car or its fitness for purpose unless the buyer was dealing as a consumer. Therefore the crucial question was whether the plaintiff company had purchased that car 'in the course of a business', which would exclude it from contracting as a consumer.

The Court of Appeal relied on the meaning of these words as they had been interpreted in the context of the Trade Descriptions Act 1968, to the effect that a contract would be made 'in the course of a business' only if the contract in question was an integral part of the business, or such contracts were entered into with such regularity that it could be treated as integral. Applying this test, the Court held that the plaintiff company was dealing as a consumer (and not in the course of a business) because purchasing cars was not integral to the company's business; and since they had bought only one or two cars in this way, there was also not the necessary regularity to render this a contract entered into in the course of a business.

This decision has rightly been criticised. It seems strange that the same expression used in s. 1(3) of UCTA 1977 appears to have been interpreted on the basis of the identity of the party without embarking upon the sort of analysis of the transaction, which is called for under the *R & B* test (see, for example, *St Albans and District Council* v *International Computers Ltd* [1995] FSR 686 — assumption that a local authority was contracting 'in the course of a business' because it fell within the s. 14 definition of a business).

It may also be criticised as introducing potential uncertainty, and because it is far from clear that s. 12 was intended to give protection to companies in this way (see also comparison with the Unfair Terms in Consumer Contracts Regulations 1999, which are inapplicable to regulate terms used against a company). However, in terms of result, the *R & B Customs* decision may be no bad thing, in that it does allow for a measure of discretion to allow the protection of s. 6(2) (and also s. 3) to small businesses who have not made the individual contract as an integral part of the business. Of course, some contracts will be integral, e.g., garage business purchases cars for resale when the garage company would be a non-consumer when entering into such contracts. The effect of s. 12(1)(c), requiring that in the context of sale contracts the goods supplied must be of a type ordinarily supplied for private use and consumption, will also limit the scope of a finding that a company has purchased goods as a consumer.

The result in *R & B Customs* may be easier to justify on the basis that the car was purchased for both business and personal use. This means that it is possible to rationalise the decision as being in line with the position under s. 5, UCTA 1977 (exclusions in guarantees of consumer goods; see 6.6.2.3). Such exclusions are totally unenforceable if the goods prove defective 'while in consumer use' and by s. 5(2); goods are defined as being 'in consumer use' when they are being used 'otherwise than exclusively for the purposes of a business'. On the facts in *R & B Customs*, since the car was not exclusively for business use, it would have been 'in consumer use', and hence it is feasible to consider the purchasing company as a consumer for the purposes of s. 6(2) and s. 3 of the 1977 Act. On this basis, the position ought to be different if the car is purchased exclusively for the use of the husband and wife for business purposes. However, this is not the test in *R & B Customs*.

More recently, the Court of Appeal had to consider the meaning of the words 'in the course of a business' in the context of s. 14 of the SGA 1979 (see 5.5.3.2). In *Stevenson* v *Rogers* [1999] 2 WLR 1064, it was argued that the sale of a trawler by a fisherman was not 'in the course of a business' so that there was no implied term as to quality. The Court of Appeal held that, under the 1979 Act, a sale would be in the course of a business unless it was a purely private transaction outside the scope of any business carried on by the seller. Accordingly, there was such an implied term in this contract. Significantly, the test applied by the Court of Appeal would bring the contract within the expression 'in the course of a business' where the sale is incidental to the seller's business. There was also no requirement to establish regularity.

There has been support for adopting the *Stevenson* v *Rogers* interpretation in the context of UCTA 1977 (see MacDonald (1999) 3 Web JCL 1), especially because it is difficult to justify different results under the two statutes arising from analysis of the same transaction, but *R & B Customs* remains good law in relation to s. 12 of UCTA at the present time.

Section 3: general contractual liability   Section 3 of the 1977 Act will apply to breaches of strict contractual obligations, other than the implied goods obligations covered by ss. 6 and 7, but only if one of the qualifying conditions is applicable. The qualifying conditions in s. 3(1) are that either one party deals as consumer (see above discussion of the meaning of this expression in s. 12(1)), or one party deals on the other party's written standard terms of business.

'Written standard terms of business' is not defined in the Act. Many contracts are in standard form, and s. 3 is clearly intended to apply to such contracts. It has not been clear, however, how much 'individualisation' of such standard forms is permitted before the section ceases to apply. For example, many standard forms leave blanks in the clauses relating to quantity and to price which must be filled in for each particular contract. The policy behind the Act ought to mean that such forms are still within the meaning of the section. Traditionally, however, it has been less clear whether a standard form in which the original offeree had deleted certain terms and then sent it back (as a counter-offer), and which had then been accepted by the original offeror, would still be within the meaning of the section. In *Chester Grosvenor Hotel Co. Ltd* v *Alfred McAlpine Management Ltd* (1991) 56 BLR 115, Judge Stannard said:

> What is required for terms to be standard is that they should be regarded by the party which advances them as its standard terms and that it should habitually contract in those terms. If it contracts also in other terms, it must

be determined in any given case, and as a matter of fact, whether this has occurred so frequently that the terms in question cannot be regarded as standard, and if on any occasion a party has substantially modified its prepared terms, it is a question of fact whether those terms have been so altered that they must be regarded as not having been employed on that occasion.

The question of what constitutes written standard terms was considered at length by Judge Thayne Forbes, acting as an official referee in the High Court, in *Salvage Association v CAP Financial Services Ltd* [1995] FSR 654. There were two contracts. The first was contained in a document produced in advance by the defendants; the conditions of business stated were accepted without any attempt to renegotiate any of them. The defendants argued that they would have been willing to renegotiate, but the judge did not allow this to deflect him from finding that this contract was concluded on the defendants' written standard terms of business. The second contract took as its point of departure the first, but was further negotiated and, seemingly, amendments made. The mere fact that the parties started with a document prepared by one of them in advance did not make this a standard-form agreement. It was a question of fact, taking into account the degree of negotiation and variation, and alternatively the degree of imposition of terms, in the light of the relative bargaining power of the parties. In this case, the second contract had moved sufficiently away from the original written standard terms of business for s. 3 not to apply.

In *St Albans City & District Council v International Computers Ltd* [1996] 4 All ER 481 (for full treatment see 6.6.2.7), the defendants had submitted their own standard form for negotiation, but the Court of Appeal held, affirming the decision of Scott Baker J on this point ([1995] FSR 686), that the local authority had contracted on the defendants' written standard terms of business because the standard form 'remained effectively untouched'. In particular, Nourse LJ stressed the fact that the section referred to 'dealing', which meant 'making a deal' and could thus be distinguished from any negotiations preceding it. If the terms are amended as a result of negotiations, Scott Baker J considered that, assuming the amendments were not too substantial, the contract could remain as standard-form as long as there was no negotiation over the 'relevant exempting terms'. Such negotiation would appear to be fatal.

A very generous interpretation was adopted by Judge Bowsher QC in *Pegler v Wang (UK) Ltd* [2000] BLR 218. The problem on the facts was that it was not the contract itself, but the exclusion and limitation clauses inserted in it, which were standard-form clauses used by the defendant. The Judge held that as the defendant considered these clauses to be non-negotiable, in relation to these material clauses, the claimant had clearly contracted on the defendant's 'written standard terms of business'. On this interpretation, it was not necessary for the whole contract to be in standard form. What mattered was whether there had been negotiation of the relevant clauses. It therefore appears that it may be sufficient that the only standard clause is the exemption.

A less controversial example is provided by the first instance decision in *Watford Electronics Ltd* v *Sanderson CFL Ltd* [2000] 2 All ER (Comm) 984. Judge Thornton QC had to consider whether the addition of a clause committing the defendant to use its best endeavours to allocate appropriate resources to the project, precluded the application of s. 3 of UCTA 1977. The judge held that the test was whether the written standard form was relied upon 'without *material* variation' (emphasis added). He concluded that the standard term had not been varied because the amendment was no more than a vague and unenforceable obligation. However, even if the amendment had been enforceable, it would have to be considered against the totality of the standard conditions which otherwise remained unaltered. As such an amendment would have been narrow and insubstantial, the contract would still have been made on the basis of the defendant's written standard terms of business. (The decision on reasonableness was overturned on appeal to the Court of Appeal (see 6.6.2.7), but no appeal was heard on the general application of s. 3.)

The importance of establishing that the contract was made on 'the other's written standard terms of business' has become increasingly clear. Often the application of UCTA 1977 will turn on this finding. Two conclusions emerge from the recent case law: (i) there must be no negotiation of the relevant exempting terms; and (ii) any amendment of other terms will have to be considered against the totality of the standard conditions.

The Law Commission made a deliberate decision not to recommend a definition of 'written standard terms of business' on the basis that any definition would provide businesses with the ability to draft to avoid it (Law Commission Report on *Exemption Clauses*, Law Com No. 69, para. 157), but the current position is generating a good deal of judicial argument on the matter. There are also potential problems in the requirement that the standard terms be 'written' for electronic contracting and the Electronic Communications Act 2000 (see MacDonald and Poyton [2000] 3 Web JCL 1). No doubt the Law Commission will examine these, and other questions, in its review of the law regulating unfair terms.

Where a party deals as consumer, or on the other's standard terms, that other may not exclude or limit his or her liability for breach of contract by means of a term in the contract except in so far as the term satisfies the requirement of reasonableness (s. 3(2)(a), UCTA 1977). The 'reasonableness' test is considered below (6.6.2.6).

Terms which modify expected contractual obligations   In general, exemption clauses operate to exclude or limit liability for breach. However, careful drafting of a contract may result in the performance obligation being such that a performance which might normally be regarded as defective does not amount to breach. In this case it is said that the term defines the performance obligation, rather than simply exempting liability for breach. Indeed, some commentators (notably D. Yates, *Exemption Clauses in Contracts*, 2nd edn, Sweet & Maxwell, 1992 pp. 123–33, see 6.4) argue that in most circumstances exemption clauses should be read in the context of the whole agreement, rather than as separate from the rest of the agreement, so that most so-called exemption clauses are obligation-defining rather than liability-exempting. As we saw at 6.4, there is some support for this approach in the speech of Lord Diplock in *Photo Production Ltd v Securicor Transport Ltd* [1980] AC 827.

The approach assumes that where the parties have defined the obligations in a particular way, there is no reason to exert the kind of control thought to be desirable where one party seeks to exempt liability. The difficulty with this assumption is that it appears to fail to take account of the fact that many contracts are perceived as being standardised, so that there is a general expectation, independent of any particular contract, of the content of such contracts. To vary the terms from those generally expected may be just as undesirable as to exclude liability, if the effect is to deprive one party of what was reasonably expected under the contract. It is only if contracts are exclusively the product of the will of the parties, rather than constructed from common intention and certain obligations imposed by law, that it would be reasonable to suggest that the proper expectation of the content of a contract can be determined by an examination of its particular terms and nothing else. Modern contract theory does not generally accept such a proposition. The orthodox approach, then, is to treat exemption clauses generally as separate from the rest of the contract, and therefore not as defining the obligations, and that approach is taken by UCTA 1977. The orthodox approach was also adopted by the Court of Appeal in *Phillips Products Ltd v Hyland* [1987] 1 WLR 659 (see also *Smith v Eric S. Bush* [1990] 1 AC 831). Slade LJ said (at 664):

> In our judgment, in considering whether there has been any breach of any obligation . . . the court has to leave out of account, at this stage, the contract term which is relied on by the defence as defeating the plaintiffs' claim for breach of such obligation or duty. . . .

In addition, the 1977 Act attempts to restrict the use of unreasonable obligation-defining clauses. By s. 3(2)(b) of the Act, a party may not claim to be entitled:

> (i)   to render a contractual performance substantially different from that reasonably expected of him; or
> (ii)   . . . to render no performance at all,
> except in so far as the contract term satisfies the requirement of reasonableness.

Of course, these provisions apply only in the case of contracts where one party deals as consumer or on the other's written standard terms (s. 3(1), UCTA 1977; see above).

Section 3(2)(b)(ii) is something of a red herring. If one party is defined by the contract as being under no obligations at all, the contract must surely fail for want of consideration (4.3). Where the absence of obligation affects only part of the contract, it can be dealt with under s. 3(2)(b)(i).

Section 3(2)(b)(i) assumes that it is possible to identify a performance which is reasonably to be expected. This assumption might be realised in two ways. In the first place, the contract might be of a recognised and standardised type. For example, a contract for the provision of domestic decorating services is rarely negotiated in detail. In particular, it is unlikely that the parties will discuss measures to be taken to protect existing decoration which is not to be replaced. Rather, the customer will assume that the decorator will take reasonable care to avoid damage to existing decorations, and such a term would normally be implied in law (*cf.* s. 13, Supply of Goods and Services Act 1982). If the decorator's order form, which was signed by the customer, included a term making protection of existing decorations the responsibility of the customer, such a term would have defined the contractual obligations in a way other than would generally have been expected. Section 3(2)(b)(i) does not say that it is not permitted to redefine the contractual obligations in such a way; it merely says that it is not permitted unless reasonable. This test might be satisfied relatively easily in such a case by showing that the customer was fully aware of the effect of the clause, and possibly by showing that the price charged was lower than would be charged where it was the decorator's contractual responsibility to take such precautions.

Alternatively, there may be a conflict between the apparent main purpose of the contract and the performance one party is entitled to tender under the terms contained in the fine print of the agreement. For example, in *Anglo-Continental Holidays Ltd* v *Typaldos Lines (London) Ltd* [1967] 2 Lloyd's Rep 61, the plaintiffs made particular holiday arrangements through a travel agent. The contract contained a clause stating that 'Steamers, sailing dates, rates and itineraries are subject to change without notice.' The Court of Appeal refused to allow the defendants to rely on the clause to escape liability for breach of contract when the original arrangements were changed unilaterally. Russell LJ pointed out, however, that the clause was not an exemption clause but a clause defining the contractual liability. In his view, 'the propounder of that clause cannot be enabled thereby to alter the substance of the arrangement'. Under s. 3(2)(b)(i) of the 1977 Act, assuming the qualifying conditions of s. 3(1) were met, the issue would have been whether the clause was unreasonable in allowing changes to be made unilaterally from what had apparently been agreed under the main provisions of the contract.

6.6.2.5 Special provisions An indemnity clause in a contract is a clause under which one party agrees to indemnify the other for any liability incurred. Such a clause may have the same effect as an exemption clause, and in any case often transfers liability away from the party who would normally be liable. Such a clause is effective against a person who deals as consumer only in so far as it satisfies the requirement of reasonableness (s. 4, UCTA 1977). On the other hand, a transfer of liability between potential defendants, neither of which deals as a consumer, is apparently a form of duty-defining clause which is not subject to control under the Act at all, on the basis that it leaves the claimant's right to a remedy untouched (*Thompson* v *T. Lohan (Plant Hire) Ltd* [1987] 1 WLR 649).

Section 10 of the UCTA 1977 is intended to prevent the evasion of the provisions of the Act by means of a secondary contract. Since the main provisions of the Act are concerned with terms in contracts which exclude or restrict liability arising under those contracts, it was feared that imposing such exclusions and restrictions by means of separate contracts might thwart the purpose of the Act. Section 10 attempts to close that loophole. A typical situation addressed by this provision would be where a maintenance contract, entered into in connection with the purchase of goods, purports to exclude or restrict rights arising under the purchase contract. In *Tudor Grange Holdings Ltd* v *Citibank NA* [1992] Ch 53, Browne-Wilkinson V-C held that s. 10 only applies to 'attempts to evade the Act's provisions by the introduction of such an exemption clause *into a contract with a third party*' (emphasis added). Consequently, in terms of the situation described above, s. 10 would apply where the maintenance service contract, which provides the vehicle for the exemption clause, is entered into with a party other than the supplier of the goods; it does not apply where the supplier is also the principal party to the maintenance agreement.

It must therefore be asked whether this interpretation of s. 10 leaves a loophole in cases where the secondary contract which exempts liability is entered into by both parties to the original contract. It is submitted that it does not, because the other provisions of the Act are drafted sufficiently widely to catch terms in secondary contracts between the original parties which purport to exempt liability under the original contract. That is, the Act does not presuppose or require that the foundation of liability and any purported exemption be contained in a single contract for its provisions to apply.

The careful construction of s. 10 of the 1977 Act by Browne-Wilkinson V-C in *Tudor Grange Holdings Ltd* v *Citibank NA*, arose out of a challenge to a settlement of a claim. The plaintiffs claimed breach of contract by the bank, and argued that the bank's defence, based on a contractual settlement of the claim, was ineffective because the settlement was unenforceable under s. 10, UCTA 1977. However, as we have already seen, since the contract settling the claim was between the original parties to the banking contract, s. 10 did not apply. Moreover, Browne-Wilkinson V-C saw the possibility of compromises or settlements being challenged under the Act as most undesirable as a matter of policy, and accordingly would interpret the Act as not extending to such transactions, relying upon what he took to be Parliament's intention and the mischief aimed at by the Act.

6.6.2.6 The 'reasonableness' requirement: s. 11
The requirement of reasonableness imposed by the 1977 Act is highly, and arguably unnecessarily, complex. In addition, although the policy objective appears to be fairly clear in the context of consumer contracts, it is far from straightforward in the context of commercial contracts, and discernible differences in policy can be identified in the case law (see Adams and Brownsword (1988) 104 LQR 94).

It is important to appreciate at the outset that the reasonableness requirement is not always the applicable test under the Act (see, e.g., s. 2(1), UCTA 1977) and the temptation to apply it to all clauses must therefore be resisted.

Section 11(1) defines the test for determining reasonableness as whether the term is a fair and reasonable one to have been included in the light of circumstances known (or which ought to have been known) to the parties at the time of contracting. In other words, the court may not take into account subsequent events, and in particular the actual effect of breach, in determining whether the exemption clause was reasonable. Nevertheless, it seems likely that the courts will be able to have regard to the effect of the breach if they wish. Under s. 11(1), UCTA 1977, they may consider circumstances which should have been in the contemplation of the parties at the time of contracting. If a particularly serious breach has occurred, a court could hold that the parties should have realised the possibility of such a serious breach, and then find that it was unreasonable at the time of contracting to exclude liability for such consequences.

Section 11(5) provides that the burden of proving reasonableness lies on the party seeking to rely on the exemption clause.

6.6.2.7 Factors relevant in the assessment of reasonableness

The approach   In *George Mitchell (Chesterhall) Ltd* v *Finney Lock Seeds Ltd* [1983] 2 AC 803, Lord Bridge set out the approach to be taken by the courts in assessing reasonableness. Although Lord Bridge rejected the notion that such a decision was 'an exercise of discretion', he accepted that the courts 'must entertain a whole range of considerations, put them in the scales on one side or the other, and decide at the end of the day on which side the balance comes down'.

It follows that each case must necessarily turn on its own particular facts, so that cases have limited significance in terms of their precedent value. In *Phillips Products Ltd* v *Hyland* [1987] 1 WLR 659, the Court of Appeal made this clear. Slade LJ, speaking for the whole court, said (at 668–669):

> The question for the court is not a general question whether or not condition 8 is valid or invalid in the case of any and every contract of hire entered into between a hirer and a plant owner who uses the relevant CPA conditions. The question was and is whether the exclusion of Hamstead's liability for negligence satisfied the requirement of reasonableness imposed by the Act, in relation to *this particular contract* . . . . It is important therefore that our conclusion on the particular facts of this case should not be treated as a binding precedent in other cases where similar clauses fall to be considered but the evidence of surrounding circumstances may be very different. (emphasis in original)

The significance of this denial of precedent value for judicial decisions on the reasonableness of exemption clauses soon became apparent when the same clause was treated quite differently (in a different fact situation by a differently constituted Court of Appeal) in *Thompson* v *T. Lohan (Plant Hire) Ltd* [1987] 1 WLR 649. (It is therefore preferable to speak of a clause being 'unenforceable' because of the application of the reasonableness test in UCTA 1977, rather than void.)

Nevertheless, in *Smith* v *Eric S. Bush* [1990] 1 AC 831, the House of Lords appears deliberately to have attempted to set down a general rule on the unacceptability of exclusions of liability by professional surveyors towards private house buyers. In confronting the question of reasonableness, Lord Templeman and Lord Griffiths both considered 'the general pattern of house purchases' and the impact of their finding on other transactions of the same type, while limiting their 'ruling' to domestic house purchases and reserving their position on exclusions of liability in respect of surveys of commercial property. The real significance of this decision appears to be that it represents a rare reported example of the application of the reasonableness requirement to a consumer contract and as a matter of policy the objectives of UCTA 1977 in this context are much clearer than is the case in the context of commercial contracts.

Until fairly recently, there were few reported decisions involving the reasonableness test. This was partly attributable to the fact that many of the consumer cases would be decided by the county courts, and also because editors of law reports presumably considered there to be little value in reporting case law which had no real value as a precedent. Although there are signs that this position may be changing because it is possible to identify trends and recurring factors in the case law, the decisions reported tend to have concerned commercial contracts. This is probably because of the size of the claims involved and the significance in financial terms of a finding that the exemption clause is reasonable or unreasonable. However, it may also be because the approach of the courts in the context of commercial contracts is more interesting because there is no obvious policy objective (as clearly exists in the consumer context).

The role of appellate courts   In *George Mitchell*, Lord Bridge also explained that in the light of the essentially fact-based exercise undertaken by the courts, and on the basis that the court at first instance will have heard all the evidence and witness statements relevant to the factors, 'the appellate court should treat the original decision with the utmost respect and refrain from interference with it unless satisfied that it proceeded upon some erroneous principle or was plainly and obviously wrong'. For a recent example where the Court of Appeal overturned a first instance finding on reasonableness, see *Watford Electronics Ltd* v *Sanderson CFL Ltd* [2001] EWCA Civ 317, [2001] 1 All ER (Comm) 696.

Factors identified by the legislation   In the first place, under s. 11(4) of the UCTA 1977, there is a special test applicable to limitation clauses (i.e., clauses restricting liability to a specified sum of money). In such cases the court must have particular regard to whether the person seeking to limit his or her liability could expect to have resources available to meet such liability should it arise, and to the extent to which it was possible for him or her to have obtained insurance cover for such liability. It is important to note that the cost and availability of insurance has been applied more generally as a factor (e.g., *Photo Production Ltd* v *Securicor Transport Ltd* [1980] AC 827 —

the House of Lords stressed that the cost of the patrolling service was modest and that it was reasonable for the factory owners to cover this risk by taking out insurance cover).

Under s. 11(2), in the case of exemptions of implied terms in the sale or supply of goods (ss. 6 and 7, UCTA 1977; see 6.6.2.4), the court is referred to a set of guidelines on reasonableness, set out in sch. 2. Among the factors to be taken into account are: the relative strengths of the bargaining positions of the parties; whether in agreeing to the exemption a party received an inducement (e.g., a lower price); whether any condition for the enforcement of liability (e.g., claiming within seven days of performance) could practicably be complied with; and whether the goods were specially made at the request of the buyer.

Although in theory this list of factors applies only in the context of exclusions of implied terms in sale and supply contracts, these factors have been applied more generally by the courts (as confirmed by Stuart Smith LJ in *Stewart Gill Ltd v Horatio Myer & Co. Ltd* [1992] 1 QB 600 at 608). Their application has now become a matter of course in case law involving an assessment of reasonableness; so much so, that judgments are frequently structured around their application.

Factors identified by the courts   Bearing in mind the limitations of decided cases in this area as precedents, it is proposed to examine some of these cases in an attempt to identify recurring factors and themes which may be of assistance in terms of giving advice.

In their article ((1988) 104 LQR 94), Adams and Brownsword identify two different approaches to reasonableness in the commercial context. In the first place there is the *Photo Production* approach of freedom of contract and ability to allocate risks bearing in mind the availability of insurance cover. This approach has gained prominence in recent decisions — see, for example, *Monarch Airlines Ltd v London Luton Airport Ltd* [1997] CLC 698 and *Watford Electronics Ltd v Sanderson CFL Ltd* [2001] EWCA Civ 317, [2001] 1 All ER (Comm) 696 (below). On the other hand, there is a more interventionist approach exemplified by the decision in *George Mitchell*.

In *George Mitchell (Chesterhall) Ltd v Finney Lock Seeds Ltd* [1983] 2 AC 803, the defendants had supplied cabbage seed at a contract price of approximately £200. The cabbages did not grow properly, causing lost production to the value of £61,000. The contract purported to limit liability for defective seeds to the amount of the contract price. The contract did not fall under UCTA 1977 because it was entered into before 1 February 1978, but it was subject to the reasonableness test applicable under s. 55(3) of the SGA 1979, which for these purposes was essentially similar to the UCTA 1977 test.

In the Court of Appeal ([1983] QB 284), in finding the clause to be unreasonable, Kerr LJ reasoned as follows (at 313–314):

The balance of fairness and reasonableness appears to me to be overwhelmingly on the side of the plaintiffs . . . Farmers do not, and cannot be

expected to, insure against this kind of disaster; but suppliers of seeds can
. . . I am not persuaded that liability for rare events of this kind cannot be
adequately insured against. Nor am I persuaded that the cost of such cover
would add significantly to the cost of seed. Further, although the present
exemption clause has been in existence for many decades, the evidence
shows that it was never negotiated. In effect, it was simply imposed by the
suppliers, and no seed can in practice be bought otherwise than subject to
its terms. To limit the supplier's liability to the price of the seed in all cases,
as against the magnitude of the losses which farmers can incur in rare
disasters of this kind, appears to me to be a grossly disproportionate and
unreasonable allocation of the respective risks.

This decision can be compared with that in *R.W. Green Ltd v Cade Brothers
Farms* [1978] 1 Lloyd's Rep 602, where a supply of potatoes had been infected
with a virus but a limitation clause in the contract purported to limit liability to
the price (£634), although the actual loss of profit on the crop was around
£6,000. This limitation clause was held to be reasonable because the parties
were of equal bargaining power, the clause had been negotiated between
relevant trade bodies and had been in use for many years. In addition, the
buyers could have paid more to obtain a guarantee against the virus.

In the commercial context the most important factors pointing to the
reasonableness of a clause appear to be equality of bargaining position,
whether the clause is a generally accepted clause in the industry in question
and whether, on this basis, it is essentially a clause allocating a particular risk
between two commercial parties thereby avoiding the risk of duplicate
insurance. These factors were cited in *Monarch Airlines Ltd v London Luton
Airport Ltd* [1997] CLC 698, in support of a finding that a clause, excluding
the liability of the airport for unintentional damage to aircraft, was reasonable. They were also used in the context of a 'no set-off' clause in a
commercial agreement in *Schenkers Ltd v Overland Shoes Ltd* [1998] 1 Lloyd's
Rep 498. The clause in question was in common use (having been arrived at
following negotiations between the relevant representative bodies). It was also
well known in the trade and by these parties who were in roughly equal
bargaining positions.

In *Watford Electronics Ltd v Sanderson CFL Ltd* [2001] EWCA Civ 317,
[2001] 1 All ER (Comm) 696, there was a claim for damages for breach of
a contract to supply a bespoke integrated software system. The contract
contained the defendant's standard terms, including a clause purporting to
exclude any liability for indirect or consequential losses and a clause limiting
liability in a general sense to the price paid under the contract (£104,600).
The contract also contained entire agreement clauses (see 5.2.4). The system
proved to be faulty and the claimant sought damages amounting to £5.5m
for breach of contract (namely loss of profits, the increased costs of working
and reimbursement of the cost of replacement), or alternatively £1.1m for
misrepresentation and negligence.

At first instance ([2000] 2 All ER (Comm) 984) the judge held the
exemption clauses to be unreasonable in their entirety. However, the Court

of Appeal considered that the judge had reached his conclusion on an incorrect basis as he had failed to consider them as separate clauses (i.e., as a term excluding indirect losses and as a term limiting liability for direct loss), to distinguish the relevant liability and to consider reasonableness in relation to each clause. The Court of Appeal reversed the judge's decision so that the clauses were considered to be reasonable.

The Court stressed the need to consider reasonableness in the light of the contract terms as a whole, including the entire agreement clauses whereby the claimant had agreed that it had no reliance on any pre-contractual statements or representations. The judge had therefore been wrong to conclude that the exemption clause could cover liability for misrepresentation since the intention behind the entire agreement clause was to prevent that liability arising in the first place.

The clauses were reasonable because the contract had been negotiated between experienced businessmen of equal bargaining power and skill. Both should have appreciated the party which was to bear the risk of loss and would anticipate that the price would reflect that risk. Chadwick LJ stated (at [54]):

> In circumstances in which parties of equal bargaining power negotiate a price for the supply of product under an agreement which provides for the person on whom the risk of loss will fall, it seems to me that the court should be very cautious before reaching the conclusion that the agreement which they have reached is not a fair and reasonable one.

He went on to state that

> . . . experienced businessmen representing substantial companies of equal bargaining power . . . should . . . be taken to be the best judge of the commercial fairness of the agreement which they have made; including the fairness of each of the terms in that agreement . . . Unless satisfied that one party has, in effect, taken unfair advantage of the other — or that a term is so unreasonable that it cannot properly have been understood or considered — the court should not interfere.

This 'freedom of contract' approach of the Court of Appeal is very much in line with that of the House of Lords in *Photo Production* and, as Peter Gibson LJ stated in his judgment (at [55]), in these circumstances there will be 'little scope for the court to unmake the bargain made by commercial men'.

However, as the decision in *Overseas Medical Supplies Ltd* v *Orient Transport Services Ltd* [1999] CLC 1243 illustrates, it is still possible for a clause to be unreasonable in a commercial contract where it undermines a contractual allocation of risk. The plaintiff contracted with the defendant freight forwarders for the transportation to Iran and back of equipment for an exhibition. The contract provided that the defendant was to insure the equipment. However, the defendant failed to take out the insurance and, in response to a claim by the plaintiff when the equipment was lost, sought to rely on a limitation clause limiting recovery to an amount per kilo (approximately £600 when the actual loss was £8,590).

The judge held that the limitation was reasonable in respect of liability for loss of the goods, but not in relation to liability for breach of the obligation to insure. The Court of Appeal agreed and stressed that the plaintiff had not contracted on equal terms with the defendant with full knowledge of the risks involved. In particular, the plaintiff failed to realise the implications or consider the possibility that the defendant would fail to fulfil the obligation to insure. The failure to insure, when taken with the limitation, would have meant that the customer lost both the goods and the insurance which would otherwise have compensated him. In addition, the plaintiff had no real choice other than to use the defendant, a specialist firm.

This is very similar to the approach in *Edmund Murray Ltd* v *BSP International Foundations Ltd* (1992) 33 Con LR 1. The contract in this case involved the purchase of a drilling rig built to the purchaser's specification. The contract purported to exclude liability for breaches of express terms, including the specification. Neill LJ found the clause unreasonable: the defendants could not promise to build to the purchaser's specification but then deny any right to compensation or redress for failure to meet that specification. The reasoning here is very similar to that of Sir Donald Nicholls V-C in *Lease Management Services Ltd* v *Purnell Secretarial Services Ltd* (1993) 13 Tr LR 337.

For the purposes of assessing the approach in the context of consumer contracts, it is necessary to consider the decision of the House of Lords in *Smith* v *Eric S. Bush* [1990] 1 AC 831. The House of Lords held that a disclaimer contained in a mortgage valuation given in respect of a domestic dwelling was unreasonable because of the lack of equal bargaining power (at least in the context of modest domestic purchases) and because the burden of insurance would be better placed on the valuers than on individual purchasers. It was no answer to argue that the purchasers could have paid more to obtain another, more detailed survey, since it was not a realistic option to pay twice for the same thing and purchasers of domestic dwellings could not afford this extra expense. As one might expect, this is very protectionist in its approach, although the House of Lords made clear that the position might well be different in the case of expensive dwellings or business premises.

Another interesting 'quasi-consumer' case example is the decision in *St Albans City and District Council* v *International Computers Ltd* [1995] FSR 686; [1996] 4 All ER 481. Although the contract was made by a local authority and the clause in question was a limitation clause (as opposed to a total exclusion), there was a clear inequality of bargaining power and clear evidence of a protectionist approach being taken by the courts.

The contract concerned the supply of a computer database for the purposes of calculating local tax rates. A serious error caused the Council a loss of more than £1m, while the contract purported to limit recovery to £100,000. The limitation clause was unreasonable, taking into account the unequal bargaining position of the parties, the extensive resources of the defendant and the small limitation figure relative to the potential actual loss. In addition, the defendant had adequate insurance, whereas reasonably priced insurance cover would probably not have been available to the plaintiff. In practice, the company's customers bore the cost of the insurance cover: if the clause had been effective the loss would have been borne by the taxpayers.

6.6.2.8 The effect and scope of a finding of unreasonableness Each substantive provision of the 1977 Act which subjects an exemption clause to the requirement of reasonableness is drafted in such a way as to make clear that, if the requirement of reasonableness is not met, the clause may not be relied upon to exclude or restrict a liability which would otherwise arise under the contract. Thus, the simple effect of a finding of unreasonableness is to cause the contract to be applied and interpreted without reference to the offending element.

Difficulties may arise in respect of this 'simple' consequence where the exemption clause is in a composite form, relating to several different possible breaches of the contract in question, or purporting to exclude or restrict liability, remedies or procedural rights in more than one way. In such a case the question arises whether a failure to satisfy the requirement of reasonableness in respect of one particular dimension of the clause will cause the whole clause to fail, or whether an offending element may be severed from the remainder of the clause, where that remainder does satisfy the requirement of reasonableness. The question was confronted directly in *Stewart Gill Ltd* v *Horatio Myer & Co. Ltd* [1992] 1 QB 600.

The relevant clause purported to prevent the buyer withholding payment of any amount due to the supplier 'by reason of any payment credit set off counterclaim allegation of incorrect or defective Goods or for any other reason whatsoever which the Customer may allege excuses him from performing his obligations'. The plaintiffs claimed the final instalment due under the contract, which the defendants had withheld because of a counterclaim in respect of an alleged breach. The plaintiffs therefore sought to rely upon the set off and counterclaim element in the exemption clause to show that withholding the sum due was not allowed under the contract, even if the alleged breach by the plaintiffs could be established. The defendants argued that the element in the exemption clause relating to payments and credits was unreasonable, so that the whole clause failed.

Lord Donaldson MR (with whom Balcombe LJ agreed) appears to have been willing to believe that a clause preventing a right of set off might be reasonable, but was unwilling to believe that it might be reasonable to prevent withholding payment where the plaintiffs owed the defendants money as a result of pre-existing payments or credits. The question therefore was whether the unreasonable part relating to payments and credits could be severed from the remainder of the clause. The court was unanimous that it could not: Lord Donaldson relied upon the wording of s. 11(1), which states that the requirement of reasonableness 'is that *the term* shall have been a fair and reasonable one' (emphasis added). Stuart-Smith LJ (with whom Balcombe LJ and Lord Donaldson agreed) relied upon the fact that the assessment of whether the clause is reasonable is to be made in the light of circumstances known to the parties at the time of contracting. He pointed out that it is impossible to know at the time of contracting which part of a composite and potentially severable exemption clause will be relied upon at some indeterminate time in the future, so that unless the entire clause is the subject of scrutiny and stands and falls as a whole, the reasonableness test cannot be applied as laid down by the Act. The decision is criticised by Brown and Chandler ((1993) 109 LQR 41: although their suggestion that the contract was 'negotiated freely' appears to run counter to Lord Donaldson's description of the contract as being on the other's written standard terms of business). They rightly suggest that the response of contract draftsmen to the decision must be to separate composite or omnibus exemption clauses into their distinct parts, so that the unreasonableness of a single part does not render ineffective parts which on their own would not be regarded as unreasonable.

6.6.3   Unfair terms in consumer contracts

In April 1993, the EC Council of Ministers adopted Directive 93/13 on Unfair Terms in Consumer Contracts (OJ 1993 L 95/29). This Directive was originally implemented in English law by subordinate legislation, the Unfair Terms in Consumer Contracts Regulations 1994 (SI 1994 No. 3159), which substantially reproduced the wording, if not the order of presentation, of the Directive itself. However, no attempt was made to tackle any clear overlap or potential conflicts between the Directive, the existing legislation (UCTA 1977) and common law rules. One of the criticisms frequently made is that the implementation of the Directive was rushed (despite the fact that the deadline for its implementation was 31 December 1994 and the Regulations did not take effect until 1 July 1995), and this may explain why there was no attempt to consolidate the Directive and the existing law.

Although the 1994 Regulations have been repealed and replaced with the 1999 Regulations (SI 1999 No. 2083), the only differences of substance relate to so-called pre-emptive challenges to unfair terms by 'qualifying bodies' (see 6.6.3.7) and there is no attempt to rationalise legislative regulation in this area. The potential therefore remains for the English courts to be presented with a series of complex questions about the interplay of the sometimes parallel, sometimes overlapping and potentially conflicting rules. One welcome development is that the Law Commission is currently examining this area of the law. This also coincides with a review of the application of the Directive being conducted by the European Commission (see DTI Consultation Paper, *European Commission Review of Directive 93/13/EEC on Unfair Terms in Consumer Contracts*, July 2000; European Commission Report on Unfair Terms, Com (2000) 248), since it is important to assess whether the Directive has achieved the desired harmonisation of treatment.

6.6.3.1   Scope of the 1999 Regulations   The purpose of the Directive was said to be to harmonise the law relating to 'unfair terms in contracts

concluded between a seller or supplier and a consumer'. The Unfair Terms in Consumer Contracts Regulations 1999 (SI 1999 No. 2083) (which apply to contracts made after 1 October 1999) make this scope clear in reg. 4(1). Regulation 3(1) defines a seller or supplier as 'any natural or legal person who . . . is acting for purposes relating to his trade, business or profession, whether publicly owned or privately owned', and 'consumer' is defined as 'any natural person who is acting for purposes which are outside his trade, business or profession'. Thus, the Regulations are in this sense narrower than the UCTA 1977 because they apply only to consumer contracts. The 1977 Act can apply to commercial contracts (e.g., s. 2, s. 3 (where one party contracts on the other's written standard terms of business), s. 6(3) and s. 7(3)). The definition of 'consumer' in the Regulations means that a company can never qualify as a consumer since companies (and limited liability partnerships) are legal entities. Thus the Regulations cannot apply to terms in contracts entered into between two companies. Technically, a sole trader and a general partnership would fall within the definition of 'natural persons', but in order to gain the protection of the Regulations the individual or individuals in question would need to be acting for purposes which are outside their business purposes. The definition of 'in the course of a business' discussed earlier in the context of UCTA 1977 (6.6.2.4), may well as applicable here, so that if the contract in question is not an integral part of the business, or if only incidental to the carrying on of the business, the contract would need to be entered into with sufficient regularity (see *R & B Customs Brokers & Co. Ltd* v *United Dominions Trust Ltd* [1988] 1 WLR 321).

As we have already seen (6.6.2.4), 'consumer' is defined more generously under the UCTA 1977, and in some circumstances a company may be 'dealing as a consumer' within s. 12(1) of that Act (see *R & B Customs* and discussion at 6.6.2.4).

The 1999 Regulations are narrower than the UCTA 1977 in another sense, since the Regulations will apply only where the term in question is 'not individually negotiated'. By comparison, the 1977 Act may apply to negotiated terms.

On the other hand, the Regulations are also wider in one important respect, namely the fact that they apply to 'unfair terms' in general. For example, the Regulations contain protection against unreasonable deposits and penalty clauses overlapping with previous common law control provided by 'the penalty rule' (13.10.2), although the latter are not limited to consumer contracts, or to contracts which are not individually negotiated. Although the Regulations do apply to exemption clauses (see sch. 2, para. 1(a) and (b) for examples), their coverage also extends beyond this to terms in general (although not those terms covered by reg. 4(2) and reg. 6(2), see below). UCTA 1977 applies only to exemption clauses (as defined by s. 13(1), UCTA 1977). The Regulations do not apply to contractual terms which 'reflect mandatory statutory or regulatory provisions' (reg. 4(2)(a)), the assumption being that if Member States have by legislative act given approval to particular contract terms, those terms cannot by definition be deemed to be unfair (see the Preamble to the Directive, recital 13). The Preamble envisages that 'default' obligations such as s. 14(2) of the SGA 1979 (implied condition that goods sold be of satisfactory quality: 5.5.3.2) would be excluded. This would accord with the treatment of attempts to exclude or limit liability for breach of such terms as against a consumer under s. 6(2), UCTA 1977. Regulation 4(2)(b) also expressly excludes 'the provisions or principles of international conventions', such as the Warsaw Convention limitations on liability towards passengers in aircraft.

In addition, the 1999 Regulations expressly exclude from their scope those terms which define the main subject-matter of the contract and questions relating to the adequacy of the contract price in relation to the performance to be provided by the other party, provided that such terms are in 'plain intelligible language' (reg. 6(2)). These elements are central to the idea of freedom of contract, which is espoused by all Member States, so that it was unacceptable that there should be any attempt to regulate the content of such terms.

6.6.3.2 The term must not be individually negotiated

The control of unfair terms applies only to contractual terms which have not been individually negotiated. Of course, it is most often the case that consumer contracts are in such form. In any event, however, the expression is given the very broadest definition in the 1999 Regulations. Regulation 5(2) provides a presumptive test of when a term is not individually negotiated, that is to say, 'where it has been drafted in advance and the consumer has therefore not been able to influence the substance of the term'. It is also expressly provided (by reg. 5(3)) that a contract may as a whole be treated as a pre-formulated standard form despite the fact that certain aspects of a term or one specific term have been individually negotiated. The intention is clear: the fact that the consumer has been able influence the content of the contract in a minor way does not prevent the remainder of the contract not so influenced from being treated as not individually negotiated and so potentially containing unfair terms. (Compare with the approach to 'other's written standard terms of business' in s. 3(1), UCTA 1977 (6.6.2.4). Difficulties can arise under s. 3(1) if a standard form is used as the basis for negotiation and there is some variation. No such difficulties can arise under the Regulations.) In addition, the burden of proving that a term was individually negotiated (and therefore outside the Regulations) falls on the seller or supplier.

Where the consumer has had an influence on the content of a term through individual negotiation, it is assumed that the term will not be unfair, so that the Regulations apply only to the rest of the contract. Although the logic of this provision may be understood, it is possible to imagine individual negotiation itself being affected by the inequality of bargaining power between parties where one is a consumer, so that it may be a false assumption to believe that individual negotiation is a fail-safe guard against unfairness.

6.6.3.3 Determining unfairness and the meaning of good faith

The contractual term shall be regarded as unfair if 'contrary to the requirement of good faith, it causes a significant imbalance in the parties' rights and obligations arising under the contract, to the detriment of the consumer' (reg. 5(1)).

This provision is the key to the control mechanism adopted by the Directive and introduces the concept of good faith into English law. The most important factor to appreciate is that it is the consumer who will have the burden of proving unfairness under the Regulations. It appears that the notion of 'detriment to the consumer' is unlikely to cause great difficulty; it is subordinate to the notion of 'significant imbalance', and its only purpose is to indicate for whose benefit the control is to be exercised. In the unlikely event of an imbalance *in favour* of the consumer, the term would clearly not be 'unfair'.

The key notion, therefore, is a 'significant imbalance in the parties' rights and obligations arising under the contract' which is in some way contrary to the 'requirement of good faith'. These are vague and ill-defined criteria, and the Regulations fail to make clear the relationship between them. In particular, the drafting of reg. 5(1) does not make clear whether the requirement of lack of good faith is additional to the condition of imbalance between the parties, or whether imbalance is to be regarded in itself as evidence of a lack of good faith. Neither the Directive nor the Regulations provide clear guidance on this matter, or on what constitutes a significant imbalance.

Some assistance in relation to 'good faith' can be gained by referring to recital 16 of the Preamble to the Directive, which defines compliance with the requirement of good faith as being satisfied by dealing equitably and fairly with the consumer, whose legitimate interests must be taken into account. However, in its Further Consultation Document, September 1994 (for details see 6.6.3.7), the DTI stated: 'So far as the directive is concerned, good faith cannot be further elaborated on. It is more than a combination of the factors set out in Recital 16 to the Directive.'

In the 1994 Regulations (now repealed and replaced by the 1999 Regulations), the substance of recital 16 was repeated in the previous sch. 2 to the Regulations, but with the significant omission of any reference to the consumer's legitimate interests. In fact, the old sch. 2 to the Regulations was similar in content to sch. 2 to UCTA 1977, with the exception of old sch. 2(d), having regard to 'the extent to which the seller or supplier has dealt fairly and equitably with the consumer'. However, this assistance has been dropped altogether from the 1999 Regulations (on the grounds that it was not included as a provision of the Directive itself), and the only assistance provided is the general provision contained in reg. 6(1) (old reg. 4(2)) which refers to unfairness as being assessed 'taking into account the nature of the goods or services for which the contract was concluded and referring, at the time of the conclusion of the contract, to all circumstances attending the conclusion of the contract and to all the other terms of the contract or of another contract on which it is dependent'. In summary, therefore, unfairness is determined in the light of the subject-matter, the circumstances surrounding formation and the other terms of the contract. This guidance is very evidently rather general in its nature.

Consequently, identification of the criteria for compliance with the terms of the Regulations is a process of deduction from what is termed (in reg. 5(5)) an 'indicative and non-exhaustive list of the terms which may be regarded as unfair' and which is contained in sch. 2 to the Regulations. That list is too long (17 items) to reproduce here, but it is possible to indicate its main themes. As might be expected, it includes terms which are plainly within the scope of UCTA 1977. Other items on the list appear well beyond the reach of the 1977 Act, such as terms 'enabling a seller or supplier to terminate a contract of indeterminate duration without reasonable notice except where there are serious grounds for so doing' (sch. 2(1)(g)), and terms 'enabling the seller or supplier to alter the terms of the contract unilaterally without a valid reason which is specified in the contract' (sch. 2(1)(j)). Such terms have not been subject to control under English law until now, although it might be argued that in some circumstances they might be classified as terms which modify expected contractual obligations and so are subject to the requirement of reasonableness under s. 3(2)(b)(i) of the 1977 Act (see 6.6.2.4) and some of them might fall within the application of the penalty rule (see 13.10.2).

From this list it appears possible to deduce that imbalance and lack of good faith are distinct elements in the test. For example, a power to alter terms unilaterally constitutes an imbalance in the rights and obligations of the parties: but that in itself is not deemed to be unfair. There must also be no valid reason specified in the contract for such unilateral alteration, and it appears to be the absence of valid reason which constitutes the lack of good faith. Nevertheless, although the two-part mechanics of the test appear to be clearly established, the list also demonstrates the extent to which both imbalance and lack of good faith will always be questions of fact in each particular case, thereby leaving a very considerable element of discretion to the courts.

It will be interesting to see how the English courts tackle this concept of good faith. It seems likely that they will draw on both traditional sources and European influences. Although English law did not formally recognise any concept of 'good faith' as such, the Chancery courts in the exercise of their 'equitable' jurisdiction, developed principles based on conscience and unconscionability which are closer to the notion of good faith in the civil law than any common law concepts. Equally, in the US, the Uniform Commercial Code has developed the idea of unconscionability into a significant regulatory device for contracts. In that context it is said that the purpose of the rule is to prevent oppression or unfair surprise. Since we are back to fairness, there is a danger of circularity. But if the English judges are to be persuaded to mount this latest unruly horse (see Burroughs J in *Richardson* v *Mellish* (1824) 2 Bing 229 at 252), it will surely encourage them if they feel that they have been on similar horses before. It is not in the nature of the common law to develop a new concept overnight and proceed immediately to draw principles therefrom. The common law thrives on experience and analogy, and we should not be surprised if, rather than trying to learn the meaning of good faith from our European partners, English law turns for inspiration to its past.

The only reported decision of the higher courts examining the Regulations (1994 version) is *Director General of Fair Trading* v *First National Bank plc* [2000] 2 WLR 1353. A term in a loan agreement regulated by the Consumer

Credit Act 1974, provided for interest to be paid at the contractual rate on sums owing 'after as well as before any judgment (such obligation to be independent and not to merge with the judgment)'. This meant that interest was paid on any outstanding amount until the judgment was discharged by payment. The Director General of Fair Trading sought an injunction to prevent the continued use of this term, arguing that it was 'unfair' within the Regulations. The Court of Appeal held that the term was unfair because of the imbalance of bargaining power and the fact that the term would create 'unfair surprise'. The problem with this term was that, following a judgment on the debt, the borrower would be required to pay the debt in instalments; but if he complied with that order, he would then find that he had to pay additional sums to cover the contractual interest. However, at no stage was the borrower's attention drawn to this fact.

The Court of Appeal considered that there was a substantial overlap between significant imbalance and absence of good faith. It is also clear that the Court equated 'good faith' with the promotion of 'fair and open dealing', 'prevention of unfair surprise and the absence of real choice'. Peter Gibson LJ (giving the judgment for the Court) referred to the following comment by Professor H. G. Beale in 'Legislative Control of Fairness: The Directive on Unfair Terms in Consumer Contracts' in J. Beatson and D. Friedmann (eds), *Good Faith and Fault in Contract Law*, Oxford University Press, 1995:

> I suspect that good faith has a double operation. First, it has a procedural aspect. It will require the supplier to consider the consumer's interests. However, a clause which might be unfair if it came as a surprise may be upheld if the business took steps to bring it to the consumer's attention and to explain it. Secondly, it has a substantive content: some clauses may cause such imbalance that they should always be treated as unfair.

Peter Gibson LJ then went on to say that 'A term to which the consumer's attention is not specifically drawn but which may operate in a way which the consumer might not reasonably expect and to his disadvantage may offend the requirement of good faith'.

6.6.3.4 Comparison of regulation of exemption clauses under UCTA 1977 and the 1999 Regulations

Note that this discussion relates only to regulation of exemption clauses in consumer contracts, where there may well be overlap in the regulatory provisions available. The Directive permits Member States to provide higher levels of consumer protection so that it is envisaged that there may be additional regulation. The consequence is that distinct bodies of rules, each with a different scope and a different test of what is acceptable in the consumer interest, apply to the same general issues of consumer protection. The result is that consumers are faced with two layers of complex regulation in a vital area of contracts.

The significant difference between UCTA 1977 and the 1999 Regulations is the burden of proof. Whereas under UCTA 1977 either the clause will be totally unenforceable or the burden of proving that the clause is reasonable will fall on the party seeking to rely on the clause, under the 1999 Regulations the consumer (or 'qualifying body' in the case of claims under reg. 12) will have to prove that the term is 'unfair'.

If the clause in question purports to exempt liability in negligence for death or personal injury, it will be unenforceable under s. 2(1) of the 1977 Act. Under the Unfair Terms in Consumer Contracts Regulations 1999, this liability is specifically mentioned as an event which may be regarded as unfair under sch. 2(1)(a), although the Regulations would not apply if the term was individually negotiated. However, it would be most unlikely that this would be the case. Therefore, the main difference under the Act is that the protection against the effect of such a clause is absolute, whereas under the Regulations unfairness would have to be proved for the clause not to be binding on the consumer (reg. 8(1)); albeit that in practical terms the position under the Act and general policy considerations would make it fairly easy to discharge the burden of proof in relation to such a clause.

In relation to a clause exempting liability in negligence for loss or damage (to which s. 2(2), UCTA 1977 would apply), the consumer would need to establish that the clause was 'unfair' within reg. 5(1).

It would appear that the implied terms in sale and supply contracts relating to the goods cannot be 'unfair' under the Regulations because they are mandatory provisions which are not capable of being excluded or limited (reg. 4(2) and ss. 6(2) and 7(2) of UCTA 1977). Other attempts to exclude contractual liability may be 'unfair', assuming that the term was not individually negotiated. This may involve reliance on the illustrative list of terms which may be regarded as unfair contained in sch. 2. However, the consumer would still need to establish the unfairness (reg. 5(1)) on the particular facts.

In relation to clauses which modify or exclude the contractual obligation in a consumer contract and which would be subject to the reasonableness test under UCTA 1977, s. 3(2)(b), sch. 2(1) to the Regulations 1999 makes clear that, in respect of terms to which the Regulations apply, certain terms which allow the non-consumer party to vary expected contractual obligations unilaterally (sch. 2(1)(j), (k)), or which result in an imbalance in the extent to which the parties are contractually bound (sch. 2(1)(c), (o)), may be regarded as unfair terms, although it would be for the consumer to prove that, contrary to the requirement of good faith, there was a significant imbalance in the parties' positions to his or her detriment.

In this respect protection for consumers under the Regulations may prove less effective than under the Act. Although the reasonableness test and the test for unfairness are not the same, they may well lead to the same result in practice, despite the fact that the precise scope and meaning of good faith in English law has yet to be determined. There is some established guidance on reasonableness under the 1977 Act (see 6.6.2.6 and 6.6.2.7). The Bulletins published by the Office of Fair Trading (6.6.3.7), may provide some guidance in relation to unfairness under the Regulations, but to date there has only been one Court of Appeal decision applying the Regulations, namely *Director General of Fair Trading* v *First National Bank plc* [2000] 2 WLR 1353; see 6.6.3.3.

6.6.3.5 Plain, intelligible language   Under reg. 7(1), there is a duty placed on the seller or supplier to ensure that terms offered to the consumer in writing are 'expressed in plain, intelligible language'. This expression is not defined in the 1999 Regulations, and its real value as a requirement may be doubted. The principal reason is that there is no real sanction for not using such language, except that where there is doubt 'the interpretation which is most favourable to the consumer shall prevail' (reg. 7(2)). This rule is similar to the existing rule in English law of *contra proferentem* interpretation of exemption clauses (6.5.2.1), although under the Directive it applies to all terms. Since the only sanction is to be found in the construction of the language of the doubtful term, it is perhaps overstating the case to say that terms must be in plain language: the obligation cannot be effectively enforced. Regulation 7 therefore amounts to no more than a legislative exhortation to use plain language.

6.6.3.6 The consequences of a term being unfair   The principal sanction for the main substantive obligation under the 1999 Regulations is to make unfair terms unenforceable (or not binding) on the consumer (reg. 8(1)). As is noted at 6.6.3.5 above, this sanction does not apply to the obligation to use plain, intelligible language; in such circumstances its operation might render the contract meaningless. Where a term is unfair and so not binding on the consumer, the remainder of the contract 'shall continue to bind the parties if it is capable of continuing in existence without the unfair term' (reg. 8(2)). This appears to imply that where a term contains an unfair element the whole term is affected so that the contract must be read without the whole term. It will be seen later, in the context of illegality, that English law is willing to consider severing the offending parts from terms where that is grammatically possible and consistent with the public policy issues at stake (12.7.10). The severance rule might be thought to contribute to the preservation of contracts; the deletion of whole terms must increase the risk that the commercial balance of the contract will be upset, or that the contract will become too vague to be enforceable. Against this must be balanced the overall purpose of consumer protection, which is perhaps more likely to be guaranteed if unfair terms are completely outlawed (see also 6.6.2.8 in the context of UCTA 1977).

6.6.3.7 General challenges to unfair terms   Article 7 of the Directive requires Member States to ensure that adequate and effective means exist to prevent the continued use of unfair terms, including powers under which persons or organisations having a legitimate interest under national law in protecting consumers shall be able to bring representative 'actions' to determine whether contractual terms drawn up for general use are unfair.

In the first Consultation Document on implementation of the Directive (October 1993), the then UK Government considered that no response to this could be required because representative actions were not possible under English law due to the doctrine of privity of contract. However, this approach was severely criticised and amounted to totally ignoring an article of the

Directive. In particular, the Consumers Association lobbied for the right to bring such representative actions.

The Government gave some ground in the Further Consultation Document (September 1994) by advocating a mechanism for pre-emptive challenges, but it focused solely on the Director General of Fair Trading, who was to be placed under a statutory duty to consider terms in use and was also to be given the right to obtain an injunction to prevent the continued use of such unfair terms. This position was implemented in the 1994 Regulations (old reg. 8), with the effect that two courses of action were open to consumers who considered that their contracts contained unfair terms: court action with reference to the Regulations to prevent the other relying on the clause; or referral to the Office of Fair Trading to ensure that use of the term was discontinued (although with no other direct remedy for the consumer). In fulfilment of its duty of dissemination of information and advice (reg. 15), the Office of Fair Trading has published regular Bulletins (structured in accordance with sch. 2 to the Regulations) in which it gives information on complaints received as well as general policy. These Bulletins also contain examples of terms which the Office considers to be unfair and in relation to which it has obtained undertakings to cease use and/or reformulate. (For further information, refer to the Office of Fair Trading's website at http://www.oft.gov.uk/.)

The 1994 Regulations contained no direct power for any other 'organisation having a legitimate interest under national law in protecting consumers' to take action intended to prevent the continued use of terms found to be unfair. The Consumers' Association commenced proceedings for judicial review in relation to implementation of the Directive (see *R v Secretary of State for Trade and Industry, ex parte Consumers' Association* (unreported), 28 February 1996). The Government decided to take some action, and in January 1998 the Department of Trade and Industry issued a Consultation Paper ('Widening the scope for action under the Unfair Terms in Consumer Contracts Regulations') seeking views on allowing representative actions by other bodies. It was these changes that were included in the 1999 Regulations.

By reg. 10(1), the Director General of the Office of Fair Trading (DGFT) has a duty to consider any complaint made to him alleging that a term is unfair, unless he considers the complaint to be 'frivolous or vexatious' or unless a 'qualifying body' has notified the DGFT that it agrees to consider the complaint. 'Qualifying bodies' are listed in sch. 1 to the 1999 Regulations and are divided in to two types: Part 1 'qualifying bodies' include utility regulators, the Rail Regulator and, as amended by the Unfair Terms in Consumer Contracts (Amendment) Regulations 2001 (SI 2001 No. 1186), the Financial Services Authority; the Part 2 qualifying body is the Consumers' Association. If a Part 1 qualifying body has notified the DGFT that it agrees to consider a complaint, that body will then be under a duty to consider it (reg. 11(1)).

The DGFT (or any qualifying body if it has notified the DGFT) may apply for an injunction to prevent the use of unfair terms in consumer contracts. If the court decides to grant such an injunction, it may relate to any similar term or terms which have the same effect as any term in use or recommended for use.

The DGFT (or other qualifying body if applicable) must give reasons for any decision to apply or not to apply for an injunction under reg. 12 (reg. 10(2) and reg. 11(2)). However, reg. 10(3) recognises that the seller or supplier in question may give an undertaking not to continue use of a term, and that such undertakings may be considered when making the decision whether or not to apply for an injunction. In practice, undertakings have staved off action in all but one case (*Director General of Fair Trading* v *First National Bank plc* [2000] 2 WLR 1353). These undertakings are recorded in the Office of Fair Trading Bulletins, which are likely to prove the main source of information on the concept of 'unfairness' in the future. Even in the *First National Bank* case, in the light of the Court of Appeal's decision, the bank gave an undertaking to amend the term in order to provide consumers with better information and undertook not to enforce the term unless it first considered whether to reduce or relinquish the contractual interest payable. The guidance given in this case will be very helpful in terms of its general approach to the meaning of 'unfair term'. In addition, it is a vitally important decision for the Office of Fair Trading in confirming its position that the term was unfair. Failure in the first such case might have led to greater resistance amongst sellers and suppliers to the giving of undertakings to cease the use of a clause or to amend it.

SEVEN

Discharge by performance, agreement and breach

7.1 BACKGROUND

The primary obligations of a contract are those which determine the performance obligations of the parties (see Lord Diplock in *Photo Production Ltd* v
Securicor Transport Ltd [1980] AC 827). Discharge of a contract is the process
whereby the primary obligations (i.e., the obligations to perform: see 7.2)
under a contract, which is validly formed, come to an end. In many
circumstances the secondary obligation to pay damages to compensate for
losses also ends (e.g., discharge by frustration: see 8.8), but that is not always
the consequence of discharge. In the case of discharge by breach, a secondary
obligation to pay damages for loss caused (or a secondary obligation to pay
the contract price) continues (7.5.1).

It is vitally important to maintain a distinction between the discharge of
valid contracts and the processes by which invalid contracts come to an end
or are invalidated. These are largely dealt with in Part III of this book. A
contract may be invalid because it is affected by mistake (Chapters 3 and 9),
by misrepresentation (Chapter 10), by incapacity (4.6), by duress or by
undue influence (Chapter 11), or by illegality (including restraint of trade:
Chapter 12). In many circumstances no legal process is necessary in the case
of an invalid contract. Since a void contract is automatically of no effect from
the very beginning, and hence gives rise to no obligation to perform, it is
sufficient for the party asserting its invalidity to do nothing, and plead the
invalidity as a defence to a claim for breach.

Where a contract is voidable (e.g., for misrepresentation), the contract
remains valid until set aside by the party who has the right to set it aside. This
process is known as 'rescission' and is very different to discharge of a contract,
because if a voidable contract is rescinded, the contract is then treated as

having no effect from the beginning, whereas discharge of the contract does not destroy the contract itself. It merely brings the primary obligations to an end (see above).

Most commonly, the discharge of a contract will occur on performance of both parties' primary obligations (7.2). However, as an alternative, a contract may be discharged by agreement of the parties. This chapter will briefly examine both discharge by performance and discharge by agreement before focusing on the central issue of the chapter, namely discharge for breach. It is important to bear in mind that there is another form of discharge of a contract, where the operation of the doctrine of frustration discharges both parties from their future obligations. This doctrine is discussed in Chapter 8.

7.2 DISCHARGE BY PERFORMANCE

A contract is discharged by the performance by both parties of all the primary obligations, express and implied, which they owed under the contract. An obligation will be performed only where the performance meets the standard of performance required. Consequently, a failure to reach the required standard will constitute breach.

7.2.1 The standard of performance

Contractual obligations require one of two standards of performance. The general rule is that the performance obligation is strict, so that the contractual obligation must be completely and precisely performed. There is no defence for failure to meet this strict obligation. For example, if a seller fails to deliver the goods to the buyer on the contractual date set for delivery by the seller, it will not avail the seller to argue that he or she could not deliver the goods because his or her own supplier let him or her down. There is a strict contractual breach by the seller in failing to deliver the goods on time, although the seller may have a remedy under the terms of the separate contract with his or her supplier. The only exception to this is for what may be regarded as 'microscopic' deviations (the *de minimis* rule). However, if the failure to meet the strict performance standard falls outside *de minimis*, there will be a breach.

The obligations as to description, fitness for purpose, satisfactory quality and correspondence with sample in a sale of goods contract (ss. 13–15, SGA 1979, at 5.5.3.2) are strict contractual obligations. That is, any failure of performance to match the contractual undertaking, however slight, is still breach. For example, in *Arcos Ltd* v *Ronassen* [1933] AC 470, timber staves of half an inch in thickness were purchased to make into cement barrels. In fact most of the timber was one-sixteenth thicker than the contractual description, although it was still perfectly useable for the purpose of making cement barrels. Nevertheless, this amounted to a breach of contract. Since it amounted to a breach of condition (s. 13, SGA 1979; 7.5.3), the buyer could reject the timber.

In some circumstances the performance obligation is not strict but qualified. If an obligation is qualified there is no requirement to achieve a guaranteed result; instead the obligation is only to exercise reasonable care and skill. An example of a qualified contractual obligation is s. 13 of the Supply of Goods and Services Act 1982 (see 5.5.3.2). At common law this standard of performance has long been regarded as the appropriate standard for professional people such as doctors and lawyers, whose work makes it impossible to guarantee a result. A further example of an implied qualified obligation is provided by the decision of the House of Lords' in *Liverpool City Council* v *Irwin* [1977] AC 239 (obligation to take reasonable care to keep the common parts of a tower block in reasonable repair, and on the facts the local authority had met this standard of performance: see 5.5.3.1). Any failure to exercise reasonable care and skill (i.e., to fail to meet the qualified standard) would amount to breach.

7.2.2   Tender of performance

A party tenders performance when he or she attempts to perform his or her primary obligations under the contract by offering the stipulated performance to the other party. Where the performance obligation requires the party actually to do something (e.g., to deliver goods), the tender of performance may be the best way for a party to show that he or she is ready and willing to perform, in order to be able to treat the other party's non-performance as a repudiation of the contract (see 7.5.2). In this sense, it is the tender of performance which discharges that party's obligation.

   Where the performance obligation requires the party merely to pay for something done by the other party, tender of payment relieves him or her of some obligations but it does not discharge the debt. That party remains obliged to pay the contract debt, and must remain ready and willing to pay to avoid repudiating the contract.

   The payment obligation is a strict obligation, so that in theory the exact amount must be made available unconditionally and in legal tender (*Betterbee v Davis* (1811) 3 Camp 70). For those reasons payment by cheque, unless otherwise agreed, is only a conditional payment, which does not discharge the debt until the cheque has been cleared. It seems likely that today, given the general access to bank accounts and automatic transfers of money, the courts will be willing to imply agreements for means of payment other than physical delivery of cash in most circumstances.

7.3   DISCHARGE BY AGREEMENT

7.3.1   General

A contract may be discharged by agreement between the parties. Where the discharge occurs with the free consent of both parties and without subsequent change of heart, there is no need for any particular form of agreement. The parties may simply abandon performance. In practice, however, in order to guard against a change of heart by the other party, it will be desirable to adopt some form of legally binding agreement to discharge all future performance obligations.

7.3.2 The requirement of consideration

In addition to demonstrating the existence of an agreement to discharge future obligations (*cf. The Hannah Blumenthal* [1983] 1 AC 854, discussed at 2.1.2), the parties must also demonstrate that it is legally enforceable. The best way of so doing will be to establish the existence of a second contract to discharge the first, which will require the existence of consideration (see 4.3.5.1). The detailed rules of the consideration doctrine are considered at 4.3.

Where both parties have performance obligations remaining under the contract, mutual abandonment of those obligations is enough to satisfy the requirement of consideration (i.e., each party agrees to give up his or her right to receive the other's performance), so that such discharge is legally enforceable (4.3.5.1). The position is the same where both parties breach obligations under their contract and then agree to discharge it. However, where one party's obligations are executed, so that only the other party needs to be discharged from further performance, the requirement of consideration may not be satisfied by mere abandonment of the contract.

The parties may enter into a binding release in a document under seal, whereby the party whose obligations have been executed agrees to discharge the other from his or her performance obligations. No consideration is required because this is a document under seal (see 4.1).

It is possible to have an agreement which amounts to *a release and replacement*, which is the total discharge of the original contract followed by the substitution of a new contract between the parties, assuming that there is the necessary consideration present (*cf. Morris* v *Baron & Co.* [1918] AC 1).

Alternatively, there may be a separate agreement supported by new consideration (so-called 'accord and satisfaction') to discharge (or vary) a particular contractual term. For example, one party may agree to release the other from his or her liability to pay damages for that other's breach, if that other pays £200 in compensation. However, it is clear that the 'satisfaction' (i.e., the consideration) cannot be a lesser form of what was due under the contract (*Pinnel's Case* (1602) 5 Co Rep 117a; see 4.3.5.2). In other words, payment of a smaller sum cannot discharge the obligation to pay the full amount owed. This remains the position because the principle in *Williams* v *Roffey Bros & Nicholls (Contractors) Ltd* [1991] 1 QB 1, which identifies consideration as constituted by a practical (or subjective) benefit to the promisor arising from an alteration promise, applies only to alteration promises to pay more and does not apply to alteration promises to accept less than the sum owed (*Re Selectmove Ltd* [1995] 1 WLR 474; 4.3.5.2). Therefore, in order for there to be the necessary 'satisfaction' to support the variation in the contract terms, the promisee will need to supply something extra, such as agreeing to pay a smaller sum on an earlier date or at a different place at the creditor's request.

In the absence of the necessary consideration to support a general release or variation of a contract term, a promise to discharge one or more obligations may have some limited effect because of the operation of the doctrine of equitable (or promissory) estoppel or as a 'waiver'. Since the development of the promissory estoppel doctrine (4.4.2), waiver has become indistinguishable from promissory and equitable estoppel (4.4). The courts have often used the two expressions interchangeably, since both are concerned with forbearance or giving up legal rights. As a result, it may be that it would be better if use of the term 'waiver' were dropped to avoid confusion. In any event, it will be recalled that the effect of promissory estoppel is said to be only to suspend contractual rights and not to terminate them (4.4.5). It might be thought, then, that it has no relevance to the discharge of contracts. Nevertheless, since it may cause instalment obligations to fall into permanent abeyance (4.4.5), in this limited sense it can be said that a contract may be discharged by estoppel.

7.4   SELF-TERMINATING CONTRACTS

A contract may also be discharged by the realisation of a condition subsequent (5.4) stipulated by the parties. The condition may be an event beyond the control of either of the parties (e.g., attainment of a certain point on a cost-of-living index), or may be entirely within the control of one of the parties (e.g., giving and serving a stipulated period of notice). Indeed, where the contract on its face has no provision for termination then, in the absence of any indication of an intention that the contract be perpetual, the courts will imply a term that the contract is terminable upon reasonable notice (*cf. Staffordshire Area Health Authority* v *South Staffordshire Waterworks Co.* [1978] 1 WLR 1387).

7.5   BREACH AND REPUDIATORY BREACH

7.5.1   Introduction

A breach of contract will occur where, without lawful excuse (e.g., frustration; Chapter 8), a party either fails or refuses to perform a performance obligation imposed upon him or her under the terms of the contract. Alternatively, a party may perform his or her contractual obligations but may do so defectively, in the sense of failing to meet the required standard of performance (see 7.2.1).

In general terms, the non-breaching party is entitled to be compensated for the loss he or she suffers which was caused by this breach. This is because the failure to perform a primary obligation under the contract gives rise to a secondary obligation to pay damages or to pay the contract price (see Lord Diplock in *Photo Production Ltd* v *Securicor Transport Ltd* [1980] AC 827). Note, however, that the right to damages may be effectively excluded or limited by an exemption clause in the contract (see Chapter 6), or the case may fall within the limited category of situations in which specific performance is available as a remedy (see generally, Chapter 14). This apart, the secondary obligation to pay damages or the contract price will arise on proof of breach.

The consequences of breach by one party for the other party's performance obligations depend largely upon the nature of the obligation breached (see below, 7.5.2), and upon whether the parties' performance obligations are 'concurrent conditions' (see 7.5.4).

7.5.2 Repudiatory breach

Unless the breach of contract constitutes a repudiatory breach, the contract will remain in force and both parties must continue to perform their obligations under it. However, a repudiatory breach allows the non-breaching party to treat the contract as repudiated. This slightly cumbersome expression is the most accurate description of the effect of such breach. It is often said that such breach discharges or terminates the contract, but neither expression is technically accurate since the primary obligations do not automatically come to an end; and even if the primary obligations cease, secondary obligations under the contract exist after breach (*Photo Production Ltd* v *Securicor Transport Ltd*). It is sometimes said that such breach entitles the non-breaching party to 'rescind' the contract, and this terminology appears to have been approved by some members of the House of Lords (e.g., Lord Roskill in the *Photo Production* case, and Lord Diplock in *Gill & Duffus SA* v *Berger & Co. Inc.* [1984] AC 382). Nevertheless, this meaning of 'rescind' is very different from the meaning of this expression which is applied in the context of misrepresentation (10.5.1), under which a contract is unravelled and treated as if it had never existed from the very beginning. The use of 'rescission' in the context of breach has been attacked several times by Lord Wilberforce (in *Johnson* v *Agnew* [1980] AC 367, and in *Photo Production*). To avoid confusion, it is better to restrict the notion of rescission to misrepresentation, and in the case of breach of contract to use the more cumbersome formulation used above.

The non-breaching party *may* treat the contract as repudiated: he or she is not obliged to. Thus, in the event of a repudiatory breach of contract, the non-breaching party has the option (or 'election') to treat both parties' future obligations to perform as terminated or to affirm the contract (see *Decro-Wall International SA* v *Practitioners in Marketing Ltd* [1971] 1 WLR 361).

If the non-breaching party elects to accepts the breach as terminating the contract, only the parties' future obligations are discharged. The contract itself survives and its terms may be relevant for the purposes of assessing remedies, e.g., any exemption clauses and/or agreed damages clause will remain and will be relevant to the assessment of damages.

The alternative option to termination is for the non-breaching party to affirm the contract. This obliges both parties to continue to perform all remaining obligations due under the contract. Irrespective of whether the non-breaching party decides to terminate or affirm, the breach will cause the secondary obligation to pay damages in compensation to accrue.

It is crucially important to appreciate that if, after a repudiatory breach, the non-breaching party affirms the contract, effectively the 'slate is wiped clean' as far as future performance is concerned. Consequently, defective or non-performance by the party electing to affirm the contract in turn becomes a breach (e.g., *Motor Oil Hellas (Corinth) Refineries SA* v *Shipping Corporation of India, The Kanchenjunga* [1990] 1 Lloyd's Rep 391, HL). It may even be a repudiatory breach entitling the other party, who was originally at fault, to treat the contract as at an end.

7.5.2.1 The election to treat the repudiatory breach as terminating the contract

Until such time as the non-breaching party elects to treat the contract as repudiated, it must be regarded as subsisting. A difficult question of fact may be to ascertain whether the non-breaching party has elected to accept the repudiation and treat the contract as at an end. A clear and unequivocal communication to that effect will resolve the matter, but what if the non-breaching party simply does nothing, and continues to do nothing when the time comes for its next act of performance? In *Vitol SA* v *Norelf Ltd, The Santa Clara* [1996] QB 108, the Court of Appeal held that, as a matter of law, an election to accept the repudiation could not be inferred from the non-breaching party's inaction, with the result that the contract was found to be subsisting. This decision was reversed on appeal by the House of Lords ([1996] AC 800) and the decision of the arbitrator reinstated. In the opinion of Lord Steyn (at 811), whose speech was unanimously supported by the other members of the House of Lords, the question whether the election to treat the contract as repudiated had been communicated was a question of fact, depending on 'the particular contractual relationship and the particular circumstances of the case'. However, he was prepared to accept that 'a failure to perform may sometimes signify to a repudiating party an election by the aggrieved party to treat the contract as at an end'. Lord Steyn then gave two examples of situations where non-performance could be interpreted as an election to treat the contract as at an end. In his first example, an employer informs a contractor that his services are no longer required and that the contractor need not return the next day. If the contractor never returns then, in the absence of any other explanation, this, in Lord Steyn's words, would 'convey a decision to treat the contract as at an end'. The second example concerns an overseas sale with shipment of the goods on a specified vessel sailing on a specified date, where the seller is under a contractual duty to obtain the necessary export licence. If the buyer repudiates the contract before any loading starts and the buyer knows that the seller does not apply for the export licence, 'it may well be that an ordinary businessman . . . would conclude that the seller was treating the contract as at an end'.

On the facts in *The Santa Clara*, the buyers had sent a telex which amounted to a repudiatory breach, and the question was whether that repudiation had been accepted by the sellers who had then not performed any of their own obligations, including tendering the bill of lading (which would be necessary to give rise to the obligation for the buyers to pay the price). One might wonder whether, on the particular facts of this case, the non-breaching party's inaction was sufficiently unequivocal to be treated as communication of the election (and that may have been the motivation of the judgment in the Court of Appeal), but this case arose out of an arbitration, so that questions of fact were within the exclusive jurisdiction of the arbitrator and were not open to review by the courts.

In the rare event of simultaneous breaches by each party, no such election can be inferred, and there will be no effect upon the parties' mutual obligations until one accepts the other's repudiatory breach (*State Trading Corporation of India* v *Golodetz Ltd* [1989] 2 Lloyd's Rep 277).

7.5.2.2   The election to affirm the contract   It is clear that in order for an affirmation to be valid, the non-breaching party must know of the facts giving rise to his or her right to accept the repudiatory breach as terminating the contract and of his or her right to choose between affirming the contract and treating the contract as discharged.

The election to affirm must also be unequivocal and make it clear that the non-breaching party is committing to continuing with performance of the contract. In *Yukong Line Ltd of Korea* v *Rendsburg Investments Corporation of Liberia* [1996] 2 Lloyd's Rep 604, the response to a repudiatory breach indicated that it was 'totally unacceptable' and 'strongly requested' the party in breach 'to honour their contractual obligations' and confirm that this would occur. This was held to be insufficient to convey an intention to continue with the contract. Moore-Bick J (at 608) stated that:

> Considerations of this kind are perhaps most likely to arise when the injured party's initial response to the renunciation of the contract has been to call on the other to change his mind, accept his obligations and perform the contract. That is often the most natural response and one which, in my view, the court should do nothing to discourage. It would be highly unsatisfactory if, by responding in that way, the injured party was to put himself at risk of being held to have irrevocably affirmed the contract.

7.5.2.3   Loss of the right to accept the repudiatory breach as terminating the contract   There is a danger that a party who has not yet affirmed but is still deliberating what to do, may lose the right to treat the contract as terminated because of the operation of estoppel (see *Clough* v *London and North Western Railway Co.* (1871) LR 7 Ex 26). In order for such an estoppel to operate, the position of the breaching party must have been prejudiced in the meantime. In *Peyman* v *Lanjani* [1985] Ch 457, May LJ (at 495–6) adopted the following passage from the judgment of Sholl J in the Australian decision in *Coastal Estates Pty Ltd* v *Melevende* [1965] VR 433, at 443:

> If the defrauded party does not know that he has a legal right to rescind, he is not bound by acts which on the face of them are referable only to an intention to affirm the contract, unless those acts are 'adverse to' the opposite party, i.e., unless they involve something to the other party's prejudice or detriment . . . This is a form of estoppel, for the other party has in such a case acted upon a representation, made by the defrauded party's conduct, that the latter is going on with the contract.

The application of these principles is well illustrated by the facts of *Peyman* v *Lanjani*. The defendant entered into an agreement for the assignment to him of a lease, expressed to be non-assignable, without the true consent of the landlord. The landlord's consent was obtained by deception. The plaintiff then agreed to purchase the lease from the defendant, and again an attempt was made to obtain the landlord's consent by deception, although the plaintiff was not a party to this. On discovering the deception, the plaintiff consulted the solicitor acting for both parties, who urged him to proceed with the purchase. The plaintiff therefore paid the first £10,000 of the purchase price. A month later the plaintiff consulted new solicitors, who advised him of his right to terminate the agreement on account of the defect in the defendant's title caused by the original deception.

The Court of Appeal held that the plaintiff had not lost the right to treat the contract as repudiated. The payment of £10,000 was not an irrevocable election because it had been made before the plaintiff was aware of the full facts, including that he had a right to treat the agreement as at an end. Neither did it give rise to an estoppel preventing the plaintiff from treating the contract as repudiated, most particularly because there was no detriment to the defendant.

In the context of sale of goods, the option to terminate the contract for repudiatory breach will be lost once the buyer has accepted the goods (s. 11(4), SGA 1979). Section 35(1) and (2) define this acceptance to include express indication of acceptance or, once the goods have been delivered, any act by the buyer which is inconsistent with the seller's ownership after the buyer has had a reasonable opportunity to inspect the goods to determine their conformity with the contract, or to compare the bulk with the sample. A buyer is also deemed to have accepted the goods after the lapse of a reasonable time in which he or she has retained the goods without indicating an intention to reject them (s. 35(4)). The availability of a reasonable opportunity to inspect the goods is a material factor in determining whether the 'reasonable' time has passed so as to constitute a lapse of time. However, the buyer is not deemed to have accepted the goods by asking for or agreeing to repair (s. 35(6)(a)), or delivering the goods to a third party under a sub-sale (s. 35(6)(b)), or by accepting part of a delivery of goods (most probably a part unaffected by the breach) while claiming to be entitled to reject the rest (s. 35A(1)).

Except as described above in the case of the sale of goods, the right to treat the contract as repudiated is not lost by mere lapse of time. The contrary view is canvassed in *Antaios Cia Naviera SA* v *Salen Rederierna AB, The Antaios* [1983] 1 WLR 1362 (affirmed on other grounds [1985] AC 191), but the argument there, that there is an implied term that notice of withdrawal must be given within a reasonable time, relates to the particular context of a charter-party and should not necessarily be regarded as being of any wider application.

Nevertheless, in a limited number of circumstances lapse of time might result in prejudice to the breaching party, or might be regarded as evidence of an intention to continue with the contract, in which case the right to treat the contract as repudiated would be lost (*per* Fenton Atkinson LJ in *Allen* v *Robles* [1969] 1 WLR 1193).

7.5.3 Classification of terms and repudiatory breach

As explained in Chapter 5 (at 5.4), the remedies available to the non-breaching party depend upon the type of term broken. This is because breaches of certain types of terms constitute repudiatory breaches, giving rise to the option to accept the breach as terminating the contract, or to affirm.

For this purpose there are three basic types of terms: conditions, warranties and innominate (or intermediate) terms. As discussed in Chapter 5, the term 'condition' has a number of different meanings. In this context we are using the term 'condition' in a promissory sense, i.e. as an obligation to ensure that a promised result will be achieved, as opposed to 'contingent' conditions, such as conditions precedent and conditions subsequent (explained at 5.4). In this promissory sense, 'condition' is sometimes used generically to mean all promissory obligations. However, for our present purposes, the term 'condition' has a more specific meaning.

A *condition* is an important term in the contract which is said to 'go to the root of the contract'. As such, breach of a condition is always a repudiatory breach entitling the non-breaching party to treat future obligations under the contract as having come to an end.

A *warranty* is a less important term which does not go to the root of the contract and is such that its breach can be adequately compensated by an award of damages. Breach of warranty is therefore not a repudiatory breach of contract. There is no option to terminate or affirm, and the only remedy for the non-breaching party will be damages.

An *innominate term* is a term which defies rigid classification, but is a term which may be broken in a number of ways, not all of which would be serious. Therefore, whether a breach of an innominate term constitutes a repudiatory breach will depend upon the effects of the breach and whether these are serious. If the effects of the breach are serious, the breach will be repudiatory, giving rise to the option to terminate or affirm. On the other hand, if the effects of the breach are not serious, the only remedy will be damages.

There is a further classification of obligations which can be made and which is relevant in determining if a repudiatory breach has occurred, namely the distinction between breach of an entire obligation and breach of a severable obligation. This distinction is discussed at 7.5.5 below.

7.5.3.1 Identifying promissory conditions
Breach of a promissory condition (used in the specific sense) entitles the non-breaching party to treat both parties' future obligations under the contract as discharged, so that the contract is brought to an end for the future (see 7.1). For this reason, not all the terms of the contract are classed as conditions. The parties rarely intend that breach of relatively unimportant terms should cause the entire agreement to collapse. Equally, the courts will not lightly classify terms as conditions because of the consequence of breach of such terms, irrespective of the actual effects of the breach in question.

In the absence of a statutory classification of the term in question (see, for example, ss. 14(6) and 15(A), SGA 1979, discussed at 5.5.5), the starting point for identifying promissory conditions is the intention of the parties. Generally, description of a term as a condition, or as entitling a party to terminate the contract (or reject the goods) upon breach, will result in the court following the parties' own classification (e.g., *Lombard North Central plc v Butterworth* [1987] 1 QB 527; the point is very carefully considered by Mustill LJ at 535–7). Mustill LJ stated that 'A stipulation that time is of the essence, in relation to a particular contractual term, denotes that timely performance is a condition of the contract. The consequence is that delay in performance is treated as going to the root of the contract, without regard to the magnitude of the breach'.

Nevertheless, the court may be unwilling to accept the parties' classification if the court considers that a breach of this term could not have been intended by the parties to give rise to the option to terminate the contract. In *L. Schuler AG v Wickman Machine Tools Sales Ltd* [1974] AC 235, the House of Lords refused to treat as a condition a term which was expressly stated to be 'a condition of this agreement'. The clause went on to provide for weekly visits over a four and a half-year period to six named firms (some 1,400 visits in total). The House of Lords did not believe that a single failure to make one of the visits should entitle the other party to bring the contract to an end. Lord Reid said (at 251):

> We must remember that we are seeking to discover intention as disclosed by the contract as a whole. Use of the word 'condition' is an indication — even a strong indication — of such an intention but it is by no means conclusive.
>
> The fact that a particular construction leads to a very unreasonable result must be a relevant consideration. The more unreasonable the result the more unlikely it is that the parties can have intended it . . .

There is further evidence of this approach in the decision of the Court of Appeal in *Rice (T/A The Garden Guardian) v Great Yarmouth Borough Council* (2000) *The Times*, 26 July, although the problem in this case was that the term in question was not expressly stated to be a condition. A clause of the four-year contract to provide leisure management and grounds maintenance services stated that 'if the contractor committed a breach of any of its obligations . . . the council may . . . terminate the contractor's employment . . . by notice in writing'. The Court of Appeal held that a literal interpretation of this would entitle the council to terminate 'for any breach of any term' and that this 'flies in the face of commercial common sense' (see also the discussion of interpretation at 5(B)). The breach in question would have to constitute a repudiatory breach in order to justify the ability to terminate. In the light of this decision it would seem sensible to avoid such open termination provisions, and to spell out the status of individual potential breaches.

Diplock LJ suggested, in *Hong Kong Fir Shipping Co. Ltd v Kawasaki Kisen Kaisha Ltd* [1962] 2 QB 26, that a condition exists only in the case of a term 'where every breach . . . must give rise to an event which will deprive the party not in default of substantially the whole of the benefit which it was intended that he should obtain from the contract'. That definition of a condition was rejected by Megaw LJ in the Court of Appeal in *Bunge Corporation v Tradax Export SA* [1981] 2 All ER 513, and his view was affirmed by the House of Lords. It is too strict a test to say that every breach must deprive the other party of substantially the whole benefit for a term to qualify as a condition. Nevertheless, the formulation does give a good indication of the nature of terms which are conditions. They are those terms which contain the main obligations, and which are central to the existence of the contract. The determination of whether a clause is a condition may require the court to make a 'value judgment about the commercial significance of the term in question' (*per* Kerr LJ in *State Trading Corporation of India Ltd v Golodetz Ltd* [1989] 2 Lloyd's Rep 277 at 283, approved by Lord Ackner in *Compagnie Commerciale Sucres et Denrées v C. Czarnikow Ltd, The Naxos* [1990] 1 WLR 1337, 1347–8).

In *Bunge Corporation v Tradax Export SA* [1981] 1 WLR 711, Lord Wilberforce expressly approved the *dictum* of Roskill LJ in *The Hansa Nord* [1976] QB 44, to the effect that the courts should not be too ready to interpret contractual clauses as conditions. The usual alternative will be to classify the term as *innominate*, which may be more appropriate if the term is such that breach may involve either serious or trivial consequences; in such cases the courts are unwilling to allow the serious legal consequences of breach of condition (7.5.3) to operate in instances where the practical consequences of breach are trivial. In *Barber v NWS Bank plc* [1996] 1 All ER 906, Sir Roger Parker in the Court of Appeal clearly had this distinction in mind when ruling upon whether a term, by which a finance company asserted that it would be the owner of a particular car at the time of its eventual sale to a buyer, was a condition of the contract. In concluding that it was, he used two tests. First of all, he said that the term was 'fundamental to the transaction'. He continued at p. 911: 'This term is not one which admits of different breaches, some of which are trivial, for which damages are an adequate remedy, and others of which are sufficiently serious to warrant rescission. There is here one breach only.' Expressions such as 'fundamental to the transaction' can be problematic because they mean different things to different judges. It is not difficult to see, however, how in this case the two tests led to the same conclusion.

7.5.3.2 Time stipulations as conditions Certain terms which are in common use in commercial contracts have acquired, by custom and the operation of the doctrine of precedent, definitive classification as conditions. The main explanation for this is the requirement of commercial certainty. Business people need to know what the effect of a contractual term is, and more particularly need to know what the effect of breach will be. When words have been interpreted in a certain way by the courts, therefore, it is generally desirable that that interpretation be consistently maintained. It is particularly true of time conditions (see *United Scientific Holdings Ltd v Burnley Borough Council* [1978] AC 904). A striking example of the strictness of the approach to time clauses is provided by the decision in *Union Eagle Ltd v Golden*

Achievement Ltd [1997] AC 514. A delay of ten minutes caused the contract to be lost, and the only real issue in the Privy Council was whether relief could be granted (see further, 13.10.5.3).

In commercial contracts the normal rule is that stipulations as to time of performance are crucial ('time is of the essence'), so that any breach entitles the other party to treat the contract as repudiated without assessing whether the term in question 'goes to the root of the contract'. For example, in *The Mihalis Angelos* [1971] 1 QB 164, a charterparty (contract to hire a ship) stated that the vessel was 'expected ready to load' on 1 July 1965 at Haiphong. The charterers purported to cancel the charter because their cargo was unavailable after the American bombing of the railway line to Haiphong. Such cancellation was not allowed under the terms of the contract. However, unknown to the charterers when they cancelled, at the time of entering the contract the owners had no reason to believe the ship would be ready to load on the date stated. The phrase 'expected ready to load' was held to be a condition, breach of which entitled the charterers to treat the contract as repudiated irrespective of the consequences of the breach.

The point was forcefully made for time clauses generally by Megaw LJ in the Court of Appeal in *Bunge Corporation* v *Tradax Export SA* [1980] 1 Lloyd's Rep 294 at 306:

> I think it can fairly be said that in mercantile contracts stipulations as to time not only may be, but usually are, to be treated as being 'of the essence of the contract', even though this is not expressly stated in the words of the contract. It would follow that in a mercantile contract it cannot be predicated that, for time to be of the essence, any and every breach of the term as to time must necessarily cause the innocent party to be deprived of substantially the whole benefit which it was intended that he should have.

This approach to time clauses was confirmed by the House of Lords in *Compagnie Commerciale Sucres et Denrées* v *C. Czarnikow Ltd* [1990] 1 WLR 1337, in which Lord Ackner cited with approval Lord Wilberforce's statement in *Bunge Corporation* v *Tradax Export SA* [1981] 1 WLR 711, that time clauses in mercantile contracts should 'usually' be treated as conditions.

Despite the strength of the authorities indicating that time stipulations in commercial contracts will be treated as conditions, it appears that the position is not conclusive in the light of the decision of the House of Lords in *Torvald Klaveness A/S* v *Arni Maritime Corporation, The Gregos* [1994] 1 WLR 1465, concerning the obligation to redeliver a vessel on time at the end of a time charterparty. The majority of the House of Lords considered this obligation to be an innominate term, and only Lord Templeman (dissenting) considered that as a time stipulation it amounted to a condition because it was of the essence of the contract. The majority was clearly concerned to achieve flexibility in terms of remedy in the event of a short delay, whereas Lord Templeman's judgment emphasises the commercial importance of this provision and the need for commercial certainty. This tension is evident throughout this area of law. The underlying basis for this decision appears to be the more general justification for innominate terms, namely the avoidance of a classification of a term as a condition in order to prevent a party using such a breach as justifying escape from the contract for other (normally economic) reasons (see, for example, *Reardon Smith Line Ltd v Hansen Tangen* [1976] 3 All ER 570). As Lord Mustill stated (at 1475):

> [A]lthough it is well established that certain obligations under charterparties do have the character of conditions I would not . . . wish to enlarge the category unduly, given the opportunity which this provides for a party to rely on an innocuous breach as a means of escaping from an unwelcome bargain.

In *Universal Bulk Carriers Ltd v Andre et Cie SA* [2000] 1 Lloyd's Rep 459, it was a term of a charterparty that the laycan (i.e., the period before which laytime would not commence) would be narrowed to a ten-day spread 32 days prior to the first layday. The charterers failed to specify this period by this date. The owners claimed that the term was a condition so that they were no longer under any obligation to nominate a vessel to perform the charterparty. The charterers sought damages for this breach. It was held that the clause in question was not a condition having considered the appropriate test, namely whether the nature of the subject-matter of the contract or the surrounding circumstances indicate that the clause was intended to be a condition. Since the provision conferred no advantage on the owners, it was difficult to see how they could be disadvantaged by its non-performance. Accordingly, it could not have been intended that any breach of the term should give rise to the option to terminate. In addition, the owners could be adequately compensated in damages for any losses resulting from its breach.

In non-commercial contracts, time is not generally regarded as being of the essence unless expressed to be so by the parties. In the absence of express agreement, the equitable rule prevails over the strict approach of the common law (*cf.* s. 41 Law of Property Act 1925), so that failure to abide by a time clause does not entitle the other party to treat the contract as repudiated. These rules are considered at length in *United Scientific Holdings Ltd v Burnley Borough Council* [1978] AC 904.

It should be noted, however, that in some circumstances, even where the original contract makes no stipulation about the time for performance, time may be made of the essence by the service of a notice to complete. In *British & Commonwealth Holdings plc v Quadrex Holdings Inc.* [1989] QB 842, at 857, Lord Browne-Wilkinson V-C ruled that

> . . . three requirements have to be satisfied if time for completion is to be made of the essence by the service of a notice, *viz.*: (1) the giver of the notice (the innocent party) has to be ready, willing and able to complete; (2) the other party (the guilty party) has to have been guilty of unreasonable delay before a notice to complete can be served; and (3) the notice when served must limit a reasonable period within which completion is to take place.

Lord Browne-Wilkinson's second requirement has provoked some comment. In the case in question, no time for performance was stipulated, and so unreasonable delay is an obviously necessary condition for the legitimate service of notice. In cases where a time for performance is stipulated, without it being a condition, it used to be thought that unreasonable delay beyond the time stipulated was required before notice could be served. Lord Browne-Wilkinson clearly did not like the rule, but did not feel he could overturn it. In *Behzadi* v *Shaftesbury Hotels Ltd* [1992] Ch 1, the Court of Appeal ruled that notice could be served as soon as the date stipulated for performance had passed. The Court was aware of the previous rule, but felt able to reinterpret the older authorities. That is not, however, the end of the matter. The assumption has been that service of such notice, followed by non-compliance, would allow the party serving the notice to treat the contract as repudiated. However, in *Re Olympia & York Canary Wharf Ltd (No. 2)* [1993] BCC 159, Morritt J said that the possibility of repudiation would arise only where the failure to comply with the time notice went to the root of the contract (7.5.3). This restrictive view reflected the judge's concern not to allow a unilateral variation of the contract, which in his view a time notice might otherwise amount to, since it would make time for performance a condition without that being the original agreement of the parties. Although there is much to this argument, it must be said that it undermines the utility of the time notice. It could be argued, however, that if the time allowed is reasonable, failure to comply will normally go to the root.

7.5.3.3 Warranties   A warranty is a term of a contract containing a minor (or less important) primary obligation. Breach of such a term gives rise to a secondary obligation to pay damages, but does not constitute a repudiatory breach presenting the non-breaching party with the option of accepting the breach as terminating the contract or affirming.

The distinction between conditions and warranties is traditionally demonstrated by contrasting two cases with similar facts. In *Poussard* v *Spiers* (1876) 1 QBD 410, a singer, hired to perform during the entire run of an operetta, did not arrive until after one week of the run, when a substitute had been taken on. It was held that the singer's obligation to appear as from the first night was a condition, the breach of which entitled the show's producer to dispense with her services. However, in *Bettini* v *Gye* (1876) 1 QBD 183, a singer, hired to perform during an entire season, had agreed to arrive six days in advance for rehearsals, but was three days late. The court did not believe that the clause relating to rehearsals was so central to the main purpose of the contract as to constitute a condition. The singer's breach, therefore, did not allow the contract to be treated as repudiated, but only allowed recovery of damages for whatever loss had been suffered.

In the past the courts maintained that the distinction between condition and warranty was to be made without considering the actual results of breach, and was to be determined on the basis of the relative importance of the term in the context of the contract as a whole at the date when it was drafted. Today, it is still the case that where the parties have expressly designated a term to be merely a warranty, or where the term is classed as a warranty by statute, the consequences of the actual breach ought not to be taken into account. But where there is no express classification of the term by either of these means, it seems unlikely that the court would class a term as a warranty without first considering the result of the breach under the innominate term doctrine (below, 7.5.3.4).

7.5.3.4 Innominate or intermediate terms   The innominate term was introduced in *Hong Kong Fir Shipping Co. Ltd* v *Kawasaki Kisen Kaisha Ltd* [1962] 2 QB 26, because although a classification of either condition or warranty had the advantage of certainty of remedy in the event of breach, once a term was classified as a condition it allowed the non-breaching party to rely on a trivial breach of that term in order to escape from the contract for other reasons, such as the fact that the contract had turned out to be a bad bargain. In other words, the certainty was inflexible.

In *Hong Kong Fir Shipping*, clause 1 of a contract for the charter of a vessel for a period of two years (commencing in February 1957) described the vessel as 'being in every way fitted for ordinary cargo service'. When delivered to the charterers the vessel was unseaworthy, because her engines were old. On her first voyage under the charter she needed repairs, and the vessel was not properly seaworthy until mid-September 1957. However, in June the charterers had treated the breach as repudiatory and terminated the charter. The question for the Court of Appeal was whether the breach of clause 1 entitled the charterers to treat the contract as repudiated, or only entitled them to damages. Diplock LJ said (at 70):

> There are, however, many contractual undertakings of a more complex character which cannot be categorised as being 'conditions' or 'warranties'. Of such undertakings all that can be predicated is that some breaches will, and others will not, give rise to an event which will deprive the party not in default of substantially the whole benefit which it was intended that he should obtain from the contract; and the legal consequences of the breach of such an undertaking, unless provided for expressly in the contract, depend on the nature of the event to which the breach gives rise and do not follow automatically from a prior classification of the undertaking as a 'condition' or a 'warranty'.

Such terms were christened 'innominate' (there being no technical name for them) or 'intermediate' (since they lay somewhere between conditions and warranties in terms of relative importance). A finding that a term is innominate rather than a condition has been said to 'repress sharp practice' (Weir [1976] CLJ 33) since it will prevent a trivial breach of the term being used to justify termination and withdrawal from the contract for other reasons (e.g., *Reardon Smith Line* v *Hansen Tangen* [1976] 1 WLR 989; and see also *The Gregos* [1994] 1 WLR 1465 (discussed above at 7.5.3.2)).

Identifying innominate terms   The analysis proposed by Diplock LJ in *Hong King Fir* was immediately welcomed by the courts (*cf.* Lord Wilberforce in

Reardon Smith Line v *Hansen-Tangen* [1976] 1 WLR 989, at 998). Neverthe-less, there has been some reaction against the uncertainty the doctrine can introduce into commercial contracts because of the need to wait and see whether the consequences of the breach are sufficiently serious to render it a repudiatory breach.

In *Bunge Corporation* v *Tradax Export SA* [1981] 1 WLR 711, buyers agreed to purchase 15,000 tons of soyabean meal from the sellers. The contract provided for three shipments of 5,000 tons, one of which was to be made during June 1975. Under the contract the buyers were to provide a vessel at a nominated port, and were to give 15 days' notice of expected readiness of the vessel. For shipment in June, therefore, notice had to be given by 13 June. Notice was in fact given on 17 June. The Court of Appeal and House of Lords both found the delay in giving notice to be a repudiatory breach of the contract. Lord Wilberforce said that certain contractual terms, especially those agreed by the parties to give rise upon any breach to a right to treat the contract as repudiated, were not amenable to being classified as innominate terms. He said that the contrary proposition would be 'commercially most undesirable . . . It would fatally remove from a vital provision in the contract that certainty which is the most indispensable quality of mercantile contracts'. However, as noted at 7.5.3.2, this did not prevent the majority of the House of Lords in *Torvald Klaveness A/S* v *Arni Maritime Corp, The Gregos* [1994] 1 WLR 1465, from determining that an obligation under a time charter to redeliver a vessel on time was only innominate.

The identification of innominate terms is therefore a process of elimination, in the sense that all terms which are not so important that breach will always entitle the non-breaching party to treat the contract as repudiated (condi-tions), and which equally are not so unimportant that their breach would never entitle the non-breaching party to treat the contract as repudiated (warranties), are innominate or intermediate terms. Hale LJ, in *Rice* v *Great Yarmouth Borough Council* (2000) *The Times*, 26 July (for facts see 7.5.3.1), defined an innominate term as 'one which can be broken in so many different ways and with such varying consequences that the parties cannot be taken to have intended that any breach should entitle the innocent party to terminate the whole contract'.

Upjohn LJ, in *Hong Kong Fir Shipping* [1962] 2 QB 26 (at 62–63), discussed the reasons why the seaworthiness clause in the charterparty constituted an innominate term:

Why is this basic and underlying condition of seaworthiness not, in fact, treated as a condition? It is for the simple reason that the seaworthiness clause is breached by the slightest failure to be fitted 'in every way' for service. Thus . . . if a nail is missing from one of the timbers of a wooden vessel, or if proper medical supplies or two anchors are not on board at the time of sailing, the owners are in breach of the seaworthiness stipulation. It is contrary to common sense to suppose that, in such circumstances, the parties contemplated that the charterer should at once be entitled to treat the contract as at an end for such trifling breaches.

In practice, the essential distinction to be made is that between conditions and innominate terms (discussed above at 7.5.3.1 and 7.5.3.2), since, except in the case of terms expressly designated as warranties, there will be no point in finding a term to be a warranty before considering the result of breach. This has led to the suggestion that there are two types of contractual terms: conditions (repudiatory) and non-conditions (which will be repudiatory only if the effects of breach are serious) — see Reynolds (1981) 97 LQR 541. This also appears to be the approach adopted by Upjohn LJ in the *Hong Kong Fir* case.

The distinction between conditions and innominate terms is far from obvious on occasion. For example, in *BS & N Ltd (BVI)* v *Micado Shipping Ltd (Malta) No. 1, The Seaflower* [2001] 1 Lloyd's Rep 341, [2001] 1 All ER (Comm) 240, although the judge at first instance held that a clause guaranteeing to obtain approval for a vessel was an innominate term, the Court of Appeal considered it to be a condition. This type of uncertainty does little to assist business people in determining their options, especially in view of the possible dangers of wrongful repudiation.

The effect of breach of an innominate term   The essential flexibility, or fatal uncertainty, of innominate terms stems from the fact that it is not possible to predict before the time of the breach what the effect of breach of such a term will be. Thus, where the result of the breach is substantially to deprive the non-breaching party of the benefit he or she was intended to obtain under the contract, the breach of the innominate term will be treated as repudiatory. Where, however, the effects of the breach caused loss to the non-breaching party but were not so serious as to deprive him or her of the benefit of the contract, the non-breaching party would be limited to the remedy of damages. For example, in *Hong Kong Fir Shipping*, after the repairs to the ship, 17 months of the original 24-month charter remained and therefore the effects of the breach were not considered to deprive the non-breaching party of substantially the whole benefit of the contract.

The innominate term is a focal point of the tension which always exists in the law of contract between the sometimes conflicting interests of certainty and fairness. It is for the parties, if they value certainty so highly, to ensure by careful drafting of their contracts that the consequences of breach of every term are clearly stated, thereby seeking to avoid the possibility of the court treating a term as innominate.

7.5.4   Independent or concurrent conditions

Promissory conditions are of three types (*per* Lord Mansfield in *Kingston* v *Preston* (1773) 2 Doug 689). They may be independent, in which case breach by one party does not entitle the other to cease performance of his or her obligations under the contract. Independent conditions are rare in modern contracts. Alternatively, performance of one obligation may be a condition precedent of the other, so that one party is not obliged to perform until the other has performed his or her obligation under the contract. Lastly, they may be concurrent, in the sense that the performance obligations are more or less simultaneous, and it is not certain which party is obliged to act first. In this case, a party must be ready and willing to perform his or her obligations in order to be able to maintain a claim against the other party for breach. The latter two categories may both be described as dependent conditions. Of these, concurrent conditions are the more common.

Whether conditions are dependent or independent is to be determined by construction of the contract. The law is very unwilling to treat conditions as independent, since to do so removes an important security under the contract from the party to whom the obligation expressed in the condition is owed. That is, if the parties' obligations to perform are concurrent, each has an important lever he or she can use to ensure the other's performance, since each may withhold his or her own performance until the other party is ready and willing to perform. Where a condition is classed as independent it changes the effect of breach, so that the non-breaching party must continue to perform his or her obligations under the contract. Thus, to class a condition as independent has much the same effect as classing a term as a warranty (7.5.3.3). When it was stated that the effect of breach of condition was to entitle the non-breaching party to treat the contract as repudiated (7.5.3), it was assumed that the condition was a dependent condition.

Possibly the only relevant modern example of an independent condition is the landlord's covenant to repair premises, which is said to be independent of the tenant's obligation to pay the rent (*Taylor* v *Webb* [1937] 2 KB 283; and see also *Liverpool City Council* v *Irwin* [1977] AC 239). As a result, the tenant may not withhold payment of rent in order to force the landlord to perform his or her obligation to repair.

An example of the more normal situation of dependent concurrent conditions is afforded by the main primary obligations of the contract of sale, as expressed in s. 28 of the SGA 1979:

> Unless otherwise agreed, delivery of the goods and payment of the price are concurrent conditions, that is to say, the seller must be ready and willing to give possession of the goods to the buyer in exchange for the price and the buyer must be ready and willing to pay the price in exchange for possession of the goods.

7.5.5   Entire or severable obligations

Some contracts involve very simple exchanges. A consumer sale for cash in a shop, for example, involves the exchange of money for goods, with possibly no other terms than an implied condition of quality. In such a contract it is easy to see, assuming that the conditions are concurrent (7.5.4), that the whole of each party's side of the bargain is the necessary condition for the performance of the other side. Any breach would destroy the commercial point of the exchange, and so would entitle the non-breaching party to treat the contract as repudiated.

Many contracts, however, do not involve such simple exchanges. Sales on credit terms of industrial machines, long-term requirements contracts, construction contracts, among many others, all involve complex sets of obligations on both contracting parties. This complexity gave rise to the standard form, and the difficulties it creates in the formation of contracts (2.6.3.2). In some such cases it is still true that any breach would destroy the commercial point of the exchange, so that the whole of each party's side of the bargain is the necessary condition for the performance of the other. In such cases the obligations are described as 'entire' and breach of an entire obligation will constitute a repudiatory breach.

However, in many complex commercial contracts it is possible to see that breach of an important term may not destroy the whole commercial point of the exchange. The obligations in such a contract are described as 'severable' (or 'divisible'), and the result is that breach of such an obligation does not entitle the non-breaching party to treat the whole contract as having been repudiated. It will entitle that party to damages, and may entitle him or her not to perform an obligation which was dependent upon the obligation breached. However, it may be that a series of breaches of severable obligations could have a cumulative effect amounting eventually to a repudiation of the whole contract (e.g., *Alexander Corfield* v *David Grant* (1992) 59 BLR 102). In *Rice (T/A The Garden Guardian)* v *Great Yarmouth Borough Council* (2000) *The Times*, 26 July (for facts see 7.5.3.1), in the context of a long-term contract for leisure services where no single breach was repudiatory but there were a number of repeated breaches, the Court of Appeal held that the correct approach to determine whether there was a repudiatory breach would be to look at the contractor's performance over one year (of the four-year contract period) to determine whether the Council was substantially deprived of the benefit that it had contracted for in that period. It was possible that there would be some aspects of the contract which were so important 'that the parties would be taken to have intended that any deprivation would be sufficient in itself' to justify termination. However, subject to this, the test required an examination of the cumulative past breaches to see whether they were such as to justify an inference that the contractor would continue to deliver a sub-standard performance in the future. On the facts the cumulative effect was considered to be insufficient.

7.5.5.1 Severable obligations

A simple example of a contract consisting of severable obligations is a contract for sale and delivery of goods in instalments which are to be paid for separately. Section 31(2) of the SGA 1979 actually states that in the case of delivery by instalments which are to be paid for separately, 'it is a question in each case depending on the terms of the contract and the circumstances of the case whether the breach of contract is a repudiation of the whole contract or whether it is a severable breach giving rise to a claim for compensation'.

In *Regent OHG Aisestadt* v *Francesco of Jermyn Street Ltd* [1981] 3 All ER 327, the contract called for the supply of 62 suits in a number of instalments. After delivery of several instalments which were accepted, one instalment was defective, being one suit short. The buyers claimed to be entitled to treat the whole contract as repudiated on the basis of breach in respect of the single instalment (the shortfall of one suit being outside *de minimis*, 7.2.1). Mustill J rejected that argument. The obligation to supply was severable so that each instalment was a separate delivery. Therefore, a breach in respect of one instalment did not entitle the non-breaching party to treat the whole contract as repudiated. The judge did not say, as seemingly he should have, that the breach did, however, entitle the buyers to reject the whole instalment affected by the short delivery (*cf. Jackson* v *Rotax Motor and Cycle Co.* [1910] 2 KB 937).

7.5.5.2 Entire obligations The classic example of an entire obligation is *Cutter* v *Powell* (1795) 6 TR 320. A sailor was hired as mate for the voyage from Jamaica to England. He was to be paid a lump sum on completion of the voyage, and it appears that the payment was considerably in excess of the normal amount for such a voyage. He died before reaching England, and his widow sued to recover a reasonable sum as payment relative to the period of the sailor's service before his death. The court refused her claim. Lord Kenyon CJ regarded the contract as 'a kind of insurance', with the result that the sailor's entitlement was 'all or nothing'. Moreover, the court was unwilling to allow the remedy of *quantum meruit* under an implied contract where there was an express contract governing relations between the parties. Ashhurst J said (at 325):

> This is a written contract, and it speaks for itself. And as it is entire, and as the defendant's promise depends upon a condition precedent to be performed by the other party, the condition must be performed before the other party is entitled to receive anything under it.

Thus, the result of failure to perform an entire obligation completely and precisely may be to deprive the party in breach of any payment for whatever performance there has been. It is for this reason that the courts are often unwilling to find that the obligations under a contract are entire. Nevertheless, certain types of contract are usually found to consist of entire obligations, especially lump sum contracts for domestic building or other similar services (e.g., *Bolton* v *Mahadeva* [1972] 1 WLR 1009 — lump sum contract to install central heating in a private house). An advantage of the entire obligations rule in such cases is that it gives the consumer a useful means of ensuring that work is completed, since until it is completed no payment is due (see 7.5.5.4).

7.5.5.3 Entire and severable obligations in the same contract Although the courts sometimes refer to entire or severable *contracts*, it is important to note that it is *obligations* which are either entire or severable, and not the contracts themselves. A contract may well consist of both entire and severable obligations. For example, although *Cutter* v *Powell* (1795) 6 TR 320 is the classic example of an entire 'contract', the court's reflections on the nature of entire obligations did not suggest that every minor breach of the deceased's duties as a mate during the voyage would have entitled the employer to deny him any payment for his services (*per* Somervell LJ in

Hoenig v *Isaacs* [1952] 2 All ER 176). A further example can be seen in the case of sale of goods contracts. The general rule is that the seller's obligation to deliver the correct quantity in a *consumer* sale of goods contract is entire so that an excess or shortfall will, subject to *de minimis*, entitle the buyer to refuse to accept the goods and pay for them. (As we saw at 7.5.5.1, this rule does not apply, however, to a contract for delivery in instalments. If one instalment is short, the buyer is not entitled to refuse to accept further deliveries.) However, obligations as to quality are not entire (although a breach of s. 14(2) or (3) of the SGA 1979 would be a repudiatory breach in a consumer sale of goods contract, that has nothing to do with the entire obligation rule).

7.5.5.4 Avoiding the 'entire obligation' rule Apart from the obvious means of avoiding the 'entire obligation' rule, by classing the obligations in question as severable (7.5.5), two other means exist to prevent the party in breach being denied any payment where that party's performance, although not exactly matching his or her contractual undertaking, has nevertheless bestowed a substantial benefit on the non-breaching party.

Acceptance of the benefit by the non-breaching party The party in breach of an entire contract may be entitled to reasonable payment for the value of his or her actual performance if the non-breaching party accepts such performance as has been given and determines to keep whatever benefit he or she may have derived from it. 'Acceptance' in this sense does not mean an indication that the non-breaching party will not treat the contract as repudiated (which is the sense in s. 11(4) of the SGA 1979: see 7.5.2.3); it means simply that the non-breaching party, while regarding the breach of the entire obligation as bringing the original contract to an end, wishes to keep a benefit conferred and is willing to pay the 'going rate' for it. In other words, although the contract may be discharged for the breach of the entire obligation, a new contract to pay a reasonable sum for the benefit which has been accepted will be implied.

The rule is explained in *Sumpter* v *Hedges* [1898] 1 QB 673. The plaintiff builder had contracted to build two houses on the defendant's land for a lump sum of £565. After completion of just over half the work, the builder abandoned the project. He had in fact received some payment, but not the entire value of the work. The defendant completed the building work, using materials left on the site by the plaintiff. At first instance the plaintiff was awarded the value of the materials used by the defendant to complete the building, but was awarded nothing for the work done but not finished. The first instance judgment was upheld on appeal. Collins LJ said (at 676):

> There are cases in which, though the plaintiff has abandoned the perform-ance of a contract, it is possible for him to raise the inference of a new contract to pay for the work done on a *quantum meruit* from the defendant's having taken the benefit of that work, but, in order that that may be done the circumstances must be such as to give an option to the defendant to take or not to take the benefit of the work done.

Therefore, such payment depends upon finding a new, implied contract, and such a contract will not be found where the non-breaching party has no real choice about whether to accept the benefit or not. In the case of a half-finished building erected on the non-breaching party's own land, there is no choice over whether to accept the benefit; the building cannot be knocked down and 'returned' to the builder in any meaningful way. The builder could not recover for his part-performance. On the other hand, building materials not incorporated into the unfinished building could have been returned, so that a positive choice had been made to keep them. On this basis the builder was entitled to payment representing the reasonable value of such building materials.

It has been suggested that the fact that payment for an accepted benefit depends upon the availability to the beneficiary of a real choice of whether to accept it, has made this rule too strict and that there should be more general recovery in respect of benefits conferred (Law Commission Report No. 121, *Pecuniary Restitution for Breach of Contract* (1983)). A case such as *Bolton* v *Mahadeva* [1972] 1 WLR 1009 (7.5.5.2) is a striking modern example. The plaintiff had agreed to install central heating for a lump sum of £560. It proved to be defective, but the plaintiff would not put it right, which would have cost a further £174. The plaintiff was not allowed any payment for the work done, although he had conferred a net benefit on the defendant of £386.

Nevertheless, as was pointed out in a note of dissent in the Law Commission's Report, the main value of classifying an obligation as entire is that it places in the hands of the other party powerful means of ensuring proper performance of the obligation, namely, the refusal of payment. Were that possibility to be removed, it might do harm to the interests of a significant number of people who are probably among the least likely to be willing to resort to litigation; that is, since most complex construction contracts are now designed for performance in stages, with interim payments, and so are severable, most contracts involving entire obligations will be between small builders and domestic consumers. Therefore, entire obligations, which may once have been thought to have been oppressive to the less powerful in society (*cf. Cutter* v *Powell* (1795) 6 TR 320), may now serve a useful purpose in consumer protection. The recommendation in the Law Commission's Report, which would have reversed cases like *Bolton* v *Mahadeva*, has not yet been implemented (see Burrows (1984) 47 MLR 76 for discussion of these issues).

Substantial performance The rigours of the 'entire obligation' rule may also be avoided by means of the doctrine of substantial performance. Where performance is incomplete or defective (the breach), but the extent of the failure to match the contractual undertaking is trivial by comparison with the primary obligations which have been satisfactorily performed, the court may be prepared to find that there has been substantial performance. The result is to prevent the non-breaching party from treating the contract as repudiated, although he or she will still be entitled to damages, or to a set-off against the contract price, for any loss caused by the fact that there has been a breach of contract.

   In *Hoenig* v *Isaacs* [1952] 2 All ER 176, the plaintiff had agreed to decorate and furnish the defendant's flat for a lump sum of £750. Some progress payments were made, but upon completion of the work £350 was outstanding. The defendant claimed that the plaintiff could not recover this amount since this was an 'entire contract' (*sic*, at 177) and the plaintiff was in breach in that some of his workmanship was defective. It was found as a fact that some of the work was defective, but that it would cost in total no more than £55 to put it right. It is not surprising, in these circumstances, that the Court of Appeal was unwilling to find that the plaintiff was not entitled to further payment. This very minor breach would have resulted in a large windfall for the defendant as a result of not having to make full payment under the contract. Therefore, the Court held that the plaintiff had substantially performed the contract and could recover, less a deduction to cover the cost of remedying the defects. The result was not to overlook the plaintiff's breach, but to limit the consequences of that breach to the creation of a secondary obligation to pay damages rather than to allow it to operate to excuse the defendant from performing his obligations.

   Although this doctrine plays a useful role in mitigating the effects of the 'entire obligation' rule, it should be realised that it is limited to minor failures to match the contractual undertaking. In *Bolton* v *Mahadeva* [1972] 1 WLR 1009, for example, the breach was far too serious to fall within the substantial performance rule.

   It will be seen that there is much similarity between the doctrine of substantial performance and the category of innominate terms, the consequences of breach of which depend upon how serious the breach was (7.5.3.4). This similarity is by no means coincidental. In *Hoenig* v *Isaacs*, Somervell LJ traced the origin of the substantial performance doctrine to the judgment of Lord Mansfield in *Boone* v *Eyre* (1779) 1 H Bl 273; 126 ER 160. In *The Hansa Nord* [1976] QB 44, Lord Denning MR traced the origin of the innominate term to the same source.

7.5.6 Breach by anticipatory repudiation

It has been assumed so far that breach is constituted either by non-performance, or by defective (including late) performance once the time for performance stipulated in the contract has arrived. Where one party indicates in advance of the time for performance, either expressly or by conduct, an intention not to perform, or to perform in a manner inconsistent with the contractual undertaking, special rules apply; or, at least, the usual rules apply somewhat differently to this particular situation. Such an indication is sometimes called 'anticipatory breach', but should more properly be referred to as 'breach by anticipatory repudiation', since it is the announcement of intention rather than the non-performance which is in advance of the stipulated time. In *Yukong Line of Korea* v *Rendsburg Investments Corporation of Liberia* [1996] 2 Lloyd's Rep 604, 607, Moore-Bick J accepted the following clear principle:

A renunciation of the contract by one party, prior to the time for performance is not itself a breach but it gives the other party, the injured party, the right to treat it as a breach in anticipation and thus to treat the contract as discharged immediately. In other words, if a person says he will not perform, the law allows the other to take him at his word and act accordingly.

The doctrine is well illustrated by the early leading case of *Hochster* v *De La Tour* (1853) 2 E & B 678, 118 ER 922. The defendants had contracted to employ the plaintiff as a courier as from 1 June 1852. However, on 11 May the defendants informed the plaintiff that his services would not be required. The plaintiff immediately commenced an action for breach of contract. The defendants argued that the plaintiff was not entitled to a remedy unless he could show that on the due date for commencement of performance of his services he was ready and willing to perform his side of the contract (*cf.* 7.5.4). The court rejected that argument, saying that the plaintiff was free to choose whether to await the time for performance, in which case he must then be ready and willing to perform, or to treat the contract as immediately repudiated, in which case the concurrent condition was discharged. The main justification given for the rule was that it was better for both parties that the plaintiff should avoid the wasteful expenditure of preparing for a performance which he had already been told would not be accepted.

It is clear that the court took the view that the right to an immediate remedy was based on the fact of repudiation, and not on any notional 'acceleration' of the contract date for performance. Lord Campbell CJ explained this finding on the basis of an implied term that between the time of contracting and the due date for performance neither party would 'do anything to the prejudice of the other inconsistent with' the contractual relationship which had been created. This rule is confirmed by subsequent cases. For example, even where performance is contingent upon a condition that may never materialise, anticipatory repudiation entitles the other party to an immediate remedy (*cf. Frost* v *Knight* (1872) LR 7 Ex 111). Nevertheless, if it is clear beyond doubt that the contingency cannot materialise, so that the repudiation cannot be said to deprive the other party of any reasonably expected performance, no remedy will be available (*The Mihalis Angelos* [1971] 1 QB 164).

From the perspective of the non-breaching party, it is essential to be able to identify whether a repudiation has occurred. The repudiation must be — within evidential limits — unequivocal. Clearly, an express statement that no further performance will be undertaken will suffice. Where the repudiation is deduced from conduct, it is not enough simply that performance is unlikely to match the contractual undertakings. It must be apparent that on the balance of probabilities the party in question cannot perform his or her obligations (*Alfred Toepfer International GmbH* v *Itex Itagrani Export SA* [1993] 1 Lloyd's Rep 360). As Lord Wilberforce stated in *Woodar Investment Development Ltd* v *Wimpey Construction (UK) Ltd* [1980] 1 WLR 277, at 280: '. . . in considering whether there has been a repudiation by one party, it is necessary to look at his conduct as a whole. Does this indicate an intention to abandon and to refuse performance of the contract?' The majority of the House of Lords in *Woodar* v *Wimpey* (see 15.6.3) held on the facts that there was no renunciation (i.e. repudiation) of the contract because instead of the necessary intention to abandon the contract, Wimpey was relying on a contractual term as justifying the right to terminate. (This term gave a right to terminate where compulsory purchase had been commenced, and that was precisely what had occurred on the facts.)

7.5.6.1 The election to terminate or affirm

On the basis that the breach is repudiatory, the usual election will apply so that the non-breaching party will have the option of accepting the breach as terminating the contract, or affirming and awaiting performance on the contractual date set for that performance to begin (*Fercometal SARL* v *Mediterranean Shipping Co. SA* [1989] AC 788).

However, the non-breaching party's right of election upon receiving notice of the other's intention not to continue with the contract is not completely without limit. It seems that an element of the distinction which for ease may be described as that between conditions and warranties (7.5.3), also applies to anticipatory repudiations. In *Decro-Wall International SA* v *Practitioners in Marketing Ltd* [1971] 1 WLR 361, the question arose whether late payment on a particular instalment, where such late payment was known to be likely to be repeated in the future, entitled the other party to treat the whole contract as repudiated. The plaintiff argued that a single late payment, which was likely to be repeated, amounted to an anticipatory repudiation of the whole agreement. The Court of Appeal accepted that the late payment was breach, and that there was every likelihood of that breach being repeated in the future, but did not accept that the plaintiff was thereby discharged from further performance under the contract. The term in question was not sufficiently serious to amount to repudiation if broken, thereby justifying bringing the whole contract to an end.

There is also some limit on the power of the non-repudiating party to elect to affirm the contract. In *White & Carter (Councils) Ltd* v *McGregor* [1962] AC 413, the appellants had agreed with the respondents to advertise the respondents' business on litterbins to be supplied to local authorities. On the same day the respondents repudiated the agreement, but the appellants went ahead, performed their side of the contract for the full three years agreed and claimed the contract price. The House of Lords (by a majority of 3:2) held that they were entitled to recover the contract price. There was no requirement that they minimise (or mitigate) their loss by finding an alternative business or product to advertise on the litterbins.

This decision has proved controversial because of the wastage involved. Consequently, subsequent courts have seized upon statements by Lord Reid in order to limit the potential scope of the principle in *White & Carter* (indeed, Megarry J in *Hounslow* v *Twickenham* [1971] Ch 233 (see below) considered them to be part of the *ratio* in *White & Carter*). Lord Reid said that the general power to affirm the contract could not be exercised by a person who had no 'legitimate interest, financial or otherwise, in performing the contract rather than claiming damages'. It would not be sufficient that it was merely 'unreasonable' to affirm; something more than this was required.

Lord Reid's statement was adopted and applied in *Clea Shipping Corp* v *Bulk Oil International Ltd, The Alaskan Trader* [1984] 1 All ER 129. The principle is clearly aimed at preventing very obvious wastage when the other party does not require performance. On the facts in *The Alaskan Trader*, it was held that the owners had acted 'wholly unreasonably' when, despite the charterers' rejection of a two-year charter after one year of the term when the vessel had to undergo extensive repairs, the owners carried out repairs and kept the vessel and the crew ready to receive sailing instructions from the charterers.

In *Stocznia Gdanska SA* v *Latvian Shipping Co.* [1996] 2 Lloyd's Rep 132, Staughton LJ suggested, *obiter*, that the test of legitimate interest must take account not only of the 'innocent' party, but also the interests of the wrongdoer. He seems to have intended to indicate that the fact that payments due will be significantly higher if the contract is kept alive is not alone a legitimate interest.

In *White & Carter* v *McGregor*, Lord Reid also discussed a further limitation on the principle in that case. However, it is a limitation on the ability of the non-breaching party to claim the contract price, rather than a limitation on that party's ability to affirm following a breach by anticipatory repudiation. In this sense it is a different limitation to the need to have a 'legitimate interest' in continuing performance. This second limitation requires that the affirming party must be able to continue with his or her performance of the contract without the cooperation of the breaching party if he or she is to be able to claim the contract price (otherwise he or she will be limited to a remedy in damages). Cooperation in this context includes both active and passive cooperation of the renouncing party (e.g. *Hounslow London Borough Council* v *Twickenham Garden Developments Ltd* [1971] Ch 233 — following renunciation by the local authority employers, contractors had no right to insist on continuing to perform the contract because the work was being done on local authority property and they were unable to gain access to the site without the local authority's permission). In the context of a sale of goods contract, the seller can bring a claim for the price only where property in the goods has passed from the seller to the buyer. This in turn is determined by the principles contained in ss. 17 and 18 of the SGA 1979. If the sale is for specific goods, property passes immediately to the buyer (s. 18, r. 1). Specific goods are 'identified and agreed upon at the time the contract is made' (s. 61, SGA 1979). On the other hand, if the sale is for 'unascertained or future goods by description', property cannot pass until the goods are 'unconditionally appropriated to the contract' with the buyer's consent (s. 18, r. 5). Unascertained goods includes generic goods such as 1,000 gallons of diesel. Future goods are defined as 'goods to be manufactured or acquired by the seller after the making of the contract of sale', and so would include, for example, a yacht to be manufactured to the buyer's specification. Therefore, in the case of unascertained or future goods, the buyer who has indicated in advance that he or she does not want the goods, can prevent the seller who affirms being entitled to claim the contract price because the buyer's assent is required for property in the goods to pass to him or her. In a practical sense, the buyer would refuse to accept delivery and therefore prevent property in the goods from passing (*per* Lloyd J in *The Alaskan Trader*).

For further discussion of the *White & Carter* principle and its limitations, see J. W. Carter, A. Phang and S-Y Phang, 'Performance Following Repudiation: Legal and Economic Interests' (1999) 15 JCL 97.

7.5.6.2 Termination As discussed at 7.5.2.1, it must be clear to the party in breach that the non-breaching party has accepted the conduct as terminating the contract; and although it is possible as a matter of law for this to occur simply by the non-breaching party failing to perform his or her own contractual obligations, whether it will do so is 'a question of fact depending on the particular contractual relationship and the particular circumstances of the case' (see generally *Vitol SA v Norelf Ltd, The Santa Clara* [1996] AC 800, at 811 *per* Lord Steyn; discussed at 7.5.2.1 above). In practice, however, it would seem to depend on whether the non-breaching party's failure to perform his or her own contractual obligations is explicable to a reasonable person only on the basis that the non-breaching party has terminated.

If the non-breaching party has terminated following the renunciation, it is clear that he or she can claim damages from that time and does not need to wait until the date fixed for performance under the contract (*Hochster v De La Tour* (1853) 2 E & B 678). However, the non-breaching party would be under a duty to mitigate his or her loss as from the date of termination.

7.5.6.3 Affirmation An election to affirm the contract means that all the obligations of both contracting parties remain alive. In order to constitute an affirmation of the renunciation there must be evidence of a clear and unequivocal intention to continue with the contract (see the earlier discussion of affirmation in *Yukong Line Ltd of Korea v Rendsburg Investments Corporation of Liberia* [1996] 2 Lloyds Rep 604, at 7.5.2.2, which is authority for the fact that a request to the renunciating party to change his mind and honour his obligations on the contractual date will not suffice for affirmation).

One of the reasons for the strict approach to identification of affirmation as requiring clear and unequivocal evidence of an intention to continue with the contract, is frequently stated to be that the election is irrevocable, i.e. having affirmed, the non-breaching party cannot change his or her mind in the period between affirmation and the contractual date for performance (although following non-performance on the contractual date there would be a new opportunity to elect to terminate or affirm for that repudiatory breach). However, it has long been recognised that where the breach is a continuing one (i.e., it continues after affirmation) and is repudiatory, the fact of the earlier affirmation will not prevent the non-breaching party from choosing to terminate. This was recognised recently by Thomas J (*obiter*) in *Stocznia Gdanska SA v Latvian Shipping Co.* [2001] 1 Lloyd's Rep 537, when he stated (at p. 565; para. 172):

To require an innocent party, who has by pressing for the contract affirmed it, to wait until there is an actual breach by the party in breach before he can bring the contract to an end might well . . . have required that innocent party to engage in performance that is entirely pointless and wasteful as the party in breach would, when he became under an obligation to accept performance, refuse to do so.

This approach is in line with the general approach of preventing wasteful performance which the other party does not want. It is a different emphasis (and different result), as Thomas J recognised, to the approach taken by Colman J in the *Stocznia* litigation ([1997] 2 Lloyd's Rep 228). Colman J considered it important that, following affirmation, the breaching party needs to be able to rely on the fact that he or she is to have a further opportunity to perform. Thomas J's approach recognises that the non-breaching party must continue with his or her own performance obligations (see also Lord Ackner in *Fercometal* v *Mediterranean Shipping* [1989] AC 788: '. . . there is no third choice . . . to affirm the contract and yet be absolved from tendering further performance unless and until [the breaching party] gives reasonable notice that he is once again able and willing to perform'). It is the existence of these two differing positions that makes this such a difficult area of law, and much may depend on the importance attached by some future appellate court to the question of allowing further opportunities to rescue initial non-performance (i.e., the possibility of curing the 'breach'). Of course, it is difficult to justify the approach of Colman J where, following affirmation, the breaching party keeps making it quite clear that he or she will not pay an instalment when it falls due and, in the meantime, the non-breaching party is incurring substantial expenses by continuing performance. In essence, there is no realistic possibility of cure in this situation. Although the award of damages (in *Stocznia* the remedies were limited by a contractual provision so that common law damages were held to be inapplicable) would be aimed at compensating the non-breaching party for the loss suffered, such a party is under no duty to mitigate following the affirmation and this does seem extremely wasteful where the indications of non-payment are so clear (*cf. White & Carter (Councils) Ltd* v *McGregor* [1962] AC 413).

Following affirmation the non-breaching party is also exposing himself or herself to a number of risks in the period between affirmation and the contractual date for performance, which might seriously affect his or her position and remedies following the earlier renunciation. If the non-breaching party does have to accept these risks, it is at least arguable that he or she should have further opportunities to terminate in this period where the renunciation is continuing.

The risks placed on the affirming party are not insignificant. For example, if the non-breaching party should find himself or herself in breach of contract, he or she cannot argue, at least not unless estoppel operated, that the initial renunciation by the other party excuses his or her own subsequent breach. In *Fercometal SARL* v *Mediterranean Shipping Co. SA, The Simona* [1989] AC 788, charterers of a ship gave notice of cancellation of the contract which was not in accordance with the terms of the charterparty and amounted to repudiation. The shipowners did not accept the repudiation, but instead gave notice of readiness to load. This notice complied with the terms of the charterparty and constituted an affirmation, but was false, and so in turn constituted a breach. The charterers consequently rejected the notice and gave further notice of cancellation, which on this occasion complied with the terms of the charterparty. The shipowners sued the charterers. The House of Lords rejected this claim. Once the contract was treated as being still in force, it was 'kept alive for the benefit of both parties', and the party affirming could not both keep it alive and seek to justify his own non-performance by reference to the earlier repudiation.

Similarly, if the contract is frustrated (see Chapter 8) in the period between the affirmation and the due date for performance, the frustration will discharge the contract and the non-breaching party will lose the remedy of damages for the breach. In *Avery* v *Bowden* (1855) E & B 714, the master of a ship had been told in advance of the last possible date for loading that there was no cargo available, which may have amounted to repudiation. He elected to affirm the contract, and remained in port hoping that a cargo would eventually be provided. Before the last possible date for performance of the contract it was frustrated by the outbreak of the Crimean War, thus depriving the shipowners of a remedy they might have had for the failure to provide a cargo, had that repudiation been accepted as terminating the contract.

7.5.6.4 The risk of over-reaction   A party faced with what he or she thinks is an anticipatory repudiation must take careful stock before acting. If that party is mistaken in thinking that the other party has repudiated the contract, his or her own purported election to accept the discharge of his or her obligations may itself amount to an anticipatory repudiation (*cf. Federal Commerce and Navigation Ltd* v *Molena Alpha Inc.* [1979] AC 757).

Some doubt was cast on this proposition by the House of Lords in *Woodar Investment Development Ltd* v *Wimpey Construction (UK) Ltd* [1980] 1 WLR 277. Lord Wilberforce said that a party's mistake as to his or her rights, in the absence of bad faith, would not lead the court to regard a purported termination of the contract as a repudiation. With respect to their Lordships, the other party may be unable to tell whether an apparent repudiation stems from a mistake as to rights, or from a simple decision not to proceed with the contract. *Woodar Investment* is thus a source of considerable uncertainty in the law, and may best be regarded as limited to the situation in which the question is whether the conditions of an express termination clause have been met, when the other party would usually be able to determine the reason for the termination. Where the purported termination is for an alleged breach of condition (or its equivalent), the risk should remain with the party making the election.

Regrettably, this argument was not accepted by the Privy Council in *Vaswani* v *Italian Motors (Sales and Services) Ltd* [1996] 1 WLR 270. It was accepted that merely to assert a claim based on an erroneous but good faith interpretation of the contract would not amount to a repudiation. However, there would necessarily be a repudiation if the assertion went beyond any position consistent with being willing to continue with the contract. In many instances a party who, believing that a repudiatory breach has occurred, wishes to escape from the contract, will make it perfectly clear that he or she wants no more to do with the contract (see *Hong Kong Fir Shipping Co. Ltd v Kawasaki Kisen Kaisha Ltd* [1962] 2 QB 26, and *Cehave NV v Bremer Handelsgesellschaft mbh, The Hansa Nord* [1976] QB 44, where the goods were wrongfully rejected). Lord Woolf in *Vaswani* expressly relied upon the statement of Lord Wilberforce in *Woodar Investment* that 'repudiation is a drastic conclusion which should only be held to arise in clear cases of a refusal, in a matter going to the root of the contract, to perform contractual obligations'.

However, in *Vaswani*, the mistaken interpretation of the contract resulted in a demand for a purchase price significantly higher than that agreed originally or permissible under a price variation clause. It was not inconsistent with a willingness to continue the contract, apparently because the party making the excessive claim never indicated that it would be pointless to tender the correct sum (although they did say that failure to pay the amount claimed would result in loss of a deposit). Although the desire not to visit the drastic consequences of repudiation on a mistaken but good-faith party is understandable, it fails to take account of the altogether more difficult position of the other party, who may not be in a position to differentiate between mistaken good faith and repudiation.

To remove some of the uncertainty from that risk, English law would do well to imitate the provision of the American Uniform Commercial Code which enables a party who has reasonable ground for insecurity with respect to the other's performance to demand an assurance of the performance due, and if it is not forthcoming then to treat the contract as repudiated (UCC § 2-609). There is a similar provision in the UNIDROIT *Principles of International Commercial Contracts* (Article 7.3.4) and in PECL (Article 8:105). Such a procedure might have avoided some of the difficulty in *Alfred Toepfer International GmbH v Itex Itagrani Export SA* [1993] 1 Lloyd's Rep 360. In effect, under two separate contracts, the buyers had nominated a ship to carry more cargo than it could manage. It was true that there must be a breach or renegotiation of one of the contracts, but there was nothing to say which one. The seller treated the double booking as a repudiation, but the court disagreed. The seller's position, which was to say the least difficult, would have been improved had he been able to force the buyer to say which undertakings he proposed to honour.

The position of a party confronted by conduct which is ambiguous and may amount to a repudiation, is improved a little by the common-sense approach of Moore-Bick J in *Yukong Line Ltd v Rendsburg Investments Corporation* [1996] 2 Lloyd's Rep 604. On this approach, a party's legal position should not be adversely affected if the first steps taken are to verify the precise intentions of the other, since this will not necessarily amount to treating the breach as repudiatory and electing to affirm.

EIGHT

Discharge by frustration: subsequent impossibility

8.1 INTRODUCTION

As we saw in Chapter 7, in general, the performance obligation in contracts is strict (7.2.1): the promisor guarantees to achieve a stipulated result, and any failure to achieve that result constitutes a breach. Such a rule would cause injustice if, through no fault of either party, the promisor were prevented from performing and yet was held to be liable for the breach. Of course, where the performance obligation is to do no more than to exercise reasonable care and skill, the fact that the stipulated result is not achieved because of some extraneous factor will not matter, provided the promisor has exercised such care and skill. But where the performance obligation is strict, the promisor must overcome extraneous interference in his or her performance unless the law provides some doctrine of excuse.

In English law a doctrine of excuse is provided by the law relating to frustration (see generally, G. H. Treitel, *Frustration and Force Majeure*, Sweet & Maxwell 1994). It provides residual rules governing intervening events the effect of which on further performance of the contract is so emphatic that the contract is automatically brought to an end. However, it is important to appreciate that the frustration doctrine is a residual doctrine and will therefore not apply if the parties have provided in their contract that it will terminate upon some contingency, or at least that the parties will not be liable for loss arising out of an incident which is beyond the control of the parties. Such clauses are usually referred to as *force majeure* clauses and are express risk allocation provisions. *Force majeure* clauses are usually enforced by the courts (e.g., *J. Lauritzen AS* v *Wijsmuller BV, The Super Servant Two* [1990] 1 Lloyd's Rep 1). It is possible that if such a clause were to allow a party to escape a liability which would otherwise usually be regarded as falling on him or her under the contract, the clause might be subject to control under the UCTA 1977 (see 6.6.2).

8.2 HISTORY OF THE FRUSTRATION DOCTRINE

Until the middle of the nineteenth century English law had no general doctrine of excuse of contractual performance. The leading case was *Paradine* v *Jane* (1647) Al 26, 82 ER 897. To an action of debt for rent due on certain land the defendant had argued by way of defence that he had been deprived of possession of the land by the action of an enemy army. The defence failed; the defendant had promised to pay rent, and if he sought to be excused in particular circumstances he should have made provision for the circumstances in his contract.

It need hardly be said that this reasoning was somewhat unrealistic, for if contracts were to contain express provision for every possible eventuality which might interfere in the contractual performance they would become very long documents indeed! The important change in the law came in *Taylor* v *Caldwell* (1863) 3 B & S 826.

In *Taylor* v *Caldwell*, the defendants had agreed to allow the plaintiffs to use their hall for four concerts for a fee of £100 for each day. After this contract was entered into but before the day of the first concert, the hall was destroyed by fire. The plaintiffs were without a venue for the concerts, for which preparations were well advanced. The plaintiffs sought to recover for their loss from the defendants, who pleaded the accidental destruction of the hall as an excuse for their non-performance. The contract contained no express provision for such an eventuality. The court found for the defendants. The principle of cases like *Paradine* v *Jane* was said to be limited to 'positive and absolute' contracts, which were contracts in which one party had guaranteed his or her performance irrespective of all risks. Not all contracts were of that type. Blackburn J said (at 833–834):

> Where, from the nature of the contract, it appears that the parties must from the beginning have known that it could not be fulfilled unless when the time for fulfilment of the contract arrived some particular specified thing continued to exist, so that, when entering into the contract, they must have contemplated such existence as the foundation of what was to be done; there, in the absence of any express or implied warranty that the thing shall exist, the contract is not to be construed as a positive contract, but as subject to an implied condition that the parties shall be excused in case, before breach, performance becomes impossible from the perishing of the thing without default of the contractor.

From this carefully guarded statement of law has grown a general doctrine of excuse. The 'absolute contracts principle' has become very much the exception, although it is possible for the parties to create an absolute contract by specifying that all the risks of performance are to fall on a named party (see 8.6).

8.3 LEGAL NATURE OF THE FRUSTRATION DOCTRINE

In *Taylor* v *Caldwell* (1863) 3 B & S 826, Blackburn J based his finding that performance had been excused upon an implied term of the contract between the parties that the concert hall should continue in existence until the time for performance. It is not particularly surprising that he chose to base his reasoning on an implied term, since at that time the courts were adamant that it was not their role to interfere in the contracts of the parties (see 1.4.2.2). Reasoning based on an implied term, enabled the court rather to say that it was doing no more than enforcing what was the true agreement of the parties, including such terms which were so obvious that they had not been expressed (see 5.5.2). The implied term basis for the frustration doctrine continued well into the twentieth century (e.g., *F.A. Tamplin Steamship Co. Ltd* v *Anglo-Mexican Petroleum Products Co. Ltd* [1916] 2 AC 397, *per* Lord Loreburn). There is no doubt that at that time what was intended was a term implied in fact (see 5.5.2) between the parties.

However, as the frustration doctrine developed and the courts were willing to apply the doctrine of excuse to an increasingly wide range of circumstances, the notion of the doctrine resting on a term implied in fact between the parties became something of a fiction. This was acknowledged by the House of Lords in *Davis Contractors Ltd* v *Fareham UDC* [1956] AC 696. Both Lords Reid and Radcliffe pointed out that in many circumstances in which it was admitted that the frustration doctrine should apply, the test for the implication of a term in fact would not be satisfied. Thus, when asked whether in given circumstances the contract would be discharged the parties would not reply 'Oh, of course' (*Shirlaw* v *Southern Foundries (1926) Ltd* [1939] 2 KB 206: 5.5.2); rather, they would be likely to consider whether the risk was one which had been or ought to be allocated between them by their contract.

The modern view of the frustration doctrine is generally regarded as expressed in the speech of Lord Radcliffe, who said (at 728–729):

[P]erhaps it would be simpler to say at the outset that frustration occurs whenever the law recognises that, without default of either party, a contractual obligation has become incapable of being performed because the circumstances in which performance is called for would render it a thing radically different from that which was undertaken by the contract . . . But, even so, it is not hardship or inconvenience or material loss itself which calls the principle of frustration into play. There must be as well such a change in the significance of the obligation that the thing undertaken would, if performed, be a different thing from that contracted for.

Lord Radcliffe was anxious to make the point that, although in many cases it made no difference whether the legal basis was said to be an implied term or the application of an objective rule of contract law independent of the parties' intention, in some circumstances it might. If in implying a term the parties' intention was the guiding factor, in many circumstances the court would be unable to agree to the discharge of further performance since cases of this kind arise precisely when the parties have no intention because they have not addressed their minds to the issue. In Lord Radcliffe's view there was good authority that actual intention was not relevant (*cf. Hirji Mulji* v *Cheong Yue Steamship Co. Ltd* [1926] AC 497). Today, Lord Radcliffe's concern is less important, because the law of implied terms has also been modernised, so that the courts now recognise a power to imply terms in law on the basis that such terms would be reasonable in contracts of a particular type (5.5.3). Such terms are no more than obligations imposed on the parties independently of intention, and there may be little difference between Lord Radcliffe's proposed basis for the frustration doctrine and a basis of a term implied in law. In either case, the difficulty of the absence of actual intention on the part of the parties is overcome.

8.4 FRUSTRATING EVENTS

It is usually said that the question of whether an event frustrates the contract is a question of law. That may be a confusing statement. In the first place, it draws attention away from what is really inevitable, that in every case it is largely dependent upon the relevant facts whether or not a contract is frustrated. The question of law is whether the relevant facts render the performance demanded 'radically different' from the performance which was undertaken by the contract (*Davis Contractors* v *Fareham UDC* [1956] AC 696; see 8.4.3). It may also be confusing in that, since such cases are not heard by a jury but by a judge sitting alone, it might be thought that the distinction between law and fact is of little consequence. It is relevant, however, to the question of whether an appellate court will be willing to overturn the finding of a first instance judge, or of an arbitrator. Nevertheless, it is crucial to realise that most frustration cases involve sometimes complex issues of fact which relate to the central question of whether the contractual performance required has been so changed by circumstances beyond the control of the parties that one party should be excused from that performance. It is, therefore, almost impossible to provide a comprehensive list of the circumstances in which a contract will be held to be frustrated. All that may be attempted is to outline some common categories of frustrating event.

8.4.1 Impossibility

Subject to any express allocation of the risk (8.6), the most straightforward examples of frustrating events are those where performance of the contractual undertaking has become impossible. In some cases the impossibility is due to physical causes, as in the leading case of *Taylor* v *Caldwell* (1863) 3 B & S 826, where the destruction of the concert hall made performance impossible (8.2). For a modern equivalent, consider *Gamerco SA* v *ICM/Fair Warning (Agency) Ltd* [1995] 1 WLR 1226, where the stadium at which the band Guns N' Roses was to play was declared unsafe, and no other venue could be made available in time, so that the contract to promote the concert was frustrated.

Similar to the physical destruction of something which is essential to performance of the contract is the death or illness of one of the parties in a personal contract. Many contracts, such as contracts for the sale of goods, do not require that the performance be made by any particular person, so that death or illness does not prevent actual performance. But certain contracts, especially those for the performance of some skilled service, demand performance by a stipulated person, who is usually one of the parties to the contract. In such a case it is clear that death of that party makes performance of the contract impossible (*Stubbs* v *Holywell Railway Co.* (1867) LR 2 Ex 311). It may also be the case that a temporary illness will frustrate the contract if the contract calls for performance on a particular day and on that day the party in question is unable to perform. In *Robinson* v *Davison* (1871) LR 6 Ex 269, the defendant's wife had been engaged to play the piano at a concert but was unable to play on the particular day through illness. The defendant was able to plead his wife's illness as a defence to an action for breach of contract.

In some cases performance remains physically possible but the contract is still frustrated, in that since the time of contracting there has been a change in the law which makes further performance of the contract illegal. The most obvious instance of such illegality is where there has been subsequent legislation (*Denny, Mott & Dickson* v *James B. Fraser & Co. Ltd* [1944] AC 265). Where the illegality exists before the time of contracting there is no scope for the operation of the doctrine of frustration, and the case falls to be determined according to the rules relating to illegal contracts (12.2). Nevertheless, in the case of the outbreak of war, a potential existing illegality intervenes to frustrate certain contracts. It is against the law to trade with the enemy (Trading with the Enemy Act 1939). If at the time of contracting the other party is not 'the enemy' such a contract is not, of course, illegal; but it may become so by subsequent declaration of war. If war is declared before the time for performance, the contract will be frustrated (*Fibrosa SA* v *Fairbairn Lawson Combe Barbour Ltd* [1943] AC 32).

Greater problems are caused when the impossibility is only temporary. For example, although it is clear that incapacitating illness on the single day for performance of the contract amounts to frustration (see *Robinson* v *Davison*, above), it is less easy to state with certainty the effect of prolonged illness on a contract of employment which may call for performance over a period of months or years. It is clear that such illness will excuse the employee's performance for the period of the illness, and it may give the employer the possibility of terminating the employment contract upon notice. Whether it will immediately frustrate the contract, however, will depend upon the particular circumstances. Unless the nature of the incapacity, or the anticipated duration of the illness in relation to the contractual period of employment, suggests that any performance which may subsequently be rendered will be radically different from that which was undertaken, the contract will not be frustrated (*Marshall* v *Harland & Wolff Ltd* [1972] 2 All ER 715). Similar considerations arise where performance of a contract is prevented by a strike, whether it be a strike by the workforce of one or other of the parties or by the workforce of a third party. For example, in *Pioneer Shipping Ltd* v

BTP Tioxide Ltd [1982] AC 724, a charterparty for six or seven voyages to be made during a nine-month period was reduced to half that number of voyages by a strike at the port where the ship was to be loaded. The contract was held to be frustrated because the performance actually possible bore no relation to the performance contracted for.

8.4.2 Unavailability

In some circumstances contractual performance is prevented because something essential to performance is unavailable. Performance is not strictly impossible, because the thing still exists, but for reasons beyond the control of the parties, it may not be put to the use which they had intended. Common examples of frustration of this kind arise in shipping contracts. Thus, where a ship has been requisitioned so that it will be unavailable to the charterer on the delivery date, the contract is frustrated (*Bank Line Ltd* v *Arthur Capel & Co.* [1919] AC 435).

Here again the more difficult problems in determining the existence of frustration arise in cases where the unavailability is only temporary. In *Jackson* v *Union Marine Insurance Co. Ltd* (1874) LR 10 CP 125, a ship was chartered to proceed with all possible dispatch from Liverpool to Newport, and there to load a cargo to be shipped to San Francisco. The ship ran aground one day out of Liverpool, and was not ready to load until eight months later. The contract had imposed no particular time limit for performance. The court held that there was an implied term that the ship should arrive in Newport in time for completion of the contract within a reasonable time, so that the contract was frustrated by such a long delay. It would have constituted 'a different voyage'.

Nevertheless, where the charter of the ship is expressed to run for a given length of time, temporary unavailability will frustrate the contract only if it takes up a disproportionate amount of the whole contract period. It must be remembered that the court is supposed to decide the issue of frustration without taking account of developments after the frustrating event. No doubt in many cases the courts allow themselves a little surreptitious hindsight, but they must sometimes decide before the period of the contract has come to an end. For example, in *F.A. Tamplin Steamship Co. Ltd* v *Anglo-Mexican Petroleum Products Co. Ltd* [1916] 2 AC 397, the court had to determine whether the requisition of a ship in February 1915, which was under charter until December 1917, frustrated the contract. The court said that it did not, no doubt in the belief that the war which had occasioned the requisition would be over in time to allow a substantial period of the charter to be used as intended. With hindsight it is easy to see that the court was unduly optimistic!

Where there is an agreed means of performance and this means is unavailable, the contract will be frustrated. For example, in *Nickoll & Knight* v *Ashton, Edridge & Co.* [1901] 2 KB 126, the unavailability of a particular ship which was specifically named in the contract, was held to frustrate the contract. However, what if, in a contract of sale, the seller's anticipated source of supply fails without the fault of the parties. Does this amount to a failure of the agreed means of performance so that the contract is frustrated? Where that source of supply is in no way a condition of the contract, but merely represents the seller's planned means of meeting his or her obligations, the contract will not be frustrated by failure of that source (*Blackburn Bobbin Co. Ltd* v *T. W. Allen & Sons Ltd* [1918] 2 KB 467). The reason is that, unless otherwise agreed, the risk of failure of a source of supply lies with the seller, who is expected to arrange alternative supplies if his or her planned supply is unavailable. There is no reason why the buyer should know of, or be affected by, the seller's planned mode of performance. Where the seller is concerned about sources of supply, and wishes to commit only in so far as the seller believes he or she has available sources, the seller may make the source of supply a condition of the contract. For example, in *Howell* v *Coupland* (1876) 1 QBD 258, the seller specified that the crop to be sold (200 tons of potatoes) was to be grown in a particular field. The crop in this field failed so that the seller was able to deliver only 80 tons. It was held that the seller was not liable for non-delivery of the remainder since it had become impossible to perform in accordance with the contract term.

Given this term of the contract, it would have been a breach of contract to supply from any other source, although the buyer might have agreed to a variation in the contract terms if the seller had proposed it. The matter is, however, more complicated where the contract envisages two possible sources of supply, one of which is destroyed, but only after contract performance has been allocated to it, and where the other source will be exhausted by other contracts. In such circumstances, in the absence of a *force majeure* clause, it may be that the party's choice of which contract to allocate to the source which was destroyed will operate to prevent the contract from being frustrated (*J. Lauritzen AS* v *Wijsmuller BV, The Super Servant Two* [1990] 1 Lloyd's Rep 1; 8.7).

8.4.3 Impracticability

Impracticability is the term used to describe circumstances in which, although contractual performance is technically still possible, it would impose a burden on one party quite different from that contemplated at the time of contracting. In the United States, the Uniform Commercial Code has adopted a standard of impracticability rather than impossibility for all cases (UCC § 2-615), with the express intention of replacing the absolute test of impossibility with a test of what is 'commercially impossible'. In other words, where performance under the contract is theoretically possible but commercially out of the question, the contract would be frustrated. English law has largely been unwilling to accept that impracticability frustrates the contract, although there are indications that some extreme forms of impracticability might. The cases on unavailability are an example of this ambivalence. In *Jackson* v *Union Marine Insurance Co. Ltd* (1874) LR 10 CP 125 (above, 8.4.2), the contract could ultimately have been performed but was nevertheless held to be frustrated. In *Blackburn Bobbin Co. Ltd* v *T. W. Allen & Sons Ltd* [1918] 2 KB 467, however, the court was unwilling to find the contract frustrated despite the fact that not only had the seller's anticipated supply failed, but it was effectively impossible to get supplies of the kind of timber required.

The leading authority on impracticability in English law is *Davis Contractors Ltd v Fareham UDC* [1956] AC 696. The contractors agreed to build 78 houses for the council over a period of eight months for a fixed price. A shortage of skilled labour caused the work to take a further 14 months. The contractors argued that the contract had been frustrated by the delay, and that they were therefore entitled to payment on the basis of *quantum meruit* (14.4.5), rather than the agreed price. The House of Lords held that the contract was not frustrated. As has already been noted (8.3), Lord Radcliffe said: '[I]t is not hardship or inconvenience or material loss itself which calls the principle of frustration into play.'

It is now accepted that the fact that performance of the contract will cost more than was originally anticipated is not, of itself, enough to frustrate the contract. This principle was demonstrated by cases arising out of the closure of the Suez Canal, after the Anglo-French invasion in 1956. In *The Eugenia* [1964] 2 QB 226 (see also *Tsakiroglou & Co. Ltd v Noblee Thorl GmbH* [1962] AC 93), a charterparty provided for a voyage from Genoa via the Black Sea to India. The contract did not expressly provide, but both parties assumed, that the voyage would be made through the Suez Canal. The charterers claimed that the contract was frustrated by the closure of the canal. The Court of Appeal held that the contract was not frustrated. However, the reasoning of the Court suggests that some degrees of impracticability falling short of impossibility would frustrate the contract. Although the ship was actually trapped in the canal, the case was argued on the basis that it would have been possible not to enter the canal and to complete the voyage by going the long way round via the Cape of Good Hope. The Court might simply have said that since performance was not impossible the contract must stand. Instead, Lord Denning MR compared the total length in days of the voyage via Suez (108 days) with the length via the Cape (138 days), and found that the latter was not entirely disproportionate to the former. He said that the fact that performance was more onerous or more expensive was not enough to frustrate the contract, but that it would be frustrated where it would be 'positively unjust to hold the parties bound'. From this reasoning it may be implied that Lord Denning MR did not believe impossibility to be the only test of frustration.

A party who is concerned that the cost of performance may in some circumstances prove greater than anticipated may protect himself by making express provision in the contract that performance in a particular way is a condition of the contract. Thus, in a case like *The Eugenia*, if the contract had stipulated that performance was to be via the Suez Canal, closure of the canal would have made performance impossible, rather than impracticable, and the contract would have been frustrated.

The issue of whether a contract is frustrated by impracticability is of particular importance during a period of severe inflation, such as that experienced by most western economies during the mid-1970s after the oil crisis. It is possible to view the increased cost of performance resulting from inflation as making the contractual performance something radically different from that which was originally undertaken. The law appears to exclude frustration in most cases while admitting the possibility that a small number of cases might be so severely affected as to qualify. In *British Movietonews Ltd* v *London & District Cinemas Ltd* [1952] AC 166, Viscount Simon said (at 185):

> The parties to an executory contract are often faced, in the course of carrying it out, with a turn of events which they did not at all anticipate — a wholly abnormal rise or fall in prices, a sudden depreciation of currency, an unexpected obstacle to execution, or the like. Yet this does not in itself affect the bargain they have made. If, on the other hand, a consideration of the terms of the contract, in the light of the circumstances existing when the contract was made, shows that they never agreed to be bound in a fundamentally different situation which has now unexpectedly emerged, the contract ceases to bind at that point.

This statement is illustrative of the policy to use the frustration doctrine 'with great caution' and not allow it to 'become an escape route whenever there is an unexpected turn of events' (J. N. Adams and R. Brownsword, *Understanding Contract Law*, 3rd edn, Sweet & Maxwell, 2000, p. 124).

One problem of finding a contract to be frustrated by inflation is that the remedy of discharging the parties from further performance may be as harsh on the other party as the extra cost of performance was on the party alleging that the contract has been frustrated. A more sensible remedy might be to preserve the contract at a reasonable price in the new circumstances (*cf.* Downes (1985) 101 LQR 98), but English law enjoys no such power. It is noticeable, however, that in one of the few cases in which the courts have held a contract to be terminated in circumstances of severe inflation, the statutory background to the litigation enabled the court to insist upon the renegotiation of a reasonable price (*Staffordshire Area Health Authority* v *South Staffordshire Waterworks Co.* [1978] 3 All ER 769). The contract in question had run without any change in the price since 1927, so that the price payable was far below the cost of performance or the going rate for such a service. The Court of Appeal was unanimous in finding that the contract had come to an end. The majority took the view that a power to terminate upon reasonable notice should be implied into the contract, which on its face was valid in perpetuity. Lord Denning MR, however, said that the contract should cease to bind because the present circumstances were 'outside the realm' of the speculations of the parties at the time of contracting. He appeared to believe that the case fell within the exceptional category of cases referred to by Viscount Simon in *British Movietonews Ltd* v *London & District Cinemas Ltd*. Lord Denning's reasoning was followed by a majority of the Court of Appeal in *Pole Properties Ltd* v *Feinberg* (1982) 43 P & CR 121.

8.4.4 Frustration of the common purpose of both parties

In some circumstances, performance of the contract may still be possible but it would be radically different performance from that originally envisaged by both parties. In other words, the event has destroyed the purpose of the contract for both parties thereby frustrating the contract. The classic case examples of this failure of the common purpose are the so-called 'coronation' cases, in which a series of contracts became devoid of purpose when the celebrations connected with the coronation of King Edward VII were cancelled because of the King's illness. In *Krell v Henry* [1903] 2 KB 740, the plaintiff sued the defendant for the balance due on a contract for the hire of rooms from which to view the coronation procession. The procession was cancelled after the hire contract was entered into. The Court of Appeal held that the contract was frustrated, although Vaughan Williams LJ laid considerable emphasis upon the fact that it was known to both parties that the subject of the contract was not merely the hire of a room, but was the provision of a view of the coronation procession. On this basis, viewing the coronation procession was the 'foundation of the contract' for both parties so that its cancellation destroyed this common foundation.

In *Herne Bay Steam Boat Co. v Hutton* [1903] 2 KB 683, however, the Court of Appeal reached a different conclusion. The contract was for the hire of a boat to observe the King's review of the Navy and for a day's cruise round the fleet. The naval review was cancelled because of the King's illness but it was still possible to cruise round the fleet. The distinction between the cases appears to be that in *Herne Bay* the particular purpose was not the subject of the contract, i.e. the contract was not intended by the parties to stand or fall upon whether the naval review took place. The distinction is also sometimes explained in terms of the fact that part of the purpose in the latter case (the cruise round the fleet) was not frustrated (*per* Stirling LJ). The approach of the Court of Appeal in the *Herne Bay* case appears to be consistent with the approach of the courts to impracticability (above, 8.4.3), so that *Krell v Henry* may be something of an exceptional case.

A modern example of this problem can be found in *Amalgamated Investment & Property Co. Ltd* v *John Walker & Sons* Ltd [1977] 1 WLR 164. This case concerned a contract for the purchase of property which had been advertised as suitable for redevelopment and which had been purchased for that purpose. This purchase contract was held to be not frustrated despite the fact that development was more or less impossible because the property had become subject to a form of preservation order.

8.5   CONTRACTS CONCERNING LAND

It has been a matter of doubt over many years whether the doctrine of frustration applies to contracts relating to interests in land. These doubts were expressed by the House of Lords in the case of a lease of which the purpose would clearly have been frustrated for a period, but in all probability not for very long by comparison with the full 99 years of the lease (*Cricklewood Property and Investment Trust Ltd* v *Leighton's Investment Trust Ltd* [1945] AC 221). The particular lease was held not to have been frustrated, but the House of Lords was divided in its reasoning. For two of their Lordships the doctrine was potentially applicable but would rarely apply, since in most cases the frustration of purpose would be of short duration relative to the period of the lease. However, two members of the House of Lords considered that the doctrine could never apply since a lease created a legal interest in land. It was this interest which constituted the subject-matter of the lease contract, and it would survive even if it became impossible to use the premises which had been leased.

The matter was reconsidered by the House of Lords in *National Carriers Ltd* v *Panalpina (Northern) Ltd* [1981] AC 675. A ten-year lease of a warehouse was deprived of its purpose for a period of 20 months by the closure of the only street allowing access by lorries. It was claimed that the lease had been frustrated. The House of Lords rejected that claim on the ground that after the disruption there would still be some three years of the lease to run. A majority of their Lordships, however, accepted that in 'rare' circumstances a lease might be frustrated. Such occasions would be very infrequent for two reasons. In the first place, since many leases run for terms of several years it is unlikely that a potentially frustrating event would take a sufficiently significant 'bite' out of the full term for actual frustration to occur. Further, the kind of major disaster which might frustrate even a long-term lease is usually provided for by an express term of the contract (see 8.6). It appears to be implicit in the reasoning in *Amalgamated Investment & Property Co. Ltd* v *John Walker & Sons Ltd* [1977] 1 WLR 164 (above, 8.4.4) that the doctrine of frustration may apply to contracts for the sale of land.

Nevertheless, its operation in this context is subject to the fact that such contracts are affected by risk allocation rules (see 8.6). Although the normal rule is that risk will pass on exchange of contracts, conveyancers may expressly delay the passing of risk until completion so that, for example, the risk of destruction of the property between contract and completion remains with the vendor and he or she would need to ensure appropriate insurance cover. Even where there is no such express provision, this is still a matter of risk allocation, and the purchaser would cover the risk from exchange of contracts by taking out appropriate insurance.

8.6 FORESEEABILITY AND RISK ALLOCATION

When circumstances intervene to frustrate a contract it may be said that a potential risk of the contract has materialised. Thus, when one enters into a contract to hire a concert hall in several months' time, there is a risk that the concert hall will be destroyed in the meantime. The court must then decide whether that risk was to be borne by one or other of the parties (see also 8.7). Thus, the mere fact that performance turns out to be impossible will not result in the contract being frustrated where one party took upon itself an obligation to perform in all the circumstances (see *Eurico SpA* v *Philipp Brothers* [1987] 2 Lloyd's Rep 215). In the absence of very clear express provision, the courts may be faced with difficult questions of construction of the contract to determine what was undertaken.

Where one party is anxious not to have to bear a particular risk, he or she may insert an express term in the contract, assuming the other party agrees, allocating the risk to the other party. For example, where a manufacturer is anxious not to bear the risk of increased costs of performance in a long-term supply contract, he or she may provide that the price to be paid is to vary in proportion to some suitable index, such as an index of raw material costs. Equally, the contract may require one party to obtain an import or export licence. If the licence is refused by the authorities, it is then a question of construction whether the contract was frustrated or whether the party who failed to obtain it is liable for breach (see *Pagnan SpA* v *Tradax Ocean Transportation SA* [1987] 3 All ER 565). In *Bangladesh Export Import Co. Ltd* v *Sucden Kerry SA* [1995] 2 Lloyd's Rep 1, BEI entered into contracts with SK for the import of sugar into Bangladesh. Import licences were required. The contract contained a term which said that licences were to be obtained by BEI, the buyer, and that 'the inability to obtain [an] import licence shall not be justification for declaration of *force majeure*'. BEI took steps to obtain the necessary licences, but eventually licences were revoked and the imports prohibited. The Court of Appeal treated the express term as placing beyond doubt the possibility of frustration of the contract. The contract provided that the risk was to fall on BEI.

Where the contract contains an express provision for the particular event which is alleged to have frustrated the contract, the courts will not intervene. The only limit on this rule is that as a matter of construction of the express terms of the contract a court may hold that the provision in question was not intended to apply to a supervening event of the gravity which actually occurred (*cf. Metropolitan Water Board* v *Dick Kerr & Co. Ltd* [1918] AC 119).

8.6.1   Unforeseen and unprovided for events

It follows from the above that frustration applies only to contracts affected by events which have not been foreseen, in the sense that they have not been expressly provided for in the contract. In the law generally, however, the notion of foreseeability embraces not only things which have been provided for, but also those which a reasonable person would have foreseen even if the particular parties did not foresee them (*cf.* the test for remoteness of damage: 13.9.2). This idea has been extended in some cases to the doctrine of frustration, so that it is said that not only does frustration not apply to contracts in which the parties have made express provision, but it also does not apply to contracts in which the parties *could have made* express provision, in the sense that the risk was foreseeable. In *Davis Contractors Ltd* v *Fareham UDC* [1956] AC 696, Lord Radcliffe treated the foreseeability of the risk as one of the main reasons for finding the contract not to have been frustrated. In such circumstances it is presumed that failure to allocate the foreseeable risk is evidence of an intention that the risk be allocated to lie where it falls 'naturally'. Thus, in the case of a manufacturer's long-term contract to supply goods, in the absence of indexation of the price the risk of increased cost of performance falls naturally on the manufacturer, since the contract is for a fixed price.

Nevertheless, it must be doubted whether the fact that the risk is foreseeable will in every case exclude the operation of the doctrine of frustration. In the first place, many risks are 'foreseeable' without the probability of their occurrence being so great that the parties ought to provide for them (see 8.6.2). Contracts are not planned to provide for every extreme and remote eventuality. If this were the position, it would make contract drafting a very lengthy process and it would be commercially very inefficient. Moreover, in some cases it has been held that the fact that the parties actually foresaw a particular risk but made no express provision for it did not prevent the frustration doctrine intervening to prevent the risk lying where it fell naturally. In *The Eugenia* [1964] 2 QB 226 (the facts are given at 8.4.3), Lord Denning MR said (at 239):

> It has frequently been said that the doctrine of frustration only applies when the new situation is 'unforeseen' or 'unexpected' or 'uncontemplated', as if that were an essential feature. But it is not so. It is not so much that it is 'unexpected', but rather that the parties have made no provision for it in their contract. The point about it, however, is this: If the parties did not foresee anything of the kind happening, you can readily infer that they have made no provision for it. Whereas, if they did foresee it, you would expect them to make provision for it. But cases have occurred where the parties have foreseen the danger ahead, and yet made no provision for it in the contract . . . see *W.J. Tatem Ltd v Gamboa* [1939] 1 KB 132.

In this case, the parties knew of the danger that the Suez Canal might be closed but, unable to agree on what provision should be put in the contract, had agreed to 'leave the problem to the lawyers' should it materialise. If an actually foreseen but unprovided for risk may constitute a frustrating event, the same must be true of a risk which was foreseeable but not actually foreseen by these parties.

8.6.2 Foreseeability as an aid to construction

It seems unlikely, in the light of *The Eugenia*, that there is a rule of law that frustration cannot apply where the risk was foreseeable. The same would appear to be true even where the more qualified test of 'reasonably foreseeable' risk is used. In any case, that test is too vague to provide proper guidance. Nevertheless, there is no denying the relevance of foreseeability to the question of allocation of risk. The courts are entitled to assess the degree of foreseeability of a risk in determining whether the parties intended the risk to lie where it falls naturally. The greater the probability of the risk materialising, the more likely it is that the parties did intend the inherent risk allocation of their contract. On the other hand, where the degree of probability is close to zero, the difficulty of determining the nature of the risk and of agreeing on its allocation may outweigh the likelihood of the risk maturing. As in *The Eugenia*, the parties may prefer to leave the matter to be sorted out later. In those circumstances a presumption of allocation of the risk based on foreseeability would defeat the intentions of the parties, and it would be preferable to find the contract frustrated.

8.7 FAULT

The doctrine of frustration applies only where the supervening event is beyond the control of the parties. It goes without saying that where performance has become impossible because of one party's breach, that party cannot claim that the contract is frustrated, and the other party will almost certainly be entitled to treat the contract as repudiated (7.5.2) and to claim damages for any loss caused (7.5.1). The law goes further, however, and says that even in the absence of breach of contract, a party may not rely on the frustration of the contract when the supervening event results from some positive action of that party.

The leading authority is *Maritime National Fish Ltd* v *Ocean Trawlers Ltd* [1935] AC 524, a decision of the Privy Council on appeal from Canada. Fishing boats using 'otter trawls' required a licence from the Minister of Fisheries. The defendants wished to operate five such boats, one of which was chartered from the plaintiffs. They duly applied for five licences, but were granted only three. They were invited by the Minister to nominate the boats to which the licences would apply, and did not nominate the boat chartered from the plaintiffs. They then claimed that the charter of that boat was frustrated. Their claim was rejected. If they had wanted they could have applied one of their three licences to the boat in question, so that it was their choice rather than the action of the Minister which deprived the charter of the boat of its purpose. The supervening event was not beyond their control, and so did not frustrate the contract.

It might be assumed that if the defendants had chartered all their boats, so that two charters would have been without purpose whichever boats were nominated, the court might have been more willing to find that the two had been frustrated. However, in *J. Lauritzen AS* v *Wijsmuller BV, The Super Servant Two* [1990] 1 Lloyd's Rep 1, the Court of Appeal took a very strict line, and indicated that any act of choice by one of the parties would prevent the supervening event from being beyond that party's control, and so prevent the contract being frustrated. Once the impossibility of performance was attributable to the decision of one of the parties, whether or not amounting to breach of contract or negligence, it would be self-induced and so not frustration.

It follows from that analysis that a negligent act which results in impossibility of performance may not frustrate the contract. In *Taylor* v *Caldwell* (1863) 3 B & S 826, Blackburn J clearly believed that if the destruction of the concert hall had been caused by the negligence of the owners then they could not have been excused. In many cases, however, the issue may be decided simply on the basis of the burden of proof, since a party alleging that a contract is not frustrated because the impossibility is caused by the default of the other party must prove that default (*Joseph Constantine Steamship Line Ltd* v *Imperial Smelting Corporation Ltd* [1942] AC 154). In this case, the appellants chartered a ship to the respondents, with the intention that the ship should proceed to Australia to load. Before the ship could sail its boiler exploded, causing such a delay that there could be no doubt that the contract was discharged. The reason for the explosion was never discovered, although the respondents suspected that the appellants had been negligent and sought to argue that the frustration doctrine should not apply unless the appellants could prove that they had not been negligent. The House of Lords rejected this argument. On the contrary, the burden of proving a negligent breach of the contract lay on the respondents, and in the absence of proof, the contract was discharged by frustration. Although the House of Lords did not commit itself to any firm view on whether a negligent act could frustrate a contract, Viscount Simon suggested that some minor forms of negligence might certainly be overlooked, but his statements were *obiter* and must be read in the light of the judgments of the Court of Appeal in *J. Lauritzen AS* v *Wijsmuller BV, The Super Servant Two* [1990] 1 Lloyd's Rep 1.

In *The Super Servant Two*, the defendants agreed to transport the plaintiffs' oil rig on one of two named barges. By an internal management decision, not communicated to the plaintiffs, the defendants allocated the task to the *Super Servant Two*, and allocated other tasks to the sister vessel. The *Super Servant Two* then sank, and the defendants claimed that the contract was frustrated, while the plaintiffs claimed that the contract was still physically capable of being performed but for the defendants' choice of vessel. As noted above, the Court of Appeal held that there was an alternative so that the sinking of *The Super Servant Two* did not automatically bring the contract to an end. It was the defendants' choice or election to allocate the other vessel to another contract. Accordingly, the defendants remained liable even though the loss was not due to any breach of contract or negligence. The Court does not appear to have considered whether that would be the case where the choice between the modes of performance lay entirely with the defendants, and the choice was made and communicated to the plaintiffs before the time of the allegedly frustrating event. The Court also indicated that the defendants could have altered their risk by including a *force majeure* clause to provide for what was to happen in these circumstances, but had not done so. Therefore, the risk of being unable to perform and having no excuse rested on the defendants. This decision illustrates the courts' preference for express provision rather than reliance on the frustration doctrine and its associated consequences.

8.8   LEGAL EFFECTS OF FRUSTRATION

The basic effect of frustration is automatically to bring the contract to an end for the future, irrespective of the wishes of the parties (*Hirji Mulji* v *Cheong Yue Steamship Co. Ltd* [1926] AC 497). In this respect discharge by frustration is significantly different from discharge by breach, where the party adversely affected may elect whether or not to treat the contract as repudiated (7.5.2). In the *Hirji Mulji* case, a ship the subject of a charterparty was requisitioned, but the owners asked the charterers if they were willing to wait a little longer, because they believed the ship would soon be released. The charterers agreed, but when release eventually came, later than anticipated, they refused to take the vessel. The owners argued that the charterers had elected to affirm the contract, despite the potentially frustrating event. The House of Lords held that there was no scope for such an election. If the event were sufficiently serious to frustrate the contract, the effect was automatic discharge of all further obligations.

8.8.1 Financial implications of the common law rule

The original common law rule was that frustration caused all primary obligations (to perform) and secondary obligations (to pay damages) which had not accrued to terminate as from the time of the frustrating event, while obligations which had matured before the time of the frustrating event remained to be performed. Under this rule the distribution of loss resulting from frustration might appear quite arbitrary.

Where the contract called for full performance on one side before payment by the other, the result of frustration was to leave the party who had partially performed before the time of the frustrating event without any payment for the work done. In *Appleby* v *Myers* (1867) LR 2 CP 651, the plaintiffs had contracted to install and maintain all machinery in the defendant's factory, payment to be made upon completion. Before the task of installation had been completed, the factory and machinery were destroyed by fire so that the contract was frustrated. Because the payment obligation was not due to be performed by the time of the frustrating event, the plaintiffs were not entitled to any payment for the work done. In this case the defendants received no lasting benefit from the plaintiffs' performance, since the machinery was destroyed, but the same result would apply at common law where a lasting benefit was conferred. In *Cutter* v *Powell* (1795) 6 TR 320 (see 7.5.5.2), the contract was frustrated by the seaman's death before completion of the voyage. His services before death were a benefit to his employer, but his estate was still unable to recover any payment since the contract provided for payment only on completion.

Where the contract provided for a payment (not necessarily full payment) in advance of performance, the original rule was that money paid could not be recovered in the event of frustration, and if not actually paid would remain payable despite the frustration (*Chandler* v *Webster* [1904] 1 KB 493). However, the House of Lords in *Fibrosa SA* v *Fairbairn Lawson Combe Barber Ltd* [1943] AC 32, held that an advance payment could be recovered where there had been a total failure of consideration. The appellants ordered machinery from the respondents to be delivered to the appellants' factory in Poland. The appellants paid £1,000 in advance under the contract. The contract was frustrated by the German invasion of Poland, and the appellants sought the return of the £1,000. The respondents resisted their request because they had already expended large sums in partial performance of the contract.

The appellants were successful in recovering their advance payment. There had been a total failure of consideration in the sense that the appellants had received none of the performance they had contracted for, and on that basis they were entitled to a restitutionary remedy to recover the money paid. The problem with this analysis was that in remedying the hardship which would otherwise have fallen on the party making the advance payment, the House of Lords imposed as great a hardship on the recipient of the advance payment, who had incurred expenses in part performance. It was very likely that the contract had provided for advance payment as a form of insurance against precisely the kind of risk which materialised. The court had interfered in the allocation of risk agreed between the parties, depriving the manufacturers of that insurance.

The common law rule on the effect of frustration was regarded as unsatisfactory for the above reasons, and so changes were made to the parties' pre-frustration obligations by the Law Reform (Frustrated Contracts) Act (LR(FC)A) 1943. Nevertheless, it is still important to understand the common law background, and to remember that the Act has no impact on the issue of whether a contract has been frustrated. It is also important to remember that the automatic discharge of future obligations where frustration occurs, is a common law principle.

8.8.2 The Law Reform (Frustrated Contracts) Act 1943

8.8.2.1 Money paid or payable in advance: s. 1(2) Where the contract provides that all or part of the price shall be payable in advance then, by s. 1(2) of the LR(FC)A 1943, money actually paid is recoverable, and money payable but not yet paid at the time of the frustrating event need not be paid. It is not necessary to demonstrate a total failure of consideration for this rule to operate. Section 1(2) is, however, subject to an important proviso intended to meet the objection to the *Fibrosa* case noted at 8.8.1 above. Where the person entitled to advance payment under the contract has incurred expenses directly related to the performance of the contract before the frustrating event occurs, the court has a discretion to allow the recipient of the advance payment to retain or recover such part of the advance payment as the court considers just having regard to all the circumstances.

The court's discretion is limited in two ways. First, the sum may not exceed the total amount payable in advance under the contract. If the parties are to be assumed to have agreed to the advance payment as insurance for the party who has the substantial performance obligation, their estimate of the necessary insurance cover should be adhered to. Secondly, the sum may not exceed the value of the actual expenses incurred. The need for such provision is unclear, since it seems unlikely that a court should find it just to allow retention or recovery of a sum greater than the actual expenses incurred. The limitation appears to be intended to prevent the advance payment being regarded as automatically forfeit upon frustration, and may also be intended to prevent recovery of any allowance for profit as opposed to actual cost of performance, although in practice the distinction may be hard to draw (*cf.* s. 1(4), LR(FC)A 1943).

One factor likely to affect the court's assessment of what is just in the circumstances is whether the expenses incurred may be recovered in some other way. For example, in the *Fibrosa* case, it may be that the machinery was not so peculiar to the appellants' needs that it could not be sold to an alternative buyer. Such a sale would 'mitigate' the loss caused by frustration (*cf.* 13.9.3) so that the expenses should not be allowed to be retained or recovered out of the advance payment. It has been suggested (see, for example, Haycroft and Waksman [1984] JBL 207 and E. McKendrick, 'Frustration, Restitution and Loss Apportionment' in Burrows (ed), *Essays on the Law of Restitution*, Oxford University Press, 1991) that it might in many circumstances be 'just' to divide the loss between the parties, allowing retention or recovery of half of the expenses incurred. However, where the advance payment is a genuine form of insurance for one of the parties, freely negotiated between the parties, such an approach would seem to be undue interference in the parties' contract.

Until comparatively recently there was no reported decision on the operation of s. 1(2) and its proviso. However, the issue arose in *Gamerco SA v ICM/Fair Warning (Agency) Ltd* [1995] 1 WLR 1226. A contract to promote a rock concert was frustrated by the closure of the stadium on safety grounds. Some US$412,000 had been paid in advance to the defendants, who were assumed, for want of concrete evidence, to have had preparatory expenses of US$50,000. The plaintiff promoters had themselves incurred expenses of around US$450,000. The only issue for Garland J was how to apply the proviso. He considered the suggestions which had been put forward concerning how this discretion should be exercised, namely 'total retention' and 'equal division', before coming to the conclusion that the invitation to do what he considered just left him 'a broad discretion . . . to do justice . . . and to mitigate the possible harshness of allowing all loss to lie where it has fallen'. Putting this into practice, and mindful of the relatively low level of expenses incurred by the defendants by comparison with the losses faced by the promoters, the judge ordered repayment of the full amount paid in advance, without deduction. He was reluctant to believe that the advance payment stipulated for was intended to be a form of insurance against loss under the contract. Consequently, he did not believe he was depriving the defendants of a bargained-for advantage under the contract. It is possible to imagine that the judge was influenced in part by the failure of the defendants to prove in detail the exact extent of their lost expenditure. (This result has, however, been criticised: and see *Carter and Tolhurst* (1996) 10 JCL 264, who argue that there is no discretion to award a nil expenses sum once expenses are proved.)

8.8.2.2 Performance conferring a valuable benefit and the award of a just sum: s. 1(3)   Where no advance payment is provided for under the contract, there is no entitlement to compensation for expenses incurred in performance of a contract which has been frustrated. However, by s. 1(3) of the LR(FC)A 1943, if performance confers a valuable benefit on the other party before the frustrating event occurs, the court may award the performing party such sum as it considers just in the circumstances. The sum may not exceed the value of the benefit to the party receiving it. In assessing what would be just, the court must consider expenses incurred by the party receiving the benefit (including the question of whether an advance payment was made and whether the performing party was allowed to retain some or all of this to cover his or her expenses under the proviso to s. 1(2)). The court must also consider the effect of the frustrating event on the benefit received.

The practical relevance of this provision is limited by the fact that the performance must have conferred a valuable benefit, in the sense of a tangible or long-term benefit. For example, there could be no s. 1(3) claim in *Gamerco v ICM* in respect of the plaintiffs' expenditure incurred in preparing the stadium for the concert, because that expenditure had not resulted in any tangible benefit to the defendants at the time of discharge for frustration. In addition, the drafting of this subsection is somewhat complex. However, the operation of s. 1(3) was considered in *BP Exploration Co. (Libya) Ltd v Hunt (No. 2)* [1979] 1 WLR 783. The important judgment is that of Robert Goff J at first instance, which was subsequently affirmed by the House of Lords ([1983] 2 AC 352).

The case arose out of a contract between the concessionaire of a potential oil field in Libya and the oil company who were to do the prospecting and development of the field. Four years after oil production began, the contract was frustrated by the Libyan Government's nationalisation of the plaintiff oil company's interest in the oil field. The oil company sought a just sum from the defendant concessionaire for benefits allegedly conferred by its performance under the contract before the time of nationalisation. Robert Goff J said (at 801):

> First, it has to be shown that the defendant has, by reason of something done by the plaintiff in, or for the purpose of, the performance of the contract, obtained a valuable benefit (other than a payment of money [to which s. 1(2) applies]) before the time of discharge. That benefit has to be identified, and valued, and such value forms the upper limit of the award. Secondly, the court may award to the plaintiff such sum, not greater than the value of such benefit, as it considers just having regard to all the circumstances of the case. . . .

According to Robert Goff J, the correct approach is therefore to identify and value the benefit to the party receiving it. This value forms the upper limit of any award under s. 1(3). The court must then decide what just sum, up to that limit, to award to the party conferring that benefit.

A key matter not entirely clear under s. 1(3) was whether the destruction of the benefit by the frustrating event, as in *Appleby v Myers* (1867) LR 2 CP 651 (above, 8.8.1), was relevant to the valuation of the benefit or to the assessment of the just sum. Robert Goff J said that the purpose underpinning the 1943 Act was the prevention of unjust enrichment, and he identified the benefit as being the end product of services rather than the services themselves. Therefore, if the end product was destroyed by the frustrating event, there would be no valuable benefit and there could be no award under s. 1(3) because there would be no unjust enrichment to remedy. Accordingly, in a case like *Appleby v Myers*, there would be no mechanism for recovery (in the absence of an advance payment under s. 1(2) and the exercise of the discretion under the proviso to allow retention of some or all of the advance payment to cover expenses). Thus *Appleby* v *Myers* would be decided the same way under the 1943 Act.

It can be argued, however, that Robert Goff J's approach does not coincide with the true construction of the Act, since s. 1(3) speaks of a valuable benefit obtained 'before the time of discharge', which suggests that the valuation is to be made on the basis of circumstances existing immediately prior to the frustrating event. Moreover, s. 1(3)(b) provides that the effect of the frustrating event on the benefit is to be considered in assessing what 'the court considers just'. As Treitel points out (*Law of Contract*, 10th edn, Sweet & Maxwell, 1999, at p. 853), this alternative reading of the section leaves a wider discretion to the court without eliminating the possibility of following the narrower construction in appropriate circumstances. The court might award no sum at all if in its view that was what was just; but in other circumstances it would be able to award a just sum if justified. By linking destruction of the benefit to the setting of the upper limit to any award, rather than to the discretion to fix the sum payable, Robert Goff J perhaps unduly restricted that discretion.

8.8.2.3 Excepted contracts The LR(FC)A 1943 does not apply to all contracts. It does not apply where the parties have made express provision for the consequences of frustration (s. 2(3)). Neither does it apply to wholly performed contractual obligations which may be severed from those which are affected by the frustrating event (s. 2(4)). Certain types of contract for the carriage of goods by sea (s. 2(5)(a)), and contracts of insurance (s. 2(5)(b)), are excepted from the scope of the Act, since such contracts are themselves largely concerned with the allocation of risk, and it was not intended that the courts should interfere with such allocations. Lastly, contracts for the sale of specific goods, which are frustrated by the goods perishing, are outside the terms of the Act (s. 2(5)(c)). The confusing wording of this final exception appears to reflect excessive caution on the part of the draftsman (see P. S. Atiyah, J. N. Adams and H. MacQueen, *The Sale of Goods*, 10th edn, Longman, 2001, at pp. 361–4).

PART III METHODS OF POLICING THE MAKING OF THE CONTRACT

This Part considers those principles of the law of contract which prevent a contract apparently validly made from being enforced. Much of this policing has the effect of rendering the contract either void or voidable (see 3.2.2) so that these doctrines are 'vitiating factors'. However, illegality (Chapter 12) renders the contract unenforceable. Technically this Part should also include an examination of the capacity rules, dealt with in Chapter 4 (4.6). The capacity rules, as a general rule, also have the effect of rendering the contract unenforceable, at least for the party affected by the lack of capacity.

Chapter 9 examines non-agreement or 'common' mistake which, if the contract has made no provision for the risk in question, and if fundamental, will render the contract void at common law or voidable in equity. In the case of such mistakes, the parties are not denying that they reached agreement but allege that the contract was impossible from the outset so that the basis on which they entered into the agreement has been destroyed. (This is linked to subsequent impossibility (frustration) discussed in Chapter 8, because both deal with contractual risks, i.e. events outside the control of the parties. However, the legal treatment of initial and subsequent impossibility is very different.)

Chapter 10 examines the law of misrepresentation which renders contracts voidable if false statements were made (short of contractual promises) in order to induce the contract. Chapter 11 examines the doctrines of duress and undue influence, which also regulate unfairness in the way in which the contract was made ('procedural unfairness'). These doctrines will also render the contract voidable if established. The related concept of whether there is a general doctrine of unfairness in bargaining or unconscionable bargaining is also discussed in this chapter.

Chapter 12 examines those instances where the law will regard the contract as tainted with illegality and therefore unenforceable. It also examines the effect of that illegality on the parties' positions, in particular the question of whether money or property passing under an illegal contract can be recovered.

NINE

Non-agreement mistake

9.1 INTRODUCTION

As discussed at 3.2.1, there is no single coherent doctrine of mistake. This reflects the different contexts in which mistake may be said to exist. There are recognised categories of mistake where the mistake negatives consent (i.e., mistakes which prevent agreement), such as cross-purposes (mutual) mistake and unilateral mistake as to term (see 3.3.1 and 3.3.2). However, there is another category of recognised mistake in English law, namely mistakes which are said to nullify consent. These mistakes are most often referred to nowadays as 'common mistake', although in past decisions the courts often referred to such mistakes as 'mutual mistakes'. This type of mistake should not, however, be confused with agreement cross-purposes mistakes, which were termed 'mutual' mistake in Chapter 3.

The type of mistake discussed in this chapter is a non-agreement mistake (i.e., the parties are not denying that they reached agreement), and it can be termed a 'common' mistake because it is claimed that in entering into the agreement the parties both made the same mistake and the true state of affairs was discovered only after objective agreement had apparently been reached. The common 'mistake' must have related to a matter which was 'fundamental' to their respective decisions to enter into the agreement and (*per* Steyn J in *Associated Japanese Bank (International) Ltd* v *Credit du Nord* [1989] 1 WLR 255) any party who is seeking to rely on common mistake must have reasonable grounds for his or her belief. The existence and consequences of this type of mistake will arise for court decision where one of the parties wishes to withdraw from the agreement on this ground but the other denies the existence of such a 'fundamental' common mistake, perhaps because the contract has proved advantageous to him or her.

Traditionally, the definition of 'fundamental mistake' for these purposes has been narrow so that the operation of the common mistake doctrine at common law has been very limited. This appears to be because such a mistake renders the contract void and therefore of no effect from the very beginning. Accordingly, as there is no contract, the parties are excused all performance. Not surprisingly, therefore, the courts have been anxious not to extend the operation of such a doctrine because of the effect of such a finding on both the positions of the parties and, in particular, on the position of innocent third parties (see the discussion at 3.2.2). It has been suggested, however, that equity provides a more extended and flexible remedy in some circumstances (see 9.5).

9.2 CATEGORIES OF COMMON MISTAKE AT COMMON LAW

The categories of common mistake at common law are based on a restrictive interpretation of mistakes which can be classified as 'fundamental' for this purpose. These categories appear to equate with situations which are so acute that they constitute 'initial impossibility', i.e. unknown to the parties, the contract (as agreed) is impossible to perform. Usually this will be because the subject-matter has ceased to exist *at* the time the contract was entered into (*res extincta*).

9.2.1 Mistake as to subject-matter

In *Strickland v Turner* (1852) 7 Ex 208, a contract of annuity was void because, unknown to the parties, the annuity related to the life of a person who was already dead at the time the contract was entered into. A further example of this type of impossibility is provided by *Galloway v Galloway* (1914) 30 TLR 531. In this case a separation agreement was void because it was entered into in the mistaken belief that the parties were married to each other and therefore needed a formal separation. However, it transpired that the husband's previous spouse was still alive.

The case of *Associated Japanese Bank (International) Ltd v Credit du Nord* [1989] 1 WLR 255, would appear to be a further example of *res extincta*. Funds were raised against the security of certain non-existent machines on a 'sale and lease back', i.e. the non-existent machines were sold to the plaintiff bank for over £1 million and then immediately leased back. The defendant bank had guaranteed the payments due under this lease. When the perpetrator of the fraud defaulted on the lease payments and disappeared with the £1 million, the plaintiff bank sought to enforce the guarantee given by the defendant. However, it was held that the guarantee was subject to an implied condition that the machines existed, thereby treating the subject-matter of the guarantee as the machines rather than the lease obligations. (In fact, it can be argued that the mistake was a mistake as to quality, i.e. that the lease related to machines which existed: see discussion of mistake as to quality, at 9.3.)

In a sense, therefore, this type of mistake is similar to frustration because both doctrines apply, in the absence of a contractual allocation of the risk in question, to instances of contractual impossibility (destruction of the subject-matter: 8.4.1). However, whereas the frustration doctrine applies where the impossibility occurs *after* the contract was entered into, common mistake will apply where the impossibility is initial (i.e., unknown to the parties, the contract was impossible to perform at the time that it was entered into). This can lead to some fine distinctions of fact which mean significantly different consequences follow. For example, in *Amalgamated Investment & Property Co. Ltd v John Walker & Sons Ltd* [1977] 1 WLR 164, the plaintiffs had agreed to purchase property from the defendants which had been advertised as suitable for redevelopment. Unknown to both parties, a decision had already been taken to list the property as a building of special architectural or historical interest, although the actual listing did not take place until after the purchase contract had been signed. The listing seriously affected the value of the property and the plaintiffs sought to have the contract set aside on the basis of mistake, or alternatively claimed that the contract had been frustrated. It was held that this was not a case involving a common mistake because the listing had not taken place until *after* the contract was made. In addition, the doctrine of frustration did not apply on the facts because this was a risk which was to be borne by the purchaser.

The fine distinction can also be illustrated by comparing two cases involving very similar facts. In *Griffith v Brymer* (1903) 19 TLR 434, the contract was void for common mistake so that the advance payment had to be repaid. The contract in question was to hire a room to view the coronation procession of Edward VII. It was made at 11 am on 24 June 1902 but, unknown to the parties, the decision to cancel the procession had been taken at 10 am that morning. This can be compared with *Krell v Henry* [1903] 2 KB 740, involving a similar contract to hire a room to view the coronation procession, but this contract was entered into on 20 June so that the cancellation of the procession amounted to frustration. At common law the loss lay where it fell so that the deposit could not be recovered. (For a discussion of how the position would differ under the LR(FC)A 1943, see 8.8.2.1.) It is worth noting that *Griffith v Brymer* is not a case of impossibility because of non-existence of the subject-matter unless the contract purpose was specifically to hire rooms to view the procession. If it was merely to hire rooms, the contract would still be physically possible. However, the purpose of the parties had clearly become impossible in both cases given that the rooms were advertised for this purpose (see 8.4.4).

The basis for *res extincta* may also be similar to the origins of the frustration doctrine which, as we saw in Chapter 8, was based on the implication of a term ('a condition') that the subject-matter should continue to exist (e.g., *Taylor v Caldwell* (1863) 3 B & S 826; see 8.3). In other words, the existence of the subject-matter at the time of the contract may be interpreted as a condition precedent to the other party's obligation to perform (see *Associated Japanese Bank (International) Ltd v Credit du Nord* [1989] 1 WLR 255). For further discussion of this theoretical basis, see J.C. Smith (1994) 110 LQR 400.

In the context of contracts for the sale of goods, the starting point for discussion is s. 6 of the SGA 1979. Section 6 provides that 'where the contract is for the sale of specific goods' which have 'perished' by the time the contract is made, the contract is void. This section, as originally drafted in the Sale of Goods Act 1893, was said to be based on *Couturier v Hastie* (1856) 5 HL 673. However, it is doubtful that such a wide interpretation can be put on this decision.

In *Couturier v Hastie*, a cargo of corn was shipped from a Mediterranean port to England. At a time when the cargo owner believed the corn to be in transit, the cargo was sold by him to the buyer. It later emerged that, because the cargo had begun to deteriorate, the master of the ship had sold it at a port en route *before* this contract of sale had been entered into. Neither party was aware of this position at the time of contracting. The seller argued that the buyer was liable to pay the price for the cargo on the basis that the buyer had purchased the cargo and all inherent risks. The House of Lords held that there was no such liability, because the contract was for the sale of existing goods but the seller no longer had the corn to sell at the time when the contract of sale was made. It might be thought that this would mean that, if there was an implied term that the goods existed, the seller would be in breach. However, if the basis of the decision is that the contract was void for common mistake then there is no contract to breach. It has been assumed by subsequent commentators that the basis of the decision is common mistake, but the alternative interpretation (placing the risk of non-existence on the seller) is equally consistent with the decision in *Couturier v Hastie*.

The other problem with s. 6 is that it appears to require the goods to have existed at one time but to have subsequently 'perished' or ceased to exist. It is arguable, therefore, that s. 6 will not apply to situations where the goods never existed. For further discussion, see P.S. Atiyah, '*Couturier v Hastie* and the Sale of Non-existent Goods' (1957) 73 LQR 340. At common law, it should equally be the case that a contract to purchase non-existent goods should be void for common mistake because there is no logical reason to distinguish it from goods which have perished. The shared misconception will be the same and it must surely be fundamental if the goods have never existed.

The decision of the High Court of Australia in *McRae v Commonwealth Disposals Commission* (1951) 84 CLR 377, concerned the sale of property which had never existed. However, the decision can be distinguished on the basis that the contractual risk of the non-existence was placed on the seller so that the non-existence constituted a breach of contract.

The Commission had invited tenders for a shipwrecked oil tanker, which was said by the Commission to contain oil and to be lying at a particular location. The plaintiffs' tender was accepted and they went to considerable expense in equipping a salvage expedition and sailing to the specified location. However, no tanker could be found, and it became apparent that none had ever existed. The Commission sought to resist the plaintiffs' claim for damages by arguing that, since the subject-matter did not exist, the contract was void and they were not liable. However, the High Court of Australia held that there was a contract since the Commission had assumed contractual responsibility for the existence of the tanker. The judgment of the court reads:

[T]he Commission cannot in this case rely on any mistake as avoiding the contract, because any mistake was induced by the serious fault of their own servants, who asserted the existence of a tanker recklessly and without any reasonable ground. There was a contract, and the Commission contracted that a tanker existed in the position specified. Since there was no such tanker, there has been a breach of contract, and the plaintiffs are entitled to damages for that breach.

Having found there to be a contract, the court was able to award damages to the plaintiffs to compensate them for their expenses in conducting the salvage expedition. The plaintiffs were also able to recover the price paid (see 13.2.3).

Therefore, it is important not to jump to the conclusion that, in a sale of goods contract, in the event of either non-existence or perishing of the subject-matter the contract will always be void. It may be that the risk of existence has been placed on one of the parties so that there is a contract and the non-delivery of these goods will amount to a breach (see 9.4).

9.2.2   Mistake as to ownership

In addition to *res extincta*, there is another category of fundamental common mistake at common law, namely mistakes concerning the ownership of property (*res sua*). Such a mistake occurs, for example, where a person contracts to purchase property which, unknown to both parties, he or she already owns.

In *Cooper* v *Phibbs* (1867) LR 2 HL 149, Cooper agreed to lease a salmon fishery from Phibbs, both parties believing that the fishery belonged to Phibbs. In fact, Cooper was already entitled to enjoyment of the fishery as a life tenant. That is, although not absolute owner, so that he could not dispose of the fishery, Cooper was effectively owner during his lifetime. He had no need to take the lease, and Phibbs had no power to grant it. It was held that the contract could be set aside (i.e., it was voidable), but the court allowed Phibbs compensation for money mistakenly spent on the fishery.

In *Bell* v *Lever Bros Ltd* [1932] AC 161, Lord Atkin relied on this decision of the House of Lords as an example of mistake operating to nullify a contract, and he expressly stated that the effect of such a mistake was to render the contract void and not merely voidable. The significance of this remark, which it is submitted is the correct position in law, will become clear below (see 9.5). Lord Atkin did not regard *Cooper* v *Phibbs* as depending on any special equitable doctrine.

9.3   MISTAKE AS TO QUALITY AT COMMON LAW

9.3.1   Is it fundamental?

A mistake as to quality made by both parties will not generally be sufficiently fundamental to render the contract void at common law since such a mistake does not render performance, as originally agreed, impossible. The emphasis at common law appears to be placed on the sanctity of contract in the absence of clear impossibility.

It is important at the outset to explain the distinction between mistakes as to quality and promises as to satisfactory quality which are implied in sales contracts where the seller sells in the course of a business (e.g., s. 14(2), SGA 1979). 'Quality' in the context of mistake refers to some special quality as opposed to the basic overall minimum quality of the goods which is implied by s. 14(2). For example, mistakenly believing that the contract relates to a high grade of tea or to a particular manufacturer's pottery.

The leading case on mistake as to quality is *Bell* v *Lever Bros Ltd* [1932] AC 161. Bell and another were made executive officers of a subsidiary of Lever Bros. Subsequently, the subsidiary was closed down and a further contract made between Lever Bros and the executive officers, terminating their appointments in return for substantial compensation. It was then discovered that the officers had earlier engaged in private dealings in breach of their service contracts (which the officers themselves had forgotten about). Therefore, at the time of the contracts to terminate their appointments, Lever Bros could have terminated the service contracts for these breaches, without having to pay any compensation. Accordingly, Lever Bros claimed that the termination contracts were void for mistake.

The House of Lords (by a majority of 3:2) refused this claim. The mistake was merely as to a quality of the service contracts, namely whether they needed to be terminated by the payment of compensation, and did not render the contract void. (The consequence was that the compensation paid was not recoverable because the agreement under which the compensation was payable, remained valid.)

Therefore, such mistakes will not generally be sufficiently fundamental in nature to render the contract void. Lord Atkin (giving what is generally acknowledged to be the leading speech for the majority) stated that a mistake as to quality 'will not affect assent unless it is the mistake of both parties, and is as to the existence of some quality which makes the thing without the quality essentially different from the thing as it was believed to be'. In *Associated Japanese Bank (International) Ltd* v *Credit du Nord SA* [1989] 1 WLR 255, Steyn J at first instance regarded this statement by Lord Atkin as forming the *ratio* of the case.

As a broad test it might be considered that this test of essential difference would provide great scope for judicial discretion in evaluating the facts in mistake cases and that in many instances a mistake as to quality would render 'the thing without the quality essentially different from the thing as it was believed to be'. However, it would be wrong to jump to this conclusion and the case law does not support such an interpretation. In particular, this test appears to be inconsistent with at least one of the cases on which Lord Atkin relied: *Kennedy* v *Panama, New Zealand and Australian Royal Mail Co.* (1867) LR 2 QB 580. The plaintiff had bought shares in a company in the belief, also held by the company, that the company had recently won a contract from the New Zealand Government for the delivery of mail. However, the New Zealand Government failed to ratify the agreement, and so the shares were worth much less. The court said that there was nevertheless a contract. Such a difference in quality, however severe, did not destroy the agreement. It is difficult to accept that there was no essential difference in this case.

In addition, despite the existence of this broad principle of 'essential difference', Lord Atkin himself gave a number of examples (see [1932] AC 161, at 224) of mistakes which would not be sufficiently fundamental which indicate that 'essential difference' will be very narrowly construed. These examples included the following:

> A buys a picture from B; both A and B believe it to be the work of an old master, and a high price is paid. It turns out to be a modern copy. A has no remedy in the absence of representation or warranty.

In essence, Lord Atkin was saying that it will not suffice to state, 'If I had known the true facts I would not have entered into this contract'. If a quality is important to one of the parties, he or she should ensure that its existence becomes a contractual promise or a false statement of fact (see 9.3.3). Lord Atkin justified this position (at 224) by stating that:

> [I]t is of paramount importance that contracts should be observed, and that if parties honestly comply with the essentials of the formation of contracts — i.e., agree in the same terms on the same subject-matter — they are bound, and must rely on the stipulations of the contract for protection from the effect of facts unknown to them.

Lord Atkin put forward another formulation for the test: 'Does the state of the new facts destroy the identity of the subject-matter as it was in the original state of facts?' In Lord Atkin's example, he would still identify the subject-matter as 'the old master'. It is interesting, however, to compare this with the suggested approach of Treitel (*The Law of Contract*, 10th edn, Sweet & Maxwell, 1999, at pp. 267–8). Treitel argues that the test should be whether the particular quality is so important to the parties that they actually use this quality in order to identify the subject-matter, e.g., if in the example of the sale of 'the old master' the parties used the name of the artist to describe the subject-matter itself. However, this argument was rejected by the Court of Appeal (*obiter*) in *Leaf* v *International Galleries* [1950] 2 KB 86, on the basis that there was no express term to this effect.

In *Leaf*, the plaintiff had bought a painting believed to be by Constable, and it had also been represented as having been painted by Constable by the seller. Five years later, when the plaintiff tried to sell the painting, it was discovered that the painting was not a Constable. The plaintiff therefore argued that the original contract of sale should be set aside. His action for misrepresentation failed because of the lapse of time (see 10.5.2.2), and in passing the Court of Appeal reiterated that no alternative remedy for mistake would be available as this was only a mistake as to quality. The fact that the mistake could be described as essential or fundamental did not change the fact that the contract as originally agreed continued to be capable of performance (and indeed had been performed). Lord Evershed MR rejected the argument that the plaintiff had 'contracted to buy a Constable' by stating that '[w]hat he contracted to buy and what he bought was a specific chattel, namely, an oil painting of Salisbury Cathedral' and 'it remains true to say that the plaintiff still has the article which he contracted to buy'.

Similarly, in *Frederick E. Rose Ltd* v *William H. Pim Junior & Co. Ltd* [1953] 2 QB 450 (the full facts are given at 3.4.1.1), the contract was for the sale and delivery of horsebeans, although both parties were under a mistake as to whether horsebeans were suitable for the plaintiffs' purposes in fulfilling a contract for the supply of 'feveroles'. It turned out that they were not, but the parties had agreed on the sale and purchase of horsebeans so that the contract as agreed was capable of performance and therefore was not void.

Lord Atkin's test in *Bell* v *Lever Bros* has generated a good deal of discussion concerning the meaning of 'essential difference'. There is one *obiter* statement in an English case which applies Lord Atkin's test more literally and suggests that the mistake as to a quality would have rendered the contract void. This is a statement by Hallett J in *Nicholson & Venn* v *Smith-Marriott* (1947) 177 LT 189, in the context of a sale of napkins and tablecloths described as the 'authentic property' of Charles I. In fact the linen was Georgian, and it was held that there was a breach of contract since this was a sale by description for Charles I linen. Hallett J stated that 'a Georgian relic . . . is an 'essentially different' thing from a Carolean relic' so that the goods purchased were 'different things in substance from those which the plaintiffs sought to buy and believed they had bought'. This view was subsequently doubted by Denning LJ in *Solle* v *Butcher* [1950] 1 KB 671 and is generally regarded as weak support for arguing that a contract can be void for mistake as to quality in the light of the decision in the case that the description amounted to a contractual term, which would undoubtedly have influenced the finding of 'essential difference'.

The English approach can be compared with the approach exemplified by the decision of the Supreme Court of Michigan in *Sherwood* v *Walker* 33 NW 919 (1887), where the mistake, relating to whether the cow being sold was barren at the time of the sale, was held to relate to 'the very nature of the thing', i.e. it was held to relate to the subject-matter being sold and not merely to a quality possessed by that subject-matter. This case illustrates the difficulties of divorcing the question of value from the determination of 'essential difference' e.g., one would undoubtedly pay a higher price for a painting by a famous artist. In *Sherwood* v *Walker*, the essential difference was that a cow in calf was worth considerably more than a barren cow, which would be sold for its meat. Therefore, a buyer would expect to pay a higher price for a cow in calf and, arguably, the only way to untangle the contract was to hold the contract to be void for common mistake. The English courts have not shown the same willingness to take account of price paid and the position on the facts (see, for example, *Bell* v *Lever Bros Ltd*, where the compensation paid could not be recovered). It seems that it is this problem of 'result' which led Lord Denning to find that a contract could be voidable in equity for mistake as to quality and be set aside on terms (see discussion below at 9.5).

9.3.2 Total failure of consideration

As far as common mistakes are concerned, the position would therefore seem to be that such mistakes nullify contracts only where one party is unable to deliver what the other party has contracted to receive, such as to amount to a total failure of consideration. This appears to be the real test used by Lord Atkin. In seeking to interpret *Bell* v *Lever Bros Ltd*, Denning LJ came to a very similar conclusion in *Solle* v *Butcher* [1950] 1 KB 671. He said (at 691):

> The correct interpretation . . . is that, once a contract has been made, that is to say, once the parties, whatever their inmost states of mind, have to all outward appearances agreed with sufficient certainty in the same terms on the same subject-matter, then the contract is good unless and until it is set aside for failure of some condition on which the existence of the contract depends . . . The cases where goods have perished at the time of sale, or belong to the buyer, are really contracts which are not void for mistake but are void by reason of an implied condition precedent, because the contract proceeded upon the basic assumption that it was possible of performance.

It is true that there is a subtle conceptual difference between total failure of consideration (see 14.4.2) and failure of an implied condition precedent. It may be that Denning LJ's explanation was over-elaborate, since each party's consideration is the performance to be supplied, and each party's obligation to perform is conditional upon that of the other (see 7.5.4). Thus it is not necessary to search for any further implied condition. Nevertheless, both Lord Atkin's and Denning LJ's explanations result in only one conclusion: only a common mistake which renders performance as originally agreed impossible will operate to render a contract void.

9.3.3 Relationship with other possible claims

It is important to make clear the relationship between mistake and the express undertakings or statements of the parties. The fact that a mistake as to quality does not result in the contract being a nullity means, as Lord Atkin made clear in *Bell* v *Lever Bros Ltd*, that the claimant's only remedies lie in establishing either an express term of the contract by which the promisor undertakes to guarantee that the quality in question is present, or a pre-contractual representation that the desired quality is present. In these cases, absence of the desired quality will provide a remedy respectively for breach of contract or for misrepresentation. In other words, by their contract, or as a result of the pre-contractual negotiations, the parties have allocated the risk that the quality will not be present to one or to the other (see, for example, *Nicholson & Venn* v *Smith-Marriott* (1947) 177 LT 189 (sale by description within s. 13, Sale of Goods Act) and *Leaf* v *International Galleries* [1950] 2 KB 86).

In these instances it would be inappropriate for the courts to intervene by means of the doctrine of common mistake, and it must be remembered that common mistake may be very much a last-ditch argument because more effective remedies may be obtainable for breach of contract or the misrepresentation. This principle is sometimes expressed in terms of the rule that mistake must not be the 'fault' of either party.

9.4 MISTAKE AND ALLOCATION OF RISK

In the case of mistakes which go beyond mere quality, and which genuinely make performance of the contract as originally agreed impossible, it is still possible for the risk that the assumed state of facts will not materialise to be allocated to one or other party. Whether such an allocation of the risk of the relevant mistake to one or other of the parties has taken place must be determined before considering the operation of the doctrine of common mistake. As Steyn J stated in *Associated Japanese Bank (International) Ltd* v *Credit du Nord SA* [1989] 1 WLR 255 (at 268):

Logically, before one can turn to the rules as to mistake . . . one must first determine whether the contract itself, by express or implied condition precedent or otherwise, provides who bears the risk of the relevant mistake. It is at this hurdle that many pleas of mistake will either fail or prove to be unnecessary. Only if the contract is silent on the point is there scope for invoking mistake.

This point was emphatically reaffirmed by Hoffmann LJ in *William Sindall plc* v *Cambridgeshire CC* [1994] 1 WLR 1016, at 1035. In *William Sindall*, the contract to purchase land contained an express term stating that the land was sold 'subject to easements, liabilities and public rights affecting it'. The purchaser later discovered that, unknown to the parties, there was a foul sewer buried under the land. They sought to argue common mistake (for the argument relating to misrepresentation, see 10.5.3.4). The Court of Appeal held that the contract term allocated the risk of such incumbrances to the purchaser, and this therefore excluded the operation of the doctrine of mistake.

Therefore, where an allocation of the risk has occurred, the fact that the contract as agreed cannot be performed may simply be something the claimant has to accept as not being within the promise made by the other party, for which, therefore, no remedy is available (as in the *William Sindall* case), or may amount to breach of the contract (as in *McRae* v *Commonwealth Disposals Commission* (1951) 84 CLR 377, discussed above at 9.2.1 and, as to the measure of damages, at 13.2.3). This point was stressed again in *Associated Japanese Bank (International) Ltd* v *Credit du Nord SA* [1989] 1 WLR 255 and more recently in *Kalsep Ltd* v *X-Flow BV* (2001) *The Times*, 3 May. The judge in the *Kalsep* case applied *Associated Japanese* and held that before concluding that an agreement was based on mistake, it was first necessary to determine whether the contract provided for either party to suffer the risk of the relevant mistake.

9.5 COMMON MISTAKE IN EQUITY

As discussed above, there has been some dissatisfaction with the rule that common mistakes, falling short of those which make performance of the contract as agreed impossible, do not render the contract void. Common mistakes as to quality are often fundamental in the sense that, in the absence of the mistake, the parties would not have entered into the contract. Thus, a mistake over the authenticity of a painting is no doubt one which is central to the contract. It is a very narrow interpretation to say that the contract (for the sale of a specific painting) can still be performed and is therefore not void.

As suggested at 3.2.2, the explanation for the narrow interpretation is that any other rule would leave third-party interests unduly exposed to disputes between parties to transactions over which the third party has no control. Nevertheless, this explanation raises the possibility that a remedy for common mistake as to quality might be acceptable if it operated between the original parties to a transaction but did not operate to defeat third-party interests. This effect would be achieved if the impact of mistake on the contract were to make it merely voidable rather than void (see 3.2.2). Lord Denning had sought to achieve just such a rule, and recent decisions indicate that such a doctrine has reached a level of judicial acceptance despite the absence of any House of Lords authority to confirm it.

9.5.1 Voidable in equity

Denning LJ (as he then was) first restated the law relating to common mistake in *Solle* v *Butcher* [1950] 1 KB 671. The defendant agreed to lease a flat to the plaintiff for seven years at £250 per annum. The parties only arrived at this figure for the rent because both believed that the property was not subject to rent control under the Rent Acts. The plaintiff subsequently discovered that the property was subject to rent control, and the rent payable would only have been £140 per annum. Nevertheless, had the defendant served the necessary statutory notices, the basic rent could have been increased to approximately £250 to take account of repairs and improvements to the property. The plaintiff sought to recover the overpaid rent over a two-year period, and sought a declaration that he was entitled to continue in occupation for the rest of the lease at an annual rent of £140. The defendant counter-claimed for the lease to be set aside for mistake.

The Court of Appeal gave the plaintiff the choice between surrendering the lease, or continuing in possession but paying the full amount of rent allowable (i.e., about £250) once the necessary statutory notices had been served. In effect, these terms amounted to enforcement of the original contract term, and arguably this may have been because it was the plaintiff (surveyor) who had supplied the defendant with the information on the rent he could charge.

Denning LJ began his analysis of the law of mistake by referring to the statement of the law by Lord Atkin in *Bell* v *Lever Bros Ltd* [1932] AC 161, and by accepting the orthodox interpretation of what Lord Atkin said (see 9.3.1). He went on to suggest, however, that *Bell* v *Lever Bros Ltd* is not the whole law on common mistake. He said that there was a doctrine of equity, not referred to in the House of Lords in *Bell* v *Lever Bros Ltd*, by which a contract may be set aside on terms on the basis of common mistake, including in circumstances where the mistake is only one of quality. (Subsequent commentators have expressed surprise that such a talented House of Lords, addressed by such eminent counsel, should have failed to take account of this equitable doctrine if such existed. The most likely explanation is that the doctrine was Denning LJ's own creation. The evidence suggests that this was the case).

9.5.2 The evidence

The argument in favour of a doctrine allowing for a mistake as to quality to be voidable in equity rests on a series of cases, of which a representative sample of two will illustrate that there is little foundation in precedent for it, however desirable the doctrine may seem. Perhaps the most important case is *Cooper* v *Phibbs* (1867) LR 2 HL 149. It was suggested above (see 9.2.2, where the facts are stated) that this was an example of the *res sua* principle of common mistake, which Lord Atkin in *Bell* v *Lever Bros Ltd* [1932] AC 161 treated as making the contract void. Denning LJ pointed out that, despite this comment, in *Cooper* v *Phibbs* Lord Westbury had stated that the contract was voidable, that the action was brought in the Chancery Court, where, had the contract been void at common law, that would have been the end of the matter, and that the court set the contract aside only after imposing terms on the parties.

The circumstantial evidence is impressive, but can be explained consistently with Lord Atkin's interpretation of the case. The essential fact is that the plaintiff had to show that he was really the owner of the fishery in question. As life tenant he was not full legal owner but had only an equitable interest. Before the Judicature Act 1873, such an interest would be recognised only in the Chancery Court. But the rule of mistake applied by the Chancery Court was the common law rule that a contract to acquire an interest in one's own property is void as impossible of performance. The court imposed terms because the would-be lessor had spent money on the land, and was entitled to be compensated for the improvements made, probably on the basis of some form of proprietary estoppel (see 4.4.6).

The second case relied on by Denning LJ was *Huddersfield Banking Co. Ltd* v *Henry Lister & Son Ltd* [1895] 2 Ch 273. The bank was a secured creditor of the defendant company, its security being the business property and all fixed assets. The defendant company was in liquidation, so that a receiver held all the company's assets on trust for the creditors. The plaintiffs agreed to the sale of certain machinery, having determined that it was not fixed. It turned out that it had been improperly loosened, and so should have been treated as fixed assets and thus part of the plaintiff bank's security. The plaintiffs applied to have the agreement set aside.

The reason the bank had to apply to the Chancery Court was that the agreement was made under its auspices as supervisor of the liquidation, but the court treated the agreement not as voidable but as void. It relied on two cases (*Cooper* v *Phibbs* and *Strickland* v *Turner* (1852) 7 Ex 208 — see 9.2.1), which have been analysed as examples of the application of the common law common mistake rule. The reason why the contract was void in this case was that at the time when the agreement for the sale of the unfixed machinery was made there was no unfixed machinery to sell. There is no suggestion that an equitable doctrine of mistake was operating.

It seems, therefore, that the legal foundation for the proposed equitable doctrine of common mistake is very insubstantial. Nevertheless, there is Court of Appeal authority and statements indicating that the doctrine is recognised by eminent members of the judiciary, including Steyn J, who subsequently became a member of the House of Lords. Thus, although there is no House of Lords authority applying this doctrine, there would seem to be justification for the belief that a subsequent House of Lords would not disown it. In addition, the doctrine is not without merit. It is certainly much closer to the continental conception of mistake found in the writings of Pothier (see 3.2.1) than the other elements of the narrow English doctrine.

There are a number of judicial decisions where the equitable doctrine has either been applied or accepted in judgments. For example, in *Grist* v *Bailey* [1967] Ch 532, Goff J set aside a contract for the purchase of a house believed to be subject to a protected tenancy whereas in fact it was available with vacant possession, making a difference of some £1,400 to the value of the property. The contract was set aside because the mistake was regarded as being sufficiently fundamental in equity on the basis that the vendor undertook to give the purchaser the chance to buy the property at the true value. Similarly, in *Magee* v *Pennine Insurance Co. Ltd* [1969] 2 QB 507, the majority of the Court of Appeal set aside a contract of settlement of an insurance claim on the ground that the parties had been mistaken about the insured's entitlement to claim as a result of material misstatements in the original insurance proposal. (It is interesting that the terms in this case did not require the insurance company to return the insurance premium.) In this case there was a spirited dissenting judgment from Winn LJ, who considered the case indistinguishable on its facts from *Bell* v *Lever Bros Ltd*.

Perhaps most significantly, there was clear recognition of the equitable jurisdiction in the judgment of Steyn J (as he then was) in *Associated Japanese Bank (International) Ltd* v *Credit du Nord* [1989] 1 WLR 255, although he clearly recognised that Lord Denning's interpretation of the majority judgments in *Bell* v *Lever Bros Ltd* was rather selective. Steyn J stated (at 267–268):

> No one could fairly suggest that in this difficult area of the law there is only one correct approach or solution. But a narrow doctrine of common law mistake (as enunciated in *Bell* v *Lever Bros Ltd*), supplemented by the more flexible doctrine of mistake in equity (as developed in *Solle* v *Butcher* and later cases), seems to me to be an entirely sensible and satisfactory state of the law.

Steyn J clearly recognised the tension in the approaches of the common law and equity and sought to clarify the relationship. He stated that the correct approach would be first to consider whether the contract was void for mistake at common law. If the contract were valid at common law then it would be necessary to consider any plea that it was voidable in equity. Thus he recognised that the role of the equitable doctrine was to mitigate the hardships of the strict approach at common law.

Although Steyn J did not make clear the circumstances in which the equitable jurisdiction would be exercised, he did make clear that a contract will not be set aside in equity for common mistake in favour of a party who is 'at fault'.

It may well be that the existence of such an equitable doctrine achieves the desired balance between fairness between the parties and protection of subsequently created third-party rights. This was certainly the view of Steyn J, who would have been willing to apply the 'more flexible doctrine of mistake in equity' had he not found the contract to be void for mistake at common law.

In *William Sindall* v *Cambridgeshire County Council* [1994] 1 WLR 1016, Evans LJ also discussed (*obiter*) the law governing common mistake at common law and in equity, and made a number of helpful comments. First, he attempted to assist in determining instances where the subject-matter is 'essentially and radically different' as a result of the mistake by equating this with circumstances 'which may lead to frustration of the contract where there has been a change in the circumstances due to a supervening event'. He then went on to specifically consider, albeit *obiter*, the application of the doctrine of equitable mistake, and stated (at 1042):

It must be assumed, I think, that there is a category of mistake which is 'fundamental' so as to permit the equitable remedy of rescission, which is wider than the kind of 'serious and radical' mistake which means that the agreement is void and of no effect in law . . . The difference may be that the common law rule is limited to mistakes with regard to the subject-matter of the contract, whilst equity can have regard to a wider and perhaps unlimited category of 'fundamental' mistake.

It is easier to relate this test to the facts of the *Sindall* case than to apply it more broadly. In *Sindall*, the alleged mistake related to whether the land was subject to any incumbrances (quality) rather than to the existence of the land itself. The actual problem with the land was not significant because the sewer could have been diverted at a cost of £20,000, as compared to a contract price of £5 million. Clearly, this event would not have justified frustration of the contract as the land was not 'essentially different' from the land as it was believed to be. It would also be doubtful whether the mistake would have been fundamental in equity, even if the test in equity is merely one of whether the mistake is material to the parties' positions.

It is important to note, however, that Evans LJ cannot have been implying that equitable relief for mistake might be available in instances where the mistake does not relate to the subject-matter or other terms of the contract. A misinterpretation of this comment may have led to the argument for rescission in *Clarion Ltd* v *National Provincial Institution* [2000] 2 WLR 1888. Rimer J made it clear (at 1899) that equity cannot grant relief in cases of alleged mistake where the mistake relates only to the commercial effect or impact of the agreement, and he dismissed (at 1904) the comment by Evans LJ as 'at most a somewhat tentative *obiter* comment which Evans LJ did not elaborate'. (Note that the *Clarion* principle has general applicability in the context of equitable relief in the context of mistake since it will also be relevant to the remedy of rectification (*cf.* 3.4.1).)

It seems that one factor which may influence a finding that a mistake is fundamental in equity will be a considerable discrepancy in the applicable price (see, e.g., *Grist* v *Bailey* [1967] Ch 532 and *Solle* v *Butcher* [1950] 1 KB 671 — where the price difference was clearly material to the parties' positions).

The Court of Appeal's decision in *Nutt* v *Read* (2000) 32 HLR 761, (1999) *The Times*, 3 December (see also (1999) 96 (42) LSG 44) involves an express application of the equitable jurisdiction. However, on the facts, although rescission on terms might have been appropriate, it had not been ordered by the judge and the Court of Appeal did not therefore have to deal with this matter. The claimants had agreed to sell a chalet on a caravan park to the defendants. It was also agreed that the defendants were to pay a monthly rent to occupy the pitch (the tenancy agreement). The defendants failed to pay this and the claimants sought to eject them from the site. The defendants' defence was that the agreement had been entered into under a common mistake, namely that both parties mistakenly believed that the chalet could be sold separately from the site pitch on which it stood. The defendants had made some improvements to the chalet increasing its value from £12,500 to £28,750, and it may seem odd that they chose to rely on a defence based on mistake.

The two agreements were treated as separate, so that the judge at first instance held the agreement for the sale of the chalet to be void for fundamental mistake, i.e. that the chalet could be sold separately from the pitch it occupied. Accordingly, the purchase price had to be returned to the defendant. (In essence, this is because the agreement was impossible in law.) However, as the Court of Appeal made clear, there was no entitlement to compensation for the money spent on improvements unless the contract was rescinded on terms. The judge at first instance had rescinded the separate tenancy agreement and this decision was appealed. The only question for the Court of Appeal was whether there were grounds on which the occupancy agreement (i.e., the tenancy) could be rescinded. The Court of Appeal held that the parties were under the common misapprehension that the pitch could be used independently of the chalet upon it and, as neither party was at fault, agreed that the tenancy was voidable. However, the issue of rescission on terms had not been appealed so that, although the Court of Appeal accepted that the claimants might have been ordered to pay compensation to the defendants for the improvements, it did not make such an order.

Of course, if the arrangements had been treated as a single agreement, there would not even have been the possibility of rescinding in equity, because the agreement would have been void at common law and the equitable jurisdiction would not have arisen. The judge's decision to separate them was therefore vital.

It can be seen from this decision that a great advantage of the equitable jurisdiction is the ability to set aside on terms, since it enables the court to mitigate the harshness of the void or valid approach at common law. However, it is important to bear in mind that rescission in equity for common mistake is different to rescission for misrepresentation since it requires the intervention of the court to rescind the contract for mistake and make any order for rescission on terms. However, the ability to rescind will be subject to the same bars that affect the general remedy of rescission (see 10.5.2).

TEN
Misrepresentation

10.1 INTRODUCTION

Misrepresentation comprises the law relating to the effect of a contract (and hence the parties' positions) where that contract was entered into on the basis of a false statement made during the course of contractual negotiations. A contract made as the result of a misleading representation is, subject to the limitations described in this chapter, voidable at the instance of the person to whom the misrepresentation was made (the misrepresentee). In other words, the primary remedy for misrepresentation will be for the misrepresentee to rescind the contract (set it aside). That person may also (or in the alternative) be able to recover compensation for loss sustained.

Once the essential conditions for recovery for misrepresentation have been established (10.2), the combination of remedies available (10.5) depends upon the type of misrepresentation in question, whether fraudulent, negligent or innocent (10.4). The law applicable is a complex blend of common law, equity and statute.

Although misrepresentation is a separate body of law, requiring individual treatment, it should be noted that it enjoys close relations with, and indeed sometimes overlaps with, several other important areas of contract law. When confronted with a factual scenario, which at first sight appears to raise issues of misrepresentation, it is important to consider whether any other doctrine is also relevant, and especially to consider whether another doctrine might provide a better remedy for the victim.

In the first place, since misrepresentation relates to misleading statements made in the course of contractual negotiations, it is possible for such a statement to take on even greater significance and, by operation of the rules of offer and acceptance and incorporation of terms (see generally Chapter 5), to become an express term of the contract (see 5.1.3 and 5.3.2). The consequences of being a term are explained below (10.3), but the most obvious is that the falsity of the statement will inevitably result in a breach of the contract, giving rise to remedies quite different from those available for misrepresentation (see generally Chapter 5, at 5.1.1).

In addition, the circumstances giving rise to a claim of misrepresentation may also substantiate a claim of mistake (Chapter 9). For example, to incorrectly state that a piece of furniture is a genuine antique is a misrepresentation, however innocent, and may also give rise to relief in equity for common mistake (9.5). Equally, to enter a contract masquerading as some other person is a fraudulent misrepresentation, while it may also give rise to relief on grounds of a (unilateral) mistake of identity (3.3.3). The advantage of mistake over misrepresentation in many situations (but not where the doctrine of common mistake in equity applies) is that, if established, it renders the contract void and not merely voidable (3.2.2), so that the party seeking relief may be able to recover property even after it has passed into the hands of a third party.

As we shall see (10.4.3.1), contractual misrepresentation is very closely linked to negligent misstatements in the law of tort, and a set of facts may raise the possibility of claims for both negligent misstatement in tort and negligent misrepresentation in contract. It is important, therefore, in order to give the most appropriate advice, to be fully aware of the differences between these claims and the remedies available in each case.

When considering action to be taken in the event of discovering a misleading pre-contractual statement, it is important to remember regulatory legislation, which is also intended to police such behaviour. In the case of the Trade Descriptions Act 1968 and the Property Misdescriptions Act 1991, the making of false statements is an offence, but there is no complementary civil liability incurred (although the law of misrepresentation as described in this chapter may well apply). In the case of the Package Travel, Package Holidays and Package Tours Regulations 1992 (SI 1992 No. 3288), there is no civil liability arising out of the main regulations relating to false and misleading statements, but reg. 4 provides that organisers or retailers must compensate consumers for loss resulting from the supply of misleading information.

Lastly, and more generally, it is important to be able to place misrepresentation in the wider context of regulation of contracts. Misrepresentation is an example of a doctrine designed to police the formation process (i.e., the circumstances surrounding the making of the contract) and achieve 'procedural fairness' by providing remedies for fraudulent and negligent misrepresentation, as opposed to fairness in terms of the content of the contract ('substantive fairness'; see, for example, regulation of unfair terms (Chapter 6) and the penalty rule (13.9.5). Other examples of doctrines aimed at achieving procedural fairness are the doctrines of duress and undue influence (discussed in Chapter 11).

10.2 ACTIONABLE MISREPRESENTATIONS

For an action for misrepresentation to succeed there must have been an unambiguous, false statement of existing fact, which induced the claimant to enter into the contract.

10.2.1 False statement of fact

10.2.1.1 False and unambiguous It might be assumed that identifying the fact that the statement is false would be an easy matter. However, falsity is sometimes a matter of degree. In *Avon Insurance plc* v *Swire Fraser Ltd* [2000] 1 All ER (Comm) 573, [2000] CLC 665, Rix J adopted the test applicable under s. 20(4) of the Marine Insurance Act 1906, namely, whether the statement is 'substantially correct' so that any difference between what was represented and the correct position would not have been likely to induce a reasonable person to make the contract.

This is linked to the requirement that the misrepresentation be unambiguous. A party making a representation, which on a reasonable construction is true, will not be liable for misrepresentation simply because the representee has put some other construction on it which is not true. In *McInerny* v *Lloyd's Bank Ltd* [1974] 1 Lloyd's Rep 246, the purchaser of a business defaulted on the contract, causing loss to the plaintiff seller. The seller claimed to have been induced to enter the contract by a statement in a telex sent at the purchaser's request to the seller by the defendant bank. The statement in question was an opinion expressed to the purchaser about whether the seller would be likely to find the financing arrangements acceptable, and could not reasonably be construed as advising the seller to agree to the deal proposed. The Court of Appeal held that the bank was not liable for an unreasonable interpretation put on its statement by the plaintiff seller. Thus, conduct will give rise to a claim for misrepresentation only if the meaning attached to the conduct by the claimant is a reasonable conclusion to be drawn from the defendant's actions.

10.2.1.2 Statement The requirement for a 'statement' has in one sense been interpreted fairly broadly, because the courts have shown a willingness to find the existence of a misrepresentation based on conduct, without the need for words (*Curtis* v *Chemical Cleaning & Dyeing Co. Ltd* [1951] 1 KB 805 (see 6.5.2.2), *per* Denning LJ: '. . . any behaviour, by words or conduct, is sufficient to be a misrepresentation if it is such as to mislead the other . . . If it conveys a false impression, that is enough').

In *Gordon* v *Sellico* (1986) 278 EG 53, concealment of dry rot was held to amount to a representation to the plaintiffs, who purchased the property in question following an inspection, that the property did not suffer from dry rot. This case can usefully be compared with *Horsfall* v *Thomas* (1862) 1 H & C 90 (see also 10.2.2.2), where concealing a serious defect in a gun by inserting a metal 'plug' amounted to representation by conduct. However, since the purchaser did not inspect the gun before purchase, he could not have been induced by it, and therefore there was no actionable misrepresentation.

A recent example of a misrepresentation by conduct is provided by the facts in *Spice Girls Ltd* v *Aprilla World Service BV* [2000] EMLR 478. The defendant, a motor scooter manufacturer, had agreed to sponsor the tour of the pop group, the Spice Girls. The group had participated in a photo shoot and other promotional material before the agreement was signed at a time when it was found that they knew that one member of the band had declared an intention to leave the group before the expiry of the term of the sponsorship agreement. The defendant sought damages for misrepresentation. Arden J held that taking part in the promotions amounted to a misrepresentation by conduct, namely a misrepresentation that the group did not know and had no reasonable grounds to believe that any member of the group had the intention to leave before the end of the agreement.

In another sense the requirement that there be a false 'statement' has been strictly interpreted. In most situations mere silence or non-disclosure does not amount to an unambiguous, false representation, and therefore will not give rise to a claim for misrepresentation. Of course, as can be seen from the discussion at 10.2.2.2, where the non-disclosure goes beyond merely remaining silent and involves active steps taken to conceal a defect, it may amount to misrepresentation (see *Horsfall* v *Thomas* (1862) 1 H & C 90).

The general rule is usually said to be that there is no duty to disclose facts which if known might affect the other party's decision to enter the contract (*Keates* v *The Earl of Cadogan* (1851) 10 CB 591). The rule reflects the attitude of classical contract law that the parties must look after their own interests in making contracts. It may also be justified by saying that a general duty of disclosure would be too vague, since it would be impossible to specify precisely what should be disclosed. Nevertheless, the general rule is subject to certain exceptions.

Half-truths   It is a misrepresentation to make statements which are true but which do not reveal the whole facts, and so are misleading. Thus, to describe property which is the subject of negotiations for sale as fully let, without disclosing that the tenants have given notice to quit, is a misrepresentation (*Dimmock* v *Hallett* (1866) LR 2 Ch App 21).

Change of circumstances   Where a truthful statement of fact is made but is subsequently rendered misleading by a change of circumstances, there is a duty to correct what has become a false impression. The classic example is *With* v *O'Flanagan* [1936] Ch 575. The defendant wished to sell his medical practice, and gave information to the plaintiff about the income to be derived from the practice. This information was true at the time it was given. The defendant then fell ill and the income from the practice fell away to almost nothing. The sale took place five months after the original information had been given, and without the defendant disclosing that the income had fallen dramatically. On discovering the state of the practice, the plaintiff sought rescission of the contract of sale. He was successful. He was entitled to continue to believe the truth of the statement made until the time of the sale or until it was corrected, so that failure to correct it amounted to a misrepresentation.

In *Spice Girls Ltd* v *Aprilla World Service BV* [2000] EMLR 478, it was held that there was a duty to correct the representation by conduct, namely, that the group did not know of the intention of one member to leave before the period of the sponsorship agreement ended. Nothing had been done to correct this continuing representation.

It is less clear whether a change of circumstances causing a person to amend an opinion voiced in the course of negotiations imposes a duty to disclose the change of opinion. It might be thought that since in some circumstances an opinion is treated as a statement of fact (10.2.1.3), in those same circumstances at least there would be a duty of disclosure where the opinion changed. Indeed, an argument could be made for extending the duty further, since an opinion will be treated as a statement of fact where there are no reasonable grounds for the opinion held. A change of circumstances would bring a once honestly held opinion into that category, and would appear to justify a duty of disclosure.

The same argument appears to apply to statements of future intention when the intention changes but is not disclosed before the time of contracting. However, despite some authority to the contrary (*Traill v Baring* (1864) 4 D J & S 318), more recent authority suggests that there is no duty to disclose a change of intention. In *Wales v Wadham* [1977] 1 WLR 199, the plaintiff and the defendant, formerly husband and wife, agreed in the course of divorce proceedings that the plaintiff would pay the defendant £13,000 from his share of the sale of their house in return for her promise not to seek a maintenance award. The defendant had stated several times that she would not remarry. By the time of this agreement she had changed that intention, but did not reveal the fact to the plaintiff, who subsequently claimed that he would not have entered into the agreement had he known she was to remarry. His action for rescission failed. The defendant was under no obligation to communicate her subsequent change of intention since her original statement of intention was honestly held and did not amount to a representation of fact (see 10.2.1.3 for a discussion of the effect of statements of intention).

Fiduciary or confidential relationship   A fiduciary relationship is a relationship of special confidence between certain classes of people, imposing particular duties of care on those to whom confidence is entrusted. Typical examples of such relationships are solicitor and client, agent and principal (Chapter 16) and partnership. In such a relationship there is a duty of disclosure of all material facts. There is a close relationship between this duty of disclosure and the doctrine of undue influence, as can be seen from the case of *Tate v Williamson* (1866) LR 2 Ch App 55 (see 11.2).

Contracts uberrimae fidei   Certain types of contract impose a duty of disclosure irrespective of the nature of the relationship between the parties. They are called contracts *uberrimae fidei* (of utmost good faith), and the most common example is the contract of insurance. The insured is under a duty to disclose all material facts at the time of making the contract of insurance, and failure to disclose such facts entitles the insurer to refuse to pay when a claim is made (i.e., the insurance contract is voidable at the option of the insurers). The rule may be explained as necessary to enable the insurer to make a proper assessment of the risk it is to underwrite, and the duty is placed on the insured because he or she is the person in possession of the relevant information. However, it does mean that a person seeking insurance is placed in a difficult position because of the need correctly to identify those facts which are material and therefore to be disclosed.

The position until fairly recently had been that facts must be disclosed which a reasonable or prudent insurer might treat as material (*Lambert* v *Co-operative Insurance Society Ltd* [1975] 2 Lloyd's Rep 485). On this test it was held that a spouse's conviction for handling stolen goods was material to a contract of insurance of valuables (*Lambert* v *CIS Ltd*, above), and that a conviction for theft was material to a contract of fire insurance (*Woolcott* v *Sun Alliance & London Insurance Ltd* [1978] 1 All ER 1253).

However, the House of Lords has reconsidered the law on non-disclosure in insurance contracts (*Pan Atlantic Insurance Co. Ltd* v *Pine Top Insurance Co. Ltd* [1994] 3 All ER 581). Their Lordships approached the matter from the particular angle of enquiry into what circumstances would permit an insurer to avoid liability on grounds of non-disclosure. There was some difference of opinion on the test of materiality. A minority (Lords Lloyd and Templeman) would have found non-disclosure to be material only if it would have had *decisive* influence on the mind of a prudent underwriter. However, the majority (in agreement with the principal speech of Lord Mustill) found that a non-disclosure would be material if it would have some (not necessarily decisive) effect on the mind of a prudent underwriter.

Their Lordships were, however, unanimous in deciding that materiality was only half the test. Rescission would be available only if it could be shown that the non-disclosure did in fact induce the making of the contract. As explained by Evans LJ in *St Paul Fire and Marine Insurance Co. (UK) Ltd* v *McConnell Dowell Constructors Ltd* [1996] 1 All ER 96, at 103, the decision in *Pan Atlantic* v *Pine Top* restores the special case of non-disclosure in insurance contracts to the mainstream of the law on misrepresentation. There remains, of course, the duty of disclosure not otherwise applying; but for non-disclosure to be actionable it is no longer enough that the facts were 'material'. They must also actually have induced the particular contract (see 10.2.2.1).

Family settlements are also contracts *uberrimae fidei* (*Gordon* v *Gordon* (1819) 3 Swan 400). Certain contracts, such as contracts of suretyship, for the sale of land or for the sale of shares, are sometimes treated as being *uberrimae fidei*. The correct view is that they are not, but in each case there may be a limited duty of disclosure greater than that applying to ordinary contracts.

10.2.1.3 Statement of fact If there is a false statement, it must also be a statement of fact as opposed to a statement of belief or opinion, a statement of future conduct or intention, or a statement of law. This is because a fact can be true or false and because a representee is only justified in relying on facts. However, it is worth noting at the outset of this discussion that if a statement is made fraudulently (see 10.4.1), it is likely to be treated as a statement of fact.

Statements of opinion or belief A statement of opinion is not normally treated as a statement of fact. For example, in *Bisset* v *Wilkinson* [1927] AC 177, the owner of land told the subsequent purchaser that, in his opinion, if properly worked, the land would support 2,000 sheep. However, to the knowledge of the purchaser, the owner had not worked the land himself as a sheep farmer, and the statement was no more than an honest estimate, made without particular expertise, as to the capacity of the land. The fact that the land did not have such a capacity did not therefore result in the owner's statement constituting a misrepresentation. The significant factor was that the statement maker was in no better position to know the facts than the purchaser.

In *Economides* v *Commercial Union Assurance Co. plc* [1997] 3 WLR 1066, it was held that there was no misrepresentation when a son incorrectly stated the value of his parents' belongings for the purposes of a contents insurance policy. They were not his belongings so that he was not in any better position than the insurers to know their true value. Significantly, it was also held that there is no duty imposed upon such a person to carry out inquiries to establish an objectively reasonable basis for that statement of belief, i.e. to obtain independent valuations. To hold otherwise would clearly have been inconsistent with *Bisset* v *Wilkinson* and with the decision in *Hummingbird Motors Ltd* v *Hobbs* [1986] RTR 276, to the effect that statements of opinion by a person with no special knowledge of the subject-matter will not constitute misrepresentations even if the belief is unreasonable.

However, what of the situation where the statement maker is in a better position to know the truth? The Privy Council in *Bisset* v *Wilkinson* pointed out that if a reasonable man, *with the state of knowledge of that person*, could not have held the same opinion as was stated, the fact that the statement was made in the form of an opinion will not protect its maker from a claim for misrepresentation (followed by Jacob J in *Thomas Witter Ltd* v *TBP Industries Ltd* [1996] 2 All ER 573). This is because the statement maker is representing that his or her statement is based on a reasonable belief and that he or she has reasonable grounds for making it.

Where in fact there is no reasonable ground for an opinion made by a person who is in a better position to know the true facts, such a statement amounts to a misrepresentation. Thus, in *Smith* v *Land & House Property Corporation* (1884) 28 ChD 7, the vendor described the tenant of property sold as 'a most desirable tenant', which was far from being the case. It was argued on the vendor's behalf that his statement had been no more than an expression of opinion. This argument was rejected by Bowen LJ, who said that a statement of opinion by a person who is in the best position to know the true position would often be a statement of fact because there is an implicit assertion that the statement maker knows of facts that justify his opinion.

It may be that the rule, that statements of opinion are not normally representations of fact, may be no more than a particular application of the rule that a representation is not actionable unless made with the intention that it be relied upon by the representee (10.2.2.3). Thus, it is common practice to preface a remark by saying, 'It is only my opinion', when it is intended that no reliance should be placed upon it.

In some circumstances a statement will be made which can only be an opinion, in that conclusive proof of its truth is unavailable at the time when the statement is made. Nevertheless, the courts would be prepared to impose liability for misrepresentation if the statement was made negligently, by an apparent 'expert', and with the intention that it be relied upon (see *Esso Petroleum Co. Ltd* v *Mardon* [1976] QB 801).

Statements of future conduct or intention A misrepresentation as to the future is not, in general, a representation of existing fact, and is therefore not actionable. Thus, a person may state an intention to follow a certain course of conduct in the future. It is not misrepresentation if he or she is prevented from following that course of conduct or later changes his or her mind (see 10.2.1.2). Nevertheless, if at the time of stating the intention the person did not in fact have any such intention then that would be treated as misrepresentation, since a present intention is a fact which can be falsely described. For example, in *Edgington* v *Fitzmaurice* (1885) 24 ChD 459, the directors of a company offered debentures for sale, saying that the purpose of the issue of debentures was to raise money for alterations and additions to premises, and for other purposes implying an expansion of the company's business. In fact, the money was needed to meet the company's liabilities. Bowen LJ noted that a representation as to the future would not normally form the basis of an action for misrepresentation, but had no hesitation in finding that where the state of a man's mind can be ascertained (and this is likely to be difficult to prove), it is 'as much a fact as the state of his digestion'. As a result, a misstatement as to the state of a man's mind is an actionable misrepresentation, and the directors in *Edgington* v *Fitzmaurice* were held liable.

Statements of law A misstatement of law will not found a claim for misrepresentation. The point was acknowledged in passing in *Solle* v *Butcher* [1950] 1 KB 671 at 703, although the case is more relevant as an example of the fact that it is rare for a person to make a simple representation of general law. A representation of law is abstract and made without reference to particular facts (e.g., 'rent control does not apply to premises which have been substantially altered so that they are in effect new premises'). It is more common for the representation to combine law and facts, so that it is a statement of the *effect* of the law in a given situation (e.g., 'the alterations done to these premises have made them new premises in the eyes of the law, so that rent control will not apply'). Such a statement, if false, is often described as a misrepresentation of private rights, and is actionable.

10.2.2 Induces the other party to contract

For the representation to be said to have induced the contract, four conditions must be satisfied:

(a) the representation must be material;
(b) it must be known to the representee;

(c)   it must be intended to be acted upon; and
(d)   it must be acted upon.

10.2.2.1 Material representation   A representation will induce a contract only if it is material. It must represent a fact which would positively influence a reasonable person, considering entering the contract, to decide positively in favour of so doing. In many circumstances the requirement of materiality may be something of a formality, serving only to exclude trivial misstatements from actionability, or to enable the court to infer actual inducement (10.2.2.4). Thus, where a statement is made with the intention of inducing a contract (10.2.2.3), and was such as would influence a reasonable person to agree (that is, was *material*), it is not difficult to infer actual inducement (*Smith v Chadwick* (1884) 9 App Cas 187 at 196, and *Avon Insurance plc v Swire Fraser Ltd* [2000] 1 All ER (Comm) 573, at 633). Alternatively, if a representee does not act unreasonably in actually being induced to contract, it may be assumed that the representation was material.

10.2.2.2 Known to the representee   It need scarcely be stated that a representation cannot be said to have induced a contract unless it was known to the representee. Thus, in *Horsfall v Thomas* (1862) 1 H & C 90, active concealment was held to be a misrepresentation, but the plaintiff's failure to inspect the subject-matter (a gun) meant that the misrepresentation never came to his attention, and so did not induce the contract. Consistent with the general law of agency (see Chapter 16), a representation made to an agent is 'known' to the principal, whether actual knowledge exists or not (e.g., *Strover v Harrington* [1988] 1 All ER 769). In addition, a representation made by one party to another, which induces a third party to enter a contract, is actionable by the third party provided the first party knew or ought to have been aware that the representation would be likely to be communicated to the third party (*Pilmore v Hood* (1838) 5 Bing NC 97 and *Yianni v Edwin Evans & Sons* [1981] 3 All ER 593). This principle was recently applied in *Clef Aquitaine SARL v Laporte Materials (Barrow) Ltd* [2000] 3 WLR 1760. The first plaintiff company had been induced to enter into distribution agreements by a fraudulent misrepresentation based on the price list. However, the second plaintiff company had subsequently taken over the agreements (by novation). It was held that the second plaintiffs could rely on the misrepresentation because the defendants knew that the first plaintiffs were '[notionally] repeating to the [second plaintiffs] the misrepresentations which [the defendants] had made' but had 'stood by and allowed them to complete the novations without disillusioning them'.

10.2.2.3 Intended to be acted upon   To be actionable, a misrepresentation must be intended to be acted upon. For example, in *Peek v Gurney* (1873) LR 6 HL 377, the promoters of a company issued a prospectus containing material misstatements. The intention had been to induce people to apply for the allotment of shares on formation of the company. The plaintiffs claimed to have been induced by the statements in the prospectus to purchase shares on the market. They were unable to recover their losses, since there had been no intention on the part of those issuing the prospectus that it should be relied upon by those dealing in the shares subsequent to the original allotment. It is worth noting, by contrast, that in the different but analogous context of an action for negligent misstatement (see 10.4.3.1), it was held that a duty of care could be owed to purchasers of shares in the 'after market' (i.e., after the original allocation) if the misleading prospectus had been intended to be relied upon by such purchasers (*Possfund Custodian Trustee Ltd v Diamond* [1996] 1 WLR 1351; though this was the trial of a preliminary issue, before the relevant facts were proved).

As noted above (10.2.1.3), the qualification of a statement as merely an opinion is often taken to indicate that it is not intended that the statement be relied upon.

10.2.2.4 Actually acted upon To establish that the representation induced the contract, it may not be enough merely to show that it was made and known and material, and that the representee entered the contract. It is open to the representor to attempt to prove that the representee did not actually rely on the misrepresentation in deciding to enter the contract, but was persuaded by some other factor. It seems, however, that in practical terms this will be possible only where the alleged misrepresentation is not fraudulent (*County Natwest Ltd v Barton* [1999] Lloyd's Rep Bank 408).

With the exception of instances of fraudulent statements (*S. Pearson & Son Ltd v Dublin Corporation* [1907] AC 351), if the representee chooses to test the truth of the statement made by making his or her own investigations then he or she is held to rely on his or her own judgment and not upon the misrepresentation. For example, in *Attwood v Small* (1838) 6 Cl & F 232, the plaintiffs sought to rescind a contract for the purchase of a mine, citing in evidence false statements made by the defendant seller about the mine's potential. However, the plaintiffs had sought to verify the seller's claims by appointing their own agent to examine the mine, and the agent had reported in similar terms. The House of Lords held that the contract could not be rescinded since the plaintiffs had relied on their own expert and not on the word of the seller. The fact that the expert had failed to discover the truth did not make the seller liable.

However, the mere fact that the representee fails to avail himself or herself of an opportunity to discover the truth, for example by inspection of goods or property, does not prevent reliance on the misrepresentation. Such a person will still be induced by the misrepresentation. In *Redgrave v Hurd* (1881) 20 ChD 1, an elderly solicitor wished to sell his house and a share in his practice. He told a prospective younger partner that the income of the practice was about £300 a year, showing him ledgers covering some £200 a year and stating that the balance was made up by income not shown in the ledgers but derived from other work represented by a bundle of papers which were available. The prospective partner did not examine the bundle of papers; had he done so, he would have discovered that the income they represented was minimal. At first instance, it was held that failure to take the opportunity of inspecting the papers indicated that there had been no reliance on the misstatement. On appeal that finding was unanimously overturned. This decision, while remaining unchallenged, must now be read in the light of the developing law governing negligent misrepresentation and the application thereto of the doctrine of contributory negligence (see 10.5.5).

Significantly, a representation will be found to have induced the contract even if it is not the only factor to have contributed to the decision to enter the contract. In *Edgington* v *Fitzmaurice* (1885) 24 ChD 459 (above, 10.2.1.3), the representee entered the contract partly as a result of misrepresentations made, and partly as a result of his own mistake in thinking that the benefits of the contract were greater than was really the case. Nevertheless, the remedy of rescission was available to the representee.

10.3   REPRESENTATIONS WHICH BECOME TERMS

As noted above (10.1), a misrepresentation may in some circumstances become a term of the contract. In other words, the representation can be incorporated as a term. For detailed consideration of the circumstances in which representations become terms, see 5.1.

At one time it was particularly important to attempt to establish that a representation had become a term of the contract because, unless fraud could be established (10.4.1), the remedies for misrepresentation compared very unfavourably with the remedies for breach (see 5.1.1). It has become less important following the availability of a remedy of damages for negligent misrepresentation (10.4.3). Moreover, it is no longer the case that the fact that a representation has become a term extinguishes the right to rescission for misrepresentation (s. 1, Misrepresentation Act 1967). Nevertheless, it will still be important to be able to determine whether a representation has become a term of the contract. As discussed in Chapter 5, this is because damages are available for misrepresentation only on proof of fault, whereas damages are available as of right for breach of a term. Further, a different measure of loss applies to misrepresentation from that applying to breach and the remoteness rules are different (see 5.1.1 for this discussion).

Where a representation becomes a term, the injured party will have two possible claims: in breach of contract, and in misrepresentation. A skilful lawyer may be able to manipulate the distinctions between remedies for breach of contract and remedies for misrepresentation to his client's advantage. However, it is not possible both to rescind for misrepresentation and to claim damages in contract (expectation measure, see 13.2) because the effect of rescission is to treat the contract as if it had never been made and it is therefore not possible to obtain damages for its breach. Assuming it to be available, it is however possible to obtain rescission for misrepresentation and damages for misrepresentation.

10.4   TYPES OF MISREPRESENTATION

The remedies available for misrepresentation depend upon the type of misrepresentation, i.e. upon the state of mind of the statement maker in making the statement which induced the contract. There are three types of misrepresentation: fraudulent, negligent, and innocent. This distinction is particularly important in determining the damages for misrepresentation. In this section the elements of each type of misrepresentation are considered, while 10.5 considers the remedies of rescission and damages.

10.4.1 Making the basic distinction

Fraud was defined by the House of Lords in *Derry* v *Peek* (1889) 14 App Cas 337, as a false statement, 'made knowingly, or without belief in its truth, or recklessly, careless whether it be true or false'. The essential ingredient for fraud is the absence of an honest belief that the statement is true. It is on this basis that it is possible to distinguish recklessness (fraud) and mere lack of care (negligence). Lord Herschell, who provided the above definition, went on to say that, in order to constitute fraud, recklessness must amount to an absence of belief in the truth of the statement made. In *Thomas Witter Ltd* v *TBP Industries Ltd* [1996] 2 All ER 573 at 587, Jacob J construed Lord Herschell's remarks as requiring a 'disregard for the truth' amounting to 'dishonesty'. In other words, a statement maker would be reckless if he or she had no knowledge whether the statement was true or false but asserted that it was true and thereby took a risk. This can be distinguished from a negligent statement where the statement maker believes the statement to be true (i.e., he or she is honest) but has been careless in reaching that conclusion. If the statement maker honestly believes that his or her statement is true and has reasonable grounds for that belief, the statement will be classified as an innocent misrepresentation.

10.4.2 Fraudulent misrepresentation and remedies available

In *Thomas Witter Ltd* v *TBP Industries Ltd* [1996] 2 All ER 573, it was alleged that a failure to disclose a change in accounting method where there was a duty to disclose this fact (*cf. With* v *O'Flanagan* [1936] Ch 575) amounted to a change of circumstances misrepresentation. It is certainly easy to jump to the conclusion that such a failure will be deceitful. However, Jacob J explained that the failure to disclose may be attributable to a failure to realise that there is a duty to disclose. It is important, therefore, to consider whether the failure was in fact deliberate or dishonest (in which case it will amount to a fraudulent misrepresentation), or whether there is no dishonesty and it is negligent. Such a misrepresentation would, it seems, have to be at least negligent, because under s. 2(1) of the Misrepresentation Act 1967, the burden of disproving negligence requires the misrepresentor to prove that the facts represented were true 'up to the time the contract was made'. In instances involving a failure to disclose a change of circumstances, the misrepresentor will be unable to discharge this burden.

At one time being able to establish fraud was crucial, since damages could not otherwise be claimed for misrepresentation. Today, a right to damages also exists in the case of negligent misrepresentation (10.4.3), but the distinction is still important in some cases, since proof of fraud *may* permit a greater measure of recovery (10.5.3.2) and takes the situation outside the scope of the court's discretion to award damages instead of rescission under s. 2(2) of the Misrepresentation Act 1967 (10.4.4).

Fraud provides the strongest combination of remedies for misrepresentation. Rescission and damages are available, and it is generally accepted that in the case of fraud the courts will compensate all loss which is a direct result of the transaction (*Doyle* v *Olby (Ironmongers) Ltd* [1969] 2 QB 158). Damages for fraudulent misrepresentation are discussed in detail at 10.5.3.2.

A note of caution   It was suggested above that there are still advantages, in terms of the remedies available, to a representee who can establish the existence of fraud rather than mere negligence. Against those advantages must be weighed the fact that the courts regard fraud as a very serious allegation, and may demand more than the usual civil burden of proof from the party seeking to demonstrate its existence and may penalise in costs a party failing to make out his or her claim. On the other hand, the remedies for negligent misrepresentation are often as good as those for fraud, and under s. 2(1) of the Misrepresentation Act 1967, the burden of proof is reversed so that it is the representor who has to establish that he or she was not negligent (10.4.3.2). In these circumstances, bringing a claim for fraud is not something which should be undertaken lightly.

10.4.3   Negligent misrepresentation

Misrepresentations which were made without due care, but were not reckless in the sense of being fraudulent (10.4.1), were once treated as innocent misrepresentations. As a result, although rescission was available, no damages could be recovered. It was a rule which was regarded by many lawyers and commentators as unsatisfactory, and led to sometimes artificial interpretations to the effect that a representation had been incorporated in a contract, in order to allow the recovery of damages for what would then be breach (5.1). Eventually the position changed, but as a result of almost simultaneous, parallel common law and statutory developments, the law relating to negligent misrepresentation has become unnecessarily complicated. These developments have resulted in two possible claims for damages being available in many instances to a party to whom a negligent misstatement has been made. The first such claim is in tort for negligent misstatement, and the second claim is for damages under s. 2(1) of the Misrepresentation Act 1967.

10.4.3.1   Negligent misstatement at common law   In *Hedley Byrne & Co. Ltd* v *Heller & Partners Ltd* [1964] AC 465, the House of Lords extended the common law tort of negligence to the field of negligent statements which cause loss. The plaintiffs had been asked for credit by a company, and had sought advice on the financial standing of the company from its bankers, the defendants. The defendants, who had known the purpose of the plaintiffs' request, had carelessly said that the company was financially sound. The House of Lords stated that the defendants owed a duty of care to the

plaintiffs, but that since in the particular case the advice had been given expressly 'without responsibility', there was no liability.

In *McCullagh* v *Lane Fox and Partners Ltd* [1996] 1 EGLR 35, Hobhouse LJ explained the impact of the disclaimer in a different way. Proceeding from Lord Bridge's formulation of the test for a duty of care in *Caparo Industries plc* v *Dickman* [1990] 1 All ER 568 (foreseeability, proximity, and whether it is fair, just and reasonable that the law should impose a duty), he found that the case turned on the last of these three, which in turn he found was essentially a question of whether the defendant had 'assumed responsibility' for the statement made (thus following Lord Goff in *Henderson* v *Merrett Syndicates Ltd* [1995] 2 AC 145 at 181). The impact of the disclaimer, according to Hobhouse LJ, is to negative the assumption of responsibility for the statement: 'It . . . tells the recipient of the representation . . . that the maker is not accepting responsibility for the accuracy of the representation.' In other words, if effective, it prevents a duty of care arising. The disclaimer must, to be effective, satisfy ss. 2 and 11 of UCTA 1977, which Hobhouse LJ found to be the case here (see further, 6.6.2.2).

Therefore, at common law, liability arises where there is a duty of care to do all that is reasonable to ensure that the statement made is correct. The House of Lords said that the duty exists where there is a 'special relationship' between the parties, although their Lordships were not clear as to what constituted a special relationship. It seems certain at least that particular types of adviser, commonly regarded as professional (such as solicitors, barristers, accountants, surveyors, etc.), have a special relationship with their clients and so owe the duty of care to those to whom they give advice.

The House of Lords has subjected common law negligent misstatement to very thorough scrutiny. In *Caparo Industries plc* v *Dickman* [1990] 1 All ER 568, their Lordships reaffirmed that liability for negligent misstatement may be imposed, but were most anxious to make clear that it would be imposed only where there is a close degree of interrelationship between the party making the statement and the party subsequently complaining. In particular, those making statements do not owe a duty of accuracy to the whole world, or to anyone who may happen to have the statement communicated to them. Lord Oliver said (at 589):

> The necessary relationship between the maker of a statement or giver of advice (the adviser) and the recipient who acts in reliance on it (the advisee) may typically be held to exist where (1) the advice is required for a purpose, whether particularly specified or generally described, which is made known, either actually or inferentially, to the adviser when the advice is given, (2) the adviser knows, either actually or inferentially, that his advice will be communicated to the advisee either specifically or as a member of an ascertainable class, in order that it should be used by the advisee for that purpose, (3) it is known, either actually or inferentially, that the advice so communicated is likely to be acted on by the advisee for that purpose without independent inquiry and (4) it is so acted on by the advisee to his detriment.

The House of Lords clearly intended to place a restrictive interpretation on the doctrine, and that lead was followed in subsequent cases (e.g., *James McNaughton Papers Group Ltd* v *Hicks Anderson & Co.* [1991] 1 All ER 134; in *Morgan Crucible Co. plc* v *Hill Samuel Bank Ltd* [1991] 1 All ER 148, a duty was found to exist, but the Court of Appeal expressly relied upon the strict test outlined above). More recently the courts have placed this analysis within the broader test of 'assumption of responsibility' for a statement (e.g., *Henderson* v *Merrett Syndicates Ltd* [1995] 2 AC 145, *Spring* v *Guardian Assurance* [1995] 2 AC 296 and *Williams* v *Natural Life Health Foods Ltd* [1998] 2 All ER 577).

It appears that the English courts may be willing to find a special relationship wherever the person giving advice holds himself or herself out as possessing some expertise or special skill, and knows that the other party will rely on the advice given, irrespective of whether he or she is in fact a 'professional' adviser. In *Esso Petroleum Co. Ltd* v *Mardon* [1976] QB 801 (see 5.1.3) the Court of Appeal found the duty of care to exist where an expert valuer for the oil company made a representation about the petrol sales potential of a garage to a prospective tenant. The statement maker clearly possessed special skill and knowledge concerning the subject-matter of the contract. In addition, since the valuer was experienced and knew much more about the business than did the tenant, he could reasonably foresee that the tenant would rely on his judgment.

Thus, the common law negligent misstatement doctrine is not limited to representations which result in a contract between representor and representee (*Hedley Byrne & Co. Ltd* v *Heller & Partners Ltd*) but can apply to representations which induce a contract between representor and representee (*Esso Petroleum Co. Ltd* v *Mardon*).

The real difficulty with the claim for damages for negligent misstatement at common law is that the misrepresentee has the burden of proving the both existence of the duty of care (special relationship) and that the duty of care has been broken.

10.4.3.2 Section 2(1) of the Misrepresentation Act 1967   Section 2(1) of the 1967 Act provides:

> (1)   Where a person has entered into a contract after a misrepresentation has been made to him by another party thereto and as a result thereof he has suffered loss, then, if the person making the misrepresentation would be liable to damages in respect thereof had the misrepresentation been made fraudulently, that person shall be so liable notwithstanding that the misrepresentation was not made fraudulently, unless he proves that he had reasonable ground to believe and did believe up to the time the contract was made that the facts represented were true.

This statutory right to damages for negligent misrepresentation is in one sense wider than that existing at common law, since it does not depend upon the existence of any kind of special relationship. In another sense, however, it is narrower, since it applies only where the representee has been induced to enter a contract with the representor by the misrepresentation. Thus, a case like *Hedley Byrne & Co. Ltd* v *Heller & Partners Ltd* [1964] AC 465 (above, 10.4.3.1) does not fall within the ambit of the section because the negligent misstatement did not result in a contract between the party giving the advice and the party seeking it. It is potentially narrow in another sense, in that it may not apply to the exceptional cases of representation by silence (10.2.1.2), on the ground that such a misrepresentation is not 'made' within the terms of s. 2(1). There is an obiter statement to that effect in *Banque Financière de la Cité SA* v *Westgate Insurance Co. Ltd* [1989] 2 All ER 952 at 1004, although such an approach appears unduly literal and may be inconsistent with the general purpose of s. 2(1).

Where the representation does fall within the ambit of the section, it is likely that the representee will choose to base the claim on s. 2(1) of the 1967 Act rather than the common law, since the burden of proof is reversed as regards negligence. Once the claimant has established the existence of a false statement which induced him or her to enter the contract, it is for the defendant to show that in making the representation 'he had reasonable ground to believe and did believe up to the time the contract was made that the facts represented were true'. This reversal of the burden of proof is a considerable advantage to the claimant. It is also not merely a matter of disproving negligence. As a result of the decision of the Court of Appeal in *Howard Marine & Dredging Co. Ltd* v *A. Ogden & Sons (Excavations) Ltd* [1978] QB 574, the defendant has to prove positively that he or she had reasonable grounds for his or her belief. In *Spice Girls Ltd* v *Aprilla World Service BV*, [2000] EMLR 478, Aprilla was held to be entitled to receive damages because under s. 2(1) the onus was on the Spice Girls to show that they had reasonable grounds to believe and did believe at the date of the agreement that the representation was true. Since it was found that they knew that one member intended to leave, they were not able to discharge that burden.

Thus, in cases in which it is not clear whether the representor acted reasonably, at common law the claim for damages will fail; but in the same circumstances under s. 2(1) of the 1967 Act the claimant will succeed (*cf. Howard Marine & Dredging Co. Ltd* v *A. Ogden & Sons (Excavations) Ltd* [1978] QB 574).

However, s. 2(1) of the Misrepresentation Act 1967 is rather clumsily drafted, being based on what has been described as the 'fiction of fraud' (Atiyah and Treitel (1967) 30 MLR 369). Liability is said to exist where it would exist had the misrepresentation been made fraudulently, even though in the particular case it was not made fraudulently. It is far from clear why this formulation was used. It may be that it was intended to indicate that the same measure of damages as for fraud should apply (see 10.5.3.3), although this appears unlikely. It is not thought that it is intended to import any of the other special rules applying to fraud (see 10.5.5). It is seems more likely that the intention was to indicate the basic circumstances for liability in damages by no more than an analogy with the established circumstances for the availability of damages for the tort of deceit.

10.4.4   Innocent misrepresentation

An innocent misrepresentation must today be regarded as a false statement which was made neither fraudulently nor negligently. In fact, as a result of the wording of s. 2(1) of the Misrepresentation Act 1967, the representee must not only have believed the statement, but also must be able to prove that he or she had reasonable grounds for believing it (see 10.4.3.2).

The victim of an innocent misrepresentation is entitled to rescission of the contract, assuming none of the bars to apply (10.5.2), and to an indemnity intended to help restore the parties to the position before the contract was made (10.5.4). There is *no right* to damages for innocent misrepresentation. However, the court has a discretion under s. 2(2) of the Misrepresentation Act 1967 to award damages in lieu of (instead of) rescission. The weight of authority supports the view that this discretion is available only where the right to rescission has not been lost (*Floods of Queenferry Ltd* v *Shand Construction Ltd* [2000] BLR 81 and *Government of Zanzibar* v *British Aerospace (Lancaster House) Ltd* [2000] 1 WLR 2333, [2000] CLC 735, see 10.5.3.4), although this might result in there being no available remedy in a case of innocent misrepresentation, and it is therefore questionable that this would have been intended.

10.5   REMEDIES FOR MISREPRESENTATION

In addition to the positive remedies of rescission (10.5.1), damages (10.5.3) and indemnity (10.5.4), it is important to remember that misrepresentation affords a defence to a claim for breach of contract brought by the representor. This defence may be subject to the same limitations as the right to rescind (10.5.2).

10.5.1   Rescission

Rescission is available in principle for all types of misrepresentation. The effect of misrepresentation is to make a contract voidable, not void (see 1.5.3), and a claim for rescission is a claim to have the contract set aside, restoring the parties to the position they were in before the contract was made. Although in *TSB Bank plc* v *Camfield* [1995] 1 WLR 430, the Court of Appeal held (in the context of a guarantee) that rescission was total and partial rescission on terms was not possible, the High Court of Australia in *Vadasz* v *Pioneer Concrete (SA) Pty Ltd* (1995) 130 ALR 570, preferred a more flexible approach. The guarantee in question covered all monies owing, in respect of both existing and future debts, when it had been represented that it would cover only future debts. The High Court of Australia was prepared to rescind the guarantee as regards the existing debt but to enforce it in relation to future indebtedness. This severing of objectionable parts of a contract is essentially also what occurred in *Barclays Bank plc* v *Caplan* [1998] FLR 532. The Privy Council in *Far Eastern Shipping Co. Ltd* v *Scales Trading Ltd* [2001] 1 All ER (Comm) 319 discussed these cases but found that, on the facts, it was unnecessary to decide between the competing authorities.

In theory, rescission may be effected without recourse to legal action, but in practice a party is likely to prefer to have the backing of a court order, especially where it is intended to recover property. The essential requirement of rescission, apart from satisfying the conditions of liability, i.e. establishing the actionable misrepresentation (10.2), is that notice be given to the other party. Where it is impossible to trace the other party the requirement of giving notice may be waived, provided all necessary steps have been taken to recover the goods. For example, in *Car and Universal Finance Co. Ltd* v *Caldwell* [1961] 1 QB 525, the owner of a car had been fraudulently persuaded to sell it to a rogue, who resold it to the finance company and then disappeared with the proceeds. Once aware of the true facts, the owner notified the police and the Automobile Association and asked for their help in recovering the car. These actions were found to have been enough to rescind the contract, and since they preceded the sale to the finance company the latter did not acquire good title to the car.

The rule may be explained in terms of the injustice of denying rescission simply because a rogue perpetrated a deliberate fraud and then absconded, so that notice could not be given. On the other hand, allowing rescission in those circumstances may cause hardship to a third party who has innocently acquired goods, if, as here, it is found that the rescission occurred before the third party acquired them.

10.5.2 Loss of the right to rescind

The remedy of rescission may be lost (or barred) if any of the following apply.

10.5.2.1 Affirmation The right to rescind is lost if the contract is affirmed by the representee after discovering the true state of affairs (*Long* v *Lloyd* [1958] 1 WLR 753). Affirmation is an indication to the representor that it is intended to continue with the contract, despite the misrepresentation. Affirmation may be indicated by express words, or by conduct. In *Long* v *Lloyd*, the plaintiff purchased a lorry which had falsely been represented to be in good condition. On its first journey several serious faults were discovered; they were drawn to the attention of the seller who offered to pay half the cost of repairs. On a second journey the lorry broke down again, revealing more serious faults. The plaintiff was held to have lost the right to rescind the contract. The first journey did not constitute affirmation, since the buyer was entitled to a 'test drive' to check the accuracy of the representation. The second journey, however, was made in the knowledge that the vehicle when sold was not in good condition, and therefore amounted to affirmation of the contract. The result on the facts was that the plaintiff had no remedy at all for misrepresentation, since damages were unavailable at this time for such non-fraudulent misrepresentations.

10.5.2.2 Lapse of time In some cases the right to rescind is lost through lapse of time. The bar to rescission through lapse of time represents one instance where it is relevant to consider the type of misrepresentation when

determining the ability to rescind. In the case of fraudulent misrepresentations, time will run from the time when the fraud either was, or could with
reasonable diligence have been, discovered. However, if the misrepresentation is non-fraudulent (i.e. negligent or innocent), time will run from the date
of the contract. A good illustration of the operation of this principle is
provided by the facts and decision in *Leaf* v *International Galleries* [1950] 2
KB 86 (9.3.1). A painting was sold. It had been misrepresented as having
been painted by Constable. Five years later the misrepresentation was
discovered, and the purchaser sought to rescind the contract of sale. His
action failed because of the lapse of time since the sale.

The misrepresentation in this case was innocent (which at the time
embraced both negligent and wholly innocent misrepresentation) so that time
ran from the date of the contract. For a recent example of the remedy of
rescission being lost due to lapse of time (delay), see *Government of Zanzibar*
v *British Aerospace (Lancaster House) Ltd* [2000] 1 WLR 2333, [2000] CLC
735 (10.5.3.4).

10.5.2.3 *Restitutio in integrum* The right to rescind is lost if *restitutio in
integrum* is no longer possible; that is, if it is no longer possible to restore the
parties to their positions before the contract was made. Such will be the case
where the nature of the subject-matter has been changed (*Clarke* v *Dickson*
(1858) EB & E 148 — misrepresentation induced purchase of shares in a
company which was subsequently wound up), or it has declined in value. For
example, a contract for the purchase of a bottle of wine, induced by a
misrepresentation about its quality, cannot be rescinded once the wine has
been opened and drunk.

Nevertheless, although a limited form of rescission was available at common law for fraud, it is essentially an equitable remedy and the Chancery
Court did not allow minor imperfections in the restoration of the original
position to stand in the way of the remedy. For example, in *Armstrong* v
Jackson [1917] 2 KB 822, a major depreciation in value of shares sold under
a misrepresentation did not bar rescission, since it was possible to return the
shares. In ordering rescission, the court may impose terms, for example to
account for profits and to allow for deterioration, in order to do what has
been described as 'what is practically just' (*per* Lord Blackburn in *Erlanger* v
New Sombrero Phosphate Co. (1878) 3 App Cas 1218 at 1278). The court is
much more likely to be willing to overlook imperfections in the process of
restoring the original positions in the case of fraudulent than in the case of
negligent or innocent misrepresentations (*per* Lord Wright in *Spence* v
Crawford [1939] 3 All ER 271 at 288).

It appears from the decision in *Thomas Witter* v *TBP Industries Ltd* [1996]
2 All ER 573, that rescission of a contract to purchase a business may be
particularly difficult to achieve because, according to Jacob J, it may well not
be the same business by the time the question of the availability of rescission
comes before the courts. The judge stressed that it was almost inevitable that
there would have been changes in personnel and third-party mortgages would
be affected. He also rejected the argument that it was for the misrepresentor

to avoid rescission by demonstrating that third parties would be actually affected on the facts. Thus, this case also illustrates another bar to rescission, namely third-party interests.

10.5.2.4 Third-party interests Rescission is a personal remedy so that the right to rescind will be lost if third-party rights intervene (see 1.5.3). Since a contract affected by misrepresentation is only voidable, not void, a person acquiring goods under such a contract may pass good title at any time before rescission to an innocent third-party purchaser who has no notice of the misrepresentation (s. 23, SGA 1979; and see 3.2.2). Many of the recent cases in which wives have sought to avoid contracts in which they have agreed to provide security in the form of the matrimonial home in order to cover their husband's business debts, rest as much on misrepresentation as they do on undue influence. Consequently, what has previously been said about third-party rights and notice applies in this context as well (see *TSB Bank plc* v *Camfield* [1995] 1 WLR 430; and see generally 11.2.3.2).

10.5.2.5 Misrepresentation Act 1967, s. 2(2) In the case of negligent and innocent misrepresentation, the right to rescind will be lost if the court exercises its discretion to award damages in lieu of rescission under s. 2(2) of the Misrepresentation Act 1967 (see 10.5.3.4).

10.5.3 Damages for misrepresentation

10.5.3.1 Background The original common law position was that damages were available only for fraudulent misrepresentation, by way of a tortious action for deceit (10.5.3.2). A non-fraudulent misrepresentation might be rescinded in equity, but gave rise to no common law right to damages. Instead, as part of the process of rescission, an indemnity might be awarded (see 10.5.4).

It is still the case that a wholly innocent misrepresentation gives no general right to damages (but see the discretion to award damages in lieu of rescission under s. 2(2) of the Misrepresentation Act 1967, at 10.4.4). However, as discussed above 10.4.3, the development of the tort of negligence (see 1.2) eventually gave rise to an action (now claim) for negligent misstatement which exists in tandem with the statutory right to damages for negligent misrepresentation (see 10.4.3).

Subject to s. 2(2) of the Misrepresentation Act 1967 (10.4.4), the right to damages is additional to the right to rescission. Provided there is no double recovery, a representee is entitled to rescission *and* damages. This would be appropriate where, for example, despite rescission the misrepresentee was not restored to his or her original position because of expenditure he or she incurred as a consequence of entering into the voidable contract. In such a situation the claimant would also need to claim damages for misrepresentation (and the courts would have to consider the application of the relevant remoteness rule to the loss in question).

If the remedy of rescission has been lost, it follows that (apart from misrepresentations to which s. 2(2) of the Misrepresentation Act 1967 applies), the remedy of damages will remain and will represent the only mechanism for restoring the misrepresentee to his or her original position. In *Production Technology Consultants Ltd* v *Bartlett* [1988] 1 EGLR 182, the Court of Appeal held that the right to damages remained, where a party went ahead with a contract with knowledge of the misrepresentation, thereby losing the right to rescind (10.5.2.1).

10.5.3.2 Measure of damages in the tort of deceit Since the claim for fraudulent misrepresentation (10.4.1) is the tortious claim for deceit, the measure of damages is the usual tortious measure of out-of-pocket loss, rather than the contractual measure of expectation loss (*cf.* 13.2). Thus, the representee is to be put into the position he or she would have been in had the representation not been made (*Derry* v *Peek* (1889) 14 App Cas 337).

The remoteness rule in claims in the tort of deceit allows the misrepresentee to recover for all direct loss incurred as a result of the fraudulent misrepresentation, regardless of foreseeability (*Doyle* v *Olby Ironmongers Ltd* [1969] 2 QB 158). The sum payable is usually calculated by reference to the difference between the amount paid and the actual value of the subject-matter of the contract judged at the date of the contract (*Smith New Court Securities Ltd* v *Scrimgeour Vickers (Asset Management) Ltd* [1997] AC 254 at 265 and 267, *per* Lord Browne-Wilkinson). So, if as a result of a misrepresentation, £2,500 was paid for a car that was actually worth only £1,500 at the date of the contract, damages would be assessed at £1,000. In addition, as noted above, in the case of fraud the courts award damages for all loss, including consequential loss such as expenses incurred as a result of entering the contract (*Doyle* v *Olby (Ironmongers) Ltd* [1969] 2 QB 158).

In *Smith New Court Securities Ltd* v *Scrimgeour Vickers (Asset Management) Ltd* [1997] AC 254, the difference in value rule and the *Doyle* v *Olby* 'all loss directly flowing' rule came into potential conflict because of the particular facts. The defendant induced the plaintiff to purchase shares in a company by a misrepresentation found to have been fraudulent. Thereafter, a further massive fraud by a third party against the company in question was discovered, causing the value of the shares to plummet. Since the plaintiff had purchased the shares as a long-term 'market making' investment, and had paid more than their market value even at the date of the contract, there was no possibility of immediately reselling the shares. The question for the House of Lords was whether the plaintiff could recover the difference between the price paid for the shares and their eventual sale price which reflected the massive third-party fraud (around £11 million), or whether the plaintiff was limited to recovering the difference between the price paid and the actual value of the shares at the date of the contract (just over £1 million). Put another way, the issue was which of the parties should have to bear the effects of the third party's fraud.

If difference in value at the date of the contract was the correct measure, the actual value of the shares *at the date of the transaction* between plaintiff and defendant would be assessed without taking into account the third-party fraud, which had not then been discovered. However, it was equally persuasively arguable that the catastrophic loss was a direct consequence flowing from the defendant's fraud, since the plaintiff would not have been exposed to the risk at all but for the inducement that fraud provided.

The House of Lords decided that the risk was the defendant's, and allowed the plaintiff full recovery of its claim. According to Lord Browne-Wilkinson, the general rule is that loss is to be assessed at the date of the transaction. However, that rule was 'not to be inflexibly applied where to do so would prevent [the misrepresentee] obtaining full compensation for the wrong suffered'. Accordingly, the general rule had to give way if 'the plaintiff is, by reason of the fraud, locked into the property' ([1997] AC 254 at 267). The same would also be true if the fraudulent misrepresentation continued to operate after the date of the contract so that the misrepresentee was 'induced to retain the asset'. Therefore, since the fraud induced the plaintiff to make a long-term investment, without the immediate prospect of reselling the shares, the loss was to be assessed as the actual loss suffered (i.e., the difference between price paid and the price at which the shares were eventually sold). Lord Steyn adopted a less technical analysis: the only question was, what loss did the plaintiff truly suffer? The transaction date valuation rule generally reveals this, but where on the facts it does not, it need not be used.

Thus, the policy appears to be that, where the statement maker has been fraudulent, he or she should be responsible for all the losses resulting from the other party having made the contract (i.e., losses from the 'transaction'). This greater potential liability might be seen as a deterrent to fraudulent inducements. This was the interpretation placed on the decision in *Doyle* v *Olby* by Lord Browne-Wilkinson.

Lord Browne-Wilkinson also stated that the misrepresentee had a duty to mitigate his or her loss once he or she discovered the fraud. In *Downs* v *Chappell* [1997] 1 WLR 461, the Court of Appeal applied this duty to mitigate in the context of damages for fraudulent misrepresentation. The fraudulent misrepresentation related to the value of a bookshop business. The business was purchased for £120,000, and eventually sold for less than £60,000. However, the misrepresentee had earlier refused two offers of £76,000. The Court of Appeal held that damages were limited to £44,000, namely, the difference between £120,000 and £76,000. The plaintiff was entitled to damages for his loss to the date when he could have avoided further losses. The offer of £76,000 had been unreasonably refused and broke the chain of causation. As a result, the further loss (an extra £16,000) was not direct loss flowing from the misrepresentation. The test for mitigation is the same as that applicable for breach of contract claims (i.e., a duty to take reasonable steps to minimise the loss; see 13.9.3) (*Standard Chartered Bank* v *Pakistan National Shipping Corp.* [1999] 1 Lloyd's Rep 747 — if the loss could reasonably have been avoided, it would not be regarded as having been caused by the misrepresentation). The Court of Appeal in *Standard Chartered Bank* v *Pakistan National Shipping (Assessment of Damages)* [2001] EWCA Civ 55, [2001] 1 All ER (Comm) 822, confirmed that in the tort of deceit the concepts of mitigation and causation could not be separated and were 'two sides of the same coin' (*per* Potter LJ, at [41]).

The decision in *East v Maurer* [1991] 1 WLR 461 (for facts see below) represents a further application of recovery of the difference between the price paid and the price at which the property was eventually sold, plus consequential sale expenses.

An interesting question arose in *Clef Aquitaine SARL v Laporte Ltd* [2000] 3 WLR 1760. If the contract entered into as a result of a fraudulent misrepresentation is profitable for the misrepresentee, can that misrepresentee nevertheless claim damages in deceit on the basis that he or she would otherwise have entered into a more profitable contract on better terms? On the facts the plaintiff company had agreed to purchase goods from the defendant. The defendant had fraudulently stated that the price list applicable represented the lowest prices at which the defendant's salesmen could sell the goods. The plaintiff managed to resell the goods at a profit, but wanted damages representing the difference between the price paid and the price that probably could have been negotiated but for the misrepresentation. In essence, the issue was whether 'all the damage (actual loss) directly flowing from the transaction' encompassed this situation. The argument against this was that it represented an attempt to create a contractual (loss of bargain) claim. The Court of Appeal held that there was no absolute rule to the effect that damages in deceit could be recovered only if the transaction was loss making. If the plaintiff could prove that he would have entered into a different and more favourable transaction with the misrepresentor or a third party but for the deceit, he could recover for his loss on that basis. Simon Brown LJ considered that allowing recovery on these facts gave effect to 'the overriding compensatory rule', i.e. that it represented damages for loss of an opportunity which the plaintiff would otherwise have had to agree better terms. Ward LJ stressed the importance of avoiding a position where only nominal damages would be payable for this fraudulent misrepresentation unless a broad approach was taken to the 'loss suffered'. He also, however, adopted a different approach to the other two members of the Court of Appeal by applying the basic difference in value measure, judged at the date of the contract, but comparing the price paid with the lowest possible price that might have been obtained at that time.

Loss of profits The Court of Appeal in *East v Maurer* [1991] 1 WLR 461, held that it was possible in principle to recover for loss of profits following a fraudulent misrepresentation on the basis of the *Doyle v Olby (Ironmongers) Ltd* formula allowing for recovery of 'all the actual damage directly flowing from the fraudulent inducement', even though loss of profits is normally associated with a claim in contract for expectation loss.

However, the Court of Appeal also held that loss of profits in the context of fraudulent misrepresentation could not be calculated on an expectation basis (i.e., as if the representation was true) because that would amount to converting the representation into a contractual promise (i.e., a term) that the statement was true. Instead, the loss of profits was to be calculated on a tortious basis, namely the profit which might have been made had the representation not been made at all. Of course, this raises all sorts of questions relating to calculation of this loss of profits, and it is far too uncertain and speculative without further refinement. The Court of Appeal in *East v Maurer* therefore calculated the loss of profit as the profit the plaintiffs would probably have made if they had purchased another *hypothetical* hair salon at that price (and calculated this figure as £10,000).

East v Maurer was approved, in respect of fraud cases, by Lord Steyn in *Smith New Court Securities Ltd v Scrimgeour Vickers (Asset Management) Ltd* [1997] AC 254 at 282. On Lord Steyn's analysis, the recovery of *hypothetical lost profit* is 'classic consequential loss', and is to be distinguished from the contractual measure of damage, which would allow recovery of the profit as represented in fact.

The Court of Appeal in *Davis v Churchward* (unreported), 6 May 1993, considered the question of recovery of loss of profits for fraudulent misrepresentation relating to the purchase of a public house. In this case, however, the Court compared the public house purchased with an *actual* public house and came to the conclusion that, as there was no difference between the actual turnover in both, there could be no recovery for lost profits.

On the basis of *East v Maurer*, as applied in *Downs v Chappell* [1997] 1 WLR 426, because recovery for loss of profits for fraudulent misrepresentation is not based on the representation being true, in order to be entitled to claim loss of profits, the misrepresentee must have been making a loss in practice (as opposed to less than the profit figure represented). In both *East v Maurer* and *Davis v Churchward* the purchasers suffered a net loss and so the question of loss of profits was considered. However, in *Downs v Chappell*, the purchaser was making a profit, albeit that the profit was not as high as represented, so that no loss of profits claim could be entertained. In practical terms this will limit the availability of this head of damages for fraudulent misrepresentation.

10.5.3.3 Damages for negligent misrepresentations Clearly, damages for negligent misstatement at common law under the principle in *Hedley Byrne v Heller* [1964] AC 465 are tortious, and the remoteness test is whether the loss is a reasonable foreseeable consequence (albeit foreseeable only as a remote consequence) of the tort (*The Wagon Mound (No. 1)* [1961] AC 388). Unlike the position with regard to fraudulent misrepresentation, it is clear that liability is limited to the position assessed at the date of the wrong.

In *South Australia Asset Management Corporation v York Montague Ltd* [1997] AC 191, in the context of a negligent survey, the House of Lords held that damages had to be assessed as the difference between the price paid and the actual value of the property at the date of the purchase contract. The surveyor was responsible only for the consequences of the information in his survey being inaccurate and could not be made responsible for subsequent falls in property values. (The same principle will apply to a claim for breach of contract. Comparison of the position for fraudulent misrepresentation (*Smith New Court Securities v Scrimgeour Vickers* [1997] AC 254) might therefore encourage a claim to be made in misrepresentation rather than contract in order to allow recovery of damages for losses subsequently incurred as a result of entering into the transaction.)

For negligent misrepresentation, s. 2(1) of the Misrepresentation Act 1967 does not expressly state the applicable measure of damages. However, since the section is based on what is known as 'the fiction of fraud' (10.4.3.2), it seems the statutory right to damages, as the common law right (10.4.3.1), is based in tort, and so the tortious (out-of-pocket) measure applies. In the past, the case law had not been entirely consistent on this question and occasionally the courts did allow recovery of expectation loss. However, the point now appears to have been finally settled by the Court of Appeal decision in *Royscot Trust Ltd* v *Rogerson* [1991] 2 QB 297. *Royscot Trust* has proved to be a very controversial case, but not in respect of the basic measure of damages being tortious (i.e., out-of-pocket loss) since if the common law and statutory claims for negligent misstatement are truly alternatives, the basis measure of damages should be the same. Instead, the decision has proved controversial because of the literal interpretation of s. 2(1) of the Misrepresentation Act 1967 (the 'fiction of fraud') adopted by the Court of Appeal. In other words, the Court of Appeal stated that damages under s. 2(1) of the 1967 Act are to be assessed in the same way as damages for fraudulent misrepresentation, even though the misrepresentation is not fraudulent. In particular, the Court would not go against the express literal words of the statute (this 'fiction of fraud') in order to apply the general test of foreseeability for negligence, but allowed the more generous test in fraud (*cf. Doyle* v *Olby* — all direct loss regardless of foreseeability) to govern.

This aspect of the decision in *East* v *Maurer* is easy to criticise because it treats negligent misrepresentations (honest statements) in the same way as fraudulent ones (dishonest statements). It also means that the remoteness tests applicable under the common law claim (*Hedley Byrne* v *Heller*) for negligent misstatement and under s. 2(1) of the 1967 Act for negligent misrepresentation, are very different. Taken to its logical conclusion, the 'fiction of fraud' ought also to mean that the principle in *Smith New Court* v *Scrimgeour Vickers* [1997] AC 254 (10.5.3.2) on the measure of damages, and *East* v *Maurer* [1991] 1 WLR 461 on loss of profit damages for fraudulent misrepresentation, ought also to apply to the assessment of damages under s. 2(1). This would seem to be a staggering conclusion, especially when the significance of fraud in *Smith New Court* is considered. It must be doubtful whether the same policy considerations should apply to negligent misrepresentations (see R. Hooley, 'Damages and the Misrepresentation Act 1967' (1991) 107 LQR 547).

Nevertheless, in *Spice Girls Ltd* v *Aprilla World Service BV (Damages)* [2001] EMLR 8, Arden J had to assess damages under s. 2(1) of the Misrepresentation Act 1967 and was bound to follow *Royscot Trust*. It was accepted that the damages had to be calculated as if the misrepresentation was fraudulent and on the basis of compensating Aprilla for losses flowing from the contract (i.e., the *Smith New Court* approach). Thus all direct loss and consequential loss was recoverable, but not payment of sponsorship fees made to the Spice Girls before the contract was concluded since this payment had not been induced by the misrepresentation.

It is submitted that it might not be long before the decision in *Royscot Trust* on the issue of remoteness is overruled. There are clear signs of judicial discontent in the higher courts, although as yet no action. It may be that the judiciary is waiting for the Law Commission to investigate the Misrepresentation Act 1967, prior to legislative reform (see comments advocating this course of action by Jacob J in *Thomas Witter* v *TBP Industries Ltd* [1996] 2 All ER 573).

The position has now become so acute that in *Avon Insurance plc* v *Swire Fraser Ltd* [2000] 1 All ER (Comm) 573, another first instance judge, Rix J, considered that because of application of the fraud rules to negligent misrepresentations under s. 2(1), a court should not be too willing to find there to be an actionable misrepresentation where the court had some room for the exercise of judgment. The judge continued (at 633, para. 201):

> If, on the other hand, the rule in *Royscot Trust Ltd* case were one day to be found to be a misunderstanding of the 1967 Act, and the way were to become open to treat an innocent misrepresentation under section 2(1) as though it was a case of negligence in *Hedley Byrne*, so that in the typical case of the provision of negligent information it would be possible to tailor the damages to the risk undertaken by the negligent representor . . . then there would be nothing to be said against adopting a more closely focused approach to the proof of misrepresentation.

In *Smith New Court Securities Ltd* v *Scrimgeour Vickers (Asset Management) Ltd* [1997] AC 254 at 267 and 283, both Lords Browne-Wilkinson and Steyn noted the serious doubts about the correctness of the decision in *Royscot Trust Ltd* v *Rogerson*, but did not expressly overrule it since it was not necessary to the decision in the case. Lord Steyn did, however, make clear that in his view fraud and negligence should be treated differently, in that whereas remoteness for fraudulent misrepresentation allows for the recovery of all losses resulting from having entered into the contract, its application in the context of negligent misrepresentation would be limited to allowing for recovery of losses resulting from that negligent statement (which may be significantly narrower). As mentioned elsewhere (*cf.* J. Poole, *Casebook on Contract*, 5th edn, Blackstone Press, 2001, p. 584), this may be very significant where there is more than one misrepresentation.

Until such time as *Royscot* is overruled, the remoteness test under s. 2(1) will be the test of all direct loss resulting from the misrepresentation, so that essentially the test will be to establish that the loss was caused by the misrepresentation. The causal link between the misrepresentation and the loss must be preserved. The applicable test will involve determining whether any subsequent action was reasonable and to be expected in the circumstances. For example, in *Naughton* v *O'Callaghan* [1990] 3 All ER 191, the judge allowed recovery of the difference between the price paid for a thoroughbred colt, intended to be run as a race horse, and its actual value after the horse's value had fallen dramatically due to poor racing performances. The plaintiff's actions in training and racing the horse were exactly the conduct that would have been expected, and were reasonable in the circumstances given that the colt had been purchased as a racehorse. Similarly, if the negligent misrepresentation induces the purchase of a business, it will have to be considered whether any consequential expenditure amounts to a reasonable and expected expense, taking into account the circumstances and, in particular, the nature of the business, or whether it is attributable to the independent whim of the purchaser. Thus, if the loss is caused not by the misrepresentation but by the misrepresentee's independent intervening action, it will not be recoverable (*Hussey* v *Eels* [1990] 2 QB 227).

10.5.3.4 Damages in lieu of rescission Section 2(2) of the Misrepresentation Act 1967 provides:

> (2) Where a person has entered into a contract after a misrepresentation has been made to him otherwise than fraudulently, and he would be entitled, by reason of the misrepresentation, to rescind the contract, then, if it is claimed, in any proceedings arising out of the contract, that the contract ought to be or has been rescinded, the court or arbitrator may declare the contract subsisting and award damages in lieu of rescission, if of the opinion that it would be equitable to do so, having regard to the nature of the misrepresentation and the loss that would be caused by it if the contract were upheld, as well as to the loss that rescission would cause to the other party.

The aim of this provision is to prevent the use of the remedy of rescission, which has the very serious consequence of rendering the contract void and thereby unravelling the contract, in the case of trivial misrepresentations for which compensation would be an adequate remedy (see *William Sindall plc* v *Cambridgeshire CC* [1994] 1 WLR 1016 at 1045, *per* Evans LJ).

It should be noted that s. 2(2) does not apply to fraudulent misrepresentation, since the law never treats fraud as trivial, and in practice it is most likely to be relevant where the misrepresentation is wholly innocent. The remedy is entirely within the discretion of the court, neither party having the right to insist upon its application. In exercising that discretion the court must weigh the seriousness of the misrepresentation, whether the representee will suffer greatly if not allowed to rescind, and whether the representor would suffer unduly if rescission were allowed (*William Sindall plc* v *Cambridgeshire CC* at 1036–7, *per* Hoffmann LJ).

An example of the kind of situation covered by the section might be an innocent misrepresentation, inaccurate by only one year, concerning the age of a second-hand cooker. Assuming the misrepresentation was sufficiently material to have induced the sale, it might be thought that the remedy of rescission would be unduly harsh in these circumstances; but for s. 2(2), it would be the only remedy available.

It has traditionally been considered that the discretion to award damages instead of rescission could be exercised only if the right to rescind had not been lost (or barred), because the section as drafted appears to require that rescission be possible. Section 2(2) clearly refers to the discretion as existing where the injured party would otherwise be entitled to rescind. However, the consequence of the application of such a principle is that no useful remedy will exist, rescission having been lost and there being no discretion to award damages in its place. This interpretation was therefore criticised, but not really doubted, by Atiyah and Treitel ((1967) 30 MLR 369) at the time the Act was passed. The conventional interpretation was challenged by Jacob J in *Thomas Witter Ltd* v *TBP Industries Ltd* [1996] 2 All ER 573 at 590. The judge clearly found such a limit on the discretion to award damages in lieu of rescission to be unattractive. He suggested that it might have been drafted in this way simply to require that the contract should have been open to rescission at some point, without requiring rescission to be a continuing possibility. He was offered support by counsel who had carried out a search of *Hansard* to discover what Parliament's intention had been. In the House of Commons, the Solicitor General had clearly indicated that the intention was to provide a damages remedy where the right to rescission had been lost (Hansard HC, 20 February 1967, coll. 1388–9). Jacob J needed no further encouragement, and he duly found that '. . . the power to award damages under section 2(2) does not depend upon an extant right to rescission — it only depends upon a right having existed in the past'.

However, this approach has not been followed in two recent cases. In the first place, Judge Humphrey Lloyd QC in *Floods of Queenferry Ltd* v *Shand Construction Ltd* [2000] BLR 81 at 93, considered that for the discretion to be exercisable, the remedy of rescission had to exist at the date of the hearing. Secondly, in *Government of Zanzibar* v *British Aerospace (Lancaster House) Ltd* [2000] 1 WLR 2333, [2000] CLC 735, Judge Raymond Jack QC, sitting as a High Court judge, adopted the same approach (at 2341–4), relying on the express words of the subsection, and refused to follow *Thomas Witter* v *TBP Industries Ltd* on this point. The significant differences of interpretation (and hence of result) again highlight the need for some reconsideration of the Misrepresentation Act 1967 (*cf.* 10.5.3.3).

The measure of damages under s. 2(2) It may be that the measure of damages awarded in lieu of rescission is more restricted than either the out-of-pocket or lost expectation measures. The inference from s. 2(3) of the 1967 Act is that it is anticipated that damages under s. 2(2) will be lower than damages under s. 2(1), since the former are to be taken into account in assessing the latter, and this much is accepted by Hoffmann LJ (*obiter*) in *William Sindall plc* v *Cambridgeshire CC* [1994] 1 WLR 1016 at 1037.

However, if the purpose of the damages is to compensate for the loss of the right to rescind, it would seem that that loss is best measured as the difference between the contract price paid (which cannot now be recovered) and the actual value of the thing, which is the tortious measure of damages. This was the approach suggested *obiter* by the Court of Appeal in *William Sindall plc* v *Cambridgeshire CC*. Hoffmann LJ said that s. 2(2) allowed the court to uphold the contract and compensate the claimant for the loss he or she has suffered on account of the property not having been what it was represented to be.

Section 2(2) damages could not be the difference between the price paid and the market value of the property on the basis that this was a loss flowing from having entered the contract. That would be the appropriate measure for fraud, but s. 2(2) damages are different and represent the loss caused by the misrepresentation if the contract is upheld. Evans LJ said that under s. 2(2), the loss caused by upholding the contract would be compensated by the award of 'the cost of remedying the defect, or alternatively . . . the reduced market value attributable to the defect' (at 1044). For Hoffmann LJ, the difference between s. 2(1) and s. 2(2) lay in the availability of damages for consequential loss, which would not be awarded under s. 2(2). This view was also supported by Jacob J in *Thomas Witter* v *TBP Industries Ltd* [1996] 2 All ER 573. It is submitted that this is the correct view of the section in view of the purpose of s. 2(2) damages, although Evans LJ in the *Sindall* case seems to contemplate the award of damages to compensate for consequential losses 'if appropriate'.

On the facts in *Sindall* (see 9.4), the Court of Appeal considered (*obiter*) that the loss that would be caused to the misrepresentee if rescission were refused (and the contract was upheld) was not the full extent of the loss due to entering into the contract, i.e. taking account of the dramatic fall in the price of land, since that was not a loss caused by the misrepresentation if the contract was upheld. Instead, the misrepresentee's loss on this basis would be the cost of diverting the sewer which had been discovered, the loss of one plot and interest charges for any consequent delay.

10.5.4 Indemnity

As was noted earlier (10.4.4), there is no general right to damages for a wholly innocent misrepresentation. Instead, where rescission is available it may be possible to recover an indemnity, which falls short of any measure of damages. An indemnity provides compensation for expenditure occurring as a result of 'obligations which have been created by the contract into which' the representee has been induced to enter (Bowen LJ in *Newbigging* v *Adam* (1886) 34 ChD 582 at 593).

The difference between an indemnity and damages may be demonstrated by reference to the facts of *Whittington* v *Seal-Hayne* (1900) 82 LT 49. The plaintiffs were induced to take a lease of a farm, intending to use it for poultry, by an innocent misrepresentation that the water supply was healthy. This proved not to be the case, a farm manager became ill and the poultry died. The plaintiffs were ordered by the local council to renew the drains, and they lost profits and spent money on medical care, rent, rates, outbuildings and other business expenses. They sought to recover an 'indemnity' for all these costs. They were able to recover compensation for rent, rates and renewing the drains, since these were obligations created by the fact of taking the lease. However, they could not recover the other expenses; these were items of damages, but did not qualify for an indemnity. They were expenses resulting from operating a poultry farm, and there was no *obligation* to run a poultry farm *created by* the contract.

10.5.5 Contributory negligence

Now that damages for negligent misrepresentation may be awarded, the question arises whether the misrepresentee's own negligence, which has contributed to his or her decision to enter the contract, operates to reduce the misrepresentee's damages award.

Needless to say, there is no scope for the application of contributory negligence where the misrepresentations were fraudulently made (*Alliance and Leicester Building Society* v *Edgestop Ltd* [1994] 2 All ER 38, *Corporacion Nacionale del Cobre de Chile* v *Sogemin Metals Ltd* [1997] 1 WLR 1396). If the statement maker has been fraudulent, he or she should not be protected against the consequences of his or her statements by claiming that the misrepresentee was negligent.

Older authorities suggest that contributory negligence has no effect in the case of misrepresentation (*Redgrave* v *Hurd* (1881) 20 ChD 1; 10.2.2.4). These cases, however, predate the establishment of a separate category of negligent misrepresentation and the Law Reform (Contributory Negligence) Act 1945. In the general tort of negligence, s. 1(1) of the 1945 Act provides for apportionment of damages to take account of the claimant's contributory negligence. Common law liability for negligent misstatement is clearly tortious (10.5.3.3), so that the 1945 Act will apply to claims based on *Hedley Byrne* v *Heller*. Since negligent misstatement at common law and the statutory claim for damages under s. 2(1) of the Misrepresentation Act 1967 are alternatives, and the basic aim of damages in both cases is tortious, it might be thought that in the case of a claim for damages under s. 2(1), the misrepresentee's damages ought also to be reduced to take account of his or her contributory negligence. However, the *Royscot Trust* 'fiction of fraud' would suggest that damages under s. 2(1) should be assessed as if the misrepresentation were fraudulent. On this basis, there should be no apportionment for contributory negligence if the claim is brought solely under s. 2(1).

This latter interpretation would lead to all sorts of fine distinctions, especially since in *Gran Gelato Ltd* v *Richcliff (Group) Ltd* [1992] Ch 560, Nicholls V-C stated that where there are concurrent claims under *Hedley Byrne* and s. 2(1), the claimant's damages could be reduced in respect of both claims where there was contributory negligence by the claimant. Sir Donald Nicholls V-C said (at 573):

> It would be very odd if contributory negligence were available as a defence to a claim for damages based on a breach of a duty to take care in and about the making of a particular representation, but not available to a claim for damages under the 1967 Act in respect of the same representation.

It should therefore make no difference to the position if the claim is framed only under s. 2(1). A different interpretation would allow the 1945 Act to be avoided by claiming damages under s. 2(1) only, even though the facts might also justify a claim based on *Hedley Byrne*.

Interestingly, in *Gran Gelato*, Nicholls V-C decided not to make any reduction in the damages awarded, on the ground that the defendants intended that the plaintiffs should act in reliance on the misrepresentation, so that they could not complain when liability was imposed precisely because the plaintiffs did act in the way the defendants intended. The judge suggests that his approach is supported by the decision in *Redgrave v Hurd*, but we have already seen that the relevance of that decision to the issue of damages for negligent misrepresentation is questionable. In fact, it has already been suggested (see 10.2.2.3) that a misrepresentation will not be taken to have induced the contract unless it was intended to be acted upon. Accordingly, this limitation on the application of contributory negligence appears inevitably to apply whenever liability can be established!

What is the position, however, if the misrepresentation was fraudulent and the allegation is that the misrepresentee was not negligent but deceitful? In *Standard Chartered Bank v Pakistan National Shipping Corporation (Reduction of Damages)* [2001] QB 167 (note: reported as *(No. 4)* [2000] 3 WLR 1692, *(No. 2)* [2000] CLC 1575 and as *(No. 3)* [2000] 2 All ER (Comm) 929; decision of 27 July 2000), the defendant ship owners had issued a bill of lading, which they knew bore a false shipment date. The plaintiff bank made payment to the seller of the goods shipped under a letter of credit and claimed repayment from the issuing bank, concealing the fact that the documents (the bill of lading) had been presented late. The issuing bank refused payment because of unrelated discrepancies in the documents. The plaintiff bank then sought damages for deceit from the ship owners. (Findings had already been made by Cresswell J ([1998] 1 Lloyd's Rep 684, confirmed by the Court of Appeal (judgment of 3 December 1999, [2000] CLC 133) that the bank had a good cause of action in deceit and that the bank had also committed a deceit because it had been intended that the issuing bank should act on the false statement. The Court of Appeal had left open the question of contributory deceit for further argument and it was this question that was being considered here.) The question was: could the fact that the plaintiff bank had itself tried to deceive the issuing bank be taken into account as reducing the damages which the plaintiff was entitled to recover against the ship owners? The majority of the Court of Appeal (Evans LJ dissenting) held that the plaintiff's damages could not be apportioned under the Law Reform (Contributory Negligence) Act 1945, because the bank's conduct did not fall within the definition of 'fault' in the Act.

10.6 EXCLUDING OR LIMITING LIABILITY FOR MISREPRESENTATION

It is possible, in some circumstances, to exclude liability for pre-contractual misrepresentations, by means of an express term in the contract which was allegedly induced by the misrepresentation. In many respects such exclusions are subject to the same constraints as exclusions of contractual liability (see Chapter 6). For example, the clause will be interpreted restrictively, and will apply only if it covers the representation in question. So, in *Toomey v Eagle*

Star Insurance Co. Ltd (No. 2) [1995] 2 Lloyd's Rep 88, Colman J found that a clause which purported to exclude the remedy of rescission, but which did not expressly refer to rescission on the basis of negligent misrepresentation, applied only to wholly innocent misrepresentation, and did not apply to negligent misrepresentation in the sense of the 1967 Act. Similarly, a clause which excludes or limits liability for misrepresentation will have no operation to a misrepresentation which has become a term (Jacob J in *Thomas Witter* v *TBP Industries Ltd* [1996] 2 All ER 573). However, there are also statutory controls of the use of such clauses, namely the UCTA 1977 and the Unfair Terms in Consumer Contracts Regulations 1999 (see 6.6).

Some particular rules apply in the case of misrepresentation. In the first place, the law will not accept the exclusion of liability for a person's own fraud (*S. Pearson & Son Ltd* v *Dublin Corporation* [1907] AC 351), although it is possible to exclude liability for the fraud of employees and others. Secondly, s. 3 of the Misrepresentation Act 1967 (as amended by s. 8, UCTA 1977) provides as follows:

> 3. If a contract contains a term which would exclude or restrict—
>   (a) any liability to which a party to a contract may be subject by reason of any misrepresentation made by him before the contract was made; or
>   (b) any remedy available to another party to the contract by reason of such a misrepresentation,
>   that term shall be of no effect except in so far as it satisfies the requirement of reasonableness as stated in section 11(1) of the Unfair Contract Terms Act 1977; and it is for those claiming that the term satisfies that requirement to show that it does.

It should be noted that this section applies to both negligent and innocent misrepresentations, and will apply to clauses which purport to deny that there is any actionable misrepresentation at all (*Cremdean Properties Ltd* v *Nash* (1977) 244 EG 547 — no statement of truth being made). The exclusion clause will be effective only if the party seeking to rely on it to avoid liability can satisfy the burden of proving that, at the time of contracting, it was reasonable, having regard to the circumstances within the contemplation of the parties (s. 11(1), UCTA 1977). The operation of the reasonableness test is considered in more detail in relation to clauses excluding contractual liability (6.6.2.7). However, as two general points, it appears in the first place that a clause is more likely to be unreasonable where the statement maker is seeking to exclude liability for representations based on facts which are only within his or her knowledge and not that of the other party, e.g., *Howard Marine & Dredging Co. Ltd* v *A. Ogden & Sons (Excavations) Ltd* [1978] QB 574. Secondly, it may be the case that where the clause purports to exclude liability in respect of all types of misrepresentations (fraudulent, negligent and innocent), it may be held to be unreasonable because it *could* apply to exclude liability for fraud (*Thomas Witter* v *TBP Industries Ltd* [1996] 2 All ER 573; but a different conclusion was reached on this point by Judge Raymond Jack

QC in *Government of Zanzibar* v *British Aerospace Ltd* [2000] 1 WLR 2333 at 2346–7). This is yet a further point which would benefit from consideration by a higher court.

A clause which excludes or limits liability for misrepresentation in a consumer contract (6.6.3.1) may be voidable as an unfair term under the Unfair Terms in Consumer Contracts Regulations 1999 (see 6.6.3).

It may be possible to avoid the impact of UCTA 1977 on clauses excluding liability for misrepresentation by careful drafting. For example, if the term in question limits or excludes the authority of an agent to make representations which will bind the principal, that amounts to a clause restricting the authority of agents and does not therefore come within the definition of an exclusion or limitation clause under UCTA 1977 (*Overbrooke Estates Ltd* v *Glencombe Properties Ltd* [1974] 1 WLR 1353). Such clauses are, for example, fairly common in contracts for the sale of new homes, in an effort to exclude liability for any statements made by site agents. In the context of consumer contracts to which the Unfair Terms in Consumer Contracts Regulations 1999 apply, it may be that a clause 'limiting the seller's or supplier's obligation to respect commitments undertaken by his agents or making his commitments subject to compliance with a particular formality', such as approval of the principal, may be an unfair term and voidable under the Regulations (sch. 2(1)(n)). This may depend on whether the word 'commitment' is interpreted narrowly, so as to be limited to a contractual undertaking, or whether it covers a representation by such an agent which induces the making of the contract but which does not become incorporated as a term.

Contracts also frequently contain a statement that the written document comprises all the terms of the contract between the parties and that no representations have been made which are not represented by the written terms. These clauses are often referred to as 'entire agreement' clauses. The effect of such clauses has recently been the subject of judicial explanation by Lightman J in *Inntrepreneur Pub Co.* v *East Crown Ltd* [2000] 2 Lloyd's Rep 611. In particular, Lightman J made an important distinction between the two elements of such a clause by clearly separating the effect of an 'entire agreement' clause which defined where the terms of the contract could be found (in the written document only) from the second part of the clause which purported to exclude there being any liability for actionable misrepresentation. The first part of the clause stated that the agreement represented the 'entire agreement between the parties', and the second part amounted to an agreement that the party had 'not relied upon any advice or statement of the Company or its solicitors' before executing the agreement. *Inntrepreneur Pub Co. Ltd* v *East Crown Ltd* was discussed in more detail at 5.2.4 in respect of the decision that the entire agreement clause prevented the other party from alleging that there was a collateral warranty based on a pre-contractual statement. The entire agreement clause had the effect of ensuring that the full contractual terms between the parties were to be found in the contractual document containing that entire agreement clause. Any other pre-contractual promises would therefore not have any contractual effect.

However, in the context of a clause which does not simply seek to state where the contractual terms are to be found but also seeks to exclude or limit liability for misrepresentation, Lightman J considered that the clause was not a true entire agreement clause and could not operate to exclude such liability. He said (at 614): '. . . an entire agreement provision does not preclude a claim in misrepresentation, for the denial of contractual force cannot affect the status of a statement as a misrepresentation.'

The same approach has also been adopted by Judge Raymond Jack QC in *Government of Zanzibar* v *British Aerospace (Lancaster House) Ltd* [2000] 1 WLR 2333. He distinguished the entire agreement clause [A] from clause [B] which excluded liability for misrepresentation.

On the facts in *Inntrepreneur* (see 5.2.4), it was held that the clause did seek to exclude liability in misrepresentation and was therefore an exclusion clause. If there were to be an actionable misrepresentation, s. 3 of the Misrepresentation Act 1967 would apply to such a clause seeking to exclude liability for misrepresentation (but not to the entire agreement clause which defined the terms of the contract) and the clause would have be shown to be reasonable in order to be relied upon. Ironically, there may therefore be some point in 'threshing through the undergrowth' (p. 614) in search of a misrepresentation in preference to a pre-contractual promise.

ELEVEN

Duress, undue influence and unconscionable bargains

This chapter examines doctrines relating to circumstances surrounding the making of the contract. In the context of commercial contracts, Parliament has stepped in to protect consumers against various high-pressure sales techniques, in particular, by allowing consumers a 'cooling off' period during which time the agreement can be cancelled (see, for example, Consumer Credit Act 1974, Consumer Protection (Cancellation of Contracts Concluded away from Business Premises) Regulations 1987 (SI 1987 No. 2117)) and other cancellation rights (e.g., Consumer Protection (Distance Selling) Regulations 2000 (SI 2000 No. 2334)).

There are also recognised general doctrines applying to instances where unfair and illegitimate pressure or threats have been applied, or unfair advantage has been taken by one party over the other in order to persuade a party to contract or to agree a variation of the contract on these specific terms. Where this is the case and either the doctrine of duress or undue influence applies, the contract is voidable (i.e., it can be set aside by the victim or complainant). The doctrine of duress, in particular, is likely to be highly relevant in the context of commercial contracts. However, there is fine line to be drawn here, because some commercial pressure in negotiating is both normal and acceptable.

11.1 DURESS

11.1.1 The limited early doctrine

The common law always accepted that some forms of coercion in the making of contracts resulted in the victim of the coercion being afforded a remedy, in that the contract would be set aside and any money paid could be recovered. However, the forms of coercion recognised as having such an effect were very limited. There was no doubt that duress to the person had such an effect, whether it took the form of threatened or actual violence (*Barton* v *Armstrong* [1976] 1 AC 104), or a threat of imprisonment (*Williams* v *Bayley* (1886) LR 1 HL 200), although the latter rule arose only after the intervention of equity. As such, the doctrine was of little significance, since the number of cases of duress to the person has always been small.

It has now also been settled that a threat to seize another's property or to damage it (duress to property), will justify a claim of duress and result in the ensuing contract being set aside (see Lord Goff in *Dimskal Shipping Co. SA* v *International Transport Workers' Federation, The Evia Luck* [1991] 4 All ER 871, 878).

In addition, in the mid-1960s the courts, led by Lord Denning, started to pay far greater attention to the requirement of fairness in bargaining. Thus, in *D & C Builders* v *Rees* [1966] 2 QB 617 (see 4.4.4), Lord Denning MR refused to apply the promissory estoppel doctrine to enforce a promise to accept a payment in final settlement of a debt, on the express ground that the promise had been extracted by unfair pressure and the creditor had been 'held to ransom'. The result of these developments has been the emergence of a new and far more significant doctrine of economic duress.

11.1.2 Economic duress

The idea that mere economic duress (threats to a person's financial or business interests) might be a ground upon which a contract could be set aside was first canvassed by Kerr J in *Occidental Worldwide Investment Corporation* v *Skibs A/S Avanti, The Siboen and The Sibotre* [1976] 1 Lloyd's Rep 293. The typical situation raising the possibility of a claim of economic duress is where one party threatens breach of contract unless the contract is renegotiated, and the other agrees rather than face disastrous consequences as a result of breach. The area is fraught with difficulty, however, since companies who deal with each other on a regular basis will often agree quite voluntarily to renegotiate a contract, and such agreements are the essence of the level of cooperation necessary in the business world. It would be unfortunate if they were threatened by the economic duress doctrine. On the other hand, changes to the law relating to consideration, particularly in the area of variation of commercial contracts (see *Williams* v *Roffey Bros & Nicholls (Contractors) Ltd* [1991] 1 QB 1; 4.3.4.3 and 4.3.5.2), have increased the need for such a clear and recognised doctrine in English law.

In the past, contract changes achieved by means of unfair pressure or extortion could be resisted on the formal ground of absence of consideration (see *Stilk* v *Myrick* (1809) 2 Camp 317, 6 Esp 129 (4.3.4.3) and *Atlas Express Ltd* v *Kafco (Importers & Distributors) Ltd* [1989] 1 All ER 641, where absence of consideration was the alternative ground for the decision). A restrictive approach to the definition of consideration was required to achieve this (i.e., the performance of an existing duty could not be a good consideration because there was no additional legal benefit or detriment). However, in

Williams v *Roffey Bros* (4.3.5.2) the Court of Appeal cited the availability of the doctrine of economic duress as the mechanism for preventing the enforceability of promises obtained as a result of extortion in order to justify their more relaxed approach to finding consideration. The result of this development is that the emphasis has now shifted from the doctrine of consideration to the doctrine of economic duress in order to prevent promises obtained by extortion, or improper threats, from being enforceable. It is vital, therefore, that the doctrine be clearly defined. However, as we shall see, the doctrine is a comparatively recent development in English law and, as such, is still developing.

11.1.2.1 Establishing economic duress In *Pao On* v *Lau Yiu Long* [1980] AC 614 (see also 4.3.3.2), the Privy Council approved the doctrine of economic duress and attempted to identify its essential ingredients. Lord Scarman identified two essential conditions for the operation of the doctrine:

(a) 'coercion of the will that vitiates consent'; and
(b) the pressure or threat must be illegitimate.

In *DSND Subsea Ltd* v *Petroleum Geo Services ASA* [2000] BLR 530, Dyson J identified the ingredients of actionable duress, as they have subsequently developed:

> [T]here must be pressure, (a) whose practical effect is that there is compulsion on, or lack of practical choice for, the victim, (b) which is illegitimate, and (c) which is a significant cause inducing the claimant to enter into the contract.

11.1.2.2 Coercion of the will that vitiates consent The question in *Pao On* v *Lau Yiu Long* was whether there had been the necessary coercion of the will vitiating consent. Under the terms of a contract, the plaintiffs were to sell their shares in a company which owned a building under construction to the Fu Chip Company and were to receive shares in the Fu Chip Company in return. The defendants, the majority shareholders in the Fu Chip Company, had been concerned that if the plaintiffs chose to sell all these shares at one time, there would be a fall in the value of their shareholdings. The plaintiffs therefore agreed with the company that they would not sell 60 per cent of their shares for one year. The plaintiffs then threatened not to perform this promise unless the defendants agreed to indemnify them against any loss in the value of their shares in this one-year period. Fearing delays, and a loss of confidence in their company if the deal were not completed, the defendants signed an indemnity agreeing to compensate the plaintiffs if the value of these shares fell below $2.50 a share. The share price fell and the plaintiffs sought to rely on the indemnity. However, the defendants claimed that the indemnity had been obtained as a result of duress.

Lord Scarman, giving the advice of the Privy Council, said that there was nothing wrong in principle in recognising economic duress as a factor making contracts voidable. The essence of the rule, he said, was that 'there must be a coercion of will such that there was no true consent . . . it must be shown that the contract entered into was not a voluntary act'. It was essential to distinguish between mere commercial pressure, which is an everyday incident of the hard-nosed bargaining which goes on in the business world, and duress. On the facts in *Pao On*, Lord Scarman emphasised the question of whether there was a realistic alternative open to the defendants. It was held that the defendants had coolly analysed the options and had taken a commercial decision that the risk to their company of non-performance was greater than the risk of the need to pay under the indemnity. Accordingly, there was no coercion of the will and no duress.

However, it would seem to be incorrect to argue that duress is based upon consent being vitiated so that the agreement is not voluntary. Atiyah ((1982) 98 LQR 197) strongly criticised this requirement. More recently, Lord Goff has stated in *The Evia Luck* [1991] 4 All ER 871 that he doubts whether it is helpful to speak of a person's will being coerced. The victim of duress knows exactly what he or she is doing and submits intentionally. In the criminal law, the House of Lords has been clear in saying that the defence of duress does not depend upon the absence of a voluntary act, but rather depends upon intentional submission in the face of no other practical alternative (*Lynch* v *DPP for Northern Ireland* [1975] AC 653). The same must be true of contract, so that duress does not negate the existence of consent but is based upon a finding that the victim had no other realistic option available to him or her other than to agree. This reasoning is borne out by the fact that duress renders a contract voidable, and not void. In *Universe Tankships Inc. of Monrovia* v *International Transport Workers' Federation, The Universe Sentinel* [1983] 1 AC 366, Lords Diplock and Scarman admitted that duress in contract law does not involve the destruction of will but intentional submission to the inevitable. It is a pity, therefore, that the first ingredient for duress in *Pao On* is not explicitly reformulated as 'no realistic choice', rather than in terms of 'coercion of the will vitiating consent'. However, the statement of the necessary ingredients cited in the judgment of Dyson J in *DSND Subsea Ltd* v *Petroleum Geo Services ASA* [2000] BLR 530, does refer instead to compulsion and lack of practical choice.

B & S Contracts & Design Ltd v *Victor Green Publications Ltd* [1984] ICR 419 provides a useful example of a situation where there was no practical choice other than to agree. The plaintiffs were to erect exhibition stands for the defendants who had let these stands to various exhibitors. However, a week before the date of the exhibition, the plaintiffs' workers refused to work unless a pay demand was met. The defendants therefore paid £4,500 in order to avoid serious losses, which would have resulted from the claims against them by disappointed exhibitors. However, the defendants then deducted this figure from the contract price paid to the plaintiffs. The plaintiffs claimed the balance. The Court of Appeal held that the defendants had been affected by duress because they had no realistic choice other than to pay. An action for breach of contract against the plaintiffs, although technically possible, was unrealistic because it would have been too damaging. (For a recent example, see *Carillion Construction Ltd* v *Felix (UK) Ltd* [2001] BLR 1 — threats to withhold deliveries when under a contractual obligation to use best endeavours to prevent delay amounted to illegitimate threats and it was held to be unrealistic to expect the other party to seek a mandatory injunction.)

Similarly, in *Atlas Express Ltd* v *Kafco (Importers & Distributors) Ltd* [1989] 1 All ER 641, the defendant had no realistic choice other than to sign a revised contract for carriage of its goods because it could not, at such short notice, have obtained alternative carriage for the goods; and without the ability to deliver, it would have lost the contract to supply its major customer (Woolworth).

11.1.2.3 Illegitimate pressure or threat In a claim for economic duress there must be pressure or a threat. This can lead to fine distinctions of fact. For example, in *Williams* v *Roffey Bros & Nicholls (Contractors) Ltd* [1991] 1 QB 1, it was vitally important that the impetus for the promise to pay more money came from the main contractor and so had not been obtained as a result of threats of non-performance from the subcontractor. It is less clear, however, what the position would be where one contracting party simply advises the other of the possibility of non-performance.

Any improper pressure must be 'decisive or clinching' (*per* Mance J (*obiter*) in *Huyton SA* v *Peter Cremer GmbH & Co.* [1999] 1 Lloyd's Rep 620). It must be established that the victim would not otherwise have made such a contract, or would not otherwise have contracted on those terms.

The pressure must also be illegitimate. It is far from clear where the line between legitimate and illegitimate pressure is to be drawn. In *DSND Subsea Ltd* v *Petroleum Geo Services AS* [2000] BLR 530, Dyson J stated that 'illegitimate pressure must be distinguished from the rough and tumble of the pressures of normal commercial bargaining'. Some pressure is clearly legitimate.

In *Universe Tankships Inc. of Monrovia* v *International Transport Workers' Federation, The Universe Sentinel* [1983] 1 AC 366, the issue of the legitimacy of the pressure exerted hinged upon the interpretation of the Trade Union and Labour Relations Act 1974. The case concerned threats by a trade union to 'black' vessels, in the sense that no tugs would be provided to assist the vessels to leave harbour unless the ship owners made a payment to the trade union. If the vessels were unable to leave the harbour, the losses would have been considerable, so the ship owner paid and then claimed the return of this money. The trade union argued that their actions were protected as actions 'in contemplation of a trade dispute' under the 1974 Act. The majority of the House of Lords considered that the threats were illegitimate because the trade union was not protected by this legislation. The minority (Lords Scarman and Brandon) thought that the trade union was protected by the legislation, so that the threat was *prima facie* lawful. However, a lawful threat would constitute duress if used, as here, to further an illegitimate purpose such as blackmail.

More recently, the Court of Appeal has had to address the question of whether there is a more general category of lawful act duress, i.e. whether lawful (if ultimately unreasonable) demands can amount to illegitimate pressure. In *CTN Cash and Carry Ltd* v *Gallagher Ltd* [1994] 4 All ER 714, the defendants had mistakenly sent a shipment of cigarettes to the wrong place of business for the plaintiffs. The plaintiffs undertook to remedy the situation, but before the cigarettes could be moved there was a burglary and they were stolen. The defendants genuinely but mistakenly believed that the cigarettes were at the plaintiffs' risk, and so invoiced them for the price, threatening to withdraw credit facilities if the price was not paid. Under the terms of their arrangement the credit facilities could lawfully be withdrawn at any time. Faced with a choice between two evils, the plaintiffs opted to pay the price, and subsequently reclaimed the money paid on the basis that the payment had been made under duress.

In finding for the defendants, Steyn LJ pointed to three key elements: the arm's length commercial dealings between two trading companies; the lawful nature of the threat; and the *bona fide* belief in their entitlement on the part of the defendants. To allow a claim based on lawful act duress in such circumstances would inevitably cause uncertainty in commercial dealings. Steyn LJ was reluctant to say that 'lawful act duress' could never be established, but it seems that a commercial concern engaged in apparently arm's length bargaining will find it very difficult to base a claim on lawful act duress. It is arguable that the same might not be true in the context of a consumer contract.

Inevitably, the good or bad faith of the person making the threat will be a relevant factor even in cases where the pressure is regarded as illegitimate. However, Mance J, in *Huyton SA* v *Peter Cremer GmbH & Co.* [1999] 1 Lloyd's Rep 620, stated that he did not consider that good faith on the part of a party making an illegitimate threat would always give protection against a claim based on duress. Thus good faith alone will not suffice.

11.1.2.4 The need to protest at the time or shortly thereafter The remedy for duress will be lost unless the victim of duress ensures that it takes action to 'protest at the time, or shortly thereafter' and seek to reopen the issue (Kerr J in *Occidental Worldwide Investment Corporation* v *Skibs A/S Avanti, The Siboen and the Sibotre* [1976] 1 Lloyd's Rep 293). The application of this requirement is well demonstrated by the decision in *North Ocean Shipping Co. Ltd* v *Hyundai Construction Co. Ltd, The Atlantic Baron* [1979] QB 705.

In *The Atlantic Baron*, the defendants threatened to breach a contract for the construction of a tanker unless the plaintiffs agreed to pay 10 per cent on top of the contract price. Consideration for this agreement was furnished by the defendants agreeing to provide an additional letter of credit as security of performance. The plaintiffs agreed to make the extra payment because if the tanker had not been available they would have lost a very valuable charter. Eight months after delivery of the tanker the plaintiffs attempted to recover the extra payment. Mocatta J held that the defendants' demand would have amounted to economic duress making the contract voidable. However, the failure to protest or reopen the issue for such a long time amounted to constructive affirmation of the contract. Therefore, the plaintiffs were no longer entitled to a remedy based on duress.

However, the difficulty with this requirement is that it leaves the victim of alleged duress with a difficult choice when deciding what course of action to take. To sit back and fail to perform, relying on the duress as a defence to any claim by the other party, runs the risk of being interpreted as affirmation of the contract. On the other hand, if the danger perceived by the victim is sufficient to persuade him or her to enter the contract despite its disadvantageous terms, it will also very likely be the case that the victim will not want to risk causing the other party to abandon performance by making an ill-timed protest. It seems that the courts will have to accept that the economic duress itself will prevent anything but mild protest until performance is complete. At that time the victim will have to take almost immediate action to avoid constructive affirmation of the contract. (In *The Atlantic Baron*, of course, it was considered that once the plaintiffs had taken possession of the tanker there was no further danger in registering a protest, and therefore waiting for eight months before doing so amounted to the affirmation.)

11.1.2.5 Conclusion   Although the number of judicial decisions examining economic duress has grown over recent years, key elements of the doctrine clearly require further elaboration. In *Huyton SA* v *Peter Cremer GmbH & Co.* [1999] 1 Lloyd's Rep 620 at 637, Mance J noted that the ingredients for establishing a claim in economic duress were 'minimum ingredients, not ingredients which, if present, would inevitably lead to liability'. He continued by stating that: 'The recognition of some degree of flexibility is not . . . fairly open to the reproach that it introduces a judicial "discretion". The law frequently has to form judgments regarding inequitability or unconscionability, giving effect in doing so to the reasonable expectations of honest persons.'

It is nevertheless helpful to have some recognised and clearly defined ingredients for the operation of the doctrine of duress, especially as in future it will operate as the primary mechanism in English law preventing the enforceability of alteration promises obtained by extortion.

11.2 UNDUE INFLUENCE

Undue influence is an equitable doctrine which provides relief from contracts entered into under improper pressure not amounting to duress. The courts will intervene where there is some relationship between the parties which has been exploited and abused to gain an unfair advantage. The precise basis of the court's intervention is a matter of debate. It might be thought to be clearly within the scope of the public policy concern for fairness in contract bargaining, and that rationale was put forward by Nourse LJ in *Goldsworthy* v *Brickell* [1987] 1 All ER 853 at 856. Lord Browne-Wilkinson appeared to have some sympathy for this view in *CIBC Mortgages plc* v *Pitt* [1994] 1 AC 200 at 209. He saw an obvious parallel between the undue influence cases and cases on abuse of confidence. The latter are based on public policy, and his Lordship expressed some doubt whether the two lines of cases were founded on distinct principles. However, as his Lordship recognised, in *National Westminster Bank plc* v *Morgan* [1985] AC 686, the House of Lords had expressed the view that undue influence was not based on considerations of public policy.

The courts have further clarified the nature of the requisite exploitation of a relationship. In *Barclays Bank plc* v *O'Brien* [1994] 1 AC 180, Lord Browne-Wilkinson approved a classification of types of undue influence put forward by the Court of Appeal in *Bank of Credit and Commerce International SA* v *Aboody* [1990] 1 QB 923:

- *Class 1* undue influence refers to actual influence exerted by one party over the other.
- *Class 2* undue influence refers to undue influence which is presumed to have been exerted because of a relationship of trust and confidence between the parties; it is then for the party alleged to have exercised undue influence to rebut this presumption.
  Class 2 undue influence may be further subdivided between those cases where a relationship of trust and confidence will be held always to exist (*Class 2A*), so that the presumption of undue influence arises automatically, and, on the other hand, those where its existence is not inevitable but is possible (*Class 2B*). Class 2B undue influence requires evidence that, on the facts, there was a special relationship of confidence between the parties so that the presumption of undue influence will apply.

Although in theory the distinction between Class 1 and Class 2B is clear enough, in practice it may not be easy to draw the line. So, as we shall see below, while husband and wife cases can never fall within Class 2A, they have been treated both as Class 1 cases and as Class 2B cases, depending on the particular facts.

11.2.1   Class 1: actual undue influence

In these cases the allegation is that actual influence was in fact exercised and induced the complainant to enter into the transaction. *CIBC Mortgages plc* v *Pitt* [1994] 1 AC 200 was treated by the House of Lords as a case of this kind. The defendant had been induced to agree to a second mortgage on the family home as security for a loan to finance share purchases. She had not wanted to go ahead with the scheme, but had given in to a campaign of sustained pressure. The principal issue for decision in that case was whether her claim of undue influence could succeed without her being able to prove that the transaction was to her manifest disadvantage. The House of Lords held that in a Class 1 case of actual undue influence, the transaction need not be one that is disadvantageous to the party affected (overruling *Bank of Credit and Commerce International SA* v *Aboody* [1990] 1 QB 923 on this point). Manifest disadvantage had been held to be a necessary ingredient of *presumed* undue influence (Class 2) by the House of Lords in *National Westminster*

Bank Plc v *Morgan* [1985] AC 686. In such cases it would be good circumstantial evidence to support the inference of undue influence. But in the case of actual undue influence it has no necessary role. According to Lord Browne-Wilkinson, actual undue influence is a 'species of fraud', and 'like any other victim of fraud, a person who has been induced by undue influence to carry out a transaction which he did not freely and knowingly enter into is entitled to have that transaction set aside as of right'.

Thus, these Class 1 undue influence cases, which are sometimes referred to as the 'domination' cases, do not require the complainant to show that there was any kind of special relationship or that there was a manifest disadvantage resulting from the transaction. On the other hand, complainants have the difficult task of proving that their free will to enter or to decline a particular contract was in some way overcome by the influence of another. There are unlikely to be many such cases in the modern era. In the past, cases of domination frequently involved dubious spiritual advisers. In *Morley* v *Loughnan* [1893] 1 Ch 736, action was brought by executors to recover £140,000 paid by the deceased to a member of a religious sect. Wright J, in finding for the plaintiffs, said that there was no need to show a special relationship between deceased and defendant, because 'the defendant took possession, so to speak, of the whole life of the deceased, and the gifts were . . . the effect of that influence and domination'.

11.2.2   Class 2: presumed undue influence

In these cases the allegation is simply that there was 'a relationship of trust and confidence between the complainant and the wrongdoer of such a nature that it is fair to presume that the wrongdoer abused the relationship in procuring the complainant to enter into the impugned transaction' (*Barclays Bank plc* v *O'Brien* [1994] 1 AC 180 at 189, per Lord Browne-Wilkinson).

In *National Westminster Bank plc* v *Morgan* [1985] AC 686, it was suggested that in these cases it is necessary to show that there was a manifest disadvantage to the complainant on the basis that the presumption of undue influence is derived from the reasoning that a party making an unfettered decision would not freely choose to enter into a manifestly disadvantageous contract. In *CIBC Mortgages plc* v *Pitt* [1994] 1 AC 200, Lord Browne-Wilkinson appeared to be less than certain that even in Class 2 cases there was an absolute requirement to establish manifest disadvantage, but he was not required to rule upon the matter in that case. In *Royal Bank of Scotland* v *Etridge (No. 2)* [1998] 4 All ER 705, Stuart-Smith LJ made the point that evidence of manifest disadvantage is 'a powerful evidential factor'. In other words, if the transaction is clearly disadvantageous to the complainant, it will be easier to establish that the contract was improperly obtained.

The requirement of 'manifest disadvantage' in cases of presumed undue influence was reconsidered by the Court of Appeal in *Barclays Bank plc* v *Coleman* [2000] 3 WLR 405 but it was bound to apply it. Nourse LJ (delivering the leading judgment) commented that 'a serious question mark' has been put 'over the future of the requirement of manifest disadvantage in cases of presumed undue influence'. It was important, pending reconsideration by the House of Lords, to consider what is really meant by 'manifest disadvantage' and not to enlarge its significance. Nourse LJ stated that the disadvantage must be 'clear and obvious'. However, he added, 'that does not mean that it must be large or even medium-sized. Provided it is clear and obvious and more than *de minimis*, the disadvantage may be small'. In addition, it was made clear that the question of whether a transaction was manifestly disadvantageous was to be determined by taking an objective view at the date the transaction was entered into.

On the facts, the charge in question covered not only money borrowed under the existing transaction, but also any future ventures which the husband might have embarked upon. The wife might therefore have been exposed to a much greater financial risk than she thought, and for this reason the transaction was to her manifest disadvantage.

The unusual feature in this case was that the security related to a new business venture rather than to secure existing and future debts of the husband's business. On the facts of this case it is possible to argue that there would be some potential advantage to the wife if the investment succeeded. However, in the usual scenario of security for the husband's business debts, the fact that the wife might benefit indirectly, in the sense that the household finances would be stronger if further funds were released on the company's overdraft, has not been considered as a sufficient 'advantage' in itself. This must be the correct position, since adopting a wider approach and accepting such indirect benefits as 'advantage' would seriously limit the possibility of establishing presumed undue influence. In turn it would also fit uneasily with the comments of the Court of Appeal seeking to avoid enlargement of the importance of the 'manifest disadvantage' requirement in this context.

11.2.2.1 Class 2A: relationships automatically giving rise to the presumption There are certain relationships which the law regards as special, and as always incorporating elements of trust and confidence, so that the presumption of undue influence would always be in issue. Typical of such relationships are solicitor and client, doctor and patient, parent and child. Relations between husband and wife are said not to give rise to a special relationship, and so do not automatically raise the presumption of undue influence (*Midland Bank plc* v *Shephard* [1988] 3 All ER 17). The relationship of banker and customer is also outside Class 2A (*National Westminster Bank plc* v *Morgan* [1985] AC 686).

11.2.2.2 Class 2B: *de facto* relationships of trust and confidence Where the relationship does not fall into any of the recognised special categories automatically giving rise to the presumption of undue influence, it is still possible for a complainant to show that the particular relationship in fact was one based on trust and confidence.

This analysis has been applied to the relationship between bank and customer. In *National Westminster Bank plc* v *Morgan* [1985] AC 686, Lord Scarman accepted that the relationship between bank and customer may be one of confidence, but that in the particular situation the bank 'had not crossed the line' into the realm of confidence.

However, in *Lloyds Bank Ltd* v *Bundy* [1975] QB 326, the Court of Appeal held that the facts did justify the presumption of undue influence between banker and customer. There was a special relationship of confidence because of the fact that old Mr Bundy had banked at this branch for many years and relied on the bank manager for all his financial advice. The manager was aware of this confidence placed in him. In addition, whereas the transaction in *Lloyds Bank Ltd* v *Bundy* was very evidently not in the interests of old Mr Bundy, the transaction in *National Westminster Bank Ltd* v *Morgan* was beneficial to Mrs Morgan because it allowed her to stay in her home, which would otherwise have been repossessed by the then mortgagee.

Of course, where the relationship between bank and customer is the ordinary commercial one, and not a special relationship of confidence, it must be remembered that the bank may still owe an ordinary duty of care to give accurate advice which may be the basis of liability towards a customer (see *Cornish* v *Midland Bank Ltd* [1985] 3 All ER 513, and see 10.4.3.1).

It has also been accepted that *de facto* relationships of trust and confidence (Class 2B) may exist between husbands and wives, and indeed between other cohabitees or persons between whom there is an emotional involvement. In particular it was recognised by Lord Browne-Wilkinson in *Barclays Bank plc* v *O'Brien* [1994] 1 AC 180 at 190–91:

> In those cases which still occur where the wife relies in all financial matters on her husband and simply does what he suggests, a presumption of undue influence within class 2B can be established solely from proof of such trust and confidence without proof of actual undue influence. . . . [T]he sexual and emotional ties between the parties provide a ready weapon for undue influence: a wife's true wishes can easily be overborne because of her fear of destroying or damaging the wider relationship between her and her husband if she opposes his wishes.

He also accepted (at 198) that similar considerations apply whenever there is an emotional relationship between cohabitees, whether married or unmarried, heterosexual or homosexual. In *Massey* v *Midland Bank plc* [1995] 1 All ER 929, Steyn LJ extended the category further by including a couple enjoying a long-term emotional and sexual relationship, who had children but who did not in fact cohabit. The presumption of influence has also been held to apply between a son and his elderly parents (*Avon Finance Co. Ltd* v *Bridger* [1985] 2 All ER 281).

Thus, although there is no automatic presumption of undue influence in such cases, it is tempting to conclude that the modern approach has been to be very ready to find *de facto* relationships of confidence between husband and wife and other cohabitees.

11.2.2.3 Rebutting the presumption The most straightforward defence in Class 2 cases, at least until Lord Browne-Wilkinson's doubts expressed in

CIBC Mortgages plc v *Pitt* (11.2.2, above) have been resolved, will be to show that there was no manifest disadvantage to the complainant (see discussion of the scope of 'manifest disadvantage' in *Barclays Bank plc* v *Coleman* [2000] 3 WLR 405 and discussion at 11.2.2 above).

Where there is manifest disadvantage, the presumption of undue influence arises but in principle may be rebutted. Rebuttal will require the defendant to show that that complainant was not in fact induced to enter the contract through the defendant's improper influence, but rather entered into it fully aware of what he or she was doing. In many cases this may be achieved by showing that the complainant chose to go ahead even after receiving independent advice about the true nature of the transaction, including the potential for disadvantage.

11.2.3 Effect of undue influence

Contracts affected by undue influence are voidable, not void. As with duress, this consequence seems to support the view that the doctrine is not concerned with the reality of consent, but with the protection of victims of improper behaviour. Since a tainted contract is only voidable, the victim must bring a claim for rescission to avoid it, and property passes under it. The effect of undue influence must be considered in more detail according to whether only the original parties to the contract are involved, or whether third party rights have intervened.

11.2.3.1 Effect between the original parties The right to rescission may be lost if the complainant has affirmed the contract in some way after the undue influence has ceased. In particular, failure to act within a fairly short time of it ceasing may be interpreted as constructive affirmation. In *Allcard* v *Skinner* (1887) 36 ChD 145, the plaintiff, under the influence of her spiritual adviser, joined an order called the 'Sisters of the Poor', to which her spiritual adviser was confessor. During the eight years she was a member the plaintiff gave some £7,000 to the defendant, who was head of the order. Six years after leaving the order she sought to recover the balance of that sum remaining unspent (about £1,700). The gift to the defendant was held to have been made under undue influence, because the plaintiff had not been independently advised. The plaintiff was, nevertheless, unable to recover the balance of her money because she had allowed such a long time to elapse before claiming, during which time she had been unaffected by the undue influence and when independent advice was presumably available to her.

An interesting question is whether partial rescission is possible, i.e. can we separate parts of the contract affected by either misrepresentation or undue influence and enforce the remainder, or will the entire contract have to be rescinded? In *TSB Bank plc* v *Camfield* [1995] 1 WLR 430, it had been argued that the charge in question should be set aside only to the extent that it provided security for a debt in excess of £15,000, the amount that the wife considered was her maximum liability. However, the Court of Appeal held that it had no power to impose terms and, insisting that rescission had to be total, set aside the charge in its entirety.

In *Vadasz* v *Pioneer Concrete (SA) Pty Ltd* (1995) 130 ALR 570, the High Court of Australia was prepared to enforce the part of a guarantee covering future debt, but not that part covering the existing debt, on the basis that it had been represented that the guarantee would cover only future debt. The High Court regarded this as no more than holding the party in question to what he was prepared to agree to independently of any misrepresentation. Although this authority may be limited to rescission of guarantees, it is submitted that this approach would be generally preferable since it allows the court to do justice and recognise the realities of the parties' positions. This issue was discussed by the Privy Council in *Far Eastern Shipping Co. Public Ltd* v *Scales Trading Ltd* [2001] 1 All ER (Comm) 319, but determination of this question was not necessary for the Privy Council's decision on the facts before it.

In any event, it appears that it may exceptionally be possible to sever objectionable parts of an instrument and enforce the remainder. However, it is clear from *Barclays Bank plc* v *Caplan* [1998] FLR 532, that this will be possible only where the parts can be separated cleanly without affecting the substance of the part enforced, i.e. first guarantee separated from later guarantees.

It is very likely that some form of restitutionary relief will be required in association with rescission of the contract (*Dunbar Bank plc* v *Nadeem* [1998] 3 All ER 876). Where complete restitution is not possible because, for example, property values have gone down, the net balance is to be divided *pro rata* between the parties according to their original contributions to the transaction (*Cheese* v *Thomas* [1994] 1 WLR 129). Where the normal remedy of restoring the parties to their original positions, with an account of profits, is impossible, for example because property has passed into the hands of a third party, the court has jurisdiction to impose a 'common-sense and . . . fair remedy' in order 'to achieve practical justice between the parties', at least where the undue influence involves a breach of fiduciary duty (*per* May J in *Mahoney* v *Purnell* [1996] 3 All ER 61 at 88, relying on *O'Sullivan* v *Management Agency and Music Ltd* [1985] QB 428). In the particular case, practical justice was achieved by 'an award . . . akin to damages' giving to the plaintiff as compensation a sum equal in value to what had been given up under the tainted transaction, but making an allowance for sums received thereunder.

11.2.3.2 Effect where third party rights intervene

Where third party rights intervene the right to rescission may be lost. If, however, the third party has knowledge of the undue influence it will take subject to the right of the victim of the undue influence. These principles have become of considerable importance in relation to the modern doctrine of undue influence, which has been invoked many times in recent years in an attempt to avoid an interest acquired by a bank (the third party) as an indirect result of a transaction between husband and wife (or other cohabitees) which was affected by undue influence (normally Class 2B).

Where one cohabiting partner has misled or influenced the other into granting rights over the 'matrimonial' home to a bank by way of surety in respect of the first party's business liabilities, the victim will understandably be reluctant to give up the home if the business fails. The courts have had to try to find a balance between the rights of parties who risk being dispossessed and the rights of banks who have legitimately sought to protect their investments in business ventures and who might be forced to rethink their lending policies in relation to couples if they were always liable to lose their security at a later date.

After a number of false starts, in *Barclays Bank plc* v *O'Brien* [1994] 1 AC 180, Lord Browne-Wilkinson held that the key to such questions lay in the doctrine of notice, and the significance of the decision of the House of Lords is that it provides guidance for lenders as to how they might avoid being fixed with notice of a contracting party's undue influence. Of course, one would be surprised to find that a bank had actual notice of undue influence; the critical issue therefore is whether the bank has constructive notice (i.e., in the circumstances the bank ought to have known of the undue influence and so is fixed with notice).

A bank will be put on inquiry if it knew of the relationship and the transaction was not obviously of any financial advantage or benefit to the wife (or other cohabitee). Once put on inquiry, the bank will be fixed with constructive notice of the undue influence exercised by the contracting party, unless the bank had taken reasonable steps to satisfy itself that the wife had entered into the transaction freely and with knowledge of the true facts. The bank could satisfy this requirement by warning the wife (at a meeting not attended by the husband) of the amount of her potential liability and the risks involved and by advising the wife to obtain independent legal advice. It is important to note that the wife (or other surety) will have the burden of proving that the bank or lender had the necessary constructive notice, and the formulation of the claim will need to make clear the facts upon which the notice argument is based (*Barclays Bank plc* v *Boulter* [1999] 4 All ER 513).

Interpretation of O'Brien Although the decision in *O'Brien* was clearly intended to clarify the law, it has given rise to a growing catalogue of decisions which in some way interpret its findings.

In *CIBC Mortgages plc* v *Pitt* [1994] 1 AC 200, the question was whether the circumstances of the particular case were such as to put the bank on inquiry so that the necessary steps needed to be taken in order for the bank to avoid being fixed with constructive notice of the husband's undue influence. The House of Lords decided that the bank was not put on inquiry because the form applying for the loan indicated that it was a joint loan for the purpose of paying off the outstanding joint mortgage and to purchase a holiday home. In fact, the loan was to enable the husband to speculate on the stock market and he had pressurised his wife into declaring that it was for these other purposes. However, on the face of the application form there was some apparent financial benefit to the wife. Accordingly, the bank could not be fixed with constructive notice of the husband's actual undue influence. There was nothing particularly suspicious about the transaction in this case; indeed; if the bank had been on notice in this case then arguably banks would be on notice in every case involving husband and wife clients.

Although the decision may be justifiable on its facts, it is perhaps regrettable that the law seems now to turn upon the form of the transaction and does not invite the court to look behind the form at the substance of the transaction.

What is the position if the loan is used partly for joint purposes and partly to guarantee the husband's business debts? *Dunbar Bank plc* v *Nadeem* [1998] 3 All ER 876 differs from *CIBC* v *Pitt* because the allegation of actual undue influence failed. It was therefore necessary to rely on presumed undue influence by the husband, which requires that the transaction be shown to be manifestly disadvantageous to the wife. The problem, therefore, in most instances of declared joint purpose (i.e., where there is no actual undue influence established on the facts) will be that the transaction will be of *some* obvious benefit to the wife which may prevent undue influence being established. Much will depend on whether the courts will be prepared to assess the level of disadvantage on the individual facts.

It is important to distinguish the requirement of 'manifest disadvantage', which is required to establish the existence of the presumed undue influence, from the requirement that the transaction on its face is not to the advantage of the complainant (thereby putting the bank on inquiry and in danger of losing its security). In *Bank of Cyprus (London) Ltd* v *Markou* [1999] 2 All ER 707, the judge made this distinction clear when he said (at 717):

> The question of manifest disadvantage is to be approached from the position of the two parties who are involved in the initial transaction. It is not to be approached from the position of the creditor, and therefore the knowledge of each of the husband and the wife is relevant in deciding whether there is manifest disadvantage. Wider factors are going to be brought into play and will necessarily be brought into play where the question is whether the bank is put on inquiry. At the same time the matter will be more circumscribed because it will depend upon the facts as presented to the bank.

On the facts, the judge found that although the wife had one share in the husband's company, he controlled the company and she took no active role in it. Accordingly, the transaction, whereby she gave an unlimited guarantee for the company's debts secured on the matrimonial home, was to her manifest disadvantage. (Compare this with the apparent approach to indirect benefit in *Barclays Bank plc* v *Coleman* [2000] 3 WLR 405, at 11.2.2.) However, under normal circumstances, if the fact of share ownership was presented to the bank, it might consider that the transaction was to the financial advantage of the wife. On the facts, the bank's knowledge of the realities of the background was more extensive, so that it was put on inquiry.

A number of subsequent decisions have sought to explain the steps which a bank will need to take when put on inquiry. In *Royal Bank of Scotland* v *Etridge (No. 2)* [1998] 4 All ER 705, Stuart-Smith LJ considered the first requirement set down by Lord Browne-Wilkinson in *O'Brien*, that the bank should first advise the wife in a private interview. Stuart-Smith LJ considered that banks would be unwilling to adopt this procedure because such an interview 'is likely to expose the bank to far greater risks than those from which it wishes to be protected' such as claims for misrepresentation. In practice the courts have been satisfied that the bank has taken reasonable steps where it has advised the wife to obtain independent legal advice and has obtained a solicitor's certificate to the effect that this has been done. Stuart-Smith LJ noted the importance of laying down a settled practice so that the lending institutions could rely upon the requirements with some certainty that they would be protected. He then continued by setting out the relevant principles as they appear from recent case law. The basic effect of these principles is to shift the responsibility to solicitors and protect the banks, because banks are entitled to rely on the professional integrity of the advising solicitors to give proper advice. It therefore appears that as a general rule, at least where the lender has no reason for suspicion and so to make further enquiry, the lender is entitled to rely on a solicitor's certificate that independent advice has been given (*Bank of Baroda* v *Rayarel* [1995] 2 FCR 631).

The following is a summary of the current principles as they appear in judgment of Stuart-Smith LJ:

(a) If the wife deals with the bank through a solicitor, the bank is entitled to assume that the solicitor has considered the question of specific advice on the transaction and does not need to ask the solicitor to give this advice or to confirm that he or she has done so (*Bank of Baroda* v *Rayarel* [1995] 2 FCR 631).

(b) In other cases, the bank need only urge the wife to obtain legal advice before entering into the transaction. The bank is entitled to rely on a confirmation from the solicitor that he or she has explained the transaction and that the wife appears to understand it.

(c) The bank is entitled to assume that the solicitor will act exclusively in the wife's interests when giving her advice, even if he or she is also the husband's solicitor or acting as the bank's agent at completion (*Massey* v *Midland Bank plc* [1995] 1 All ER 929, *Banco Exterior Internacional* v *Mann* [1995] 1 All ER 936, *Barclays Bank plc* v *Thomson* [1997] 4 All ER 816). The bank is not concerned to question the solicitor's independence.

(d) Accordingly, the bank cannot be fixed with imputed notice of any thing the solicitor learns in this capacity of advising the wife, even if he or she is also the bank's solicitor (*Halifax Mortgage Services Ltd* v *Stepsky* [1996] Ch 207). The lender in this case was found not to have notice of the borrower's misrepresentation both to the lender and the borrower's wife, despite the fact that the lender's solicitor knew of it.

(e) The bank is also not concerned with the sufficiency or quality of the advice given.

There was also no requirement to obtain confirmation that the advice had been given and no requirement for the solicitor to confirm that the wife appeared to understand the advice. However, if the bank asks the solicitor to confirm that the advice has been given and such confirmation is not received, the bank is put on inquiry as to whether the wife has in fact been advised and will need to make further inquiry to ascertain that it has happened.

These principles will apply equally to instances where the surety is advised by a legal executive, as long as the advice is given with the authority of the solicitor as principal (*Barclays Bank plc* v *Coleman* [2000] 3 WLR 405).

The 'Etridge' exception   The only exceptional circumstances where the bank would need to do more (as recognised in *Royal Bank of Scotland* v *Etridge (No. 2)* [1998] 4 All ER 705) would be where the bank is in possession of material information which is not available to the solicitor, or where the transaction was 'one into which no competent solicitor could properly advise the wife to enter'. These instances will turn largely on the particular facts of the cases indicating that the bank or lender not merely ought to have been alert to a risk of undue influence, but was aware of facts making the whole transaction particularly dubious. Such a transaction arose on the facts in *Credit Lyonnais Bank Nederland NV* v *Burch* [1997] 1 All ER 144.

In *Credit Lyonnais Bank*, the defendant was a junior employee of a company and was a family friend of the plaintiff, the company's main shareholder. The plaintiff asked her to provide security to cover the company's overdraft, which involved charging her flat and giving an unlimited guarantee to the bank. Although the bank had advised her to obtain independent legal advice, she had not done so. When the company went into liquidation, the bank sought possession of the defendant's flat. The bank argued that it had discharged its responsibility by advising the defendant to take legal advice and could not be responsible for her failure to do so. The Court of Appeal held that, as the bank knew the nature of the employment relationship, it should have realised that undue influence was probable. Therefore, it should have ensured that the defendant obtained the independent legal advice and explained the potential extent of her liability. Accordingly, the bank was fixed with notice of the undue influence and the transaction was set aside. (In *O'Brien*, Lord Browne-Wilkinson had stated that where undue influence was *probable* in the circumstances, the bank would need to ensure that independent advice was obtained. *Credit Lyonnais Bank* may therefore be no more than an application of this principle.)

The Court of Appeal in *Barclays Bank plc* v *Goff* [2001] EWCA Civ 635 (unreported), 3 May 2001, expressed some unease with the scope of this exception, which has been seized upon in subsequent cases. Pill LJ stated (at para. 66) that

. . . family members do sometimes enter into unwise arrangements to assist their nearest and dearest. I do not consider that the exception was intended to cover all cases in which a solicitor would be expected to decline to give positive advice to enter into the transaction or to all cases in which the solicitor would be expected to advise that the transaction was unwise.

He went on to explain the extreme nature of the facts of *Credit Lyonnais Bank* which he considered to be the origin of the *Etridge* exception. *Credit Lyonnais*

Bank was referred to as involving a transaction which 'shocks the conscience of the court' (*per* Millett LJ). The decision in *Portman Building Society* v *Dusangh* [2000] 2 All ER (Comm) 221 (see below, 11.3) also indicates that the test for the exception to apply will be whether the conscience of the court is shocked by the transaction. In other words, the transaction must give rise to 'moral outrage' (*per* Ward LJ).

11.3   A DOCTRINE OF UNCONSCIONABLE BARGAINING?

At the root of both the doctrines of duress and undue influence lie considerations of fairness between the parties and a desire to prevent one party taking unfair advantage of the other. In *Lloyds Bank Ltd* v *Bundy* [1975] QB 326, Lord Denning MR argued that these doctrines were not really independent doctrines but rested on 'a single thread' of 'inequality of bargaining power'. Lord Denning MR stated (at 339):

> English law gives relief to one who, without independent advice, enters into a contract upon terms which are very unfair or transfers property for a consideration which is grossly inadequate, when his bargaining power is grievously impaired by reason of his own needs or desires, or by his own ignorance or infirmity, coupled with undue influences or pressures brought to bear on him for or for the benefit of the other.

Thus the doctrines of duress and undue influence were seen as part of a general power of equity to intervene where there has been an abuse of unequal bargaining power between the parties. (As noted above at 11.2.2.2, the majority of the Court of Appeal in this case based their decision on a finding of undue influence by the bank because of the special relationship of confidence between bank and customer which had arisen on the facts.)

In *National Westminster Bank Ltd* v *Morgan* [1985] AC 686, Lord Scarman referred with approval to the conventional analysis provided by Sir Eric Sachs in *Lloyd's Bank* v *Bundy*. Lord Denning's broader principle was firmly rejected. Lord Scarman has also expressly disapproval of such a doctrine in his judgment in *Pao On* v *Lau Yiu Long* [1980] AC 614 (see 11.1.2.2) on the basis that it 'would render the law uncertain' because it would have to be determined on the facts of each case whether the use of the bargaining position was unfair.

Nevertheless, it may be that there is scope for a single principle as the basis for policing the fairness of bargains in the light of their content. In *Schroeder Music Publishing Co. Ltd* v *Macaulay* [1974] 1 WLR 1308 (12.7.8), Lord Diplock used the idea of inequality of bargaining power to assess what he considered to be fair between the parties. The same principle may be found in the test of reasonableness of an exclusion clause set out in sch. 2 to the UCTA 1977 (see 6.6.2.7), which includes a reference to 'the strength of the bargaining positions of the parties relative to each other'. Clearly, there is also more direct consumer protection legislation, such as the Consumer Credit Act 1974, and the Unfair Terms in Consumer Contracts Regulations 1999 which regulates unfair terms (6.6.3) but takes account of all the circumstances surrounding the making of the contract.

There are limited signs that English law would be prepared to recognise a general right of intervention to prevent a weaker party (see, e.g., *Alec Lobb (Garages) Ltd* v *Total Oil GB Ltd* [1985] 1 WLR 173). In *Lloyd's Bank Ltd* v *Bundy*, Lord Denning MR was careful to avoid defining inequality of bargaining power only in terms of the obvious disparity between commercial enterprises and individual consumers. He defined it as existing whenever a party's bargaining power is 'grievously impaired by reason of his own needs or desires, or by his own ignorance or infirmity'. In this sense even economic duress against a large corporation would fall under the inequality of bargaining power principle. A weak bargaining position might be caused by other commercial commitments. In order to succeed, however, the corporation would also have to show abuse of that position by exertion of undue pressure on the part of the other contracting party. One of the criticisms made of Lord Denning's doctrine by Lord Scarman in subsequent cases (*Pao On* v *Lau Yiu Long* [1980] AC 614 and *National Westminster Bank Ltd* v *Morgan* [1985] AC 686) is that it exposes a risk that any contract, resulting from bargaining in which one party had the upper hand, might be overturned by the courts, thereby causing great uncertainty. However, it seems that any such doctrine would have to be based on the concept of 'abuse' of the unequal bargaining power and not merely its existence.

Something very like a doctrine of abuse of unequal bargaining power already exists in § 2-302 of the American Uniform Commercial Code, which reads:

> (1)   If the court as a matter of law finds the contract or any clause of the contract to have been unconscionable at the time it was made the court may refuse to enforce the contract, or it may enforce the remainder of the contract without the unconscionable clause, or it may so limit the application of any unconscionable clause as to avoid any unconscionable result.

The Code itself does not define 'unconscionable', but the commentary published with it says that the section is aimed at preventing 'oppression and unfair surprise' (see discussion of the Unfair Terms in Consumer Contracts Regulations 1999 at 6.6.3.3) and is not intended to disturb normal allocations of risk resulting from disparities in bargaining power. It is a question to be determined by the court in each case whether the behaviour of one party has crossed the line between the free play of market forces and oppression. The relevance of bargaining power in the doctrine is that what may in some circumstances amount to oppression will be regarded between parties of more equal bargaining power as legitimate negotiating tactics. Australia also has a recognised doctrine of unconscionability as a ground for intervention (see *Commercial Bank of Australia Ltd* v *Amadio* (1983) 151 CLR 447).

The closest that English law comes to such intervention is the Unfair Terms in Consumer Contracts Regulations 1999 (SI 1999 No. 2083), where a term will be unfair if 'contrary to the requirement of good faith' it 'causes a significant imbalance in the parties' rights and obligations under the contract to the detriment of the consumer'. Many of the terms which are listed as indicative of unfairness in sch. 2 are based on this imbalance; and in *Director General of Fair Trading* v *First National Bank plc* [2000] 2 WLR 1353, in assessing unfairness the Court of Appeal stressed both inequality of bargaining power and the element of 'unfair surprise' which can be key ingredients in a wider doctrine of unconscionability.

There have also been increasing references in recent cases involving allegations of undue influence to a link between unconscionability and undue influence (*Credit Lyonnais Bank* v *Burch* [1997] 1 All ER 144 and *Dunbar Bank plc* v *Nadeem* [1998] 3 All ER 876). However, other cases have refuted such a link on the basis that undue influence is 'concerned with the prior relationship between the contracting parties and whether that was the motivation or reason for which the bargain was entered into' (*per* Buxton LJ in *Irvani* v *Irvani* [2000] 1 Lloyd's Rep 412). In other words, undue influence might be regarded as 'plaintiff-sided', whereas unconscionability might be regarded as 'defendant-sided' because it was concerned with abuse of position by the defendant.

Ward LJ in *Portman Building Society* v *Dusangh* [2000] 2 All ER (Comm) 221 considered the sides to the debate (Capper (1998) 114 LQR 479 and Birks and Chin, 'On the Nature of Undue Influence' in Beatson and Friedmann (eds), *Good Faith and Fault in Contract Law*, Oxford University Press, 1995), but did not consider it necessary to determine which position was correct. Instead, he regarded unconscionability as a legal wrong for the purposes of the application of *O'Brien*, i.e. in the same way as undue influence and misrepresentations were legal wrongs. Ward LJ also cited Mason J in the High Court of Australia in *Commercial Bank of Australia* v *Amadio* (1983) 151 CLR 447, 461 to the effect that all of the reasons for setting aside contracts on equitable grounds 'constitute species of unconscionable conduct'. Mason J had also stated that:

> Relief on the ground of 'unconscionable conduct' is usually taken to refer to the class of case in which a party makes an unconscientious use of his superior position or bargaining power to the detriment of a party who suffers from some special disability or is placed in some special situation of disadvantage . . . Although unconscionable conduct in this narrow sense bears some resemblance to the doctrine of undue influence, there is a difference between the two. In the latter the will of the innocent party is not independent and voluntary because it is overborne. In the former, the will of the innocent party, even if independent and voluntary, is the result of the disadvantageous position in which he is placed and of the other party unconscientiously taking advantage of that position.

This passage was also cited with approval by Mantell LJ (at para. 33) in *Barclays Bank plc* v *Goff* [2001] EWCA Civ 635 (unreported), 3 May 2001, although he recognised that the two remedies might both arise on the facts of a particular case (such as *Credit Lyonnais Bank*).

In English law the recognition of a principle of unconscionability has its origins in *Fry* v *Lane* (1888) 40 ChD 312. This doctrine derives from a right of equity to set aside transactions at a considerable undervalue and without independent advice against the 'poor and ignorant'. The presumption of fraud, which arises in these circumstances, may be rebutted by evidence that the bargain was 'fair, just and reasonable'. This principle has gradually been extended in its scope (e.g., *Cresswell* v *Potter* [1978] 1 WLR 255), so that 'poor and ignorant' is a matter of relative perspective and old age appears to come within its ambit (*Boustany* v *Pigot* (1993) 69 P & CR 298). In *Credit Lyonnais Bank* v *Burch* [1997] 1 All ER 144, Nourse LJ would, it seems, have been prepared to extend the doctrine still further, i.e. to a junior employee influenced by employer and family friend. However, the key ingredient of any doctrine of unconscionability, as explained in *Boustany* v *Pigot*, is not that the transaction is unreasonable or unfair, but there has been an 'abuse' of the position. Millett LJ in *Credit Lyonnais Bank* referred to the need for 'some impropriety, both in the conduct of the stronger party and in the terms of the transaction itself'. In *Kalsep Ltd* v *X-Flow* (2001) *The Times*, 3 May, it was stressed that a party seeking to set aside an agreement as an unconscionable bargain had to show more than just improvidence. Pumfrey J stated that although it would be difficult, '[I]t is necessary to prove impropriety, and that is to say not merely harshness but impropriety, both in the terms of the agreement and in the manner in which the agreement was arrived at'. On the facts there was no evidence of any coercion or other improper pressure, although the judge accepted that it was an 'exceptionally improvident agreement, ignorantly and foolishly entered into'. It seems, therefore, that to succeed in a claim based on unconscionability, there must be procedural and substantive 'impropriety' which extends beyond mere unfairness.

In *Portman Building Society* v *Dusangh* [2000] 2 All ER 221 the Court of Appeal refused to grant relief based on an argument of unconscionability of the bargain. The defendant was aged 72. He was illiterate in English and spoke the language poorly. The claimant building society granted him a mortgage, guaranteed by his son, covering 75 per cent of the value of his property over 25 years in order to release the equity in the property. The money was given to the defendant's son to enable him to purchase a supermarket. The son was later declared bankrupt so that the guarantee was worthless. The building society sought to enforce their security, but the defendant claimed that because of the nature of the agreement it could be set aside as an unconscionable bargain, both in respect of unconscionable conduct by the son exploiting his father's weakness which affected the building society, and in respect of unconscionable conduct by the building society itself based on the principle in *Fry* v *Lane*.

The Court of Appeal rejected the argument based on the son's unconscionable conduct, distinguishing *Credit Lyonnais Bank*, because the building society had not exploited the situation and had not acted in a 'morally reprehensible manner' (*per* Simon Brown LJ). The father had merely sought to assist his son in what he hoped would be a profitable venture. Ward LJ stated that 'it may be that the son gained all the advantage and the father took all the risk, but this cannot be stigmatised as impropriety. There was no exploitation of father by son such as would prick the conscience and tell the son that in all honour it was morally wrong and reprehensible'.

Undue influence was potentially relevant because of the finding that unconscionability was 'a legal wrong' within *O'Brien*. However, there was no undue influence on the facts, the transaction was not manifestly disadvantageous and legal advice had been received. The case also would not have fallen within the *Etridge* exception (11.2.3.2) where the lender would have been placed under a higher duty of inquiry and the solicitor would be under a duty to refuse to act unless his advice not to enter the transaction was adopted. Neither of the two criteria for the operation of this exception was present on the facts. The building society was not in possession of material information unavailable to the defendant's solicitor. Neither was the transaction one which no competent solicitor could have advised the defendant to enter so that the solicitor ought to have refused to act.

In addition, although the defendant fell within the 'poor and ignorant' requirement for the operation of the principle in *Fry* v *Lane* and the transaction was an improvident one, Simon Brown LJ stated that building societies were not required to police transactions to ensure the wisdom of parents' actions in seeking to assist their children.

The development of a doctrine of unconscionability is therefore likely to be hampered by the practical reality that few cases will justify intervention by the courts; and where they do so, they are also likely to give rise to a claim based on undue influence which may be conceptually more certain and therefore easier to satisfy. For example, in *Credit Lyonnais Bank* v *Burch*, there was no plea of unconscionable bargain, although the Court of Appeal considered there to be a sufficient basis for intervention on this ground. On the facts in *Portman* v *Dusangh*, there was no evidence of undue influence and the required unconscionable conduct was also missing.

TWELVE

Illegality

12.1 INTRODUCTION

As a general principle it can be said that the courts will not enforce contracts which are tainted with illegality. There are two basic questions to consider:

(a) what will constitute an illegal contract; and
(b) what will be the effect of that illegality?

In respect of this second question: will the illegality operate as a defence to a contractual claim or a claim in restitution to recover money paid or other benefit conferred under the contract? Will it act as a defence to a claim to enforce a proprietary right created or transferred by such a contract? Alternatively, will there be any relief available to a party to an illegal contract? The type of illegality will inevitably influence the attitude of the courts to the question of whether relief is possible.

The notion of illegality covers a wide spectrum of factors, which have been said at one time or another to deprive contracts of legal force. The factors have little in common other than that they are for the most part within the compass of the category of public policy where the public interest prevails over whatever may be the intentions of the parties. Since the general public interest is the predominant concern, illegality is an exception to the normal rules on drafting claims and defences. The court is not obliged to wait for one or other party to raise the matter, but may raise the issue of illegality of its own motion (*Northwestern Salt Co. Ltd* v *Electrolytic Alkali Co. Ltd* [1914] AC 461).

It has always been difficult to classify the separate heads of illegality, and the courts have not sought a conceptual basis for intervention but have simply stepped in whenever there was a reason of public policy to do so. It is certainly the case that the factual situations giving rise to judicial intervention on the ground of illegality are so varied that they defy conceptual classification. Some traditional categories may be used for ease of exposition, but it should be remembered at all times that the categories are only descriptive, and few if any legal consequences derive from them. It should also be noted that contracts in restraint of trade are usually treated as a type of illegal contract. They are treated under a separate heading in this chapter partly to ease the organisation of material, but also because the public policy issues therein extended beyond the general need to protect the public interest.

It is interesting to note at the outset that in its Consultation Paper, 'Illegal Transactions: The Effect of Illegality on Contracts and Trusts', LCCP No. 154 (1999), the Law Commission used a wide definition of illegal contracts as including 'any contract which involves (in its formation, purpose or performance) a legal wrong (other than the mere breach of the contract in question) or conduct otherwise contrary to public policy' (para. 7.70). (Compare this definition with the recognised categories of illegality discussed in this chapter.)

It has sometimes been suggested that the types of illegality may be broken down according to their effect (i.e., (a) and (b) above are interdependent), some contracts being illegal and void, others being merely void and yet others not being void but only 'unenforceable'. These categories reflect a more complex situation, which is that the effect of illegality varies according to the nature and gravity of the illegality in question, and so is dependent upon the facts in each case (see 12.5 and 12.6). This attitude of the courts is well summarised by the following passage from the judgment of Bingham LJ in *Saunders* v *Edwards* [1987] 2 All ER 651 at 665–6:

> Where issues of illegality are raised, the courts have (as it seems to me) to steer a middle course between two unacceptable positions. On the one hand it is unacceptable that any court of law should aid or lend its authority to a party seeking to pursue or enforce an object or agreement which the law prohibits. On the other hand, it is unacceptable that the court should, on the first indication of unlawfulness affecting any aspect of a transaction, draw up its skirts and refuse all assistance to the plaintiff, no matter how serious his loss or how disproportionate his loss to the unlawfulness of his conduct.
>
> . . . on the whole the courts have tended to adopt a pragmatic approach to these problems, seeking where possible to see that genuine wrongs are righted so long as the court does not thereby promote or countenance a nefarious object or bargain which it is bound to condemn.

The House of Lords in the important decision in *Tinsley* v *Milligan* [1994] 1 AC 340 at 358, condemned any approach to illegality of contracts which suggests that the courts simply have a discretion as to whether to grant or refuse relief. However, the Law Commission has more recently recommended that the courts should have such a discretion (albeit within stated guidelines) to decide whether illegality should act as a defence to a claim in contract, in restitution or in respect of property rights (Law Commission,

'Illegal Transactions: The Effect of Illegality on Contracts and Trusts', LCCP No. 154 (1999), discussed in more detail at 12.6.5).

12.2 STATUTORY ILLEGALITY

The rule against illegal contracts is a common law doctrine, but the courts have had to adapt it to prohibitory rules contained in statutes, which in the twentieth century had a major impact on our legal system. The only issue in relation to such prohibitory rules is to determine their precise effect on the contract.

12.2.1 Express prohibition

Sometimes the statute expressly prohibits the type of contract in question, in which case it is clear that neither party can enforce the contract, even if one of them is innocent. In *Re Mahmoud and Ispahani* [1921] 2 KB 716, the statute prohibited unlicensed dealing in linseed oil. The defendant misrepresented to the plaintiff that he had a licence, but subsequently refused to accept delivery arguing that the contract was illegal because he did not possess the required licence. Despite the plaintiff's innocence, the contract could not be enforced.

This principle was applied more recently by the Court of Appeal in *Mohamed* v *Alaga & Co. (A Firm)* [2000] 1 WLR 1815, where the agreement (whereby a firm of solicitors would pay an introduction fee from its legal aid fees to a person introducing refugees requiring legal services) was expressly prohibited by subordinate legislation. Public policy precluded relief under the contract or by means of a claim in restitution for the services of introduction. However, the Court of Appeal did grant leave for the claim to be amended to a claim for a *quantum meruit* for services rendered (interpreting) as the plaintiff was blameless (in the sense that he was not aware of the breach of rules) and no public policy was infringed by allowing him to recover for these services.

This case was distinguished in *Awwad* v *Geraghty & Co. (A Firm)* [2000] 3 WLR 1041, where the distinguishing feature was that it was the firm of solicitors who were trying to recover a fee chargeable under the terms of a contract prohibited by subordinate legislation. On these facts, the Court of Appeal held that any claim for a *quantum meruit* also failed because such a claim was trying to achieve the same purpose, i.e. recovery of a fee which was contrary to public policy.

Some statutes are interpreted by the courts as being intended to regulate the activities of a particular class of persons, in which case only the party belonging to that class is disbarred from enforcing the contract. In *Bloxsome* v *Williams* (1824) 3 B & C 232, the defendant sold a horse to the plaintiff, giving a warranty as to its age and fitness. The sale contravened Sunday trading laws, and the defendant sought to resist an action for breach of warranty by relying on the illegality of the contract. He was unsuccessful. The Sunday trading laws were not aimed at all persons making contracts but at *traders*.

12.2.2 Contracts not expressly or impliedly prohibited but performed by one party in illegal manner

In *Archbolds (Freightage) Ltd* v *Spanglett Ltd* [1961] 1 QB 374, the defendants agreed to carry a cargo of whisky to London for the plaintiffs, who were unaware that the defendants did not have the required licence. The whisky was stolen, and when the plaintiffs claimed damages for the loss the defendants pleaded illegality. The plaintiffs were allowed to sue on the contract for the defendants' loss of the goods en route. The contract was not expressly or impliedly prohibited by statute (i.e., not illegal on its formation) and so was not illegal. It was performed by the defendants in an illegal manner, but the plaintiffs were not party to that illegal performance and so could enforce it.

This case can be usefully compared with *Anderson Ltd* v *Daniel* [1924] 1 KB 138, where the contract was illegal in performance because the seller had failed to give the required invoice. As the party who had performed the contract illegally, the seller was therefore held to be unable to enforce the contract and recover the price. (It is interesting to compare these cases, which indicate that the contract in question is not illegal but only unenforceable by the illegal performer, with the definition of 'illegal contracts' employed by the Law Commission in its 1999 Consultation Paper, No.154, at 12.1 above.)

Lastly, in some cases the penalty provided for by the statute is thought to be sufficient sanction for the infringement in question, so that the contract may be enforced by both innocent and guilty parties. In *St John Shipping Corporation* v *Joseph Rank Ltd* [1957] 1 QB 267, statute made it an offence to load a ship to such an extent that the load line was below the water. The offence was punishable by payment of a fine. The plaintiff charterers committed this offence and the defendants sought to withhold freight on the basis that it was an illegal contract. However, Devlin J held that the contract was not prohibited from the outset. It would be illegal in performance only if the contract, as it was performed, were prohibited by statute. The statute did not, however, prohibit contracts of carriage performed in breach of the load line rule. A similar conclusion was reached in *Hughes* v *Asset Managers plc* [1995] 3 All ER 669, where penalties were imposed on those dealing with share purchases without the necessary licence but the purchase contracts made by such persons were not void as illegal contracts. This view was supported by the need to give effect to the protection intended by Parliament in imposing the licensing requirement. This purpose would be destroyed if the contracts themselves were void.

12.3 GAMBLING CONTRACTS

A gambling contract is a contract under which two persons mutually agree that upon the determination of some uncertain (and normally future) event, one shall pay to the other, the winner, a sum of money or other stake (*Carlill* v *Carbolic Smoke Ball Co.* [1892] 2 QB 484 at 490). A contract will be treated in the same way if its purpose is gambling even if the parties have dressed the contract in the guise of a sale (*Brogden* v *Marriot* (1836) 3 Bing NC 88).

Gambling includes 'gaming' (betting on the outcome of games, including horseracing) and other wagers, but the two are sometimes treated differently. There is little good reason of policy why they should be.

At common law such contracts were valid, but a series of statutes have very largely reversed that rule. Since the unenforceability in this area extends also to securities (12.3.2) and loans (12.3.3), detailed treatment must be left to practitioners' works (*cf. Chitty on Contracts*, 28th edn, Sweet & Maxwell, 1999, Vol. II, Chapter 40).

Below is a brief summary of the law.

12.3.1 Gaming Act 1845

Section 18 of the Gaming Act 1845 provides:

> All contracts or agreements, whether by parole or in writing, by way of gaming or wagering, shall be null and void; and no suit shall be brought or maintained in any court of law and equity for recovering any sum of money or valuable thing alleged to have been won upon any wager, or which shall have been deposited in the hands of any person to abide the event on which any wager shall have been made. . . .

The effect of this section is threefold. In the first place, recovery on the basis of a gambling contract is impossible. Secondly, collateral contracts associated with gambling contracts are also unenforceable. Thus a contract to pay gambling debts in return for not being posted as a defaulter, although not itself a gambling contract, is unenforceable since any claim would be brought to recover a sum alleged to have been won on a wager (*Hill v William Hill (Park Lane) Ltd* [1949] AC 530). Lastly, money deposited with a stakeholder cannot be recovered as winnings, although the section has been interpreted as allowing a party to recover his or her own deposit before it has been paid over to the winner (*Diggle v Higgs* (1872) 2 ExD 422).

12.3.2 Securities

Sometimes a winner receives a security, such as a cheque, in payment. Such a security has been unenforceable in the case of gaming winnings since the passing of the Gaming Act 1710. This rule caused hardship in the case of negotiable instruments (see 15.4.4) given as security, since they might subsequently be given in payment to a third party who would be deprived of their value for no good reason. Relief was provided by the Gaming Act 1835, which said that such securities were to be deemed to be given for illegal consideration. The result was that a third party receiving the negotiable instrument would be able to enforce it if able to show that consideration had been given for it without notice of the illegality. In the case of securities given for non-gaming winnings, after the Gaming Act 1845 a similar rule applies, but the burden of proof in this case is on the person drawing the instrument to show that no value has been given (*Lilley v Rankin* (1887) 56 LJ QB 248).

The Gaming Act 1968 legalised some forms of gaming, and by s. 16, cheques which are not post-dated and which are given in exchange only for the face value of the cheque in order to be able to take part (e.g., a cheque to purchase chips) are enforceable by the holder of an appropriate licence under the Act.

12.3.3 Loans

Loans made in connection with gambling contracts are also irrecoverable, although the court may be faced with a difficult question of fact as to whether the loan is for gambling or merely for the general use of the gambler. Under s. 1 of the Gaming Act 1892, a loan to pay off gambling debts is irrecoverable if paid directly to the winner by the lender, as is a loan paid to the loser and specifically earmarked for gambling debts (*Macdonald* v *Green* [1951] 1 KB 594). But where the money is paid to the loser who retains control over how it shall be spent then the transaction does not have a sufficient link with the illegal gambling contract and so the money is recoverable (*Re O'Shea* [1911] 2 KB 981).

It is probably also the case that a loan made to finance future gambling contracts is irrecoverable. That would seem to be the case for an earmarked loan by virtue of s. 1 of the 1892 Act. In the case of non-earmarked loans there is authority in *Carlton Hall Club Ltd* v *Laurence* [1929] 2 KB 153 to the effect that these too are unenforceable, by virtue of the Gaming Acts of 1710 and 1835. However, the decision has been almost universally criticised and the authority is unreliable. The Gaming Act 1968 imposes further restrictions on the giving of credit for the purposes of gaming.

12.4 PUBLIC POLICY UNDER THE COMMON LAW

As a discretionary tool in the hands of judges, public policy has been used and abused, and its strength and weakness can be measured by the quality of those who apply it. It is traditional for judges to deprecate resort to public policy (*cf.* Burrough J in *Richardson* v *Mellish* (1824) 2 Bing 229 at 252) and to point to the adverse effect on freedom of contract of allowing public policy arguments to prevail (*cf.* Jessel MR in *Printing & Numerical Registering Co.* v *Sampson* (1875) LR 19 Eq 462 at 465). Nevertheless, the different heads of public policy under which courts have declared contracts to be unenforceable are numerous, and despite judicial statements there is no reason to think that they may not increase still further. Listed below are the more common heads of public policy so far identified.

12.4.1 Contracts to commit crimes or civil wrongs

A contract to commit a crime is self-evidently illegal (see *Bigos* v *Boustead* [1951] 1 All ER 92: contract contrary to exchange control regulations). Contracts to defraud the revenue are also illegal (see *Alexander* v *Rayson* [1936] 1 KB 169: contract designed to make the value of property seem less to the rating authority). A contract which envisages the commission of a civil wrong, which is not also criminal, is nevertheless tainted by illegality (*Clay* v *Yates* (1856) 1 Hurl & N 73: contract to publish a libel). Contracts of indemnity for unlawful acts may also belong to this category, and are equally unenforceable (*Gray* v *Barr* [1971] 2 QB 554: insurance claim refused because the loss followed directly upon threatening violence with a gun).

12.4.2 Contracts prejudicial to the administration of justice

Contracts are illegal by which a party promises to give false evidence (*R* v *Andrews* [1973] QB 422) or promises to withdraw a prosecution (*Keir* v *Leeman* (1846) 6 QB 308). Under s. 5(1) of the Criminal Law Act 1967, however, it is no longer an offence to withhold information which might secure a conviction if it is withheld in return for reparation for loss caused by the offence. It may be, therefore, that such a contract is no longer unenforceable.

Contracts which oust the jurisdiction of the courts are illegal. However, arbitration clauses in contracts are enforceable (*Scott* v *Avery* (1855) 5 HL Cas 811), provided no attempt is made to oust the supervisory role of the courts. Maintenance agreements between husband and wife in which one party agrees not to apply to the court for maintenance have been held to be contrary to public policy (*Hyman* v *Hyman* [1929] AC 601), but the impact of that decision is considerably reduced by legislation (s. 34, Matrimonial Causes Act 1973).

12.4.3 Contracts prejudicial to the family

Contracts of marriage brokage, by which one party is to procure the marriage of another for a fee, are illegal (*Hermann* v *Charlesworth* [1905] 2 KB 123). The same is true of agreements restraining marriage (*Baker* v *White* (1690) 2 Vern 215). A separation agreement between parties currently cohabiting or prior to marriage is invalid (*Cartwright* v *Cartwright* (1853) 3 De G M & G 982), but where the agreement is made after or immediately before separation it is valid. There are statutory prohibitions on relinquishing the obligations of a parent (e.g., s. 2(9), Children Act 1989). A surrogacy agreement (whereby it is agreed that the surrogate mother will relinquish parental responsibility in favour of another) is unenforceable under s. 36 of the Human Fertilisation and Embryology Act 1990.

12.4.4 Contracts prejudicial to (sexual) morality

It is sometimes said that contracts contrary to public morals are unenforceable. The rule is probably limited to sexual morality. Thus, a promise of payment in order to induce a woman to become one's mistress is unenforceable (*Benyon* v *Nettlefold* (1850) 3 Mac & G 94). The position must be the same if the sexual roles were to be reversed. Contracts ancillary to immoral purposes are equally affected (*Pearce* v *Brooks* (1866) LR 1 Ex 213: contract of hire of a carriage for the known purpose of prostitution). It should be noted, of course, that attitudes to sexual morality change, and the law is less severe than it once was on unmarried cohabitees whose relationship is stable.

12.4.5 Contracts prejudicial to foreign relations

Contracts which involve doing illegal acts in foreign friendly countries are unenforceable (*Regazzoni* v *Sethia (1944) Ltd* [1958] AC 301), as would be a contract hostile to such a country's interests to be performed elsewhere. In a similar vein, trading with an enemy is illegal (*Potts* v *Bell* (1800) 8 TR 548; Trading with the Enemy Act 1939). In *Lemenda Trading Co.* v *African Middle East Petroleum Co. Ltd* [1988] 1 All ER 513, Phillips J suggested that an English court should not enforce a contract governed by English law which would be contrary to English public policy, where the same public policy applies in the country of performance, making the contract unenforceable there.

12.4.6 Public corruption

Contracts which further corruption in public life are illegal. The rule is most commonly applied in the case of sales of public offices or honours. For example, in *Parkinson* v *College of Ambulance Ltd* [1925] 2 KB 1, the plaintiff was encouraged to believe that if he were to make a substantial donation to a certain charity, the officers of the charity would be able to obtain a knighthood for him. The sum of £3,000 was agreed and paid, but no knighthood was forthcoming. The plaintiff sued to recover the amount paid, but was unable to succeed because the contract was found to be illegal (see also the Honours (Prevention of Abuses) Act 1925). It is clear from *Lemenda Trading Co. Ltd* v *African Middle East Petroleum Co. Ltd* [1988] 1 All ER 513 (above, 12.4.5) that illegality of this kind does not rest on the fact that the party promising to exercise influence in return for payment occupies a public office.

12.5 GENERAL EFFECT OF ILLEGALITY

The effect of illegality varies according to the gravity with which the illegality is viewed by the court. For examples of this eminently sensible principle one need only reconsider the cases on statutory illegality (see 12.2).

The general principle that illegal contracts are unenforceable may be traced back to *Holman* v *Johnson* (1775) 1 Cowp 34, and the primacy of this long-standing authority was reaffirmed by Lord Goff and Lord Browne-Wilkinson in *Tinsley* v *Milligan* [1994] 1 AC 340 at 355 and 363.

The defence of illegality does not exist for the benefit of the defendant, but for the benefit of society as a whole, and rests on public policy. Consequently, if claimant and defendant were to reverse roles, the defence might still apply. In particular, a claimant will not succeed if his or her claim is based on an illegal contract, or if the illegality of the contract must be pleaded to support the claim. Equally, a claimant will not succeed if to do so would result in him or her benefiting from his or her own illegal contract.

It is sometimes said that these particular aspects of the rule must not be seen as exhaustive in stating the effect of illegality, and the overriding public policy element may result in the courts refusing relief to a claimant where illegality is disclosed even if there is no direct reliance on an illegal contract or any benefit from the claimant's wrongdoing. It was in this sense, in a case not relating to a claim in contract, that Hutchison J in *Thackwell* v *Barclays Bank plc* [1986] 1 All ER 676 employed what has been described as the 'public conscience test'; he accepted counsel's argument that in circumstances where there was no technical bar to the claimant's action, the nature of the illegality might nevertheless be such that no court would be willing to assist the claimant, for fear of appearing to assist or encourage criminal acts. In other words, the court had to apply a test of balancing the consequences of refusing relief or granting it on the basis of the facts of the particular case.

In a series of subsequent cases in the Court of Appeal the notion of a 'public conscience test' was very considerably developed, and eventually its meaning distorted, so that ultimately in *Howard* v *Shirlstar Container Transport Ltd* [1990] 3 All ER 366 a claimant was permitted to benefit from his own illegal acts, and to rely upon an illegal contract in making his claim. In this case, therefore, the public conscience test, rather than providing a further residual ground upon which the claimant's action might be refused, became an argument to overturn the general principle of public policy against enforcement of illegal contracts, because of what the court deemed to be an absence of affront to the public conscience on the particular facts.

This development was roundly condemned by the House of Lords in *Tinsley* v *Milligan* [1994] 1 AC 340. Although Lord Goff was in the minority in respect of the final outcome of the appeal, Lord Browne-Wilkinson, who gave the principal speech for the majority, agreed with his trenchant criticisms of the Court of Appeal's development of the law. Lord Goff said (at 361):

> This development has been allowed to occur without addressing the questions (1) whether the test is consistent with earlier authority, (2) if it was not so consistent, whether such a development could take place consistently with the doctrine of precedent as applied in the Court of Appeal, or (3) whether the resulting change in the law, if permissible, was desirable.

In particular, Lord Goff was not convinced that the public conscience test would be any better than the existing rules. He went on to make clear that in his view it would not be appropriate for the House of Lords to adopt such a rule, albeit that it was technically possible for the House of Lords to do so. In *Nelson* v *Nelson* (1995) 184 CLR 538, the High Court of Australia also rejected this test on the basis that it allowed the courts an unstructured discretion.

It appears that a claimant may clearly succeed if his or her claim does not require any reliance on the illegal contract. This would be the case where the claim made is not contractual at all (e.g., *Saunders* v *Edwards* [1987] 2 All ER 651: claim in tort for fraud giving rise to a contract which was tainted with illegality; and see *Hughes* v *Clewley (No. 2)* [1996] 1 Lloyd's Rep 35 at 63), or where the illegality does not affect the contract upon which the claim was based but some related transaction (e.g., *Euro-Diam Ltd* v *Bathurst* [1988] 2 All ER 23: claim on a contract of insurance in respect of goods stolen in the course of a transaction tainted with illegality) or where the defendant does not have to plead the illegality but is merely asserting a property right (*per* Lord Browne-Wilkinson in *Tinsley* v *Milligan*: claim to have an equal share in property, despite the house having been put in only one name as a device to contribute to a fraud on the Department of Social Security; see further 12.6.4).

Sometimes, although it seems only exceptionally, in order to ensure that 'genuine wrongs are righted' the courts will go so far as to allow recovery on a collateral contract, thereby avoiding, by use of a fiction, the problem of allowing a claim founded upon an illegal contract. In *Strongman (1945) Ltd* v *Sincock* [1955] 2 QB 525, a builder was informed by his client that the client would obtain the necessary licences, which the client then failed to do. A contract to build without a licence was absolutely prohibited by statute. Although the builders could not recover the contract price because the contract was prohibited, the assurance that the client would obtain the necessary licences constituted an enforceable collateral contract to obtain the licences. Therefore the Court of Appeal held the client liable for breach of this collateral contract.

The limit on this doctrine is that a remedy under a collateral contract must not be the equivalent of enforcing the illegal contract. This difficulty might have been avoided in *Re Mahmoud and Ispahani* [1921] 2 KB 716, which on its facts is not easy to distinguish from *Strongman* v *Sincock*, by bringing an action for misrepresentation, for which a different measure of loss would apply (see 12.2.1).

This (fictitious) kind of enforceable collateral contract must be kept separate from other transactions collateral to illegal contracts. For example, security given in respect of payment for, or performance of, an illegal contract is tainted by the illegality of the main transaction (*Fisher* v *Bridges* (1854) 3 El & Bl 642). Where one party is not involved in the illegal intention, as for example in the case of a class-protecting statute (*cf. Bloxsome* v *Williams* (1824) 3 B & C 232; see 12.2.1), that party may enforce the contract or recover under a restitutionary remedy.

Lastly, where one party adopts an illegal mode of performance without there ever having been any illegal intention at the time of contracting, he or she may still enforce the contract, provided he or she does not have to rely on the illegal element. So, in *Skilton* v *Sullivan* (1994) *The Times*, 25 March, the Court of Appeal allowed recovery of the price under a contract of sale, despite the fact that the seller had presented an invoice which falsely described the goods in order to delay payment of VAT, on the basis that he could establish liability to pay by relying only on the contract itself.

12.6 RECOVERY OF MONEY OR PROPERTY

The general rule stated in *Holman* v *Johnson* (1775) 1 Cowp 341 (see 12.5) applies equally to claims brought to recover money or property passing as a result of an illegal contract as it does to enforcement of the contract itself. Thus, where the parties are equally guilty even a restitutionary remedy is barred. Nevertheless, the rule may be avoided in a number of situations where either the parties are not regarded as being equally guilty, or the illegality need not be pleaded in order to obtain the remedy.

12.6.1 Where one party withdraws from the illegal transaction

Restitution may be available where one party withdraws before the illegal purpose is carried into effect (the so-called doctrine of *locus poenitentiae*). It appears that repentance is not necessary (*Tribe* v *Tribe* [1996] Ch 106; although compare with the Law Commission's provisional recommendation (Law Commission Consultation Paper No. 154 (1999)) which requires the court to consider whether the repentance is genuine and the serious of the illegality before permitting withdrawal, paras 7.58–7.69). In *Taylor* v *Bowers* (1876) 1 QBD 291, Mellish LJ suggested that withdrawal is allowed at any time before completion, and the decision in that case is only really consistent with that interpretation. However, in *Kearley* v *Thomson* (1890) 24 QBD 742, it was suggested that restitution would be denied once performance of the illegal purpose had started, irrespective of whether it was ever completed. The *Kearley* v *Thomson* principle appears to be more consistent with the public policy requirements inherent in the control of illegal contracts.

For similar reasons, the withdrawal from the transaction must be voluntary. In *Bigos* v *Boustead* [1951] 1 All ER 92, restitution was refused because the plaintiff had 'withdrawn' from the transaction only after the illegal purpose had been frustrated by the duplicity of the other party. A slightly different version of this rule emerged in *Tribe* v *Tribe* [1996] Ch 107. The illegal purpose was never carried into effect because the 'need' for the illegal scheme (which was designed to defraud creditors by transferring property to another) was avoided. When it became clear that the illegal scheme was not required, the transferor claimed the property back. To the defence that the transaction was illegal so that restitution was not allowed, the transferor replied that he had withdrawn before it was carried into effect. The Court of Appeal accepted this argument, which is perhaps surprising since the first element of the illegal transaction had been performed, i.e. the transfer of the property. The best explanation is probably that the transfer was not *necessarily* referable to an illegal purpose, and so should not be regarded as commencing the illegal performance. Such reasoning is technical and artificial: there is little doubt that the Court was also influenced by the view it took of the conduct of the party (who was the son of the transferor) who sought to retain the property, contrary to what had been their original plan.

12.6.2 Class-protecting statutes

In some cases a statute is intended to protect one class of contracting party against exploitative behaviour by another. The Rent Act 1977, s. 125, provides for recovery of a premium paid to secure a lease. Before the 1977

Act the courts had held that such a premium was recoverable under the common law. The parties were not equally guilty because the rule against payment of a premium was intended to protect lessees (*Gray* v *Southouse* [1949] 2 All ER 1019).

12.6.3   Fraud, duress or undue influence

Where one party is induced to enter into an illegal contract by fraud, duress or undue influence, that party is clearly not as guilty as the other. While it would be undesirable in such circumstances to enforce the contract, some remedy may be provided by permitting the victim to recover money or property passed as a result of the contract. In *Hughes* v *Liverpool Victoria Legal Friendly Society* [1916] 2 KB 482, the plaintiff was fraudulently induced to take out a policy of insurance on the life of someone in which she had no insurable interest. She was able to recover the premiums paid.

The suggestion that recovery in such cases depends on the fraud of the defendant rather than the innocence of the claimant (*cf. Harse* v *Pearl Life Assurance Co.* [1904] 1 KB 558) is difficult to reconcile with the basis of this right to recovery, which is that the parties are not equally guilty. Insurance companies might take proper care in such cases if a negligent misrepresentation (10.4.3) by their agent, inducing an innocent party to enter a contract, were also to entitle that party to recover premiums paid.

12.6.4   Proprietary remedy not relying on the illegal contract

Restitution will be allowed where the defendant is merely asserting a property right and need not rely on the fact that the contract is illegal. In the case of the sale of goods, it is established that property passes despite the illegality (*Singh* v *Ali* [1960] AC 167). Therefore, a proprietary remedy would not be available in a sales case, since there would be no property right to assert (see 1.5). However, where something less than full title is passed, as in the case of a lease, bailment or pledge, there may be scope for restitution. Nevertheless, if, in order to assert that property has not passed to the other party, it is necessary to plead the illegality of the transaction under which physical possession was transferred, then no remedy is available (*Taylor* v *Chester* (1869) LR 4 QB 309).

A common form of bailment is the hire-purchase agreement. In *Bowmakers Ltd* v *Barnet Instruments Ltd* [1945] KB 65, goods were delivered to the defendants under an illegal hire-purchase agreement. The defendants had failed to make payments and had sold some of the goods. The plaintiffs claimed damages for conversion; that is, they brought an action to recover the value of the goods, asserting their property right. The Court of Appeal allowed this claim. In the case of the goods which had been sold, their right to them could be asserted without reference to the terms of the contract, by virtue of the common law of bailments. However, the decision has been criticised for also allowing recovery for the goods retained by the defendants, since any right to their value, resulting from the failure to make the payments, must have depended on the terms of the contract, on which the court was not entitled to rely.

In *Tinsley* v *Milligan* [1994] 1 AC 340, Lord Browne-Wilkinson, speaking for the majority in the House of Lords, took the view that an action brought to assert a joint interest in a house, which had been put into the name of only one of the parties in order to assist in a fraud against the Department of Social Security, did not involve any reliance on an illegal contract but was simply an action to enforce a property right in the form of a trust. He did not believe that the fact that the property right asserted was in the form of an equitable rather than a legal interest had any impact on the case. Lord Browne-Wilkinson accepted that at some time in the past an equitable property right might have had to be treated differently, but was persuaded that the fusion of law and equity allowed the plaintiff to avoid the consequences of the illegal contracts rule by relying on a property right whether legal or equitable.

By comparison, Lord Goff, in the minority, took the view that an equitable property right could not be used in this way to avoid the consequences of the illegal contracts rule, because of the distinct maxim of equity that 'he who comes to equity must come with clean hands'.

As is clear from *Tribe* v *Tribe* [1996] Ch 107, this analysis will be ineffective between family members, since the transfer of property will not give rise to a resulting trust as it did in *Tinsley* v *Milligan* but rather will be subject to the presumption of advancement, i.e. it will be presumed that the intention was to make a gift to the transferee. That presumption can be rebutted only by disclosing the illegal purpose, so that any claim will be denied. In *Tribe* v *Tribe*, that consequence was avoided by the plaintiff showing to the satisfaction of the Court of Appeal that he had withdrawn from the illegal purpose before it was carried into effect.

12.6.5 Reform

In *Tinsley* v *Milligan* [1994] 1 AC 340 at 363–4, Lord Goff advocated reform of this area of the law on the basis that the present rules are 'indiscriminate in their effect, and are capable therefore of producing injustice'. The Law Commission examined this issue in its 1999 Consultation Paper, 'Illegal Transactions: The Effect of Illegality on Contracts and Trusts', LCCP No. 154, and also concluded that the law was 'unnecessarily complex', 'uncertain' and 'may give rise to unjust decisions'. It therefore recommended that the present rules be replaced by giving the courts a discretion to decide whether to enforce the illegal contract or permit a claim in restitution, or to recognise property rights either created or transferred under an illegal contract. The discretion would be circumscribed, in the broadest sense, by requiring the courts to consider a number of factors:

(a) the seriousness of the illegality involved;
(b) the knowledge and intention of the party claiming relief;
(c) whether denying the claim would deter the illegality;
(d) whether denying the claim would further the purpose of the rule which rendered the transaction illegal; and

(e)   whether denying the claim would be proportionate to the illegality involved (para. 7.43).

It is also proposed that this discretion should not exist for contracts which do not involve any legal wrong but are illegal because they are otherwise contrary to public policy.

These factors are important because they emphasise the policy objectives underlying illegality. However, almost inevitably, they would still allow a good deal of discretion to the courts in individual cases and hence promote uncertainty in this area of the law. See R. A. Buckley, ' "Illegal Transaction": Chaos or Discretion?' (2000) 20 LS 155 and N. Enonchong, 'Illegal Transactions: The Future?' (LCCP No. 154) [2000] RLR 82.

12.7   CONTRACTS IN RESTRAINT OF TRADE

Unlike the elements of the illegality doctrine previously dealt with, contracts in restraint of trade require reference both to the public policy which seeks to protect the public interest over the parties' individual interests and to the public policy which deems it unfair to enforce the agreement between the parties. Thus, such contracts may be subject to the intervention of the court on the ground either of protecting the general public interest, or of maintaining fairness between the parties.

Moreover, the illegality doctrine causes the public interest to be brought into conflict with the countervailing interest in freedom of contract. In the case of restraint of trade, the intervention takes place precisely to protect the public interest in freedom of contract. Contracts in restraint of trade are contracts whereby one or both parties agree to limit their individual freedom to contract. The common law will not tolerate such limitations if the public interest in free competition is adversely affected, or if the limitation is unfair between the parties.

12.7.1   General principles

During the nineteenth century the restraint of trade doctrine barely existed. Unless the agreement imposed a total restraint, the view was that no harm would be done, and that freedom of contract was the more important policy to pursue (*Printing & Numerical Registering Co.* v *Sampson* (1875) LR 19 Eq 462). This attitude neglected, or at least lagged behind, the progress of industrialisation and commercial agglomeration which had taken place. However, in *Nordenfelt* v *Maxim Nordenfelt Guns and Ammunition Co. Ltd* [1894] AC 535, the House of Lords restated the restraint of trade rule, and its decision in that case is the foundation of the modern law.

Nordenfelt concerned a restraint upon the seller of an ammunition and arms manufacturing company, which prevented him engaging in such business anywhere in the world for 25 years. The leading speech is that of Lord Macnaghten. His statement of the law may be summarised as follows: There is an initial presumption that contracts in restraint of trade are void. The courts may of their own motion refuse to enforce such a contract (see 12.1). The presumption may be rebutted only by showing special justifying circumstances. Whether the circumstances alleged to justify the restraint do so, is a question of law for the court. For a restraint to be justified it must be reasonable both in the interests of the parties and in the public interest. Generally, the burden of proof in relation to what is reasonable between the parties rests on the party seeking to enforce the contract. If that burden is sustained, the party resisting enforcement has the burden of showing that the restraint is contrary to the public interest.

It has been argued that the presumption that such contracts are void is inconsistent with the fact that the burden of proof in relation to the public interest rests on the party resisting enforcement. In *Attwood v Lamont* [1920] 3 KB 571, it was suggested that the more accurate presumption might be that such contracts were valid until proved otherwise. However, that suggestion was firmly rejected by the House of Lords in *Mason v Provident Clothing and Supply Co. Ltd* [1913] AC 724.

The conclusion must therefore be that of the two streams of public policy in relation to contracts in restraint of trade, fairness between the parties is predominant, since once that has been established the presumption switches to one of validity. In *Schroeder Music Publishing Co. Ltd v Macaulay* [1974] 1 WLR 1308 at 1315–6, Lord Diplock went so far as to suggest that the doctrine was concerned only with fairness between the parties. It is submitted that his view must be open to considerable doubt.

12.7.2 Reasonable between the parties

What is reasonable between the parties must be determined in each individual case. However, the decision of the House of Lords in *Herbert Morris Ltd v Saxelby* [1916] AC 688 provides guidance on how the issue is determined. In that case the defendant was employed as engineer by the plaintiffs, a leading manufacturer of hoisting machinery. His contract of employment contained a seven-year restraint on carrying on a wide range of related trades anywhere in the United Kingdom should he leave the plaintiffs' employment. The plaintiffs sought to enforce the clause. They failed. The House of Lords identified two different types of contract in restraint of trade in which different policy considerations apply. In the sale of a business, restraints are permitted which seek to preserve the value of the 'goodwill' of the business by preventing the vendor setting up in competition with the purchaser. In *Kall-Kwik Printing (UK) Ltd v Rush* [1996] FSR 114, restrictive covenants in a franchise agreement were treated as being analogous with those employed in the sale of a business. In contracts of employment it would not normally be reasonable to prevent a former employee from working in any capacity for a competitor, but restraints to prevent the loss of trade secrets or the poaching of customers to whom the employee had access are permitted. In each case, the identification of a legitimate interest to be protected is only the first stage in the process of justification.

It must also be shown that the duration and geographical extent of the restraint are not out of proportion to the interest identified. It was suggested in *Allied Dunbar (Frank Weisinger) Ltd* v *Weisinger* [1988] IRLR 61 that it was not appropriate to import the doctrine of proportionality into the field of restraint of trade. It is respectfully submitted that the point is largely semantic: in assessing reasonableness by weighing the severity of the restraint against the need to protect legitimate interests, the test is inevitably one of proportion.

While at first sight it may seem difficult to imagine how any restraint can be reasonable to the party upon whom it is imposed, it is essential to consider the whole contract in its economic context. In many cases, but for the restrictive terms, the contract as a whole might never have been made, or at least the person accepting the restraints might not have succeeded in obtaining such favourable terms. It is acknowledged, therefore, in *Esso Petroleum Co. Ltd* v *Harper's Garage (Stourport) Ltd* [1968] AC 269, that what is fair between the parties can be assessed only in the light of the consideration paid. To give a simple example, if in the sale of a business the vendor seeks to place a high value on the goodwill of the business, the purchaser will be entitled to restraints to ensure that the vendor cannot subsequently undermine that value by competing for his or her former customers. Such restraints might not be permitted at all if in the sale no value was allocated to the goodwill.

12.7.3 Reasonable in the public interest

It has sometimes been suggested that no contract reasonable between the parties can be unreasonable in the public interest. Lord Diplock was an advocate of that view in *Schroeder Music Publishing Co. Ltd* v *Macaulay* [1974] 1 WLR 1308; see 12.7.8), although the impact of his statement may be limited by interpreting what he said as meaning no more than that in contracts of employment of individuals (and analogous transactions) it is rare that a restraint will have any perceptible effect on the competitive structure of the market as a whole. It is certainly the case that there are *dicta* contradicting the wider view (i.e., that no contract reasonable between the parties can be unreasonable in the public interest) in the House of Lords decision in *Esso Petroleum Co. Ltd* v *Harper's Garage (Stourport) Ltd* [1968] AC 269.

The public interest is an important consideration, especially in those cases falling outside the employment contract and sale of business type of restraint identified in *Herbert Morris Ltd* v *Saxelby* [1916] AC 688. When two companies, as a result of arm's-length bargaining, agree not to compete with each other, one may assume that both think that the contract is reasonable. In such a case it is the public which is likely to suffer, and control by the courts in the public interest is essential.

12.7.4 Employment contracts

Restraints in employment contracts are usually subject to attack only in so far as they purport to operate after the period of employment has terminated.

Moreover, if the contract is terminated by a repudiatory breach by the employer, and the employee accepts the repudiation and treats the contract as at an end, restrictive covenants cease to bind the employee (*per* Simon Brown and Morritt LJJ in *Rock Refrigeration Ltd* v *Jones* [1997] 1 All ER 1; relying upon *General Bill Posting Co. Ltd* v *Atkinson* [1909] AC 118, HL). Thus, in the terminology devised by Lord Diplock in *Photo Production Ltd* v *Securicor Transport Ltd* [1980] AC 827 (see 7.1), restrictive covenants are primary conditions and so terminate once the repudiation is accepted. As discussed at 7.1, secondary obligations which govern what happens after termination survive repudiatory breach.

Since restrictive covenants in employment contracts are designed to govern post-termination conduct, there is obviously an argument for them to be classified as secondary obligations. The refusal to do so appears to reflect the general policy against such clauses. During employment the employer is entitled to control the activities of the employee, unless the nature of the restraint is to stifle rather than utilise the employee's skills. In this respect there may be an analogy between contracts of employment and restraints on those who engage in professional sport or in popular entertainment (see 12.7.8).

The common legitimate interests which may be protected are trade secrets and clients or customers to whom the employee may have had access during his or her employment. However, the restraint must not go beyond the scope of the type of activity carried on by the particular employee. In *Home Counties Dairies Ltd* v *Skilton* [1970] 1 WLR 526, a milk roundsman agreed not to sell milk or dairy produce to his former employer's customers. The restraint was found reasonable only upon an interpretation of 'dairy produce' limiting it to the kind of products with which he had dealt during the course of his employment.

In *Mason* v *Provident Clothing & Supply Co. Ltd* [1913] AC 724, the constraint purported to prevent the employee entering into a similar business within 25 miles of London. His employment had been in a small shop in Islington, and for that reason the restraint was too wide to be reasonable.

As noted above, it is rare that a restraint in such a contract will be contrary to the public interest, although this was the basis of the somewhat anomalous decision in *Wyatt* v *Kreglinger and Fernau* [1933] 1 KB 793. Nevertheless, it is possible that in the case of a person eminent in their field, such as a surgeon or scientist, the public interest might be adversely affected in a perceptible way. In *Oswald Hickson Collier & Co.* v *Carter-Ruck* [1984] 2 All ER 15, Lord Denning MR (with whom the other members of the Court of Appeal agreed) had suggested that it would not be in the public interest for a solicitor to be restrained from acting for his client, especially in view of the fiduciary relationship between them. However, in *Deacons* v *Bridge* [1984] 2 All ER 19, the Privy Council refused to recognise this as a general rule, and this view was followed in respect of a doctor in general practice within the National Health Service by the Court of Appeal in *Kerr* v *Morris* [1986] 3 All ER 217. These later decisions do not seem to detract from the proposition that a restraint upon a particularly expert specialist in a given field may be contrary to the public interest.

12.7.5 Sale of a business

In the case of sale of a business, equality of bargaining power is more likely to exist between the parties, and so fairness between the parties might be thought to be a less crucial, and the public interest a more prominent, concern. The classic case is *Nordenfelt* v *Maxim Nordenfelt Guns and Ammunition Co. Ltd* [1894] AC 535. The House of Lords identified the goodwill of the business as the interest entitled to protection. Lord Macnaghten stressed that the public have 'an interest in every person's carrying on his trade freely', and that restraints which are fair between the parties must not be 'injurious to the public'.

It is slightly surprising that there appear to be no cases of this kind where the public interest has been found to be the reason for the contract being void. Courts have usually referred to the public interest as an important factor to be considered, but have not matched their words with action. It may be that courts have not been sufficiently vigilant in this area since the changes supposedly wrought by the decision in *Nordenfelt's* case.

12.7.6 Cartels

Cartels are agreements between supposedly competing undertakings at the same level in the commercial chain. They are sometimes known as horizontal agreements. At least at the time of contracting it must be assumed that the parties believe they are beneficial to them both, and there is little chance of an inequality of bargaining power being exploited. On the other hand, where cartels consist of agreements not to compete, the conventional economic wisdom (and current political judgment) is that the public may well be harmed if competition is unnaturally impaired.

The reluctance of the courts to interfere with freedom of contract led in the past to the Privy Council suggesting that cartels are not injurious to the public (*Attorney-General of Australia* v *Adelaide Steamship Co.* [1913] AC 781). This reluctance to take necessary measures against these harmful agreements led to intervention by Parliament. Cartels are now largely controlled by statutory regulation; the relevant rules are now contained in the Competition Act 1998, in particular the Chapter 1 prohibition which is to be interpreted in line with case law under Article 81 (ex 85) of the Treaty of Rome. For example, s. 2(2)(a) of the Act prohibits agreement which 'directly or indirectly fix purchase or selling prices or any other trading conditions'. However, such an agreement will be prohibited only if it has an 'appreciable' effect on competition. (See the discussion of statutory control of anti-competitive agreements below, at 12.7.9.)

12.7.7 Exclusive dealing agreements

Exclusive dealing agreements are agreements between undertakings at different stages in the commercial chain which provide for a closer tie between the undertakings than a mere contract of supply. They are sometimes known as vertical agreements. They may well have advantages for both parties in terms of forward planning, but where one party is a retailer and the other a manufacturer, the security of supply for the retailer may be provided at too high a price. The leading case is *Esso Petroleum Co. Ltd* v *Harper's Garage (Stourport) Ltd* [1968] AC 269.

The parties made a contract, known as a solus agreement, under which the garage owners agreed to purchase petrol only from the company. In the case of one garage the tie was to last for four years and five months, and in return the garage owners received a discount on the price of petrol supplied to them. In the case of a second garage the tie was to last for 21 years, and in return the garage owners received a mortgage loan of £7,000. The House of Lords made it clear that there is no overall ban on such contracts. An investigation must be made in every case into whether there is a legitimate interest to be protected, and if so whether the restraints imposed are reasonable to protect the interests in question. On the particular facts, their Lordships found the shorter restraint to be reasonable, but the 21-year restraint was unreasonable and unenforceable.

There are *dicta* in the *Esso* case suggesting that an agreement for these kinds of restraints, if contained in a lease, would always be considered valid. It was apparently feared that to say otherwise might cause unnecessary interference in the law of real property relating to restrictive covenants. That opinion has been questioned by subsequent commentators, and it was made clear in *Alec Lobb (Garages) Ltd* v *Total Oil (GB) Ltd* [1985] 1 WLR 173 that the restraint of trade doctrine did apply, in principle, to leases. However, on the facts the particular exclusive dealing agreement linked to the lease was reasonable.

12.7.8 Restraints on professional sportspeople and entertainers

In some circumstances restraints are imposed to ensure that a person provides services only for one recipient. Such contracts are common in the world of professional sport and entertainment. The individual who is restricted may not have a contract of employment with the beneficiary of the restriction, but he or she is nevertheless unable to supply his or her services to anybody else. They are often referred to as 'exclusive service agreements'. This category includes those agreements where employers agree to regulate employment in a particular sector, and especially agree not to employ those who have previously worked for other parties to the agreement. Such agreements may be equivalent in effect to the restraints contained in contracts of employment (see 12.7.4), and for that reason they are within the restraint of trade doctrine.

In *Greig* v *Insole* [1978] 1 WLR 302, the organisers of international and English county cricket sought to exclude from their matches those players who participated in games promoted by a private cricketing 'circus' established in a battle over television rights. The plaintiff, who until this time had been captain of the England team, successfully challenged the ban imposed on the ground that it interfered with freedom of employment.

The most striking cases are those where the bodies responsible for the organisation of professional sport impose a rule upon their members intended to prevent large clubs poaching the best players from small clubs. Often such rules are alleged to be justified in the interests of the sport-watching public. The employees of the clubs can find that they are unable to make the best commercial exploitation of their skills. The cases make it clear that such rules are in restraint of trade and thus invalid (*cf. Eastham* v *Newcastle United Football Club Ltd* [1964] Ch 413). It should be noted that trade unions are given special protection in that the restraint of trade doctrine does not in itself justify a finding that, because of the purposes of a trade union, any agreements it enters into are void or voidable (Trade Union and Labour Relations (Consolidation) Act 1992, s. 11).

There have also been a number of cases concerning exclusive service agreements between musicians/pop groups and their management. In *Schroeder Music Publishing Co. Ltd* v *Macaulay* [1974] 1 WLR 1308, an unknown songwriter entered into a contract with a music publisher whereby they engaged his exclusive services for five years; and if royalties exceeded £5,000 the contract was to be automatically extended for a further five years. The contract was terminable at the option of the music publisher, who had copyright in all compositions, but not at the option of the songwriter. The publisher was not obliged to publish any songs. The songwriter sought to escape the confines of the contract after achieving considerable popular success, alleging that the agreement was contrary to public policy. The House of Lords held that such agreements fell within the restraint of trade doctrine. The restrictions in this agreement were one-sided and removed all incentive to creativity. Accordingly, the agreement was an unreasonable restraint of trade.

12.7.9 Statutory control of anti-competitive agreement

Restrictive agreements were subjected to statutory control by the Restrictive Practices Act 1956 and the Competition Act 1980. However, on joining the European Community in the early 1970s, the United Kingdom also became subject to the competition law of the EC, namely Articles 85 and 86 (now 81 and 82) of the Treaty of Rome. (That Treaty and all law made under it becomes part of English law by virtue of the European Communities Act 1972.) Article 81 (ex 85) prohibits agreements and concerted practices 'which have as their object or effect the prevention, restriction or distortion of competition between Member States'. It is therefore designed to control contracts in restraint of trade in so far as they prevent the realisation of the aims of the common market by hindering trade between Member States. However, because Article 81 (ex 85) refers to agreements 'between undertakings', it cannot apply to restraint of trade clauses in individual employment contracts where the common law rules prevail.

Any agreement contravening Article 81 (ex 85) is void and unenforceable (Article 81(2)), although it is possible (under Article 81(3)) to gain exemption from the operation of this rule. However, such exemptions may be granted only by the Commission, and not by the national courts of the Member States. Until an exemption is given the agreement remains unenforceable, however harmless it may appear (*Brasserie de Haecht SA* v *Wilkin (No. 2)* [1973] CMLR 287). Article 82 (ex 86) prevents the abuse of a dominant position.

Some EC law operates only at the level of governments, but where provisions are of 'direct effect' they create rights in individuals which may be protected and enforced by direct legal action in the national courts. By the decision of the European Court of Justice in *Belgische Radio en Televisie* v *SABAM* [1974] ECR 51, Article 81 (ex 85) is of direct effect. Thus, agreements which infringe Article 81 (ex 85) may not only be subject to investigation and possible fines imposed by the EC Commission, they may also be unenforceable by legal action by the parties in the English courts even before the Commission has ruled against them.

Although Article 81 (ex 85) regulates agreements affecting trade between Member States, it should not be thought that a purely domestic agreement cannot have such effect. In *Brasserie de Haecht* v *Wilkin (No. 1)* [1968] CMLR 26, the European Court of Justice was asked whether a brewery solus agreement affected trade between Member States. It answered in the affirmative, on the ground that where the agreement was a small part of a large network of similar agreements, such that most bars in the country were tied in a similar manner to breweries established in that country, the opportunities for imports to that country by foreign brewers were so minimal that it was correct to regard trade between Member States as affected. Thus, an agreement in restraint of trade need not relate directly to imports or exports to fall foul of Article 81 (ex 85).

In domestic law, the Restrictive Trade Practices Acts and Competition Act 1980 have now been repealed and replaced by the Competition Act 1998. The Chapter 1 prohibition in the 1998 Act prohibits various anti-competitive agreements in very similar terms to Article 81 (ex 85) of the Treaty of Rome, although the anti-competitive agreement must be one which may affect trade within the United Kingdom. Article 81 (ex 85) will apply where it may affect trade between Member States. The link between the two measures is reinforced by the requirement that the Chapter 1 prohibition be interpreted in line with the existing case law on Article 81 (ex 85).

It has long been held that Article 81 (ex 85) applies to both horizontal agreements (agreements between parties at the same level of production or supply) and to vertical agreements (between parties operating at different levels of supply) (*Consten & Grundig* v *Commission* [1966] ECR 299). Vertical agreements would include exclusive dealing agreements. The European Commission has issued a single block exemption (Regulation 2790/1999; [1999] OJ L 336/21) for vertical agreements such as petrol solus agreements and other exclusive dealing agreements based on a test of market share. This Regulation will operate from 1 June 2000 until 31 May 2010. Vertical agreements have been *excluded* from the Chapter 1 prohibition in the Competition Act 1998 by subordinate legislation (the Competition Act 1998 (Land and Vertical Agreements Exclusion) Order 2000 (SI 2000 No. 310)).

Having briefly examined these statutory provisions, it is important to note that where an agreement falls outside them, e.g., because the agreement does not have an 'appreciable' effect on competition, the agreement may be invalid as a restraint of trade at common law (as discussed above at 12.7.1).

12.7.10   Severance of the offending parts

In some circumstances illegal contracts remain enforceable by both parties provided changes are made by removing the offending parts. The rule is especially relevant in the case of contracts in restraint of trade which is why it is dealt with at this point.

Severance is allowed only if it is consistent with the public policy which made the contract containing the offending part illegal. If the whole contract is tainted by the illegality, severance cannot save it. In *Napier v National Business Agency* [1951] 2 All ER 264, a contract of employment contained provisions on pay and expenses which were clearly designed to defraud the Inland Revenue. The plaintiff was not allowed to enforce it in order to recover his salary by severing the part relating to the payment of expenses.

The illegal portion of the contract must be capable of being verbally and grammatically separated from the rest. This principle is usually called the 'blue pencil test'. In *Goldsoll v Goldman* [1915] 1 Ch 292, the plaintiffs were dealers in imitation jewellery, and entered into an agreement with the defendant, a competitor, to the effect that the defendant would no longer compete with them in any capacity, either in his own right, or as an agent or employee of others, for a period of two years. The clause purported to cover 'the county of London, England, Scotland, Ireland, Wales, or any part of the United Kingdom of Great Britain and Ireland and the Isle of Man or France, the United States of America, Russia or Spain, or within twenty-five miles of Potsdamerstrasse, Berlin, or St Stefans Kirche, Vienna'. The Court of Appeal was willing to enforce the contract but for the unreasonable geographical extent of the restraint, and did so after severing the words from 'or France' to the end of the clause.

The illegal part of the contract must not be the main subject-matter, since its severance would totally unbalance the agreement, making it essentially different from the original bargain. In *Bennett v Bennett* [1952] 1 KB 249, husband and wife separated, and the wife commenced divorce proceedings in which she applied for a maintenance order against her husband. Before the trial she entered into an agreement with the husband by which he undertook to pay her an annuity and to convey property to her, in return for which she promised not to pursue any claim for maintenance in the courts. The husband did not keep his side of the bargain. The promise not to seek maintenance was illegal (12.4.2), so that the whole of the consideration to be furnished by the wife failed.

Even where the illegal part is not the main subject-matter of the contract, the courts will not sever it and enforce the rest if to do so would alter entirely the scope and intention of the agreement. This rule appears to be the most satisfactory explanation of *Attwood v Lamont* [1920] 3 KB 571, which is otherwise not easily distinguished from *Goldsoll v Goldman*. In *Attwood v Lamont*, the respondent was the owner of a department store which carried out tailoring and general outfitting. The appellant was employed as a cutter in the tailoring department, and his contract of employment contained a clause restraining him from working at any time in the future within ten miles of the store in the 'business of a tailor, dressmaker, general draper, milliner, hatter, haberdasher, gentlemen's, ladies' or children's outfitter'. The restraint was found to be too wide, since the appellant's only significant skill was as a tailor, and the question arose whether the other functions on the list might be severed. The Court of Appeal held that the rest of the clause could not be severed, and that this was a covenant 'which must stand or fall in its unaltered form'.

Whether in any particular case the scope and intention of an agreement will be so altered by severance is a question of fact. Consequently, the application of the principle will vary from case to case. *Marshall* v *NM Financial Management Ltd* [1995] 4 All ER 785 provides an unusual and illuminating example. The clause providing the plaintiff with the right to certain payments for work done in the capacity of agent itself contained a provision found to be an unreasonable restraint of trade. The court was faced with a dilemma: if the whole clause was unenforceable, the plaintiff's right to payment would be lost; on the other hand, severance of the offending elements of the clause turned a conditional right to payment into an automatic right, which was a more than trivial change to the contract. Nevertheless, the judge agreed to sever the offending parts in order to protect the plaintiff's rights.

In *Carney* v *Herbert* [1985] 1 All ER 438, the Privy Council identified two limits on severance. In the first place, the significance of the illegal term or terms in relation to the whole of the transaction is to be judged not at the time of contracting, but at the time of trial. Consequently, the fact that a party would not have been willing to enter the contract but for the illegal term may be irrelevant. Secondly, where the parties enter into a lawful contract, and there is an illegal ancillary provision which exists solely for the benefit of the claimant, which the claimant may waive without prejudicing the substance of his or her claim, the court will normally permit the provision to be severed, provided there will be no overriding affront to the public conscience. On the other hand, the courts have expressed considerable reluctance to go out of their way to rescue employers from the consequences of having drafted restrictive covenants in terms that were excessively broad (*Living Design (Home Improvements) Ltd* v *Davidson* [1994] IRLR 69; *J.A. Mont (UK) Ltd* v *Mills* [1993] IRLR 172). Quite properly, the effect of these decisions ought to be to force employers to draft clauses properly and reasonably in the first place.

12.7.11 Remedies where a restraint is valid

Where it is sought to enforce a valid restraint of trade clause, the party for whose benefit the clause was included will usually be more concerned to prevent breach of the clause than to recover damages. Indeed, since restraints which are reasonable are often quite short in duration, he or she will require immediate protection (by the time the matter comes to a full trial the period of restraint may be close to expiry). Such immediate protection may be provided by the grant of an interim injunction (for jurisdiction of courts to grant interim injunctions, see s. 37(1), Supreme Court Act 1981 and s. 38, County Courts Act 1984; see also CPR, r. 25 and PD 25).

Where the covenant is *prima facie* valid, i.e. reasonable in geographical area, scope and duration, as in *Office Overload Ltd* v *Gunn* [1977] FSR 39, the court will grant the injunction. However, there will frequently be some dispute or doubt about the claimant's case. In *Lawrence David Ltd* v *Ashton* [1991] 1 All ER 385, the Court of Appeal held that, in such circumstances, the test to be applied in respect of an application for an interim injunction would be the usual test set out in *American Cyanamid Co.* v *Ethicon Ltd* [1975] AC 396. According to that test, such an injunction would be granted only where:

(a)   there was a serious issue to be tried;
(b)   damages at the time of full trial would not be an adequate remedy; and
(c)   the balance of convenience was in favour of granting it.

In *Lansing Linde Ltd* v *Kerr* [1991] 1 All ER 418, the Court of Appeal held that in respect of the first part of the test, where the full hearing would be held only at or about the time of the expiry of the period of restraint, an interim injunction would be granted only where there was not only a serious issue to be tried but the claimant was more likely than not to succeed at the full trial. Once the case for an injunction is made out, the claimant will normally be granted an injunction covering the whole scope of the restraint clause.

Injunctions to restrain breaches of restrictive covenants in employment contracts may be combined with an injunction restraining the misuse of confidential information obtained as a result of the employment. In the case of the latter type of injunction, the *American Cyanamid* principles will also apply (*Lock International* v *Beswick* [1989] 1 WLR 1268).

PART IV ENFORCEMENT OF CONTRACTUAL OBLIGATIONS

The notion of enforcement

The definition of contracts as 'legally enforceable agreements' (1.1) assumes that there exist mechanisms for the enforcement of those agreements which are identified by the law as creating legal obligations of performance. The mechanisms of enforcement of contractual obligations are the subject of the next two chapters. In fact, very few contractual obligations are 'enforced' in the sense of compelling actual performance, or in the sense of deterring non-performance by the threat and imposition of penalties.

Although compulsion and penalty probably represent the popular notion of enforcement, the basic legal means of enforcement of contractual obligations is by compensation for loss caused; in other words, by the payment of damages for breach of contract (Chapter 13). It is enforcement in the sense that the party who should have performed but did not, is compelled to pay the extra cost of obtaining substitute performance.

Penalties for breach of contractual obligations

English law has always denied any role for punishment in the enforcement of contracts. Although theorists have at times attributed the binding force of contractual undertakings to the moral obligation to keep one's promises, the law does not seek to punish promise-breakers, just as it is not directly concerned to enforce morality. Punishment is regarded as an instrument of social control, so that the law punishes criminals and may in limited circumstances award punitive (or 'exemplary') damages against those who are particularly callous or deliberate in the commission of torts (*Cassell & Co. Ltd v Broome* [1972] AC 1027), although even in tort the scope of recovery of exemplary damages is very limited (see *AB v South West Water Services Ltd* [1993] 1 All ER 609). There is little scope for social control in English contract law, however; the focus is rather on enabling private transactions, and in the last resort on remedying grievances. For these reasons there is no penalty for breach of contract (*Perera* v *Vandiyar* [1953] 1 All ER 1109).

Where breach occurs but no loss is sustained, in most circumstances only nominal damages will be awarded (*Surrey County Council* v *Bredero Homes Ltd* [1993] 1 WLR 1361; but see 13.5). The *Bredero Homes* case reveals essential truths about remedies for breach of contract. The breach was deliberate, and made with the intention of increasing the profitability of the transaction, which intention was duly realised. It might be thought that such conduct would invite censure from the courts, but, crucially, the non-breaching party could not been shown to have suffered a loss. The Court of Appeal was unanimous in refusing any award of damages, although the House of Lords in *Attorney-General* v *Blake* [2000] 3 WLR 625, has recently held that in very exceptional circumstances, it may be possible to obtain an order whereby the party in breach has to account for profits made as a result of the breach. The exact scope of this principle in *AG* v *Blake* is unclear but, because of the specific facts of the case, it is unlikely to have more general application and will be very tightly circumscribed.

Another aspect of the non-punitive approach to contractual damages is the policy of the courts denying enforcement to contractual clauses purporting to impose penalties for non-performance (13.10).

Compelling actual performance

The political and economic liberalisms which were the foundations upon which nineteenth-century contract law was built (1.4.2.2) were inconsistent with the idea of compelling a person to perform a contract against his or her will in circumstances in which suitable equivalent alternative performance is available. In the case of contracts for goods or services in which there is an available market, the non-breaching party can obtain substitute performance. The price the party in breach must pay for not being compelled to perform against his or her will is whatever is the extra cost of obtaining that substitute performance. For example, if A promises to cut B's hedge on Tuesday for £5, but then arranges to cut C's lawn on the same day for £10, making performance of his contract with B impossible, there is undoubtedly a breach of contract. A will not be punished, neither will he be forced to revoke the contract with C in order to perform his contract with B. B must find someone else to cut his hedge, and if the market price for the services of a hedge-cutter is higher than £5, A must pay the difference. The contract has been enforced only in the sense that at the end of the day B will have received the promised contractual performance at the cost to him agreed in his contract with A.

This result can be justified in terms both of the relationship between the parties and of economic efficiency. No doubt B would not be happy to accept A's services, since he believes A to be unreliable; equally, it may be impossible to force A to perform at his best if his performance is given against his will. In these circumstances substitute performance is probably more acceptable to both. Alternatively, if A is to pay B's extra costs, B will be no worse off by allowing A not to perform, while A may be better off if B's extra cost is less than the extra profit A will make on his contract with C. That is, if B's substitute performance costs £7 then A must pay B £2 for B to be no worse off. A makes an extra profit, by contracting with C for £10, so that after paying B he will be £3 better off. For one party to be better off while no party is worse off is, in economic terms, an efficient result. This simple example assumes that B incurred no costs in finding substitute performance.

It is therefore only where substitute performance is irrelevant or inadequate that the law will compel actual performance. Substitute performance is irrelevant where the contractual obligation that is unperformed is to pay the price (see 14.1), since compulsion of payment of the price is no different from compulsion to pay damages for the cost of substitute performance. However, substitute performance will be inadequate where the promised contractual performance is in some way unique, or at least exceedingly rare, so that substitution is impossible. For example, a contract to sell the Mona Lisa is a contract for a unique item, and if breached the buyer could obtain no substitute. In such circumstances damages are inappropriate, and the court will compel actual performance (14.2). Substitute performance may also be inadequate where the contractual undertaking is in the form of a promise to refrain from some activity. If A pays £50 to B, his neighbour, in return for B's promise to refrain from making loud noises during the period while A is revising for an examination, calculating A's loss should B disturb his work may be impossible. A needs to be able actually to prevent the disturbance occurring. Again, in such circumstances damages are inappropriate, and the court will compel actual performance (14.3).

Compensation

Except in those cases where substitute performance is irrelevant or inadequate, the method of enforcement of contractual obligations is by compensation for losses caused by their breach. The claimant may have suffered loss in any of three broad areas of interest, and the interest to be compensated determines the measure of damages payable. The *expectation* interest refers to whatever is necessary to put the claimant into the position he or she would have been in had the contract been performed. Compensation for lost profit is compensation of an expectation interest, as is payment of damages for the cost of substitute performance. The *reliance* interest refers to whatever is necessary to put the claimant into the position he or she was in before the contract was made rather than seeking to compensate for loss of an anticipated gain. Compensation for expenditure made towards performance of the contract is compensation of this reliance interest. This reliance interest is the same as the standard measure of damages for tort. Lastly, the *restitutionary* interest refers to the restoration to the claimant of a benefit conferred on the defendant to which the defendant is not entitled. The basis for this recovery is that the defendant would otherwise be unjustly enriched at the claimant's expense. Compensation for work done in anticipation of entering a contract, which in fact never materialises, is compensation of a restitutionary interest, as is the return of an advance payment under a contract which is void for mistake, or discharged by frustration.

THIRTEEN

Damages for breach of contract

13.1 THE AIM OF CONTRACTUAL DAMAGES

In *Photo Production Ltd* v *Securicor Transport Ltd* [1980] AC 827 (see 6.5.3 and 7.5.1), Lord Diplock said at 849:

> Every failure to perform a primary obligation is a breach of contract. The secondary obligation on the part of the contract-breaker to which it gives rise by implication of the common law is to pay monetary compensation to the other party for the loss sustained by him in consequence of the breach. . . .

Thus damages for breach of contract are available as of right, on proof of breach. In some circumstances breach may also give the non-breaching party the option of bringing the outstanding primary obligations to a premature end (see 7.5.2). In this chapter, however, we shall consider the rules applicable to the secondary obligation to pay compensation for loss caused which arises whenever there is a breach of contract. Essentially we will be examining how these damages are quantified.

As we saw above, 5.1.1, the basic aim of contractual damages is to compensate the claimant for the loss he or she has suffered as a result of the breach of contract. Therefore, in calculating these damages the focus should be placed on the claimant's loss. The claimant cannot recover more than his or her actual loss; and if he or she suffers no loss, he or she will be constrained to recovering only nominal damages. This principle also means that because it is not part of the loss suffered by the claimant, the claimant cannot, as a general rule, recover any profit made by the defendant even if that profit resulted from a deliberate breach of contract by the defendant (*Surrey County Council* v *Bredero Homes Ltd* [1993] 1 WLR 1361; although see the discussion at p. 374 and 13.5 relating to the possible recovery of profits as restitutionary damages and the decision in *Attorney General* v *Blake* [2000] 3 WLR 625).

The basic rule of recovery of compensation in the case of breach of contract is that the non-breaching party is to be put into the position he or she would have been in had the contract been performed as agreed (*Robinson* v *Harman* (1848) 1 Ex 850; and see *Surrey County Council* v *Bredero Homes Ltd* [1993] 1 WLR 1361). This general measure of loss was described above as compensating the claimant's expectation interest (p. 375), i.e. compensation for loss of the benefit of the promised performance (the expected gain under the contract).

Lost expectation may therefore comprise loss of a profit which would have been made but for the breach. For example, if A bought machinery from B with the intention of making goods and selling them at a profit to C, then B's failure to deliver the machines will result in A losing the profit to be made on the sale of the goods. Subject to certain limitations (see 13.9), quantification of such a loss should not present great difficulty.

Lost expectation may also occur without any intention to profit from the contract, and in those circumstances quantification of the loss is more difficult. It may be measured either by reference to the diminished value to the claimant (13.2.1), or by reference to the cost of achieving the agreed performance (13.2.2).

In some cases the claimant may prefer, or may be obliged (13.2.3), to recover compensation for his or her reliance interest (13.3), such as out-of-pocket expenses arising from his or her performance of the contract, and other expenses which it was intended would be recovered if the contract had been performed. There is no reason why both lost profit and out-of-pocket expenses should not both be recovered, provided there is no double compensation (13.4).

13.2 QUANTIFICATION OF LOSS: LOST EXPECTATION

Expectation loss will normally be compensated on the basis of the difference in value measure, i.e. the difference in value between the promised performance and the actual performance. Difference in value damages are often calculated using the 'market price' rule. However, where there is no market, these damages will be calculated as the difference between the value of the performance as contracted for and the actual value of the performance received. Alternatively, in some circumstances, it may be possible to recover the cost of achieving the expected performance ('cost of cure').

13.2.1 Difference in value

13.2.1.1 The market price rule The best example of the measurement of expectation loss in terms of difference in value is the process of assessment of damages for the seller's breach by non-delivery of goods in a contract for the sale of goods: the market price rule. Where the goods are freely available upon demand, there is no difficulty in identifying a 'market' and the price at which goods may be bought or sold. However, it seems that the definition of what constitutes a market may be much more limited. In *Shearson Lehman Hutton Inc.* v *Maclaine Watson & Co. Ltd (No. 2)* [1990] 3 All ER 723, Webster J said, in the context of a breach by the buyer, that a market would exist where either:

(a)   the seller actually offers the goods for sale and there is one actual buyer on that day at a fair price; or
(b)   there is no actual offer for sale but there are sufficient traders potentially in touch with each other to evidence a market in which the actual or notional seller could, if he or she wished, sell the goods.

The market price of the goods (which represents their real value) is then said to be either:

(a)   the 'fair price' obtained by the actual sale; or
(b)   in the absence of an actual sale, a fair price for the total quantity of goods sold on the market on the relevant date, or such price as might be negotiated 'within a few days with persons who were members of the market on that day and who could not be taken into account as potential buyers on the day in question only because of difficulties of communication'.

These principles would apply *mutatis mutandis* in the case of seller's breach.
    The law assumes that the buyer will mitigate his or her loss (see 13.9.3) by immediately going to the market and buying similar goods from another source. The buyer will then suffer a loss only if he or she has to pay more for the substitute goods on the open market than he or she had originally contracted to pay. The buyer's damages will, therefore, be assessed by subtracting the contract price from the market price at the time of breach (s. 51(3), SGA 1979). Where the buyer had anticipated making a profit on the transaction by reselling the goods at a price higher than the market price, his or her damages are nevertheless restricted to the difference between market price and contract price, since he or she would have been able to make the resale, and thus the profit, by obtaining substitute goods on the market (*Williams* v *Reynolds* (1865) 6 B & S 495).
    The converse of this measure of expectation loss applies to the buyer's breach by non-acceptance of the goods in a contract for the sale of goods. Where there is an available market, it is assumed that the seller will immediately be able to sell the goods to a substitute buyer, so that he or she will suffer a loss only if the market price is below the price he or she had originally contracted to receive. The seller's damages will, therefore, be assessed by subtracting the market price at the time of the breach from the contract price (s. 50(3), SGA 1979).
    In the case of the seller's remedy, the market price rule will often result in no loss being revealed, for the reason that standard items are sold at standard prices, so that there will be no difference between market price and contract price. For example, if A has three sacks of coal to sell, and contracts to sell

them to B at the standard (market) price of £4 per sack, if B later wrongfully refuses to accept the coal, A will almost certainly be able to sell them to C at the same price. B will assert that he is entitled to benefit from A's mitigation of the loss (see 13.9.3) so that no damages are payable, while A will assert that he has lost the profit on the sale to B since he would have been able to sell another three bags of coal to C.

The expectation loss claimed by A is usually referred to as created by 'lost volume'. The claim will succeed in cases where supply is greater than demand. That is, if A has unlimited access to supplies of coal then it is true that he could have made sales to both B and C, so that there is genuinely one lost sale, and A should recover the profit he would have made on that sale (*Thompson (W.L.) Ltd* v *R. Robinson (Gunmakers) Ltd* [1955] Ch 177: the case involved the sale of a new 'Vanguard' car, which cars were readily available so that supply exceeded demand and the breach resulted in a lost sale). However, where demand is greater than supply, the claim will not succeed. That is, if the three sacks of coal were A's last three available sacks, and no further supplies were obtainable, A could not have made sales to both B and C, and the sale to C was genuinely a substitute for the sale to B. In such a case there will be no lost profit (*Charter* v *Sullivan* [1957] 2 QB 117, also a new car sale). These rules do not apply in the case of unique goods, since in that case there is no market for such goods and no scope for a substitute sale (*Lazenby Garages Ltd* v *Wright* [1976] 1 WLR 459, concerned the sale of a second-hand car, but there is scope for doubting whether every second-hand car is 'unique').

13.2.1.2 Alternative measures of difference in value

The market price rule will not be used as the measure of loss either where there is no available market, or where, in the circumstances, the non-breaching party is not expected to avail itself of the market to mitigate its loss.

There may be no available market for a number of reasons, and it will be a question of fact in each case whether a market exists. A good example of absence of a market is where goods are specially manufactured to the order of the buyer, so that it is very unlikely that a different buyer would have ordered precisely the same goods. Another is where there is a serious disequilibrium between supply and demand. Thus, in ascertaining a seller's loss there may be no market price if supply so far outstrips demand that the seller cannot reasonably make an alternative sale. Equally, in ascertaining a buyer's loss, there may be no market price if demand so outstrips supply that the buyer cannot reasonably make an alternative purchase.

Where there is no market, the basic principle is that the market price rule formula (13.2.1.1) should continue to be used, but the court must put its own estimation of the actual value of the goods in question into the formula in the place of the market price. Such estimations will sometimes be highly speculative, but the court may have some evidence available from actual contracts of resale of the goods. In some circumstances, where measurement of the expectation loss is so uncertain the claimant may prefer to claim his or her reliance losses (13.3).

Defective performance   A claimant buyer will not be expected to avail himself or herself of the market to mitigate a loss when he or she is obliged to keep the goods despite the breach, which will occur when the breach relates only to a warranty (see 7.5.3.3), or is a non-serious breach of an innominate term (see 7.5.3.4) or where the breach once entitled the buyer to reject the goods but that right has been lost (7.5.2.3). The buyer will still seek to be compensated for his or her lost expectation through the defective performance, which in this case will normally be represented by the difference in value of the goods as warranted in the contract and as actually delivered. Here again, the estimation of values may be somewhat speculative, although where there is a market, the warranted value will be taken to be the same as the market price.

An interesting question arises where the buyer's actual loss resulting from the supply of defective goods is less than the difference in value. In *Slater* v *Hoyle & Smith Ltd* [1920] 2 KB 11, the contract was for the sale of 3,000 pieces of cotton of a particular quality. The cotton delivered was not of this quality, but the buyers had already contracted to sell 2,000 of the pieces to a sub-buyer and the buyers managed to use some of the cotton supplied partially to perform this sub-sale. The price applicable to the sub-sale was higher than the market value of the cotton supplied. The Court of Appeal held that the buyers could obtain damages based on the difference between the value of the cotton as warranted and as supplied without taking account of the price received under the sub-sale. However, the majority of the Court of Appeal in *Bence Graphics International Ltd* v *Fasson (UK) Ltd* [1998] QB 87, distinguished *Slater* and said that damages should be the loss directly and naturally arising. Accordingly, the majority decided that where it is within the contemplation of the parties at the time of contracting that, after substantial processing, goods will be resold, the loss caused by the seller's breach of warranty will be measured by reference to the buyer's potential liability to sub-buyers.

Late delivery   Where the delay in delivery constitutes a repudiatory breach and the buyer rejects the goods for this reason, damages are assessed as if the breach constituted non-delivery (s. 51(3), SGA 1979). However, where the delay in delivery is affirmed or does not constitute a repudiatory breach, the measure of damages will differ depending upon the intended purpose for those goods. Damages will normally be assessed on the basis of the difference in market value where goods intended for income-generation (e.g., manufacturing machinery) are delivered late, and the lost expectation will be the profits lost during the period when the machinery should have been in operation (see *Victoria Laundry (Windsor) Ltd* v *Newman Industries Ltd* [1949] 2 KB 528; see 13.9.2). However, where the intention was to sell the goods in the market, the loss will be the difference between the market price on the date when the goods should have been delivered and the market price on the date when they were delivered.

Cancellation of a contract to supply   The normal measure of damages where a contract to supply is cancelled with be the lost net profit on the contract. (It may be possible, in addition, to recover for wasted expenditure incurred in seeking to perform prior to the date of cancellation (see 13.3).) In exceptional circumstances, the supplier may, in addition to net profit, be able to recover an element of the gross profit to cover fixed overheads where (in this case due to a business recession) it is not possible to defray these overheads by obtaining a substitute contract (*Western Webb Offset Printers Ltd* v *Independent Media Ltd* [1996] CLC 77).

13.2.2 Cost of cure

Cost of cure is the other possible way of calculating expectation loss. In some circumstances, awarding cost of cure may be the only way of ensuring that the claimant's expectation under the contract is fulfilled. In a contract for the sale of goods the buyer will probably want performance in order to put the goods into immediate use, or in order to resell them and make a profit on the sale. The seller's failure to deliver may be cured by the buyer obtaining substitute goods on the market. In such a case, difference in value, as measured by the market price rule (13.2.1.1), and cost of cure are one and the same thing. In other circumstances, the claimant may have wanted performance for other 'subjective' reasons, so that a damages award based on an objective difference in value will not compensate him or her. Harris, Ogus and Phillips ((1979) 95 LQR 581) refer to these 'subjective' reasons for wanting performance as 'the consumer surplus'. The 'consumer surplus' is defined as 'the excess utility or subjective value over and above the market value of the performance contracted for' and which would have been secured had the contract been properly performed. For example, if A contracts with B for B to build a wall on A's land in order to act as a boundary and reduce noise, but B fails to build the wall, it is arguable that the only way to compensate A (and achieve A's purpose under the contract) will be to award the cost of achieving that promised performance.

However, the measure of cost of cure may be significantly greater than the measure of difference in value. The question, therefore, is whether the courts should give effect to the consumer surplus and award higher cost of cure damages. In the famous American case of *Jacob & Youngs* v *Kent* (1921) 230 NY 239, the plaintiffs had inserted an express clause in the contract that a particular make of piping be used in the plumbing work during the construction of a house. A different make of piping of identical quality was in fact used. The court refused to allow damages on the basis of cost of cure, and allowed only the difference in value, which was purely nominal.

The courts have to balance two competing issues here. In the first place, awarding cost of cure may appear to be out of all proportion to the consequences of the breach, and there is a risk of unjust enrichment if the claimant is awarded cost of cure damages but then does not use this damages award to carry out the repair. On the other hand, if a building owner has specified a particular means of performance, the building contractor may save costs of performing by not complying with the specification but only have to pay a small difference in value measure of damages. This might send the wrong signals to the construction industry.

In order to seek to achieve this balance, the courts have imposed some limitations on the ability to recover cost of cure damages in such circumstances. However, there has been very clear recognition of this non-financial interest in performance, for example, in *Radford* v *De Froberville* [1977] 1 WLR 1262, *Ruxley Electronics and Construction Ltd* v *Forsyth* [1996] 1 AC 344 and *Attorney-General* v *Blake* [2000] 3 WLR 625. For example, in *AG* v *Blake*, Lord Nicholls stated (at 636) that 'The law recognises that a party to a contract may have an interest in performance which is not readily measured in terms of money'. Thus, the mere fact that the claimant has stipulated for a particular kind of performance which others would regard as having no value, or as not enhancing the value of the property, will not of itself prevent the recovery of cost of cure damages. In *Ruxley Electronics*, Lord Jauncey referred to the construction of a folly in a garden and stated that, if the folly collapsed, it would be irrelevant to the determination of the loss suffered to argue that the construction of the folly, which did not increase the value of the land, 'was a crazy thing to do'.

A further example is provided by the facts of *Radford* v *De Froberville* [1977] 1 WLR 1262. The defendant had contracted to build a wall on her land to mark the boundary, but failed to perform. The plaintiff was entitled to the cost of building a wall on his own land to mark the same boundary, and it was irrelevant that a less costly structure such as a fence would have done the job equally well.

However, cost of cure damages will be recoverable only where it is reasonable to award such damages in the sense that the cost of cure is not out of all proportion to the benefit to be obtained (as in *Jacob & Youngs* v *Kent* (1921) 230 NY 239). In addition, no cost of cure damages will be awarded where either the rebuilding had not been completed, or, at the very least, it is not intended to carry out the rebuilding. This is because, unless this is the case, cost of cure will not be an actual loss needing to be compensated by a payment in damages. These limitations were confirmed by the House of Lords in *Ruxley Electronics*, although they can be traced back to *Radford* v *De Froberville* (reasonable on the facts to award cost of cure) and *Tito* v *Waddell (No. 2)* [1977] Ch 106 (the court was not convinced that the damages award would be used to cure the breach).

In *Ruxley Electronics and Construction Ltd* v *Forsyth* [1996] 1 AC 344, the defendant employed the plaintiff to construct a swimming pool in his garden. It was to be of a maximum depth of 7' 6". The finished pool was only 6' deep at the point where people dive in. However, at first instance it was found that the pool, as constructed, was safe for diving. The failure to meet the contractual specification could be remedied only by demolishing the existing pool and starting again, at a cost of £21,560. At first instance the judge found that there was no difference in value between the pool as specified and that actually built. He awarded £2,500 for lost amenity. The Court of Appeal awarded the full cost of curing the defect.

The House of Lords was unanimous in holding that, in the circumstances, the cost of cure was not recoverable, so that the Court of Appeal's decision was reversed and the original award for loss of amenity, which had not been challenged, was allowed to stand. Lord Lloyd referred to the judgment of Cardozo J in *Jacob & Youngs* v *Kent* in stating as a general principle that the cost of cure can be recovered only 'if it is reasonable for the plaintiff to insist on that course'. In assessing whether it was reasonable to allow the cost of cure it was appropriate to consider the personal preferences of the buyer in stipulating for a particular performance as this assisted in identifying the loss suffered. However, personal preferences 'cannot *per se* be determinative of what that loss is' (*per* Lord Jauncey).

The conclusion is that there is a line to be drawn between circumstances in which cure is reasonable and those in which it is not. In his judgment in *Ruxley Electronics* Lord Bridge gave an example, which was also referred to by Lord Jauncey. In the example, a house is to be built and the owner specifies that one of the lower courses of brick should be blue. The house as built conforms to the specification except in relation to the colour of this course of bricks. Yellow bricks have been used instead of blue. To conform to the requirements of the owner would involve knocking down the house and rebuilding, at great cost. This is an example where it would clearly be unreasonable to award cost of cure. Lord Jauncey contrasted this with the position where a building is constructed so defectively that it is of no use for its designed purpose; it would clearly be reasonable to award cost of cure in such a case. Of course, these examples are extremes and the majority of cases will fall somewhere in between.

The House of Lords has confirmed that it is also important to take into account the likelihood of the cure actually being effected, otherwise the cost of rebuilding is not a loss actually suffered.

In addition to these general principles, we know that cost of cure will be awarded only where such a remedy is appropriate to the liability assumed by the defendant. For example, if the obligation undertaken is a qualified obligation (reasonable care and skill), awarding cost of cure would amount to treating it as if it were a breach of warranty. In *Watts* v *Morrow* [1991] 1 WLR 1421, the purchasers of a house brought an action against a surveyor for breach of a contract to exercise care and skill in preparing a report on the house purchased. Defects were found which were not revealed by the defendant's report. The difference in value between what the plaintiffs paid and what the house would have been worth had the defects been known, was put at £15,000. The plaintiff paid nearly £34,000 to remedy the defects and sought the larger sum in damages for breach of contract. In the Court of Appeal, Ralph Gibson LJ (at 1436) said that to award damages for the cost of cure would amount to compensating the plaintiff for breach of a warranty by the defendant that the condition of the house was correctly described by the surveyor. No such warranty was given in a case such as this. Relying on the judgment of Denning LJ in *Philips* v *Ward* [1956] 1 WLR 471, Ralph Gibson LJ stated that compensation was limited to the amount which would 'put the plaintiff into as good a position as if the contract for the survey had been properly fulfilled'. Had the survey been properly carried out, either the plaintiff would not have bought at all (in which case there would have been no loss), or he would have bought at the lower value (so that the difference in value was the proper measure of the loss). Where no particular benefit to the claimant can be identified in the defendant's contractual undertakings, cost of cure will not be allowed if it exceeds the diminution in value.

13.2.3 Expectation loss speculative and uncertain

There can be no doubt that the measurement of expectation loss may be a speculative and uncertain process, especially in cases where it must be assessed by reference to difference in value and where the assumed value of the market price is unavailable as a guide. Nevertheless, as a general principle, damages for lost expectation may always be recovered, subject to the various limitations considered below (see 13.9). The fact that measurement of the loss is difficult or speculative will not prevent the court attempting such measurement and awarding damages accordingly. In *Simpson* v *London and North Western Railway Co.* (1876) 1 QBD 274, the plaintiff sent specimens for exhibition at a trade show by rail, clearly indicating the date by which they had to arrive. They arrived after that date, and the plaintiff claimed damages for loss of the profits he would have made had he been able to exhibit his specimens. He was entitled to succeed, despite the speculative nature of his loss.

The court will attempt to put some value on an expectation even when what is lost is no more than an opportunity to take the risk of making a profit, rather than a certain loss of a speculative profit. For example, in *Chaplin* v *Hicks* [1911] 2 KB 786, there was an agreement between the defendant, a theatrical manager, and the plaintiff that, if the plaintiff would attend for an interview, he would select 12 out of 50 interviewees for employment. He then failed, in breach of contract, to give the plaintiff a reasonable opportunity to attend. She was able to recover damages for that lost opportunity, although there was no certainty that she would have been successful. In those circumstances the loss was said to depend upon the chances of her succeeding at interview, which were quantifiable. The court said, 'where by contract a man has a right to belong to a limited class of competitors, he is possessed of something of value, and it is the duty of the jury to estimate the pecuniary value of that advantage if it is taken from him'.

In some cases, however, the estimation of the lost expectation may be so speculative that the courts will refuse to award damages on the standard basis, and will instead only compensate the claimant's out-of-pocket expenses in attempting to perform the contract. The classic example of this principle is the Australian case of *McRae* v *Commonwealth Disposals Commission* (1951) 84 CLR 377 (see also 9.2.1).

In *McRae*, the plaintiffs and defendants had contracted for the recovery of a shipwrecked oil tanker, said by the defendants to be lying at a specified place. The plaintiffs mounted an expedition to salvage the tanker, but no tanker could be found and it became apparent that none had ever existed. The plaintiffs claimed lost profit as the measure of their lost expectation resulting from the defendants' breach. The High Court of Australia considered that recovery of lost profit on the vessel would be too speculative, since no details had been given at the time of contracting about the size of the tanker, or whether it still held its cargo of oil, and it could not be known whether the salvage operation would have been successful. Instead, the court awarded the plaintiffs' reliance loss, that is, the wasted cost of mounting the salvage expedition. They also recovered the price they had paid under the contract (the restitutionary interest: see 14.4).

The distinction between *McRae* and *Chaplin* v *Hicks* is that in *Chaplin* v *Hicks* there was a real or tangible loss of a chance of obtaining the prize, while in *McRae* the plaintiffs could not demonstrate that any profit would have been made so that the loss was purely speculative. This distinction was confirmed by the Court of Appeal in *Allied Maples Group Ltd* v *Simmons & Simmons (a firm)* [1995] 4 All ER 907. The loss suffered by the plaintiff as a result of the defendant's breach depended on the hypothetical action of a third party, in that the plaintiff argued that if it had been properly advised by the defendant it would have had the opportunity of negotiating a better deal with target companies during an acquisition. The Court of Appeal held that the plaintiff was entitled to succeed in its action since it had established on the balance of probabilities that there was a 'substantial chance' of negotiating a better deal and not merely a speculative chance. The plaintiff did not need to establish that the negotiations would definitely have succeeded. This test was reaffirmed in *Bank of Credit and Commerce International SA (in liquidation)* v *Ali (Stigma Claims)* [1999] 4 All ER 83, in relation to loss of the chance of employment. This question, and the applicable test, is to be considered by the House of Lords (see *Bank of Credit and Commerce International SA (in liquidation)* v *Ali (Permission to Appeal)* (unreported), 4 May 2001 (CA)).

13.3   QUANTIFICATION OF LOSS: RELIANCE LOSS

As discussed at p. 375, reliance loss will arise where the claimant has expended money either in preparation for, or in partial performance of, the contract which is then wasted because of the breach. Damages which compensate for reliance loss are intended to compensate for this wasted expenditure.

In some circumstances the claimant may prefer to claim reliance loss rather than the expectation loss. Where expectation loss is too speculative to recover because it is impossible to say what the profit on the contract would have been, reliance loss will necessarily have to be claimed (see above at 13.2.3: *McRae* v *Commonwealth Disposals Commission* (1951) 84 CLR 377: reliance loss measure imposed by the court; *Anglia Television Ltd* v *Reed* [1972] 1 QB 60: reliance loss claimed because it was not possible to prove what the profits on the contract would have been). In *Anglia Television Ltd* v *Reed*, the plaintiff television company had been forced to abandon its project to make a film when the lead actor withdrew from the project in breach of contract. The company was able to recover for wasted expenditure, including expenditure incurred before the contract with the actor had been made. Pre-contractual expenditure which has been lost as a result of the breach will be recoverable as reliance loss provided that 'it was such as would reasonably be in the

contemplation of the parties as likely to be wasted if the contract was broken'
(see remoteness rule, at 13.9.2).

In general, it appears that the claimant can choose to claim reliance loss
subject to an important limitation. The essence of the limitation is that such
a claim must not result in the compensation of a loss which is not the result
of the defendant's breach. In other words, the claimant cannot claim damages
for reliance loss if this would amount to compensating him or her for having
made a 'bad bargain', because he or she would not even have recovered
expenses. To award reliance loss in these circumstances would amount to
putting the claimant in a better position than he or she would have been in
had the contract been properly performed. In the case of bad bargains, the
loss results from the claimant having made the contract rather than from its
breach by the defendant. Of course, this is just the situation where the
claimant would want to recover for wasted expenditure, and the courts will
therefore be extremely wary of such claims.

This difficulty is well illustrated by *C & P Haulage* v *Middleton* [1983] 1
WLR 1461. The plaintiff was entitled under a series of six-month contracts
to the use of a garage for the purposes of his business. He had spent some
money on equipping the garage for his needs, but under the contracts
the equipment installed became the property of the garage owner once the
plaintiff's use of the garage ceased. Ten weeks before the end of one of
the six-month contracts, the garage owner ordered the plaintiff out of the
garage in breach of contract. The local planning authority allowed the plaintiff
to use his own garage for more than ten weeks, with the result that he saved the
weekly rental on the garage. His profits were, therefore, greater than if the
contract had not been breached. He brought an action to recover the costs of
equipping the garage from which he had been ejected. The Court of Appeal
rejected that claim on the ground that the cost of the equipment would have
been lost had the contract been performed as agreed and lawfully terminated at
the end of a six-month period. The loss did not, therefore, result from the
breach but from the terms of the contract itself, and so was not to be
compensated. The plaintiff could recover only nominal damages for the breach.

Nevertheless, the Court of Appeal in *C & P Haulage* v *Middleton* did not
rule out the possibility of a claim for reliance loss succeeding simply because
it cannot be shown that the contract would have been profitable. The very
specific test of the recoverability of reliance loss must be whether the actual
loss which is claimed results from expenditure wasted as a result of the breach
where this expenditure would be recovered out of the income produced by
performance of the contract. Put in rather simplified terms, provided the
contract would have resulted in the claimant breaking even on the venture,
wasted expenditure is recoverable. It is irrelevant to such a claim that the
claimant would not have made a net profit. If the contract had been properly
performed and yet the claimant would not have broken even, reliance loss
claimed would have to be reduced by the amount of expenditure the claimant
would have failed to recover out of income produced by performance.

The burden of proof on this issue is quite complex. In *Dataliner Ltd* v
Vehicle Builders and Repairers Association (1995) *Independent*, 30 August, the

Court of Appeal held that the claimant had the burden of establishing on the balance of probabilities that, but for the defendant's breach, he would have recouped this expenditure. On the facts in *Dataliner*, this meant establishing that but for the defendant's breach in failing to promote a trade show, the plaintiff would have recouped his expenses in attending by obtaining sales at the trade show.

Where the nature of the breach makes it impossible for the claimant to establish that he or she would otherwise have recouped this expenditure, the burden then shifts to the defendant to establish that the claimant would not have recouped his or her expenditure irrespective of the breach. In *CCC Films (London) Ltd v Impact Quadrant Films Ltd* [1985] 1 QB 16, the contract was discharged by the defendant's breach, so that the plaintiff was deprived of the two films which, it was anticipated, would have generated sufficient profits to cover the plaintiff's costs. Therefore, as a result of the defendant's breach, the plaintiff was unable to prove that he would otherwise have recovered his expenditure.

This burden of proof, although complex, is sensible because the claimant will normally be in the better position to discharge the burden of establishing that its costs would have been recouped. However, where the defendant's breach makes this impossible, the burden should shift to the defendant to prove that the claimant would not have recovered.

13.4 QUANTIFICATION OF LOSS: AVOIDING DOUBLE COMPENSATION

In *Anglia Television Ltd v Reed* [1972] 1 QB 60, Lord Denning MR said that a claimant may elect whether to claim for loss of profits or for wasted expenditure, but that the claimant cannot claim for both. That statement, although capable of rational explanation, may be misleading. Lord Denning MR did not indicate whether he was speaking of gross or net profits. It is true that a claimant may not claim both the reliance loss of wasted expenditure and the gross profit expected under the contract, since the claimant would expect to recover expenditure out of such gross profit, and to award both would be double compensation of the reliance loss (*Cullinane v British 'Rema' Manufacturing Co. Ltd* [1954] 1 QB 292). But if it is advantageous to the claimant to divide the claim between expenditure on performance and the lost net profit, there seems to be no good reason why the claimant should not do so, since the net profit is calculated by deducting expenditure from the gross profit (*cf. Hydraulic Engineering Co. Ltd v McHaffie, Goslett & Co.* (1878) 4 QBD 670, where such a claim was allowed). To award only net profit and the expenditure wasted would involve no double compensation.

13.5 QUANTIFICATION OF LOSS: RESTITUTIONARY DAMAGES

It was suggested at the beginning of this Part that among the interests which may be protected by the law is the restitutionary interest. The modern law of

Damages for breach of contract

restitution is now firmly based in the notion of unjust enrichment (*Lipkin Gorman* v *Karpnale Ltd* [1991] 2 AC 548). In the general field of contracts, unjust enrichment will usually take the form of a benefit accruing to one party which for some reason may be regarded as 'belonging' to another, and the purpose of a restitutionary remedy would be to restore the benefit to its 'rightful owner'. Such cases are often referred to as instances of enrichment by subtraction from the claimant (P. Birks, *Introduction to the Law of Restitution*, Clarendon Press, 1989; G. McMeel, *The Modern Law of Restitution*, Blackstone Press, 2000). A classic example would be the rendering of some performance, in anticipation of a contract being made, only to have that expectation come to nothing because of a failure to agree terms. The recipient of the performance has received a benefit which must have cost the other party something to provide, and it would be unjust to allow the benefit to be retained without payment of some kind. Situations of this kind are considered in greater detail in Chapter 14 (14.4).

There may also be an enrichment, which in some circumstances might be considered unjust, where one party receives a benefit as a result of a wrong done to the other party, without there being any 'subtraction' from that party; and the question then posed is whether a restitutionary remedy (sometimes referred to as 'restitutionary damages') should be available in such a case.

The question was central to the decision of the Court of Appeal in *Surrey County Council* v *Bredero Homes Ltd* [1993] 1 WLR 1361. The Council sold land to the defendant property developer, who covenanted not to build more than 72 houses on it. Without seeking a variation of the covenant (for which it would certainly have had to pay), the developer built an additional five houses. The Council claimed damages based on its estimate of what the defendant would have had to pay as the 'price' for variation of the covenant.

Inevitably, there is some sympathy for the Council's case: the developer had deliberately breached the covenant in order to make a greater profit. On the other hand, the Council could not be shown to have suffered a loss. Thus, there was an enrichment of the defendant without there being any subtraction from the plaintiff in this case. Normal contract damages were not recoverable, because the plaintiff was already in the position it would have been in had the contract not been breached. The question was simply whether the deliberate breach of the contract should in some way be sanctioned by making the defendant disgorge a part of its profit. The Court of Appeal did not think it should. Case law rejected this possibility. For example, in *Tito* v *Waddell* *(No. 2)* [1977] Ch 106 at 332, Megarry V-C stated: 'The question is not one of making the defendant disgorge what he has saved by committing the wrong, but one of compensating the claimant.' The only previous case in which recovery had been permitted in similar circumstances (*Wrotham Park Estate Co. Ltd* v *Parkside Homes Ltd* [1974] 1 WLR 798) was approved but distinguished by Steyn LJ (on the basis that it concerned an interference with property rights). In *Wrotham Park Estate Co. Ltd* v *Parkside Homes Ltd*, in breach of a restrictive covenant in favour of an adjoining estate, the defendant had built houses on his land. The estate owners sought an injunction but were unsuccessful. However, they were awarded damages based on the profit which the defendant made from the breach of covenant on the basis that this related to the sum the estate owners might reasonably have required to relax the covenant. This decision might therefore be distinguished as an award of damages in lieu of an injunction, and this was the conclusion of Dillon and Rose LJJ in *Surrey* v *Bredero*. Therefore, if a claimant could have obtained specific performance or an injunction, and might have negotiated to release the defendant from such an order at a price, damages may clearly be awarded in lieu of the order (see 14.2 and 14.3). The problem in *Surrey* v *Bredero* was that the Council had not sought specific enforcement.

There were arguments of policy against an extension of the law to provide for a general right to restitutionary damages, such as the difficulty in defining which breaches of contract would allow a claimant to claim a part of the defendant's profits and which would not. Steyn LJ in *Surrey* v *Bredero* also considered that such damages would lead to 'greater uncertainty in the assessment of damages in commercial and consumer disputes' and would 'have a tendency to discourage economic activity in relevant situations'. There were also arguments of principle: the purpose of damages in contract is to compensate for losses suffered. Once the idea that the Council had suffered a loss by not being able to bargain for a 'price' in return for variation of the covenant had been rejected, there was no loss and no reason to award compensation.

It is not the case that damages are never awarded on the basis of a benefit to the defendant as opposed to a loss to the claimant, but the *Bredero Homes* case indicated a judicial reluctance to develop a new general principle of contractual damages from the existing instances. The few cases where such recovery is possible are explained by Dillon and Steyn LJJ as resting on wrongful interference with property rights (seemingly by analogy with tort cases of trespass, under which a person who uses land without permission must pay for that use, even if no harm has been done to the land: e.g., *Whitwham* v *Westminster Brymbo Coal and Coke Co.* [1896] 2 Ch 538). The existing exceptions are stated in *Chitty on Contracts*, 28th edn, Sweet & Maxwell, Vol. 1, at para. 27–018, to be situations where the claimant 'has a remedy in tort or in restitution or can enforce a fiduciary obligation, or has an interest in property used by the defendant without permission'.

However, it has been argued that a more general right to restitutionary damages could solve many of the existing dilemmas in the application of principles governing breach of contract. For example, it has been suggested (see Poole (1996) 59 MLR 272) that in cases where there is no difference in value but cost of cure damages would be disproportionate (cases of 'skimped performance'), a suitable remedy would be to require the defendant contractor (say) to disgorge his or her savings in costs through constructing the swimming pool at less than the required depth. This would send a more appropriate signal to the construction industry and achieve a better balance of the respective interests.

In its 1997 Report, 'Aggravated, Exemplary and Restitutionary Damages' (Law Com. No. 247, at paras 3.38–3.47), the Law Commission rejected suggestions advocating a legislative formulation for such restitutionary damages on the basis that this would 'freeze' the position. Instead, the Law Commission recommended that the availability of such damages should be left to common law development.

The question was discussed again in *Attorney-General v Blake* [2000] 3 WLR 625, and some common law development occurred, although the exact scope of this development is uncertain and appears very limited (see Hedley (2000) 4 Web JCL 1). The majority of the House of Lords considered that in 'exceptional circumstances', restitutionary principles could be used to enable one party to recover the profits made as a result of the other's breach of contract. Lord Nicholls put the position as follows (at 638):

> When, exceptionally, a just response to a breach of contract so requires, the court should be able to grant the discretionary remedy of requiring the defendant to account to the plaintiff for the benefits he has received from his breach of contract. In the same way as a plaintiff's interest in performance may make it just and equitable for the court to make an order for specific performance or grant an injunction, so the plaintiff's interest in performance may make it just and equitable that the defendant should retain no benefit from his breach of contract.

Blake had worked for the intelligence services but had become an agent for the Soviet Union. He had been tried and imprisoned for treason, but had escaped from prison to Moscow, where he had written his autobiography. This book had been published in England and (although by this time none of the material it contained was confidential) publication was in breach of a term of Blake's former employment contract that he would not divulge official information. The Attorney-General wanted to prevent payment of the royalties to Blake.

The facts of *Blake* were exceptional because of the nature of the wrong involved, and the majority considered that it justified an order that the Attorney-General was entitled to an account of these profits. Lord Nicholls expressly approved the reasoning in *Wrotham Park* and stated that 'in so far as the *Bredero* decision is inconsistent with the approach adopted in the *Wrotham Park* case, the latter approach is to be preferred'.

This still leaves open the question of precisely what will constitute an 'exceptional case'. The House of Lords laid down no detailed guidance and stated that 'no fixed rules can be prescribed' (*per* Lord Nicholls, at 639). The only real comments are the following statements by Lord Nicholls (at 639):

> The court will have regarded to all the circumstances, including the subject-matter of the contract, the purpose of the contractual provision which has been breached, the circumstances in which the breach occurred, the consequences of the breach and the circumstances in which relief is being sought.

This is not terribly helpful because it is far too general. Lord Nicholls added the following as a possible qualifying condition:

A useful general guide, although not exhaustive, is whether the plaintiff has a legitimate interest in preventing the defendant's profit-making activity and, hence, in depriving him of his profit.

Lord Nicholls examined the two instances which had been suggested by the Court of Appeal, namely 'skimped performance' (see above) and instances where the profit was made by the defendant doing the very thing he had contracted not to do. He considered that neither could be covered by the account of profits which had been permitted, and implied that the situations of skimped performance might be addressed in other ways and that the second possibility was far too wide because it extended to all negative stipulations. It therefore seems that the possibility of recovering restitutionary damages for skimped performance has been ruled out for the time being.

The factors which had been identified by Lord Woolf in the Court of Appeal (i.e., cynical and deliberate breach, breach enabled the defendant to enter into a more profitable contract elsewhere, defendant had put it out of his power to perform his contract with the claimant) were rejected as grounds for ordering an account of profits.

Thus, although *Blake* is an important decision in recognising the possibility of restitutionary damages (in the sense of an account of profits), the circumstances in which this remedy might operate are uncertain. The majority clearly considered the remedy's practical scope to be extremely limited. Only Lord Hobhouse warned against the potential consequences of this apparent recognition of non-compensatory damages for breach of contract if applied to commercial contracts, arguing that such a step would require 'very careful consideration before it is acceded to'. However, this is unlikely to deter the making of commercial claims including an account for profits.

13.6 CONSEQUENTIAL LOSS

The courts sometimes speak of the award of damages for 'consequential loss' resulting from the breach of the contract. The phrase has no very precise meaning, but it usually indicates loss which does not result directly from the breach but which is still an inevitable consequence of the breach. For example, in a contract for the sale of an animal feed hopper, if the ventilation of the hopper is defective there is a breach of the contract. The loss directly resulting is that the hopper is not worth as much as promised in the contract, and that loss may be compensated by an award of damages for the difference in value (assuming the hopper was not, or could not be, rejected: 7.5.2) or for cost of cure (13.2.2). Where, in addition, the livestock became ill and the herd had to be destroyed through eating animal feed which had become mouldy due to the defective ventilation on the hopper, there is a *consequential* loss of the value of the herd resulting from the breach. In such a case the difference in value or cost of cure may be minimal, but the consequential loss is considerably greater.

To describe the loss as consequential is, however, of little significance except to find a convenient label for a loss which purists do not regard as strictly belonging to either the expectation or the reliance categories. What must be remembered is that such loss raises particular questions of causation (did the loss actually result from the breach which occurred? See 13.9.1.1) and of remoteness of damage (was this consequence of the breach within the contemplation of the parties at the time of contracting, so that the defendant in promising to perform can be taken to have promised not to cause such loss? See 13.9.2).

13.7   TIME FOR ASSESSMENT OF LOSS

The basic rule is that damages are to be assessed at the time of breach, which usually occurs at the time when performance became due. For example, the buyer's damages for the seller's non-delivery in a contract for the sale of goods are to be assessed according to the market price for the goods (13.2.1.1) at the time when the goods ought to have been delivered (s. 51(3), SGA 1979). This rule is based on the obligation placed on the claimant to mitigate his or her loss (13.9.3), and assumes that he or she will do so by taking immediate action.

The basic rule is only a presumptive rule, however, and it is now clear that where it would be reasonable for the claimant to do something other than to take immediate steps to mitigate the loss, the court will postpone the time for assessment of damages until whatever date is more appropriate. In particular, the courts appear to be anxious to prevent rigid adherence to the breach-date assessment rule causing contracts to be abandoned which might, with a little patience on the part of the non-breaching party, have been saved. That is, the non-breaching party may be allowed time to seek confirmation that no performance will be forthcoming, or that defective performance will be cured, before being expected to mitigate the loss. In *Radford* v *De Froberville* [1977] 1 WLR 1262 (see 13.2.2), it was suggested that when at first it seems probable that the defendant will make good his default, damages will be assessed at the time when that probability ceases to exist, since the duty to take steps of mitigation arises at that point. In some circumstances it may be reasonable to take no action in mitigation right up to the time of trial. In *Wroth* v *Tyler* [1974] Ch 30, the defendants had repudiated a contract for the purchase of a house, and in the particular circumstances the plaintiffs could not reasonably have done anything to mitigate the loss by purchasing a different house. When damages were awarded in lieu of specific performance (14.2.4), they were assessed at the time of the hearing. Similarly, in *Johnson* v *Agnew* [1980] AC 367, the vendors agreed to sell a house and land to the purchaser, but the purchaser failed to complete the transaction on the day appointed. The vendors then obtained an order for specific performance, but it was not drawn up for some five months, by which time specific perform- ance had become impossible. The vendors sought discharge of the order for specific performance, and to recover damages in its place. The House of Lords found for the vendors, holding that damages were to be assessed at the date when specific performance became impossible. Lord Wilberforce said (at 401):

In cases where a breach of a contract for sale has occurred, and the innocent party reasonably continues to try to have the contract completed, it would to me appear more logical and just rather than tie him to the date of the original breach, to assess damages as at the date when (otherwise than by his default) the contract is lost.

In *Janred Properties Ltd v Ente Nazionale Italiano per il Turismo* [1989] 2 All ER 444, Nourse LJ suggested that Lord Wilberforce's words must be understood in the context of the special facts of the case, and should not be taken as a statement of general principle in respect of reasonable attempts to secure actual performance. There appears to be no good reason to urge such a limitation on his statement of principle.

Equally, in some cases it may be impossible at the time of performance for the non-breaching party to discover that a breach has occurred. For example, it is breach of a contract of sale of goods to deliver goods which are defective, but the breach may remain undetected if the defect does not immediately manifest itself (e.g., a car with a latent fault which will inevitably cause it to break down after 1,500 miles of driving). In such a case the damages will be assessed at the time when the breach could first reasonably have been discovered (*East Ham Corporation* v *Bernard Sunley & Sons Ltd* [1966] AC 406).

Where there is a breach by anticipatory repudiation (7.5.6), establishing the time for assessment of damages is more complex. Where the non-breaching party elects to affirm the contract despite the repudiation, damages fall to be assessed according to the principles discussed so far in this Part. There is no duty to mitigate the loss until the time for performance. Where, however, the non-breaching party accepts the repudiation, the breach-date assessment rule is subject to the crucial proviso that the duty to mitigate in such a case arises upon acceptance of the repudiation (7.5.6.2). Damages will then be assessed not at the time for performance stipulated in the contract, but at the time when the claimant could reasonably have arranged an alternative contract (*Garnac Grain Co. Inc.* v *H.M.F. Faure & Fairclough Ltd* [1968] AC 1130). Where the claimant, acting reasonably, ought to have arranged an alternative contract by a given date but had failed to do so, his delay was at his own risk: damages would be assessed according to the market price on the date the alternative contract ought to have been made (*Kaines (UK) Ltd* v *Osterreichische Warrenhandelsgesellschaft Austrowaren GmbH* [1993] 2 Lloyd's Rep 1).

13.8 EFFECT OF TAX ON QUANTIFICATION

Where the claim is for lost gross profit under a contract, the court must take into account the effect of tax liability before making its award. Where damages awarded in judicial proceedings for breach of contract are not subject to taxation, while profits earned through the agreed performance of the contract would have been, the latter liability for tax must be accounted for. The court must not award more than the net amount which the claimant would have been able to keep as a result of performance of the contract, after tax had been deducted from the gross income.

This principle is best demonstrated by the decision of the House of Lords in *British Transport Commission* v *Gourley* [1956] AC 185. The case involved an action in tort for loss of earnings resulting from personal injury, but the reasoning applies equally to actions for breach of contract. The plaintiff suffered gross loss of earnings of nearly £38,000, which, had he received it as income, would have been reduced by liability for tax to under £7,000. The court awarded only the lower sum, since damages for loss of earnings are not taxable while income is.

This rule does not apply to loss of a capital asset, since there is no general liability for tax on the acquisition of capital assets. Neither does it apply to many claims for lost profit, since damages for lost commercial profits are themselves taxable as income.

13.9   LIMITATIONS ON THE ABILITY TO OBTAIN COMPENSATION

13.9.1   Causation and contributory negligence

13.9.1.1   Causation   Damages will not be awarded to compensate loss which was not caused by the breach. We have already encountered an example of this principle in operation in the case of *C & P Haulage* v *Middleton* [1983] 1 WLR 1461 (13.3). The user of a garage claimed his wasted expenditure in equipping the garage when the garage owner wrongfully terminated his contract to use the premises. The Court of Appeal rejected the claim, because ten weeks later the owner could have rightfully terminated the contract, whereupon the equipment would in any case have become the property of the garage owner. The loss by wasted expenditure was not caused by the breach of contract, therefore, but by a term of the contract, which in this respect was inherently disadvantageous to the plaintiff. On the other hand, the fact that the contractual provision is inadequate to provide a perfect solution to a given problem does not deprive the non-breaching party of compensation sufficient to achieve the imperfect solution, provided that is some real benefit. In *Dean* v *Ainley* [1987] 1 WLR 1729, the purchaser of a house stipulated for repairs to be carried out to prevent leaks from a patio to a cellar below. The repairs were not carried out. It became apparent that had they been carried out, they would have excluded only 70 per cent of the water penetration, since 30 per cent was due to a problem which could not be prevented by the repairs provided for by the contract. The purchaser was nevertheless entitled to recover the cost of the work which should have been carried out.

In all cases the question whether the loss was caused by the breach will largely be a question of fact, on which it is difficult to give any guidance. In contract claims the breach must be shown to be the effective cause of the claimant's loss, and it is not sufficient that the breach merely provided the claimant with an opportunity to sustain losses (*Galoo Ltd* v *Bright Grahame*

Murray [1995] 1 All ER 16). In the majority of cases causation is not a difficult issue; greater difficulty arises from the question whether loss, which admittedly results from the breach, is too remote to be compensated (13.9.2).

However, causation may sometimes present difficulty when it appears that the loss was caused partly by the breach and partly by some other factor. The general rule is that where breach can be shown to be an actual cause of the loss, the fact that there is another contributing cause is irrelevant. The breach will entitle the non-breaching party to damages. For example, in *Wroth* v *Tyler* [1974] Ch 30 (13.7), the plaintiff's loss was caused partially by the defendant's breach of contract and partially by the fact that the plaintiff lacked the financial resources to take active steps to mitigate the loss. The loss was nevertheless recoverable. Similarly, in *County Ltd* v *Girozentrale Securities* [1996] 3 All ER 834, the Court of Appeal said that the trial judge had been wrong, having identified two contributing causes to the loss sustained, to choose which of them was the effective cause by enquiring which had been of 'greater efficacy' in causing the loss. That the breach of contract might have had a lesser role in causing the loss did not mean that it was not a cause for the purposes of the recovery of damages. It was sufficient in a claim in contract that the cause in question was *an* effective cause of the loss.

However, where one of the contributing causes of the loss was an adverse movement in the market, the House of Lords has ruled that the full amount of the loss is not necessarily to be regarded as having been caused by the breach: see *South Australia Asset Management Corporation* v *York Montague Ltd* [1997] AC 191, reversing the decision of the Court of Appeal *sub nom. Banque Bruxelles Lambert SA* v *Eagle Star Insurance Co. Ltd* [1995] QB 375. Reducing complex facts to simple form, mortgage companies were induced to lend money by a negligent overvaluation of the property which was being purchased and which was the security for the loan. The borrower defaulted, and the lender's position was made even worse by a very sharp decline in property values. The essential question was whether the extra loss resulting from the fall in property values could be said to have been caused by the breach, and to be recoverable as damages. The additional amounts at stake were sometimes several million pounds. The Court of Appeal said they were recoverable: but for the negligent valuation, the lender would not have lent the money at all, and it was entitled to be compensated for all the loss suffered, including that resulting from the fall in the market. However, the House of Lords disagreed. The most significant element in the reasoning was that Lord Hoffmann did not regard the essential issue as one of causation at all. The issue was the extent of liability, which in turn depended upon just what the defendant had undertaken to do. In these cases, the defendants had only undertaken to provide information, not to provide advice about the transactions contemplated. Their liability was therefore limited to the direct consequence of the information being wrong, which was that the lenders had inadequate security, but did not include the disastrous consequences of the fall in the market. At best, that was an indirect consequence of the information being wrong, and the law does not impose liability for such loss unless there are grounds of policy to show strong disapproval, as in fraud (compare with *Smith New Court Securities Ltd* v *Scrimgeour Vickers (Asset Management) Ltd* [1997] AC 254: damages for fraudulent misrepresentation could include subsequent loss in value of shares due to other causes on the basis that locked into the transaction by the fraud). The point of policy may be clear, but the reasoning is fragile. There is no response to the Court of Appeal's main contention that, but for the negligently inaccurate valuation, no loss would have been sustained because the lender would not have entered into the transaction at all, so that the defendant should be liable for the whole loss. In such cases it is not true to say that these were 'losses which would have occurred even if the information which he gave had been correct'. We must conclude that the House of Lords wished to limit liability for policy reasons and therefore restricted considerations of loss to the date of the transaction.

Where the act of a third party or parties is a factor contributing to the loss, in addition to the breach by the defendant, the question whether the act by the third party will excuse the breaching party from the obligation to pay damages is largely a question of whether the contract has been frustrated (see Chapter 8). The court is likely to be especially concerned to know whether the intervening act was so foreseeable that steps could have been taken to avoid it. For example, in *The Eugenia* [1964] 2 QB 226 (see 8.4.3 and 8.6.1), the charterers of a vessel breached their contract by taking the vessel into the Suez Canal at a time when it was a 'dangerous' zone. The effect of that breach was made many times worse by the act of a third party in closing the canal. Nevertheless, the charterers were not excused the obligation to pay compensation for their breach.

13.9.1.2 Contributory negligence Where the claimant is negligent and that negligence is a *novus actus*, it provides a complete defence because it breaks the chain of causation. For example, in *Beoco Ltd* v *Alfa Laval Co. Ltd* [1994] 4 All ER 464, the defendants supplied a defective machine. It was inadequately repaired. The plaintiffs put the machine back into service without carrying out tests, and it exploded, causing much more serious damage and a loss of production. The Court of Appeal held that although at one time the plaintiffs had a right of recovery for breach of contract against the defendants because of the original defect, any loss resulting from that breach was extinguished by the explosion which destroyed the machine and was not therefore attributable to the defendants.

However, where the claimant has been negligent but his or her negligence is not so great as to break the chain of causation, the position is quite complex. In the law of torts, where injury is caused by the negligence of the defendant and by the contributory negligence of the claimant, the damages payable by the defendant to compensate the claimant will be reduced proportionately to the amount by which the claimant's negligence contributed to the injury (Law Reform (Contributory Negligence) Act 1945). The question is whether the provisions of that Act apply equally to the law of contract. The difficulty is the definition of 'fault' in s. 4 of that Act. 'Fault' is defined as meaning 'negligence, breach of statutory duty or other act or omission which gives rise to a liability in tort or would, apart from this Act, give rise to the defence of contributory negligence'. In *AB Marintrans* v *Comet Shipping Co. Ltd, The Shinjitsu Maru No. 5* [1985] 1 WLR 1270, a ship was chartered for a voyage from New Zealand to West Africa. The cargo was badly stowed, and the ship had to return to port for the cargo to be restowed. The charterers made deductions from the hire payable and claimed further compensation to account for the delays and extra costs involved. The owners claimed that the loss was partly attributable to the fault of the charterers, and argued that compensation recoverable should be reduced proportionately in accordance with the terms of the 1945 Act. Neill LJ (sitting as a judge of the Commercial Court) held that on its true construction, the 1945 Act did not apply to actions for breach of contract. The wording of the Act was directed only to tortious liability and was not suitable to cover breaches of contractual duties of care. Although only a first instance judgment, this decision might be thought to be of considerable authority, but it was not followed in *Forsikringsaktieselskapet Vesta* v *Butcher* [1986] 2 All ER 488, which was itself affirmed by the Court of Appeal ([1989] AC 852), and it was also not followed at first instance in *Lipkin Gorman* v *Karpnale Ltd* [1987] 1 WLR 987.

In *Butcher*, the plaintiffs were insurers of a fish farm. They had effected reinsurance of 90 per cent of the risk through the defendant brokers. It was a condition of the contract of reinsurance that the farm be under a 24-hour watch. The owners of the farm informed the plaintiffs that it was impossible to comply with the condition, and the plaintiffs in turn informed the defendants. The defendants took no action, and the plaintiffs failed to follow up their first telephone call. The farm lost 100,000 fish, and the reinsurers denied liability because of the absence of a 24-hour watch. The plaintiffs brought an action against the defendants for breach of contract, alleging negligence. The defendants pleaded the plaintiffs' contributory negligence in failing to follow up the first telephone call as a defence to this claim.

Hobhouse J did not accept that the contributory negligence doctrine had no application to actions for breach of contract. He preferred to divide claims for breach of contract into three categories, and concluded that in at least one of these cases apportionment for contributory negligence was applicable. Many claims for breach of contract depend upon contractual terms imposing a strict standard of performance on the defendant (7.2.1). Hobhouse J stated that where the defendant has breached a term imposing a strict standard of performance (Category 1 case), there is no scope for the operation of the contributory negligence rule. This is because the defendant's negligence, if any, is irrelevant to his or her liability for breach of such a term, so that any negligence by the claimant should also be irrelevant.

The Law Commission's Working Paper No. 114, *Contributory Negligence as a Defence in Contract* (1990), provisionally recommended that contributory negligence should apply to Category 1 cases (breach of strict obligation by the defendant), but this would undoubtedly be an undesirable development in the law, since it would undermine the nature of strict liability. The Law Commission abandoned its proposal in its final Report, *Contributory Negligence as a Defence in Contract* (No. 219, 1993), and the existing law was robustly reaffirmed by Nourse LJ in *Barclays Bank plc* v *Fairclough Building Ltd* [1995] QB 214.

Where the contract term broken imposes only an obligation to exercise reasonable care and skill, which may be classed as a 'negligence standard' (*cf.* 7.2.1), but there is no duty of care existing independently of the contract (Category 2 cases), it is a matter of debate whether the claimant's damages can be apportioned to take account of his or her contributory negligence. Neill LJ appeared to treat *AB Marintrans* v *Comet Shipping Co. Ltd* as a case of this kind, and said the 1945 Act did not apply, although the claim may in fact have been within Category 1. In *De Meza* v *Apple* [1974] 1 Lloyd's Rep 508, at first instance it was stated that the 1945 Act did apply to such a case, but the matter was left open by the Court of Appeal.

Some contracts impose a duty to exercise reasonable care (qualified contractual obligation), the breach of which would in any case amount to an independent tort (Category 3 cases). *Vesta* v *Butcher* belonged to this category, and the judge found no difficulty in holding that the 1945 Act did apply to such a claim. As Neill LJ remarked in the *AB Marintrans* case, there is 'great force in the contention that the same rule should apply to claims whether they are based in contract or tort where the act complained of involves the breach of a duty of care'. In *Forsikringsaktieselskapet Vesta* v *Butcher* [1989] AC 852 in the Court of Appeal, Neill LJ accepted that this might be achieved under the analysis offered by Hobhouse J at first instance, although he continued to have doubts about whether the wording of s. 4 of the 1945 Act was capable of such an interpretation. This objection might be met by a very minor amendment of the 1945 Act to include a definition of negligence as contained in s. 1(1) of the UCTA 1977, which covers 'any obligation, arising from the express or implied terms of a contract, to take reasonable care or exercise reasonable skill in the performance of the contract'.

In its 1993 Report the Law Commission recommended that contributory negligence should apply in all cases of contractual negligence (i.e., where the defendant's breach of contract was a breach of a qualified contractual obligation: Categories 2 and 3). The Law Commission also recommended that the parties should be able to exclude apportionment for contributory negligence if they so wished. It was proposed that this could be achieved expressly or by implication, e.g., using an agreed damages clause would impliedly exclude apportionment for contributory negligence. However, it was proposed to implement these recommendations by means of a separate Bill relating to contributory negligence in contract claims, rather than by amendment to the wording of the 1945 Act. No progress has yet been made with this proposal, although the decision of the Court of Appeal in *Barclays Bank plc* v *Fairclough Building Ltd* [1995] QB 214 is in line with the recommendations contained in the 1993 Report in relation to breaches of strict contractual obligations. The position with regard to Category 3 cases seems reasonably settled. However, it will be interesting to see whether future courts will be prepared, pending legislation, to treat Category 2 and Category 3 cases in the same way and how they justify their actions under the 1945 Act.

13.9.2 Remoteness of damage

The defendant is not liable for all losses which result from his or her breach of contract. Some losses are too remote a consequence of the breach to be recoverable, in the sense that they are regarded as too improbable and therefore not within the scope of the contractual responsibility undertaken. The remoteness rule in contract is therefore designed to prevent the defendant having to compensate a loss attendant upon a risk which was not his or hers to bear. In *Hadley* v *Baxendale* (1854) 9 Ex 341 at 354, Alderson B said:

> Where two parties have made a contract which one of them has broken, the damages which the other party ought to receive in respect of such breach of contract should be such as may fairly and reasonably be considered either arising naturally, i.e., according to the usual course of things, from such breach, of contract itself, or such as may reasonably be supposed to have been in the contemplation of both parties, at the time they made the contract, as the probable result of the breach of it.

This rule, which is the test of the remoteness of damage, is intended to ensure that the defendant was aware when making the contract that he or she must avoid causing the kind of loss which occurred. The rule can be analysed in economic terms and is concerned with optimising the allocation of risks between the parties to the contract. If a party knows that he or she must bear the risk of losses occurring naturally ('in the usual course of things'), that party can take preventative action with the aim of avoiding that loss. In addition, if a party knows that he or she must bear a particular risk then that party can take out appropriate insurance cover for that risk. Uncertainty over allocation of risk often leads to duplicate insurance which is economically inefficient. The fact that the breaching party will also be responsible for unusual losses where knowledge of the relevant facts has been disclosed, encourages the parties to address the risks and to give relevant information.

The test of remoteness of damage established in *Hadley* v *Baxendale* is frequently described as consisting of two rules, or a single rule with two limbs (*Victoria Laundry (Windsor) Ltd* v *Newman Industries Ltd* [1949] 2 KB 528). Under the first limb, damages may be recovered for loss arising 'according to the usual course of things' from the breach of contract (i.e., normal loss). The intention of this rule is to identify those losses which *must inevitably* have been within the contemplation of the parties as likely to result in the event of breach of contract. The likelihood of such losses is a reasonable deduction from the nature of the contract, and the defendant cannot simply assert that he or she did not know of that risk to avoid having to compensate such loss. Knowledge of such losses is therefore imputed, and consequently the loss must have been within the reasonable contemplations of both parties.

Under the second limb, damages may also be recovered which result from special circumstances, provided the defendant knows of those circumstances (see, for example, *Seven Seas Properties Ltd* v *Al-Essa (No. 2)* [1993] 3 All ER 577: no actual knowledge of the sub-sale and so could not recover lost profit on that sub-sale). Only if there is knowledge of the relevant facts giving rise to the special damage can it be said that the loss was within the reasonable contemplations of *both* parties. In *Hadley* v *Baxendale*, Alderson B said (at 354–355):

> Now, if the special circumstances under which the contract was actually made were communicated by the plaintiffs to the defendants, and thus known to both parties, the damages resulting from the breach of such a contract, which they would reasonably contemplate, would be the amount of injury which would ordinarily follow from a breach of contract under these special circumstances. . . .

It is almost certain that Alderson B did not intend to establish two rules of remoteness of damage. Rather, there is a single test which requires greater knowledge on the part of the defendant as the degree of likelihood of the particular loss resulting from the breach diminishes (*The Heron II* [1969] 1 AC 350 at 385). Usual (or normal) loss and loss resulting from special circumstances (abnormal loss) are no more than the polar positions of that test, and there are intermediate positions where the loss is recoverable only if the defendant has some knowledge, but without requiring communication by the claimant of the precise loss at risk (*cf.* Neill LJ in *Lips Maritime Corporation* v *President of India* [1987] 1 All ER 957 at 968).

The operation of the contractual remoteness rule is well illustrated by the decision of the Court of Appeal in *Victoria Laundry (Windsor) Ltd* v *Newman Industries Ltd* [1949] 2 KB 528. The defendant engineering company contracted to sell a boiler to the plaintiff laundry company. The boiler was to be delivered on 5 June. The defendants were aware of the nature of the plaintiffs' business and had been informed by letter that the plaintiffs intended to put the boiler to immediate use. The boiler was delivered late. The plaintiffs sought damages for the profit they would have earned through the use of the boiler in their business during the period of the delay and for the profit on a number of highly lucrative Government contracts which they 'could and would have accepted'.

The plaintiffs were not entitled to recover for the loss of profit on the Government contracts since the defendants had no knowledge of these contracts or of their terms. However, that did not mean that the plaintiffs could not recover damages for general lost profit from the expansion of their business intended as a result of purchasing the boiler. Once the defendants knew that the boiler was intended for immediate use they should have been able to work out for themselves that late delivery was likely to lead to loss of business. These general profits are usually treated as normal loss, and it is submitted here that this is the correct conclusion. Every loss depends on some fact, but the fact in question is not a special fact but very common (see, e.g., *The Heron II* [1969] 1 AC 350: fall in market price of sugar due to delay in shipment was normal loss but on the basis that the shippers knew they were shipping sugar for sugar merchants to a port where there was a sugar market). Arguably, therefore, if a business purchases machinery or equipment, the natural conclusion is that it is intended to be used immediately on receipt. Another view can be adopted, namely that the loss of profits in this case was dependent on knowledge of the special fact that the plaintiffs intended to put the boiler to immediate use in their business and so amounted to abnormal loss. If this is the case, had the defendants not known the boiler was intended for immediate use, the Court might have found that even damages for loss of general profits were too remote.

Remoteness on the facts of *Hadley* v *Baxendale* turned on a special fact and the lack of knowledge of that special fact. The plaintiffs, mill owners in Gloucester, engaged the defendant carriers to take a mill shaft to Greenwich as a pattern for a new shaft. In breach of contract, delivery was delayed so that the stoppage at the mill was extended. The plaintiffs claimed damages for their loss of profit caused by the delay. It was held that this loss of profit was not recoverable because it was too remote a loss. The loss did not arise naturally because the plaintiffs might have had a spare shaft. The fact that the mill had a spare shaft would not be a natural inference from the circumstances, and on this basis that case can be distinguished from the *Victoria Laundry* loss of general profits. *Hadley* v *Baxendale* indicates the importance of informing the other party of circumstances which affect performance and the risk where full recovery is required.

It can be seen, therefore, that it is often difficult to divide losses into two simple categories of normal losses (those arising in the usual course of things) and abnormal losses (those arising out of special circumstances). As mentioned earlier, it might be preferable therefore to see the rule as a single rule whereby, as the likelihood of the loss occurring diminishes, the degree of knowledge on the part of the defendant must increase for the loss to be recoverable in damages. This was certainly the preferred approach of Evans LJ in *Kpohraror* v *Woolwich Building Society* [1996] 4 All ER 119 at 127–8, who considered that the question of remoteness should focus on the shared knowledge of the parties. He considered that if this approach were adopted it would be 'unnecessary to draw a clear line of demarcation' between the first and second limbs in *Hadley* v *Baxendale*.

The identification of 'normal loss' or loss arising naturally may remain pivotal, and it is significant that the approach evidenced in the case law is to restrict normal loss, thereby encouraging greater disclosure of the factual background (see, e.g., *Balfour Beatty Construction (Scotland) Ltd* v *Scottish Power plc* (1994) 71 BLR 20: actual knowledge of the construction process of continuous pour was required and could not be imputed). Much may depend on the context in which the question of 'normal loss' arises. It can arise in the context of construction of exemption clauses which exclude liability for 'indirect or consequential loss' and the determination of whether the particular loss falls within this definition. There is often a policy incentive to limit the scope of such a clause and hence find that the loss falls outside its scope. For example, in *Hotel Services Ltd* v *Hilton International Hotels (UK) Ltd* [2000] 1 All ER (Comm) 750, the question was whether such a clause exempted the supplier of defective electronic minibars from liability for the cost of their removal and the loss of profit on their use suffered by the hotel.

The Court of Appeal held that neither of these losses depended on special facts. Both losses were direct and natural consequences of the breach, because it was obvious that if the minibars were dangerous they would have to be removed and it was clear that when in use such minibars would generate a profit.

It remains to determine what must be the likelihood of a loss resulting from breach for the claimant not to have needed to spell the matter out to the defendant at the time of contracting. In *Victoria Laundry (Windsor) Ltd* v *Newman Industries Ltd*, Asquith LJ impliedly suggested that the test was the same as the test of foreseeability in the tort of negligence, since he said that the claimant may recover 'such part of the loss actually resulting as was at the time of the contract *reasonably foreseeable* as liable to result from the breach' (emphasis added). This formulation was called into question, however, by the House of Lords in *The Heron II*. Lord Reid said that the claimant may only recover 'loss arising naturally' or 'in the usual course of things' (echoing Alderson B in *Hadley* v *Baxendale*); and he or she may not recover loss which, although a real possibility, was likely to occur only 'in a small minority of cases'. He went on to stress that the test of remoteness in contract is stricter than the test of remoteness in tort, for the reason that the communication of special circumstances is irrelevant to many torts but in contract allows the defendant to modify his or her contract or performance according to the known risks of the contract. The remoteness test must therefore encourage such communication.

In *H. Parsons (Livestock) Ltd* v *Uttley Ingham & Co. Ltd* [1978] 1 QB 791, the Court of Appeal was faced with the task of making sense of the very vague tests of remoteness which were available. The contract was for the sale of an animal feed hopper. The ventilation of the hopper was defective, amounting to breach of the contract. The farmer's livestock became ill through eating animal feed which was mouldy because the ventilation was defective, so that the herd had to be destroyed. The particular illness and its consequence would have been considered an unlikely result of the breach in question at the time when the contract was made. The farmer claimed the loss of the value of the herd. The Court of Appeal concluded that the farmer could recover. However, the approaches of the majority (Scarman and Orr LJJ) and Lord Denning MR differed.

Lord Denning MR found the various formulations of the test of remoteness confusing and 'a sea of semantic exercises'. He accepted that sometimes the test is stricter than at others, but rather than distinguishing between contract and tort he distinguished between claims for economic loss (such as lost profit) and claims for physical loss (as in this case). In the case of physical loss, he considered that the less strict test of remoteness applied. Provided some physical injury might be envisaged, its precise nature was irrelevant.

Scarman LJ (with whom Orr LJ agreed) rejected Lord Denning's distinction between economic and physical loss, and ultimately decided that the remoteness tests in contract and tort were the same. This reasoning must be doubted, however, in view of Lord Reid's clear statement in *The Heron II* that the test in contract is stricter than the test in tort. Scarman and Orr LJJ decided the case on the basis that since the type of loss was within the parties' contemplations, the extent of it need not be.

Further confusion, or perhaps integration, of the contract and tort tests of remoteness occurred in *Brown* v *KMR Services Ltd* [1995] 4 All ER 598. The case arose out of the disastrous losses made by Lloyd's 'names' and was one of several actions brought against those who had encouraged (or not discouraged) such 'names' taking on excessive liabilities. The losses were, of course, financial not physical; they were of a type which it could readily be 'foreseen' might be incurred as a result of the breach of contract, but their extent went well beyond that which might in any year arise 'in the usual course of things'. The Court of Appeal said that such losses were recoverable, and dismissed this part of the appeal. Gatehouse J, the trial judge, had expressly relied upon *H. Parsons (Livestock) Ltd* v *Uttley Ingham & Co. Ltd* for application of the type-extent dichotomy in contract cases, but the Court of Appeal did not. Nevertheless, it lies at the heart of the reasoning. Stuart-Smith LJ cited with approval *Chitty on Contracts* (27th edn, 1994, Vol. 1, para. 26-023; now 28th edn, 1999, para. 27-042), to the effect that only the type of loss needs to be 'foreseeable', and Hobhouse LJ relied upon the following clear *dictum* of Sir Thomas Bingham MR in *Banque Bruxelles Lambert SA* v *Eagle Star Insurance Co. Ltd* [1995] 2 WLR 607 at 620 (now reversed on other grounds: see 13.9.1.1):

The test is whether, at the date of the contract or tort, damage of the kind for which the plaintiff claims compensation was a reasonably foreseeable consequence of the breach of contract or tortious conduct of which the plaintiff complains. If the kind of damages was reasonably foreseeable it is immaterial that the extent of the damage is not.

The difficulty with this reasoning is likely to be that in the case of financial loss it will not be easy to differentiate kinds of loss (see, e.g., *Victoria Laundry* v *Newman Industries*: general loss of profits and profits on specific contracts were not treated as part of a generic class of loss of profits), although counsel may seek to exploit this argument. For example, in *Kpohraror* v *Woolwich Building Society* [1996] 4 All ER 119, the question arose of the extent of liability for breach of a banking contract where the bank had wrongfully dishonoured the plaintiff's cheque. Counsel for the plaintiff sought to rely on *Brown* v *KMR Services Ltd* to establish that once it was known to the defendant that the account would be used in export-import transactions, the particular extent of financial loss in such transactions was of no concern and the full loss should be recoverable. The Court of Appeal baulked at such reasoning, perhaps not surprisingly since the cheque was for £4,550 while the total loss claimed was more than £57,000. In refusing to award such extensive compensation the Court clearly proceeded on the basis that knowledge of the particular risk, or that generic risks of a similar extent might arise, was necessary for such loss not to be too remote.

The law on remoteness of damage remains unclear, and may require an authoritative statement by the House of Lords to settle it. In favour of Lord

Reid's approach is the argument that contracts enable the parties to allocate risks between themselves, and that such allocation will work only if the parties have proper information about the risks involved. The strict remoteness test in contract would encourage the provision of such information, since unless the information is provided, the loss will not be recoverable. The approach advocated by Lord Denning has the advantage that it would prevent the result of the case depending upon the artificial classification of the claim as either contractual or tortious. It would also impose a stricter test on those claims which are inherently speculative (lost profits), while allowing a more lenient test for claims where the loss is more readily measured (physical loss). However, it begs another question, namely whether it is possible clearly to distinguish financial and physical loss.

13.9.3 Mitigation

The claimant is under a 'duty' to mitigate his or her loss in the sense that the claimant may not recover damages for losses which could have been avoided by taking reasonable steps. In *British Westinghouse Electric and Manufacturing Co. Ltd* v *Underground Electric Railways Co. of London Ltd* [1912] AC 673, Viscount Haldane LC said (at 689):

> The fundamental basis is . . . compensation for pecuniary loss naturally flowing from the breach; but this first principle is qualified by a second, which imposes on a plaintiff the duty of taking all reasonable steps to mitigate the loss consequent upon the breach, and debars him from claiming in respect of any part of the damage which is due to his neglect to take such steps . . . [T]his second principle does not impose on the plaintiff an obligation to take any step which a reasonable and prudent man would not ordinarily take in the course of his business.

The mitigation principle is central to many other aspects of the law relating to damages. For example, we have already seen how the market price rule for quantification of difference in value damages is based on an assumption of immediate mitigation of loss (13.2.1.1).

The duty to mitigate is limited by the fact that the claimant is only required to take *reasonable steps* to minimise his or her loss. Thus, loss will not be recoverable if it could be avoided by taking reasonable steps. The market price rule for quantifying difference in value damages embodies this limitation, in that where there is a market it is reasonable for the claimant to seek substitute performance via the market, and loss greater than that represented by the market price formula cannot be recovered.

What is reasonable will very largely depend upon the facts of individual cases. In *Pilkington* v *Wood* [1953] Ch 770, it was held that there was no duty to embark on 'a complicated and difficult piece of litigation' in order to attempt to remedy the consequences of the defendant's breach of contract. However, in some circumstances it may be reasonable to accept the performance offered by the defendant even when that performance amounts to breach of the original contract. If it remains the best substitute performance available then it will be unreasonable not to go to that source (*Payzu Ltd* v *Saunders* [1919] 2 KB 581). What is reasonable may also depend upon the circumstances of the claimant. In *Wroth* v *Tyler* [1974] Ch 30, the plaintiff was unable to mitigate because he lacked the financial resources to make a substitute purchase. His failure to mitigate was not unreasonable in the circumstances.

The claimant must not by unreasonable action on his or her part increase the loss resulting from the breach and reasonableness of the action is judged at the time when the need to take such action arises. However, if the claimant takes reasonable steps in an attempt to minimise the loss but these reasonable steps increase it, the claimant can recover for that increased loss. In *Banco de Portugal* v *Waterlow* [1932] AC 452, the defendant's breach resulted in large numbers of forged banknotes circulating in Portugal. The plaintiffs undertook to honour the face value of all such notes, although they were able to detect the forgeries. The plaintiffs' action increased the loss resulting from the breach, but was held to be reasonable because to have done otherwise would have caused a crisis of confidence in the paper currency.

Conversely, if the mitigating act has the effect of wiping out the loss resulting from the breach, the claimant will be entitled to only nominal damages for that breach. In the *British Westinghouse* case, the appellants were to supply electricity turbines to the respondents' specification. The turbines never met that specification, and after a time were replaced by turbines of a different manufacture. These turbines were much more efficient to run, so that the savings over the original turbines were such that the replacement machines paid for themselves in a short time. The respondents claimed damages for the cost of replacing the original turbines, but the House of Lords refused that claim. The respondents had rightly mitigated their loss, and had been so successful that most of the losses had been eliminated. The respondents were not entitled to anything more than the compensation already received for the period of time when the original turbines were running inefficiently. However, the rule that benefits from actions taken in mitigation of the loss must be set off against the loss, even to the point of eliminating it, applies only where there is a demonstrable link between the original breach, the mitigating steps, and the benefit accruing. A merely collateral benefit accruing as a result of a new contract entered into in an effort to mitigate would not be set off against loss claimed as a result of the breach (*Famosa Shipping Co. Ltd* v *Armada Bulk Carriers Ltd* [1994] 1 Lloyd's Rep 633).

The mitigation principle applies to breach by anticipatory repudiation (7.5.6) as it applies to ordinary breach, but in some instances the effect of its application is rather different. Where the non-breaching party accepts the repudiation as terminating the contract, loss sustained is subject to the mitigation principle from the moment of that acceptance. Thus, where the claimant misses an opportunity to mitigate, the loss will be assessed at the date of the missed opportunity rather than at the date for performance (*Kaines (UK) Ltd* v *Osterreichische Warrenhandelsgesellschaft Austrowaren*

GmbH [1993] 2 Lloyd's Rep 1). However, where the non-breaching party affirms the contract following an anticipatory breach, the rule that the loss must not be increased by taking unreasonable steps is reflected in the rule that a party may not affirm the contract and continue performance in the face of a repudiation unless he or she has a legitimate interest in so doing (7.5.6.1). Where the contract is affirmed, the obligation to take steps to reduce the loss which will be sustained when the time for performance comes, arises only at the time for performance. This rule is conceptually logical, in that the mitigation principle expects the claimant to take steps to reduce the loss resulting from breach. If the contract is affirmed there will be no breach until non-performance on the due date, and until then both breach and loss are only potential, so that there is no scope for the mitigation principle to apply. Nevertheless, this rule seems rather wasteful, since it allows the claimant to take no action even when it is clear that performance will not take place and it is also clear that some of the loss is avoidable. Avoiding such waste may be preferable to the conceptual purity of the existing rule (see also 7.5.6.1).

13.9.4 Non-pecuniary loss

13.9.4.1 General limitation As a general rule, damages cannot be re-covered in contract for losses which do not affect a pecuniary interest of the claimant, and to this extent contractual damages may under-compensate a claimant. For example, in addition to financial loss a claimant might suffer disappointment, hurt feelings or distress as a result of breach, but damages for such non-pecuniary losses are generally not recoverable in contract. This general rule stems from the House of Lords authority of *Addis* v *Gramophone Co. Ltd* [1909] AC 488, where it was held that it was not possible to recover damages for the distress caused by the nature of a dismissal from employment (i.e., caused by the *manner of the breach*), as opposed to directly caused by the breach itself.

It follows from this that damages for distress are recoverable where that distress is directly consequent on physical inconvenience caused by the breach. In *Perry* v *Sidney Phillips & Son* [1982] 1 WLR 1297, the Court of Appeal held that damages for distress caused by repairs necessitated following a negligent property survey were recoverable on the basis that this loss was foreseeable. This principle was also applied in *Watts* v *Morrow* [1991] 1 WLR 1421, to allow recovery for distress caused by the physical inconvenience of living in a property during repairs. This also appears to be the basis for recovery in *Hobbs* v *London & South Western Railway Co.* (1875) LR 10 QB 111, where the plaintiff and his family were taken to the wrong station by the railway company, necessitating a walk of several miles on a wet night. He recovered damages for that inconvenience. However, had the plaintiff mitigated his loss by hiring a cab (which, assuming one could be found, would have been reasonable), his expenditure would clearly have been recoverable. Thus, although the loss was in fact non-pecuniary, it might just as well have been very specifically quantifiable in financial terms. It is where the loss bears no relation to a financial loss that the general principle is that courts will not award such damages.

In addition to distress consequent on physical inconvenience, there are two other recognised instances where such damages may be recovered. These exceptions were recognised by the Court of Appeal in *Bliss* v *South East Thames Regional Health Authority* [1987] ICR 700, which also reinforced the authority of *Addis* v *Gramophone* as the central principle. Dillon LJ stated that there were exceptions 'where the contract which has been broken was itself a contract to provide peace of mind or freedom from distress: see *Jarvis* v *Swans Tours Ltd* [1973] QB 233 and *Heywood* v *Wellers* [1976] QB 466'.

In these exceptional situations, where the contract is specifically intended to confer a benefit other than a pecuniary gain, damages for disappointment can be justified on the basis of compensating for the loss of expectation of that benefit. Again, these exceptions can be seen as covering distress caused by the breach rather than the manner of the breach. For example, in *Jarvis* v *Swans Tours Ltd* [1973] QB 233, the plaintiff booked a winter holiday which the defendants promised in their brochure would be like a 'houseparty', with special entertainments and proper facilities for skiing. The skiing facilities were in fact inadequate, the entertainments were far from special, and in the second week the 'houseparty' consisted of the plaintiff alone. The Court of Appeal held that he was entitled to recover not merely the cost of the holiday, but a similar amount again as general damages for the disappointment suffered and the loss of the entertainment he had been promised in the brochure. Lord Denning MR pointed out that the plaintiff had entered the contract not merely to purchase the travel facilities and the board and lodging, but in order to enjoy himself, and he was entitled to compensation for the loss of that part of his expectation.

A similar rationale appears to underlie those cases where the court awards damages on the basis of cost of cure, even when the difference in value is small relative to that cost, in order to meet the claimant's particular expectation or 'consumer surplus' (*cf. Radford* v *De Froberville* [1977] 1 WLR 1262, at 13.2.2). In *Ruxley Electronics and Construction Ltd* v *Forsyth* [1996] 1 AC 344, Lord Mustill recognised the need to 'cater for those occasions where the value of the promise to the promisee exceeds the financial enhancement of his position which full performance will secure'. Lord Lloyd believed that in this case the owner's subjective appreciation of the benefit of the contract could be catered for by making a modest award (for loss of amenity) precisely in reliance on the *Jarvis* case (and see *Jackson* v *Horizon Holidays Ltd* [1975] 1 WLR 1468). Lord Lloyd stated that he could live with this conclusion as 'a further inroad on the rule in *Addis*', although he 'preferred to regard it as a logical application or adaptation of the existing exception to a new situation'. The argument was that Mr Forsyth had contracted for a swimming pool for reasons of pleasure, and in this sense his expectation had not been fulfilled. However, the amount awarded was relatively small, and significantly less than the cost of cure. In *Johnson* v *Gore Wood & Co. (a firm)* [2001] 2 WLR 72, the House of Lords commented on this aspect of the decision in *Ruxley Electronics* v *Forsyth*. Lord Bingham did not consider that it affected the general applicability of *Addis* on the facts before him (a claim for distress damages by a company shareholder in relation to the management of the company).

With the exception of these situations, the courts have refused to award damages for non-pecuniary loss and they have consistently refused to extend the recognised scope of these exceptions despite encouragement to do so from counsel in a number of cases. In *Watts* v *Morrow* [1991] 1 WLR 1421, the Court of Appeal, placing considerable reliance on the decision in *Hayes* v *James & Charles Dodd* (below), declined to give more than a very narrow scope to the category of contracts 'to provide peace of mind or freedom from distress', and refused to regard a surveyor as having any such contractual obligation towards the purchaser of a house for whom he had prepared a report on the basis that 'peace of mind' was not the subject-matter of such a contract. This position was confirmed in *Farley* v *Skinner (No. 2)* [2000] PNLR 441, [2000] EGCS 52, where a surveyor failed adequately to assess the impact of aircraft noise on a property. Damages for distress were not available for the reasons cited in *Watts* v *Morrow*, unless the distress was consequent on physical inconvenience (above), and there was no physical inconvenience on these facts. This decision is somewhat disappointing in itself given that the surveyor was actually instructed to report on this matter precisely because the house was close to the airport and this specific purpose might have been separated from the general nature of the surveying contract. Clarke LJ (dissenting in relation to the question of physical inconvenience) stated that 'I do not see that we are bound to hold that the question depends upon the object of the contract as a whole. I can, however, see that it is at least arguable that we are and it seems to me that this is an area of law which is ripe for consideration by the House of Lords or the Law Commission'. A further, more understandable example, set in a different context, is provided by *Alexander* v *Rolls Royce Motor Cars* [1996] RTR 95, where it was held that a contract for car repair was not a contract to provide freedom from worry and anxiety since this was not the subject-matter of the contract.

The reluctance to extend the scope of the exceptions may be explained in part by the difficulty of quantification of such losses, by the fear of unfounded claims (since such feelings are hard to prove or disprove), and by the fear of double compensation (in that disappointment, etc. may be adequately compensated by an award of damages for any pecuniary interest injured by the breach). In particular, the courts have consistently refused to allow recovery of damages for disappointment and distress in the context of commercial contracts. In *Hayes* v *James & Charles Dodd* [1990] 2 All ER 815, Staughton LJ was very robust in dismissing such a claim. In his view the reason for disallowing the claim was not merely a question of remoteness of damage, but one of policy. The policy was to limit recovery for mental distress to categories of contract in which it was a central obligation to provide peace of mind or to relieve a source of distress (see more recently *Johnson* v *Gore Wood & Co.* [2001] 2 WLR 72 confirming this position).

Although the decision in *Addis* v *Gramophone* was re-examined in *Johnson* v *Unisys Ltd* [2001] 2 WLR 1076 (see 13.9.4.2), the reconsideration was essentially focused on the question of whether, despite *Addis*, it is possible to claim damages for financial loss (i.e., loss of earnings/loss of employment prospects) based on the manner of a wrongful dismissal. Lord Steyn expressly stated that the question before the House of Lords was no wider than this, i.e. it was not an authority on the question of damages for anxiety and mental stress resulting from the manner of the dismissal, and it would be 'wrong to express any view on it'. Lord Millett admitted that these facts did not represent 'an appropriate occasion on which to revisit' *Addis*, but explained that there could be no damages for injured feelings in the context of breaches of commercial contracts on the basis that such loss would be too remote. He also explained the 'exceptional' cases, such as *Jarvis* v *Swans Tours Ltd* [1973] QB 233, not as exceptions but as falling outside the principle in *Addis* altogether, because the loss (distress and disappointment) in such cases is the direct result of the breach itself, rather than the manner of the breach.

Only Lord Hoffmann (with whose judgment Lord Bingham agreed) goes as far as to suggest that if the question had been concerned with non-pecuniary loss (damages for distress, damage to reputation) resulting from the dismissal, he would have been prepared to 'circumvent or overcome the obstacle of *Addis*'.

13.9.4.2 Damages for loss of reputation   Traditionally it has not been possible, as a general rule, to recover contractual damages for loss of reputation. Quite apart from the inevitable difficulties of causation, the problem is that such a loss could not be formulated in terms of financial interests. *Addis* v *Gramophone Co.* [1909] AC 488 has been interpreted as authority for the fact that a plaintiff wrongfully dismissed in a particularly abrupt way could not recover damages for injury to his reputation by the manner of his dismissal. Lord Loreburn went on to suggest that damages were not recoverable for the increased difficulty of obtaining alternative employment and this has also been interpreted as part of the *ratio* in the case, although in *Johnson* v *Unisys Ltd* [2001] UKHL 13, [2001] 2 WLR 1076 Lord Steyn regarded the headnote as 'arguably wrong' in so far as it states that it is never possible to sue for loss of employment prospects resulting from the manner of a dismissal. In a general sense, it is possible to distinguish this type of loss since it can be identified as financial loss and in general the law will allow damages for lost opportunity (13.1), and loss of this kind is sufficiently similar for it to be difficult to justify any distinction being made. It is on this question that there has been a radical re-evaluation in recent decisions.

Such damages for financial loss caused by difficulty in obtaining alternative employment (so-called 'stigma compensation') were awarded by the House of Lords in *Malik* v *Bank of Credit and Commerce International SA (in liquidation)* [1998] AC 20 (also known as *Re Mahmud* v *BCCI*; '*Mahmud's* case') on the basis that the employer in this case was in breach of an implied term not to conduct the business in a dishonest and corrupt way. Exceptionally, on the facts of this case, it was reasonably foreseeable that such a breach would prejudice the future employment prospects of these employees. This was seen as an extremely limited decision because the claim in *Malik* was not a claim for true distress damages and it was not based on wrongful dismissal. It was limited to a claim for continuing financial loss ('special damage') due to an inability to obtain alternative employment resulting from breach of this particular implied term in the operation of the business.

In *Johnson* v *Unisys Ltd*, the claimant tried to use the principle in *Malik* but to extend it to such damages resulting from the manner of a wrongful dismissal. The Court of Appeal ([1999] 1 All ER 854) had considered that such a claim was precluded by *Addis* and that *Malik* could not apply to a claim based on the manner of dismissal. There is also a legislative regime for compensation for unfair dismissal under which compensation is capped at a maximum amount. The claimant had been summarily dismissed from his employment and had obtained the statutory maximum for unfair dismissal from an employment tribunal (just under £11,700). He claimed that, as a result of the manner of the dismissal, he had suffered psychiatric illness and considerable distress and had been unable to obtain employment. Accordingly, he sought to recover £400,000 in lost earnings relying on the *Malik* argument, i.e. that by dismissing him in this way his employers had breached the implied term not to conduct themselves so as to damage the relationship of trust and confidence. Basing the argument on breach of an implied term of trust and confidence does seem illogical, in that in the context of dismissal there will inevitably be this breakdown in the relationship, although it may be easier to argue if this obligation is limited to the manner of actually carrying out the dismissal. The majority of the House of Lords considered that the implied term of trust and confidence was an obligation in a continuing relationship rather than one relating to the termination of that relationship (although Lord Steyn would have extended the obligation to all aspects of the relationship and Lord Hoffmann would have considered a different implied term in relation to termination corresponding with a duty to act fairly). However, the principal difficulty for the majority in accepting any common law right to such damages lay in the fact that Parliament had already put in place a statutory regime governing this compensation. Only Lord Steyn did not consider this a difficulty, but agreed with the majority that the claimant could not recover at common law by citing the difficulties of establishing that the loss was not too remote and had actually been caused by the manner of the dismissal rather than the fact of dismissal. It is unlikely, therefore, that an argument such as that in *Johnson* v *Unisys Ltd* will ever get very far because of these practical difficulties of proof (see *Bank of Credit and Commerce International SA (in liquidation)* v *Ali (Stigma Claims)* [1999] 4 All ER 83, for evidence of the difficulties of causation even where the claim falls within *Malik*).

The principle in *Malik* has therefore been confirmed as limited in its operation and it cannot currently apply to losses claimed to result from the manner of a wrongful dismissal; this is not, however, because of the decision in *Addis*, but because of the existing legislative regime and practical problems of proof. Nevertheless, there is clear evidence in *Johnson* v *Unisys Ltd* that the House of Lords wishes to see further movement away from *Addis*, on the basis that the employer-employee relationship has moved on in the past 90 years (see Lord Steyn's judgment), and Lord Hoffmann's suggestion of a willingness to get around *Addis* in the context of distress damages indicates that we may yet see further relaxation of the principle where the circumstances permit. Nevertheless, the House of Lords has also recently applied *Addis* in the context of a claim by company shareholders in *Johnson v Gore Wood & Co. (a firm)* [2001] 2 WLR 72, although even in this decision Lord Cooke (at 109) suggested that *Addis* may not be a permanent feature of English law.

There are a number of recognised instances of damage to an existing reputation. One such instance applies in the case of breach of a banking contract by the wrongful dishonouring of a cheque, which traditionally was limited to dishonouring the cheques of traders (*Wilson v United Counties Bank Ltd* [1920] AC 102). In *Kpohraror v Woolwich Building Society* [1996] 4 All ER 119, the Court of Appeal extended this to non-trader clients of banks on the basis that the exception existed to protect the reputation for creditworthiness of the client. A reputation for creditworthiness is 'as important for their personal transactions' for individuals as it is for traders, given the existence of central registers of credit ratings. Individuals might also suffer loss if their reputations were damaged by the wrongful dishonouring of cheques. Accordingly, in today's society, there was no good reason for limiting this recovery to traders.

Damages for loss of reputation may also be recoverable for breach of an advertising or publicity contract, where the main purpose of the contract is to promote and publicise. If the breach has the opposite effect, there is a failure of the main purpose of the contract. A good illustration of this is *Aerial Advertising Co. v Batchelors Peas Ltd (Manchester)* [1938] 2 All ER 788 (the 'one' contract law case that every law student seems to remember!) The plaintiffs were to advertise the defendants' peas by flying over towns trailing a banner reading 'Eat Batchelors' Peas'. In breach of contract, the pilot flew over the main square of Salford during the two minutes silence on Armistice Day. This caused great upset and the defendants' products were boycotted, leading to a fall in sales.

13.10 AGREED DAMAGES PROVISIONS

As in many other areas of contract law, the nineteenth-century view that contractual obligations were founded in the will of the parties resulted in the rule that the common law provisions as to the award of damages might be displaced by express agreement. The *prima facie* rule is that if the parties provide in their contract for the amount of damages to be paid upon breach, that term of the contract will be enforced to the exclusion of whatever might be the common law measure of damages. Such clauses are common in commercial contracts, especially to deal with delay in performance.

There are advantages for both parties in the use of such clauses. The non-breaching party is spared the effort and possible expense of proving his or her loss, together with the added complexities of remoteness and mitigation, so that a claim for compensation will be relatively straightforward. In addition, the party who must perform has clear notice of the extent of the risk upon non-performance. The existence of such contractually agreed damages should avoid much of the disruption to the continuing relationship between the parties and the associated costs of a dispute on quantum, so that such clauses are generally regarded as efficient and desirable.

The courts have nevertheless been unwilling to allow their unfettered use on the basis that there is a danger that where the damages payable are set too high, the clause will have a punitive effect, which would be contrary to the essential purpose of enforcement of contractual obligations (see p. 373). Further, there is a danger that disadvantageous terms as to damages might be forced by the stronger party on the other, rather than be freely negotiated.

The distinction between clauses which will be enforced and those which will not is expressed as a distinction between *liquidated damages clauses* (enforceable) and *penalty clauses* (unenforceable).

13.10.1   Liquidated damages clauses

The essence of a liquidated damages clause is that it should be a genuine attempt to pre-estimate the loss which will be suffered by breach (*Dunlop Pneumatic Tyre Co. Ltd* v *New Garage and Motor Co. Ltd* [1915] AC 79). Once that definition is established, however, it must be said that the identification of liquidated damages clauses is rather a process of elimination; that is, the clause will be enforced by the courts unless it falls foul of the rule against penalties (13.10.2). Once a clause is classified as a liquidated damages clause, the liquidated sum will be payable whether the actual loss is greater or smaller than this stipulated sum. In *Cellulose Acetate Silk Co. Ltd* v *Widnes Foundry (1925) Ltd* [1933] AC 20, the contract contained a term providing for damages for late performance to be paid 'by way of penalty' at a rate of £20 per week. The actual loss for a delay of 30 weeks was £5,850. The House of Lords held that despite the designation of this clause as a penalty, it was in fact a genuine pre-estimate of the likely loss resulting from delay and so was a liquidated damages clause. It therefore followed that the non-breaching party could recover only £600 (£20 × 30).

As this decision illustrates, one function of a liquidated damages clause may be to keep the compensation payable upon breach below the amount of the loss actually sustained. For the party who must perform, the advantage of knowing the precise extent of the risk of non-performance usually lies in knowing that the risk is limited. Thus, in *Cellulose Acetate Silk Co. Ltd* v *Widnes Foundry (1925) Ltd*, damages payable under the clause amounted to £600, while the actual loss was £5,850. Ironically, it was the non-breaching party who sought to avoid the clause on the ground that it was a 'penalty', a threat to compel him to perform, so that he could recover his actual loss.

Cases of this kind raise the question whether liquidated damages clauses are a class of exemption clause, subject to the panoply of controls now existing over such clauses (see generally 6.6). In *Suisse Atlantique Société d'Armement Maritime SA* v *NV Rotterdamsche Kolen Centrale* [1967] 1 AC 361 (6.5.3) it was suggested that such a clause was not a limitation clause, since it fixed the amount payable irrespective of loss, so that the sum would be payable even if the loss were less than the amount stipulated. A limitation clause simply puts a ceiling (or upper limit) on the loss recoverable, and if the loss is below that amount only the actual loss is recoverable. On the other hand, it would seem that a clause fixing damages at an amount below the lowest possible loss which can be envisaged at the time of contracting is a form of limitation clause. It may be that the area of overlap between limitation clauses and liquidated damages clauses requires further examination, and perhaps reform (see 13.10.4).

13.10.2 Penalties

A clause is a penalty if the sum fixed is not a genuine pre-estimate of the loss suffered in the event of breach but is designed as a threat to compel the other to perform by penalising him or her for non-performance. An example of a penalty is the retransfer clause in *Jobson* v *Johnson* [1989] 1 WLR 1026. The defendant had contracted to purchase shares in a football club on terms whereby, if he defaulted on payment of any instalment of the purchase price, he was required to retransfer the shares for £40,000. The defendant defaulted when he had paid £140,000 of the purchase price. The Court of Appeal held that the retransfer clause was not a genuine pre-estimate of the loss on breach but a penalty payable on breach. Until this time it had largely been assumed that classification of a term as a penalty resulted in the clause being wholly unenforceable, and the non-breaching party being left to recover unliquidated damages at common law to compensate for his or her actual loss. However, in *Jobson* v *Johnson*, the Court of Appeal held that the effect was for the court, in the exercise of its equitable jurisdiction against penalties, to enforce the penal clause only to an extent commensurate with the actual loss sustained by the non-breaching party, i.e. the penalty is unenforceable beyond the actual loss suffered (*per* Nicholls LJ at 1040). Of course, in many cases the distinction is of no relevance, for the quantification of damages payable would be the same in each case. But in *Jobson* v *Johnson* the Court of Appeal relied on the exact nature of this equitable jurisdiction to impose complex terms on the plaintiff's right to a remedy, involving an election between alternative modes of proceeding, which went way beyond the mere recovery of damages.

Clearly, if the actual loss is lower than the penalty amount, only the actual loss can be recovered because the penalty is invalid. It should follow that if the actual loss is greater than the penalty amount, the non-breaching party should be able to claim his or her higher actual loss.

In the context of consumer contracts (see 6.6.3), penalties may additionally be unenforceable as 'unfair' terms. Under the Unfair Terms in Consumer Contracts Regulations 1999 (SI 1999 No. 2083), sch. 2(1)(e), a term may be unfair where it has not been individually negotiated if it requires 'any consumer who fails to fulfil his obligation to pay a disproportionately high sum in compensation'.

13.10.3 Distinguishing liquidated damages and penalty clauses

The distinction between these clauses is a vital one. It is essentially a question of construction depending upon the parties' intentions judged in the light of all the circumstances at the time of the contract. However, some guidelines to assist in determining this intention were laid down by Lord Dunedin in *Dunlop Pneumatic Tyre Co. Ltd v New Garage and Motor Co. Ltd* [1915] AC 79. The continuing authority of these guidelines was endorsed by the Privy Council in *Philips Hong Kong Ltd v Attorney-General of Hong Kong* (1993) 61 BLR 49.

The clause will be a penalty if the sum payable is 'extravagant and unconscionable' by comparison with the greatest loss which might be caused by the breach. In many cases this rule will be simple to apply. In *Philips Hong Kong Ltd v Attorney-General of Hong Kong*, it was held that comparisons must be made in respect of reasonably likely eventualities, and it would not be adequate proof that a clause amounts to a penalty to show a serious disparity between amounts recoverable and loss actually sustained in wholly unlikely, hypothetical situations. Lord Woolf stressed that in a commercial contract, in the absence of blatant domination by one party over the other, the courts should not be as ready to conclude that a clause is penal. It would be very difficult to draft a clause which would never operate in a penal way, and it was more important to ensure certainty and the ability to rely on agreed damages clauses in the context of commercial contracts. This approach was followed recently in *Cenargo Ltd v Empresa Nacional Bazan de Construcciones Navales Militares SA* (unreported), 30 January 2001, in order to reach the conclusion that an agreed damages clause in a commercial contract was a liquidated damages clause.

One difficulty is to know whether the amount which the stipulated sum must not unconscionably exceed is the total loss to the non-breaching party, or the possibly lower sum of what would be recoverable as damages at common law. For example, the clause may provide for the recovery of damages which would otherwise be too remote (13.9.2). In *Robophone Facilities Ltd v Blank* [1966] 1 WLR 1423, Diplock LJ suggested that it would be wrong to allow the penalty clause rule to be used to prevent a claimant contracting to be compensated for his or her entire loss rather than merely that which would be recoverable under the common law rules. His suggestion seems to be eminently sensible in the case of loss not otherwise recoverable because it would be too remote, since the clause would in any case amount to notice of a special loss.

Where the breach consists of not paying a sum of money, and the amount payable under the clause upon breach is greater than the sum owed, the clause will be a penalty.

Where the contract provides for the same amount to be payable as damages in the event of several different types of breach, some of which may result in serious and others only trifling damage, it is presumed that the clause is a penalty. The rationale of this presumption is simply that it is unlikely that each type of breach will result in exactly the same degree of loss, so that the clause does not represent a genuine attempt to pre-estimate the loss. On this basis, the presumption may be rebutted by showing that in all the circumstances the amount payable was a genuine pre-estimate of the loss resulting from each type of breach.

Lastly, Lord Dunedin pointed out that the fact that the loss is difficult or impossible to pre-estimate does not of itself turn every liquidated damages clause into a penalty. In the *Dunlop* case itself, the contract contained a provision providing for a payment of £5 per tyre in 'liquidated damages' if any tyre was sold at below the list price. The House of Lords held that this was a liquidated damages clause despite the fact that precise quantification of Dunlop's loss in these circumstances would have been difficult and the £5 figure was only a rough and ready way of estimating it. The £5 figure was reasonable in the circumstances and represented 'the true bargain between the parties'.

One of the main values of liquidated damages clauses is that they enable a precise figure to be put on the risk of breach, and the court should intervene in such an agreement between the parties only where it appears one is taking unfair advantage of the other.

13.10.4 Critique of the scope of the penalty rule

Sometimes it seems that the distinction between liquidated damages and penalty clauses is merely used to justify the court's decision about whether a particular clause should be enforced, and does not enable the parties to predict whether an agreed damages clause will be enforceable. Equally, it may strike down a clause intended as an incentive to performance even when the clause has been freely negotiated between the parties. A better approach might be to follow the example of the UCTA 1977 (see generally 6.6.2), and to treat contracts differently according to whether they are freely negotiated or the clause has been imposed, by virtue of a standard form or the superior bargaining position of one of the parties. In the former case there seems no good reason to disallow a penalty clause, since it must be assumed that the party subject to its terms must have had good reason to agree to it. In the latter case, both penalty clauses and unreasonably low liquidated damages clauses might be disallowed.

There is some evidence of a willingness to adopt such an approach in the advice of the Privy Council in *Philips Hong Kong Ltd* v *Attorney-General of Hong Kong* (1993) 61 BLR 49, where Lord Woolf stressed the importance of not interfering with the freedom of parties to stipulate for themselves the damages recoverable upon breach, 'especially in commercial contracts'. On the other hand, he appeared to contemplate that courts should be more willing to interfere where the contract does not involve 'two parties who should be well capable of protecting their respective commercial interests'. Rather, where 'one of the parties . . . is able to dominate the other as to the choice of the terms of the contract', the courts should be more vigilant in ensuring that damages recoverable under a contract clause are not extravagant. Of course, in the context of consumer contracts, penalty clauses which have not been individually negotiated may be unenforceable as unfair terms essentially because of this imbalance in the parties' relationship (see above at 6.6.3 and 13.10.2).

It is also possible to criticise the fact that the penalty rule applies only where the sum specified as agreed damages is payable on breach. Therefore, if an agreed sum is penal in nature but payable on some event other than breach, it will remain payable (*Export Credit Guarantee Department* v *Universal Oil Products Co.* [1983] 1 WLR 399). This is unsatisfactory and leads to all sorts of fine distinctions in practice, e.g., *Alder* v *Moore* [1961] 2 QB 57 where the promise was interpreted as a promise to repay £500 if the defendant played football again, rather than a promise not to play with a £500 penalty if the promise was breached. This is little more than an exercise in semantics, although the outcome was that the penalty rule did not apply and the £500 had to be repaid.

This restriction is capable of causing particular difficulties in the context of minimum payment clauses in the event of termination of hire-purchase agreements. If the customer gives notice to terminate the agreement early, the contract may provide for the customer to make payment of a minimum sum as compensation for loss of the agreement. Since this is a non-breach event the penalty rule will not apply to this payment. However, if the customer defaulted on his or her payments under the agreement, the penalty rule would apply to this breach and render the minimum payment clause unenforceable. This was criticised in *Bridge* v *Campbell Discount Co. Ltd* [1962] AC 600 and was referred to as 'a paradox' by Harman LJ.

In its Working Paper (*Penalty Clauses and Forfeiture of Monies Paid*, WP No. 61, 1975) the Law Commission recommended the abolition of this arbitrary distinction so that the penalty rule 'should be applied wherever the object of the disputed contractual obligation is to secure the act or result which is the true purpose of the contract'. However, no action was taken on this recommendation, and the House of Lords in *Export Credit Guarantee Department* v *Universal Oil Products Co.* [1983] 1 WLR 399 confirmed the restriction on the application of the penalty rule to breaches of contractual obligations.

Schedule 2(1)(e) to the Unfair Terms in Consumer Contracts Regulations 1999 (SI 1999 No. 2083) provides that in consumer contracts a term may be unfair if it requires any consumer 'who *fails to fulfil his obligation* to pay a disproportionately high sum in compensation' (emphasis added). It therefore appears that the same restriction applies in the consumer context.

13.10.5   Deposits, prepayments and relief from forfeiture

Closely related to the rule against penalty clauses and the rules governing restitution of sums paid under contracts (14.4) are those rules which govern claims to recover various forms of advance payment made in respect of a contract. The law in this area, like the law relating to penalty clauses, is not always logically defensible, and the different rules for different categories of payment set out below would benefit from a thorough revision, and from integration with a revised set of rules on penalty clauses.

13.10.5.1   Deposits   Money paid in advance which is expressly designated as a deposit is not normally recoverable in the event of breach of the contract by the paying party even if the payee has not suffered any loss as a result of the breach. Authority for this rule is well established; in *Howe* v *Smith* (1884)

27 ChD 89, the element of penalty embodied in the rule was invoked as a desirable incentive to performance, 'an earnest to bind the bargain'. More recently, in *Damon Compania Naviera SA* v *Hapag-Lloyd International SA* [1985] 1 All ER 475, the Court of Appeal, confirming the rule, also held that if the deposit remained unpaid at the time of the breach, the non-breaching party was entitled to bring an action to recover payment.

Although the rule against recovery of deposits may be the equivalent to the enforcement of penalty clauses, in that the amount of the deposit may far exceed the actual loss to the party entitled to retain it, it had been thought (subject only to an *obiter* statement of Denning LJ in *Stockloser* v *Johnson* [1954] 1 QB 476 at 491) that the rule against penalties and the equitable jurisdiction to allow relief from forfeiture could not apply. The only exception appeared to be s. 49(2) of the Law of Property Act 1925, which provides that in contracts for the sale or exchange of interests in land the court may, if it thinks fit, order the repayment of any deposit. However, in *Workers Trust and Merchant Bank Ltd* v *Dojap Investments Ltd* [1993] AC 573, the Privy Council imposed an important limitation on the general principle. Lord Browne-Wilkinson accepted that a deposit is not normally recoverable because it is given in earnest of performance. Nevertheless, he went on to say that 'it is not possible for the parties to attach the incidents of a deposit to the payment of a sum of money unless such sum is reasonable as earnest money'. In the particular case, a deposit of 25 per cent had been demanded when the prevailing local rate was 10 per cent. The Privy Council advised that the deposit was unreasonable, and that the deposit should be repaid subject to a set-off for any loss actually sustained.

Apart from this limited instance of unreasonable deposits, the penalty rule does not therefore apply to deposits. The Law Commission's Working Paper No. 61 (13.10.4) recommended that it should do so.

13.10.5.2 Prepayments not expressed to be deposits Where part of the contract price has been paid in advance, without that payment being expressed to be in the nature of a deposit or subject to express forfeiture, the payment may be recovered upon termination of the contract, subject to any set-off there may be for performance rendered before the time of discharge (*Dies* v *British & International Mining & Finance Corporation Ltd* [1939] 1 KB 724 and *Rover International Ltd* v *Cannon Film Sales Ltd (No. 3)* [1989] 1 WLR 912). It is therefore important to be able to distinguish between deposits (above) and mere prepayments, although *Dies* v *British & International Mining & Finance Corporation Ltd* is also authority for the proposition that in the event of doubt the prepayment rule will prevail.

However, the prepayment may be completely consumed by performance in some instances, e.g., contracts for work and materials where the recipient of the advance payment is bound to incur costs in performing prior to completion. In both *Hyundai Heavy Industries Co.* v *Papadopolous* [1980] 1 WLR 1129 and *Stocznia Gdanska SA* v *Latvian Shipping* [1998] 1 WLR 574, concerning the construction of ships, the contractual obligations were held to include the design and construction of the ships as well as their delivery.

Since much of the design and construction work had been completed, it was possible to bring an action to recover a prepayment which had become due. (*cf.* discussion in Chapter 14, at 14.4.2). Much may therefore depend on the nature of the contract and the purpose behind the requirement for the making of prepayments.

13.10.5.3 Relief from forfeiture Except in the case of deposits (13.10.5.1), where breach results in the breaching party losing the benefit of all payments or rights under the contract in a manner which is disproportionate to the actual breach or the loss caused by it, the law may provide relief from forfeiture. That is, Draconian consequences provided for by the contract may be set aside. Such relief is closely related to the rule against penalties, although the technical requirements for its application are very different. In two instances relief from forfeiture is available upon a statutory basis; apart from these, there is an equitable jurisdiction in the court to provide relief from forfeiture in some circumstances, but the courts take a very restrictive view of their powers in this area. Consequently, there are considerable advantages in being able to characterise a clause as amounting to a penalty, rather than merely leading to forfeiture, since relief of some kind is then immediately available (*cf. Jobson* v *Johnson* [1989] 1 WLR 1026, 13.10.2).

(a)   Section 49(2) of the Law of Property Act 1925   Under s. 49(2) of the Law of Property Act 1925, which (by s. 49(3)) applies to sale or exchange of any interest in land:

> (2)   Where the court refuses to grant specific performance of a contract, or in any action for the return of a deposit, the court may, if it thinks fit, order the repayment of any deposit.

Courts have differed over the breadth of discretion afforded to them by this provision, but for an example of its application, in which the view taken was that repayment of the deposit should be ordered whenever that would be the fairest solution between the parties, see *Universal Corporation* v *Five Ways Properties Ltd* [1979] 1 All ER 552.

(b)   The Consumer Credit Act 1974   As an express piece of consumer protection legislation, the Consumer Credit Act 1974 contains specific provisions which are akin to measures for the relief from forfeiture, especially in relation to contract terms which purport to make the purchaser/debtor liable for all payments under the agreement in the event of early termination of the contract (e.g., s. 100(1) and (2)). This legislation applies only to 'regulated agreements', and detailed consideration of its application is beyond the scope of this book.

(c)   Relief from forfeiture in equity   Beyond the statutory provisions described above, there is a restricted equitable jurisdiction to relieve a defaulting party

from the consequences of a contract term which purports to entitle the other to treat payments (usually instalments) or other rights as having been forfeited by the defaulting party.

There appears to be no functional difference between a deposit (as described in 13.10.5.1) and an express clause allowing forfeiture of prepayments. However, it appears that the jurisdiction to relieve against forfeiture does not extend to deposits as such (although Lord Browne-Wilkinson in *Workers Trust* clearly indicates that it does apply to forfeiture of 'unreasonable deposits').

The modern foundation for the equitable jurisdiction is *Stockloser* v *Johnson* [1954] 1 QB 476. The Court of Appeal held that a clause providing for forfeiture of prepayments would not be enforced if it was penal, and if to enforce it would be oppressive and unconscionable. The relief provided will usually be the allowance of more time in which to make an overdue payment, although sometimes the repayment of sums paid may be ordered. Relief will not be granted if the primary object of the transaction would thereby be defeated (*Shiloh Spinners Ltd* v *Harding* [1973] AC 691 at 723). However, the House of Lords has subsequently ruled that the power to provide relief from forfeiture may be exercised only in relation to possessory or proprietary rights (*Scandinavian Trading Tanker Co. AB* v *Flota Petrolera Ecuatoriana* [1983] 2 All ER 763). The ruling leads to fine distinctions between types of contract where the commercial purpose of the contract and the real effect of the forfeiture clause are more or less identical (e.g., *Sport International Bussum BV* v *Inter-Footwear Ltd* [1984] 2 All ER 321: House of Lords refused relief in the case of a mere contractual licence to use trade-mark rights; *BICC plc* v *Burndy Corporation* [1985] 1 All ER 417: Court of Appeal allowed relief in the case of assignment of a patent right). Such fine distinctions are difficult to justify.

It seems that this restriction is part of a more general policy of limiting the scope of relief from forfeiture, largely for reasons of commercial certainty. The decision of the Privy Council in *Union Eagle Ltd* v *Golden Achievement Ltd* [1997] AC 514 provides a good illustration of this principle. Time was of the essence in relation to completion of the purchase of a flat, and there was a provision allowing for forfeiture of the deposit in the event of any failure to comply with the contract terms. The purchaser was ten minutes late in tendering the purchase price and sought relief against forfeiture in the form of an extension of the time for completion. The Privy Council refused this relief, citing the need for certainty. In essence it was being asked to relieve against the immediate right to terminate the contract for failure to comply with the essential time condition when it was important, for reasons of certainty, for the vendor to know whether he could resell the flat.

FOURTEEN

Remedies providing for specific relief and restitutionary remedies

This chapter is divided into two parts. The first part considers those equitable remedies which provide for specific relief. Specific relief is the general name for those remedies for breach of contract which compel actual performance rather than merely compensating for loss caused by breach. Compulsion of performance may take the form of a claim for an agreed sum (14.1), or a claim seeking specific performance (14.2), or a claim seeking an injunction (14.3).

The second part of the chapter contains a brief introduction to restitutionary remedies, namely recovery based on failure of consideration and *quantum meruit* (14.4). These are situations where one party has received a benefit at the expense of the other. This is sometimes referred to as 'unjust enrichment by subtraction'. The controversial question of the availability of restitutionary damages for breach of contract, which focuses on whether the claimant can obtain restitution of a gain made by the defendant (in excess of any loss made by the claimant) as a result of a breach of contract, was discussed at 13.5.

14.1 CLAIM FOR AN AGREED SUM

The most common form of claim for an agreed sum is a claim for the price. The purpose of the claim is to enforce the defendant's contractual obligation (his or her promise to pay). In rests on the fact that the claimant has performed his or her obligations, which gave rise to that obligation to make payment. It is therefore a claim in debt, rather than a claim for damages.

There are many advantages of such a claim, since the amount claimed is known from the beginning ('a liquidated sum'), so that many difficulties relating to actions for damages — notably, remoteness of damage (13.9.2) and mitigation (13.9.3) — are avoided. In a debt claim, the amount of the debt is the amount recovered. In addition, because the issues at trial are frequently uncomplicated, there is a streamlined procedure for claims for unpaid debts (i.e. summary judgment, CPR r. 24). In most cases the only difficulties, if there are any, are questions of fact and problems of enforcement. Questions of fact arise where the defence offered is that the obligation to pay has been discharged by a defective performance by the claimant (7.5.1). Enforcement problems arise where the defendant has not paid because he lacks the means to pay.

Greater difficulties occur where the party in breach will not allow the other to complete performance, which has the effect of preventing the latter bringing a claim for the price. The performing party will be confined to a claim for damages for his or her actual loss and will be subject to a duty to mitigate that loss.

14.1.1 Breach by anticipatory repudiation and a claim for the agreed sum

In *White & Carter (Councils) Ltd* v *McGregor* [1962] AC 413, before the appellants had commenced performance of the contract, the respondents had announced that they no longer wished to go ahead with it. The appellants nevertheless elected to affirm the contract (which they were held to be entitled to do: see 7.5.6.1 where the facts are given) and continued their performance, claiming thereby to be entitled to the price. On the facts of this case, they were able to perform without the need for the other party's cooperation, so that there was nothing to prevent them performing despite the respondents' protestations that it was pointless.

A majority of the House of Lords upheld the appellants' claim of the price, despite the absence of any attempt to minimise the loss (see 13.9.3). It therefore seems that, unlike the position in relation to a claim for un-liquidated damages, there is no obligation to mitigate in the case of an action for an agreed sum. This particular decision may have been justified on the ground either that in the particular circumstances mitigation was in any case impossible, or that the loss would have been very difficult to quantify as damages. Nevertheless, it raised the possibility that a party might be able to elect to continue performance without any substantive reason. If the performance remained unwanted by the other party then the cost of performance would be wasted. For this reason, the right to elect to affirm the contract is limited to those cases where the party wishing to affirm has a legitimate interest in so doing (7.5.6.1).

Where there is no legitimate interest in continuing to perform the contract rather than claiming damages (and assuming that the right to claim the price has not yet arisen because the necessary performance has not yet taken place), the non-breaching party will be forced to mitigate his or her loss and claim damages. For example, in *The Alaskan Trader* [1984] 1 All ER 129, the owners claimed that they could affirm and keep the vessel at the disposal of the charterers although the charterers had indicated that the vessel was not required. The judge held that this action was 'wholly unreasonable' so that the owners were not entitled to the payment of hire for the vessel during this period. In essence, the owners had to mitigate their loss because they did not have the necessary interest in continuing with performance. Thus mitigation may actually prevent a non-breaching party from performing and so having an entitlement to claim the agreed price. It seems, however, that mitigation could have no relevance where the claim for the price had already arisen.

14.1.2   Sale of goods

A particular problem may arise in the sale of goods when legal performance, which is constituted by the passing of property, is separated from the physical delivery of the goods, which may take place at a later date. This is because the SGA 1979, s. 49, provides that the seller can bring a claim for the price if the property in the goods has passed to the buyer. For example, A sells his cow 'Rose' to B for £500, promising to deliver her to B's farm five days later. Since this is a contract for the sale of specific goods, property passes immediately to B (s. 18, r. 1, SGA 1979), with the result that A has performed everything necessary to bring a claim for the price (s. 49(1), SGA 1979). If B informs A before the time for delivery that he no longer wishes to have Rose, it seems that A may still claim the price, obliging B to take on the responsibility of disposing of the cow. If B is a dealer then he may well be better able to dispose of her than A is, in which case this rule is justified. However, in a similar case in which A is a dealer and B is only a consumer, it makes little sense to leave disposal of the unwanted goods to the party less likely to be able to sell them without difficulty. Here again, the claim for the price appears to be inconsistent with the obligation for the claimant to mitigate the loss, which exists in the case of a claim for damages.

14.1.3   Non-payment — recovery of additional loss and interest

14.1.3.1   At common law   At common law, in the absence of a contractual provision fixing interest on a debt, the general rule is that interest is not payable on late payment of debts (*London, Chatham and Dover Railway Co.* v *South Eastern Railway Co.* [1893] 1 AC 429). The result is that, at common law, a debtor discharges his or her obligation by paying the amount owed even if that payment is made late. Although the Law Commission in its *Report on Interest* (Law Com. No. 88, 1978) had recommended a general right to statutory interest, Parliament had failed to take action to address this problem, and the House of Lords (in *President of India* v *La Pintada Cia Navegacion SA* [1985] AC 104), although considering that the existing law was unsatisfactory, had accepted that the matter was one for Parliament rather than the courts. (Although Parliament has now provided for a right to statutory interest, the common law position will still be relevant where, for some reason, the legislation does not apply, e.g., because the contract in question falls outside its scope.)

In practice the common law rule can be, and frequently is, avoided by expressly agreeing that interest will accrue if payment is made late. In *Minter*

(F.G.) v *Welsh Health Technical Services Organization* (1980) 13 BLR 1, the court was prepared to imply a term for the payment of interest into the agreement.

It may also be possible in some circumstances to recover damages for loss suffered where payment is made late. At common law the traditional position had been that the loss due to non-payment was simply the amount outstanding, making no allowance for consequential loss, so that it was not possible for the damages award to contain an element of damages covering loss due to late payment. However, in *Wadsworth* v *Lydall* [1981] 2 All ER 401 the Court of Appeal held that the unavailability of damages for non-payment of money applied only in the case of general damages. Where the claimant had actually communicated to the defendant at the time of contracting information about a specific loss, which would result from the non-payment of the particular debt, then damages would be available.

In *Wadsworth* v *Lydall*, the plaintiff was the vendor of land who intended to use £10,000, to be paid by the purchaser before a stipulated date, as down-payment on the acquisition of other land. The defendant purchaser was aware of this intention, but paid only £7,200 by the stipulated date, so that the plaintiff had to borrow the balance for the down-payment. The plaintiff sought as damages the interest payable on the sum borrowed to enable the down-payment to be made, and was held to be entitled to recover such damages. In this case it was vital that the plaintiff was claiming for a loss he had actually incurred by paying interest on the sum he had to borrow. He was not claiming interest on the amount unpaid by the defendant.

In *Lips Maritime Corporation* v *President of India, The Lips* [1988] AC 395, the House of Lords limited the no damages rule to non-recovery of 'general' damages or normal loss arising naturally, under the first limb in *Hadley* v *Baxendale* (1854) 9 Exch 341. This left open the possibility of recovering damages for loss suffered as 'special' damages; and the House of Lords in *President of India* v *La Pintada Cia Navegacion SA* [1985] AC 104, endorsing *Wadsworth* v *Lydall* as an application of this principle, acknowledged that such damages could be recovered where the creditor could establish that the non-payment had resulted in special damage within the second limb of the rule in *Hadley* v *Baxendale*, i.e. that the loss in question was within the reasonable contemplations of the parties because the debtor had actual knowledge of the special facts making this damage likely.

Thus, under the second limb in *Hadley* v *Baxendale* (13.9.2), unless the defendant knows or has reason to know that the claimant will suffer a particular loss by the non-payment of money, no such damages will be recoverable. 'Reason to know' may be inferred from the terms of the contract and the surrounding circumstances, including facts of which other people doing similar business may have been aware (*Lips Maritime Corporation* v *President of India* [1987] 1 All ER 957 at 968, reversed on other grounds *sub nom. President of India* v *Lips Maritime Corporation* [1988] AC 395).

14.1.3.2 Interest under statute For some time now the courts have had a statutory discretion to award interest on judgments in claims for an agreed sum. This discretion covers both interest on debts for which judgment has been given, and interest on sums paid before judgment but after the proceedings have commenced (s. 35A, Supreme Court Act 1981 or s. 69, County Courts Act 1984, as amended by the Administration of Justice Act 1982). However, until recently, there was no statutory provision dealing with the situation where the debtor paid late but before the commencement of proceedings, despite the fact that late payment of debts had become widespread and almost a matter of commercial practice. There is now a right to statutory interest arising under the Late Payment of Commercial Debts (Interest) Act 1998. This Act has made interest payable on late payment of debts arising from sale and supply contracts where both parties act 'in the course of a business'. (This phrase has caused difficulties in other contexts (see 6.6.2.4). The Act will have greater scope if the interpretation in *Stevenson* v *Rogers* [1999] 2 WLR 1064 is adopted.)

At present the Act only applies to contracts where one party is a small business supplier, defined as a business with 50 or fewer employees. Statutory interest will run from the contractual date for payment or, where there is no such date, 30 days after (whichever is the later of) either performance by the supplier or the giving of notice of the debt. Section 5 provides for the court to remit this statutory right to interest where the interest of justice so requires because of the conduct of the supplier.

Any contract term which purports to exclude or vary this statutory right to interest for late payment is unenforceable unless the contract provides a 'substantial remedy' for late payment. A contractual remedy is regarded as 'substantial' unless it is insufficient either as a compensation for late payment, or as a deterrent to late payment, or if allowing the contractual remedy to operate in place of the statutory remedy would not be 'fair or reasonable'. This is judged by considering factors similar to those in sch. 2 to the UCTA 1977, such as strength of bargaining positions, whether the term was imposed by one party to the detriment of the other and whether there was any inducement to agree to the term. In addition, in assessing the fairness and reasonableness of the alternative, the court is to consider 'the benefits of commercial certainty'. In order to prevent more complex attempts to avoid the 1998 Act, s. 14 also provides that any term purporting to postpone the date when the qualifying debt would be created (even if not contained in written terms of business) will be subject to the UCTA 1977 test of reasonableness (see 6.6.2.6).

The 1998 Act is an important measure, but its effectiveness will need to be judged in the light of the evidence on whether businesses feel able to enforce their statutory right to interest against large public companies or public authorities with whom they have a long-term business relationship.

14.2 SPECIFIC PERFORMANCE

An order of specific performance is a court order compelling actual performance of the substantive primary obligations under the contract (i.e., the obligations to perform rather than those merely to pay the price: see 14.1).

The court ensures compliance with its order by deterring non-compliance with threats of punitive measures against the person to whom the order is addressed. These measures include committal to prison for contempt of court, sequestration of property and fines.

At common law the only remedy for breach of contract was by way of damages to compensate loss caused. The Chancery Court made specific performance available, by way of exception. It remains an exceptional remedy even after the amalgamation of law and equity, in that damages are available as of right upon breach if loss can be proved, while the availability of specific performance is subject to a number of restrictions, including that damages be an inadequate remedy.

14.2.1 Inadequacy of damages

The principle whereby damages may compensate the non-breaching party's cost of obtaining substitute performance has already been explained (pp. 374–75). In such circumstances damages may be said to be an adequate remedy, and it is for this reason that in the ordinary run of cases specific performance will not be awarded. For example, in many contracts for the sale of goods, it is possible to purchase substitute goods in the market, and therefore damages will be an adequate remedy (*Société des Industries Metallurgiques SA* v *The Bronx Engineering Co. Ltd* [1975] 1 Lloyd's Rep 465). Nevertheless, it is open to a party to demonstrate that for some reason damages would be an inadequate remedy. It is impossible to list every eventuality allowing specific performance, but the more common situations in which the remedy will be available can be identified.

The most obvious case is where substitute performance is unavailable. Thus, where goods are in some way unique no substitute for them will satisfy the buyer, and in such circumstances specific performance is the better remedy (*cf.* s. 52, SGA 1979). The example of a valuable painting has already been suggested (p. 373); another example of a unique good might be a family heirloom. Perhaps more significantly, it appears that the courts may be willing to accept a commercial definition of the unavailability of substitute goods. In such circumstances rarity in absolute terms may not be necessary, if within the relevant time limits of the particular contract substitute performance cannot be obtained. In *Sky Petroleum Ltd* v *VIP Petroleum Ltd* [1974] 1 All ER 954, the plaintiff company had contracted to purchase all its requirements of petrol and diesel fuel from the defendant at fixed prices for a ten year period. During a time of worldwide shortages of petroleum products the defendant purported to terminate the contract, leaving the plaintiff with no realistic prospect of obtaining alternative supplies. The plaintiff sought an injunction to prevent termination of the contract. Goulding J accepted that by granting an injunction he would be specifically enforcing the contract, and that petrol and diesel fuel were not of themselves unique. Nevertheless, he granted the injunction because in the particular circumstances damages were an inadequate remedy, since 'for all practical purposes' substitute performance would not be available in time to prevent the plaintiff going out of business.

Contracts for the sale of land merit separate attention. As a matter of law all land is unique, so that specific performance is available upon breach of a contract for the sale of land. This rule does not vary according to the facts of each case, so that even a contract to purchase a modest house, of a kind which may be duplicated several times in a single development, is regarded as subject to the remedy of specific performance. The rule extends not only to purchasers of land, but also to vendors. It is not clear that the purchaser's obligations to pay the purchase price and to take conveyance of the land are in every case unique, and it seems likely that the extension of specific performance to claims brought by the vendor is based in the principle of mutuality (14.2.3.2).

Specific performance may also be granted when the quantification of damages is difficult for some reason (for example, it was accepted in *Co-operative Insurance Society Ltd* v *Argyll Stores (Holdings) Ltd* [1997] 2 WLR 898 that damages would not be adequate because of difficulties in quantifying the plaintiff's loss over the full term of the lease, although the House of Lords refused specific performance for other reasons (see 14.2.2)), and especially where there is a risk that the claimant will not be properly compensated if he or she is restricted to the remedy of damages. For this reason, it will also be available where for technical reasons damages would only be nominal, so that the sole means of protecting the claimant's expectation is by compelling performance. In *Beswick* v *Beswick* [1968] AC 58, a contract between uncle and nephew provided for the sale of the uncle's business to the nephew in return for payment of a pension to the uncle, which was to continue after the uncle's death as payment to his widow. After the uncle's death the nephew ceased making the payments. The widow was prevented from suing in her own right because of the application of the doctrine of privity (15.6.1, although compare with the position now under the Contracts (Rights of Third Parties) Act 1999). However, she could succeed in an action as administratrix of her husband's estate. The difficulty was that the estate had suffered no loss as a result of the breach of contract, since Mr Beswick's interest, and so the estate's, ceased upon his death. The widow had suffered the loss in her personal capacity. However, her husband's estate could not recover damages on behalf of someone who was not a party to the contract (discussed at 15.6.3). Nevertheless, the House of Lords was able to avoid the obvious injustice of allowing the nephew to break his promise by awarding specific performance of the contract.

In some circumstances, specific performance may even be awarded simply because the defendant is unlikely to be able to come up with the money to pay damages (*Evans Marshall & Co. Ltd* v *Bertola SA* [1973] 1 All ER 992).

14.2.2 Contracts not specifically enforceable

Certain contracts, which might otherwise satisfy the tests for the availability of specific performance, cannot be enforced in this way because of the nature of the obligations undertaken.

It was once thought that contracts requiring considerable supervision of performance would never qualify for specific performance. For example, in

Ryan v *Mutual Tontine Westminster Chambers Association* [1893] 1 Ch 116, a lease contained a term by which the landlords undertook to provide a resident porter in constant attendance at a block of flats. The person appointed had other employment, and so was often absent from the flats. The court refused specific performance of this term of the lease because it would require a level of constant supervision beyond that which the court was able to provide.

This principle has been invoked in a number of different situations, including building contracts. Nevertheless, it may well be that the unavailability of specific performance on this ground can always be avoided by careful drafting. The decision in *Ryan* v *Mutual Tontine Westminster Chambers Association* was effectively distinguished in the similar case of *Posner* v *Scott-Lewis* [1986] 3 All ER 513, on the ground that, in the particular circumstances, what was necessary to comply with the contract could easily be defined and did not require excessive supervision. Thus, it is not that the court lacks the power to ensure that the terms of the contract are properly being carried into effect; rather, the difficulty usually stems from the fact that the contract does not state sufficiently precisely the performance intended by the parties. Vagueness in an alleged contract does not necessarily make it unenforceable through the remedy of damages (but see 3.1.2), but it may prevent the court supervising its performance. Thus building contracts can be specifically enforced provided 'the particulars of the work are so far definitely ascertained that the Court can sufficiently see what is the exact nature of the work (*per* Romer LJ in *Wolverhampton Corporation* v *Emmons* [1901] 1 KB 515). Megarry J in *C.H. Giles & Co. Ltd.* v *Morris* [1972] 1 All ER 960, expressed dissatisfaction with any absolute restriction based on the difficulty of supervision, as much will clearly depend upon the drafting of the term in question and the background circumstances.

These surrounding circumstances appear to have been crucial in the decision of the House of Lords in *Co-operative Insurance Society Ltd* v *Argyll Stores (Holdings) Ltd* [1997] 2 WLR 898, to refuse specific performance because of difficulties in supervising compliance. The defendant, a supermarket chain, had a lease of a unit in the plaintiff's shopping centre. It was a term of the lease that the defendant covenanted to keep the premises open for retail trade during the usual hours of business. Although the lease was for a 35-year term, after less than six years the defendant closed the supermarket and moved out of the centre. The plaintiff sought specific performance of the covenant to compel the defendant to continue to operate the supermarket. Despite that fact that damages would clearly have been an inadequate remedy on the facts (14.2.1), the House of Lords refused to order specific performance on the basis that its effect would be to order the carrying on of an uneconomic business. Thus the loss which might then be suffered by the plaintiff, would be out of all proportion to the loss suffered due to the breach of the covenant. In addition, it would be difficult both to formulate a suitable order and to supervise it.

This decision may be compared with that in *Rainbow Estates Ltd* v *Tokenhold Ltd* [1998] 2 All ER 860, which concerned breach of a tenant's covenant to repair. This could be specifically enforceable because it would be an order to achieve a specified result (which was capable of supervision), rather than an order to carry on an activity (as in *Co-operative* v *Argyll*).

More clearly excepted from the scope of the remedy of specific performance are contracts of personal service. The reason is usually said to be that it would be an infringement of liberty to oblige one party to work personally for the other (*De Francesco* v *Barnum* (1890) 45 ChD 430: facts given at 4.6.1.2), or to have to employ a particular person. Thus, in *Page One Records Ltd* v *Britton* [1968] 1 WLR 157, 'The Troggs', a pop group, appointed the plaintiffs as their sole agent and manager for a period of five years. The contract contained an express negative covenant whereby the group agreed not to engage anyone else to act as their manager during that period. The judge refused to enforce this covenant by means of an injunction because such a group could not work at all without a manager, and so an injunction would have had the same effect as an order of specific performance of the management contract. It would be wrong to force the group to continue to employ as their manager and agent any person in whom they had lost confidence. (See also *Warren* v *Mendy* [1989] 1 WLR 853: no injunction to compel a boxer to use the exclusive services of a particular manager. The position in question necessitated mutual trust and confidence, and it would therefore be wrong to force the boxer to employ as a manager a person in whom he had lost confidence.) Thus, an injunction is unlikely to be issued to force one person to employ another where the relationship is based on the maintenance of confidence.

There is now a statutory provision preventing specific performance (or a compelling injunction) against an employee in relation to the general obligation to work for an employer (s. 236, Trade Union and Labour Relations (Consolidation) Act 1992). Although, in general, an injunction will not be issued to prevent a person working for any other person in breach of covenant, it may be granted where there is an express term of the contract preventing the party in question from taking up *specified* alternative employment. For example, in *Lumley* v *Wagner* (1852) 1 De GM & G 604, the plaintiff engaged the defendant to sing at his theatre, and the contract contained an express clause forbidding the defendant from singing anywhere else for the period of the contract. The defendant then entered another contract to sing elsewhere, and refused to perform under her contract with the plaintiff. Specific performance was not available to the plaintiff because the contract was for personal service, but the express negative covenant could be enforced by injunction thereby preventing the defendant from singing elsewhere. Similarly, in *Warner Brothers Pictures Incorporated* v *Nelson* [1937] 1 KB 209, an injunction was granted to prevent the film actress, Bette Davis, appearing in any film or stage production for anyone other than Warner Brothers without their consent. The important point was that Warner Brothers did not seek enforcement of a positive performance obligation, which would have been refused. Counsel for Miss Davis had argued that if the injunction was granted she would effectively be placed in the position of having to work for Warner Brothers or starve. The judge rejected this argument on the basis that Miss Davis could earn money in other ways.

There is an evident tension here between avoiding forcing a person to work for a particular employer and yet giving effect to stipulations in their contracts which were freely agreed to and which have significant financial implications for the employer. In practice, the courts are unlikely to apply the test in *Warner Bros* when considering whether to grant an injunction. It is far more likely that they will have regard to the circumstances in which the restraint is asked for, including matters such as the duration and likely effect on the reputation and general prospects of the person being restrained, as well as the commitment and ability to pay salary for the period covered by the injunction.

14.2.3   Equitable limits: discretion, mutuality and volunteers

14.2.3.1   Discretion   Specific performance is an equitable remedy. This fact is significant in that equitable remedies are not available as of right, unlike the common law remedy of damages. Even where the claimant can demonstrate that his or her claim satisfies the conditions of availability of the remedy outlined above, the court has a discretion to refuse specific performance. Of course, the discretion is not entirely arbitrary. The principles of equity have developed as rules very similar to those of the common law. The extent of the discretion is that if the claim falls within certain loosely defined categories, the court may refuse to award specific performance if in the circumstances it believes that would be the right thing to do. In the first place, the court may consider the conduct of the claimant, and if he or she has not behaved entirely properly it may refuse specific performance. The claimant's conduct need not amount to a legal wrong; mere 'trickery' will suffice to allow the court to consider exercise of the discretion (*Quadrant Visual Communications Ltd* v *Hutchinson Telephone (UK) Ltd* [1993] 1 BCLC 442). The remedy has also been refused where the plaintiff sought to take advantage of an obvious mistake by the defendant (*Webster* v *Cecil* (1861) 30 Beav 62; see 3.3.1.3), and where the plaintiff rushed the defendant into signing the contract before he had had a proper chance to consider its terms (*Walters* v *Morgan* (1861) 3 DF & J 718). This principle is sometimes colourfully stated in the terms that 'he who comes to equity must come with clean hands'. Any provision of the contract which purports to prevent the application of the 'clean hands' rule will be ineffective: the parties cannot fetter the discretion of the court (*Quadrant Visual Communications Ltd* v *Hutchinson Telephone (UK) Ltd*).

The remedy may also be refused where it would be unfair to the defendant. In *Shell UK Ltd* v *Lostock Garage Ltd* [1976] 1 WLR 1187, an injunction to prevent a tied garage from obtaining petrol from another supplier was refused on the ground that the plaintiff supplier had granted discounts to all garages in the area other than the defendant's, so that it had become impossible for the garage to compete. No injunction could therefore be granted while this discount scheme for other garages was in place. Evidence of unfairness may also be found in the undue hardship which would be caused to the defendant by specific performance (*Denne* v *Light* (1857) DM & G 774).

14.2.3.2 Mutuality Specific performance may also be refused where there is no mutuality of remedy between the parties. It was once thought that this requirement meant that specific performance would not be available if at the time of contracting it could not also have been available to the other party. There was little sense in such a strict rule, and there were a number of exceptions to it.

The rule was subsequently clarified by the Court of Appeal in *Price v Strange* [1978] Ch 337. The defendant promised to grant a lease to the plaintiff in return for the plaintiff's promise to do some internal and external repairs. The plaintiff's promise could not be specifically enforced. By the time of the trial the internal repairs had been completed, and the plaintiff had wrongfully been prevented from doing the external repairs by the defendant (who had carried them out herself). The court considered that the crucial time at which mutuality must be tested is the time of the trial. At that point the claimant must have performed all of his or her obligations, or these obligations must themselves be capable of specific performance, or non-performance of those obligations must be adequately compensatable by an award of damages (14.2.1). The purpose of the rule is to protect a defendant from the risk of being obliged to perform the actual contractual undertakings only to find that he or she will be inadequately compensated for the claimant's own non-performance. As such, it may be no more than a particular application of the undue hardship principle. In *Price v Strange*, the plaintiff's contractual undertakings were not capable of specific performance, but by the time of the trial they had all been performed, so that there was no risk of hardship to the defendant in granting specific performance.

14.2.3.3 Volunteers It is a general principle of equity that it will not 'assist a volunteer'. That is, equitable rules and remedies will not be applied in the case of a person who has not given real consideration for a promise. Thus, a promise which is binding under the common law because it was made under seal (4.1), or which was given for a nominal and symbolic consideration such as a peppercorn (4.3.2.1), cannot be specifically enforced (*Re Parkin* [1892] 3 Ch 510).

Under the Contracts (Rights of Third Parties) Act 1999, a third party who satisfies the test of enforceability will be able to enforce a contractual term even where he or she has not provided any consideration to support it, assuming that the promise is supported by consideration provided by someone (probably the promisee) so that it is not a gratuitous promise. The third party will have any remedy that 'would have been available to him in an action for breach of the contract if he had been a party to the contract' (s. 1(5)). This would, in principle, include the remedy of specific performance, although the third party would technically be a volunteer in equity.

14.2.4 Damages in lieu of specific performance

By s. 50 of the Supreme Court Act 1981, the High Court is empowered to award damages in lieu of specific performance. In the majority of cases the claimant will be unlikely to invite the court to exercise its power, since it is possible to claim damages and specific performance at the same time (s. 49, Supreme Court Act 1981). However, damages in lieu of specific performance may be awarded in circumstances in which common law damages would not be, although instances are likely to be rare. Where such damages are awarded they are to be assessed in the same way as common law damages for breach of contract (*Johnson* v *Agnew* [1980] AC 367).

14.3 INJUNCTION

An injunction is a court order restraining the defendant from a specified activity. Its use extends far beyond the law of contract, but in this context it may be used to prevent the breach of a negative stipulation in the contract. The example given earlier of such a stipulation was a promise in the form of a contract not to make loud noises during the period when the promisee was revising for an exam (p. 375), and see also restraint of trade provisions (12.7). Such promises may be enforced by means of an injunction.

The requirement that damages be shown to be inadequate before specific relief will be granted does not apply strictly to ordinary injunctions. Nevertheless, the courts will not in most circumstances allow the claimant to exploit this difference to achieve by injunction what cannot be achieved by specific performance. We have already seen how this principle applies in the case of contracts of employment (14.2.2). In other contracts the courts will be unwilling to enforce by injunction an express term which does no more than broadly prohibit breach of the positive stipulations in the contract, if the contract would not otherwise qualify for specific performance. Thus, injunctions are limited to specific restraints.

Normally, the activity to be restrained will be stipulated expressly in the contract, and the courts will be unwilling to imply a negative stipulation from the positive terms of the agreement. Such implication will occur, however, where the circumstances justify it. For example, where an exclusive dealing agreement is found not to be in restraint of trade (12.7.7), the court may imply a negative term preventing conduct which is inconsistent with the purpose of such a contract (*Evans Marshall & Co.* v *Bertola SA* [1973] 1 All ER 992). Nevertheless, it is usual for such contracts to contain explicit negative stipulations.

Prohibitory injunctions are granted to prevent future breach of contract. However, if the claimant wishes to compel the defendant to remedy an injury caused by a breach which has already occurred, he or she must obtain a mandatory injunction. The effect of such an injunction is to compel the defendant to undo work which has been done in breach of a negative stipulation in the contract. For example, a mandatory injunction might be granted to compel the defendant to cut down trees which had been planted in breach of a covenant not to restrict the plaintiff's view (*cf. Wakeham* v *Wood* (1982) 43 P & CR 40). Mandatory injunctions are subject to the same rules as specific performance. Damages must be an inadequate remedy, and grant of the injunction must not cause undue hardship to the defendant. This latter requirement may be waived where the breach was deliberately and knowingly committed (*Wakeham* v *Wood*).

14. 4   RESTITUTION

14.4.1   Introduction

It remains to consider two remedies which do not strictly fall within the scope of enforcement of the contractual obligations. Restitutionary remedies do not provide a response to one party's failure to satisfy the other party's expectation under the contract. Rather, they seek to restore money paid or the value of a benefit conferred in circumstances in which no contract exists, or in which there is no longer any obligation to perform under an admitted contract. Thus, their availability is not solely dependent upon the existence of a breach of contract, although where there has been breach the non-breaching party may have to decide whether a claim for his or her expectation loss or a restitutionary remedy would provide a better level of compensation. It should be noted that the law of restitution covers a much broader field than just the fringes of the law of contract, and in its entirety is a field of study all of its own. (For a detailed treatment, see G. McMeel, *The Modern Law of Restitution*, Blackstone Press, 2000.)

14.4.2   Total failure of consideration

A party may recover money paid in anticipation of a contractual performance which the other party has failed to provide where there has been a total failure of consideration, even in the absence of breach. Performance may be impossible because the contract has been frustrated (Chapter 8), or because unknown to the parties the subject-matter of the contract had been destroyed before the time of contracting (9.2.1). In each case the promisee may recover money paid in advance despite the fact that the failure of performance does not amount to breach. Indeed, most claims for total failure of consideration do not arise out of breach by the other party.

In the event of breach, the normal reaction will be to claim damages for lost expectation, but the restitutionary remedy is available as an alternative (see 14.4.4). Special rules apply where there is no performance because the contract is illegal (see 12.6). The special rules apply, however, only between the parties to the agreement which is tainted with illegality. In *Lipkin Gorman* v *Karpnale Ltd* [1991] 2 AC 548, the House of Lords had to deal with a claim to recover money stolen from the plaintiffs and then paid to the defendants in good faith but under a contract which was void under s. 18 of the Gaming Act 1845 (see 12.3.1). In restating the modern law of restitution, Lords Goff and Templeman agreed that the essential question was whether the defendants had been unjustly enriched. That in turn depended upon whether, irrespective of their good faith in receiving the money, the defendants had given good consideration for it. It was held that they could not have given valuable consideration, because the contract was void. The mere fact of honouring gaming debts did not amount to providing consideration; as a matter of law it was no more than a gift from the gambling club to the client. Consequently, the unjust enrichment was established, and the restitutionary claim succeeded, subject only to the defence of change of position, recognised as a general defence to restitutionary claims by the House of Lords in this case.

Similar reasoning has been applied to interest rate swap transactions which were void because they were *ultra vires* the local authorities involved (see *South Tyneside Metropolitan Borough Council* v *Svenska International plc* [1995] 1 All ER 545). The courts have considered there to be no consideration in such cases (see *Westdeutsche Landesbank Girozentrale* v *Islington BC* [1994] 4 All ER 890 at 924, and *Kleinwort Benson Ltd* v *Birmingham CC* [1997] QB 380 at 386–7), although this must be so simply on the basis that these contracts are void.

Although such contracts are void, if the payment of money was made under a mistake of law (i.e., a mistaken belief that the contract is valid), as a result of the decision of the House of Lords in *Kleinwort Benson Ltd* v *Lincoln CC* [1998] 4 All ER 513, such payments may be recovered. It was held that it made no difference that the contract had been performed by the parties. Thus, in instances of payments made under a void contract as a result of a mistake of law, the sums in question can be recovered even where there is no total (or partial) failure of consideration. The basis of the total failure of consideration rule is that the contract in question should be valid. (For further discussion of recovery in instances of mistakes of law, see *Nurdin and Peacock plc* v *D.B. Ramsden and Co. Ltd* [1999] 1 WLR 1249).

Relationship to consideration as 'promise'   It will be recalled that in relation to the formation of contracts 'consideration' was described as constituted not merely by an exchange of performances, but also by an exchange of promises. It might be thought, therefore, that where it is possible to show agreement there can never be a failure of consideration. However, where 'consideration' is used in the technical sense of giving rise to a restitutionary remedy upon total failure, it must be understood as referring to *performance* of whatever was promised in the agreement. In *Fibrosa SA* v *Fairbairn Lawson Combe Barbour Ltd* [1943] AC 32 (see 8.8.1), Viscount Simon LC explained (at 48):

> [I]n the law relating to the formation of contract, the promise to do a thing may often be the consideration; but, when one is considering the law of failure of consideration and of the quasi-contractual right to recover money on that ground, it is, generally speaking, not the promise which is referred to as the consideration, but the performance of the promise. The money was paid to secure performance and, if performance fails, the inducement which brought about the payment is not fulfilled.
>
> If this were not so, there could never be any recovery of money, for failure of consideration, by the payer of the money in return for a promise of future performance.

This standard explanation of the doctrine of total failure of consideration was affirmed by the Privy Council in *Goss* v *Chilcott* [1997] 2 All ER 110 at 116. The *Fibrosa* case is a classic example of the operation of the doctrine. The seller was prevented from completing performance of a contract by the outbreak of war, since the buyer was in enemy occupied territory. The buyer had paid part of the price in advance, and since it had received none of the promised performance, it was entitled to repayment of that money because there had been a total failure of consideration.

For a further, more modern example, relying on this explanation of total failure of consideration, see *Rover International Ltd* v *Cannon Film Sales Ltd (No. 3)* [1989] 1 WLR 912. The Court of Appeal held that there had been a total failure of consideration despite the fact that Rover had received the films in question. The total failure of consideration related to the fact that the promised performance for which they had contracted was the securing of a profit and this had been prevented. It will therefore be a matter of determining what performance is owed under the terms of the contract.

This was again confirmed by the House of Lords in *Stocznia Gdanska SA* v *Latvian Shipping Co.* [1998] 1 WLR 574. The House of Lords explained that for there to be a total failure of consideration, it did not need to be established that the promisee had received nothing under the contract; the issue was whether the other party had performed any part of his or her contractual duties in respect of which payment is due. The argument on the facts of this case was that because the defendants had not received the vessels being constructed under the contract, there was a total failure of consideration. The House of Lords considered that the contractual obligations, for which payment was to be made, extended beyond delivery of the vessels and included design and construction. Accordingly, since some of this work had been completed, there was no total failure of consideration. This was reinforced by the fact that payment was to be made in instalments.

14.4.3 Partial failure of performance

The general rule is that where the promisee has received some of the performance to which he or she was entitled under the contract, so that the failure is only partial, the promisee is not able to recover money paid in advance (*Whincup* v *Hughes* (1871) LR 6 CP 78). The explanation for this rule is usually said to be that it is impossible to apportion the consideration between the performed and unperformed parts of the contract. For this reason, where performance is severable (7.5.5), so that the money paid can easily be split *pro rata* among the several parts, recovery of part of the money for partial failure of consideration will be allowed (*Ebrahim Dawood Ltd* v *Heath (Est. 1927) Ltd* [1961] Lloyd's Rep 512). This rule was applied to slightly surprising effect in *Goss* v *Chilcott* [1997] 2 All ER 110.

In *Goss* v *Chilcott*, the appellants had borrowed a sum of money, but had been unable to repay any of the capital, and in fact paid only two instalments of interest. An action against them in contract was unavailable, for reasons which are not relevant here. The question was whether the capital was recoverable for total failure of consideration. The Privy Council rejected the argument that there was no failure of consideration because of the reciprocal exchange of promises at the time of making the contract. For these purposes, the existence of consideration required actual performance of some part of what had been promised (see 14.4.2). More difficulty was presented by the fact that two instalments of interest payments were made. In the light of these payments, it could be argued that there had been some performance, so that there had not been a total failure of consideration. However, the contract did not provide, as would usually be the case with a long-term loan, for the scheduled payments to combine both interest and some repayment of capital; they were only payments of interest due. As a result, Lord Goff said, it was possible to separate the elements of the contract; and, since there was no performance in respect of the capital, it could be recovered.

It may also be possible for a promisee to convert a partial failure of consideration into a total failure of consideration by returning any benefit he or she has received by such performance as has taken place. This may be a particularly desirable course of action if the promisee is of the opinion that a restitutionary remedy would be preferable to a claim for damages (14.4.4). In some circumstances, of course, restoration of the benefit will be impossible. Where building work has been done on the promisee's land, but not completed, the promisee cannot return the work done (cf. Sumpter v Hedges [1898] 1 QB 673: 7.5.5.4). If, however, it is impossible to return the performance received for some reason connected with the other party's breach, there will be no obstacle to recovery of payment on the basis of total failure of consideration.

In some circumstances restoration of any performance received will not convert partial into total failure of consideration because the promisee has had the benefit of use between the time of performance and the time of its return (Hunt v Silk (1804) 5 East 449). This rule may sometimes appear to conflict with cases in the sale of goods, where the courts will find total failure of consideration even when the goods in question have been in the possession of and used by the promisee over a substantial period of time. The reason is that in the sale of goods the essential performance is the provision of good title to the thing sold, and the courts take the view that use of the goods in question is irrelevant to the contract of sale (Rowland v Divall [1923] 2 KB 500). This rule makes good sense in the case of a dealer, who purchases to resell and who must therefore have title, but does not seem right in the case of a consumer, who purchases in order to use the goods in question.

The Law Commission in its Working Paper, Pecuniary Restitution on Breach of Contract (No. 65), had provisionally recommended that restitutionary recovery ought to be available in cases of partial failure of the consideration. However, the Law Commission changed its mind in its 1983 Report (No. 121). This may be explicable in the light of the inventiveness of the courts in enabling recovery, despite what appears to be only a partial failure of consideration.

14.4.4 Restitution versus damages

Where the total failure of consideration is due to breach by the other party, the promisee will normally claim damages for loss of expectation, since the promisee will probably wish to recover the cost of mitigating his or her loss by resort to the market, and may wish to recover damages for lost profits. If the contract was an advantageous one then the expectation measure of damages will almost certainly be more attractive than recovering money paid. If, however, the claimant had made a bad bargain, so that he or she would have made a loss on the contract had it been performed, he or she may be glad of the opportunity provided by the total failure of consideration to retrieve intact the investment made.

14.4.5 *Quantum meruit*

Quantum meruit is a remedy under which a party who has provided a benefit, and who for some reason cannot obtain payment under a contract, may recover the reasonable value of the benefit provided. It may apply where there is no contract, or where the contractual provisions as to remuneration are inapplicable.

14.4.5.1 *Quantum meruit* in the absence of contract Where one party confers a benefit on another with the intention on both sides that that benefit will be paid for, then, in the absence of any contract between the parties, the party conferring the benefit will be able to recover reasonable remuneration from the recipient under the restitutionary remedy of *quantum meruit* (*Planche* v *Colburn* (1831) 8 Bing 14). For an example of the operation of this principle, see *British Steel Corporation* v *Cleveland Bridge & Engineering Co. Ltd* [1984] 1 All ER 504 (at 3.1.4). Work had begun, at the request of the defendants, on a major construction before all the elements of the contract had been agreed. Both sides confidently expected to reach agreement without difficulty. Final agreement was never reached. The plaintiffs claimed a *quantum meruit* for the work they had done. Their claim succeeded.

The *Cleveland Bridge* decision was rightly distinguished by Rattee J in *Regalian Properties plc* v *London Dockland Development Corporation* [1995] 1 WLR 212. In *Regalian* (unlike the *Cleveland Bridge* case) the plaintiffs had not carried out the work at the request of the defendants; rather, they had done it in order to be able to win the contract from the defendants. The negotiations had been conducted on a 'subject to contract' basis so that such expenditure was at their own risk, conferred no benefit on the defendants, and was not recoverable when they failed to obtain the anticipated contract.

Remuneration on the basis of *quantum meruit* may also be recoverable where performance is rendered under a contract which, unknown to both parties, is void. In *Craven-Ellis* v *Canons Ltd* [1936] 2 KB 403, the plaintiff had worked as managing director of a company without being appointed in the legally proper manner. His contract was therefore void, but he was able to recover the reasonable value of his work.

Similar rules apply in the case of work done by companies under contracts which are void because at the time the contract was made the company had not been incorporated, and so had no legal existence (*Rover International Ltd* v *Cannon Film Sales Ltd (No. 3)* [1989] 1 WLR 912).

14.4.5.2 *Quantum meruit* **despite the contract** Where there is a contract between the parties, it is fundamental to the law of contract that payment is to be determined according to the terms of the contract. The courts must not interfere with the parties' agreement. However, in limited circumstances that general rule is displaced and the court will allow a *quantum meruit* remedy despite the existence of a contract.

In the first place, where the contract fails to provide for the payment to be made, a reasonable price is payable. This rule has now been embodied in statute (s. 8, SGA 1979; s. 15, Supply of Goods and Services Act 1982). The same rule may also apply where the contract provides a price-fixing mechanism which is regarded as a mechanism for fixing a fair price rather than an essential factor in its determination, and for some unforeseen reason this mechanism fails to work (see *Sudbrook Trading Estate Ltd* v *Eggleton* [1983] 1 AC 444, 3.1.3).

In the case of an entire obligation, partial performance does not entitle the party who breaches by abandoning performance before completion to any payment under the contract (see 7.5.5 and 7.5.5.2). Where, however, the non-breaching party voluntarily accepts a benefit conferred by partial performance before the contract has been abandoned, the party who has breached may recover the reasonable value of the benefit conferred. Conversely, where the non-breaching party confers a benefit on the other party before the latter's breach, the non-breaching party may recover the value of that benefit under a *quantum meruit* rather than bringing a claim for damages (*Slowey* v *Lodder* (1901) 20 NZLR 321, affirmed by the Privy Council *sub nom. Lodder* v *Slowey* [1904] AC 442). By so doing, the non-breaching party may be able to avoid the consequences of having made a bad bargain.

PART V WHO CAN ENFORCE THE CONTRACT?

The examination of the law of contract in the previous Parts of this book almost always assumed that the type of contract under consideration involved two parties who were each to perform a stipulated obligation towards the other. From that assumption it followed that the enforcement of the obligations promised in the contract was a principal concern of the contracting parties themselves, and the question whether any other person might be entitled to enforce performance of the contract did not occur.

This concentration on the effect of bilateral contracts between the contracting parties is inevitable, since that is the area in which most contractual disputes occur. Nevertheless, it is easy to imagine situations in which one party has stipulated in the contract that performance be made towards some other person, and examples of this type of contract have been noted in passing (see 4.3.4.2 and 14.2.1).

Part V considers the rules of the law of contract, and related rules, applicable to contracts which stipulate a benefit for a third party. This type of contract may most easily be described in terms of a triangular relationship (see Figure 1 below). The contract is negotiated and made between A and B, but B stipulates that A's performance should be made to C (the third party). The questions which arise are whether C may enforce A's promise to perform for C's benefit; and whether B may enforce A's promise for the benefit of C.

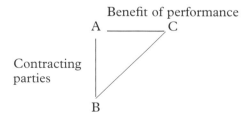

Figure 1 Contract benefitting third party

Related problems arise when B purports to stipulate not for a benefit to accrue to C from A's performance, but for C to perform B's obligations under the contract (so-called 'burdens' under the contract).

The general principle is that only the parties to the contract are bound by or are entitled to a remedy for enforcement of the obligations under the contract (15.1). This rule is known as the doctrine of privity of contract. The effect of the doctrine may be demonstrated by reference to a classic case from the law of torts. In *Donoghue* v *Stevenson* [1932] AC 562, the appellant and a friend went into a cafe, where the friend ordered a bottle of ginger beer for the appellant. The drink came in an opaque bottle. Part of the contents was poured out and the appellant consumed it. When the rest was poured out, a partly decomposed snail was found. The appellant suffered nervous shock and illness, and wished to recover compensation. She was unable to proceed against the café owner in contract because the contract to purchase the ginger beer was made with her friend and the appellant was not a party to it. Accordingly, she chose to proceed against the manufacturer of the ginger beer and established a breach of a duty of care in tort. Of course, it can be argued that in ordering the drink on behalf of the appellant, the friend had impliedly contracted for the benefit of the contract (including the statutory implied terms as to what is now satisfactory quality, 5.5.3.2) to pass to the appellant. In other words, it is possible to argue by way of implication from the facts of the case, that the café owner's contract with the friend included an undertaking to supply merchantable ginger beer to the appellant. However, the doctrine of privity of contract was a bar to the success of an action in contract by the appellant.

The unavailability of an action in contract against either manufacturer or retailer led to the development, in *Donoghue* v *Stevenson*, of the modern tort of negligence, under which the claimant may recover compensation for loss suffered as a result of breach of a duty of care owed to him or her by the defendant.

FIFTEEN

Third party rights and the doctrine of privity of contract

15.1 THE DOCTRINE OF PRIVITY OF CONTRACT

The doctrine of privity of contract states that a person may not enforce a contractual promise and obtain remedies for its breach, even when the promise was expressly made for his or her benefit, if he or she is not a party to the contract. The corollary of this is that persons who are not a party to a contract may not have their rights diminished by that contract. Both aspects of the doctrine have been subject to certain exceptions, although the exceptions to the latter rule (the 'burden' rule) are limited. Indeed, the rationale of the burden rule is easy to understand, since any other rule would be an infringement of individual liberty. However, the benefit rule is less readily explained (but see 15.2). It was confirmed in English law in the early nineteenth century (*cf. Price* v *Easton* (1833) 4 B & Ad 433). Modern authority for the rule is found in the decision of the House of Lords in *Dunlop Pneumatic Tyre Co. Ltd* v *Selfridge & Co. Ltd* [1915] AC 847.

In *Dunlop*, the appellants had sold tyres to a distributor on terms that he would not resell them at a price lower than the appellants' list price, and on terms that if sold to a trade buyer the distributor would obtain a similar undertaking from that buyer. The distributor resold some tyres to the respondents who gave the required undertaking, agreeing to pay £5 liquidated damages to the appellants for each tyre sold in breach of that undertaking. The respondents sold tyres below the list price, and the appellants sued to recover the agreed damages. In a much-quoted passage, Viscount Haldane LC said (at 853):

> My Lords, in the Law of England certain principles are fundamental. One is that only a person who is a party to a contract can sue on it. Our law

knows nothing of a *jus quaesitum tertio* arising by way of contract. Such a right may be conferred by way of property, as, for example, under a trust, but it cannot be conferred on a stranger to a contract as a right to enforce the contract *in personam*. A second principle is that if a person with whom a contract not under seal has been made is to be able to enforce it consideration must have been given by him to the promisor or to some other person at the promisor's request.

Viscount Haldane's statement of the privity doctrine has been taken as comprising two elements, one relating to the agreement component of a contract and the other relating to the consideration component.

15.1.1   The agreement component

It will not normally be difficult to establish whether a person was a party to the agreement in question. It is a simple question of fact whether the person took part as a principal in the negotiations which resulted in agreement. Occasional difficulty may arise when a beneficiary under the contract has signed the contractual document, and it is disputed whether he or she signed as a party to the agreement or merely as someone interested under the agreement (e.g., *Coulls* v *Bagot's Executor & Trustee Co.* (1967) 119 CLR 460: agreement containing a promise to pay a weekly royalty to Coulls and his wife had been signed by both but the majority of the High Court of Australia held that the wife was not a party to the contract).

15.1.2   The consideration component

The rule that consideration must move from the promisee appears to originate in the early privity case of *Tweddle* v *Atkinson* (1861) 1 B & S 393. After a marriage the partners' respective fathers entered into an agreement whereby each would pay a sum of money to the husband, and by that agreement the husband was to have the power to sue for the sums of money promised. After the death of his wife's father, the husband sued his estate to recover the sum promised. However, the action failed because the husband had given no consideration for the promise (although he was also not a party to the contract).

    The rule that consideration must move from the promisee also appears to have been the *ratio* of the decision of the House of Lords in *Dunlop Pneumatic Tyre Co. Ltd* v *Selfridge & Co. Ltd* [1915] AC 847 (above). The need to establish consideration has resulted in all kinds of complexities in devices designed to avoid the application of the privity doctrine (e.g., agency; see, for example, 15.5.4.1).

    This rule has traditionally been explained on the basis that a party not providing consideration is not part of the axis of inducement or mutual exchange, which is central to the enforceability of agreements. Nevertheless, it is not easy to discern any policy interest making such a rule necessary. As long as the promise in question is not gratuitous (i.e., the promisee has provided consideration for it), there is arguably no reason why the third party should have to provide consideration.

The fact that the third party need not provide consideration was also accepted by the Law Commission in its Report, *Privity of Contracts: Contracts for the Benefit of Third Parties* (Law Com. No. 242, 1996, Cm 3329 (see Part VI, pp. 68–73)). In its Consultation Paper (No. 121, 1993), the Law Commission had considered that the consideration requirement did not pose a problem to its suggested reform of the third party beneficiary rule because the rule only required that 'consideration must move from the *promisee*'. However, the Law Commission later accepted that this had been interpreted as 'consideration must move from the *plaintiff* [*claimant*]' or person seeking to enforce the contract. Clearly the entire reform would be ineffectual if the third party could be prevented from enforcing the contract on the basis that he or she had not provided consideration. However, the Law Commission was satisfied that this problem was met by the central provision of the legislation giving a third party the right to enforce the contract and concluded that the clause 'can only be interpreted as also reforming the rule that consideration must move from the promisee'. However, there is no provision spelling this out in the applicable legislation, the Contracts (Rights of Third Parties) Act 1999. Therefore, the position since the introduction of this legislation is that a third party seeking to enforce a contractual provision using the 1999 Act, cannot be defeated by a claim that he or she has not provided consideration to support the promise, as long as the promise is not gratuitous (i.e., as long as the promisee has supplied consideration). However, it is unclear whether there has been any alteration in the need to provide consideration in situations falling outside the Act. There has been some recognition of this position at common law, but only from the minority in the High Court of Australia. In *Coulls* v *Bagot's Executor and Trustee Co.* (1967) 119 CLR 460 (15.1.1), although the majority considered that the widow was not a party to the contract, the minority (Barwick CJ and Windeyer J) considered that the fact that the widow had provided no consideration for the promise was not fatal to her ability to enforce the promise given that the husband had provided consideration to support it.

15.2 CRITICISMS AND CALLS FOR REFORM

The reasons for the privity doctrine are not clear. In *Trident General Insurance Co. Ltd* v *McNiece Brothers Proprietary Ltd* (1988) 165 CLR 107, Toohey J (in the High Court of Australia) considered that it 'lacks a sound foundation in jurisprudence and logic'. It has sometimes been suggested that it rests on a principle of mutuality (*cf.* 15.1.2), to the effect that it would be unfair to allow a person to sue on a contract who cannot be sued by the other party (*cf. Tweddle* v *Atkinson* (1861) 1 B & S 393). It is also sometimes suggested that it would be undesirable to allow third party rights to be created by contract, since that would restrict the freedom of the parties subsequently to amend or rescind their agreement (*cf. Re Schebsman* [1944] Ch 83). Alternatively, it is suggested that third party beneficiaries are frequently gratuitous recipients of the benefit in their favour, and so the rule was closely related to the doctrine of consideration. Each of these explanations is open to objection, either on the ground that provided the contract is freely negotiated there is no particular reason why contracting parties should not undertake obligations which lack mutuality or which restrict their future freedom to act, or on the ground that the explanation does not account for the full extent of the rule.

Whatever the explanation of the rule may be, it has been strongly and consistently criticised, at least in the context of contractual provisions in favour of third parties. Thus, whereas it has generally been accepted that there must be a privity doctrine to prevent total strangers from seeking to enforce a contract, it is more difficult to justify why, in situations where a contract is expressly made for the benefit of a third party (such as the husband in *Tweddle* v *Atkinson*), that third party should not be able to enforce that benefit. It is essentially in the context of enforcement by these third party intended beneficiaries that exceptions to privity have been developed and devices invented to avoid it.

In *Dunlop Pneumatic Tyre Co. Ltd* v *Selfridge & Co. Ltd* [1915] AC 847, Lord Dunedin, who felt compelled to agree with Viscount Haldane in finding against the appellants, said (at 855):

> I confess that this case is to my mind apt to nip any budding affection which one might have had for the doctrine of consideration. For the effect of that doctrine in the present case is to make it possible for a person to snap his fingers at a bargain deliberately made, a bargain not in itself unfair, and which the person seeking to enforce it has a legitimate interest to enforce.

As long ago as 1937 the Law Revision Committee (Sixth Interim Report, Cmnd 5449, p. 31), proposed that a third party should be able to enforce a contract where the contract expressly conferred a benefit on that third party. In *Beswick* v *Beswick* [1968] AC 58, Lord Reid referred to this proposal and said that that 'if one had to contemplate a further long period of Parliamentary procrastination, this House might find it necessary to deal with this matter'. In *Woodar Investment Development Ltd* v *Wimpey Construction (UK) Ltd* [1980] 1 WLR 277, Lord Scarman regretted that nothing had been done about this 'unjust rule', and he was not alone in his criticism.

The reasons in favour of reform of the third party beneficiary rule are well rehearsed and were set out and explained by the Law Commission in its Report (pp. 39–50). The fundamental justifications for reform were also set out by Steyn LJ in *Darlington Borough* Council v *Wiltshier Northern Ltd* [1995] 1 WLR 68 at 76:

> The case for recognising a contract for the benefit of a third party is simple and straightforward. The autonomy of the will of the parties should be respected. The law of contract should give effect to the reasonable expectations of contracting parties. . . . there is no doctrinal, logical, or policy reason why the law should deny effectiveness to a contract for the benefit of a third party where that is the expressed intention of the parties.

Moreover, often the parties, and particularly third parties, organise their affairs on the faith of the contract. They rely on the contract. It is therefore unjust to deny effectiveness to such a contract. I will not struggle with the point further since nobody seriously asserts the contrary.

Thus, whereas the intentions of the parties are usually given prominence in English contract law (see classical contract law, at 1.4.2.2), in respect of the operation of the privity doctrine those expressed intentions are ignored. Not unreasonably, a third party intended beneficiary may have relied upon the promise. It is also the case that the various attempts to avoid the operation of privity in this context (15.5) have resulted in legal principles which are 'complex, artificial and uncertain'. Perhaps most significant is the fact that many of the jurisdictions in the European single market provide for the enforceability of stipulations for the benefit of third parties and the English position would cause harmonisation difficulties for the European Union (see, e.g., Article 6.110, PECL: third party's right to enforce may be expressly or impliedly agreed by the parties). Significantly, the doctrine has also either been rejected or abrogated in many Commonwealth and common law jurisdictions (a good example is the New Zealand Contracts (Privity) Act 1982), so that the English position appeared to be out of line. However, perhaps the greatest impetus for reform stemmed from the fact that the third party rule led to difficulties in commercial life. The Law Commission specifically cited and explained the problems in relation to construction contracts and insurance contracts. (However, for another view, see S. A. Smith, 'Contracts for the Benefit of Third Parties: in Defence of the Third Party Rule' (1997) 17 Oxford J Legal Stud 643, esp. 658–63.)

The debate in the early to mid-1990s focused on the format for reform (see *Tettenborn* [1996] JBL 602: 'The interesting question is, in short, not whether we ought to reform privity, but how') and, in particular, whether reform should be achieved judicially on a case by case basis, or by means of legislation. The Supreme Court of Canada in *London Drugs Ltd* v *Kuehne & Nagel International Ltd* (1993) 97 DLR (4th) 261, when faced with a situation which did not fall within the technical requirements of an existing exception (see *The Eurymedon* [1975] AC 154; 15.5.4.1), created a new exception in order to give effect to the 'true intentions of the contracting parties and commercial reality'. Iacobucci J advocated this 'incremental approach' to change in appropriate circumstances. (A further example of this approach can be seen in *Fraser River Pile & Dredge Ltd* v *Can-Dive Services Ltd* [2000] 1 Lloyd's Rep 199. The Supreme Court of Canada continued its 'incremental changes' and held that a third party who fell within the class of 'charterers' could rely on a 'waiver of subrogation clause' in an insurance policy notwithstanding the doctrine of privity of contract.) However, as Iacobucci J made clear in his judgment in *London Drugs*, 'major reforms . . . must come from the legislature'; and in *Fraser River* he again stated (at 208, para. 43):

Wholesale abolition of the doctrine would result in complex repercussions that exceed the ability of the Courts to anticipate and address. It is now a well-established principle that the Courts will not undertake judicial reform of this magnitude, recognizing instead that the legislature is better placed to appreciate and accommodate the economic and policy issues involved in introducing sweeping legal reforms.

There are distinct problems with judicial reform of the privity rule, as is evident from an examination of the decision of the High Court of Australia in *Trident General Insurance Co. Ltd* v *McNiece Brothers Proprietary Ltd* (1988) 165 CLR 107; judges may differ in their justifications for allowing third party enforcement on the facts of the case. In *The Mahkutai* [1996] 3 All ER 502, Lord Goff identified some of the problems of judicial reform, namely, having to wait for an 'appropriate' case to arise and for the question of reform to be fully argued. However, the greatest danger of judicial reform is the uncertainty that it would generate (a particular problem in the commercial context), and the Law Commission cited this uncertainty as a reason in favour of its proposed legislative reform on the question of enforcement by third party beneficiaries.

The Law Commission's proposed legislative reform has now been broadly adopted as the Contracts (Rights of Third Parties) Act 1999. However, it is important to appreciate that it does not abolish privity. There are a number of reasons why this is so. In the first place, burdens were excluded from the scope of the Law Commission's reform and the Act does not therefore allow enforcement of burdens imposed on third parties. The exceptional situations when a 'burden' may be imposed on a third party are discussed at 15.7.

The 1999 Act deals only with enforcement of benefits by third parties and, although it came into force on 11 November 1999, it only applies to contracts entered into after 11 May 2000, unless the contract was made between 11 November 1999 and 10 May 2000 and expressly stated that the 1999 Act was to apply to it. Therefore the common law may still be applicable to many existing contracts.

Even where the Act does apply to the contract, it is not every third party who can enforce a contractual provision. The test of enforceability in s. 1 of the Act must be satisfied before a third party will have rights of enforcement. This test of enforceability is vital to the scope of the legislation and, as we will see, many of the existing decisions would be unaffected if the Act were to apply to the same set of facts. However, s. 7(1) of the Act makes it clear that existing exceptions to privity and devices to avoid privity will continue to operate in this situation. It is therefore necessary to approach this topic by first examining the Act and its scope, and then examining what are now residual common law exceptions which may still be relevant in some situations falling outside the Act. It is to be hoped that the existence of the Act will not curtail judicial developments outside the scope of the Act, although it is extremely likely that the Act will have this effect.

It is also the case that the existing rights of promisees to secure remedies for the benefit of third parties are unaffected by the legislation. The Law Commission specifically left this question for judicial reform. The scope for the promisee to recover on behalf of the third party, and the limitations on this, are discussed at 15.6.

15.3 THE CONTRACTS (RIGHTS OF THIRD PARTIES) ACT 1999

(See generally, C. MacMillan 'A Birthday Present for Lord Denning: The Contracts (Rights of Third Parties) Act 1999' (2000) 63 MLR 721.)

In its Report, the Law Commission had recommended that the privity doctrine be reformed by legislation in order to 'enable contracting parties to confer a right to enforce the contract on a third party', i.e. the right to enforce remedies for breach of contract that would have been available had the third party been a contracting party, and the right to enforce an exemption clause as if the third party was a party to the contract. This basic right is contained in s. 1(1) of the 1999 Act, which states that a person who is not a party to the contract may enforce a term of the contract in his or her own right if the test of enforceability in s. 1(1)–(3) is satisfied. Section 1(5) provides that for this purpose the third party will have 'any remedy that would have been available to him in an action for breach of contract if he had been a party to the contract (and the rules relating to damages, injunctions, specific perform-ance and other relief shall apply accordingly)'. For the avoidance of doubt, s. 1(6) provides for a third party to be able to enforce an exemption or limitation clause in a contract (where the test of enforceability is satisfied). This is important to the reform as many of the difficult cases have concerned enforcement of these clauses by third parties and one of much criticised technical common law exceptions to privity was developed to deal with this situation (see 15.5.4.1). The fact that the third party has not provided consideration to support the promise will not prevent him or her enforcing the term (assuming that the promise is not gratuitous). This is not contained in the Act, but the entire reform would fail if the position were otherwise and the Law Commission made this clear in its Report. Interestingly, if a person is a party to the contract because he or she is a joint promisee but has not provided consideration for the promise, the Act cannot apply because such a person is not a third party. Such a joint promisee might therefore be unable to enforce the contractual term in his or her favour on the basis that he or she has not provided consideration. It would be anomalous for a joint promisee to be in a worse position than a third party, and the Law Commission clearly envisaged that the courts would resolve this difficulty, presumably on the basis that the particular joint promisee does not need to provide consideration for the promise as long as it is supported by consider-ation provided by another joint promisee.

By s. 3, the promisor will have the same defences and rights of set-off in a claim for enforcement brought by the third party as in a claim brought by the promisee. This is subject to any express clause in the contract giving additional or reduced defences in an enforcement claim by a third party. Section 3(6) specifically states that a third party seeking to enforce an exemption clause will be subject to the same controls on enforcement as would exist in the case of enforcement by a contracting party.

As discussed earlier, it was never intended that complete strangers should be able to enforce contractual provisions, only third parties who were intended to benefit under the relevant term of the contract. Accordingly, the test of enforceability must achieve this objective. Formulating such a test has proved to be difficult and the proposed test contained in the Report was altered from that which had originally been proposed in the Consultation Paper on the basis that it was too restrictive, since it required not only that there be an intention that the terms should confer a benefit on the third party, but also that there was an intention that it should create a legal obligation enforceable by that third party (the so-called 'dual intention test'). This dual intention test was rejected and replaced with the test now contained in s. 1(1)–(3).

There are two ways in which a third party may satisfy the test of enforceability and be able to enforce contractual terms under the Act. In the first place, the contract may expressly state that the third party is to have a right to enforce the provision (s. 1(1)(a)). Under s. 1(3), the third party 'must be expressly identified in the contract by name, as a member of a class or as answering a particular description', although he or she need not be in existence at the time the contract is made. It will be rare that the s. 1(1)(a) test of enforceability will be satisfied. It requires a particular form of drafting which, if used in the past, has not achieved its objective. Ironically, there was such a provision on the facts in *Tweddle* v *Atkinson* (1861) 1 B & S 847, so that if this set of case facts were to arise again, the husband ought to be able to enforce the promise in his favour. This does indicate the most straightforward method for conferring a right of enforcement on third parties, where this is desired, and ought therefore to affect *future* drafting practice. However, the evidence to date is that, rather than contracting to fall within the Act, many commercial parties are contracting to avoid its operation because of the uncertainties over some of its other provisions. This can be achieved by stating that the third party will not receive an enforceable right.

As an alternative to the s. 1(1)(a) test, a third party will also fall within the Act and be able to enforce contractual provisions in his or her own right where he or she is expressly identified in the contract and 'the term purports to confer a benefit on him' (s. 1(1)(b)). However, by s. 1(2): 'Subsection (1)(b) does not apply if on a proper construction of the contract it appears that the parties did not intend the term to be enforceable by the third party'. This would appear to be the case in most construction contracts, so that it will not enable a building owner (third party to the contract between main contractor and subcontractor) to sue a subcontractor directly since the intention is that the owner should sue the main contractor. Inevitably this intention proviso will cause problems of certainty for commercial parties since this is not a simple test (although it is similar to the sole test used in the New Zealand Contracts (Privity) Act 1982, s. 4). (For further discussion, see T. Roe, 'Contractual Intention under Section 1(1)(b) and 1(2) of the Contracts (Rights of Third Parties) Act 1999' (2000) 63 MLR 887.)

In a practical sense, this s. 1(1)(b) test will also be limiting because of the requirement that the third party be expressly identified in some manner in the clause. An analysis of existing case law will illustrate the limitations this imposes and the fact that it restricts the operation of the Act (see, e.g., 15.5.4.2).

One of the most controversial and difficult issues to be resolved when formulating such a legislative reform is the crucial question of whether the original parties should be able to vary or cancel the third party's benefit under the contract. This is a particular problem where the third party has relied on the rights in the contract. Section 2(1) provides that the contracting parties cannot vary or cancel the third party's rights without his or her consent where the third party had communicated his or her assent to the term to the promisor (s. 2(2) explains this assent and ousts the postal rule in the case of assent by post), or the third party had relied on the term and the promisor knew this (or ought reasonably to have foreseen this). It appears that any reliance will suffice for this purpose; this is extremely generous to the third party. This section appears to offer generous and effective protection for third parties in this situation, or at least it would offer protection but for s. 2(3) which expressly allows contracting parties to opt out of this by stipulating for a different crystallisation test (other than assent or reliance), or by reserving the right to vary or cancel the third party's right irrespective of reliance or acceptance by the third party. In accordance with the Report recommendations, there is also a specific judicial discretion to vary or cancel irrespective of reliance or acceptance by the third party in certain circumstances (s. 2(4)–(7) of the Act). These provisions shift control, and hence the balance, back in favour of the contracting parties.

Another potential difficulty posed by third party reform concerns the question of overlap with remedies of the promisee against the promisor. In other words, should the promisee lose the right of enforcement where the third party has such a right? This would require an extremely complex piece of drafting and arguably would be impossible to achieve. On the other hand, if both retain a right of action, who would have priority? The Law Commission recommended that the promisor's duty to perform should be owed to both promisee and the third party, so that (unless otherwise agreed between the parties) the promisee should retain the right to enforce a contract even if it was also enforceable by the third party. Since each has a separate right of action, there should be no priority rule (although the appropriate course would be to join the third party if the promisee sues). In addition, although it did not require legislation to say so, if the promisor fulfilled his or her duty to the third party, the promisor was, to that extent, to be discharged from his or her duty to the promisee.

The legislation is minimalist and to the point. Section 4 preserves the promisee's right to enforce the promise, and s. 5 expressly seeks to avoid double liability by explaining that where the promisee has recovered substantial damages (or agreed sum) for the third party's loss, the third party will not be entitled to a duplicate damages sum because 'the court . . . shall reduce any award to the third party to such extent as it thinks appropriate to take account of the sum recovered by the promisee'. This situation appears to be of great concern to students, who point out that if the promisee does recover damages for the third party, there is no provision of the Act requiring him or her to pass those damages to the third party. The absence of a provision is explicable because this is a question of remedies of the promisee and outside the scope of the legislation. The question of liability to account to the third party should therefore be dealt with at common law (see the discussion at 15.6.4).

The drafters of this legislation appear to have been concerned to avoid making it complex or providing provisions on matters which might become too prescriptive. However, they did include one particularly controversial provision. To what extent should UCTA 1977 protect a third party who acquires rights under this Act? By s. 7(2) of the 1999 Act, s. 2(2) of UCTA 1977 shall not apply to the breach of a qualified contractual obligation where the person seeking to challenge the contractual provision is a third party relying on s. 1 of the 1999 Act. However, s. 2(1) of UCTA 1977 will apply (as an existing right or remedy), so that any contractual provisions excluding liability for death or personal injury will remain ineffective when utilised by a third party. This was stated in the debate in the House of Lords to be 'consistent with the underlying policy of the Bill which is to enable contracting parties to confer rights on third parties but to allow them to retain control over the nature and extent of those newly conferred rights' (Lord Irvine, 11 January 1999). However, it is questionable whether UCTA, should be restricted in this way so as to exclude its protection in the context of third parties (see Lord Borrie in debate in the House of Lords, 11 January 1999), although it is clear that the Unfair Terms in Consumer Contracts Regulations 1999 cannot apply to a third party claim because the Regulations apply only to contracts between a seller or supplier and a consumer.

It is also made clear by s. 7(4) that s. 1 will not allow a third party to be treated as a contracting party for the purposes of any other enactment. Specifically, s. 3 of the UCTA 1977 applies '*as between contracting parties* where one of them deals as a consumer or on the other's written standard terms of business' (emphasis added). Thus, if an exclusion clause operated to exclude or limit a third party right, it would not be subject to regulation under s. 3 of UCTA 1977. In this sense, the third party is not treated in the same way as the promisee and it will be easier for contracting parties to exclude third parties' rights. This appears to be in conflict with the apparent purpose of the 1999 Act.

Section 6 contains an extensive list of exceptions where this Act will not apply, e.g., contracts of employment, negotiable instruments (see 15.4.4), contracts for the carriage of goods by sea (other than in relation to the benefit of exemption clauses) (see 15.5.3), and the s. 14 contract in company law.

Lastly, it is important to remember that the existing exceptions to privity are expressly preserved by s. 7(1) of the Act. Thus, although the Law Commission's Report envisaged that the reform would avoid the 'complexities of the devices presently used to circumvent the privity doctrine', these complexities will remain, at least where the device has not been overtaken by the availability of a direct right of enforcement in the legislation. It is important, therefore, to consider these exceptions and their potential usefulness in the light of the new legislation. Some of these 'exceptions' are merely means of circumventing the application of the privity doctrine using other legal concepts. Others are true exceptions to privity which exist within the law of contract. These are considered below (see 15.5).

15.4 MEANS OF CIRCUMVENTING THE PRIVITY DOCTRINE

These mechanisms exist as independent legal concepts enabling a benefit to be conferred on a third party who was not apparently a party to the making of the contract. Tort claims are clearly outside the law of contract. The other mechanisms are related to contract but represent independent concepts.

15.4.1 Claim in tort

The appellant in *Donoghue* v *Stevenson* [1932] AC 562 (p. 440) was able to avoid the effect of the privity doctrine by framing her action in tort. It is by no means always possible to avoid the doctrine in this way, since it depends upon being able to establish that the defendant was negligent, and in any case may not result in the award of compensation for expectation loss (see 5.1.1). Although English law flirted with the idea of permitting evasion of the privity doctrine by means of the tort of negligence (in the House of Lords decision in *Junior Books Ltd* v *Veitchi Co. Ltd* [1983] 1 AC 520), that development was rapidly abandoned, and Lord Brandon's dissenting speech has become the restored orthodoxy. In a line of cases culminating in the decision of the House of Lords in *D & F Estates Ltd* v *Church Commissioners for England* [1989] AC 177, it became clear that the existence of a contract between the defendant and a third party (as in a subcontractor/main contractor relationship) will usually result in the court being unwilling to find that the defendant is also liable in tort in an independent obligation to the claimant (e.g., the building owner). In any case, where such a tortious obligation is shown to exist, it will not allow the recovery of pure economic loss such as the diminished value of work done, and recovery will normally be restricted to loss resulting from physical damage.

15.4.2 Assignment and agency

The law of assignment and agency is considered further in Chapter 16. Both assignment and agency make important contributions to the commercial world. Although not strictly exceptions to the privity doctrine, they are contrary to the spirit of that rule, and were developed to meet the practical needs of those in business, for whom the privity doctrine proved unduly restrictive.

15.4.3 Trusts

The trust is a device developed by the Court of Chancery long before the Judicature Act 1875. It allows a party to pass property to a second party, while stipulating that the second party must hold the property for the benefit of a third. That stipulation is enforceable by the third party. In terms of the triangular relationship outlined at p. 439, A (the trustee) receives property from B over which B has declared a trust in favour of C (the beneficiary or *cestui que trust*). C is then able to enforce the terms of the trust to prevent A dealing with the property other than in a manner which is to C's benefit. Although the relationship between the party declaring the trust (B) and the trustee (A) is not necessarily contractual, where it is, the device is inconsistent with the privity doctrine.

The Court of Chancery had developed the trust in response to issues of property and conscience arising out of such cases. Chancery took the view that a properly constituted trust had the effect of actually transferring and splitting the ownership of the property in question. The legal owner (i.e., under the common law rules) was the trustee; but the effect of constitution of the trust was to make the third party the beneficial owner of the property. To allow the third party to enforce the trust was not, therefore, to allow the enforcement of a contractual right to acquire the property. The property belonged to the third party from the moment of constitution of the trust, and enforcement of the trust by him or her was necessary to prevent improper interference with his or her right, which was similar in nature to a property right. In turn, the trustee could not as a matter of good conscience interfere with that right. The right of the beneficial owner could be lost only by virtue of the acquisition of the trust property by a bona fide purchaser for value who had no notice, actual or constructive, of the trust over the property (*Alcher* v *Rawlins* (1872) LR 7 Ch App 259).

In order for there to be a properly constituted trust, there must be property which is capable of being subjected to a trust. Property includes not only land and goods but also rights, such as a right under a contract, which are known as *choses in action*. There must be a declaration of, or disposition on, trust by a competent person which demonstrates a certain intention that a trust be created. There must also be certainty of property and of object, i.e., it must be possible to determine the property to which the trust attaches and the purposes for which the trust was created. Lastly, the declaration or disposition must comply with any statutory requirements regarding evidence.

The most significant aspect of the trust as an exception to the privity doctrine arises where one party declares himself or herself to be a trustee on behalf of a third party of a right to performance owed to him or her by the other contracting party. That is, in terms of the triangular relationship outlined at p. 439, where B declares *himself or herself* to be trustee on behalf of C of the performance due to him or her under the contract from A. This situation is considered below (see 15.5.1).

15.4.4 Negotiable instruments

The negotiable instrument is a device originally developed by the law merchant to overcome the privity doctrine and certain commercial disadvantages inherent in the device of assignment. In the case of assignment, the assignee of a contractual right is at the very least inadequately protected unless notice of the assignment is given to the original debtor each time the right is assigned (see 16.2.2.2). Moreover, the assignee takes the right which has been assigned 'subject to equities' (16.4.1), which means that any defences enjoyed by the original debtor against the assignor are equally valid against the assignee. Thus, an assigned right may not be worth its face value if the original debtor is entitled to a set-off against the assignor. For example, returning to the triangular relationship outlined above (p. 439), if B agrees to sell goods to A for £100, but the goods delivered are reduced in value to £80 by a breach of the quality term, the fact that B has assigned to C the right to recover payment from A will not entitle C to recover any more than the £80 which B could have recovered in his own right.

If, however, A's obligation to pay is recorded in a document ('instrument') which is recognised by the law as 'negotiable', B may transfer the right to recover the amount recorded in the instrument to C by simple delivery (i.e., by handing it over), or perhaps by indorsement and delivery (e.g., by signing it and then handing it over). There is no need to give notice of the transfer to the original debtor (A), and it may be transferred several times before the debt which it represents is collected from A. Moreover, the particular advantage of the negotiable instrument is that the transferee(s) do not take 'subject to equities', provided they receive the instrument for value and without notice of any defect in title which may have arisen before they became 'holder in due course' of the instrument. Common forms of negotiable instrument are bills of exchange (of which the most familiar example is the cheque) and promissory notes (of which the most familiar example is the bank note). These are regulated by the Bills of Exchange Act 1882. It is beyond the scope of this book to list all other forms of negotiable instrument, but they include certain forms of bond and share certificates.

15.4.4.1 The requirements of negotiability   It is sometimes said that there are four requirements of negotiability:

(a)   that the right expressed in the instrument is to be transferable upon delivery (with indorsement where necessary);
(b)   that the holder of the instrument for the time being has the right to collect payment from the original debtor;
(c)   that the holder for the time being, if taking for value and without notice, does not take subject to equities; and
(d)   that the instrument is of a type recognised by the law as negotiable.

However, the first three elements are not requirements but statements of the legal effect of the recognition that the instrument is negotiable. There is really only one requirement of negotiability, which is that the instrument is recognised as negotiable. But the mere fact that an instrument falls within a category of instruments generally regarded as negotiable does not prevent a particular instrument from being denied negotiability by express words (s. 8(1), Bills of Exchange Act 1882). For example, cheques may be crossed 'not negotiable'. If they are crossed 'account payee' or 'account payee only', they are not negotiable, and are not even transferable.

15.4.4.2 The position of holder in due course   Negotiable instruments provide a means of circumventing the privity doctrine because the original contract debt is enforceable not only by the other contracting party, but also by any other person for the time being holding the instrument who has been constituted holder in due course. The position of the holder in due course is strengthened still further by the fact that if the party primarily liable on the instrument fails to pay, he or she may if necessary bring a claim against all previous signatories of the instrument (s. 38(2), Bills of Exchange Act 1882).

A party is holder in due course if he or she receives the instrument for value and in good faith, provided it is complete and regular on its face (s. 29(1), Bills of Exchange Act 1882), and is in a deliverable state (s. 31(3), (4)). The requirement that the transfer be made for value is considerably more relaxed than the requirement of consideration in contracts generally. In the first place, provided value has been given at some time, the holder for the time being is deemed to have given value (s. 27(2) of the 1882 Act). Moreover, negotiable instruments are an exception to the general rule against past consideration (s. 27(1)(b); *cf.* 4.3.3.3). The requirement of good faith is the same as that in other parts of the law: the transferee must not have acquired the instrument by fraud, duress, undue influence or other unacceptable behaviour, neither must he or she have acquired it in the knowledge that it was already tainted with such defects before it came into his or her hands (*cf.* s. 30(2) of the 1882 Act). The requirement that the instrument be complete and regular on its face poses little difficulty. It covers such defects as omission on the instrument of a payee or the amount payable. The requirement that the instrument be in a deliverable state is more complex. It relates to the need in certain circumstances for the instrument to be indorsed for the delivery to be effective. An instrument made payable to the bearer (a 'bearer bill') does not require indorsement in order to be negotiated, and so is always in a deliverable state. But an instrument made payable to a named person, or to a named person 'or order' (an 'order bill'), cannot be negotiated unless indorsed, and the fact of indorsement puts the bill in a deliverable state. Transfer of an order bill without indorsement would remove one of the essential characteristics of negotiability, i.e. that the holder acquires the instrument free from equities.

15.4.5 Collateral contract

The privity doctrine may be avoided by the collateral contract device, which gives a third party a right to enforce promises under a separate contract with the promisor. In *Shanklin Pier Ltd* v *Detel Products Ltd* [1951] 2 KB 854, the plaintiffs had hired a firm to paint their pier, and on the strength of a representation made by the defendants had instructed the firm to use the defendants' paint. The paint did not last anywhere near as long as the defendants had represented, but the contract for the purchase of the paint was between the firm of painters and the defendants, and so could not afford the plaintiffs a remedy. The court held that there was a collateral contract between the plaintiffs and the defendants to the effect that the paint would last for seven years. In this case the plaintiffs had furnished consideration for the defendants' undertaking by instructing the firm of painters to use the defendants' paint.

The collateral contract is of considerable practical significance in relation to commercial contracts as a means of avoiding the operation of the privity doctrine (see, e.g., *Andrews* v *Hopkinson* [1957] 1 QB 229: promise by car dealer enforced as a collateral contract with customer when dealer's promise had induced the making of the separate contract of hire purchase between the customer and the finance company).

15.5 EXCEPTIONS TO THE PRIVITY DOCTRINE

We have already considered devices, some of which may have had their origin in contract but all of which must now be regarded as conceptually independent, which may be used to circumvent the privity doctrine (15.4). In this section we consider genuine exceptions to the privity doctrine.

15.5.1 Trust of rights created by contract

We saw above (15.4.3) that the concept of privity is restricted to contracts and does not extend to trusts. A trust may attach to property of any kind, including a *chose in action*, which is a form of intangible property such as a right to enforce an obligation. It follows from that definition that a right under a contract is a chose in action, and thus may be subject to a trust.

The possibility is raised, therefore, that the promisee under a contract might declare himself or herself trustee of the benefit of the promise in question on behalf of a third party, and by that means avoid the privity doctrine. This device was used successfully during the nineteenth century (*cf. Lloyd's* v *Harper* (1880) 16 ChD 290), and its existence as a means of avoiding the privity doctrine was acknowledged by Viscount Haldane LC in *Dunlop Pneumatic Tyre Co. Ltd* v *Selfridge & Co. Ltd* [1915] AC 847, in the passage previously quoted (15.1).

15.5.1.1 Effect of a trust of a contractual right Where a trust of a contractual right is found to have been created, the principal effect is to permit the third party to enforce the benefit. For example, in *Les Affréteurs Réunis SA* v *Leopold Walford (London) Ltd* [1919] AC 801, a charterparty between shipowner and charterer provided that the shipowner would pay a commission of 3 per cent to the broker who had negotiated the contract for the parties. When the shipowner failed to pay, the broker brought an action to recover the commission, although he was not a party to the contract. The House of Lords accepted that it was the practice of the shipping trade in such cases for the charterer to sue to enforce the promise of commission as trustee for the broker. Since the shipowner was willing to allow the case to be treated as having been brought upon such an action, the broker succeeded in recovering the commission.

The third party's claim to enforce the contract would normally need to be brought in the name of the trustee, but as *Les Affréteurs Réunis SA* v *Leopold Walford (London) Ltd* shows, the promisor may waive that requirement, in which case the third party may bring the claim in his or her own name. If the trustee is unwilling to cooperate in bringing a claim to enforce the promise, the third party may start proceedings in his or her own name and join the trustee as co-defendant (*Vandepitte v Preferred Accident Insurance Corporation of New York* [1933] AC 70 at 79).

A further effect of the creation of a trust of a contractual right is to prevent the contracting parties from varying or rescinding the contract, since to do so would be an improper interference with the beneficiary's rights. An intention to reserve the right to vary in the future if so desired has been regarded as evidence contradicting the alleged intention to create a trust (*Re Schebsman* [1944] Ch 83).

15.5.1.2 Limits of the trust exception Despite the apparent utility of the trust device as a means for avoiding the privity doctrine, it has fallen into disuse. The reason is to be found in the requirements for the constitution of a trust (15.4.3), and especially in the requirement that there be a certain intention on the part of the person allegedly declaring the trust that a trust be created (*Vandepitte v Preferred Accident Insurance Corporation of New York* [1933] AC 70). The usual difficulty is that at the time of making the contract, and indeed at all times until the particular problem arises, the promisee has not thought at all about how the third party was to enforce the benefit to be conferred. In *Vandepitte v Preferred Accident Insurance Corporation of New York*, the plaintiff's action against an insurance company depended upon whether the insured held the promised cover under a policy of motor insurance on trust for his daughter who was a minor. Under the law of British Columbia the father was civilly liable for the torts of his minor children, so that it was almost inconceivable that he should feel it necessary to hold the benefit of insurance on his daughter's behalf since he was the person most likely to be sued, not his daughter. On that ground the Privy Council considered there to be no trust.

For some time the English courts have been unwilling to imply an intention to create a trust. In *Re Schebsman* [1944] Ch 83, Du Parcq LJ said: '[U]nless an intention to create a trust is clearly to be collected from the language used and the circumstances of the case, I think that the Court ought not to be astute to discover indications of such an intention.' In practice, therefore, unless there is an express declaration of the intention to create a trust it seems that the device of a trust of a contractual right will fail.

15.5.2 Insurance

In principle the privity doctrine applies to contracts of insurance, but there are several statutory exceptions to the doctrine in the case of common contracts which provide for benefits to be payable to third parties. For example, under s. 148(7) of the Road Traffic Act 1988, an injured third party may recover compensation from the insurance company once he or she has obtained judgment against the insured. Equally, under s. 11 of the Married Women's Property Act 1882, a spouse has an enforceable right to recover sums due on a policy of life insurance taken out by the other spouse on his or her own life.

15.5.3 Carriage of goods by sea

It is common in commercial transactions for one party (the shipper) to enter into a contract with another (the carrier) for goods to be taken and delivered to a third party (the consignee). The doctrine of privity of contract would prevent the consignee suing the carrier for damage caused to the goods in transit, since the consignee was not a party to the contract. In the nineteenth century, Parliament attempted to solve this problem by attaching the right to sue the carrier (originating in the shipper as a party to the contract of carriage) to the ownership in the goods, so that when the consignee became owner of the goods he acquired the right to sue the carrier for damage in transit (see the Bills of Lading Act 1855). More recently the complex nature of commercial transactions exposed weaknesses in this solution in the 1855 Act, especially where the consignee was for some reason regarded by law as exposed to the risk of loss in respect of the goods but had not acquired ownership (e.g., *Leigh and Sillavan Ltd* v *Aliakmon Shipping Co. Ltd* [1986] AC 785). By the Carriage of Goods by Sea Act 1992, Parliament attempted to remedy the situation. The 1855 Act was repealed, and under the 1992 Act the right to sue the carrier passes from shipper to consignee or lawful holder of a bill of lading (as defined by ss. 2 and 5) by operation of law, and independently of the passing of ownership. This statutory exception to the doctrine of privity of contract is said to be justified as a matter of commercial necessity.

15.5.4 The *Eurymedon* device: protection of third parties by exemption clause

15.5.4.1 Scope of the exception
An exemption clause is a clause which purports to exclude or to limit liability for breach of contract. We have already examined the law relating to exemption clauses in two-party contract situations (Chapter 6). However, some commercial transactions, especially those involving international trade and shipping, cannot easily be analysed in terms of the traditional bilateral contract. Since in the commercial field the attitude of the English courts has always been that contract law must be the servant, and not the master, of the needs and practices of those engaged in business (see 1.4), the law must accommodate those needs and practices as best it can without over-insisting on the purity of the conceptual framework. It was precisely in the context of an attempt to protect a third party by means of an exemption clause that Lord Wilberforce made his now well-known statement about the occasional difficulty of 'forcing the facts to fit uneasily into the marked slots of offer, acceptance and consideration' (in *New Zealand Shipping Co. Ltd* v *A.M. Satterthwaite & Co. Ltd (The Eurymedon)* [1975] AC 154: see 2.2). It was on the basis of the needs and practices of the business community that an exception to the privity doctrine, which allows the protection of third parties by means of an exemption clause, was allowed to develop. The ability to afford protection to third parties through exemption clauses is accepted as commercially efficient since in the commercial context such clauses operate

as risk allocation devices. Given this commercial rationale based on the fact that such clauses are freely negotiated between commercial parties, its scope was unlikely to be extended to consumer contracts. It should be noted, however, that even where this exception applied and the exemption clause was found to be capable of protecting a third party, the clause remained subject to all the usual controls (see generally 6.5 and 6.6).

In *Elder, Dempster & Co.* v *Paterson, Zochonis & Co. Ltd* [1924] AC 522, shipowners, who were not parties to a contract between the shippers of goods and the charterers of the vessel, which was evidenced by a bill of lading, claimed nevertheless to be protected by an exemption clause contained therein. The House of Lords upheld that claim. No reasons for the decision were given, other than that such a decision was consistent with the commercial realities of the situation, and that the alternative proposition, that the charterer was protected by the clause but the shipowners were not, was 'absurd'. The difficulty of this decision was that it was clearly inconsistent with the privity doctrine, but did not explain how the doctrine had been avoided.

A very similar situation arose for consideration by the House of Lords in *Scruttons Ltd* v *Midland Silicones Ltd* [1962] AC 446. It was apparent that such purported extensions of exemption clauses to third parties, and especially to stevedores employed to load and unload cargoes, were commonplace in the commercial world, and that the particular action was regarded as a test case. The majority of the House of Lords confirmed that commercial contracts were not as a category exempt from the requirement in the general law of contract of privity between parties. It was accepted that the privity doctrine might be avoided by means of a separate contract between the third party and the shipper of the goods, and that such a contract might arise by way of agency (see 16.6), but their Lordships would not find such a contract on this ground unless the requirements for a finding of agency were present, namely, there had to be authority to act as agent and consideration for the promise would need to be given by the third party (as principal in the agency relationship). Lord Reid (at 474) spelt out four conditions which would need to be satisfied before a third party could rely on an exemption clause in a contract to which he or she was not a party:

> I can see a possibility of success of the agency argument if (first) the bill of lading makes it clear that the stevedore is intended to be protected by the provisions in it which limit liability, (secondly) that the bill of lading makes it clear that the carrier, in addition to contracting for these provisions on his own behalf, is also contracting as agent for the stevedore that these provisions should apply to the stevedore, (thirdly) the carrier has authority from the stevedore to do that, or perhaps later ratification by the stevedore would suffice, and (fourthly) that any difficulties about consideration moving from the stevedore were overcome.

In this particular case there was nothing in the bill of lading to suggest that the exemption clause was intended to benefit the stevedores, and nothing to indicate that the carrier was contracting as agent for the stevedore to obtain the benefit of the clause. Nevertheless, the statement by Lord Reid provided a glimmer of hope to the business community, who appeared to find it commercially necessary that protection of this kind be afforded to third parties involved in the performance of their contracts. As a result, attempts were made to draft contractual exemption clauses which would meet the requirements set out by Lord Reid.

One such clause (known as a 'Himalaya clause') fell to be considered by the Privy Council in *New Zealand Shipping Co. Ltd v A.M. Satterthwaite & Co. Ltd (The Eurymedon)* [1975] AC 154. As it was aimed at fulfilling Lord Reid's criteria, the clause is particularly long and complex, but its essential ingredients are that the clause expressly grants protection to a category of persons ('servants, agents and independent contractors') in a wide range of circumstances and expressly states that for the purposes of obtaining this protection the carrier is acting as agent or trustee on behalf of these persons who, to this extent, are to be regarded as parties to the contract.

It was established without difficulty that the clause satisfied the first three requirements of the agency argument put forward by Lord Reid. The issue was whether there was any consideration for the contract between the stevedores and the shippers arranged through the agency of the carriers. The stevedores were already under a duty, by virtue of their contract with the carriers, to unload the cargo with due care, and the performance of that duty could also be consideration for the separate contract exempting the stevedores from liability to the shippers (see 4.3.4.2).

Although it was possible in *The Eurymedon* to find a contract between the shippers and the stevedores by virtue of the doctrine of agency, there was some difficulty about describing that contract as bilateral, since at the time when the carrier made the principal contract with the shipper the intended stevedore might be unaware of the actual contract envisaged (this would not affect the carrier's authority to act for the stevedore, which would have been given in general terms). The Privy Council overcame the difficulty by finding that the principal contract resulted in the shipper making an offer in the form of a unilateral contract whereby it would exempt from liability anybody undertaking to unload the cargo. This *Eurymedon* device was criticised because of its artificiality and complexity rather than because of its result.

One reason why it was relatively easy in *The Eurymedon* to find that the carriers were acting as duly authorised agents (*cf.* 16.7) for the stevedores was that the carriers and stevedores were part of the same group of companies. It was suggested (*cf. The Suleyman Stalskiy* [1976] 2 Lloyd's Rep 609) that where there was no previous relationship between the stevedore and the carrier the agency argument would not prevail over the privity doctrine. However, that suggestion was disapproved by Lord Wilberforce in a further Privy Council case on this point (*Port Jackson Stevedoring Pty Ltd v Salmond & Spraggon (Australia) Pty Ltd, The New York Star* [1981] 1 WLR 138). Lord Wilberforce thought that *The Eurymedon* principle should be regarded as of general application, and should not depend upon fine distinctions based upon the nature of the relationship between carrier and stevedore. This reasoning appears to be correct. If it is the practice of the commercial world, when exemptions from liability are included in contracts, to seek to extend the benefit of such protection to third parties necessary to the performance of the contract, then there is no undue surprise to the other party if the first claims also to contract as agent for such a third party, irrespective of whether there is any other relationship between them.

This plea to apply *The Eurymedon* generally and not to seek to distinguish it based on fine distinctions of fact was not followed by the English courts in the context of attempts by subcontractors to rely on clauses in the contract between the employer and main contractor, on the basis that there could be no authority to act as agent for a person who had not been identified to that contract at the time it was entered into. Subcontractors would not generally be appointed until after the main contract was entered into and so could not have authorised the main contractor to contract on their behalf (*Southern Water Authority* v *Carey* [1985] 2 All ER 1077 and *Norwich City Council* v *Harvey* [1989] 1 All ER 1180; although in both cases the subcontractor was protected because the clause was interpreted as a risk allocation provision and as restricting the scope of the duty of care in tort). This difficulty of non-existence in relation to the main contract was avoided by the High Court of Australia in *Trident General Insurance Co. Ltd* v *McNiece Brothers Proprietary Ltd* (1988) 165 CLR 107. The Court allowed McNiece to obtain the protection of an insurance policy on the basis that it was a subcontractor of the insured and the policy purported to extend to cover subcontractors, even though McNiece was not a subcontractor at the time the policy contract was entered into. Commercial difficulties would arise if this broad interpretation was not adopted because third parties might well rely on the fact that they were covered by insurance and neglect to take out their own cover. Equally, if they did take out their own cover, it might result in double cover which would be inefficient.

The scope of *The Eurymedon* device was nevertheless quite limited. In *The Mahkutai* [1996] 3 All ER 502, the Privy Council refused to extend its scope to jurisdiction clauses, on the basis that, unlike exemption clauses which benefit one party only, jurisdiction clauses create mutual rights and obligations. This was a neutral clause, and not one included simply 'for the benefit' of one party.

The most fundamental difficulty that could be faced in seeking to rely on *The Eurymedon* was experienced in *London Drugs Ltd* v *Kuehne & Nagel International Ltd* (1993) 97 DLR (4th) 261. There was a limitation clause in a storage contract which limited 'the warehouseman's liability'. However, the clause did not expressly cover the employees who in fact damaged the goods in storage. The Canadian Court of Appeal held that it covered the employees by impliedly extending the meaning of the clause although this amounted to extending Lord Reid's criteria in *Scruttons* v *Midland Silicones*. On appeal the Supreme Court of Canada considered that it was not possible to extend *The Eurymedon* in this way, and instead created a new exception to the privity doctrine in Canada. This exception was outside the scope of *The Eurymedon* and is limited to employees. It would apply where the clause expressly or impliedly extended the benefit of the clause to employees and the employees caused the loss in performing the very services provided for in the contract. In *Fraser River Pile & Dredge Ltd* v *Can-Dive Services* [2000] 1 Lloyd's Rep 199, the *London Drugs* exception was put in broader terms, namely that the parties must have intended to extend the benefit to the third party and the activities performed by the third party must have been the very activities contemplated as coming within the scope of the contract or the contractual provision which was being relied upon.

15.5.4.2 The effect of the 1999 Act on the ability of a third party to enforce an exemption clause   The ability of a third party to enforce a contract term (including an exemption clause (1999 Act, s. 1(6)) is determined by the test of enforceability. Therefore, if the clause in question expressly provides that the third party, who is expressly identified in the contract by name or as a member of a class, is to have the right to enforce the exemption clause, the third party will clearly have that right. However, the Himalaya clause in *The Eurymedon* (see 15.5.4.1) does not expressly give this right. Instead, it states that the stevedore (as a member of the class of independent contractors) is to have the benefit of the clause and that the carrier is acting as his agent for this purpose. Section 1(1)(b) ought therefore to apply to this clause and factual context unless 'on a proper construction of the contract it appears that the parties did not intend the term to be enforceable by the third party'. This will depend on the wording of the contract as a whole. Accordingly, and on the basis that there is nothing to indicate that the parties did not intend the term to be enforceable by the third party (as to which see 15.3), under the 1999 Act there should be a direct right of enforcement of the Himalaya clause in *The Eurymedon*. This should reduce much of the complexity of the law governing third party enforcement of exemption clauses.

The 1999 Act may also provide a direct right of enforcement in situations such as those in *Southern Water Authority* v *Carey* and *Norwich City Council* v *Harvey* (see 15.5.4.1), because of the clarity of the risk allocation clauses and because the Act specifically states that the third party (i.e., the subcontractor) 'need not be in existence when the contract is entered into' (s. 1(3)). However, it would not be available in factual situations such as *Scruttons* v *Midland Silicones* because of the absence of an *express* identification of the third party as an intended beneficiary of the clause. The same problem would exist on the facts in *London Drugs* v *Kuehne & Nagel*, namely, the fact that the clause does not *expressly* confer a benefit on the employees unless they can be said to be *expressly* identified as members of a class of 'warehouseman', when the reality is that this can be achieved only by fairly generous implication. *The Eurymedon* could not operate in either of these cases because the first criterion specified by Lord Reid is not satisfied. The 1999 Act effectively keeps that first requirement and dispenses with the remaining three, thereby eliminating the complexity. *London Drugs* can be compared with *Fraser River Pile & Dredge Ltd* v *Can-Dive Ltd* [2000] 1 Lloyd's Rep 199, which would satisfy the s. 1(1)(b) test of enforceability in the 1999 Act. On the facts, the clause extended to third party beneficiaries coming within the class of 'charterers', so that this constituted express identification in the waiver of subrogation clause.

15.6 REMEDIES AVAILABLE TO THE PROMISEE

One method of avoiding the consequences of the privity doctrine would be if the promisee could bring a claim and recover remedies which enforced the third party's rights or compensated for the third party's loss. The fundamental weakness in relying on this means of enforcement is that the third party will be dependent on the willingness of the promisee to bring a claim.

This method of avoiding the consequences of privity will be less relevant as a result of the 1999 Act if the third party can achieve a remedy directly (although the promisee's right to enforce and recover on behalf of the third party is expressly retained: s. 5). Nevertheless, as we have seen, the 1999 Act does not provide third parties with rights of enforcement in all circumstances so that the following remedies remain relevant.

15.6.1 Specific performance

Specific performance is an order which would compel the promisor to carry out the promise so that the third party obtains the intended benefit under the contract. However, as discussed in 14.2.3.1, this remedy is discretionary and will not be granted where damages would be an adequate remedy. In *Beswick* v *Beswick* [1968] AC 58, the fact that the loss suffered by the promisee was negligible, so that damages would be purely nominal, was said to be good reason for awarding the discretionary remedy of specific performance (for the facts of this case, see 14.2.1). Mrs Beswick would now be able to enforce the nephew's promise directly under s. 1(1)(b) of the 1999 Act since the contract clearly purported to confer a benefit on her as a named individual (although it did not give her an express right to enforce the promise against the nephew). There also seems to be no evidence 'on the proper construction of the contract' that she was not intended to be able to enforce the term.

This remedy is undoubtedly the best suited to achieving the promisee's original contractual intention of conferring a benefit on the third party, but it is not without limitations. In the first place, as a general remedy specific performance is subject to restrictions, such as the fact that damages must not be an adequate remedy (see also 14.2.1). Moreover, in *Beswick* v *Beswick* it was a happy coincidence that the widow had been appointed administratrix of the husband's estate, since she then had no problem in persuading the 'promisee' to bring the action for specific performance. Since it appears that the third party cannot compel the promisee to act (15.6.4), the remedy of specific performance will be available only when it suits the promisee to enforce the contract.

In addition, it is suitable as a remedy only where the performance has yet to take place (or to take place fully). It will not be appropriate where the contract has been performed, albeit defectively, and the third party seeks a remedy.

15.6.2 Enforcement of negative undertakings

Where the contractual term breached is in the form of a negative undertaking (a promise to refrain from doing something), the obvious remedy is an injunction (14.3), which is a form of specific relief similar to specific performance designed to prevent actions rather than to enforce performance. It would appear to be consistent with the reasoning in *Beswick* v *Beswick* [1968] AC 58 if an injunction were to be available to a promisee in appropriate circumstances in the same way that specific performance was in that case. Where the negative undertaking is a promise not to sue the third party, the correct procedure is not to seek an injunction but to ask the court to stay the proceedings which have been brought in contravention of the promise. In *Gore* v *Van der Lann* [1967] 2 QB 31, the Court of Appeal said that, even where there was a definite promise not to sue the third party, the promisee would be granted a stay of proceedings only if he had a sufficient interest in the enforcement of the promise. Such an interest would arise only if, for example, the promisee was under a legal obligation to reimburse the third party (the defendant to the action) in respect of any damages the third party had to pay to the claimant. However, in the subsequent case of *Snelling* v *John G. Snelling Ltd* [1973] 1 QB 87, the requirement of sufficient interest appears to have been ignored by the court.

In *Snelling*, three brothers each loaned money to the family company, and subsequently agreed among themselves not to seek to recover such loans should any of them resign his directorship of the company. The plaintiff resigned and brought an action against the company to recover money loaned to it. The other brothers applied to be joined as defendants to the action, and then counterclaimed for a declaration that the plaintiff was not entitled to recover the sums in question. In theory, the plaintiff should have succeeded against the company, since the company could not enforce the stipulation made on its behalf. On the other hand, the brothers were entitled to succeed on their counterclaim. Ormrod J resolved this apparent impasse by staying the proceedings, since in reality the plaintiff had lost his action. The two brothers were under no legal liability to the company should the third fail to keep his promise to refrain from recovering the money owing to him, so that it is not easy to see what was the sufficient interest which they had in seeking enforcement of the promise. The decision in *Snelling* would therefore appear to be more in line with the approach in *Beswick* v *Beswick*, i.e. that the nephew could not be allowed to ignore his express promise to pay Mrs Beswick on Mr Beswick's death. The brother in *Snelling* could not be permitted to do the very thing which he had contracted not to do. It may be that the sufficient interest requirement is either an alternative (where there is no express promise not to sue), or of no effect at all (given that discussion of this issue in *Gore* v *Van der Lann* was strictly *obiter*).

15.6.3 Promisee's claim for damages

The difficulty with a claim for damages in relation to breach of a contract providing for a third party benefit, is that the promisee may usually recover damages only for his or her own loss. If the performance to be provided by the other party was intended entirely for the benefit of the third party, the law takes the view that there is no loss to the promisee resulting from the breach, so that damages will be purely nominal (*Beswick v Beswick* [1968] AC 58; although compare the opinion of Lord Pearce). Of course, if the promisee were to receive some benefit from the other party's performance in addition to the benefit intended for the third party, then that loss would be recoverable under the normal rules, but the promisee would still be unable to recover for the third party's loss. It seems, however, that if the promisee were to be under a legal obligation to compensate the third party in the event of non-performance by the other contracting party (e.g., as a result of a contract between promisee and third party), then that obligation would amount to a real loss to the promisee, and substantial damages would be recoverable on that account. It is open to question whether payment to the third party by the promisee on the strength of a perceived moral obligation to provide compensation would also be a recoverable loss.

In recent years it has been suggested that the promisee should in any case be able to recover damages for the loss suffered by the third party. If the third party were then able to compel the promisee to hand over the damages recovered (see 15.6.4), such a remedy would effectively side-step any privity problems (assuming that the promisee can be persuaded to bring the claim for damages in the first place). Such a claim by the promisee appears to have been allowed by the Court of Appeal in *Jackson v Horizon Holidays Ltd* [1975] 1 WLR 1468.

In *Jackson*, the plaintiff had booked a package holiday for himself and his family. The holiday fell well short of the standard promised. The plaintiff brought an action for breach of contract. The defendant holiday company challenged the trial judge's award of damages of £1,100, which was just less than the full cost of the holiday. In the Court of Appeal the award was upheld. Lord Denning MR said that the award was excessive as compensation for the plaintiff's loss alone, but was a correct assessment of the aggregate loss suffered by the whole family. The plaintiff was entitled to recover damages for loss suffered by the family members because he had contracted on their behalf. The other members of the Court of Appeal, although upholding the award, did not openly state that it represented compensation for loss suffered by the other members of the family as well as by the plaintiff.

Lord Denning MR regarded *Jackson v Horizon Holidays Ltd* as an example of a general principle allowing the promisee to recover damages on behalf of third party beneficiaries. He claimed that it fell within the principle contained in an *obiter* statement by Lush LJ in *Lloyd's v Harper* (1880) 16 ChD 290 at 321 at 'I consider it to be an established rule of law that where a contract is made with A for the benefit of B, A can sue on the contract for the benefit of B, and recover all that B could have recovered if the contract had been made with B himself'. This reasoning and the width of this principle was disapproved (*obiter*) in *Woodar Investment Development Ltd v Wimpey Construction (UK) Ltd* [1980] 1 WLR 277.

In *Woodar Investments*, the plaintiffs agreed to sell some land to the defendants for £850,000. It was a term of the contract that the defendants should pay £150,000 of the price to a third party. The defendants failed to go ahead with the purchase, and the plaintiffs claimed damages for what they said was a repudiatory breach. The House of Lords found that the defendants had not repudiated the contract, but went on to discuss the privity issue. While being far from satisfied with the privity doctrine (see 15.2), their Lordships denied the existence of a general principle allowing the promisee to recover damages for loss suffered by the third party beneficiary, and claimed that Lord Denning MR had taken the statement of Lush LJ out of its proper context limiting this principle to situations of agency or trust. They did not, however, overrule the actual decision in *Jackson* v *Horizon Holidays Ltd*. Lord Wilberforce thought that the decision probably belonged to a special category of cases 'calling for special treatment', where one party contracts for a benefit of a group for reasons of convenience. Transactions which may fall within this special category are 'contracting for family holidays, ordering meals in restaurants for a party, hiring a taxi for a group'.

It appears from this that the person contracting on behalf of the group would also need to suffer some loss in order to be able to recover for the members of the party. This would have been of no assistance on the facts in *Woodar Investments*, because it was not a contract made on behalf of a group and there was no evidence that Woodar had suffered any loss as a result of the non-payment to the third party. In his judgment Lord Scarman suggested that had Woodar been under an obligation to pay compensation to the third party following the non-payment, this might have been included within Woodar's loss (as promisee).

Nevertheless, another exception to the general rule has been recognised in the commercial context, which allows the promisee to recover substantial damages on behalf of a third party although the promisee has not suffered any loss. In *Linden Gardens Trust Ltd* v *Lenesta Sludge Disposals Ltd* [1994] 1 AC 85 ('the St Martins Property' appeal) the question arose of what compensation was recoverable where party A engaged party B to carry out work on his property, in circumstances where both understood that A was very likely to transfer the property to party C. This transfer took place. B performed the work defectively and in breach of contract. In the absence of an assignment (which was contractually excluded) C could not sue, and it was argued that since A no longer had any interest in the property, its damages would be purely nominal. The House of Lords did not agree. Their Lordships' motivation appears to have been the desire to avoid the conclusion that the building contractor (B) would not have to pay substantial damages for the breach. Relying on Lord Diplock's explanation (in *The Albazero* [1977] AC 774) of the decision in *Dunlop* v *Lambert* (1839) 6 Cl & F 600, Lord Browne-Wilkinson said (at 114–115):

> The contract was for a large development of property which, to the knowledge of both [parties], was going to be occupied and possibly purchased by third parties . . . Therefore, it could be foreseen that damage caused by a breach would cause loss to a later owner and not merely to the original contracting party . . . In such a case, it seems to me proper, as in

the case of the carriage of goods by land, to treat the parties as having entered into the contract on the footing that [the original owner] would be entitled to enforce the contractual rights for the benefit of those who suffered from defective performance. . . .

This reasoning is referred to as 'the narrow ground' for the decision in *Linden Gardens*. It allows A to retain the right to sue for substantial damages and recover for the loss suffered by C, on the basis that it was contemplated that someone other than A would suffer loss in the event of breach of the contract but be unable to sue.

Lord Griffiths advocated 'the broad ground' to support his conclusion that the building owner could recover substantial damages, and there was some sympathy with this approach from other members of the House of Lords (Lords Keith and Bridge, although Lord Browne-Wilkinson thought that further academic consideration of this ground was required). (For this academic discussion, see Palmer and Tolhurst (1997) 12 JCL 1, (1997) 12 JCL 97 and (1998) 13 JCL 143). If the broad ground is accepted as a means of obtaining substantial damages on behalf of third parties, it has the potential drastically to alter the practical consequences of the application of the privity doctrine because the loss will be suffered by the promisee.

The 'broad ground' argument rests on the premise that in a contract for the supply of work and materials, it makes no difference whether the promisee has any proprietary interest in the subject-matter of the contract; the crucial factor is whether there has been defective performance or non-performance, since the result of the breach is that the promisee does not receive 'the bargain for which he contracted'. That is the promisee's loss and he or she can recover substantial damages on a cost of cure basis for that loss of expectation.

There was some support in the judgment of Steyn LJ in *Darlington Borough Council* v *Wiltshier Northern Ltd* [1995] 1 WLR 68 for this 'broad approach'. However, in that case it was the 'narrow ground' in *Linden Gardens* which was applied by the Court of Appeal (in relation to a claim by the third party). The contractor had contracted with the bank (which had become involved because of restrictions on local authority expenditure) to construct a recreation centre for the local authority on land owned by that local authority. Contractual rights had been assigned (transferred) to the council and the contractor was aware that that the centre was being built for the council. The local authority wanted to bring an action for defective performance of the construction contract, but could recover substantial damages only if the bank had assigned the right to substantial damages. Therefore, the question was the same as that in *Linden Gardens*, namely, could the contracting party recover substantial damages for breach of a contract when it had no property interest and had therefore suffered no loss? The Court of Appeal applied 'the narrow ground' exception and held that there was a right to recover substantial damages, because it was clear to the contractor that the centre was being constructed for the local authority on local authority land and that the local authority would suffer loss in the event of breach. This extends the application of the 'narrow ground' to instances where the promisee has never had any ownership interest in the property affected by the breach. Steyn LJ pointed to the need, recognised previously by Lord Diplock and Lord Browne-Wilkinson in *Linden Gardens*, 'to provide a remedy where no other would be available to a person sustaining loss which under a rational legal system ought to be compensated by the person who has caused it'.

However, in *Alfred MacAlpine Construction Ltd v Panatown Ltd* [2000] 3 WLR 946, the House of Lords refused to allow an employer to recover substantial damages for defective workmanship where the employer did not own the land in question and so had suffered no financial loss. Panatown had employed McAlpine to build an office block and a multi-storey car park. The construction site was owned throughout by an associate company of Panatown, UIPL. The distinguishing fact in this case was that the contractors (McAlpine) had also entered into a 'Duty of Care Deed' with UIPL (the site owner), which gave UIPL a direct remedy against the contractor for breaches of qualified contractual terms. Panatown claimed damages for defective performance of the construction contract. UIPL did not seek to bring an action under the Duty of Care Deed. The majority of the House of Lords held that, because of the existence of the Duty of Care Deed which gave the site owner a direct remedy, the 'narrow ground' exception in *Linden Gardens* could not apply; it was unnecessary because the third party had a direct right of action against the contractor. Accordingly, there was no need to depart from the general rule that substantial damages cannot be claimed by a promisee who has suffered no loss.

This decision therefore rests on its facts. However, it is a significant decision because the House of Lords modified the 'narrow ground' in *Linden Gardens* and stated that it was not based on contractual intention and what the parties contemplated (as the Court of Appeal had considered [1998] CLC 636). Instead it was a solution imposed by law, although one which was excluded on the facts in *Panatown*. This should simplify the application of the 'narrow ground' as it avoids difficult questions surrounding the determination of the intentions of the parties.

The House of Lords in *McAlpine v Panatown* also considered the 'broad ground' which had been advocated by Lord Griffiths in *Linden Gardens*. The majority (who decided the case on the basis of the Duty of Care Deed) expressed grave doubts about the broad ground, although they accepted that the promisee would be able to recover in the event of defective performance if he spent money on repairing the defects, despite the fact that he was under no legal obligation to do so. On the other hand, there was support for the broad ground from the dissenting members of the House of Lords, Lords Goff and Millett. They dissented on the Duty of Care Deed because they considered it irrelevant. Their focus was on the loss suffered by the promisee (Panatown) as a result of the defective performance for which it had contracted, whereas the Duty of Care Deed dealt with the question of third party enforceability. Lord Browne-Wilkinson (who was in the majority in that he considered that the Duty of Care Deed prevented the promisee's recovery) also appeared to accept the broad ground argument because he attempted to

link the two. He stated that because of the Duty of Care Deed, UIPL had a
remedy against McAlpine so that Panatown had not suffered a loss of bargain
(i.e., there was no damage to Panatown's performance interest). (For further
discussion of this case, see B. Coote, 'The Performance Interest, Panatown,
and the problem of Loss' (2001) 117 LQR 81.)

15.6.4 Relations with the promisee

The third party's relations with the promisee are most likely to be an issue
where after the time of contracting the promisee changes his or her mind
about the intention to confer a benefit on the third party. The result of such
a change of mind might be either a refusal to bring a claim against the
promisor for specific performance, or, if damages were recoverable on behalf
of the third party, a refusal to hand over the sum recovered. Lord Denning
MR believed that the third party could prevent both such refusals. In the
Court of Appeal in *Beswick* v *Beswick* [1966] Ch 538, he suggested that the
third party could compel the promisee to bring the claim by starting
proceedings and joining the promisee as co-defendant. However, the majority
in the Court of Appeal rejected this procedure, and their view is the more
orthodox. In *Jackson* v *Horizon Holidays Ltd* [1975] 1 WLR 1468, Lord
Denning suggested that when the plaintiff recovered damages on behalf of the
third party beneficiaries under the contract he held them as money had and
received for the use of the third parties, who in theory could therefore recover
the money from him by legal action if he refused to hand it over. Subject to
the proviso that such damages appear rarely to be recoverable (15.6.3), Lord
Denning's suggestion would seem to be correct.

   In *Darlington Borough Council* v *Wiltshier Northern Ltd* [1995] 1 WLR 68,
Dillon and Waite LJJ would have found, if necessary, that damages obtained
by the original contracting party were held on a constructive trust for the true
owner of the property, relying on an analogy with *Lloyd's* v *Harper* (1880) 16
ChD 290.

15.7 PRIVITY AND IMPOSING OBLIGATIONS UPON THIRD PARTIES

The privity doctrine provides that a third party cannot be made subject to a
burden in a contract to which he or she is not a party. There are some
recognised exceptions to this principle at common law, although, as noted at
15.2, the Law Commission Report and the Contracts (Rights of Third
Parties) Act 1999 do not extend to this aspect of the doctrine.

15.7.1 Restrictions on the use of chattels

Under a doctrine peculiar to land law, founded in the old case of *Tulk* v
Moxhay (1848) 2 Ph 774, third parties can be subject to burdens of restrictive
covenants affecting land. The vendor of land can attach restrictive covenants
to that land which 'run with the land' and regulate its future use. Such

covenants are enforceable by adjacent landowners, and bind all subsequent purchasers.

It was suggested by the Privy Council in *Lord Strathcona Steamship Co. Ltd v Dominion Coal Co. Ltd* [1926] AC 108, that this principle also applied to restrictions affecting the use of chattels in contracts which did not concern land if the third party purchased the chattel in question with notice of the restriction. In *Lord Strathcona*, it was held that where purchasers of a vessel had purchased it with knowledge of the existence of a charter relating to its use, the charterers could obtain an injunction to prevent the new owners from ignoring that charter. However, in *Port Line Ltd v Ben Line Steamers Ltd* [1958] 2 QB 146, Diplock J refused to follow *Lord Strathcona* on the basis that it was wrongly decided due to an inappropriate analogy with the land law cases which required the party enforcing the restriction to have retained an independent proprietary interest which would benefit from the restriction. The charterers in *Lord Strathcona* had no such independent proprietary interest. Diplock J also stated that even if the principle did apply, it could do so only where the remedy sought was an injunction to restrain inconsistent use and where the purchaser took with *actual* notice of the restriction.

It may be the case that *Lord Strathcona* is actually an application of the tort of knowing interference with contractual rights. This appears to have been the view held by Browne-Wilkinson J when he followed *Lord Strathcona* in *Swiss Bank Corporation v Lloyds Bank Ltd* [1979] Ch 548. A third party commits a tort if he or she interferes in an intentional or reckless manner with a contract, e.g., intentionally procuring a contractual party to break his or her contract (*Lumley v Gye* (1853) 2 E & B 216). The issue of the injunction in *Lord Strathcona* would equate with this in preventing the new owner from acting inconsistently with an existing charter contract of which he was aware when he purchased the ship.

The point was reconsidered by Hoffmann J in *Law Debenture Trust Corporation plc v Ural Caspian Oil Corporation Ltd* [1993] 1 WLR 138. The case concerned the claims for compensation of companies which had traded in Russia and whose assets had been confiscated as a consequence of the Russian revolution. The shares in these companies had been sold to L, subject to an undertaking by the purchaser that any compensation would be paid to the original shareholders and that a similar undertaking would be secured from future purchasers. The purchaser sold the shares on to H Ltd without obtaining the undertaking, and H Ltd later transferred the shares to C Ltd. The allegation was that both H and C had taken the shares with knowledge of the covenant. A significant sum in compensation was paid and the original shareholders sought to recover it. Hoffmann J had to consider whether they had an arguable case to do so. He considered there to be an arguable case on the basis of interference with a remedy which would otherwise have been available, namely the fact that H knew of the breach of covenant and could therefore had been forced to transfer the shares back to L in order to prevent the obligation between the shareholders and L being defeated. The transfer by H to C had eliminated the possibility of this remedy and constituted a tort. (The Court of Appeal ([1994] 3 WLR 1221) overturned the decision on this point on the basis that the tort could not exist unless the transfer between H and C constituted an actionable wrong and none existed.)

Hoffmann J specifically rejected a claim based on the principle in *Lord Strathcona* on the ground that the shareholders were seeking to use the principle to obtain compliance with a positive covenant when the principle could only ever permit the issue of an injunction to ensure compliance with a negative covenant. Hoffmann J stated specifically (at 144): 'One thing is beyond doubt: [the principle] does not provide a panacea for outflanking the doctrine of privity of contract.'

The decision has failed to resolve the uncertainties surrounding the relationship between the *Lord Strathcona* principle and the tort of knowing interference with contractual rights, although it appears that they can be claimed as alternatives and so may not be the same.

15.7.2 Bailment

In some circumstances the bailor will be bound by the terms of a sub-bailment entered into by the bailee, including any exemption clauses in that sub-bailment. Bailment involves the delivery of goods under a contract by a bailor to the bailee for some purpose, e.g., dry-cleaning, repairing, safekeeping, and their subsequent return to the bailor after that purpose has been fulfilled. For example, in *Morris* v *C.W. Martin & Sons Ltd* [1966] 1 QB 716, the owner of a mink stole (the bailor) sent it to a furrier (the bailee) for cleaning. The bailee sent the stole to a sub-bailee for cleaning on terms whereby the goods were 'held at the customer's risk'. Could the sub-bailee rely on this exemption clause when sued by the bailor? Lord Denning (*obiter*) considered that as the bailor had agreed that the bailee should pass the stole to the sub-bailee for the cleaning, she had impliedly consented to the cleaning taking place on the terms of that sub-bailment. This principle was applied by the Privy Council in *The Pioneer Container* [1994] 2 AC 324.

The bailor will therefore be affected by terms in a contract to which he or she is not a party where the bailor expressly or impliedly consented to those terms. In *Northern Electric Ltd* v *Econofreight Heavy Transport Ltd* (unreported), 21 December 2000, this principle was applied in relation to an express consent to the subcontracting of haulage. It was stressed that there was nothing in the contract between the claimant and the bailee which sought to control the terms of that subcontract, so that the only proper inference was that the claimant had consented to the bailee entering into a subcontract on the standard terms of transport of the sub-bailee.

SIXTEEN

Assignment and agency

This chapter considers two mechanisms which may be utilised to avoid the privity doctrine and which both have considerable commercial significance. Paragraphs 16.1 to 16.5 examine the law of assignment (or transfer) of contractual rights. Paragraphs 16.6 to 16.11 provide an introduction to the law of agency. Agency is the legal device by which one person (the *agent*: 'A') may act on behalf of another (the *principal*: 'P') in the formation of a contract between that other and a third party. The doctrine in its standard form is not really an exception to the privity doctrine, since there is no contractual relationship between the agent and the third party. Thus the agent does not stipulate for a benefit to be conferred on his or her principal: rather, the principal is a party to the contract with the third party. Nevertheless, agency may sometimes be used as a means of avoiding the impact of the privity doctrine; see *The Eurymedon* device which was designed to enable a third party to rely on an exemption clause in a contract to which he was not a party (15.5.4.1). This device proved to be very technical because of the need to meet the requirements for the establishment of the agency relationship, and its significance will be greatly reduced as a result of the Contracts (Rights of Third Parties) Act 1999 (see 15.5.4.2).

16.1 ASSIGNMENT: INTRODUCTION

Assignment is a device which enables one party to transfer the benefit of a performance, which he or she has contracted to receive, to another person in such a way that the assignee (to whom the benefit is transferred) may enforce performance. It should be noted that in this situation the original contract does not stipulate that the benefit of performance should go to a third party. In terms of the triangular relationship outlined at p. 439, a bilateral contract is made between A and B. After the contract is made, B (the assignor/ creditor) assigns the right to enforce the contract (a form of intangible personal property known as a *chose in action*) to C (the assignee), who then has a direct right of action against A (the debtor). It should also be noted that an involuntary assignment by operation of law may occur upon death or bankruptcy, but we are concerned here only with voluntary assignments.

The common law made no provision for the assignment of choses in action. A direct right of action against the debtor could be conferred on a third party only by granting a power of attorney or by a 'novation', both of which procedures had their disadvantages. The problem with the power of attorney was that it might be revoked by the original creditor, or upon his or her death, so that it could not guarantee the third party's independent right of action. Novation involves the rescission of the original contract between debtor and creditor, and the substitution in its place of a new contract between debtor and third party, and thus requires both fresh consideration on the part of the third party and the consent of the debtor.

Dissatisfaction with the common law provisions as to the transfer of choses in action led to the development in equity of a doctrine of assignment. The effect of the doctrine was to permit a right of action to be conferred on a third party, but the means whereby that was achieved varied according to the nature of the chose in action. If the right was one which before the Judicature Acts 1873–75 could be enforced only in the Chancery Court (an 'equitable chose'), the assignee could bring the action in his or her own name and need not involve the assignor since there was no risk of conflict with the common law courts. If, however, the right was one which could be enforced in the common law courts (a 'legal chose'), the assignee had to bring the action in the name of the assignor, in order to avoid the risk of the common law courts granting to the assignor a remedy different from the solution reached by the Chancery Court. In other words, by bringing the action in the name of the assignor all the parties were within the jurisdiction of the court, and their competing interests and claims could all be adjudicated upon at the same time. If the assignor was unwilling to allow his or her name to be used, the assignor would be compelled to do so by Court of Chancery.

As a result of the Judicature Acts 1873–75, assignments became enforceable in all courts, and the distinction between legal and equitable choses became blurred. Section 25(6) of the Judicature Act 1873 introduced a new form of statutory assignment. As we shall see (16.3), however, equitable assignment is still important, since an assignment which fails to satisfy the statutory provision may still take effect in equity (*William Brandt's Sons & Co. v Dunlop Rubber Co. Ltd* [1905] AC 454).

16.2   STATUTORY ASSIGNMENTS

16.2.1   Law of Property Act 1925, s. 136

Section 25(6) of the Judicature Act 1873 was replaced by s. 136(1) of the Law of Property Act 1925, which provides:

(1)   Any absolute assignment by writing under the hand of the assignor (not purporting to be by way of charge only) of any debt or other legal thing

in action, of which express notice in writing has been given to the debtor, trustee or other person from whom the assignor would have been able to claim such debt or thing in action, is effectual in law (subject to equities having priority over the right of the assignee) to pass and transfer from the date of such notice—

(a) the legal right to such debt or thing in action;
(b) all legal and other remedies for the same; and
(c) the power to give a good discharge for the same without the concurrence of the assignor. . . .

The effect of this provision is to enable the assignor to transfer the chose in action to the assignee without requiring the consent of the debtor, and in turn to enable the assignee in his or her own name to enforce the chose in action against the debtor without joining the assignor to the proceedings. Other statutes have provided for the legal assignability of particular debts and rights (e.g., Policies of Assurance Act 1867 and Companies Act 1985). However, here we examine only the requirements of general assignments.

16.2.2 Legal requirements

16.2.2.1 Absolute assignment An absolute assignment makes clear to the debtor to whom he or she should pay the debt which is owed. It is usually defined by stating what it is not. Assignment of part of a debt is not an absolute assignment (*Forster* v *Baker* [1910] 2 KB 636), since the subdivision of the debt creates the risk of the debtor being faced by claims for enforcement by more than one person. Where, on the other hand, what is assigned is the balance of the debt after part has been paid off then the assignment is absolute, since the debtor will be faced with only one potential claim for enforcement (*Harding* v *Harding* (1886) 17 QBD 442).

Assignment by way of charge is not an absolute assignment, as s. 136(1) indicates, since it only gives a right to be paid out of an identified fund, rather than transferring the whole fund to the assignee. In many cases assignments by way of charge are also conditional assignments, which again are not absolute. For example, in *Durham Bros* v *Robertson* [1898] 1 QB 765, a firm of builders borrowed money from the plaintiffs and as security assigned to the plaintiffs the sum of £1,080 owing to the builders under a contract with the defendant. The assignment was to last 'until the money with added interest be repaid'. Although the assignment was reasonable between assignor and assignee, it left the defendant debtor in a difficult position since he had no access to the information upon which the condition governing to which party he was supposed to pay the money depended. It is still possible to make an absolute assignment which is subject to a condition, provided that realisation of the condition does not merely cause the assignment to cease (the situation in *Durham Bros* v *Robertson*), but imposes a duty on the assignee to *reassign* the debt to the assignor (*Tancred* v *Delagoa Bay and East Africa Railway Co.* (1889) 23 QBD 239). In that case the position of the debtor is always protected, since once the debt is assigned to the assignee he or she is absolutely entitled to it, and the debtor may safely pay the money to the assignee until such time as the debtor receives actual notice of any reassignment.

16.2.2.2 Express notice Section 136(1) requires that notice in writing be given to the debtor. However, notice need not be given by the assignor; the notice is valid provided it actually reaches the debtor before such time as the assignee commences any claim upon the debt, and takes effect from the time it reaches the debtor (*Holt* v *Heatherfield Trust Ltd* [1942] 2 KB 1).

16.2.2.3 Debt or other legal thing in action Section 136(1) states that a statutory assignment may be made of 'any debt or other legal thing in action'. A debt is a definite sum of money due under some legal obligation, and especially for our purposes due under a contract. It might be thought that 'other legal thing in action' would correspond to the former category of legal choses (16.1), but it has been interpreted as meaning debts or rights not assignable at common law but regarded as assignable in equity, and so also includes equitable choses (*Torkington* v *Magee* [1902] 2 KB 427 at 430).

16.2.2.4 Other requirements Section 136(1) requires the assignment to be in writing and signed by the assignor.

There is no requirement of consideration for a statutory assignment to be valid between assignor and assignee, or for the assignee to be able to maintain a claim in his or her own name against the debtor (*Re Westerton* [1919] 2 Ch 104).

16.3 EQUITABLE ASSIGNMENTS

16.3.1 Introduction

An assignment which fails to satisfy the statutory requirements may still take effect as an equitable assignment (*William Brandt's Sons & Co.* v *Dunlop Rubber Co. Ltd* [1905] AC 454). The requirements of validity of equitable assignments are in some respects different from those for statutory assignments (see 16.3.2). In addition, the status of the assignee in the case of an equitable assignment is less strong, in that in some circumstances he or she may not be able to bring a claim without also involving the assignor in the proceedings. That status still depends upon the distinction which existed before the Judicature Act 1873 between equitable choses and legal choses (16.1).

In the case of the assignment of an equitable chose, the assignee may bring a claim against the debtor in his or her own name, except in those cases where the assignor has some remaining interest in the debt. For example, in the case of an assignment which is not absolute but is made by way of charge against a fund, the assignee must join the assignor to the proceedings so that all interested parties are within the jurisdiction of the court and will be bound by its decision. This procedure is essential, because an assignment by way of charge only gives a right to recover a certain sum out of a greater amount, with the balance remaining as a debt owed to the assignor (16.2.2.1).

In the case of the assignment of a legal chose, the assignee brings the claim against the debtor in his or her own name, but must always join the assignor to the proceedings, either as claimant, if the assignor is a willing participant, or as defendant if not (if, for example, the assignor disputes the validity of the assignment).

16.3.2 Legal requirements

16.3.2.1 Consideration By way of introduction, it should be pointed out that consideration is only an issue between the assignor and the assignee. It is not open to the debtor to impugn the validity of the assignment on the ground of want of consideration; the debtor's only concern is to know to which person to pay the debt alleged to be the subject of an assignment.

It is accepted without question that it is legally possible to make a gift (i.e., a gratuitous transfer) of personal property which is tangible (a chose in possession, e.g., a book). It is also recognised that it is not legally possible to make an enforceable promise to make a gift of a book at some point in the future, unless that promise is in the form of a contract, and so supported by consideration. A chose in action is a form of personal property which is intangible. It is equally capable of being the subject of a present gratuitous transfer, but a promise of a future transfer is unenforceable unless in the form of a contract and so supported by consideration. The basic principle, then, is that the question whether an equitable assignment requires consideration depends upon whether it is effective as a present gift of the chose in action (i.e., the assignment has been completed), or is effective only as a promise of a future gift (i.e., the assignment is incomplete). Only in the latter case is there a requirement of consideration.

In some cases the application of this principle is straightforward. Where there is an express agreement to make an assignment at some point in the future, it is valid only if supported by consideration (*Re McArdle* [1951] Ch 669). Moreover, it is impossible to assign property which does not currently exist. For example, an expectation of receiving a sum of money by way of damages in a court case is an expectation of 'future property', in that until judgment is made the property does not exist. An assignment of such future property can only take effect as an agreement to assign whatever interest accrues under the expectation once it has accrued (*Glegg* v *Bromley* [1912] 3 KB 474). Therefore, an assignment of future property also requires consideration (*Tailby* v *Official Receiver* (1888) 13 App Cas 523). The same would also be true of an assignment of money to be earned under a contract which, at the time of the assignment, had not been made (*E. Pfeiffer Weinkellerei-Weineinkauf GmbH & Co.* v *Arbuthnot Factors Ltd* [1988] 1 WLR 150).

In other cases where there is no express future element in the assignment, it is more difficult to determine whether consideration is required. A gratuitous equitable assignment will be invalid only if the assignment has not been completed; that is, if the assignor has not done everything in his or her power to effect the transfer to the assignee (*Fortescue* v *Barnett* (1834) 3 My & K 36). How much the assignor must do before the assignment is complete varies according to whether the subject-matter of the assignment is an equitable or a legal chose (see 16.1). Where the assignment is of an equitable chose, the only requirements are that the assignor must express an unequivocal intention that the right belong to the assignee (*Voyle* v *Hughes* (1854) 2 Sm & G 18) and the assignment must be evidenced in writing (see below, 16.3.2.2).

In the case of the assignment of a legal chose, the question whether an assignment of a legal chose is complete will depend upon the nature of the chose in action to be assigned and the nature of the particular assignment made. For example, the assignment of a right to enforce payment under a contract would not be complete if the amount due was not yet a sum certain because it remained to be computed. Equally, an assignment of a sum certain which was conditional upon an uncertain event (e.g., 'when you have completed your education to my satisfaction') would not be complete because further action is required by the assignor (approving the level of education achieved).

16.3.2.2   Other requirements   An equitable assignment of a legal chose is not required to be evidenced in writing unless the transaction by which the chose is created (e.g., a contract) expressly so stipulates. Any disposition, including an assignment, of an equitable interest or chose must be evidenced in writing and signed by the person making the disposition, who for these purposes is the assignor (s. 53(1)(c), Law of Property Act 1925).

There is no requirement to give notice to the debtor in order for an equitable assignment to be valid. However, until notice is received the debtor may pay the assignor and be discharged of the debt (*Stocks* v *Dobson* (1853) 4 De GM & G 11). Giving notice may prevent further equities interfering with the assignee's rights (16.4.1) and will be relevant to any issue of priority (16.4.2).

16.4   LIMITS ON ASSIGNMENT

16.4.1   Subject to equities

The assignee takes the chose in action 'subject to equities', i.e. he or she cannot recover more from the debtor than the assignor himself or herself might have recovered. Thus, defences available to the debtor against the assignor are, for the most part, equally valid against the assignee. For this reason, the assignee must be careful to ascertain the true value of the chose in action, including any equities against it, if the assignee is to take it in payment for the assignee's own contractual performance. It should be noted that the expression 'equities' does not merely include equitable rights; any defence, legal or equitable, will avail the debtor against the assignee (e.g., mistake, misrepresentation or breach). On the other hand, an action for recovery of an advance payment made to the assignee, which exists under the contract in the event of total failure of consideration, cannot be maintained against the assignee: the contractual duty to repay rests on the assignor (see *Pan Ocean Shipping Co. Ltd* v *Creditcorp Ltd* [1994] 1 WLR 161).

The precise scope of the rule depends upon whether the defence arises out of the transaction which is the subject-matter of the assignment. Where that is the case, the defence is valid against the assignee whether notice of the assignment was given to the debtor before or after the defence accrued. For example, in *Young* v *Kitchin* (1878) 3 ExD 127, the debtor was able to set off his claim for damages for non-performance under his contract with the assignor against the assignee's action for the contract price. One, rather anomalous, exception to this rule arose in *Stoddart* v *Union Trust Ltd* [1912] 1 KB 181, when the debtor was not allowed to set off a claim for damages for fraud by the assignor against the assignee's action. The explanation given was that the fraud was personal to the assignor, but the result was that the assignee was better off than the assignor would have been, which appears to be detrimental to the interests of the debtor. It is thought that if the debtor had sought to rescind the contract rather than merely claim damages, that defence would have prevailed against the assignee.

Where the defence arises out of an independent transaction, it is valid against the assignee only in so far as it has already accrued by the time the debtor is given notice of the assignment. For example, in *Roxburghe* v *Cox* (1881) 17 ChD 520 a sum of money in a bank account (which in legal terms is no more than a debt owed by the banker to the account holder) was assigned to the assignee. The assignor was, at the time of the assignment, indebted to the bank to the tune of some £647, and that indebtedness was set off against the claim by the assignee for the money in the account. Notice of the assignment was given to the bank the day after it was made; if the assignor had incurred any further indebtedness to the bank after that time it could not have been set off against the assignee's claim.

16.4.2 Priorities

Difficulty may arise when more than one assignment is made of the same chose in action and the chose in action is not sufficient to satisfy the several assignees' claims upon it. This situation will raise the question of priority between the assignees. Priority is determined according to the order of first giving notice to the debtor (*Dearle* v *Hall* (1823) 3 Russ 1), so that it is possible for an assignment which was second in time to take priority over the first assignment if the second assignee was first to give notice. Knowledge of the previous assignment on the part of the second assignee at the time of the second assignment will prevent the possibility of such priority arising. However, knowledge of the previous assignment on the part of the second assignee at the time of giving notice will not prevent priority being given to the second assignment (*E. Pfeiffer Weinkellerei-Weineinkauf GmbH & Co.* v *Arbuthnot Factors Ltd* [1988] 1 WLR 150). The rule is necessary to protect the debtor. The first assignee cannot complain if he or she has delayed in giving notice.

The nature of the notice which must be given is irrelevant provided it can be proved, but for that reason it is advisable that notice be given in writing.

16.4.3 Non-assignable rights

16.4.3.1 In general The law provides that certain rights may not be assigned. The most obvious example is where the contract which creates the right in question contains an express provision against assignment (*United Dominions Trust Ltd* v *Parkway Motors* [1955] 2 All ER 557). In *Linden Gardens Trust Ltd* v *Lenesta Sludge Disposals Ltd* [1994] AC 85, it was argued that a contractual prohibition on assignment of a right in property was void as contrary to public policy, in so far as it is normally contrary to public policy to render property inalienable and contractual rights were a species of property. If this argument had succeeded the effect would have been to outlaw all attempts to impose limits on the right to assign contract rights by means of contractual provisions. The argument was firmly rejected by the House of Lords.

Some rights may not be assigned because the contract which creates them is of a personal nature, or is a relationship of confidence, or is founded on particular qualities or attributes of one of the parties. For example, the benefit of a policy of motor insurance may not be assigned with the sale of a car, since that assignment might impose an entirely different risk on the insurance company (*Peters* v *General Accident and Life Assurance Corporation Ltd* [1937] 4 All ER 628).

16.4.3.2 Assignment of a bare right of action A bare right of action may not be assigned; that is, while it is permissible to assign the benefit of a contract which remains to be performed, it is not permitted to assign the unqualified right to sue for breach of contract after the contract has been breached.

The assignment will not be considered to be of a *bare* right of action where the assignee has a legitimate interest in enforcing the right in question (*Trendtex Trading Corporation* v *Credit Suisse* [1982] AC 679). For example, the assignment to the purchaser of land of the right to sue for damage done to that land by the vendor's tenants is valid (*Ellis* v *Torrington* [1920] 1 KB 399). Equally valid is the assignment, to the person who has provided finance for the transaction creating the right assigned, of the right to sue for breach where the assignment was made as a form of security for the credit facility made available (*Trendtex Trading Corporation* v *Credit Suisse* [1982] AC 679 at 696–7, 703). In this particular case there was said to be no legitimate interest in pursuing the claim since the assignment had been made with the intention of the assignee reselling the right assigned for profit.

16.5 ASSIGNMENT OF THE BURDEN OF THE CONTRACT

The general rule is that the assignment of the burden of a contract is invalid unless made with the consent of the promisee/creditor (*Robson* v *Drummond* (1831) 2 B & Ad 303). Certain apparent exceptions to this rule exist, but they are not true exceptions in that they depend upon independent legal concepts and not upon the law relating to assignment.

The promisor under a contract may subcontract the actual performance of the undertakings in the contract to another person, provided the contract does not depend upon any personal skill or quality of the main contractor (*Griffith* v *Tower Publishing Co. Ltd* [1897] 1 Ch 21). So, it would not be possible for a portrait painter to subcontract his or her obligation to paint a particular person to a third party. Where a permitted subcontract has been made, however, the original main contracting party remains principally liable on the contract and is the person entitled to sue on the contract (*Davies* v *Collins* [1945] 1 All ER 247).

Just as the common law has always allowed the transfer of the benefit of a contract by 'novation' (see 16.1), the burden of a contract may also be transferred in this way. Novation involves the rescission by consent of both parties of the original contract, and the substitution of a new contract between the original promisee and the new promisor. At that point the original promisor's interest in the transaction ceases. The new contract must meet all the usual requirements of contract, and especially the requirement of consideration.

16.6 AGENCY: INTRODUCTION

Agency is an essential ingredient of modern commercial life. It is the means by which many contracts are made, so that it is important to be aware of the basics of agency law. However, there are many detailed texts on this subject alone (see, e.g., G. H. L. Fridman, *The Law of Agency*, 7th edn, Butterworths, 1996), or texts on commercial law (such as R. Bradgate, *Commercial Law*, 3rd edn, Butterworths, 2000).

Agency may be analysed in terms of three separate relationships. The first and most important is the relationship between principal and agent, which is based on the authority given by the principal to the agent to act on behalf of the principal (see 16.7 and 16.9). In normal circumstances the authority will have been created by a contract between the principal and agent (16.7.1), but there are circumstances in which the existence of authority is entirely a matter of objective ascertainment, when the relationships of agency must be regarded not as consensually created but as imposed by law (see 16.7.3).

The second relationship is the goal of the agency which has been created: the contract between the principal and the third party (16.8).

The last relationship is the potential relationship between the agent and the third party (16.10). It is only of any significance where the normal course of agency has not been followed.

A final word of caution must be entered about technical and non-technical uses of the term 'agent'. In the legal sense an agent is someone who does not act on his or her own account but only as a legal representative of another person. In ordinary usage the term 'agent' may be used to describe someone who buys and sells on his or her own account (i.e., as principal). For example, a retailer who specialises in stocking goods made by a particular manufacturer may be described as 'agent for . . .'. The retailer is very unlikely to be an agent in the legal sense. What matters is not the term used but whether on a proper analysis the legal relationships of agency, especially the relationship of authority, have been created. It is equally irrelevant whether there is some other legal relationship between principal and agent. An agent may be an employee, an independent contractor, a partner, or any other person in whom the power of representation has been invested by authority from the principal.

16.7 FORMATION OF THE RELATIONSHIPS OF AGENCY

There are a number of different types of agency depending upon the authority involved. The agent may have actual authority (either express or implied), apparent authority, his or her authority may arise by operation of law, or there may be subsequent ratification despite the fact that there was no authority at the time of acting. We also need to make brief mention of commercial agents (Commercial Agents (Council Directive) Regulations 1993 (SI 1993 No. 3053); see below at 16.7.5). For details of these Regulations, see Bradgate, *op cit.* at 16.6 above, or specialist texts on agency.

16.7.1 Actual authority

Where agency is created by agreement between P (principal) and A (agent), it invests actual authority in A, and this is so whether the agreement is express or implied. Such agreements normally take the form of a contract, but contract is not an essential requirement of such agency.

It is always open to the agent to act gratuitously. This affects the relationship between P (principal) and A (agent) (although it has no effect on the relationship between P and the third party). In the absence of consideration A will be under no obligation to act for P. However, where A does so act and incurs losses or expenses in the process, he or she will be able to recover them from P, since the right to an indemnity in this way arises independently of any contract between the parties (*Brook's Wharf and Bull Wharf Ltd* v *Goodman Bros* [1937] 1 KB 534). Where a gratuitous agent does act, he or she may be found to owe a duty of due care and skill to his or her principal (16.9.1.2) and a duty to account (16.9.1.6).

16.7.1.1 Express actual authority   In the case of an express grant of authority, the extent of the authority granted depends upon the construction of the agreement. Where the agency relationship is created in a deed (4.1 and 4.5.2), the courts apply very strict rules of construction. For example, where the deed gives authority to do specified acts but is phrased in general terms, the authority will be construed as restricted to the minimum necessary to achieve the goals in question. In *Jacobs* v *Morris* [1902] 1 Ch 816 an Australian principal authorised his English agent to buy goods and to write bills of exchange, etc. 'in connection with his business'. This authority was held not to extend to the agent's borrowing money on the strength of bills of exchange, so that the principal was not liable for the debt when the agent had taken the money for his own use.

Nevertheless, it is possible by deed to create a general authority to act on behalf of P under the powers contained in s. 10 of the Powers of Attorney Act 1971.

Where the agency relationship is created orally, or in writing not in the form of a deed, the usual rules of construction of the general law of contract apply (see 5(B)). The court must establish the extent of authority by inference from the words used and the surrounding circumstances, and if P has not expressed himself or herself clearly, P must accept the consequences of any actions of A which are consistent with a reasonable interpretation of the authority given. In *Ireland* v *Livingston* (1872) LR 5 HL 395 P asked A to arrange shipment of a cargo of sugar. A arranged for 80 per cent of the cargo to be shipped on one vessel, and it must be assumed he intended to send the balance on another vessel. P claimed to be entitled to reject the part-cargo. The House of Lords rejected that claim. P's instructions to A had not made explicit that he required shipment of the cargo in a single instalment, and A's behaviour was reasonable in the light of the instructions given. Nevertheless, where communication is possible (which today is the usual case), A may be under an implied obligation to seek clarification from P if P's instructions are ambiguous (*European Asian Bank AG* v *Punjab and Sind Bank (No. 2)* [1983] 3 All ER 508).

16.7.1.2 Implied actual authority When we speak of implied authority it is not intended to refer to agency which is imposed by law (see 16.7.2 and 16.7.3; in particular, it is important to distinguish implied actual authority from apparent authority, since the two are not necessarily coextensive: *per* Parker LJ in *Industrie Chimiche Italia Centrale* v *Alexander G. Tsavliris & Sons Maritime Co.* [1990] 1 Lloyd's Rep 516 at 524). Rather, it is agency created by actual authority which upon consideration of all the circumstances may be inferred to have been given to A by P. The best example of such implied authority is where express authority has been given for a particular purpose or purposes, and the court finds an implied authority to do everything necessary to achieve those purposes (*Howard* v *Baillie* (1796) 2 H Bl 618, *Rosenbaum* v *Belsen* [1900] 2 Ch 267). For example, it is accepted that a lawyer has authority to bind his or her client to any agreed compromise of litigation in which the client is engaged (*Waugh* v *H.B. Clifford & Sons* [1982] 1 Ch 374).

Authority may also be implied from a particular trade usage. For example, in *Howard* v *Sheward* (1866) LR 2 CP 148, an agent who had sold a horse for a horse dealer was found to have had authority to give a warranty of quality in respect of the horse, which bound the principal horse dealer when the horse failed to match the warranty.

The effect of this authority implied from trade usage may be to grant to A greater authority than P intended. To counter that effect, P may expressly withdraw the authority usually pertaining in the circumstances. Such withdrawal of usual authority may be ineffective, however, where the third party is aware that A acts for P but is unaware of the limitation of A's authority by comparison with that usual in the trade. Thus, the usual authority may be restored by virtue of 'apparent' or 'ostensible' authority (see 16.7.2). This will apply only where the third party knows that A acts for a principal. This point appears to have been overlooked in *Watteau* v *Fenwick* [1893] 1 QB 346, in

482   Assignment and agency

which an undisclosed principal was found to be bound by the acts of his agent done under a usual authority which had been expressly withdrawn. The defendants owned a hotel which was managed by their agent, H. The defendants' ownership was in no way apparent, H's name appearing over the door as licensee. H had been forbidden to buy cigars on credit. The plaintiff, unaware of the existence of the defendants or of their instruction to their agent, sold cigars on credit to H. They were cigars of a kind usually supplied to such an establishment. The plaintiff was found to be entitled to recover the price of the cigars from the defendants.

The case is perhaps best regarded as wrongly decided, but may possibly be explained on the ground that of the two innocent parties (principal and third party) the principal was better placed to prevent the loss, and so he should bear it. He would then be able to pursue his remedy against the agent for exceeding his authority.

16.7.2   Apparent authority

If the principal represents to the third party that the agent has authority to act in the way in which he or she is acting, the principal will be unable to deny that authority in order to avoid liability on a contract with a third party apparently made by the agent on the principal's behalf. This 'apparent' or 'ostensible' authority is created by estoppel. It arises from the representation by the principal to the third party rather than from agreement between the principal and the agent.

This type of authority embraces two quite different situations. The first is the rare occurrence where the principal allows the agent to hold himself or herself out as having the principal's authority when in fact he or she has none. For example, in *Freeman & Lockyer* v *Buckhurst Park Properties (Mangal) Ltd* [1964] 2 QB 480, the defendant company was empowered by its articles of association to appoint a managing director. Although never officially appointed to this post, A acted in this capacity with the knowledge and consent of the other directors. A employed the plaintiffs to do certain work for the company, which then sought to avoid having to pay for the work on the ground that A did not have authority to make such a contract on the company's behalf. The Court of Appeal held that although A did not have actual authority, he did have ostensible authority to bind the company since the other directors on behalf of the company had allowed the plaintiffs to gain the impression that A was empowered to act as managing director (and accordingly had the usual authority of a managing director to act). In *Lease Management Services Ltd* v *Purnell Secretarial Services Ltd* (1993) 13 Tr LR 337, P had adopted a trading name very similar to that of the alleged agent, and was said by Sir Donald Nicholls deliberately to have led the third party to believe that the two were one and the same. In the circumstances P was estopped from denying the authority of the alleged agent to make representations which were binding on P.

More usually, apparent authority will arise where P fails to make known to the third party a limitation (in scope or time) imposed on A's admitted authority. For example, in *Watteau v Fenwick* [1893] 1 QB 346 (above, 16.7.1.2), there was no doubt that A had actual authority (even if the agency had not been disclosed); the difficulty in that case arose from the fact that the third party had no way of knowing that the authority was in any way limited.

In *Rama Corporation Ltd v Proved Tin and General Investments Ltd* [1952] 2 QB 147 at 149, Slade J said:

> Ostensible or apparent authority . . . is merely a form of estoppel, indeed, it has been termed agency by estoppel, and you cannot call in aid an estoppel unless you have three ingredients: (i) a representation, (ii) a reliance on the representation and (iii) an alteration of your position resulting from such a reliance.

There must first, therefore, be a representation made to the third party. As in the general law of contract (see 4.4.3.1), the representation may be express or implied from conduct. An estoppel will not arise out of the mere silence of the supposed principal, unless there are circumstances giving rise to a duty to speak (*Arctic Shipping Co. Ltd v Mobilia AB* [1990] 2 Lloyd's Rep 51). In this context representations by conduct are particularly relevant. It is crucially important that the representation is attributable to P, and is not merely an impression from A's own conduct, since only the former is sufficient evidence on which to base an estoppel (*Attorney-General for Ceylon v Silva* [1953] AC 461).

This requirement may raise difficulties when the principal is a company. Clearly the company itself cannot make a representation, but a duly authorised person may make a representation on behalf of the company. So, in *Freeman & Lockyer v Buckhurst Park Properties (Mangal) Ltd* [1964] 2 QB 480, the *acting* managing director was found to be an agent through the operation of estoppel on the strength of a representation by conduct made by the other directors, whom Diplock LJ found to have actual authority to make such representations. This analysis raises the question whether a person with actual authority to make representations can bind the company by an agency by estoppel on the strength of a representation made about his or her own authority as granted by the company (i.e., where representation and subsequent contract are made by one and the same person). Such a possibility was ruled out by the House of Lords in *Armagas Ltd v Mundogas SA* [1986] 1 AC 717. However, in *The Raffaella* [1985] 2 Lloyd's Rep 36 the plaintiff entered a contract to purchase a cargo of cement from the seller. The plaintiff became concerned about serious delays in performance, and obtained a letter of guarantee signed by the documentary credit manager of the defendant bank which was financing the seller's acquisition of the cement to fulfil the contract. The cement, when delivered, was in very poor condition, and the plaintiff sought to enforce the guarantee. The defendant bank denied liability on the ground that the manager was unauthorised to give such an undertaking. The bank was found to be liable because its agent, the manager, had been allowed to act without reference to higher authority, and so to create the impression that he needed no further authorisation for the undertaking he gave. Browne-Wilkinson LJ expressed the view that a binding estoppel would be created in those circumstances, although they come close to undermining the rule that the representation must not derive from the conduct of the agent. A similar result was reached by the Court of Appeal in *United Bank of Kuwait Ltd v Hammoud* [1988] 1 WLR 1051, where a solicitor, with actual authority to represent himself as such, gave undertakings which in the circumstances appeared to have been given in the ordinary course of business of the firm of solicitors for which he worked. It was held that he had apparent authority to give the undertakings.

The decision in *First Energy (UK) Ltd v Hungarian International Bank Ltd* [1993] 2 Lloyd's Rep 194 clearly undermines that general rule which requires that representations of authority of an agent have to be made by the principal. The case concerned a senior manager who was known not to have authority to approve a particular credit facility with the bank. He nevertheless sent a letter suggesting that head office approval to the transaction had been given, and the question was whether the bank was then bound by that communication. The Court of Appeal held that it was. Although the manager lacked authority to make the transaction, he had been put into a position in which it was usual to have authority to communicate head office decisions authorising such transactions. Steyn LJ said (at 204):

> [His] position as senior manager . . . was such that he was clothed with ostensible authority to communicate that head office approval had been given. . . . In the circumstances . . . the idea that [the plaintiffs] should have checked with the managing director in London whether [the bank] had approved the transaction seems unreal. . . . In my judgment, a decision that [the manager] did not have apparent authority to communicate head office approval would defeat the reasonable expectations of the parties. And it would fly in the face of the way in practice negotiations are conducted between trading banks and trading customers.

Secondly, there must be some reliance by the third party on the representation made. Thus, if it can be shown that the third party knew when entering the contract that A lacked the requisite authority, whatever impression P's conduct might have given, the contract will not bind P (*Overbrooke Estates Ltd v Glencombe Properties Ltd* [1974] 1 WLR 1355). There may be difficult issues of fact where the circumstances in which the contract between A and the third party was made lead to the allegation that the third party ought to have known that A lacked authority.

Lastly, there must be detriment to, or alteration of position by, the third party as a result of his or her reliance on the representation. It will be recalled that in relation to promissory estoppel there is some dispute as to the precise degree of reliance required, whether detriment or alteration of position (see 4.4.3.3). A similar dispute exists in the case of apparent authority as a result of estoppel. Since agency by estoppel results in the creation of new rights, and so is more akin to proprietary estoppel than to promissory estoppel (*cf.* 4.4.6), it may be that the more stringent requirement of actual detriment, which undoubtedly exists in the case of proprietary estoppel, applies in this case too (although this proposition was not accepted by Gatehouse J in *Arctic Shipping Co. Ltd* v *Mobilia AB* [1990] 2 Lloyd's Rep 51 at 59).

16.7.3 Authority by operation of law

These are other circumstances, outside agreement or representation of authority, where the law considers that an agency relationship should be found.

16.7.3.1 Cohabitants Agency of cohabitants depends upon three crucial factors, of which the first is cohabitation in a household (*Debenham* v *Mellon* (1880) 6 App Cas 24). Cases have involved wives (*Phillipson* v *Hayter* (1870) LR 6 CP 38) and mistresses (*Blades* v *Free* (1829) 9 B & C 167), so that it is conclusively established that this form of agency is not merely an incident of marriage. The principle enables the cohabitant to obtain 'necessaries' on credit, to be paid for, by virtue of agency, by the cohabitee as principal. The standard definition of 'necessaries' provided in *Phillipson* v *Hayter* (1870) LR 6 CP 38 at 42 (things 'suitable to the style in which the husband chooses to live, in so far as the articles fall fairly within the domestic department which is ordinarily confined to the management of the wife') is dated and offensive. It may be that if the principle is to be retained at all it would be better, as has been proposed for minors' contracts (4.6.1.2), to rely on a narrower class of goods and services defined as 'necessities'.

This form of agency is said to be a presumption which may be rebutted where the alleged principal is able to produce contrary evidence (*Debenham* v *Mellon*). Suitable evidence would be that the tradesman had been warned that the cohabitant did not have authority to contract on P's credit (*Etherington* v *Parrot* (1703) 1 Salk 118), that the cohabitant was adequately supplied with the things in question, or that the cohabitant had been expressly forbidden to make such contracts (*Debenham* v *Mellon*). These last two grounds of rebuttal suggest that agency of cohabitation depends upon a form of implied authority, since, being addressed to the agent rather than to the third party, they would not be sufficient to prevent the raising of an estoppel.

16.7.3.2 Agency of necessity Agency of necessity is an umbrella expression under which two quite distinct types of case may be found (*per* Lord Diplock in *China Pacific SA* v *Food Corporation of India* [1982] AC 939 at 958).

The first type of case raises the question of whether in some circumstances (which for the time being may be described as emergencies) a person has authority to bind a principal contractually to third parties, despite the absence of any formal agency arrangement, and despite the absence of circumstances giving rise to apparent authority (16.7.2)? This type of agency originated in the needs and practices of the shipping business. It was essential for the best interests of all concerned that the ship's master be empowered to react to all the emergencies of the voyage without incurring personal liability. So, for example, the sale of the cargo in *Couturier* v *Hastie* (1856) 5 HL Cas 673, which resulted in a second sale being void for initial impossibility (see 9.2.1), was made by virtue of the master's authority as agent of necessity.

From these beginnings the doctrine has expanded in two different dimensions. In the first place, it has been applied in cases not involving the carriage of goods by sea. Secondly, it has been applied not only to extend where necessary an existing authority (which might be no more than an example of implied authority: 16.7.1.2), but also to create an authority to act to bind P where no authority previously existed.

Despite this expansion, the requirements for the creation of an agency of necessity are sufficiently strict to suggest that it can only ever remain a limited doctrine. In particular, such agency will not be created unless A was unable to obtain express instructions from P before the time when it became necessary to act (*Prager* v *Blatspiel, Stamp and Heacock Ltd* [1924] 1 KB 566). Modern methods of telecommunication may make this a particularly severe requirement. In addition, A must have acted in good faith in P's interest in a manner reasonable in the circumstances (*Prager* v *Blatspiel, Stamp and Heacock Ltd*). Lastly, there must be circumstances of emergency or necessity, although it is not easy to define quite what this entails. It seems it is intended to be judged on commercial criteria (*Australasian Steam Navigation Co.* v *Morse* (1872) LR 4 PC 222).

The second type of case arises in similar circumstances of necessary emergency action, but raises no issue of agency. The only question is: Is a person who acted to preserve another's endangered property entitled to an indemnity for the cost to him or her of so acting? There is no issue of agency since there is no question of a principal allegedly being bound to a third party. This is really a form of restitutionary claim. However, as English law has refused to recognise any general right of recovery in such circumstances (*Falcke* v *Scottish Imperial Insurance Co.* (1886) 34 ChD 234), claims have wrongly been formulated on the basis of agency of necessity (*China Pacific SA* v *Food Corporation of India* [1982] AC 939 at 958).

16.7.4 Agency by ratification of the agent's unauthorised acts

It has long been established that the relationships of agency may be created by subsequent ratification of an agent's unauthorised acts, and, provided A purported to act for P rather than for himself or herself, the effect is the same as where A acts within an express actual authority (*Wilson* v *Tumman* (1843) 6 Man & G 236). However, for an apparent ratification to bind P, there must have been some real choice available whether to adopt the acts of A or not (*Forman & Co. Pty Ltd* v *The Liddesdale* [1900] AC 190). The exact nature of this agency is unclear since, although it is apparently consensual, it is unusual in English law to be able to create liability by consent for acts which have already occurred.

16.7.4.1 Requirements of ratification The following requirements must be fulfilled for ratification to be effective:

(a)   A third party will not be bound to P unless at the time of contracting A appeared to be acting on P's behalf, and not on his or her own account. For example, in *Keighley, Maxsted & Co.* v *Durant* [1901] AC 240, A was authorised by the appellants to purchase corn at a certain price. A bought corn above the price authorised, which would have been beyond his authority, but he bought in his own name. The appellants purported to ratify the transaction, but then failed to take delivery of the corn. They resisted the respondent's action for breach of contract by claiming not to be parties to the contract since they were not entitled to ratify an agreement which had not purported to be made in their name. This defence succeeded. (Compare with actual authority where the principal may be undisclosed; see 16.7.1.)

(b)   In order for the ratification to be effective, the principal must have been identifiable at the time the contract was made. For example, in *Kelner* v *Baxter* (1866) LR 2 CP 174, the promoters of a new company made a contract on its behalf with a third party at a time before the company had come into existence. The company once formed purported to ratify the contract, but then went into liquidation, and the promoters themselves were sued on the contract. They argued that they had contracted as agents, and that liability on the contract had passed to the company by ratification. This defence failed because the company's ratification was invalid since the company had not been in existence at the time of the contract in question.

(c)   A third party will not be bound to P unless, at the time the contract was made with A, P was competent to make the contract, and unless, at the time when P purports to ratify, P could then do the act in question. The first rule is straightforward. If at the time A makes the contract P lacks contractual capacity, he or she cannot later ratify it (*Firth* v *Staines* [1897] 2 QB 70). The second rule exists to prevent P taking advantage of A's unauthorised acts to achieve something which P has left too late to achieve himself or herself. The rule is of particular application to insurance contracts, and prevents P ratifying a contract of insurance taken out by A in excess of his or her authority once the risk insured against has occurred, since P could not then himself or herself take out insurance (*Grover & Grover* v *Mathews* [1910] 2 KB 401; there is a statutory exception in s. 86 of the Marine Insurance Act 1906, so that contracts of marine insurance can be ratified after loss of the insured goods).

In *National Oilwell (UK) Ltd* v *Davy Offshore Ltd* [1993] 2 Lloyd's Rep 582, at 607, Colman J suggested that this general rule should be relaxed. The rule was considered by the Court of Appeal in *Presentaciones Musicales SA* v *Secunda* [1994] 2 All ER 737, a case not without difficulty. The general principle that ratification is ineffective if it occurs at a time when P could not do the act in question was accepted as correct. In practice, however, the majority recognised a significant exception to the principle, because the need for P to be able to do the act in question is restricted to situations where the act to be ratified is without effect unless ratified. Where the act has a legal validity before ratification, it may be adopted by P even if at that time it would be too late for P to do the act for itself. So, although the ratification of an unauthorised issue of writ took place only after the expiry of the limitation period, the ratification was valid because the writ was not a nullity despite being issued without authority. (Of course, if A's acts are void, they may not be rescued by ratification by P.)

16.7.4.2 Effect of ratification   The effect of ratification, as the rule that P must be competent at the time the contract was made between A and the third party suggests, is to make P liable on the contract retroactively from the time it was first made (*Boston Deep Sea Fishing & Ice Co. Ltd* v *Farnham* [1957] 3 All ER 204). This rule may have difficult consequences for a third party who wishes to revoke an offer which has been accepted by A but which has not been ratified by P. Where the third party has been informed that the contract is subject to ratification by P, the third party may withdraw at any time before ratification (*Watson* v *Davies* [1931] 1 Ch 455). But where the third party does not know of the need for ratification there is some imbalance between the parties, since the third party is bound while P is free to choose whether to ratify or not (*Bolton Partners* v *Lambert* (1889) 41 ChD 295). There is no great hardship in this rule, however, since P is under an obligation to choose within a reasonable time (*Metropolitan Asylums Board Managers* v *Kingham & Sons* (1890) 6 TLR 217). Moreover, where P is unaware of the need for ratification, the third party must believe he or she is bound by the fact of A's acceptance, so that revocation of the offer would not be open to the third party. Should P fail to ratify, the third party will not be left without a remedy, since A will in any case be personally liable (16.10).

16.7.5 Commercial agents

The Commercial Agents (Council Directive) Regulations 1993 (SI 1993 No. 3053, as amended) implement the EC Directive on Commercial Agents (1986/653/EC), which creates a protective scheme for commercial agents. A commercial agent is defined as 'a self-employed intermediary who has continuing authority to negotiate the sale or purchase of goods on behalf of another person (the "principal"), or to negotiate and conclude the sale and purchase of goods on behalf of and in the name of that principal'. Essentially, therefore, commercial agents are a particular type of agent given actual authority. The 1993 Regulations introduced protection for commercial agents, which had existed for some time in other Member States. The result is that the independent commercial agent is now much more like an employee.

16.8 RELATIONSHIP BETWEEN PRINCIPAL AND THIRD PARTY

The relationship between principal and third party is the central relationship and goal of agency. Its effect varies according to whether the existence of P was disclosed to the third party by A at the time of making the contract.

16.8.1 Disclosed principal

The paradigm of agency, and its preponderant manner of expression, is the contract made by an agent acting within an express or implied actual authority on behalf of a disclosed principal. Where all those conditions are met, there is a binding agreement between P and the third party which results in a bilateral contract between those two and allows A to drop out of the relationship (16.7.1). Equally, where P is disclosed but A acts outside any possible authority existing at the time of making the contract, there can be no contract between P and the third party unless A's acts are subsequently ratified by P (16.7.4).

The exceptions to the general principle, that A's authorised contract with the third party on behalf of a disclosed P allows A to drop out of the relationship, are listed by Wright J in *Montgomerie v United Kingdom Mutual Steamship Association Ltd* [1891] 1 QB 370 at 371–2. The effect of these exceptions is to create a personal liability on the part of A (discussed below at 16.10.1). The most important exception (apart from the rules applicable in the case of an undisclosed principal: 16.8.2) is where there is an express contractual provision that A should be liable. There may also be an irresistible inference that A contracted to incur personal liability if he or she signed a written contract without qualifying that signature by words showing that he or she signed only on behalf of P, especially where there is no other reference to P in the contractual document (*Parker v Winlow* (1857) 7 El & Bl 942). In *Seatrade Groningen BV v Geest Industries Ltd* [1996] 2 Lloyd's Rep 375, the Court of Appeal accepted that in the absence of a clear indication that the signature was given as agent only, the correct approach was to find the agent liable together with the principal.

16.8.1.1 Election where agent is also liable?

The important question where the agent has incurred a personal liability is what effect that has on the liability of P to the third party. One effect which has been canvassed in the cases is that the third party has an election between enforcing the liability of P or that of A, with the consequence that once made the election is binding on the third party who may not subsequently reverse the choice made (*Debenham's Ltd v Perkins* (1925) 133 LT 252). The difficulty is to know when an election has been made. It depends upon some unequivocal act committing the third party to a single course of action. Thus, obtaining judgment against either P or A will clearly suffice (*Priestly v Fernie* (1865) 3 Hurl & C 977: see 16.8.2.2).

The doctrine of the third party's election between liability of A and that of P almost certainly originates from the law relating to undisclosed principals (see 16.8.2.2). There is no question in that situation that the third party might have understood the contract to have been made with both A and P, since the existence of P is unknown at the time of contracting. But where P's existence is disclosed and yet A has contracted for a personal liability, it might seem that the natural inference is that A and P contracted to be jointly and severally liable, with the result that judgment against the one would not be a bar to proceedings against the other unless the debt had actually been satisfied. In that case, to hold the third party bound by an election where the judgment is not satisfied (as occurred in *Priestly* v *Fernie*) would not accord with the intention of the parties, and might cause serious injustice to the third party. There are indications that the courts may be more willing today to recognise this state of affairs (*cf.* Diplock LJ in *Teheran-Europe Co. Ltd* v *S. T. Belton (Tractors) Ltd* [1968] 2 All ER 886 at 892–3).

16.8.1.2 Payment to the agent The general rule is that where the principal is disclosed, payment by either party to A does not discharge the liability of the party making payment to the other contracting party (*Butwick* v *Grant* [1924] 2 KB 483). However, this rule may be varied by actual authority, by estoppel or by ratification. This exception to the general rule applies equally to payment by P (*Heald* v *Kenworthy* (1855) 10 Ex 739) and payment by the third party, although in this case the third party must comply with the exact authority given in order to discharge his or her liability to P (*Hine Brothers* v *Steamship Insurance Syndicate Ltd* (1895) 72 LT 79). In that case A was authorised to receive payments in cash, and it was found that payment to A by bill of exchange did not discharge the debt to P. The third party's authority to P to discharge liability by payment to A most commonly arises by way of an estoppel based on the third party's conduct which has induced P to make payment to A (*Irvine & Co.* v *Watson & Sons* (1880) 5 QBD 414).

16.8.2 Undisclosed principal

In English law a contract may be established between P and a third party by virtue of agency even when the existence of P was not disclosed at the time of the negotiation of the contract between A and the third party. This rule has always been widely regarded as anomalous as a matter of legal theory, since it has been almost impossible to reconcile it with the doctrine of privity (see 15.1). It does not exist in most other legal systems, and especially not in those in which it is unnecessary since it is possible to contract for a benefit to be conferred on a third party. Herein lies the probable key to the historical existence of the doctrine: it has always been seen as a necessary commercial expedient because of the privity doctrine. It will be interesting, therefore, to assess the impact of the Contracts (Rights of Third Parties) Act 1999, which now makes it possible to contract for a benefit to be conferred directly on a third party, although under the Act there must be express identification of the intended beneficiary in the contract (15.3).

In *Keighley, Maxsted & Co.* v *Durant* [1901] AC 240, Lord Lindley said (at 261–262):

[T]here is an anomaly in holding one person bound to another of whom he knows nothing and with whom he did not, in fact, intend to contract. But middlemen, through whom contracts are made, are common and useful in business transactions, and in the great mass of contracts it is a matter of indifference to either party whether there is an undisclosed principal or not. If he exists it is, to say the least, extremely convenient that he should be able to sue and be sued as principal. . . .

A similar justification was put forward by Lord Lloyd in *Siu Yin Kwan* v *Eastern Insurance Co. Ltd* [1994] 1 All ER 213.

16.8.2.1 Limits on the doctrine It is clear that in some circumstances to hold the third party bound to an undisclosed principal will be an unfair surprise, and certain limits exist upon the doctrine which are intended to prevent that.

The third party will not be bound to an undisclosed P where from the terms of the contract it appears that A is the only possible principal. In some circumstances the impossibility of contracting as agent on behalf of P will be express. For example, in *United Kingdom Mutual Steamship Assurance Association Ltd* v *Nevill* (1887) 19 QBD 110, the contract, which was constituted by the rules of a mutual insurance association, provided that only members of the association could be made liable for premiums. The defendant, a co-owner of a vessel insured by the association, was not liable for premiums unpaid by another co-owner since the defendant was not himself a member of the association.

In other circumstances the restriction on contracting as agent may be implied from the contract. For example, in *Humble* v *Hunter* (1848) 12 QB 310, A entered into a contract in which he was described as 'owner' of a particular vessel. It was held that this description justified the inference that there was no true owner as principal behind A, so that P was unable to sue on the contract.

In subsequent cases the courts have been unwilling to make such inferences (e.g., *F. Drughorn Ltd* v *Rederiaktiebolaget Trans-Atlantic* [1919] AC 203: A described as 'charterer'), and it may be that the implied restrictions on the power to contract as agent are now confined to the situation where A describes himself or herself as owner, or otherwise asserts a full property right over the goods in question (*cf. The Astyanax* [1985] 2 Lloyd's Rep 109). This modern trend was confirmed by *Siu Yin Kwan* v *Eastern Insurance Co. Ltd* [1994] 1 All ER 213. Although Lord Lloyd declined to comment on whether *Humble* v *Hunter* was still good law, the inference was that it was not.

A further limit on the doctrine exists where the third party made the contract in the light of personal qualities of the person now alleged only to have been an agent. Where A has some personal skill (e.g., a portrait painter), P will not be entitled subsequently to perform the contract, just as rights under such a contract may not be assigned (see 16.4.3 and 16.5). Equally, where A has some particular attribute in the eyes of the third party, A may not contract on behalf of P. For example, in *Greer* v *Downs Supply Co.* [1927] 2 KB 28, the third party contracted with A in order to obtain a set-off to which he was entitled on account of a debt owed to him by A. It was held that A could not in those circumstances make the contract on behalf of an undisclosed principal.

It may also be the case that personal qualities of P make it impossible for there to be a contract on his or her behalf where P is undisclosed at the time of contracting. Contracts of insurance are said to be personal in nature, but it was doubted in *Siu Yin Kwan* v *Eastern Insurance Co. Ltd* whether they were 'personal' in the fullest sense: certainly, the Privy Council allowed an undisclosed principal to sue on a contract of insurance. Lord Lloyd drew an important distinction between the non-assignability of personal contracts, which was easily defended, and the separate case of enforcement by an undisclosed principal.

The normal rule is that the fact that the third party is unwilling to contract with P does not prevent a contract coming into existence between them by virtue of the undisclosed principal doctrine of agency (*Dyster* v *Randall & Sons* [1926] Ch 932). If, however, A misrepresents the identity or existence of P, the third party will be able to resist any claim on the contract by P (*Archer* v *Stone* (1898) 78 LT 34). Difficulty is caused by the case of *Said* v *Butt* [1920] 3 KB 497, in which P was found unable to sue on the contract despite the fact that A had made no representation as to his identity. In principle the case appears inconsistent with *Dyster* v *Randall & Sons*, but it is understandable why on the particular facts it should have been decided as it was.

In *Said* v *Butt*, P (a theatre critic) had attempted twice to enter the exact same contract with the third party, and had been refused, and so resorted to the subterfuge of an agent. In the circumstances (the sale of theatre tickets) it was impossible for the third party to ask every purchaser if they were acting for P. Such a question is usually the only means of provoking the necessary misrepresentation. It does not seem on these facts that any injustice was done to P, and it is questionable whether this contract could really be said to be 'personal'.

16.8.2.2 Legal effect The general rule is that while P remains undisclosed, A can sue and be sued on the contract with the third party. A's right to sue is lost as soon as P intervenes (*Atkinson* v *Cotesworth* (1825) 3 B & C 647). The more important question concerns the effect of P's intervention on the third party's right to sue A.

The third party must elect whether to seek to make either A or P liable, and that election is binding on the third party so that once it has been made he or she cannot go back on it (*Scarf* v *Jardine* (1882) 7 App Cas 345). Election depends upon an act which unequivocally indicates that the third party is committed to the choice made. In *Priestly* v *Fernie* (1865) 3 Hurl & C 977 (see 16.8.1.1), the master of a ship signed a bill of lading, thus making himself personally liable. Goods covered by the bill of lading were both damaged and lost in transit. The plaintiff consignee of the goods obtained judgment against the master both in Australia and in the English High Court, but the judgment was not satisfied because of the master's bankruptcy. The plaintiff then sought to bring proceedings against the owners of the vessel. The plaintiff was found to have chosen to make the master liable, and to be unable to go back on that decision.

The courts may in some circumstances be reluctant to find that anything short of actually obtaining judgment amounts to an election and have, for example, found that the issue of a writ to commence proceedings against P did not prevent the third party abandoning those proceedings in order to seek payment from A (*Clarkson, Booker Ltd* v *Andjel* [1964] 2 QB 775). The facts of this case were, however, regarded by the court as exceptional, and it indicated that in normal circumstances an election will occur when proceedings are commenced by issue of proceedings against one or other potential defendant. In *Chestertons* v *Barone* [1987] 1 EGLR 15 the Court of Appeal suggested that in the case of an undisclosed principal, election requires evidence that the third party has abandoned any possible claim against the agent. The Court then suggested that it would be difficult to imagine circumstances in which an election had been made without proceedings having been started, but that that would normally be the 'clearest evidence of an election'.

As in the case of assignment (see 16.4.1), P is able to take the benefit of A's contract with the third party only to the extent that it may be encumbered with defences available against A. In particular, any set-off available to the third party against A will continue to operate against P (*Isaac Cooke and Sons* v *Eshelby* (1887) 12 App Cas 271). In that case the set-off against A was held not to prevail against P because the third party knew that A sometimes contracted on his own account and sometimes on the account of others, without disclosing which on any particular occasion. If the third party wished to rely on the set-off, he should have enquired whether A was contracting on his own account for the contract in question. It must be doubted whether this sensible rule can really be said to rest on estoppel (as was suggested in *Isaac Cooke and Sons* v *Eshelby*), since until P is disclosed he or she cannot have made any representation.

Where the third party pays A before the existence of P is disclosed, that payment is sufficient to discharge the third party's liability (*Coates* v *Lewes* (1808) 1 Camp 444). It would seem that where P pays A before P's existence is disclosed to the third party, it would not be right for P's liability to be discharged by such payment. *Armstrong* v *Stokes* (1872) LR 7 QB 598, which takes the opposite view, was doubted in *Irvine & Co.* v *Watson & Sons* (1880) 5 QBD 414. It is true that if A fails to pay the third party in this situation then hardship will result either for P or for the third party, but in those circumstances P should perhaps suffer the loss since he or she appears better placed to have avoided it.

16.9 RELATIONSHIP BETWEEN PRINCIPAL AND AGENT

16.9.1 Agent's obligations to the principal

The agent's obligations to the principal may derive from contract, or may be imposed by law in the form of tortious or fiduciary liability. The imposition of duties independently of contract is inevitable since in some circumstances there may be no contract between an admitted agent and his or her principal.

16.9.1.1 Duty to obey instructions Where A has been authorised to act by means of a contract with P, and the contract sets out instructions which A is to follow, A is under a contractual duty to follow those instructions and will be liable for breach of contract if he or she fails to do so. It is also a breach of duty to act in excess of authority (*Fray* v *Voules* (1859) 1 El & El 839). Where there is no contract between A and P there can be no duty to obey instructions as such, but there may still be a tortious duty to exercise due care and skill.

16.9.1.2 Duty to exercise due care and skill The duty to exercise due care and skill may arise out of a contract between A and P (*cf.* 6.6.2.2), or may be imposed independently as tortious liability. In either case, the actual standard of care or skill demanded in the particular circumstances will be for the court to decide. It is sometimes said that the standard of care is greater in the case of agency made under contract than under a gratuitous agency where liability is based in tort. That statement is, however, potentially misleading. For example, it seems certain that the same standard of care and skill will be expected of a solicitor whether he or she is acting for remuneration or not, provided P knows A is a solicitor (see Stuart-Smith LJ in *Chaudhry* v *Prabhakar* [1988] 3 All ER 718 at 721). Where the existence of a contract may make a difference, however, is that in some circumstances A promises by virtue of the contract that he or she possesses some special skill not possessed by everybody, and that he or she undertakes to exercise it on P's behalf. The contract may then result in the higher standard of care expected of a skilled person being expected of A, rather than the lower standard expected of an unskilled member of the general public (*cf. Esso Petroleum Co. Ltd* v *Mardon* [1976] QB 801: 5.1.3). The same may result from a representation by an unpaid agent about the degree of skill he or she possesses (*Chaudhry* v *Prabhakar*). In *Chaudhry* v *Prabhakar*, the Court of Appeal recognised that where the gratuitous agency arises between friends there may be no legal duty owed at all, and the relationship may give rise only to social obligations. May LJ in particular took the view that, in the light of the recent restrictive attitude to the existence of tortious duties of care, the defendant may have been unwise to concede that such a duty existed in the circumstances of this case (advice to a friend about the purchase of a second-hand car).

The remaining duties of A to P are 'fiduciary' duties, which is to say that they are duties originally developed by the Court of Chancery to protect a person, who has put his or her confidence in another, from abuse of that confidence. It is generally accepted that these duties impose high standards of conduct.

16.9.1.3 Duty to act personally The agent may not delegate his or her authority to act on behalf of P unless expressly or impliedly authorised so to do (*De Bussche* v *Alt* (1878) 8 ChD 286). The power to delegate may be implied if P knows at the time of creation of the agency that A intends to delegate and does not object (*Quebec & Richmond Railroad Co.* v *Quinn*

(1858) 12 Moo PC 232). It may also be implied where it is the trade usage to allow such delegation. The courts will allow delegation where the acts delegated are 'purely ministerial' and do not involve the confidence and discretion which exists between P and A (*Allam & Co. Ltd v Europa Poster Services Ltd* [1968] 1 All ER 826: delegation of service of a notice to solicitors).

Where there is an authorised delegation there will not necessarily be a contractual relationship between P and the sub-agent. In *Calico Printers' Association v Barclays Bank* (1931) 145 LT 51, Wright J said that in such circumstances P remained entitled to hold A liable for any failure of duty and could not claim against the sub-agent. Privity would be established between P and the sub-agent only if it could be demonstrated that P authorised A to create a contract between the sub-agent and P. In *Prentis Donegan & Partners Ltd v Leeds & Leeds Co. Inc.* [1998] 2 Lloyd's Rep 326, although the delegation was authorised, the agent had no authority to create privity between the principal and the sub-agent. The result was that A was liable to pay the commission to S. Rix J stated that: 'There are good commercial reasons for such a rule. It emphasises the importance of the contractual chain.'

The sub-agent may still owe a duty of care in tort to the principal. (See *Henderson v Merrett Syndicates Ltd* [1995] 2 AC 145, where there was no direct contractual relationship between the Lloyd's 'names' and sub-agents of managing agents but it was held that the sub-agents owed a duty of care to the 'names' in accordance with the principle in *Hedley Byrne & Co. Ltd v Heller & Partners Ltd* [1964] AC 465. The existence of such a duty of care will depend on the facts and will normally be more difficult to establish where the loss is purely economic.)

16.9.1.4 Duty to act in good faith   The characteristic duty of all fiduciary relationships is the duty to act in good faith, which may be subdivided into a duty to avoid any conflict of interest with P, and a duty not to make secret profits, including bribes, from the position of agent. There is inevitable overlap between these duties and the general rule against undue influence (see 11.2).

The classic cases of conflict of interest are where A acts in his or her own right as principal as the other contracting party with P, e.g., where A buys for himself or herself goods he or she has been instructed to sell for P, or where A sells his or her own goods when he or she has been instructed to buy on behalf of P. The conflict of interest lies between A's duty to get the best possible deal for P and A's own interest in making a profit for himself or herself. For example, in *De Bussche v Alt* (1878) 8 ChD 286 the defendant was instructed to sell a ship for a minimum price of $90,000. Unable to find a buyer, the defendant finally bought it himself at the minimum price. Shortly afterwards he was able to sell it for $160,000. The defendant was forced by P to account for the profit made on this deal.

In addition, or as an alternative to recovering profits made by A, P may rescind the agency relationship. In *Logicrose Ltd v Southend United Football*

Club Ltd [1988] 1 WLR 1256, Millett J held that recovery of the profit made did not imply affirmation of the contract by the principal, so as to bar him from rescinding the contract. He also held that the *restitutio in integrum* required as an ingredient of rescission does not include restitution of the illegal profit. It should be noted that P's remedy does not depend upon proof of any intentional wrongdoing by A; it is sufficient that there is the appearance of a potential conflict of interest. For example, in *Boardman v Phipps* [1967] 2 AC 46, agents acting for trustees in relation to the shares in a company acquired extra shares in the company on their own account. It seems probable that the trustee principals in this case suffered no loss, and may have benefited, from A's actions, but A was still obliged to account for profits made from the transaction. It should also be noted that this duty may extend beyond the period of agency itself, if in all the circumstances A has acquired a standing in relation to P which itself endures (*Allinson v Clayhills* (1907) 97 LT 709).

A conflict of interest may arise where an agent has undertaken to act for more than one principal, although in such cases whether there is a conflict can be determined only by careful examination of the facts. So, in *Sears Investment Trust Ltd v Lewis's Group Ltd* [1992] RA 262, an agent was not in breach of the duty of loyalty to his principal when the agency relationship had been terminated by agreement between them, and P had actively encouraged A to take instructions from the second principal in the affair. Harman J said that there could be no duty towards two principals without the clear agreement and knowledge of both. In *Kelly v Cooper* [1993] AC 205, in the particular context of estate agency, where it is a matter of common knowledge that agents act concurrently for more than one principal, the Privy Council advised that a term should be implied into individual agency contracts permitting A to act for more than one P concurrently, and permitting A to withhold from P confidential information obtained through dealings with another principal. It is also common knowledge that the same solicitor may frequently act in a mortgage transaction for both the lender and the borrower.

16.9.1.5 Duty not to take bribes A bribe is a commission paid to A without the knowledge of P. It is not necessary to show that A was influenced by it. For example, in *Boston Deep Sea Fishing & Ice Co. v Ansell* (1888) 39 ChD 339, a company director accepted bonuses from two other companies of which he was also a director, paid on the strength of orders placed with those other companies by the first company. He was held liable to account for the bonuses.

The duty not to make secret profits extends further than the acceptance of bribes. It includes a prohibition on A's use of confidential information gained as a result of the relationship with P to make personal profit. For example, the acquisition of the shares in *Boardman v Phipps* was a secret profit made by exploiting information gained from the relationship of confidence. In either case, P's remedy is either to force A to account for the profit made, or to oblige A to pay damages for any loss sustained (*Mahesan v Malaysia Government-Officers' Cooperative Housing Society Ltd* [1979] AC 374). In that case the argument that these remedies should be available cumulatively was rejected. The decision in *Mahesan* was approved by the Court of Appeal in *Arab Monetary Fund* v *Hashim* [1996] 1 Lloyd's Rep 589.

16.9.1.6   The duty to account   It is essential to the idea of agency that where A receives money on behalf of P he or she must keep it separate from his or her own, and that A is in effect a trustee of P's money (*Foley* v *Hill* (1848) 2 HL Cas 28). A must keep proper accounts, which he or she may be required to produce for P's examination. Although there may be a contract between P and A, the duty to account is independent so that termination of the authority, or of the contract between P and A, does not end the duty to account. Where A mixes P's money with his or her own in a single fund, P may be entitled to a tracing remedy to recover his or her property, provided it is still identifiable in the mixed fund (*Re Hallett's Estate* (1880) 13 ChD 696).

16.9.2   Agent's rights against the principal

16.9.2.1   Remuneration   Where there is a contract providing for A to act on behalf of P, A is entitled to remuneration for the services he or she provides. Where A is a professional agent who usually provides his or her services for payment, the courts will be willing to assume the existence of a contract even if concrete evidence is lacking (*cf.* the past consideration rule as applied to professionals: 4.3.3.2).

In the case of an employee who, in the course of his or her employment, acts from time to time as agent for that employer, it may well be that remuneration is constituted by the salary received. The employee's contract of employment may provide for additional payments of commission, but the entitlement to the salary will not depend upon the actual negotiation of any particular number of transactions on the employer's behalf. As far as any commission is concerned, however, an employee is in the same position as that usually occupied by an independent contractor who acts as agent; that is, the entitlement to remuneration depends upon the achievement of the tasks for which remuneration was promised. In technical terms, A's right to payment is subject to a promissory condition precedent (see 5.4). A good example of this type of condition is provided by an estate agent's right to payment for negotiating the sale of a house. The usual situation is that the estate agent is not entitled to payment until there has been a completed sale. A claim to be entitled to commission where there has been no completed sale will be allowed only if the contract between the estate agent and the vendor provides for it in very clear language (*Luxor (Eastbourne) Ltd* v *Cooper* [1941] AC 108).

The entitlement to remuneration also depends upon A's performance being the cause of the transaction entered into by P. For example, in *Millar* v *Radford* (1903) 19 TLR 575, A was instructed to find a purchaser or a tenant for P's property. A found a tenant, and was paid a commission. One year later the tenant purchased the property, and A claimed to be entitled to further commission on the sale. His claim was rejected because the second transaction did not result from A's efforts on behalf of P.

A vexed question in relation to A's right to remuneration is whether P is free to interfere with A's right to earn the commission. In the case of estate agents' contracts it seems that P is under no duty to refrain from preventing A earning his or her commission. In *Luxor (Eastbourne) Ltd v Cooper*, P employed A, an estate agent, to find a purchaser for P's cinemas. A's fee was to be £10,000, payable if A introduced a purchaser who paid not less than £185,000 for the property. A introduced a purchaser who offered the stipulated amount 'subject to contract', but P withdrew from the sale. A nevertheless claimed to be entitled to the fee. The House of Lords refused to imply a term into estate agents' contracts preventing vendors from depriving agents of the opportunity to earn their commission, so that A's action failed.

It seems that today the courts may be more willing to imply a term in general contracts of agency protecting A's right to earn the commission, at least against P's breach of any contract upon which A's earning capacity rests (*cf. Alpha Trading Ltd v Dunnshaw-Patten* [1981] QB 290). The position would be quite different where the breach preventing A from earning the commission is committed by the third party (e.g., *Marcan Shipping (London) Ltd v Polish Steamship Co.* [1989] 2 Lloyd's Rep 138). It is most unlikely that a court would be willing to imply a term into the contract between P and A intended to prevent breach by the third party. In the final analysis, of course, such cases depend upon the particular facts as found by the court, but Bingham LJ made clear in *Marcan Shipping (London) Ltd v Polish Steamship Co.* that the usual tests for implication of a term as a matter of fact (i.e., business efficacy and officious bystander: see generally 5.5.2) would apply.

Special rules governing the remuneration of commercial agents are laid down in the Commercial Agents (Council Directive) Regulations 1993 (SI 1993 No. 3053).

16.9.2.2 Indemnity The agent is entitled to be indemnified by P for all liabilities reasonably incurred in A's performance of his or her duties on behalf of P (*Thacker v Hardy* (1878) 4 QBD 685). Expenses recoverable include any tortious liability incurred by A in performing P's explicit instructions (e.g., sale authorised by P of property belonging to a third party: *Adamson v Jarvis* (1827) 4 Bing 66). A is not entitled to an indemnity for liabilities incurred in the course of unauthorised acts (*Barron v Fitzgerald* (1840) 6 Bing NC 201). Neither is A entitled to an indemnity for liabilities which are incurred as a result of his or her own fault (*Lewis v Samuel* (1846) 8 QB 685), or which are illegal (*Re Parker* (1882) 21 ChD 408).

16.9.2.3 Lien An agent is entitled to a lien over P's property which is lawfully in his or her possession to secure debts arising out of the agency relationship. The lien does not entitle A to dispose of the goods in order to realise their value in satisfaction of the debt: it merely entitles him or her to keep the goods until payment is made (*West of England Bank v Batchelor* (1882) 51 LJ Ch 199). Since a lien is a possessory title only, it is lost when the goods lawfully pass out of A's possession.

The parties may contract to prevent the acquisition of such a lien (*Rolls Razor Ltd* v *Cox* [1967] 1 QB 552). Unless the parties so contract, or there is a particular custom of the trade (as, for example, in the case of solicitors and bankers), the lien operates only in respect of debts arising out of the particular agency relationship, and does not cover other general debts owed by P to A.

16.10   RELATIONSHIP BETWEEN AGENT AND THIRD PARTY

In the usual circumstances of an agency created in order to effect a contract between P and the third party, once that contract comes into existence A drops out of the relationship, and need have no further dealings with the third party. In some circumstances, however, A may have incurred personal liabilities towards and rights from the third party.

16.10.1   Personal liability of agent

16.10.1.1   Undisclosed principal   We have already seen (16.8.2.2) that if A contracts on behalf of an undisclosed principal, A is personally liable on the contract. Indeed, until the time P is disclosed, in the eyes of the third party A is the only person liable on the contract. At the point when P is disclosed the third party may elect whether to proceed against A or against P, so that A's personal liability may continue after P's existence becomes known.

16.10.1.2   Agent contracting in a personal capacity   In a number of situations the agent will be held to have contracted in a personal capacity, and so will be liable on the contract made with the third party. The most obvious example of this rule is where it is the intention of all the parties that A should be a party to the contract in addition to P, and the contract therefore expressly so provides. Contracts of this kind present difficulty only where there is a question of construction of a written document as to whether this effect was in fact intended (see 16.10.1.3).

A may also be held to have contracted in a personal capacity if A contracts on behalf of a non-existent principal. We have already seen that an agent's contracts cannot be ratified by a principal who did not exist at the time the contracts were made (*Kelner* v *Baxter* (1866) LR 2 CP 174: 16.7.4.1). In the same case it was held that since the company had not been formed and so could not ratify the contracts purportedly made on its behalf, the promoters who had made the contracts were personally liable. Except in the case of companies (see s. 36C, Companies Act 1985, which imposes personal liability in these circumstances), this personal liability of A who contracts for a non-existent P is not automatic but depends upon the construction of the particular contract. *Kelner* v *Baxter* was distinguished in *Coral (UK) Ltd* v *Rechtman* [1996] 1 Lloyd's Rep 235. The first defendant signed on behalf of a company which had ceased to exist legally, having been divided into two legally independent companies with complementary manufacturing and trading functions. The first defendant was a director of the trading division, with authority to contract on its behalf; in signing on behalf of the overall group, it was clear that he intended to bind the trading division. According to Potter J, this was not a case of a contract purported to be made on behalf of a non-existent company: it was simply a case of misdescription of the principal. Since the trading division did not deny its liability as principal on the contract, there was no reason to suppose that it had been intended that the first defendant undertook any personal liability. In the absence of an intention that A be personally liable, A may still be liable for breach of warranty of authority (16.10.1.4).

Lastly, A may be held to have contracted in a personal capacity if he or she contracts for an unnamed principal (see further 16.10.2). The usual rule in this situation is that where A contracts *as agent* he or she does not make himself or herself personally liable, but that rule may be varied as a matter of construction (*Hitchens, Harrison, Woolston & Co.* v *Jackson & Sons* [1943] AC 266).

16.10.1.3 Contracts in writing There may be an irresistible inference that A contracted to incur personal liability if he or she signed a written contract without qualifying that signature by words showing that he or she signed only on behalf of P, especially where there is no other reference to P in the contractual document (*Parker* v *Winlow* (1857) 7 El & Bl 942). The problem is that the word 'agent' on its own may be either a qualification or merely a description (*The Swan* [1968] 1 Lloyd's Rep 5 at 13). To avoid being held personally liable after signing a written contract, A must show not only that he or she is employed as agent, but that he or she signed only in that capacity (*Universal Steam Navigation Co. Ltd* v *J. McKelvie & Co.* [1923] AC 492). In that case, after A's signature the words 'as agents' appeared, and it is now generally accepted that this form will avoid personal liability on the part of A.

Difficult issues of construction may still arise if the words 'as agents' are used in association with another possible capacity. In *Seatrade Groningen BV* v *Geest Industries Ltd* [1996] 2 Lloyd's Rep 375, no qualification was attached to the signature, but elsewhere the contract referred to the party in question 'as agents for owners or as disponent owners'. In these circumstances there was nothing to negate the inference that the alleged agents contracted as principals. Greater clarity might have been achieved by qualification of the signature with the phrase 'as agents only' (*per* Evans LJ at 379).

It is much more difficult for A to avoid personal liability after signing the contract without qualification if the only evidence to suggest his or her restricted status as agent is not intrinsic to the document. Such evidence will normally be excluded by the parol evidence rule (see 5.2.1).

16.10.1.4 Agent's unauthorised acts Where A lacked authority to make the contract with the third party, unless the contract has subsequently been ratified by P, A will incur a personal liability to the third party on any one of three grounds. If A knew that he or she lacked authority A will be liable for deceit (*Polhill* v *Walter* (1832) 3 B & Ad 114). Alternatively, if A failed to act with due care in stating that he or she had authority to make the contract when in fact he or she had none, A may be liable for negligent misstatement (see 10.4.3.1).

The third party's most likely claim against A who contracted without authority, however, is a claim for breach of warranty of authority. It is said that there is a collateral contract between A and the third party in which A warrants that P exists and that A has authority from P to make the main contract in question. In *Collen v Wright* (1857) 8 El & Bl 647, the defendant, in his capacity as land agent for one Gardner, had leased land belonging to Gardner to the plaintiff for a period of 12 years. Gardner was able to prove that the defendant lacked authority to grant such a long lease, so that the plaintiff's action against Gardner failed. The plaintiff then brought an action against the agent. The defendant was found liable for breach of a collateral warranty of his authority. Consideration for this warranty lay in the third party entering the main contract.

The advantage of the claim for breach of warranty of authority is that it does not depend upon A's state of mind: A is liable even if entirely innocent in representing that he or she had P's authority (*Collen* v *Wright*). For example, in *Penn v Bristol and West Building Society* [1997] 1 WLR 1356, a solicitor who had been instructed to sell a house owned by a husband and wife impliedly warranted to both the purchaser and the building society, which advanced mortgage funds to purchase the property, that he had the authority of both the husband and the wife. In fact, he did not have the authority of the wife. The solicitor was liable to the building society for breach of the warranty of authority.

16.10.2 Rights of the agent

It is axiomatic that if A has incurred personal liability on the main contract with the third party, he or she will also acquire contractual rights against the third party. Where, therefore, in the circumstances outlined above, A incurred a personal liability, he or she would also have acquired rights.

More difficult is the question whether A may purport to contract as agent, only later to reveal that A is in fact also the principal. It is generally accepted that if A contracts on behalf of an unnamed principal, A may acquire the contractual rights against the third party by revealing himself or herself as principal, since if the third party was willing to contract without knowing who the principal was, it is highly unlikely that the third party should object to a contract with A (*Schmaltz v Avery* (1851) 16 QB 655).

Even greater difficulty is presented when A claims to be entitled to take over a contract purportedly made on behalf of a named principal. If, after being informed that A contracted as principal, the third party affirms the contract, A may then enforce it in his or her own name (*Rayner v Grote* (1846) 15 M & W 359). It will always be possible, however, for the third party to assert that the identity of the particular named principal was part of what induced him or her to make the contract, and on that ground to resist A's attempts to take over the contract rights (*The Remco* [1984] 2 Lloyd's Rep 205).

16.11 TERMINATION OF AGENCY

Agency may be terminated by the voluntary act of one or both parties, or by operation of law. In some circumstances agency may be irrevocable. The effect of termination is to bring A's actual authority to an immediate end, although P may nevertheless be bound by contracts made by A on his or her behalf after the moment of termination by virtue of an apparent authority vested in A (*Trueman* v *Loder* (1840) 11 Ad & El 589). Rights to commission or to indemnity which vested in A before the time of termination remain recoverable, but no new rights may be created.

16.11.1 Voluntary termination

Where the agency was created by contract between P and A, it may be terminated by agreement between them, just as any other contract may be rescinded by a fresh contract between the parties. More significantly, agency may be terminated unilaterally by P on giving notice, although in the case of agency created by contract, P may be required to give a reasonable period of notice (*Martin-Baker Aircraft Co. Ltd* v *Canadian Flight Equipment Ltd* [1955] 2 QB 556). Nevertheless, it seems that although a revocation of authority may be a breach of contract entitling A to damages, the revocation will be effective since A's authority is not created by the contract but depends upon P's power to confer it. P's power to terminate by notice may be affected by an implied term preventing P from interfering with A's ability to earn commission under the contract of agency (see 16.9.2.1).

16.11.2 Termination by operation of law

If there is a contract of agency it is subject to the usual rules applicable to frustration (see Chapter 8).

Since agency is regarded as a personal contract it is terminated automatically by the death of either party, even in the case where the other party has no knowledge of the death (*Campanari* v *Woodburn* (1854) 15 CB 400). Similarly, the insanity of either P or A results in the automatic termination of the agency (but see the Enduring Powers of Attorney Act 1985). It may still be possible for A to bind an insane principal by virtue of apparent authority (*Drew* v *Nunn* (1879) 4 QBD 661). It has been held in such a case that the agent was personally liable, but the case should probably be regarded as decided upon the special fact that A should have known of P's incapacity but did not, and so was effectively in breach of a warranty of authority (*Yonge* v *Toynbee* [1910] 1 KB 215). The bankruptcy of P imposes a legal incapacity, and so would automatically terminate the agency. Bankruptcy of A would not necessarily terminate the agency, but it would be likely to since it would probably make A unfit to perform his or her duties. The cessation of business by a principal will not of itself bring an agency to an end (*Triffit Nurseries (a firm)* v *Salads Etcetera Ltd* [1999] 1 All ER (Comm) 110; aff'd [2000] 1 All ER (Comm) 737).

Index

Absolute assignment 473–4
Absolute contracts 256
Acceptance of goods 232
Acceptance of offers 30–1, 32, 40–54, 59
  battle of forms 14, 44–7
  communication of 47–54
    distinction between instantaneous and
      non-instantaneous
      communications 49, 51–3
    electronic means of communication
      53–4
    implied waiver of need to communicate
      in unilateral contracts 47–8
    postal rule 48–51
  mirror image rule 42–4
  requests for further information 44
  in response to offer 41–2
  revocation and 56–7
  unilateral contracts 59
Accord and satisfaction 227
Account, duty to 497
Accounting for profits 3
Administration of justice, contracts
  prejudicial to 354
Advance payments 270–2, 417–18
  deposits 416–17, 418
Advertisements 33–5, 94–6, 152
Affirmation of contracts 229, 231, 249–50,
  251–3, 309
Age, misrepresentation of 148
Agency 300, 451, 471, 479–502
  actual authority 480–2
  agent/third party relationship 499–501
    personal liability of agent 499–501
    rights of agent 501
  apparent authority 482–5
  authority by operation of law 485–6
  commercial 488

Agency – *continued*
  disclosed principal 489–90
  formation 480–8
  indemnity 498
  lien 498–9
  principal/agent relationship 493–9
    agent's obligations to principal 493–7
    agent's rights against principal 497–9
  principal/third party relationship 488–93
    disclosed principal 489–90
    undisclosed principal 490–3
  ratification of unauthorised acts 486–8
  remuneration 497–8
  termination 502
  undisclosed principal 490–3, 499
Agreements 1, 2, 12, 26–63
  agreement to agree 14, 69
  alterations 118–22
  anti-competitive 184, 367–9
  certainty of 64–74
    generally 64–6
    recovery where contract fails to
      materialise 72–4
    where essential terms are missing
      68–72
    where essential terms are vague 66–8
  damages provisions 411–19
  determination of existence of agreement
    26–30
    objective approach 26, 27–9
    subjective approach 26, 27, 29–30, 66
    traditional and non-traditional
      approaches 30–1
    using offer and acceptance 30–1, 32
  discharge of contracts by
    agreement 226–8
    requirement of consideration 227–8
  mistake 64, 74–6

Agreements – *continued*
  cross-purposes mistake   76–9, 276
  in documents   87–90
  effect of   75–6
  as to identity   80–7
  unilateral mistake   79–87
  offers   30–1
    acceptance   32, 40–54, 56–7, 59
    communication of   40
    counter-offers   42–4
    distinguished from invitations to treat
      32–40
    firm offers   55–6
    termination of   54–7, 59–62
    unilateral contracts   58
  see also Unilateral contracts
Alteration promises   118–22
Anti-competitive agreements   184, 367–9
Anticipatory repudiation   247–54, 421–2
Apprenticeship   146
Arbitration   3, 65
Assessment of loss   392–3
Assignment   451, 471–9
  burden of contract   478–9
  equitable   474–6
  limits on   476–8
  statutory   472–4
Assumpsit   8
Attorney, power of   472
Auctions   39–40

Bailment   359, 470
Battle of forms   14, 44–7
Belief, statements of   298–9
Bills of exchange   143
Bills of sale   143
Binding alteration promises   118–22
Blue pencil test   369
Breach of contract   13–14, 228–54
  action for   7–8
  affirmation after   229, 231, 249–50,
    251–3
  anticipatory repudiation   247–54, 421–2
  classification of terms and   233–41
  entire obligations   242, 244–7
  fundamental breach   193–5
  independent or concurrent conditions
    241–2
  innominate terms   239–41
  promissory conditions   233–5
  remedies   7–8, 373–4
    claim for agreed sum   420–4
    damages   376–419, 430–1
    injunctions   431
    restitution   387–91, 432–7
    specific performance   424–31
  repudiatory breach   229–32

Breach of contract – *continued*
  anticipatory repudiation   247–54,
    421–2
  severable obligations   242, 243–5
  time stipulations   235–8
  warranties   238–9
Bribes, duty not to take   496–7
Business efficacy rule   178

Capacity   145–9
  companies and partnerships   149
  mental disorder and drunkenness   145–6
  minors   146–9
Care, duty to exercise   494
Carriage of goods by sea   457
Cartels   365
Causa doctrine   8
Causation, damages for breach of contract
  and   394–6
Certainty of agreements   64–74
  generally   64–6
  recovery where contract fails to
    materialise   72–4
  where essential terms are missing   68–72
  where essential terms are vague   66–8
Chattels, restriction on use of   468–70
Children (minors), capacity   146–9
Circumstances, change of   295–6
Civil wrongs, contracts to commit   353–4
Claim for agreed sum   420–4
  additional loss and interest   422–4
  anticipatory breach   421–2
  sale of goods   422
Classical theory of contract   10, 11–14
Cohabitants, agency of   485
Collateral contracts   60–1, 140–1, 159–60,
  357, 454–5
Collateral warranties   156–7
Collective theory of contract   15–17
Commencement, acceptance upon   60
Commercial agents   488
Commercial agreements
  intention to create legal relations   94–9
  past consideration   111–12
Common knowledge, incorporation of
  terms   168
Communication
  of acceptance of offers   47–54
    distinction between instantaneous and
      non-instantaneous
      communications   49, 51–3
    electronic means of communication
      53–4
    postal rule   48–51
  of offers   40
  of revocation   57, 61–2
Companies, capacity   149

Compensation   375
  see also Damages
Competitive tenders   37–9
Compromise   3
Conciliation   3
Concurrent conditions   241–2
Conditions   169–70, 233
  breach of   233–8
  independent or concurrent conditions
      241–2
  precedent   169
  promissory conditions   233–5
  subsequent   169, 228
Confidential relationships   296
Consent, coercion and vitiation of consent
      328–30
Consequential loss   391–2
Consideration
  assignments   475–6
  binding alteration promises   118–22
  classical theory of contract and   12–13
  definition   1–2, 101–4
  discharge of contracts by agreement
      and   227–8
  enforcement of contracts and   91, 92,
      101–25
  future of   122–5
  history of   8
  mistake and   284
  past consideration   109–12
  privity of contract and   442–3
  sufficiency and performance of existing
      duties   113–18
  total failure of   432–4
  unilateral contracts   59
  value, exchange and inducement   104–9
Consistent course of dealing, incorporation
    of terms   167–8
Construction *see* Interpretation of contracts
Constructive trust   141–2
Consumer contracts   16, 17, 179
  consumer credit agreements   142
  guarantees for consumer goods   198
  judicial attitudes to exemption
      clauses   185–6
  statutory control of exemption and
      exclusion clauses   195, 199–201,
      214–23
Content of contracts   152–79
  control of substantive content of contracts
      183–4
  implied terms   13, 16, 170–9
    blurring of categories   177–8
    classification   178–9
    implied in fact   172–3
    implied in law   173–7
  incorporation of terms   109, 161–9, 302

Content of contracts – *continued*
  common knowledge   168
  consistent course of dealing   167–8
  exemption clauses   187
  incorporation of written terms into oral
      contract   163–4
  in practice   168–9
  reasonable notice of existence of
      terms   164–7
  written documents which have been
      signed   161–3
  pre-contractual statements   152–7, 293
    collateral warranties   156–7
    distinguishing representations from
        terms   152, 153–6
  promissory and contingent obligations
      distinguished   169–70
  written contracts   157–61
    collateral contracts   159–60
    parol evidence rule   157–8, 179
    partly written and partly oral   158
Contingent obligations   169–70
Contra proferentem rule   188–9
Contract law
  globalisation of   20–3
  good faith in   22–3, 70, 74, 216–19
  history of   7–8
  role of   10–18
Contractual liability
  exemption clauses and   198–205
  nature of   1–3
Contributory negligence   321–2
  damages for breach of contract and
      396–8
Corruption   355
Costs, pre-contractual   72–3
Counter-offers   42–4
Covenant, action for   7
Credit agreements   142
Creditors, duress against   131–2
Crimes, contracts to commit   353–4
Cross-purposes mistake   76–9, 276
  fault doctrine   77–8
  objective test   77
  refusal of specific performance in
      equity   78–9
Cure, cost of   381–4
Customary terms   177–8

Damage
  remoteness of   6, 12, 312
    damages for breach of contract and
        399–404
Damages   6, 11–12
  breach of contract   376–419
    agreed damages provisions   411–19
    aim of   376–7

Damages – *continued*
 avoidance of double compensation
  387
 causation and 394–6
 consequential loss 391–2
 contributory negligence and 396–8
 expectation loss 377–85
 inadequacy of 425–6
 in lieu of specific performance 430–1
 limitations on ability to obtain
  394–411
 mitigation 404–6
 non-pecuniary 406–11
 reliance loss 377, 385–7
 remoteness of damage and 399–404
 reputation loss 409–11
 restitution 387–91, 432–7
 taxation and 393–4
 time for assessment of loss 392–3
 for deceit 312–15
 liquidated damages clauses 412–15
 for misrepresentation 153, 304, 306,
  311–20
 contributory negligence and 321–2
 in lieu of rescission 318–20
 nominal 374
 promisee's claim for 463–8
 punitive 373
 restitution compared with 435–6
Death, termination of offers 55
Debt
 action for 7–8
 claim in 420–1
Deceit, damages for 312–15
Deeds 91–2
 contracts required to be made by
  deed 138
Defences, exemption and exclusion clauses
  as defences to liability 186–95
Definition of 'contract' 1
Delegation by agent 494–5
Delivery, late 380
Deposits 416–17, 418
Detached objectivity 27, 28
Discharge of contracts 224–54, 255–74
 by agreement 226–8
  requirement of consideration 227–8
 by breach 228–54
 by frustration 255–74, 278
  common purpose of both parties
   263–4
  fault and 268–9
  foreseeability and risk allocation
   265–7
  frustrating events 258–64
  history of doctrine 256
  impossibility 258–60

Discharge of contracts – *continued*
  impracticability 261–3
  land contracts 264–5
  legal effects 269–74
  legal nature of doctrine 257–8
  unavailability 260–1
 by performance 225–6
  standard of performance 225–6
  tender of performance 226
 self-termination 228
Distance selling contracts 142
Documents
 mistakes in 87–90
 non est factum plea 87, 89–90
 rectification 87–9
Domestic arrangements *see* Social and
  domestic arrangements
Drunkenness, capacity and 145–6
Duress 23, 104, 326–32, 343, 359
 against creditors 131–2
 coercion and vitiation of consent 328–30
 economic 327–32
 illegitimate pressure or threat 330–1
 limitations of early doctrine 326–7
 to property 327
 protest at 331–2
Duties
 consideration and performance of existing
  duties 113–18
  contractual duties owed to promisor
   116–18
  duties owed to third parties 114–16
  public duties 113–14

E-commerce 144–5
Economic duress 327–32
Economic loss 6
Electronic means of communication 53–4
Electronic signatures 144–5, 161
E-mail 53–4
Employment contracts 16, 146
 restraint of trade 363–4
Enforcement of contracts 3, 373, 439–40
 capacity and 145–9
  companies and partnerships 149
  mental disorder and drunkenness
   145–6
  minors 146–9
 consideration and 91, 92, 101–25
 criteria for 90–149
 equitable estoppel and 125–6
  development of doctrine 125–6
  scope of 126
 essential ingredients of enforceability
  1–2
 intention to create legal relations 92–101
  commercial agreements 94–9

Enforcement of contracts – *continued*
  generally 92–3
  presumed intention 93–4, 96
  rebuttal of presumption 96–9, 100–1
  social and domestic arrangements
    99–101
  negative undertakings 463
  not specifically enforceable 426–9
  promissory estoppel and 127–33, 135–7
  development of 127–9
  effect of 132–3
  future of 135–7
  requirements for 129–31
  proprietary estoppel and 133–5
  by third parties *see* Third parties
  unenforceability by defect of
    form 137–45
    contracts required to be evidenced in
      writing 137, 143–4
    contracts required to be made by
      deed 138
    contracts required to be made in writing
      137, 138–43
    electronic signatures and implications of
      e-commerce 144–5
    generally 137–8
Enrichment, unjust 388, 432
Entertainers 366–7
Entire obligations 242, 244–7
Equitable assignment 474–6
Equitable estoppel 125–6, 228
  development of doctrine 125–6
  scope of 126
Estoppel
  agent's apparent authority 482–5
  equitable 125–6, 228
  loss of right to accept repudiatory breach
    as termination 231–2
  promissory *see* Promissory estoppel
  proprietary 133–5, 141
European Union
  anti-competitive agreements and 367–8
  contract law and 22, 177
  Principles of European Contract Law
    (PECL) 21, 23, 28, 31, 40, 46,
    53, 56, 57, 70, 92, 254, 445
Exchange 9
Exclusive dealing agreements 365–6
Excuse *see* Frustration
Executory contracts 2, 14–15
Exemption and exclusion clauses 5, 12, 23,
  161, 162, 183, 198–9
  as defences to liability 186–95
  fundamental terms 193–5
  incorporation 187
  interpretation 187–92
  judicial attitudes to 185–6

Exemption and exclusion clauses – *continued*
  misrepresentation and 322–5
  protection of third parties by 457–62
  purpose of 184–5
  reasonableness requirement 206–14
  statutory control of 195–223
    consumer contracts 195, 199–201,
      214–23
    nature of 195
    UCTA 1977 195, 196–214
    types and nature of 186
Expectation
  expectation loss 6, 12, 375, 377–85
    cost of cure 381–4
    difference in value 377–81
    speculative and uncertain 384–5
  protection of 15–16, 17–18

Fair dealing principle 80
False statement of fact 294–9
Family
  contracts prejudicial to 354
  settlements 297
Fault
  cross-purposes mistake and 77–8
  frustration and 268–9
Fax communication 52
Fiduciary relationships 296
Firm offers 55–6
Forbearance 107–8
Force majeure clauses 255
Foreign relations, contracts prejudicial to
  355
Foreseeability and risk allocation 265–7
Forfeiture 184
  deposits 416–17, 418
  relief from 418–19
Form of contract
  unenforceability by defect of 137–45
    contracts required to be evidenced in
      writing 137, 143–4
    contracts required to be made by
      deed 138
    contracts required to be made in writing
      137, 138–43
    electronic signatures and implications of
      e-commerce 144–5
    generally 137–8
Formalism 17
France 11, 75
Fraud 104, 140, 141, 359
  exemption clauses and 192
  fraudulent misrepresentation 81, 152–3,
    303–4
Freedom of contract 4, 7, 65, 104
Frustration 13, 255–74, 278
  common purpose of both parties 263–4

Frustration – *continued*
  fault and   268–9
  foreseeability and risk allocation   265–7
  frustrating events   258–64
  history of doctrine   256
  impossibility   258–60
  impracticability   261–3
  land contracts   264–5
  legal effects   269–74
  legal nature of doctrine   257–8
  unavailability   260–1
Fundamental breach   193–5
Future conduct, statements of   299

Gambling contracts   351–3, 432
Gap filling   68
Germany   70
Gifts, conditions imposed upon recipient
  103–4
Globalisation of contract law   20–3
Good faith   22–3, 70, 74, 216–19
  agent's obligation   495–6
  uberrimae fidei contracts   296–7
Guarantees   143–4
  for consumer goods   198

Half-truths   295
Hire purchase agreements   142, 359

Identity
  mistake as to   80–7
    general rule   81–2
    intention to deal with some other person
      82–5
    no fault by mistaken party   85–6
If contracts *see* Unilateral contracts
Illegal contracts   13, 348–71
  class-protection   358–9
  gambling contracts   351–3, 432
  general effect of illegality   355–7
  public policy under common law   353–5
  recovery of money or property   357–61
  restraint of trade   184, 349, 361–71
    cartels   365
    employment contracts   363–4
    exclusive dealing agreements   365–6
    general principles   361–2
    reasonable between the parties   362–3
    reasonable in public interest   363
    remedies where restraint is valid
      370–1
    sale of business   365
    severance of offending parts   36–70
    sportsmen and entertainers   366–7
    statutory control of anti-competitive
      agreement   367–9
  statutory illegality   350–1

Illegal contracts – *continued*
  contracts performed in illegal manner
    351
  express prohibition   350
  withdrawal by one party   358
Implied terms   13, 16, 170–9
  blurring of categories   177–8
  classification   178–9
  implied in fact   172–3
  implied in law   173–7
Implied unilateral contracts   38–9
Importance attached test   154–5
Impossibility, frustration and   258–60
Impracticability, frustration and   261–3
Incorporation of terms   109, 161–9,
    302
  common knowledge   168
  consistent course of dealing   167–8
  exemption clauses   187
  incorporation of written terms into oral
    contract   163–4
  in practice   168–9
  reasonable notice of existence of
    terms   164–7
  written documents which have been
    signed   161–3
Indemnity
  agents   498
  contracts of   143
  remedy for misrepresentation   320
  for unlawful acts   354
Independent conditions   241–2
Individualism   11, 16, 17
Inducement to contract, misrepresentation
    and   299–302
Influence *see* Undue influence
Injunctions   431
Innocent misrepresentation   303, 308
Innominate terms   170, 233, 239–41
Insurance contracts   16, 274, 456
  marine   143
  utmost good faith (*uberrimae fidei*)   296–7
Intention, statements of   299
Intention in agreements   26–30
  intention to create legal relations   92–101
    commercial agreements   94–9
    generally   92–3
    presumed intention   93–4, 96
    rebuttal of presumption   96–9, 100–1
    social and domestic arrangements
      99–101
  objective approach   26, 27–9
  subjective approach   26, 27, 29–30, 66
Interest, recovery of   422–4
International influences on contract law
    20–3
International trade contracts   16

Internet
  incorporation of contract terms 167
  websites 36–7, 54
Interpretation of contracts 179–82
  exemption clauses 187–92
  foreseeability and 267
Invitations to treat 32–40

Land
  contracts for sale or disposition of interest
    in land 138, 139–42
  frustration of land contracts 264–5
  restrictive covenants 468–70
  specific performance remedy 426
Late delivery 380
Latent ambiguity 66
Law, statements of 299
Liability
  nature of contractual liability 1–3
  see also Exemption and exclusion clauses
Lien, agency 498–9
Limitation clauses 161, 186, 191, 196
  misrepresentation and 322–5
Limitation periods 6–7, 138
Limited liability partnerships, capacity
  149
Liquidated damages clauses 412–15
Loans, gambling contracts and 353
Lock-out agreement 69, 140
Locus poenitentiae doctrine 358
Loss
  assessment of 392–3
  consequential loss 391–2
  economic loss 6
  expectation loss 6, 12, 375, 377–85
  measure of loss recoverable 6
  non-pecuniary 406–11
  of profits 314–15, 394
  reliance loss 6, 375, 377, 385–7
  reputation 409–11
  speculative and uncertain loss 384–5
  see also Restitution

Marine insurance contracts 143
Market price rule 377–9
Market system 12
Marriage, illegality in contracts 354
Maximisation of wealth 12, 13
Mediation 3
Mental disorder, capacity and 145–6
Minors, capacity 146–9
Mirror image rule 42–4
Mispricing 36–7
Misrepresentation 20, 75, 157, 292–325
  actionable 293–302
  of age 148
  contributory negligence and 321–2

Misrepresentation – *continued*
  exclusion or limitation of liability for
    192, 322–5
  false statement of fact 294–9
  fraudulent 81, 152–3, 303–4
  inducement to contract 299–302
  innocent 303, 308
  negligent 153, 293, 303, 304–7, 315–18
  remedies for 303–4, 308–22
    damages 153, 304, 306, 311–20
    indemnity 320
    rescission 304, 308–11
  representations which become terms 302
  types 302–8
Mistake 13, 20, 157, 276–91, 293
  agreements 64, 74–6
  allocation of risk and 285
  categories 277–80
  common law 277–85
  cross-purposes mistake 76–9, 276
  in documents 87–90
  effect of 75–6
  in English law 74–5
  in equity 286–91
  as to identity 80–7
    general rule 81–2
    intention to deal with some other person
      82–5
    no fault by mistaken party 85–6
  as to ownership 280
  as to quality 280–5
  as to subject matter 277–80
  unilateral mistake 79–87
    as to identity 80–7
Mitigation, damages for breach of contract
  and 404–6
Money, recovery after illegal contract
  357–61
Moral obligation 11–12, 14
Morality, contracts prejudicial to 354–5
Mutual mistake 76

Necessaries, contracts for 145, 146–7
Necessity, agency of 485–6
Negative undertakings, enforcement of
  463
Negligence 5, 6, 189
  contributory negligence 321–2, 396–8
  negligent misrepresentation 153, 293,
    303, 304–7, 315–18
  statutory control of exemption clauses
    limiting liability for 197
Negotiable instruments 112, 452–4
Nemo dat qui non habet rule 19–20
Nominal damages 374
Non est factum plea 87, 89–90
Non-pecuniary loss 406–11

Notice, reasonable notice of existence of
   terms   164–7
Novation   472

Obedience to instructions   494
Objective approach to determination of
   existence of agreement   26, 27–9
Offers   30–1
   acceptance   30–1, 32, 40–54, 59
      battle of forms   14, 44–7
      communication of   47–54
      mirror image rule   42–4
      requests for further information   44
      in response to offer   41–2
      revocation and   56–7
   communication of   40
   counter-offers   42–4
   distinguished from invitations to treat
      32–40
   firm offers   55–6
   termination of   54–7, 59–62
      death   55
      lapse of time   54–5
      revocation   55–7
   see also Unilateral contracts
Office of Fair Trading   3
Officious bystander test   173
Onerous and unusual terms   23
Opinion statements   298–9
Option contracts   67, 139–40
Oral contracts
   incorporation of written terms   163–4
   partly written and partly oral   158
Ownership   18
   mistake as to   280
   power to transfer   19–20
   void and voidable contracts and   20

Parol evidence rule   157–8, 179
Part payment   127
Part performance   140, 434–5
Partnerships, capacity   149
Past consideration   109–12
Penalties
   for breach of obligations   373–4
   penalty clauses   413–15
   penalty rule   23, 184, 414, 415–16
Performance of contracts   5–6
   compulsion   374–5
   defective   380
   discharge of contracts by   225–6
   frustration of see Frustration
   in illegal manner   351
   part performance   140, 434–5
   refusal of specific performance in equity
      78–9
   requested performance   110–11

Performance of contracts – continued
   standard of performance   225–6
   substantial   246–7
   substitute   374–5, 425
   tender of performance   226
Perishing of goods   278–9
Postal rule   48–51, 57
   avoidance of   49–51
   retraction of postal acceptance   51
Power of attorney   472
Precedent, doctrine of   13
Pre-contractual costs   72–3
Pre-contractual statements   152–7, 293
   collateral warranties   156–7
   distinguishing representations from
      terms   152, 153–6
Pre-payments   270–2, 417–18
Presumption
   intention to create legal relations   93–4
      commercial agreements   94–9
      rebuttal of presumption   96–9, 100–1
      social and domestic arrangements
         99–101
   terms of contracts   154
Prices
   claim for   420–1
   mispricing   36–7
   uncertainty as to   70–1
Privity of contract   426, 441–3
   criticisms of   443–6
   exceptions   455–62
   imposing obligations on third parties
      and   468–70
   means of circumvention   451–5
   remedies available to promisee   462–8
Profits
   accounting for profits   3
   loss of   314–15, 394
   secret   496–7
Promise   11–12, 14, 91–2, 138
Promisee, remedies available to   462–8
Promisee objectivity   27–8
Promisor, contractual duties owed to
   116–18
Promisor objectivity   27
Promissory conditions   233–5
Promissory estoppel   13, 14, 15, 59–60, 61,
   127–33
   development of   127–9
   discharge by agreement and   228
   effect of   132–3
   future of   135–7
   requirements for   129–31
Promissory obligations   169–70
Property
   duress to   327
   power to transfer ownership   19–20

Property – *continued*
recovery after illegal contract   357–61
rights   18–19
Proprietary estoppel   133–5, 141
Protest at duress   331–2
Public conscience test   356
Public corruption   355
Public duties   113–14
Puffs   152
Punitive damages   373

Quality
implied terms   170
mistake as to   280–5
Quantum meruit basis   69, 74, 436–7
Quasi-contract   147

Ratification of agent's unauthorised acts
486–8
Realism   17
Rectification   87–9, 140, 158
Redistribution of wealth   16
Release and replacement   227
Reliance
on misrepresentation   301–2
promissory estoppel and   130–1
reliance loss   6, 375, 377, 385–7
reliance-based theories of contract
14–15
Remedies   3, 13–14
available to promisee   462–8
breach of contract   7–8, 373–4, 420–37
claim for an agreed sum   420–4
discretionary   429
indemnity   320
injunctions   431
for misrepresentation   303–4, 308–22
quantum meruit basis   69, 74, 436–7
restraint of trade   370–1
see also Damages; Rescission; Restitution;
Specific performance
Remoteness of damage   6, 12, 312
damages for breach of contract and
399–404
Remuneration of agents   497–8
Representation
distinguished from terms   152, 153–6
promissory estoppel and   129
see also Misrepresentation
Repudiatory breach   229–32
anticipatory repudiation   247–54, 421–2
Reputation, loss of   409–11
Requested performance   110–11
Requests for further information   44
Rescission
misrepresentation and   304, 308–11
damages in lieu of   318–20

Rescission – *continued*
loss of right to rescind   309–11
repudiatory breach and   229
Responsibility for truth of statement   154
Restitution   72, 148–9, 375
after illegal contract   357–61
breach of contract   387–91, 432–7
Restraint of trade   184, 349, 361–71
cartels   365
employment contracts   363–4
exclusive dealing agreements   365–6
general principles   361–2
reasonable between the parties   362–3
reasonable in public interest   363
remedies where restraint is valid   370–1
sale of business   365
severance of offending parts   36–70
Restriction on use of chattels   468–70
Restrictive covenants on land   468–70
Revocation of offers   55–7
Revocation of unilateral contracts   59–61
communication   57, 61–2
Risk allocation
foreseeability and   265–7
mistake and   285
Role of contract and contract law   8–18

Sale of business, restraint of trade and   365
Sale of goods   16, 18–20
acceptance of goods   232
claim for an agreed sum   422
mistake and   75
Seals   91–2
Secret profits   496–7
Security, gambling contracts and   352–3
Self-termination of contracts   228
Settlement of claims, consideration and
106–7
Settlements, family   297
Severance
clauses   68
restraint of trade agreements   36–70
severable obligations   242, 243–5
Sexual morality, contracts prejudicial to
354–5
Shop displays   35–6
Signatures   161–3
electronic   144–5, 161
Silence, acceptance and   47–8
Skill, duty to exercise   494
Social conventions   11–12, 14
Social and domestic arrangements
intention to create legal relations   99–101
past consideration   111
Specific performance   424–31, 462
refusal of   78–9
Specification   67

Speculative loss 384–5
Sportspeople 366–7
Standard form contracts 185, 201–2
Standard of performance 225–6
Statutory assignment 472–4
Statutory illegality 350–1
  contracts performed in illegal manner
    351
  express prohibition 350
Subject matter, mistake as to 277–80
Substantial performance 246–7
Substitute performance 374–5, 425
Supermarket shelves 35–6
Supply, cancellation of contract to supply
    380–1
Surrogacy agreements 354

Taxation, damages for breach of contract
    and 393–4
Telephone communication 51, 52–3
Telex communication 51–2
Tender of performance 226
Tenders 37–9
Termination of agency 502
Termination of contracts see Discharge of
    contracts
Termination of offers 54–7, 59–62
  death 55
  lapse of time 54–5
  revocation 55–7
Terms of contracts see Content of contracts
Theory of contract 10–18
  classical theory 10, 11–14
  collective theory 15–17
  formalism and realism 17
  reliance-based theories 14–15
  significance of 10–11
Third parties 441–70
  agency and
    agent/third party relationship 499–501
    principal/third party relationship
      488–93
  duties owed to 114–16
  mistake and void contracts 75–6, 81
  privity of contract and 426, 441–3
    criticisms of 443–6
    exceptions 455–62
    imposing obligations on third parties
      and 468–70
    means of circumvention 451–5
    remedies available to promisee
      462–8
  rescission and 311
  statutory rights 447–50
  undue influence and rights of 338–43
Threat see Duress
Tickets 163, 165

Time
  lapse of time
    loss of right to rescind 309–10
    termination of offers and 54–5
  limitation periods 6–7, 138
  stipulations 235–8
Tort
  claim in tort as means of circumventing
    privity of contract 451
  relationship between contract and
    4–7
  waiver of 148
Tracing 148
Trading standards officers 3
Trespass on the case 8
Trusts
  constructive 141–2
  as means of circumventing privity of
    contract 451–2
  of rights created by contract 455–6

Uberrimae fidei contracts 296–7
Unavailability, frustration and 260–1
Uncertain loss 384–5
Unconscionability 184, 343–7
Undertakings 2, 11–12
Undue influence 23, 332–43, 359
  actual 333–4
  effect of 337–43
  presumed 334–7
  rebuttal of presumption 336–7
Unfair terms 194, 195, 196–223
UNIDROIT Principles of International
    Commercial Contracts 21, 23, 28–9,
    31, 40, 46, 53, 56, 57, 70, 92, 254
Unilateral contracts 57–63
  consideration 59
  function 62–3
  implied 38–9
  implied waiver of need to communicate
    acceptance 47–8
  offers 58
    acceptance 59
    revocation 59–61
    communication 61–2
Unilateral mistake 79–87
  as to identity 80–7
    general rule 81–2
    intention to deal with some other
      person 82–5
    no fault by mistaken party 85–6
United Nations Commission on
    International Trade Law (UNCITRAL)
    21
Unjust enrichment 388, 432
Unsolicited goods 48
Use of chattels, restriction on 468–70

Utmost good faith (*uberrimae fidei*)
  contracts 296–7

Verification, advice on 154
Void contracts 20, 64, 224
  mistake and 75–6, 86
Voidable contracts 20, 75, 81, 86, 146,
  147, 224–5, 286–7

Waiver 228
  of tort 148
Warranties 170, 233
  breach 238–9
  collateral 156–7

Wealth
  maximisation of 12, 13
  redistribution of 16
Websites 36–7, 54
Writing
  agency and 500
  contracts required to be evidenced in
    writing 137, 143–4
  contracts required to be made in
    writing 137, 138–43
  incorporation of written terms into oral
    contract 163–4
  written contracts, content of
    contracts 157–61